T. S. ALLEN
56 BRAMFORD ROAD
WANDSWORTH
LONDON SW18 1AP

(0181-870-2418)

CW01083607

THE CATALYTIC WARS

A Study of the Development of Warfare
1860–1870

Philip Howes

MINERVA PRESS

LONDON
ATLANTA MONTREUX SYDNEY

THE CATALYTIC WARS: *A Study of the Development of Warfare 1860–1870*
Copyright © Philip Howes 1998

ISBN 0 75410 203 3

First Published 1998 by
MINERVA PRESS
195 Knightsbridge
London SW7 1RE

Printed in Great Britain for Minerva Press

Dedicated to the memory of
David Craig Esq., MA (Oxon)
Head of History and Cavendish Librarian
of Eastbourne College, 1938–1962

To whose profound scholarship and ripe wit the author owes his lifelong interest in
modern history.

THE CATALYTIC WARS
A Study of the Development of Warfare
1860–1870

Biographical Note

Philip Howes, OBE

Philip Howes was educated at Eastbourne College and commissioned into the Royal Artillery from RMA Sandhurst in 1956. During thirty years in the army he served in Cyprus, Jordan, some of the Gulf States, Malaya, Germany and Northern Ireland. In his final appointment, as head of the Ministry of Defence staff section responsible for planning the support of all army operations worldwide, he devised and brought into service the Falklands Intermediate Port and Storage System, for the support of the Falklands garrison after the end of the war in 1982. This is still in service at Port Stanley.

Philip Howes lives in Surrey, and writes and lectures on the related topics of Defence and Military History. He was elected chairman of the Defence and Security Forum in 1997. *The Catalytic Wars* is his first book. Magazine articles published previously include a series on the French commanders after the Crimea, and a study of the Falklands project.

Acknowledgements

The author acknowledges with most grateful thanks the help of Mr John Montgomery, librarian of the Royal United Services Institute for Defence Studies, and Brigadier Ken Timbers and the staff of the Royal Artillery Institution Library. Major Colin Robins OBE, editor of *The War Correspondent*, the journal of the Crimean War Research Society, provided invaluable advice about source material on the state of European armies in the 1850s, and Martin and Marna Warner, at the Malden Print and Copy Centre, were instrumental in producing the final manuscript. Nor could work on the book have been sustained without the encouragement of many personal friends.

Every author is in the hands of his publishers. Throughout the whole publication process, the staff of Minerva Press have been unstinting in their encouragement and support. The author would like to thank in particular Angelina Anton, Editorial Director, Emma Rhodes, whose eagle eye and flair for detail were vital in the final proofing and indexing stages, and Gavin Toye, who drew the maps and illustrations and designed the cover.

Contents

List of Maps and Diagrams

Chapter I
The Changing Nature of Warfare

Man is a land animal and resort to force of arms is his ultimate sanction. Even in the era of the intercontinental ballistic missile, with its armoury of independently targeted nuclear warheads, there remains an element of single combat about land warfare. War is simultaneously a test to destruction and a contest for ground. In the last resort, if one man is determined to defend with his life a piece of territory which another is equally as determined to capture, the fight between them is in essence the same as that between two cavemen, however technologically advanced their weaponry.

For many years after the Second World War it was the practice for every annual course at the British Army Staff College to spend a week in Normandy studying, on the ground, the D-Day landings and the subsequent engagements which led to the fall of Paris eighty days later. This visit had a dual purpose. First, it gave the feel of a major battle to the potential future commanders and staff officers of the British Army. Attending the course in their early thirties, these officers, from 1960 onwards, though nearly all highly experienced in the practice of internal security operations, had no personal experience of the sustained battlefield management of a combined force of all arms – infantry, tanks and artillery. Secondly, the tour was structured to study in detail the German conduct of the defence. Although handicapped by flawed strategic direction, outnumbered, outgunned and faced by overwhelmingly superior Anglo-American air power, this defence was fought with enormous tactical skill. The parallel has been drawn, quite correctly, between the achievement of the Wehrmacht in Normandy and the nature of the battle which the forces of NATO's Northern Army Group would have had to undertake against the forces of the Warsaw Pact, had the latter ever invaded West Germany.[1] Lectures were given on location by surviving senior officers and others who, in the battle, had commanded at the point of contact level. Many of the latter subsequently achieved very high rank; for instance, one Lieutenant Edwin Bramall, a platoon commander in the 2nd Battalion, the King's Royal Rifle Corps at the time, was a future Chief of the Defence Staff.[2] But the unforgettable presentation of the 1968 tour was that of Company Sergeant Major Hollis, of the Green Howards, the only man to win a Victoria Cross on D-Day. After we had walked the ground of his exploit there was time for questions. A young captain, with his head full of grand strategy and the most comprehensive logistic war plan ever mounted, asked the sergeant major how much he had known at the time about the wider picture. 'Sir, all I cared about was ten yards to my left and ten yards to my right.'

An operation involving the cross-channel transportation of over 2,000,000 men and nearly 500,000 vehicles, an opposed landing on a fifty mile front from which developed a battle lasting nearly three months and fought over an area of 1,200 square miles, was fought at point of contact on both sides by men whose horizons would be no wider when the issue was win or lose, life or death.

The cavemen merged into tribes over the course of history, and instead of fighting as individuals began to do so in formed bodies of troops, which usually dissolved once the immediate crisis was over. The emergence of the nation state brought in its train the mercenary band, the palace guard and the standing army, which could be expanded in emergency by mobilisation of the fit adult male population. The introduction of the bow and arrow conferred a stand-off capability, but the trained archer could not engage more than a single individual at a time, despite a rate of fire faster than that of any firearm until the invention of automatic weapons in the mid-nineteenth century. Even the discovery of gunpowder, the consequent development of the gun and the appearance on the battlefield of the crew-served weapon did little to alter the 'single combat' nature of warfare, even though on its first introduction the latter proved able to throw a heavier and more lethal projectile further than anything in the hands of a single man-at-arms. The reason was the basic inefficiency of guns of all types, for centuries after their first use in battle. By the beginning of the nineteenth century, the personal weapon of the foot soldier in the armies of all developed nations had been some sort of firearm for at least the preceding 250 years, but even the most highly trained and battle-experienced infantryman of the armies of Napoleon or Wellington had difficulty in achieving a rate of fire of three rounds a minute, or hitting a target more than 100 yards distant, even in ideal conditions.[3] Consequently, and given the abiding reason that battle was a contest for ground, battles even as late as the Napoleonic era soon became hand-to-hand brawls in which the foot soldiers on both sides fought as pikemen with bayonets attached to their muskets, exactly as their ancestors had in the Middle Ages. For a further century the tendency to number infantry in 'bayonet strength' would continue.

Battle could remain for so long an enterprise of single combat because man is a unique balance of the five component parts of a complete fighting capability. These comprise a command communication and information-evaluating system, hitting power (or firepower), protection, mobility and endurance (or sustainability). Rudimentary improvements, such as a sword or gun to improve hitting power, and an axe or spade to construct a protective environment or to improve concealment (itself a form of protection), are achievable at little penalty, but concentrated enhancement of any one of the five components is always detrimental to one or more of the others. Mount the man on a horse and his mobility is increased at least threefold, but there is a logistic, or sustainability, penalty to be paid in terms of forage for the horse, and the man's hitting power is reduced unless, and until, he has been schooled to act in concert with others; a lengthy training process is thus essential. Hence the development and use of the tactic of shock action by units of sabre- or lance-wielding horsemen, until well into the twentieth century; given the right conditions a battle winner, but, even as much as a century earlier, the rigidly disciplined and trained infantry of Wellington's army had established that it was a mistake to use cavalry to charge unbroken squares of infantry. As the nineteenth century advanced, the breech-loading rifle, the machine-gun and the ever-increasing range and lethality of artillery laid bare the catastrophic lack of protection of the horseman. Commanders would nevertheless continue to demand feats of shock action by their vulnerable cavalry against devastating firepower generated by infantry and artillery in prepared positions, often at exorbitant cost in casualties.

The quest for improved endurance or sustainability for the man-at-arms would always reach, and quickly, the limit imposed by his carrying capacity. Throughout the ages, the combat capability of the averagely fit foot soldier is eroded rapidly if he is required to carry more than about seventy pounds, or thirty kilograms, dead weight.[4] Although on occasions supremely fit soldiers may start their approach to battle with more – the mortar men in the parachute battalions engaged in the Falklands War began a day of battle with nearly twice this load – even the standard seventy pounds carried for any length of time not only impedes tactical mobility but, by increasing the fatigue factor, reduces the endurance of the foot soldier instead of enhancing it. Planners throughout the ages have remained prone to demand the impossible in the carrying capacities of men, animals and vehicles, often despite their own experience. The French campaign in Spain in 1823 to assist the Bourbon monarchy against insurrection is devoid of modern tactical significance, but nevertheless contains an enduring lesson for the logistician. The French minister of war, Victor, responsible for logistic planning, was a Napoleonic marshal; not of the top echelon, proved in successful independent command, but nevertheless one with a good track record as commander of a subordinate formation. As one of the majority of the marshals of the First Empire who had started in the ranks – he had achieved the rank of sergeant over ten years' service in the Grenoble Artillery of the army of Louis XVI – personal experience should have taught him better than to decree that each infantryman should carry 800 cartridges. He was set to rights by Marmont, a fellow marshal and comrade of Marengo: 'If you can carry sixty you may think yourself lucky, but I doubt if you can manage even that.'[5]

Where sought-after improvement of one or more of the separate but related elements of combat capability for the individual soldier is either unachievable, inadequate, or only obtainable with an unacceptable penalty, the alternative is to produce a weapon platform from which a man or crew can operate. This not only introduces cost penalties, and a broadening of the whole spectrum of national defence procurement, but leads to a plethora of different types of hardware. The consequent number, nature and varied type of weapon platform gives rise to endless debate about design compromise, tactical organisation, integration and employment, and introduces logistic penalties in terms of support and spares backing. The prime example is the tank, introduced initially to the battlefield in the First World War as a counter to the machine-gun. The latter, protected by ever-improving techniques of entrenchment, was lethal because of its high rate of fire deriving from self-generated automatic action, its accuracy and its highly effective munition. Because the machine-gun was, and remains, predominantly a direct-fire weapon, that is engaging targets which its crew can see, it was deployed invariably on ground which an attacking force would have physically to capture, and so would have to be destroyed or overrun. The first tanks were, in consequence, infantry-support weapons and numerous conduct-of-battle memoirs of the First World War attest to their success in this role.[6] The first-generation tank was an effective compromise, given the conditions of the time, between three of the five components of a rounded fighting capability – firepower, protection and mobility.

Deep analytical study at the time and later, both of the conduct of the battles of World War I and of the potential of the tank, introduced much wider possibilities for its use on the battlefield. The pre-eminent British military intellectuals, Fuller and Liddell Hart, propounded doctrines which a German military thinker of similar calibre, Guderian, developed and which, in his own hands and those of others, gave the German Army by the end of 1941 a mastery of continental Europe from the Atlantic coast to Moscow, at least equivalent to that of Napoleon at the height of his power.

It is not that England[a] ignored the possibilities. The need to restore mobility to the land battle and to improve the protection of troops in the assault was well understood. Two men, Brooke and Wavell, who had established outstanding battlefield reputations in World War I and added to them afterwards, as trainers of troops and speakers and writers on the evolution of warfare, were given the opportunity to examine tactical concepts, tank design, organisation and employment. In 1927 the War Office allowed the establishment of a brigade-sized[b] 'Experimental Mechanised Force', but after two years the trial was discontinued as an economy measure. Wavell, a certainty at the time for future high command, as chief operations staff officer of the controlling division, had much to do with what, by any standard, was a very thorough evaluation. At the conference at Camberley devoted to analysis of the experience, Wavell stated:

> The requirements of mobility, firepower and armour [i.e. 'protection'] must always be to a certain extent conflicting. I suggest very tentatively that the respective value of these three might be assessed in the ratio of 3:2:1[7]

While at the time this may have been an absolutely correct assessment, it would soon be overtaken by progressive development of anti-tank weapons, both crew-served and individual. In 1937 Brooke, as a major general, was appointed to command the British Army's first 'Mobile Division' – mobile in the sense that the organisation embodied a brigade each of tanks and mechanised cavalry, and the artillery had replaced its horses by motor vehicles.

The consequence of British neglect, misconceived economy and disregard of previous experience and pioneering study, was disastrous, and Brooke, as chief of the imperial general staff, and Wavell, as commander-in-chief Middle East would, in 1941, at the nadir of British fortunes in World War II, pick up the bill. Until the advent of American equipment, the British Army fought its campaigns in France in 1940 and in the Western Desert with a mixed tank fleet: an 'infantry' tank, well protected and with adequate hitting power but

---

[a] For national nomenclatures, please refer to Appendix A.

[b] The reader unfamiliar with military organisation is invited to refer to Appendix B.

with mobility little better than that of the foot soldier; and a 'cruiser' tank, highly mobile but inadequate in terms of both gunpower and protection against its German adversary. In addition to the obvious inbuilt tactical disadvantage, the mixed fleet incurred logistic penalties in the form of non-compatible ammunition and spare parts, and additional non-combat manpower to maintain two quite different weapon platforms. The US Sherman, with which the Anglo/US armies fought the battles of 1944/5, at least disposed of the mixed fleet, but was markedly inferior in both firepower and protection to the Panzer Mark IV. Fortunately for the outcome, Allied numerical superiority and massive advantages in air- and artillery-delivered firepower redressed better German application of technology and tactical handling.

There followed the contest for potential battlefield supremacy in conventional armaments between NATO and the Warsaw Pact, which developed after World War II, in itself an integral part of the equation of deterrence fortunately never put to the test. This became a three-tiered competition in terms of numbers and quality of men and equipment, application of technology and battlefield technique. The area of contention embraced not only each of the five basic characteristics of combat capability, but also their optimum interrelationship and the ever-increasing types and numbers of both weapon platforms and support systems needed to produce a rounded and balanced whole.

For centuries, the ground taken up by a given battlefield could be described precisely by the word 'field'. Few battles before Waterloo were fought over an area any larger than a suburban golf course. Similarly, a single day's fighting was usually enough to decide the result of a battle fought in open ground; sieges, however, required longer. The side in possession of the field at the end of the day was demonstrably the winner, and a single battle was often all that was needed to decide the issue of the campaign. The wars of the nineteenth century saw a progressive expansion in the area of ground over which a battle was fought; thus there would be an enormous increase in the numbers engaged, the duration of a given battle tended to lengthen, and fewer battles could be seen as decisive. The reasons derive from philosophy, technology and a heightened perception of the links between policy and war by national leaders.

The Greco-Roman city states of ancient times had in emergency demanded military service from every able-bodied male, and the marauding tribes which swept across Europe at intervals throughout the first millennium AD similarly embodied all their manpower, at least until they came to settle. Nation states up to the time of the French Revolution did not, if only because even in time of war manufacture, agriculture and trade had to be maintained in order to sustain the armies in the field. All required the diversion of potential military manpower. For France in 1793, these needs had no priority compared with the overriding requirement to defend French territory and revolutionary form of government against a coalition of all Europe. In the contemporary ardour and excitement tantamount to that of a new religion to fan the flame, both the government decree and the popular acceptance of the *levée en masse* become readily comprehensible. Throughout the nineteenth century, the rising tides of nationalism and xenophobia, the doctrines of the total nature of warfare put forward by Clausewitz and the absolute primacy of the state over the individual propounded by Hegel produced an intellectual justification for universal liability to military service, which would be enacted, but not necessarily invoked, by every major power, England being the last to do so.

It is, however, one thing to decree national liability for conscription for all fit adult manpower, and even to call to the colours a significant percentage of the total number available, but quite another to equip the troops, transport them to the area where the campaign is to be fought, and maintain them once there. The simple firearms, artillery and munitions of the Napoleonic era needed only a very basic industrial infrastructure, but Napoleonic organisational genius was essential in order to relate manufacture or capture of weapons to the equipment of armies in the field and reinforcing drafts. Deployment to campaign areas would be conducted at foot pace unless a suitable river axis happened to coincide with the line of march, until the advent of the railway; first used to assist mobilisation in 1859 in the war fought in northern Italy between France and Austria. By 1870, however, the railway had become the critical mobilisation asset in the collective brain of every European Ministry of War.

From the date of the first use of gunpowder, the numbers engaged in battle developed a continuous upward trend, as the following table illustrates.

TABLE I

Date	Battle	Numbers Engaged[8]
1346	Crécy	39,000
1415	Agincourt	31,000
1513	Flodden	45,000
1515	Marignano	55,000
1525	Pavia	57,000
1590	Ivry	30,000
1643	Rocroi	50,000
1644	Marston Moor	45,000
1704	Blenheim	108,000
1745	Fontenoy	123,000
1759	Minden	96,000
1805	Austerlitz	156,000
1809	Wagram	312,000
1815	Waterloo	140,000
1859	Solferino	238,000

These battles represent the culmination of effort for the campaign in which they occurred, and were decisive for its result. The numbers brought to battle by either side were broadly similar. Battles of civil wars (Ivry), with neither army reinforced significantly by an external ally, and, by extension, battles fought between England and Scotland (Flodden) vary the trend, as do battles fought at the end of what for the time was a long campaign (Agincourt), or where significant forces were engaged elsewhere (Minden). The latter qualification applies also to Waterloo, which might in late twentieth-century terms be regarded as the right flank of a 'broad front' invasion of France. It is of interest in parenthesis that, in the last battle fought on British soil, Culloden, eleven months after Fontenoy, no more than 15,000 men were engaged and the battlefield is no larger than the Horse Guards Parade in London. The French and German Armies embattled on the Gravelotte–St Privat feature west of Metz, 124 years after Culloden, numbered 300,000.

As numbers grew and the battle area was enlarged, the support arrangements became of necessity more elaborate, and also ever more manpower-intensive. The ability of military commentators to assess accurately the numbers engaged became increasingly difficult as a result. The full number of troops on hand might not be committed to action; reserves might either not be required or might be preserved as a safeguard to meet future emergency, or might not receive their orders in time, or might misunderstand or disobey the orders received. Numbers of 'supporting' as a proportion of 'combat' troops increased as weapons became increasingly complex and artillery ammunition tonnages multiplied. Categorisation of the two became harder to define; no one would deny the right of a member of a brigade headquarters staff, the driver of an ammunition wagon replenishing a gun line, or the fitter recovering a tank when under fire, to consider himself a combat soldier.

Wagram is notable for engaging a larger number of combat soldiers than any previous battle. This, as will be seen from Chapter III, was the result of the concentration of all available forces over the preceding two months by the opposing commanders. As has been noted, Waterloo involved numbers much smaller than Wagram, or the major battles of the campaigns of 1812 and 1813, but the numbers given exclude the French right wing, under Grouchy, who failed to get into the battle, and Blucher's 89,000 Prussians, who did not arrive until the battle was over. There were separate armies of 500,000 Austrian, German and Russian soldiers moving at the same time, somewhat ponderously, towards an invasion of France across the Middle Rhine, to which France could have opposed an army equal in size to the 90,000 men of the Armée du Nord taken by Napoleon into what is now Belgium. For battles from 1914 onwards it is impossible to estimate with any precision at all how many soldiers actually took part. Not only was there the blurred distinction between 'combat' and 'supporting' troops; there is also the fact that never were all of the combat units engaged simultaneously. Suffice to say that by mid-1917 the British Expeditionary Force, under Haig in north-eastern France, had a total ration strength of 1,870,455 all ranks.[9] Haig was responsible for a continuous front of 100 miles, and his soldiers were organised as five separate armies, each of which comprised a number of corps. At any one time up to a dozen corps commanders would be conducting a battle from day to day, in charge of more soldiers than either Marlborough or Wellington ever led in battle.

Nineteenth-century philosophy and technology combined to ensure that nations would bring ever-larger numbers of soldiers to battle. This of itself expanded the land over which battles were fought and in consequence the area over which commanders-in-chief would be required to exercise control. The constantly increasing number of field guns and their progressively improving range and lethality introduced the need for dispersion and a correspondingly progressive enlargement of the battle area. A growing perception of the advantages to be gained by an intelligent use of ground also played its part in expanding the size of the battlefield beyond golf course acreage.

The increased span of command in both numbers and area made necessary continuous development of control, communication and intelligence-gathering capabilities. On the small battlefield the commander's eye could usually assess the whole situation, and orders could often be given by word of mouth. Wellington at Salamanca could judge at first-hand the exact moment at which the attempt of Marmont to outflank him had produced a dangerous weakness at the centre of the French deployment.[10] Commanders of relatively small armies did not, nevertheless, always have available such dominating real-time observation and control, nor did they show themselves always capable of immediate, unequivocal and correct decision making when they did. Seeking the necessary commanding viewpoint was sometimes an invitation to disaster. Lord Raglan's view of the British frontal attack, which decided the Battle of the Alma (1854), was from a knoll behind the enemy front line. The Russians made no effort to capture him and his staff because they could not believe that he had arrived there unsupported.[11] His view at Balaclava was equally commanding and the first cause of a real catastrophe. From an eminence 600 feet above the plain on which the battle was fought, irregularities of ground cease to be apparent, as any hunting man under his command could have advised him. Lord Raglan's subordinate commanders were manoeuvring in mutual ignorance of each other's movements, but the orders from on high assumed that the British divisions and brigades were in full view of each other. The separation of the commander from the battle introduced the need for written orders. Those issued at Balaclava were fatally ambiguous and imprecise;[12] hence the necessity for staff training to inculcate precision of language and to teach standard operating procedures which all subordinate commanders could be trusted to follow. Ten years after Balaclava, the Prussians, who remained neutral in the Crimean War, demonstrated how thoroughly their general staff had learned this lesson.

Exercise of command depends upon the prompt communication of clear orders. In the transmission of government directive to commander in the field, France led the way. A system of semaphore stations allowed the armies of the Revolution operating in the Low Countries to receive instructions from Paris within a quarter of an hour of transmission, and Napoleon expanded the system to link Paris with the Danube valley. This had a limited operational capability on a clear night, but, as will be seen in Chapter III, could not work if visibility was poor and caused potentially disastrous confusion if important messages were delayed. Orders in the field from commander to subordinate formations, and reports upwards, if they could not be given by word of mouth, were conveyed by a body of gallopers who formed the majority of the personal staff of the commander. These men needed to be of unbreakable courage, iron determination, extreme fitness, outstanding horsemanship and possess a developed eye for ground. As the size of the battlefield enlarged they were given power, at first tacit but soon codified by both Napoleon and Wellington, to speak for their commanders. This prerogative became increasingly necessary as geographic distance between commander and subordinates lengthened. The time lapse between the formulation of an order and its delivery might well outdate or render it irrelevant in changed circumstances. By 1914 a lieutenant colonel from Imperial German Supreme Headquarters, located in Coblenz, would, in the name of the chief of staff, give orders to army commanders which altered fundamentally their execution of the prepared plan designed to ensure the defeat of France before the completion of Russian mobilisation could threaten the eastern frontiers of the Central Powers. This mechanism of command pushed beyond any acceptable limit the use of the 'galloper'. It was, nevertheless, forced on the kaiser's armies because, in an advance on a 200 mile front and with the headquarters of the right wing army 250 miles distant from its superior headquarters, virtually all other contact had been lost.

Communications within the unit could remain simple as long as men remained within sight and hearing of their commanders. The colours, familiar to all ranks because of the daily 'trooping' held for precisely this reason, provided the rallying point essential after a disjointed hand-to-hand struggle, and infantry drum and cavalry trumpet reinforced orders given by voice or gesture. Senior commanders were known by sight throughout their commands. In terms of numbers engaged, over 250,000 men, Borodino was a larger battle than any fought previously except for Wagram, three years earlier. The numbers and the 'slogging match' nature of the tactics provided a foretaste of most of the battles to be fought in the coming century. The advance to contact of the French right wing corps, commanded by Davout, was thrown into confusion by difficult ground, the efficiency of the Russian skirmish line and a rumour that the corps commander had been killed; he had in fact been unhorsed and slightly wounded by a shell burst.[13] The corps was only steadied by the reappearance half an hour later of the marshal, who had not won two 'battlefield'[14] titles in the imperial nobility for nothing. The expanding battle area would continue to demand similar high courage from commanders, but their exercise of command, if it were to be successful, would need ever more elaborate control and communication mechanisms. Similarly, intelligence gathering and evaluation had to develop beyond what the commander either could see for himself or deduce from reports, the latter often imprecise in time of origin and transmission, never on a common time base and provided by observers of varying quality and trustworthiness. Nations and armies neglecting these developments, and commanders who failed to appreciate the time lapse between observation and report, did so at their peril, as battle areas, length of time in contact and numbers available all continued to increase.

In the hand-to-hand combat of the pikeman, the only important attribute of ground was a good foothold. Formed bodies of horsemen could engage each other or take the enemy infantry in flank as efficiently as the going would allow, and the stand-off weapon operated with greater security if used to the optimum limit of its range, which invariably required it to be deployed on dominating ground. Defence in the field had always derived some advantage by being conducted from a ridge or hilltop, which ruse might persuade the defenders to leave, as at Hastings. Attacks might fail because conditions of ground or weather had caused them to be launched on too narrow a front, as at Poitiers. Wellington sought to minimise the effect of French firepower and to improve the battlefield security of his own troops by taking up reverse slope positions wherever possible.[c] The parallel increases in battle area, numbers engaged and time in contact, compounded by the massive and progressive enhancement of firepower as the century proceeded, forced increasing importance to be given to the tactical use of ground. This in turn caused the development of the symbiotic relationship between target acquisition, firepower, movement and the optimum use of ground which is the basis of present-day battlefield tactics.

The student of military history comes early to realise that some comparatively small parts of the surface of the earth are fought over in almost every century.[15] The Low Countries, the Rhineland, the Danube valley, the Austrian Quadrilateral in northern Italy and the Marchfeldt north of Vienna are recurring examples of battlefield venues. The reason these particular stretches of ground attracted so often the clash of arms is because the territory was either important in its own right, as a generator of wealth or influence for whichever nation held it, or provided an essential buffer for a province of strategic or economic importance. The acknowledged importance of ground

---

[c] The reader is referred to the military glossary at Appendix B.

nevertheless produced differing perceptions of the purpose of battle between commanders of armies in the field on the one hand and, on the other, those responsible for the direction of national policy. While battle once joined was, as it remains, by definition a test to destruction, national leadership, if not in command of the army in the field, tended to view the matter from an altogether different standpoint. Battle and war need not necessarily be designed to bring about the destruction of the enemy's fighting capacity; such an extreme aim might, in any event, be unattainable because of the opposition's much greater resources of manpower or ground. The real aim of most pre-Napoleonic wars was the acquisition or retention of territory. This difference of perception and the logistic impossibility of sustaining for any prolonged length of time the armies in the field, or of reconstituting them quickly after a major battle, caused a 'unitary' design of battle comparable to the structure of classical Greek drama – fought in a single day, confined to a small area and decisive for the immediate point at issue. It follows that most battles were 'set piece' in that they were fought on ground chosen by one side, usually that on the tactical defensive. The siege, which of course lasted longer than a single day because of the defensive and logistic assets accumulated by the besieged, is the most basic example of the set-piece battle, but the majority of battles in open field fought up to the end of the eighteenth century were conducted on the same basic principle. One side stood on the defensive, on ground of its own choice, which the other side had to capture because it could not risk bypassing or masking the defenders.

While by no means the first individual to combine the functions of head of state, head of government and de facto commander-in-chief in the field, nor the first to seek the destruction of the enemy army in every battle engaged, Napoleon's control of these triple functions was unparalleled in previous history in its effectiveness, and introduced a new perception of the aim of warfare. Napoleon appreciated to a greater degree than any before him the fact that the destruction of the enemy's fighting capability brought in its train the 'territorial' objective of former wars. Napoleon would always seek to bring the enemy army to battle and, once this had been achieved, to destroy it. All manoeuvres were directed to this end, and great successes were achieved, not necessarily by frontal attack on ground of the enemy's own choice – the classic set piece in the field – but by flanking manoeuvres leading to the destruction of the enemy by encirclement. Napoleon was not the first to seek advantage from attacking in flank rather than frontally – the *manoeuvres sur les derrières* so comprehensively analysed by Chandler. The classic optimum solution of encirclement had been applied at Cannae two millennia before. Napoleon would use any combination of manoeuvres to achieve his invariable aim – the destruction of the enemy's army. The stereotyped tactics of generals and armies still thinking on eighteenth-century lines stood little chance against the Napoleonic combination of unchanging aim and flexible method.

Larger opposing armies spread out over more territory increased the confusion inherent in warfare – the fog of war – and produced, as the nineteenth century developed, a type of engagement in the field other than the set piece. 'Encounter' battles became increasingly frequent. These were battles fought on ground chosen initially by neither side. They started at a point where elements of the opposing armies, usually reconnaissance or screening forces, made contact. If neither commander was prepared to refuse action, the main bodies would be drawn in and a full-scale battle would ensue. The result of the encounter battle would be judged in exactly the same way as that of the set piece: the side retaining possession of the ground taken up during the battle would be the recognised winner, either because the opposition had been too weakened by losses to make another attempt to drive them off, or because of their need to avoid unacceptable further loss in order to retain an army in being. Mahan's doctrine of the retained threat of the fleet in being, however small, came to have equal relevance to land warfare as the time-span of conflict lengthened. Battles begun as encounter might develop into set piece. The First Battle of Ypres, in autumn 1914, started as a typical encounter battle, each side seeking to turn the flank of the other, neither desiring battle on the ground where the clash occurred. The outflanking manoeuvres having failed, the battles fought over the same ground later in the war, in 1915 and 1917, were set pieces. The trench lines which, by the first winter of the war, stretched from the Channel to the Swiss frontier caused every Western Front battle after First Ypres to be fought as a set piece, in which both sides utilised many of the tactics and techniques of siege warfare.

First World War battlefields were larger, but not significantly so, than those of the decade between 1860 and 1870. On a fine day, such as seldom occurred during the four months of the Third Battle of Ypres, there is a clear view from Tynecot Military Cemetery on Passchendaele Ridge back over the six miles of muddy farmland to the city of Ypres, in the valley of the Yser. The three battles fought over this relatively small stretch of ground cost the two sides engaged over a million casualties in killed, wounded and missing. Similarly, the holiday or business motorist of the late twentieth century bypasses, in half an hour's drive on the nearby Euroroutes, the battlefields of the Somme and Verdun, fought respectively for four and eight months in 1916, with casualties proportionately as high as those of Ypres.

It was the Second World War, initially in the North African desert and in Russia, which produced an expansion of the direct area of battle to the point at which the size of the battlefield became almost irrelevant. The vital necessity became concentration in both time and space at the enemy's most vulnerable point. Instead of the concentration at the critical point in space normally sufficient to decide battles before the Napoleonic era, the nature of battles from Marengo onwards introduced the parallel need for concentration in time. Activity levels on the battlefield changed as a result: whereas in old-fashioned battles concluded in a single day virtually every fighting man on both sides would be directly involved, in the modern land battle a significant proportion of the combat strength of both armies spends little time in direct contact with the enemy, and a great deal more in conditions of boredom and physical discomfort, but not necessarily undue danger, waiting for something to happen.

The application of the principle of concentration in time reached its ultimate state in the Gulf War of 1991. While the size of the land battle area of Operation Desert Storm, fought over four days only, is comparable to that of the Battle of Normandy, the area of strategic interest to the Allied command embraced the whole of the Middle East, from the Mediterranean to Iran, land forces were mobilised from the United States and Northern Europe, and air strikes both before and during the land battle were mounted from bases as far apart as Fairford in England and Diego Garcia in the Indian Ocean, five time zones apart. These required the most precise coordination of timing over target in the battle area. Victory in a battle fought in an area relatively small by late twentieth-century standards depended upon acquisition and communication of information and orders, of necessity both instantaneous and global.

Change in any field of human endeavour is more often the result of evolution than revolution. Although the demands of war have generated change more frequently than most other first causes, it could be argued that there was no revolutionary change in the technology of land warfare between the first use of gunpowder and that of nuclear power. The areas in which warfare adopted revolutionary inventions for its own use were many and varied throughout the six-century span between Crécy and Hiroshima, but neither the adoption of new technologies nor the evolution of those already in use proceeded at an even pace. The soldier of Marlborough's army, fighting in the Low Countries in the first decade of the eighteenth century, would have found little to surprise him in Wellington's regiments at Waterloo a century later. Tactics, organisation, equipment and weaponry had altered little. The battles fought between 1860 and 1870 showed, by contrast, an enormous increase in the lethality of firepower. Since battlefield tactics had failed to take account of this major enhancement, the price was paid in much bigger casualty lists.

A century after Waterloo, British, French and German Armies were engaged again on the same ground, but the change in the nature of the land battle which had taken place in the ninety-nine years between Waterloo and Mons had been dramatic and far greater than in any previous comparable time-span. Some touchingly archaic customs, such as the German bugles sounding the 'Cease Fire' on the first evening of the battle of Mons,[16] had survived until the start of the First World War but did not long remain thereafter. However, despite the changes in both custom and technology, the essential nature of battle at point of contact – the one-against-one fight to the death – did not change.

This fundamental alteration in the conduct of land warfare had occurred in spite of the fact that for most of the century between the Congress of Vienna and the outbreak of the First World War, the European Great Powers had remained at peace with each other. The arrangements made after the downfall of Napoleon established a peace among the nations of Europe which endured for forty years and was broken, more as a result of aberration than intent, by the Crimean War. Long periods of peace are never conducive to military reform, and seldom to improvement of combat capability. Even Prussia, dependent to a greater extent than any other European power on a standing army for her security because of her lack of natural frontiers, neglected her army. In the progress towards German unification since the first stirrings against Napoleonic hegemony, Prussia had suffered frequent humiliation. The combination which came together in 1862, of William I, a simple and straightforward soldier who had fought in the campaign of 1814, Bismarck, who viewed war as an instrument of national policy rather than as a moral crusade, Roon, an organising war minister of genius, and Moltke, disciple of Clausewitz and perhaps the pre-eminent strategic planner of all time, matched philosophy, a national sense of power, purpose and priorities to available resources and ends. By the second half of the nineteenth century the lands associated in the German customs union were already overtaking Victorian England in the application of technology, a pre-eminence which would only be surrendered to the massive quantitative resources of the United States over half a century later.

Applied technology produced almost simultaneously the railway, the electric telegraph and steel. The latter, as a substitute for bronze in gun construction, combined with rifling of barrels, breech-loading and an integrated mechanical recoil system to give greater range, rate of fire and accuracy to artillery. Concurrently, ammunition developments improved vastly its lethality. The infantryman received not only the first automatic crew-served weapons, but also the breech-loaded magazine rifle, which improved both his hitting power and his protection, because he could load his weapon either lying prone or in a trench in a way physically impossible with the muzzle-loaded musket. Concealment further improved the prospects for surprise. In consequence, the wars caused by the fundamental divergences of view within the United States and the latent conflicts of interest of the European Great Powers were fought on an unprecedented level of intensity. The boiling-over of technological improvement coincided with the acceptance of war as a legitimate instrument of national policy, without the concurrent realisation of the increasingly destructive nature of warfare.

Thus the years between 1860 and 1870 were critical, and the wars fought in this decade catalytic in the development of modern warfare. There was no thunderclap transformation: the honing of principle, practice and contemporary doctrine had begun to evolve long before, and many lessons which should have been learned from the experiences of these catalytic wars were later ignored or misapplied, to be relearned at enormous cost. The American Civil War, the Six Weeks War between Austria and Prussia in 1866 and the opening weeks of the Franco-Prussian War transformed the conduct of land warfare, provided both crucible and ingredients for the melting pot of the twentieth century, and continue to furnish fundamental lessons for the present day. But the starting point, combining the formation of the first modern army and the dawn of twentieth-century conduct of land warfare, lies in the first fifteen years of the nineteenth century, with Napoleon.

Notes

[1] Keegan, *Six Armies in Normandy*, London, Pimlico Press, 1982, in particular pp.327–30.

[2] Horne and Montgomery, *The Lonely Leader: Monty 1944–45*, London, Macmillan, 1994, p.158.

[3] Elting, *Swords Around a Throne*, London, Weidenfeld and Nicholson, Chapter XXIV.

[4] Keegan, *A History of Warfare*, London, Hutchinson, 1993, p.301.

[5] Macdonnell, *Napoleon and His Marshals*, London, Macmillan, 1934, p.335.

[6] See for example Duff Cooper, *Old Men Forget*, London, Hart-Davis, 1995, Chapter Five.

[7] Connell, *Wavell: Scholar and Soldier*, London, Collins, 1964, p.157.

[8] These figures are taken from *A Traveller's Guide to the Battlefields of Europe*, Chandler [ed.], two vols, London, Hugh Evelyn, 1965.

[9] Terraine, *Haig: The Educated Soldier*, London, Cooper, 1990, p.324.

[10] Longford, *Wellington, The Years of the Sword*, London, Weidenfeld and Nicholson, 1969, p.285.

[11] Woodham-Smith, *The Reason Why*, London, Constable, 1953, Chapters X and XI.

[12] Woodham-Smith, op.cit., p.239 and pp.264–5.

[13] Macdonnell, op.cit., Chapter XV.

[14] Napoleon I created twenty-six 'Marshals of the Empire'; eighteen in 1804 and a further eight between 1807 and 1815. Nineteen of these received further distinction as princes of the empire or dukes. Ruling principalities were conferred on the two imperial relations by marriage, Murat and Bernadotte, and the senior marshal and chief of staff of the *Grande Armée*, Berthier. Of the remaining sixteen, nine received 'province' titles, in 1807 and later, from territories, mostly in Italy, newly incorporated into the French Empire. The other seven drew their titles from battles in which they had achieved pre-eminent distinction. For an eminently readable account of who got what (and why) see Macdonnell, op.cit., Chapter X, and for more scholarly biographies of the twenty-six, see the similarly entitled *Napoleon's Marshals*, Chandler, [ed.], London, Macmillan, 1987. For the distinction between 'province' and 'battlefield' titles one cannot improve on Macdonnell:

> The marshals who received the battlefield titles were delighted because, henceforward, wherever they went or were spoken about their great feat of arms would be remembered. The marshals who got the province titles were furious because all the world would infer that they had no feats of arms worth remembering.

Three of the battlefield-titled marshals, Massena, Duke of Rivoli, Davout, Duke of Auerstadt and Ney, Duke of Elchingen, were later created princes in honour of subsequent victories, respectively of Essling, Eckmuhl and The Moskowa (the latter the name given by Napoleon to Borodino), and Berthier was created Prince of Wagram. Throughout this book all First and Second Empire-created nobility are referred to by their family names, for clarity.

[15] For an in-depth analysis of which parts of the earth's surface have been fought over most frequently, see Keegan's *History of Warfare*, 'Interlude 1 – Limitations on Warmaking'. The prize for the world's most fought-over piece of ground goes to the otherwise historically unremarkable town of Adrianople, now Edirne, in European Turkey. Keegan identifies fifteen battles or sieges on this site between AD 323 and 1913.

[16] Chandler, *The Campaigns of Napoleon*, Part Three, Chapter 15, 'Strategic Concepts', and Annex B, 'Examples of Napoleon's *Manoeuvres sur les Derrières*', London, Weidenfeld and Nicholson, 1966.

[17] Barnett, *The Swordbearers*, London, Eyre and Spottiswoode, 1963, p.64.

Chapter II
The First Modern Army: Napoleon's *Grande Armée*

The Army of the Coasts of the Ocean, formed by Napoleon in May 1803 for the invasion of England, became the finest instrument of land warfare the world had seen up to that time. The combination of battle experience, training, organisation and capacity for sustained operations was more complete, and the Army Group[a] (as it would now be termed) much larger than any comparable predecessor. It was also the first genuinely national army of modern times. The armies of the *ancien régime* had contained no permanent grouping larger than a regiment, and the regiments were in almost all respects the private property of their colonels, who were, in the main, court favourites with varying taste and aptitude for the more practical aspects of soldiering. The armies of the republic and the Directory, at war almost constantly from 1792 onwards in the Low Countries, both sides of the Rhine and in Italy, and General Bonaparte's Army of Egypt, had reflected the personalities and ambitions of their commanders. Not even the dreaded députés en mission or the cross-posting of senior officers among theatres of war had eradicated mutual jealousies or produced common organisations, concepts of operation or tactical doctrine.

The uneasy peace arrived at in 1802, producing an eighteen month interlude in the twenty-two years of war not to be ended until Waterloo, imposed a settlement in Europe which was very much to the advantage of France. Her natural frontiers, the Rhine, the Alps and the Pyrenees, were buttressed by satellite republics in the Netherlands and north-west Italy, and a neutral Switzerland. This gave France a wider and more cohesive area of sovereignty than anything achieved previously, even by Louis XIV, and caused an imbalance of power on the Continent which England, ever since the reign of Elizabeth I, had preferred to fight rather than to tolerate. The peace was also

---

[a] See Appendix B.

militarily to the advantage of France in that it returned to her the army left stranded in Egypt by Nelson's victory at Aboukir Bay and subsequent domination of the Mediterranean, and also the prisoners of war of the later campaigns in Italy and Germany. While some of the latter were no doubt broken by their experience and therefore unfit for further active service, those who had survived in physically and mentally fit condition would have become hardened to withstand almost anything. The Army of Egypt, the garrison of Genoa, which surrendered in July 1800 after a most determined defence by Massena, and the veterans of the victories of Marengo and Hohenlinden were the seed corn for the rich harvest of outstanding leaders and elite troops which formed, in due course, the core of the *Grande Armée*.

Napoleon's obsession with the invasion of England gave the new army time to perfect its organisation and training. Two years were spent waiting, in vain, for the French fleet to secure mastery of the Channel for long enough to allow the invasion force to cross, though even had this mastery been gained, a successful invasion was not a foregone conclusion. The reason is that Napoleon, by no means unique in supreme commanders before and after him, did not appreciate the particular difficulties inherent in an opposed assault landing from the sea. Of all the operations of war, this is, with the exception of a seaborne evacuation when in contact, the most difficult. The attacking force must be landed in condition to fight at once, which requires 'tactical' as opposed to 'logistic' loading of shipping,[1] and thus a greater number and variety of vessels. There is a mutual incompatibility in the design characteristics of the ships needed. While on the one hand they must be weatherly enough to withstand storm, wind and sea, if the soldiers are to be fit to fight immediately on landing, they must equally be of shallow enough draught to land the invading force dryshod. The coordination of the fire support which must be provided for troops ashore by the guns of the fleet until their own artillery is disembarked and in action with adequate ammunition stocks is a further problem, requiring highly specialised and practised procedures to resolve. Napoleon had no answer to difficulties which would not satisfactorily be overcome until the United States' operations against Japan in the Pacific theatre in the Second World War, from which derived the amphibious equipment and particular skills essential for the successful invasion of Normandy in 1944. Although Napoleon's army practised embarkation drills and, on one occasion, a full imperial review of the landing craft, undertaken against maritime advice because of a gathering storm, at a cost of 200 soldiers being drowned,[2] far more time was spent in practising the disciplines and techniques of the land battle.

The Army of the Coasts of the Ocean was deployed from Hanover, which France had occupied at once on the resumption of hostilities, to Brest, in nine operational combat groupings:[3]

TABLE II

Formation	Strength	Commander	Concentration Area
I Corps	17,000	Bernadotte	Hanover
II Corps	20,000	Marmont	Utrecht
III Corps	26,000	Davout	Bruges
IV Corps	40,000	Soult	Boulogne
V Corps	18,000	Lannes	Boulogne
VI Corps	24,000	Ney	Montreuil
VII Corps	14,000	Augereau	Brest
Imperial Guard	7,000	Bessières	Boulogne
Reserve Cavalry	22,000	Murat	Pas de Calais

A separate army of 50,000 was established under Massena in the satellite Ligurian Republic, formerly Piedmontese and Austrian territory.

The permanent corps organisation was a major step forward. Span of command is determined by the capacity and methods available to the commander to issue timely and effective orders, and is defined by the area over which he can influence the battle, by a combination of occupation of ground and domination by the firepower of the troops and weapons at his disposal. Permanent formations intended to be capable of fighting unsupported until reinforcements could arrive had existed many centuries earlier. The obvious example is the Roman legion, comprising 6,000 men when at full strength and including a small cavalry component for reconnaissance. Larger combat groupings than Napoleon's *corps d'armée*, subordinate to the command of a higher headquarters in the field, had been established in previous wars for the duration of a single battle, and even occasionally for part of a campaign. By the eighteenth century the operational grouping of regiments, which were the basic unit common to all armies, into larger battlefield formations had come to be accepted as essential if command in battle was to be exercised effectively. These formations were not intended to be permanent. In peacetime, such supervision of training of regiments as was undertaken was carried out by the inspector general of the appropriate combat arm.[4] The staff organisation essential both for preparation and transmission of orders relating to current operations and for planning ahead was minimal, and training for it virtually non-existent. Cavalry and artillery units were not integrated. The brigades and divisions into which the permanent regiments were grouped when action was likely were neither intended nor organised to fight unsupported.

Napoleon's *corps d'armée* were designed to have precisely these characteristics. Although strength was varied according to combat mission, the corps were permanent groupings of all arms, in a basic organisation of two (sometimes three) infantry divisions, one of cavalry, and integral artillery. The ability to regroup divisions between corps assisted tactical flexibility and the varying organisation of the corps provided good security cover. The capacity of a corps for independent operation short of battle was limited only by the competence of the commander to function within the resources he had been allocated to carry out the strategic directives of the emperor, even when at a riding distance of days from imperial headquarters. Each corps was intended to be capable of fighting an independent battle against an enemy of at least equal size for up to twenty-four hours, during which time a mutually supporting formation could, if necessary, be moved up in support. The relationship between composition and combat mission presaged later practice, and there is a taste of the future also in the diverse tasking of the component corps of the Army of the Coasts of the Ocean. While all were planning and preparing for the specific operation to invade England, they were at the same time training to fight a land battle in any condition of warfare. At the same time some of the corps undertook necessary internal security operations. Bernadotte was occupying conquered territory and maintaining an active watch on Prussia, Augereau provided a visible military presence and support to civil government in a part of France notoriously prone to revolt, and Davout had to seek out and destroy enemy intelligence-gathering networks.

The combination of ability and potential among the carefully chosen senior commanders also has a modern style. Massena, in independent command of the Army of Italy, had an established reputation as one of the foremost soldiers of Europe, in particular because of his victory at Zurich in 1799 and his defence of Genoa a year later. Murat's exploits as a cavalry leader had earned him similar fame. Of the corps commanders, Soult had at the time probably the highest prestige by reason of previous achievement, Lannes, Ney and Augereau had formidable records as commanders of subordinate formations on the battlefield, and Bernadotte combined this with successful administrative achievement as minister of war under the Directory. Davout and Marmont, still in their early thirties, had their reputations yet to make in high command, but had already displayed much potential. Marmont, the only principal subordinate commander not to be included in the first promotion list of marshals,[b] and thus appointed ahead of several of his seniors, had turned the Battle of Marengo at a critical moment by mounting what would, in modern parlance, be termed an all-arms battle-group counter-attack. Davout, within thirteen months of the opening of the coming campaign in Central Europe, founded at Auerstadt a renown which, by 1815, eclipsed that of any other marshal, with the possible exception of Massena. Two things were common to all the senior formation commanders of the Army of the Coasts of the Ocean. All were 'hungry boxers' – war weariness was years away in the future – and all were outstanding trainers and motivators of troops. Future high commanders would need a similar blend of combat record, well-directed energy and ability to train and administer large numbers of soldiers.

It is nearly 450 miles from Boulogne to Hanover; in those days a week's hard riding for the experienced horseman and up to twelve days by coach, provided that relays of fresh horses were in place. Brest is almost as far in the opposite direction. Berthier, combining until 1807 the functions of minister of war and chief of staff of the army,[5] produced a control mechanism in which the foundation of the staff organisation of the modern army is readily discernible. The army of Louis XVI had in 1783 formed a *'Corps d'État Major'*, which formulated rudimentary standing operational and organisational procedures, but all this disappeared in the class-war fervour of the Revolution. Nevertheless, Berthier, who had reached the rank of one-star general in the royal army, and was a prominent founder-member of the embryonic staff corps, applied the valuable experience which he had gained. Initially devising simple staff procedures when chief of staff to General Bonaparte's Army of Italy in 1796, he subsequently expanded these to provide the nervous system through which the emperor could exercise command of over a million men under arms and more than 150,000 on a single battlefield. The basic five-pronged staff organisation common to all modern armies – Operations, Intelligence, Manpower, Support and Civil Affairs – both at policy level in the government Ministry of Defence and in operational headquarters in the field, can be seen clearly to exist in Napoleonic army organisation.[6] Great emphasis was placed on the accurate preparation and prompt transmission of orders. The business of a military staff is to translate the wishes of the commander into complete, accurate, unambiguous and timely orders to subordinate units,

[b] See Note 14 to Chapter I.

and in their planning to ensure a proper relationship between resources allocated and results to be attained. The chief of staff must run an organisation capable of this achievement. Berthier was a grand master of the necessary skills. The permanent formation structure of the armies of the First Empire and the efficiency of their staff organisation produced an enormous dividend on the battlefield. This advantage was particularly apparent compared with the armies of the Habsburg Empire, who, even as late as 1809, were still handicapped by the need to prepare orders at army headquarters for each individual regiment. This was the case because the intervening levels of command were established only for the campaign and there was no body of staff officers competent and trained to provide the necessary spread of expertise at subordinate formation headquarters. And Austrian staff work, compared with that of the Russian Army, was a paragon of efficiency.

Modern battle procedure is apparent also in both the organisation and operation of Berthier's Grand Quartier Général. The already widening complexity of the technology of warfare brought with it the need for specialist advisers and staff cells, such as artillery, engineer, topographical, supply and remount, whose advice commanders and officers of the general staff disregarded at their peril. In turn, the increasing size of the headquarters introduced the requirement to hive off a small tactical element, comprising the commander, essential staff officers and communications, from which to exercise detailed control once battle was joined. Any staff officer of any army of the late twentieth century would recognise at once the clear line of authority within the Grand Quartier Général to the chief of staff, the cellular organisation and the relevance of the routine procedures instituted by Berthier.

The present-day staff officer, if translocated backwards two centuries, would have to appreciate a time lapse in the transmission of orders and reports which the real-time communication facilities, now commonplace in all modern armies, have rendered obsolete. Nevertheless, 'instant' communication has not abolished the risk of the tendency, as present now as in Napoleonic times, for higher headquarters to assume, particularly when under pressure, that an order has been carried out as soon as it has been given. At the start of the nineteenth century, orders in the field which could not be given by word of mouth or sound of drum, bugle or trumpet had to be borne by horseman.[7] Even those who were brave, lucky and competent needed travel time to their destination which might well render the order irrelevant. Worse, their luck might run out, and those without the necessary abilities might not arrive at all. Berthier laid down practices designed to minimise the risk of orders going astray which, although no more than routine common sense in present-day terms, were innovative in their time. Important orders were sent by more than one courier, instructed to take different routes, duplicates were kept and all orders time-dated, referenced and receipted by the subordinate headquarters. The meticulous chief of staff insisted on the same procedures for reports sent up the chain of command. In the age before instant communication, much depended on the skill of the aide bearing the message. Having completed his journey, probably under fire and at some risk, he might then have to adapt the order to changed circumstances, possibly have to interpret or amplify it, and then bear back an up-to-date report of the situation to his commander. At the top level the imperial aides-de-camp were men fully proved in action, who were often given command of ad hoc groupings formed on the battlefield to meet the exigencies of a particular situation, similar to the modern 'task force'. Junior officers entrusted with orders would ideally be of the calibre of the liaison officers and used in the same way as those of Montgomery, when army and army group commander, and in reporting back had the same function. The emperor himself encapsulated their operating instructions:[8] an aide-de-camp or *'officier d'ordonnance'*:

> must set down nothing by hearsay. He must see everything with
> his own eyes, report nothing but what he has seen; and, when he
> is obliged to report something which he has not seen, say that he
> has not seen it.

The multiple layers of command which developed between commander-in-chief and front line did so because the improvements in both firepower and communication enabled commanders to influence a battle with proportionately fewer soldiers for a given area of ground; one might realistically compare the area dominated by the organic firepower of a modern platoon with what could be covered by the weapons of a Napoleonic division. The disadvantage inherent in the separation of the commander from sight of the battlefield is that reports upwards always have a tendency to lose both precision and accuracy, particularly in the hands of an intervening headquarters who, of necessity, will collate, edit and summarise. The many functions and wide area of responsibility of today's senior commander prevent him from going to see for himself as often as he would wish, and the one-to-one report of a trusted intelligence with a trained pair of eyes is the best substitute. Unfortunately, and inevitably, the Napoleonic armies and those after them saw too many jobs on the headquarters staff going to sons, nephews and well-connected others, who might not necessarily be of the requisite standard of competence.[9] This notwithstanding, the integrated staff and communication system of the *Grande Armée* was the best which could be devised within contemporary human and technological resources available. So long as Berthier was there to run it, it served Napoleon well, set a pattern which has been followed to the present day and established standards not always subsequently achieved.

The Napoleonic army was the first to recruit by mass conscription, in the sense that a very high proportion of adult males eligible for military service were in fact called to the colours and served beyond the frontiers of France.[10] Although the *levée en masse* had in theory made every Frenchman liable for military service, and men had flocked enthusiastically to enlist, there had been no coherent procedure to register all those eligible, or to select and embody those needed. The disparity between numbers available and the battle strengths of the armies of France from 1792 to 1800 is an indication of the hit or miss nature of the system.[11] Berthier, in his capacity as minister of war after Marengo, devised a method remarkably similar to that used in the United States from the start of registration of manpower for the Second World War until the nation returned to all-volunteer armed forces in the aftermath of Vietnam. More soldiers were needed than could be obtained by voluntary enlistment; basic social justice required that all adult males of a given age should have a liability to serve; but the armies did not need all those who were both eligible and of acceptable physical and mental standard. Everything possible was done to encourage voluntary enlistment, re-enlistment and prolongation of service. The numbers were made up by conscription, with the process of selection made the joint responsibility of the départements and communes into which France had been subdivided by Napoleon's civil reforms, and the regimental depots created by his reorganisation of the whole military administration. The regimental depots, usually established in or near main centres of population, were a further foretaste of the future in that they provided a recruiting, conscript training and administrative base for the battalions of the regiment on active service, and a peacetime station for those not, for the time being, needed elsewhere. The Cardwell reorganisation of the British Army seventy years later would adopt much the same pattern.

The actual recruitment process was surprisingly modern in character. Each year, what would now be termed the manpower planning branch of the ministry of war, determined how many recruits would be required to reach the armies in the field a year ahead, and allotted a quota to every department/regimental catchment area. The civil administration would see to it that every adult male was registered, initially to enter the service at the age of twenty, but this limit was reduced in the later years of the empire as casualty lists lengthened and ever more soldiers were needed for service anywhere between Spain and Russia. The system thus required modern bureaucratic skills and literate and honest officials. On a specified day, and in every commune, numbers would be matched by lot to names; men drawing low numbers being taken first for enlistment. Naturally there were exemptions, such as married men, those studying for the priesthood and only sons of widows, but, because there would continue to be more in each annual class than were in fact called for by the quota, it remained possible, even up to 1814, for a young man of rich family, who had drawn a '*mauvais numero*', to purchase a substitute. As the numbers required increased and annual classes anticipated, prices of substitutes rose and the supply of voluntary recruits dried up. Nevertheless, the call-up was by no means all-embracing, notwithstanding the anticipation of future classes and the comb out of those of previous years which occurred from 1807 onwards. It has been calculated that, out of 2,646,947 Frenchmen assessed as eligible for conscription between 1800 and 1815, only about half were in fact called up for active duty.[12] The proportion is, nevertheless, high enough for the army of Napoleon to be adjudged the first national conscript army, founded upon a modern recruitment process which required relatively advanced civil/military bureaucratic techniques.

The conscript underwent an induction process which will be familiar to anyone enlisted into the armies of the developed nation states of the twentieth century.[13] He was attested, kitted out, given the necessary minimum of basic training and then in normal circumstances dispatched as a member of a reinforcement draft to his regiment. In many ways he will have found the transition from civilian to soldier easier than the present-day recruit joining the all-volunteer armies of the Western world. Particularly if he was country-bred, he was better and far more quickly suited for the life of a combat soldier. He was physically fitter, more inured to hardship and far better equipped to scrounge or forage a subsistence-level living for himself off the land. For most, the military life improved their previous hard and hand-to-mouth existence. In the army, the soldier had a regular issue of rations most of the time in most theatres: he was given a serviceable and durable uniform; the prospects for immediate recognition of worth and advancement were good; and always before him was the fact that more than half of the marshals of the empire had started army life as private soldiers, either in the royal army or as volunteers between 1789 and 1792. The army gave a man much wider horizons than the confines of his home district, and, in addition to the uplift gained from the *ésprit de corps* of his own regiment, he knew he was serving under the greatest soldier in the world. The letters quoted by Claude Manceron in his vivid study of the Austerlitz campaign[14] contain no more than the average mixture of homesickness and grumbling common in any similar correspondence. Arrangements for mail were quite modern and seem to have been remarkably efficient, except for the armies in Spain and Russia.

The infantry regiments, by 1813 numbered consecutively up to 134,[15] owed their structure more to the quasi-territorially oriented regiments of the royal army than to the chaos of the early years of the new republic. The basic organisation of the infantry regiment reached 'steady state' in 1808 and was not in principle altered thereafter. Regiments had what was intended to be a standard organisation of four combat battalions, desirably all serving together in the same formation of the field army, and a depot battalion. A combat battalion had six companies, each of 140 men when at full strength; in passing, it is remarkable how the basic military subunit, and the lowest level of battlefield command at which previous military experience is essential, has, from the time of the 'century' of the Roman legion to the present-day infantry company, had an established strength of between 100 and 150 men. Two of the companies in each combat battalion were intended to be elite troops. The tallest and fittest men, who had to have a minimum of two years' good service, formed the first, or grenadier company, and the shortest and lightest the '*voltigeur*', literally 'vaulter' company, intended to be capable of mounting behind cavalrymen. As such, the voltigeurs could flesh out a covering force or flank guard consisting mainly of cavalry, similar to the modern practice of providing armoured carrier-borne infantry to support light tanks. The soldiers of the elite companies were rewarded by higher pay and distinctions of uniform.

Successful competition in relevant skills at individual and group level, combined with prompt and obvious reward, is an essential ingredient of high military morale. Selection for the Imperial Guard was, not excepting promotion, the acme of achievement at all levels. The genesis of the Imperial Guard was the consular guard, no more than 2,000 strong at Marengo, where it fought as an elite but somewhat hairy of heel battle group. Its veterans were not, therefore, the natural showpiece household troops which Napoleon wanted as a manifestation of imperial dignity, but a succession of what would nowadays be termed good regimental officers in command, encouraged by the occasional snap inspection by the emperor in person, soon produced the required standard.[16] By 1804, a candidate for the Imperial Guard had to have a minimum of five years exemplary service and two campaigns, and his nomination required the personal approval of Napoleon. This presupposes a system of unit documentation for every individual soldier, differing in a modern army only by computerisation of records. The basis of selection for what became known as the Old Guard remained much the same throughout the duration of the First Empire, but the 2,000 strong battle group at Marengo had become, in the Army of the Coasts of the Ocean, as we have seen, a 7,000 strong composite division; by 1812 the Guard in the *Grande Armée* formed for the campaign in Russia had swollen to army corps strength, 47,000 men including twenty-eight squadrons of cavalry and 112 artillery pieces. This was numerically equivalent in effective strength, and far better founded logistically, than Bonaparte's Army of Italy of 1796, and rather larger than Marlborough's whole army at Blenheim. The expansions, first in 1806 by the addition of a four-battalion reconnaissance and skirmishing unit (the Middle Guard), and later, in 1809, by the creation of the Young Guard, formed from the pick of each year's conscripts,[16] were not wholly desirable on such a large scale. They diluted the standards in the line regiments by creaming off too many battle-experienced soldiers, and later absorbed as well the most promising recruits; no doubt to the despair of the line regimental officers. The Guard received additional pay, many extra privileges, including immediate seniority over any line officer or soldier of equivalent rank, and a much larger allocation of integral unit transport than the line regiments. This latter was not necessarily or solely a matter of perquisite. Since the operational *raison d'être* of the Guard was to provide a reserve of elite troops to be committed only at the critical moment of a battle, their place in an advance to contact would be some way from the head of the column. Logistic arrangements for resupply of food for men and fodder for horses, though much improved on anything achieved in most previous armies, tended to collapse under pressure and a line of march through countryside already thoroughly foraged by the cavalry screen and one or more line corps would yield little to supplement the basic bread ration, which was for the most part maintained remarkably efficiently; hence the provision of extra unit transport for the Guard.

The standard infantry regimental organisation was tolerant of considerable modification to suit circumstances. Grenadier companies were often detached from their parent battalion to form a strike force for special tasks. Reinforcing drafts of conscripts might be used when they arrived at their regiments either as individual reinforcements to replace battle casualties or as a formed subunit. The demands of the Spanish war in particular forced recurrent calls on the depot battalions to form 'provisional' battalions or *'régiments de marche'*. Although crisis management and overextended commitment had much to do with this flexibility of organisation, which was therefore undesirable in some of its effects, it provided nevertheless a model for the future. The twentieth-century parallels are the units of special forces who require soldiers with top-level individual combat skills, and ad hoc groupings formed to meet particular administrative or tactical situations.

Cavalry and artillery were also organised far more coherently and methodically than in any previous army. Napoleon so thoroughly comprehended the major differences between the many tactical tasks of cavalry that he forbade officer transfers between cuirassiers, dragoons and hussars.[17] Although these distinctions, together with 'carbineers', 'chasseurs' and 'lancers', survive in modern armies, if at all, only in regimental titles and idiosyncrasies of ceremonial uniform, they denoted in the Napoleonic army discrete operational functions which required men different in both physical and mental attributes, as these regimental titles would continue to do for the next century. Cuirassiers were heavy cavalry for shock action: big men on big horses, wearing body armour and helmets similar to that of today's British Household Cavalry and the French Garde Républicaine. Carbineers and dragoons were more lightly armoured, and equipped with a lighter version of the infantry musket, later rifled, as well as a sabre. They might fight either from the saddle or dismounted. Dragoons, both in 1805 and subsequently, appear to have been the poor relations of the cavalry in that they remained on foot until sufficient horses had been acquired, either by capture or requisition, to mount them.[18] Carbineer and dragoon regiments were intended for skirmishing, flank guard and lines of communication security. The light cavalry, regiments of hussars, chasseurs and later lancers, were equipped with a sabre, lighter than that of the heavy cavalry, or with a lance, and were intended for reconnaissance and pursuit. Like modern armoured car or light tank units, their task was to identify the main enemy deployment while screening that of their own army. They were not expected to fight for their information without reinforcement by something heavier, unless compelled to do so by enemy action. While recognising the degree of specialisation necessary, Napoleon insisted that no element of cavalry should deploy without the support of another.[19] Each *corps d'armée* had its division of light cavalry, while the remainder were grouped by division and operational role in the army group reserve cavalry. Later, cavalry corps would be established. As a generalisation, the strength of the reserve cavalry was usually about ten per cent of that of the army group. Napoleon's maxims, written after the event, suggested varying desirable proportions of infantry to cavalry in different theatres of war.[20]

Himself an artillery officer, Napoleon was heir to the rich legacy of the work of two French artillerists of the mid-eighteenth century, De Vallerie and De Gribeauval, who were well-ahead of their time, both in the development and standardisation of artillery equipment and in the formulation of doctrine for its tactical employment.[21] The Revolution affected the French artillery less than any other arm of the service, partly because of the meritocratic rather than aristocratic basis of its officer selection and advancement procedures. Notwithstanding previous efforts, and perhaps in part because of the relative simplicity of manufacture of muzzle-loaded artillery pieces, Napoleon had inherited non-standardised designs and uncoordinated production. This had produced a multiplicity of non-compatible types of both ordnance (barrel and firing mechanism) and gun carriage. A standardisation committee under Marmont, operating in 1802–3, reduced to four the basic calibres of field artillery guns, standardised component parts wherever possible, for example reducing from twenty-two to eight the types of wheel, and most importantly upgraded from four to six pounders the standard calibre of the guns of divisional artillery groups.[22] As this was the basic calibre of the field artillery guns of both the Austrian and Prussian armies, captured stocks both of guns and ammunition could be taken into use. Whereas before Marengo, Marmont had been able to bring into service only five guns from the enormous holdings of the Milan arsenal, the French Army before both Austerlitz and Wagram virtually re-equipped its field artillery, and in 1809 deployed a substantial number of heavier calibres from the stocks of the Vienna arsenal, which on each occasion the Austrians had neglected either to move or destroy. Artillery was fought in batteries of six or eight guns, but could be massed in grand battery to suit the tactical situation, as at Friedland and Wagram. Only the batteries supporting covering forces or cavalry formations were wholly mounted, as 'flying' or horse artillery. For the rest of the army artillery, the guns were drawn by teams of up to six horses at a foot's pace, and most of the detachments marched. The heaviest calibre guns, twelve pounders in corps and army artillery parks, produced a dead weight for movement, excluding any ammunition holding, of more than two metric tons, and were fought by detachments of eight men, with a further seven in support as drivers and ammunition handlers. The lighter guns of the divisional artillery, six and eight pounders, although slightly less in dead weight tonnage,[23] nevertheless produced serious constraints on both route selection and logistic backing for the horses. Although those manning the guns were specialists, a trained infantryman was expected to be able to replace gunner casualties and infantrymen provided the detachments for the guns, allotted permanently to each battalion from 1809 onwards. Napoleon's artillery organisation as a whole produced a system which remains fundamental to the handling of artillery in battle to the present day. Combat groupings of infantry and cavalry had available to them at all times the direct support of their own guns, which could at any time be augmented by the further allocation of guns under higher formation command.

It is not surprising that training, both for recruits and within combat units and formations, was based much more on drill than marksmanship. The live-firing musketry course for the army in training at Boulogne is said by Macdonnell[24] to have consisted of no more than three shots point-blank at a target. Later, because the serious losses in Russia and the campaign of 1813 made it necessary for the boy recruits to be sent almost straight into battle in the campaign of 1814, even this absolute minimum was eroded. Marmont at Champaubert asked a soldier why he was not firing and was told by the young recruit that he would fire as well as anyone, if only he knew how to load.[25] This notwithstanding, the inefficiency by future standards of the muzzle-loaded musket and the hand-to-hand nature of the bayonet fight into which all battles sooner or later developed, meant that physical endurance and an exact knowledge of drill movements were more important than marksmanship. The only way to train soldiers to march under load is to march them under load. The sine qua non of the execution of the concentration in time, which was the foundation of Napoleonic design for battle, was the stamina and hardihood of the marching infantry. This enabled phenomenal distances to be covered in very short time by infantry, cavalry and artillery, advancing to contact at a steady foot pace.

The spectator at the annual Queen's Birthday Parade of the Household Division in London sees a formalised version, not wholly without contemporary relevance, of the drill movements carried out on the Napoleonic field of battle. Every soldier had to have exact knowledge of drill, enabling instant execution of the evolutions which kept him within a formed body of troops. This was the line infantryman's best guarantee of survival because, detached from his comrades, he was likely to be soon cut down. The purpose of every drill movement should be either safe and effective weapon handling or controlled alteration in unison of the frontage or direction of movement of a formed body of troops. Until developments in firepower and communications and a better harnessing of individual initiative permitted dispersed infantry combat by any other than skirmishers, units from company up to division, fighting as a single cohesive entity, had to be adept at taking up the right formation at the right moment, because otherwise they would be

<u>Tactical Formations</u>
Used in advance to contact or attack

Line

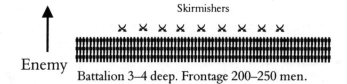

Skirmishers

Enemy

Battalion 3–4 deep. Frontage 200–250 men.

Column

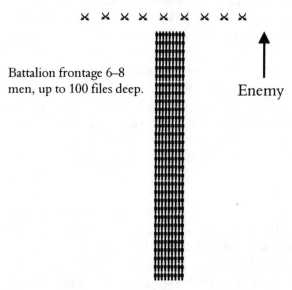

Skirmishers

Battalion frontage 6–8
men, up to 100 files deep.

Enemy

Tactical Formations

Square
Always in defence
Enemy

Formed in defence by company (up to
150 men), or battalion (up to 1,200 men).
Soldiers deployed in ranks 2 or 3 deep.

Ordre Mixte

Any combination of above.
High standard of training essential to order change of
formation.

overrun and routed. The three basic formations were the column, the line and the square, which could be combined within the division as necessary, in which case the result was known as the '*ordre mixte*'. Advance to contact would invariably be undertaken in column, to make optimum use of all available routes. The column might also be used for the assault, which, because only the outlying skirmishers and those at the head of the column could shoot, limited the firepower which could be brought to bear but, at the same time, gave troops with limited battle experience confidence deriving from operation en masse. The line, two or three deep, might be used either for assault or defence. In the assault more firepower was generated, always remembering the limitations of the muzzle-loaded musket, and the line might outflank the enemy position. In defence, the lines would ideally fire in turn by volley, which allowed each to cover the other when reloading, but in both assault and defence a break in the line risked attack in flank and defeat in detail. The square was for defensive purposes only, giving the obvious benefit of all-round defence. The battalion artillery guns, which might be overrun or captured if fought for too long at point-blank range, could be protected within the square until a local attack had been beaten off, and enemy cavalry would not care to break on the *cheveux de frises* of the bayonets of a resolute infantry square.

These formations were standard but not stereotyped and the deployments, ordered by voice or drum, had to be understood and become capable of execution as second nature by all, at every level from company to division. A commander with a well-developed tactical sense, a good eye for ground and a well-trained and practised unit could order the adoption of the correct deployment very quickly.

Chandler illustrates[26] what could be achieved by a highly competent commander of a trained and battle-hardened formation. Napoleon's design for the Battle of Jena in October 1806 envisaged that, while he engaged frontally what was thought to be the main body of the Prussian Army, the corps of Bernadotte and Davout would outflank the main enemy position right-handed, first to contain and then to destroy them in retreat from the frontal attack of the rest of the *Grande Armée*. In the event the reverse happened. Bernadotte failed, whether by accident or design, to get into action at all, and Davout found himself with a corps, no more than 25,000 strong, fighting the main body of the Prussian Army at Auerstadt, at odds of nearly three to one. Although in his post-action bulletin Napoleon treated Auerstadt as no more than the right wing of the Jena battle (Auerstadt is the only important Napoleonic battle not to be commemorated on the Arc de Triomphe), contemporaries and military historians alike are united in considering the two to be separate battles, fought as they were some fifteen miles apart. Davout and his divisional commanders, Gudin, Friant and Morand, were not men to be daunted by these odds. The *Grande Armée* had, by the autumn of 1806, reached a peak of excellence, deriving from a combination of its three years' training on the Channel coast and the campaign of the previous year, crowned by Austerlitz, which would never again be attained. Replacements for battle casualties did not have the depth of training of their predecessors and commitments became overextended. Davout had at Auerstadt the benefit of veteran soldiers whom he had personally trained. In five hours of battle, Morand's division took up five quite different deployments for advance to contact, defence and counter-attack, employing permutations of column, line, square and *ordre mixte* to achieve a total local success against greatly superior numbers. The foundation of the victory was training and discipline.

Before the French Revolution, little more had been needed to make a man a soldier than to give him a musket, bayonet and cartridges. Thereafter, success in battle came to depend increasingly on training and on disciplined and practised procedures, in order to enable armies ever-increasing in size to bring their maximum force to bear and to fight as a cohesive whole.

Notes

The author has drawn principally on six works in writing Chapters II and III:

Chandler, *The Campaigns of Napoleon*, London, Weidenfeld and Nicholson, 1966
> This magnum opus, containing a totally comprehensive analysis of Napoleon's conduct of war and detailed and well-mapped studies of all the campaigns from Toulon to Waterloo, must be accepted as the leading authority for any subsequent work touching on Napoleonic warfare. Cited in these references as 'Chandler, *Campaigns*'.

Elting, *Swords Around a Throne*, London, Weidenfeld and Nicholson, 1989
> This is an all-embracing portrayal of all aspects of the *Grande Armée*, from leadership to logistics, and is a mine of detailed but nevertheless highly readable information about the organisation, composition, equipment and battle procedures of the army.

Manceron, *Austerlitz*, translated by George Unwin, London, George Allen and Unwin, 1966

A vivid picture of the march of the *Grande Armée* from the Channel coast to Moravia, and an outstanding 'conduct of battle' account of Austerlitz.

Chandler, [ed.] *Napoleon's Marshals*, London, Macmillan, 1987

Contains short but comprehensively well-referenced biographies of each of the twenty-six marshals of the empire, and a description of a battle associated with each. Cited as 'Chandler, *Marshals*'.

Macdonnell, *Napoleon and his Marshals*, London, Macmillan, 1934

A highly readable narrative of the careers of the marshals, related to the campaigns from northern Italy in 1796 to Waterloo. Perhaps overly reliant on Marbot, some facts and assessments have been contradicted by later authors.

De Marbot, *Memoirs*, translated by Butler, London, Longmans, Green, two vols, 1892

Although of landed gentry by birth and the son of a general, Marbot joined the Army of Italy as a recruit in 1799, rising by successive exploits to command a regiment by 1812, and subsequently to lieutenant general under the Orléans monarchy. He was present at Genoa, Austerlitz, Jena, Eylau, Friedland, Aspern–Essling and Wagram. His service as an aide-de-camp to, successively, Bernadotte, Augereau, Lannes and Massena, and as colonel of a cavalry regiment in Russia and until Waterloo gave him direct experience both of exercise of command and high-level conduct of nearly all the main campaigns of the First Empire much wider than most of his contemporaries. His memoirs, written during the early years of the Second Empire, perhaps 'remember with advantage' and are occasionally prejudiced, but provide a unique record of the day-to-day life of a key member of a *corps d'armée* headquarters staff, of the personalities and abilities of his commanders, and of life in the *Grande Armée en campagne*.

[1] Shipping 'logistically loaded' makes the optimum use of the vessel's carrying capacity, without regard to any consideration other than seaworthiness. Ships loaded tactically allow troops to come ashore in the order in which they are needed for battle, i.e. the baggage wagons do not lead, and as near-ready as can be to go straight into action. The author, concerned in the planning of the operation to recover the Falkland Islands in 1982, was surprised to have to explain this principle to more senior officers of the British Army and Royal Navy.

[2] Manceron, op.cit., p.63.

[3] Strengths from Chandler, *Campaigns*, Appendix D: 'Deployment'; Macdonnell, op.cit., pp.85–94.

[4] With the notable exception of Prussia, victors and vanquished alike returned to this practice after 1815. See Chapter VII.

[5] Elting, op.cit., Prologue and Chapter V.

[6] Elting, op.cit., p.96.

[7] Marbot, op.cit. Almost every chapter contains an account of a hair's-breadth escape by this ubiquitous and fearless cavalry officer. See in particular vol. I, p.262 et seq. [Eylau] and pp.282–84 [Friedland].

[8] Watson, *By Command of the Emperor*, Cambridge, Ken Trotman Ltd, 1988, p.104. 'A Life of Marshal Berthier'.

[9] Macdonnell op.cit., p.150. See also Marbot, *op. cit.*, vol. II, p.34, for what might happen as an unforeseen consequence of nepotism.

[10] Elting, op.cit., Chapter XVI, pp.323–33.

[11] The critical battles of the years between 1792 and 1800 were Valmy, Fleurus, Napoleon's campaign of 1796 in Northern Italy, Marengo and Hohenlinden. Had any of these gone the other way, it is probable that the regime in France would have collapsed, and there would have been a Bourbon restoration. The effective strength of the Army of Italy never exceeded 50,000 and no French army in the other five battles exceeded a strength of 60,000. Notwithstanding some campaigns fought concurrently, it seems unlikely that, before Napoleon's military and civil reforms, France ever had under arms more than half the number achieved by 1809.

[12] Elting, op.cit., p.329, taken from Lachouque, *Napoleon et la Garde Impériale*, Paris, Bloud et Guy, 1956.

[13] Elting, op.cit., p.323.

[14] Manceron, op.cit., pp.99–101, from Fairon and Heuse, *Lettres des Grognards*, Liège, 1936.

[15] Elting, op.cit., Chapter X.

[16] Elting, op.cit., Chapter IX. For the expanding strength of the Guard, see Chandler, *Campaigns*, Appendix C [Marengo], Appendix D [Army of the Coasts of the Ocean, on redesignation as the *Grande Armée*], and Appendix G [Russian campaign].

[17] Chandler, *Marshals*, p.132.

[18] Elting, op.cit., pp.236–37.

[19] Phillips, *Roots of Strategy*, Harrisburg, Pennsylvania, 1985, *Napoleon's Maxims*, no.32, p.415. See also Maxim 91, op.cit., p.431.

[20] Philips, op.cit., ibid., no.91, p.435.

[21] Elting, op.cit., Chapter XII.

[22] Macdonnell, op.cit., p.201.

[23] Chandler, *Campaigns*, pp.358–59.

[24] Macdonnell, op.cit., p.91.

[25] Macdonnell, op.cit., p.293.

[26] Chandler, *Campaigns*, p.353.

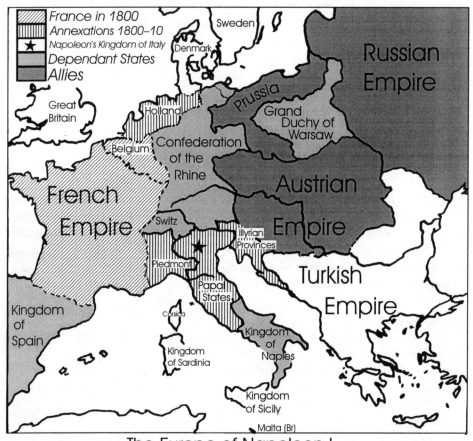

The Europe of Napoleon I

Chapter III
Napoleonic Dawn

Autumn 1805 – the Approach to Battle

The Peace of Amiens was too brittle to last and in May 1803 England and France were again at war. The immediate *casus belli* was England's refusal to evacuate Malta, as required by the terms of the peace settlement.

For neither the first nor the last time in her history, England had disarmed in precipitate haste. Her preparations for the resumption of the conflict and against the immediate threat of invasion by the Army of the Coasts of the Ocean were a blend of enthusiasm, determination, technical proficiency at unit level in such regiments of the standing army and ships of the Royal Navy as had survived the disarmament process, and bumbling and inconsistent political and higher military direction, in no way dissimilar to the recurrent circumstances of 1914 and 1939. Addington, who had replaced Pitt as prime minister in the concluding months of the first phase of the war because of the latter's irreconcilable difference of view with King George III about the need for Roman Catholic emancipation, was no war leader. Pitt resumed power in May 1804 on the understanding that he would not resurrect this controversy.

On the same day in Paris, a *senatus consultum* decreed that Napoleon, already first consul for life, should become emperor of the French. A year later he crowned himself king of Italy in Milan Cathedral. It is hard to conceive of any action which could have given greater offence to the ruling houses of divided Italy – Habsburg, Savoy, the Bourbons of the Two Sicilies and the Papacy.

While the survival of England depended upon the denial of the English Channel to the French fleet, the restoration of the balance of power in Europe required the total defeat of Napoleon, for which the acquisition of continental allies was essential. England's obvious partners in this enterprise were the Habsburg Empire, humiliated in the first phase of the war, dispossessed of territory and influence in Italy, and given fresh cause to take up arms by Napoleon's unilateral assumption of the title of king of Italy; Russia, because of the Francophobia of the new tsar, Alexander I; and Prussia, because of her concern for her scattered territories throughout Germany. Government indecision in Berlin, caused by the conflict of pro- and anti-French enthusiasm within the royal family and among the advisers of King Frederick William III, and fomented by diplomatic inferential suggestion from France that Prussia might receive Hanover as a reward for remaining neutral, was to keep Prussia out of the campaign of 1805. The coalition was thus flawed from the start, as were all its successors until 1813, by its failure to combine and coordinate the totality of the national forces available.

The failure of the French fleet to obtain mastery of the Channel and reports of the build-up of Austrian and Russian armies foreclosed Napoleon's first choice of campaign strategy; the invasion of England. His remaining options were to mount his primary effort in either Germany, where he had not campaigned before, or northern Italy, where he might repeat his triumphs of 1796, while at the same time conducting a holding operation in the alternative theatre of war. The land forces of the coalition had a similar choice. While the Austrians, for reasons of prestige if nothing else, wished to make their main endeavour in northern Italy, they would, while awaiting the arrival of the Russian masses, have to lay off significant forces in southern Germany. This would be necessary in order to neutralise the incipient hostility of the elector of Bavaria and, given the ambivalence of Prussia, secure Habsburg possessions in Bohemia, Silesia and Galicia. If the security of the latter two were to be left to the tsar, Vienna had a justifiable concern that Russian forces might never be ejected. The Russian strategic preference was for a campaign in Central Europe. This choice was perhaps not altogether uninfluenced by the traditional aim of Russian policy from Peter the Great to Yeltsin – to safeguard the western frontier of the motherland by the creation of satellite buffer states. Russia's practical considerations were that deployment in Central Europe was the simpler option, both in terms of mobilisation and approach to battle, and it would also exert pressure on Berlin sufficient to secure the neutrality at least of Prussia.

A potential and unrecognised cause for confusion in the allied councils for the campaign of 1805 was a ten day difference in date between the Gregorian calendar of Western Europe and the Julian calendar of Greek Orthodox Russia; the same numerical date in the Russian calendar lying ten days behind the Austrian. Later alliances would find that time spent in identifying discrepancies and agreeing common definitions and terminology would be time well spent. This variation, and the divergence of strategic design for the campaign, was compounded by a misappreciation on the part of the Aulic Council, a totally hidebound committee of generals, who exercised the day-today supreme command of Austrian imperial forces in the name of the emperor. This body formed the view that Napoleon would make his main effort in northern Italy, a course rendered unlikely by reason of the deployment of most of the French Army along the Channel coast. The resulting conflict of both fact and intention produced a fragmented deployment which prevented superior allied concentration on any battlefield until far too late in the campaign. The main Austrian dispositions allocated[1] 95,000 men to Archduke Charles in northern Italy; not enough to regain the lost Habsburg provinces, but too many for a containing operation in a subsidiary theatre. Archduke John and the veteran General Jellacic had 23,000 in the Tyrol; more than the number needed to ensure local security and to link the army of Archduke Charles with what was finally determined as the main concentration of troops in the Danube valley. Seventy thousand men under the nominal command of Archduke Ferdinand, but with Mack, the Austrian general, enjoying the highest contemporary reputation as his chief of staff, and by direction of Emperor Francis II in de facto command, advanced in September across Bavaria to the fortified town of Ulm, 250 miles up the Danube from Vienna and seventy-five miles west of the Bavarian capital, Munich. Bavaria thus neutralised, Mack's mission was to screen and await the arrival of three Russian armies, in all nearly 100,000 men, approaching on separate axes of advance. The tsar had promised that the first of these, 35,000 under Kutuzov, would arrive on Bavarian soil by 20th October. The ten-day disparity in dates remained unrecognised, and Ulm is in any event west of the Bavarian border, in Wurtemburg. Allowing twelve miles for a standard day's march, the junction of the armies of Mack and Kutuzov would be at least a fortnight later than expected by the Austrians, and it was not appreciated that Ulm lay nearer to the French start points than to the Russian.

Criticism of the allied dispersion of force must be tempered not only by relating it to the conditions of the time but also to the received wisdom of contemporary military hierarchies. The great commanders of the previous century had propounded[2] a limit of 50,000 men for any prolonged campaign in the field. Writing from 1818 onwards, and basing his theories on nine years' practical experience of warfare from Jena to Waterloo, Clausewitz would declare[3] that the factor limiting the size of *force en rase campagne* was the capacity of the country to provide forage for the horses. An army in the field was totally dependent on its horses, and would remain so for the next century, for reconnaissance, communications, shock action, artillery support and logistic sustainability. As this and subsequent chapters will show, a ratio of one horse to three men was required if an army in the field was to be properly balanced

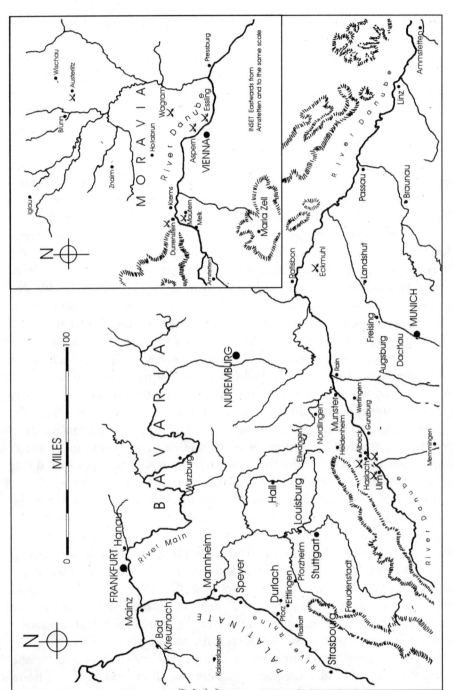

The Campaigns on the Danube

and supported. In these terms, a dispersal of force which runs totally counter to the fundamental principle of war – concentration of maximum force at the vital point – becomes explicable but not excusable. Napoleon's *corps d'armée* organisation presents the first successful solution of the problem of concentration versus maintainability because it allowed massive expansion of the 50,000 maximum on the size of an army in the field, accepted, at least tacitly, by every previous commander. It was of course the factor of sustainability which gave so much importance to the garrison towns of Europe, quite apart from their defensive attributes. Important as these were, very heavy siege guns of correspondingly poor mobility and lengthy excavation of covered approaches being essential if stone fortifications had to be breached, the fortified towns allowed the accumulation of weapons, ammunition, clothing, rations and fodder. No military commander has ever been able to ignore the fact that his men have to be fed if they are to fight – a consideration even more important for the horses, which continued to be essential in large numbers for the support of armies in the field up to the Second World War.[a] Some were better than others at achieving this. The resources of the fortified towns, which in any event were the focal points of an economy still predominantly agrarian, exercised a powerful influence on the planning of conventionally minded generals throughout the nineteenth century.

Intelligence of Austro-Russian preparations compelled Napoleon in August 1805 to finally abandon his project for the invasion of England. On 29th August, the Army of the Coasts of the Ocean was redesignated as the *Grande Armée*. French field armies having historically taken their titles from their intended area of operation, this unspecific title was a security measure to cloak Napoleon's intentions, which were also masked by his prolonged stay first at Boulogne and later in Paris.

The deployment of the seven army corps, plus the Imperial Guard, Reserve Cavalry and Artillery Park, which was to overwhelm Mack by encircling him before he had realised it, was a masterpiece of march planning and logistic support without precedent in military history, and with few subsequent parallels. Orders to the subordinate formations were prepared and issued in mid-August, and by the end of the month 210,607 men, 29,474 cavalry horses and 396 field guns, the latter with their first line ammunition limbers drawn by another 6,430 horses,[4] were en route. A decree of 2nd September requisitioned a further 14,000 horses to draw 3,500 army supply wagons,[5] but it is doubtful whether more than two-thirds of these ever materialised.

---

[a] Nowadays, oil-fuelled vehicles demand even more logistic provision.

Marches were on a carefully timed programme and along strictly designated divisional routes initially, to the first objectives; the crossing points over the Rivers Main and Rhine. These having been reached by 24th September, there followed the execution of the massive left hook which, by encircling Mack from north through east to south, isolated him from relief and led to his defeat in detail before he could be joined by Kutuzov. The whole approach to contact was screened throughout by the Reserve Cavalry, simultaneously providing Napoleon with intelligence about the enemy deployment while denying to the enemy acquisition of information about his own movements, at least to the point at which le Malheureux Mack might have arrived at a correct appreciation of the French plan.

For once, a faultless plan was matched by perfect execution. The routes of the seven corps,[6] from start points 850 miles apart to deployment areas, concentrated them around and within a circumference of no more than 100 miles from Ulm on the day first contact occurred, fourteen days after the Main/Rhine start lines had been crossed. This epic of planning and march discipline deserves to be recorded.

TABLE III

Corps and Commander	Start Point (29th Aug. or later)	Main/Rhine (24th Sept. or later)	Route via	Concentration Area (Reached 8th to 11th Oct.)
I Bernadotte	Hanover	Wurzburg	Ansbach Ingoldstadt*	Munich
II Marmont	Utrecht	Mainz	Wurzburg Feuchtwangen	Wassenfeldt*
III Davout	Bruges	Mannheim	Heidelberg Dinkelsbuhl	Neuberg*+
IV Soult	Boulogne	Germersheim	Heilbronn Obrigen Donauworth* Augsburg Memingen	Biberach
V Lannes	Boulogne	Strasbourg	Lugwigsburg Aalen Gunzberg*	Pfaffenhofen
VI Ney	Montreuil	Karlsruhe	Pforzheim Stuttgart Heidenheim Dillingen+	Elchingen
VII Augereau	Brest	Huningen (10th Oct.)	Freiburg	Donaueschingen, then SE to the Tyrol

* Danube crossing points.
+ Davout's corps deployed to face eastwards, as a covering force against the approach of the Russian armies.

The first skirmish occurred on 8th October at Wertingen, forty miles north-east of Ulm, between units of Lannes's corps and an Austrian force of nine infantry battalions and one cavalry squadron;[7] the latter in these circumstances large enough to get into trouble, but insufficiently mobile to extricate itself unsupported. At this point the French deployment around Ulm resembled a siege on a grand scale. The corps of Ney and Lannes, with Murat in command, formed the forces of circumvallation, whose mission was to capture the besieged town and army. The remainder formed the forces of contravallation, intended to prevent any relief from reaching the surrounded garrison. Bernadotte reached Munich on 12th October, thus cementing the allegiance of the elector of Bavaria to Napoleon. Marmont was placed to

64

reinforce either the besieging force or Davout. Soult had marched three-quarters of a circle round Ulm to his concentration area, south-west of the town, and Augereau was shepherding the small army of Archduke John south-eastwards towards the Tyrol. Together, the latter five ensured that Mack was isolated and could not mount a successful breakout in any direction. While Napoleon had gone to some lengths to avoid a violation of Swiss neutrality by ordering the construction of a pontoon bridge at Huningen[8] rather than use an existing bridge at Basle, only two miles south but inside Swiss territory, no such reservations were applied to Bernadotte. His march through Ansbach, a Prussian dependency halfway between Augsburg and Munich, would provide Prussia with her pretext for a declaration of war the following year. A planning nicety ensured that only once did the line of march of one corps cross that of another, the formations concerned being those of Marmont and Davout, when the latter was given his covering force task.

The corps moved by column of divisions, with the divisions within each corps one day's march apart from the others. The normal day's march was between eighteen and twenty miles, starting between four and six o'clock in the morning and over by midday, to leave the afternoon for foraging, food and rest. Infantry and cavalry moved in parallel columns either side of the road in order to leave the presumably firmer and more even road surface free for the use of artillery and the divisional supply wagons. The rate of march was a steady three miles in the hour, and an infantry division required some two and a half miles of road space; a cavalry division covered about a quarter of this distance. Manceron has established[9] that, at least in fair weather, the movement of large bodies of troops, whether on foot or horseback, presented fewer difficulties in the early years of the nineteenth century than later:

... because of the extraordinary width of some of the roads and the slight transition between them and the neighbouring ground. In some provinces of France, and in the approaches to Paris, the roads were as much as 26 yards wide,[b] and the least of them under the empire still measured from 8.5 to 15 yards between the ditches on either side, whose embankments were a good deal less pronounced than those that came later. In certain regions they did not exist at all. The land adjacent to the road was far more

---

[b] Equivalent to the width of a modern dual carriageway trunk road.

accessible to a troop of men than 100 years later;[c] the progress of industry and the rise of the working classes developed, to an extent that is hard to appreciate, walls, artificial rough stone enclosures, metal trellis-work, drainage ditches, etc. A road in those days was a broad, ill-defined strip of land on which the flood tide that rolled over it constantly overflowed to left and right.

Commissariat arrangements worked adequately enough in France and by requisition on repayment in the friendly southern German principalities, Bavaria, Wurtemburg and Baden. Their rulers would be rewarded progressively over the next ten years by promotion in degree of sovereign title (Bavaria and Wurtemburg became kingdoms) and additions of territory, usually at the expense of Austria or Prussia. For the 1805 campaign, the elector of Bavaria was asked to provide one million rations of 'biscuit';[10] hard bread with a relatively slow rate of deterioration. This was enough to feed the ration strength in the field for fourteen days. Foraging was always tacitly permitted, and divisions on the march were allocated areas twenty kilometres (12.5 miles) square round their bivouac areas. One of Manceron's grognards relates[11] the progressive despoliation of the potato crop along the route of the march of Davout's corps, despite the fact that Davout was unusual for his time in the priority and personal supervision he gave to the logistic arrangements for his command, and for the degree of severity with which he dealt with looters. Nevertheless, the tightening concentration both of and within the corps, the approach of winter (which started early in 1805) and unpractised and inevitably corrupt purchasing and distribution systems led to a progressive worsening of organised supply.

By mid-October, when the great left hook had swung south and west, an imperial aide-de-camp describes a logistic situation in the Danube valley little short of chaotic:[12]

From Gunzberg to Pfaffenhofen the army presented an aspect of the greatest disorder; the roads, which were full of ruts, were strewn with our Alsatian wagons stuck fast in the mire, with their drivers at their wits' end, and with fallen horses dying of hunger and fatigue. Our soldiers were rushing right and left, helter-

---

[c] For example, for the great feats of marching by both sides on the Western Front in August and September 1914.

skelter, across the fields; some looking for food, others using their cartridges shooting the game with which these plains abound. Hearing all this noise and the whistle of bullets, one might have fancied oneself at the advance posts, and one ran quite as great a risk.

Mack was so bemused that, on receipt of information that substantial French forces were moving westwards from the line of the River Lech, which rises in the Tyrol and joins the Danube east of Donauworth, itself fifty miles east of Ulm, he concluded that the French were in full retreat. Because Ulm then lay mostly north of the Danube, Mack's conventional brain could not conceive of an operation to assault the town from the south bank. Although once battle was joined, the French did not have matters wholly their own way, a division of Ney's corps being caught in isolation north of the river and roughly handled, the outcome was not in doubt. Mack agreed on 17th October, only nine days after the first contact, to capitulate on 25th October if he had not been relieved by that date. In the event he surrendered unconditionally five days ahead of this deadline, on 20th October, coincidentally the date by which the tsar had promised that Kutuzov's army would be on Bavarian soil. In fact, thanks alike to the confusion of the calendars and the imprecision of the planning, Kutuzov had reached Braunau, 150 miles east of Ulm and at least twelve days' march away by Russian or Austrian standards of performance, only by 23rd October.[13] Thus the first allied army was effectively destroyed, barely 8,000 of Mack's original 70,000 making good their escape for further participation in the campaign.

Nevertheless, the French had won a battle but not the war. Kutuzov retreated in good order from Braunau; not, as his allies would have wished, eastwards to cover Vienna, which could have been done by contesting the passage of any of four rivers flowing northwards into the Danube (Inn, Traun, Ipps and Traisen), but north-eastwards in order to fall back on the other two Russian armies approaching Moravia. Notwithstanding two sharp rearguard actions, first at the Danube crossing of Durrenstein and later at Hollabrunn (the latter the 'Schon Grabern' of Tolstoy's War and Peace), this master of the controlled withdrawal evaded action against the superior concentration of force which Napoleon would have brought to bear, had the pursuit been able to 'fix' Kutuzov for long enough. Murat, the logical choice as commander of the pursuing forces, both in his capacity as commander of the Reserve Cavalry and as imperial brother-in-law, blundered twice.[14] The lure of being the first to enter Vienna as conqueror was too great a temptation for the son of the innkeeper of Cahors, just as, in June 1944, the attraction of Rome diverted United States General Mark Clark from his assigned task.[d] Similarly, Murat went for Vienna. A cascade of imperial wrath realigned the axis of the impetuous cavalryman's advance, but his agreement before Hollabrunn to a short armistice, which was, as the emperor furiously reminded him, in excess of his powers, again afforded Kutuzov time to break clear.

Austerlitz

The pursuit continued, through an increasingly depressing November, into country inhospitable in winter conditions. Although the capture of Vienna and in particular its arsenal, left intact by the Austrians, had produced a rich haul of weaponry, the French Army was becoming increasingly overextended and supply arrangements markedly less reliable. The great parallelogram of the Marchfeldt,[e] bounded on the south by the Danube, and to west, north and east respectively by the mountain ranges of Bavaria, the Riesengebirge (the present-day border between the Czech Republic and Poland), and the Carpathians, while presenting few constraints to strategic movement and, in normal circumstances, the granary and market garden of Vienna, had little to offer in the depths of an early nineteenth-century winter, with the harvest long gathered in and the country already thoroughly foraged by the withdrawing Austrian and Russian forces.

Napoleon's dispositions for his advance to contact into Moravia were a very carefully calculated risk in response to a worsening operational situation. The forces immediately available to him, themselves much attenuated by three months' marching and fighting, consisted of the Imperial Guard, the reserve cavalry, gravely reduced by detachment, and the corps of Lannes and Soult only. The whole was considerably numerically inferior to the concentration of Austrian and predominantly Russian forces now assembling around the fortified garrison town of Olmutz. Napoleon had two further corps within supporting distance, given early intelligence and forced march, Davout from Vienna and Bernadotte from Iglau (now Jihlava), the latter masking Austrian forces in Bohemia. These were respectively eighty miles south and fifty miles west of Brunn (now Brno). Napoleon had secured this fortified town,

---

[d] Instead of thrusting due east out of the Anzio beach head to cut off the greater part of Kesselring's army, still holding strong defensive positions against the main Allied thrust from the south, Clark chose to drive northwards on the Eternal City.

[e] For a description of the present-day appearance of the Marchfeldt and the battlefield of Austerlitz, the latter little affected by development, the reader should glance at Appendix C.

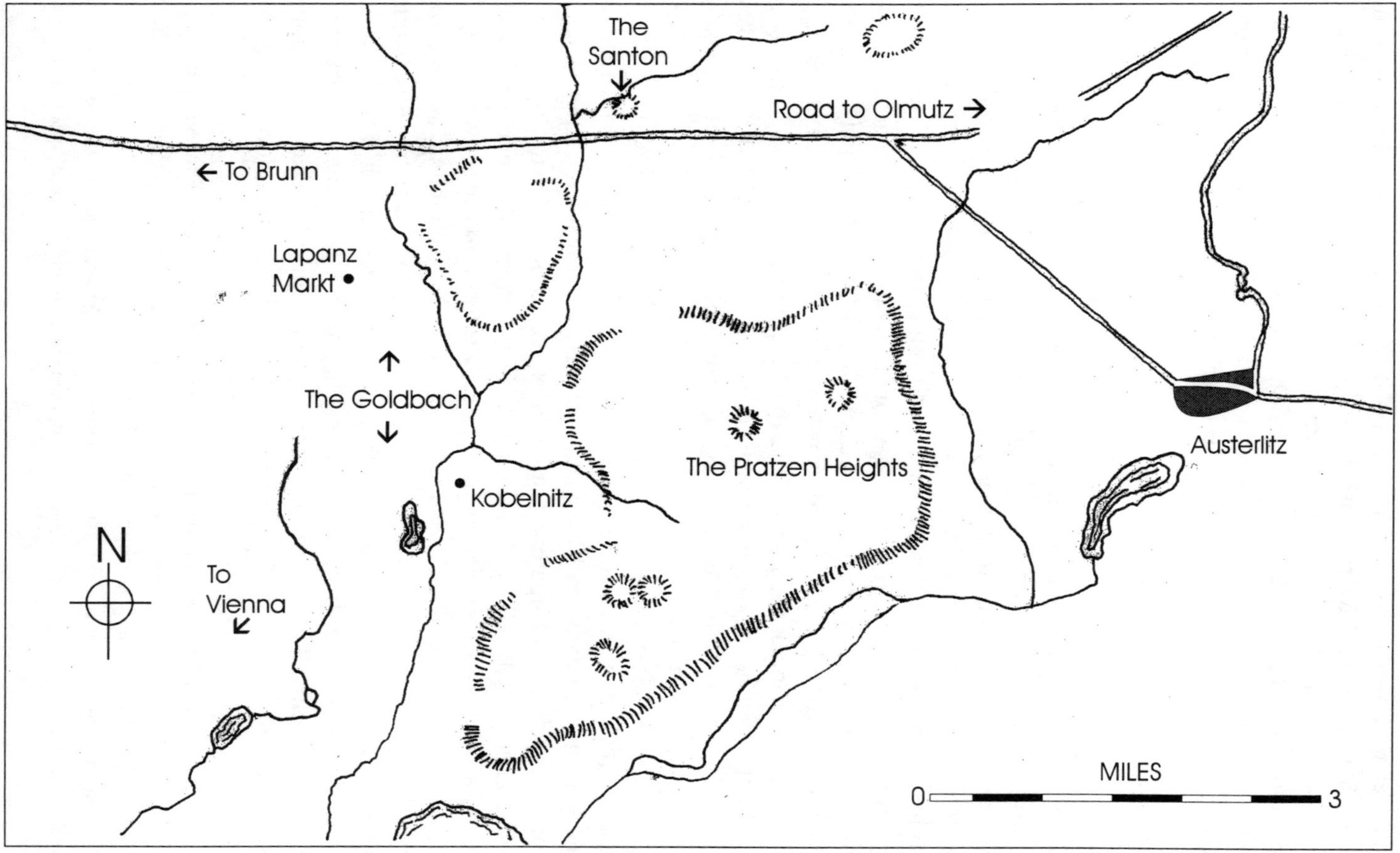

The Santon

Road to Olmutz →

← To Brunn

Lapanz Markt ●

The Goldbach

Kobelnitz ●

The Pratzen Heights

To Vienna

Austerlitz

N

MILES

0   3

Austerlitz

unopposed on 25th November. Of the other 'starters' from the Channel coast in August, Marmont was holding a blocking position at Leoben, sixty miles south-west of Vienna and 150 miles from Brunn, in order to prevent the army of Archduke Charles, pressed almost too well by Massena, from joining the allied concentration at Olmutz. Augereau was 'fixing' the force of Archduke John in the Tyrol.[15] Ney, whose corps had borne the brunt of the fighting round Ulm, was guarding the line of communication along the Danube into southern Germany, and an eighth corps, commanded by Mortier and formed by detachment of divisions from the formations of Marmont, Ney and the reserve cavalry, was securing Upper Austria. None of these four corps could be available in time for a battle in Moravia. Napoleon retained the strategic option of retreat south-westwards, gathering up the masking and blocking corps of the *Grande Armée* as he withdrew, but he could not risk the disadvantages in terms of policy and prestige implicit in withdrawal without having achieved a decisive victory. He had, therefore, to bring to battle the Austro-Russian concentration at Olmutz, notwithstanding his smaller numbers, under circumstances of his own choice.

A determined enemy under a unified command might have exposed the inherent contradiction in this situation. Unified command in the allied camp did not exist, but opinion did not divide on national lines. The Austrian emperor, Francis II, favoured further withdrawal; a man still under forty, but of prematurely elderly mindset and rendered cautious by the continual series of defeats suffered by the armies of his empire ever since 1792. As Manceron puts it:[16]

> stiff with affected gravity, ...with a face already mottled by a surfeit of good living and conjugal pleasures, with its endless pendulous chin and its large eyes ever fearful, the look of the crowned conserver of the existing order.

Austerlitz would demonstrate that the day had gone for good of the commander-in-chief who was neither a natural nor an experienced soldier. The Fabian General Kutuzov, senior Russian field commander present, shared the caution of the Habsburg emperor, but was, of course, subordinate to the twenty-eight year old Tsar Alexander of All the Russias, present with his armies for the first time, and so, like his brother-emperor of Austria, without previous battlefield experience. The tsar and his coterie of young lions, relying more on an assumed superiority of style and breeding over the Corsican upstart than on any rational military appreciation, were in favour of attack.

They had the benefit of a plan which, whatever its failings in the event, was of sensible strategic concept and, based upon comprehensive knowledge of the ground, had been prepared with Germanic thoroughness by Weirother, Austria's professional soldier foremost in reputation since the disaster befalling Mack.

If a battle had to take place somewhere in the forty miles of rolling country between Brunn and Olmutz, Napoleon had to create the conditions for success by a carefully crafted combination of deception and choice of ground. North of Brunn the flat plain of the Marchfeldt is broken by ridges and hills, but there is no geographic feature to hinder or canalise troop movement in an advance to contact. The deception plan was founded first on a series of meetings to discuss an armistice, from which the Russian representative, Prince Dolgoruki, was allowed to deduce that Napoleon was prepared to settle for anything rather than battle, and, later, on an apparently precipitate and disorganised evacuation of the high ground east of Brunn, which had been secured in the last days of November, including the dominating Pratzen Heights eight miles from the town. On 21st November, eleven days before the battle in fact occurred, Napoleon conducted the combination of reconnaissance, tutorial and briefing, which would later become known as a 'staff ride', of the Pratzen and surrounding ground for the instruction of his senior commanders and staff officers. 'Gentlemen, examine this ground carefully, it is going to be a battlefield; you will have a part to play on it.'[17]

On 27th November, some sort of order having been imposed on the multilingual chaos at Olmutz, the Russian and Austrian armies began their advance south-westwards towards Brunn. On 29th November the pseudo-preliminaries for an armistice were broken off, the French began their deployment and orders were sent to Bernadotte and Davout to concentrate east of Brunn, fast.

Napoleon had comprehended exactly the allied design for battle, which was to seek to isolate the French Army in Moravia by cutting off its retreat towards Vienna. While an advance guard of 13,600 men under Kienmayer and Doctorov had the task of fixing the right, or southern, flank of the French position, formed on and between the villages of Telnitz and Sokolnitz, two-thirds of the balance of the allied effective strength, 45,600 men, were to march in two parallel columns of divisions east of, and so concealed by, the Pratzen feature, wheeling right, first to block the French line of retreat and then to roll up their position from south to north. Command of this part of the operation was entrusted to Buxhowden. Meanwhile a further division of 13,000 under Bagration, Kutuzov's rearguard commander at Hollabrunn, was to assault the left (northern) flank of the French position on the Santon (Zuran) feature, five miles due east of Brunn, which the French had developed by field fortification into a strong point. The allies retained the Russian Imperial Guard (3,500) and cavalry (4,600) in reserve.[18] Napoleon identified the flaw inherent in this plan, which was to leave the dominating Starhe Vinobrady/Pratzen feature inadequately held once Buxhowden's columns were committed to their march southwards. But, while a blow struck firmly at the allied centre would split their army in half, everything depended upon the supports at the northern and southern flanks of the French line holding firm in the face of attack by larger enemy forces. If the French plan, based on a counterstroke which would drive a wedge into the middle of the allied position by capturing its centre of gravity, were to have any chance of working, it was essential that both Bernadotte and Davout should reach the battlefield in time.

By the afternoon of 1st December, Bernadotte's corps had come up but there was no news of the approach of Davout, who had the longer distance to march. The northern flank of the French defensive position, a frontage of 4,000 metres between the Santon and the village of Lapanz Markt (now Slapanice) was held by the corps of Lannes, on the Santon, and Bernadotte. The Reserve Cavalry, now reduced to 5,600 effectives, the Imperial Guard and the grenadier companies, the latter detached from their parent battalions and grouped separately as a task force 5,500 strong under Oudinot, were retained in army reserve to the rear of the French left. Given the timely arrival of the corps of Bernadotte and Davout, the key to a French victory lay in the two tasks entrusted to Soult's corps. The first of these was to hold, with one division only, 7,000 men commanded by Legrand, a frontage of 5,000 metres, lengthy for this strength, along the line of the Goldbach streamlet, holding as *points d'appui* the villages of Kobelnitz, Sokolnitz and Telnitz. The Goldbach was, and is, readily fordable by men on foot, but artillery and cavalry would need the use of the bridges, located in each of the villages. Although the slopes of the Starhe Vinobrady/Pratzen feature are bare open farmland, the shallow valley of the Goldbach is close country, and the Russian striking force would need at least one of the bridges if infantry attacks west of the Goldbach were to be developed with cavalry and artillery support. Thus Legrand had to hold his position at any cost. The second task, entrusted to the remaining two infantry divisions of Soult's corps, a total of 16,000 men under Vandamme and St Hilaire, was the critical counterstroke operation. The two divisions were to advance, when so ordered, from dead ground west of Lapanz Markt, making the best use of a wooded re-entrant leading to the foot of the Pratzen, and then to form up for an assault on the heights; this was not to be launched until Napoleon judged that the allied centre had been weakened sufficiently by the southward march of Buxhowden's columns, and that these were committed beyond the point of recall. The twenty-five per cent French inferiority in numbers of effectives on the ground on 1st December (66,800 against 85,400) was compounded by the fact that Davout had to come up in time to reinforce Legrand on the French right flank. If he did not, the route for a retreat southwards, should one be needed, would be secure only for so long as Legrand's division could hold the line of the Goldbach against a force potentially almost ten times its size.

In the early hours of 2nd December Napoleon received the welcome intelligence that the Iron Marshal had not failed him. Manceron quotes extensively[19] from a letter home written by one Jean-Pierre Blaise, a very literate conscript NCO in Davout's corps, which describes graphically an epic march of some eighty miles in forty-six hours:

> We left the village where we had been billeted between eight and nine o'clock in the evening [29th November, 2000–2100 hours]. We marched until two in the morning, when we made a halt in a wood. We lit fires there, and rested until five o'clock [30th November, 0500] when we set off again. We marched all day and we bivouacked in a wood at six o'clock in the evening; we did not prepare a meal because we had been warned that we would be leaving at nine [that is, after three hours' rest]. We preferred to use the time for resting. We had received bread for three days at Vienna before leaving; we were therefore not short of it: it provided our sole nourishment. On leaving this position we marched until five o'clock [1st December, 0500], when the regiment made a halt. I can assure you that that was the hour, for there was nobody left in the companies. The colonel, whose kindness towards us never flagged throughout the campaign, had wine issued to us in abundance. This restored our energies and put us in a state to continue our march. When it was judged that the majority of the men had returned to their companies, we were marched off; the colonel left an officer to collect the stragglers. We arrived at last this evening, at seven o'clock in the evening [1st December, 1900] in a village where we bivouacked with a division of dragoons. We had a false alarm caused by the cries of a woman, but we were sent back one after the other to our fires. I leave you

to imagine whether we made good use of the night to ourselves, after such a long march.

They were on foot again at six o'clock the following morning, and in action two hours later.

Eighty miles' advance to contact in forty-six hours, in battle order – the infantryman's pack, ammunition pouch and musket weighed about fifty pounds (twenty-two kilograms) – is a formidable achievement by any standard. It was more than that because the imperative equal with speed was to bring a formed body of troops straight into battle off the line of march as a cohesive unit. While foot and horse present fewer logistic problems than would a mechanised force of similar strength, the description provides conclusive evidence of a level of combat fitness, route control and march discipline not within the compass of untrained or badly led troops. The logistic arrangements, if rudimentary, were evidently adequate. The three halts, of about ten hours in all, provided a necessary minimum of rest. Units and subunits retained cohesion, and necessary provision was made for stragglers. Marbot describes[20] how Napoleon, on 23rd November, suspected that the chasseurs of the Guard were as much as one-third fewer than the 1,200 noted by the emperor as the number for duty reported in the latest regimental strength return.[f] Mounted soldiers would tend, naturally, to forage further afield than those on foot, and rest might enable horses to cover distance more quickly and in better condition than they would be if driven on regardless, but it appears from Marbot that some men of this elite regiment were at the time as far distant as Hollabrunn, sixty miles away. However, as Marbot relates:

> A messenger arriving from Vienna had fallen in with more than 100 between Znaym and Brunn, and a good many more this side of Hollabrunn, so that he [Colonel Morland, the regimental commander] was certain that within forty-eight hours the regiment would have recovered most of its losses.

The chasseurs of the Guard went into battle little short of their reported strength.

---

[f] Regiments submitted this return fortnightly, and notebooks containing the figures were kept permanently on hand for Napoleon to consult. Woe betide the commanding officer caught out in an inaccurate return.

The village Blaise referred to was Gross Raigern, now Rajhradice, eight miles across country to the French position on the Goldbach. Davout brought 6,600 men to battle, just in time to secure Napoleon's right flank against a series of assaults pressed with great courage but without any effective coordination, and later to provide the anvil against which the hammer blows of Vandamme, St Hilaire, Oudinot and the Guard, by contrast coordinated to perfection by Soult and the emperor, would destroy the allied striking force. Over-provision by Weirother for the allied left hook had unbalanced their whole deployment. The stalwart Jean-Pierre fought bravely at Telnitz, and survived the battle with what might be described as a 'lucky' wound; two of his toes being broken by a stray cannon ball.

It is tempting to describe any battle as a tidy series of related phases, but the fog of war precludes at the time any such understanding by most of the participants. Nevertheless, commanders at all levels must have clearly in their mind's eye, if not in physical view, their objectives, the resources available to them, the present effective strength of the force under their command and how they can obtain reinforcement if and when they need it. They must also have good intelligence, by which is meant properly evaluated information, independently confirmed wherever possible, about what is in front of them. This coalesces up the chain of command into a picture which may become increasingly less complete, and is inevitably of variable accuracy and time base, but the overview at the highest level of command must be essentially valid if the battle is to proceed in accordance with the commander's design for it, and if he is to be enabled to take correctly the critical decisions as the need arises. Perhaps the most critical decision common to any battle is when and where to commit a reserve, men or firepower, for which subordinates may be making competing claims.

At Austerlitz, the allied army had no such controlling brain. The two emperors, nominally commanding-in-chief, were without previous battlefield experience, and had neglected to provide themselves with any mechanism to receive and evaluate information upon which to base command decisions, should it become necessary to amend an over-rigid plan. Kutuzov was in tactical control of a plan in which he had no confidence. Weirother's plan was at the same time complex and inflexible, and no arrangements were made to coordinate the attacks of Bagration on the Santon with those of the allied advance guard and Buxhowden on the southern flank of the French position. It would have been beyond the capability of the allied army, but probably not that of the French, to reverse the movement of Buxhowden's columns once the threat to the Pratzen became evident, but no such order was ever given.

While some allied subordinate commanders made praiseworthy efforts to carry out their allotted tasks in the early part of the battle, and later to retrieve what they could from disaster, others, Buxhowden in particular, proved totally incompetent. Buxhowden had no staff or communications organisation capable of coordinating the action of five separate division-sized formations. A foggy December dawn, poor route discipline and organisation inadequate for the movement of 45,000 troops threw into confusion from the start Buxhowden's approach march. This was over a distance of no more than six miles, right-handed through Augezd Markt, now Ujezd U Brana, to Telnitz.

Napoleon, by contrast, saw the battle developing exactly as he had planned, and, despite inevitable shocks, retained throughout his control of events, which unfolded precisely as he had expected. His concern about his right allayed by the arrival of Davout, the two assault divisions of Soult's corps were launched across the Goldbach by way of Puntowitz, now Ponetovice. Making the best use of the cover afforded by the dank morning, the convenient re-entrant and the heavy grey-black smoke generated by the cannon and muskets of the time, they remained undiscovered throughout an approach march of about an hour, and formed up for their attack at the foot of the Pratzen. The corps commander was retained at army headquarters on the Santon until Napoleon judged that the main body of the Austro-Russian Army had vacated the heights beyond the point of recall. Vandamme and St Hilaire captured the ridge from the Starhe Vinobrady to the Pratzen, driving a wedge between Bagration and Buxhowden, which successive attacks by the allied cavalry and the Russian Guard proved unable to dislodge. Bagration, unable to make any impression on the Santon defences, withdrew in good order towards Olmutz, receiving very late in the day, after the disaster in the south had become all too apparent, his only orders: to keep open at all costs the road which provided the axis of retreat towards Olmutz. The destruction of Buxhowden's masses was encompassed by an advance south-westwards from the summit of the Pratzen by Soult's two assault divisions, linked by Oudinot's grenadiers to Legrand and Davout, who had maintained their positions on the Goldbach, south of Lapanz Markt, all day. Surrounded on three sides by an arc of converging enemy formations, Buxhowden's only line of retreat south-eastwards, oblique at a considerable angle away from the Olmutz road, was constrained by marshy ground and two shallow lakes, the latter since drained. On the day of the battle the lakes were iced over, and might have provided going adequate for a carefully controlled retreat, even by cavalry and artillery. Inevitably, however, all control was lost. French artillery fire was directed on to the lakes to break the ice, but the actual numbers of Russian and Austrian losses in this area of the battlefield were much magnified by subsequent report. In all, the allied army lost 77,000 men, nearly a third of its strength, in killed, wounded and prisoners.

Napoleon spent the night at the country-house château of Austerlitz, three miles east of the Pratzen, the property of Prince Kaunitz, imperial chancellor under Maria Theresa.[21] The Russians melted away eastwards, not to fight again until the early months of 1807, over a year later. Emperor Francis II was forced into a further humiliating peace.

While Austerlitz itself may be considered to be an old-style battle because the whole action was completed in a short December day, it was the culmination of a campaign entirely modern both in concept and direction. Napoleon's fundamental aim, the destruction of the enemy army, was at no point compromised or allowed to be obscured by the acquisition, for prestige reasons, of cities or territory. A superb strategic deployment plan, faultlessly executed by thoroughly trained troops ensured that the *Grande Armée* engaged the dispersed allied armies successively, leading to their defeat in detail. Basic as the resupply arrangements were, and evidently erratic from the date of arrival in the Danube valley onwards, they were nevertheless good enough to sustain prodigious feats of marching. This achievement allowed Napoleon to concentrate, east of Brunn, a force large enough to engage with good prospects of success the combined armies of the two emperors, though these were much larger than his own. The tactician taking over from the strategist, a credible deception plan and a balanced design for battle based on a totally correct appreciation of the enemy's intentions produced a concentrated thrust at the decisive point and time. Land warfare entered a new era.

The Zenith and the Decline

After Austerlitz, the *Grande Armée* was at its peak. The campaign against Prussia in the autumn of the following year foreshadowed the blitzkrieg of May 1940. In thirty-three days, Napoleon annihilated the army foremost at the time in world reputation, but one which relied too heavily on the prestige, organisation and methods of Frederick the Great, forty years earlier, and which had retained too many of his superannuated generals in high command. The concurrent battles of Jena and Auerstadt, fought on 14th October, 1806, routed the Prussian field army, and were followed by a mopping-up operation which eliminated Prussia as a great power for the next six years. Had King Frederick William III gone to war a year earlier, he would undoubtedly have severely embarrassed Napoleon's operations against Austria and Russia from the outset of the campaign on the Danube, and, with Prussia poised to strike at his rear, it is hard to see how the latter part of the campaign in Moravia, which led to Austerlitz, could have taken place at all. In the event, Prussia, fighting alone in 1806, was destroyed. Berlin, 150 miles north of the battlefields of 14th October, fell ten days afterwards, pride of place in the formal entry to the city being given to Davout's corps for their triumph at Auerstadt.

By early November the leading elements of the *Grande Armée* had reached the Baltic coast, and French garrisons occupied Hamburg, Lubeck and Stettin. The final capitulation was that of Magdeburg on 10th November. In addition to 25,000 Prussian soldiers, killed or wounded in action, 140,000 more surrendered as the pursuit developed and the national arsenals yielded up 2,000 cannon to Napoleon.[22] The collapse of Prussia was on a scale comparable with that of France in 1940, and the devastation of their army in the pursuit comparable to that inflicted on the Iraqi forces committed to the Gulf War in February 1991.

With the elimination of Prussia, and with Austria out of the war following a peace treaty which had compelled the Habsburg emperor to cede Dalmatia, Venice, the Tyrol, the Vorarlberg and Swabia to the French Empire or its satellite and client states, only England and Russia remained of the major powers of the Third Coalition, established so painstakingly three years earlier by the younger Pitt. Napoleon at no stage altered his conviction that England was not only his main but his irreconcilable enemy. The inception of the campaigns in the peninsula from 1808 onwards and in Russia in 1812, which stretched his army beyond its limit of capability and so caused his downfall, becomes comprehensible once it is appreciated that Napoleon's immutable war aim was to destroy England as a world power. Trafalgar, fought six weeks before Austerlitz, had ended for ever any prospect of a cross-channel invasion. Pitt, the architect of the Second and Third Coalitions, and Nelson also, might be dead, and the British Army too small to count for much in a continental war, but British gold would subsidise continental allies and buy mercenary reinforcements, mostly from the principalities of northern Germany, for British armies. Hence Napoleon had to deny to England access to the European markets from which his arch-enemy derived the resources to continue the war.

As we have seen, Tsar Alexander had not sought peace after Austerlitz, and the campaign of 1806 was over too soon for him to render any support in the field to Prussia. As 1806 drew into 1807, a Russian army of 70,000 under Bennigsen, not among those present at the débâcle of Austerlitz, advanced into Poland. The *Grande Armée* drew east, in increasingly vile weather, and on worsening roads and deteriorating supply arrangements, to bring him to battle. The first clash, at Eylau in February 1807, was an old-style battle of indecisive result, and thus notable as the first serious check suffered by the *Grande Armée*. The battle was begun in a blinding snowstorm, which caused the misalignment of a frontal attack by Augereau's VII Corps, intended in the classic Napoleonic style to 'fix' Bennigsen while Davout was launched on a turning movement. Caught in flank, Augereau's corps was so badly mauled that it could not be reconstituted after the battle. While the first disbandment of a *Grande Armée* formation had no tactical and little operational significance, the blow to prestige and morale was nevertheless appreciable, and even Napoleon's self-confidence was badly jolted.[23] There followed an interval for regrouping, reinforcement and detachment of a force of 25,000 men under Marshal Lefebvre for the investment and capture of Danzig. This was necessary to eliminate the fortress as a threat to the ever-lengthening lines of communication, to secure for the *Grande Armée* the substantial stocks of food and forage in the city, and to provide the prestige of a victory in independent command for the former royal guard sergeant major and staunch republican, Lefebvre. A stalwart battlefield commander, but by no means a top choice among the marshals for an important autonomous task, Napoleon needed to manufacture a victory for him to justify the first creation of a dukedom among the marshals, apart from the titles already given to Berthier and the two imperial brothers-in-law, Murat and Bernadotte. Bennigsen, however, was still in the field. The recurrent problem of day-to-day rationing for the *Grande Armée* in a poverty-stricken region, and the growing necessity for detachments to secure its lines of communication caused an ever-widening dispersion of corps on the ground. This was not only dangerous in itself, but, because it lengthened the march distances for concentration, rendered more difficult the crafting of a decisive battle to destroy the Russian Army. The latter consideration allowed Bennigsen to escape a typical 'fix and outflank' manoeuvre in early June, but a week later, on the seventh anniversary of Marengo, he appeared to have caught Lannes's V Corps unsupported. Bennigsen, in the process of withdrawing his army eastwards across the River Aller through the small town of Friedland,[24] recrossed the river. Battle was engaged at odds of three to one in his favour, but Lannes held on for a long hot summer's day while the emperor concentrated the corps of Victor (replacement for Bernadotte, wounded, in command of I Corps) and Ney, the Guard and the Reserve Cavalry. Murat and Soult had been detached to capture Konigsberg, capital of East Prussia and the last city retained in

Prussian hands, and they and Davout were too distant to be brought up in time for a battle intended to catch Bennigsen's army with its back to the river.

Acting on an impromptu but precise plan by the emperor, Ney launched an attack on Bennigsen's left (southern) flank, surprising the conventional eighteenth-century military mind of the Russian commander by the lateness of the hour as much as anything else. Supported from the centre of the French line by a massed battery of thirty-eight guns under Senarmont, Napoleon's artillery commander, Ney drove into the Russian line. With the bridges over the Aller destroyed by French artillery fire, the Russians should have been annihilated, but, in the absence of Murat, the cavalry was handled with something less than previous boldness. Nevertheless, Bennigsen lost 18,000 out of 50,000 troops committed and most of his artillery, which was caught on the wrong side of the river.

Friedland was the first Napoleonic battle in which massed artillery played a decisive part. Napoleon had always regarded the arm of the service from which he came with the importance due to it in terms of eighteenth-century warfare, but Friedland is the first battle in which a positive decision was made to mass all the available guns in a single fire unit. Senarmont's tactical handling of his artillery group foreshadowed modern practice, once allowance is made for the minimal ranges of muzzle-loaded pre-cast-steel-age cannon. Senarmont's eight and twelve pounders opened fire at the maximum range for solid-shot ball ammunition of 1,600 yards – on hard ground ricochets might add a bonus of half as much again, but are unaimed and therefore unpredictable in effect. By a wholly twentieth-century combination of fire and movement – some guns remaining in action while the others limber up, move forward and come into action to cover in their turn the advance of those originally left behind – the range was reduced progressively to 600 yards. This allowed fire to be opened with canister rounds;[g] lethal against unprotected infantry. After Friedland, Napoleon sought to compensate for the deteriorating quality of his infantry by increasing both the number of guns in direct support of units and formations, and the weight of fire developed from mass concentrations of army and army group artillery. Because of the range limitation, which would continue until the advent of rifled, breech-loaded steel cannon, guns had to deploy, wheel-to-wheel, in considerable numbers. Massed stocks of ammunition were a prerequisite, and the traffic chaos of large numbers of horses, guns and ammunition wagons would be increased in conditions of poor going or constrained routes. Massed artillery was therefore

---

[g] See the military glossary at Appendix B.

highly vulnerable after a failure by its supported infantry, either in defence, as at Leipzig, or attack, as at Waterloo. The technical development of guns in the second half of the nineteenth century produced a fivefold increase in their effective range and so permitted concentrations of fire at less hazard of capture, but the problems of fire direction at long range remained unresolved until the development of radio and techniques for the adjustment of fire by observers.

After Friedland, Tsar Alexander sought peace, and the agreements reached at Tilsit between the French and Russian emperors finally brought to an end the War of the Third Coalition. While historians consider Tilsit to represent the peak of Napoleon's power and political achievement, his military capability was already in decline at a time when its commitments had increased substantially. The satellite kingdoms of Naples, Italy, Westphalia and Holland required the support of reliable forces of occupation. A substantial containing force was needed in southern Germany because Austria was unlikely to submit permanently to the outcome of wars which, since 1796, had deprived her successively of northern Italy, Belgium, most of what is now Upper Austria and Dalmatia. Concurrently, at the other end of the continent, the need to coerce Portugal into Napoleon's continental system, intended to prohibit English trade, caused, three months after Tilsit, the first French deployments into Spain. Chandler has evaluated[25] the total effective strength of the Armée d'Espagne in October 1808, exactly a year after the first incursion into the peninsula, as nearly 250,000 men and 600 field guns. It will be noted that, while the manpower strength was only slightly larger than that of the Grande Armée on first designation, there were two-thirds again as many cannon. This force was grouped into four separate formations, not entitled 'armies' but which may be considered as such, comprising eight corps d'armée, the Imperial Guard, now up to a strength of 12,000, Reserve Cavalry, and a central reserve of infantry. Allowing for sick and detached, the summed strength return in this one theatre was 314,612; a far cry from the 50,000 of the Army of Italy commanded by General Bonaparte in 1796.

The need to hold down the empire produced a requirement for soldiers in numbers which could not be sustained by the manpower of France alone. Napoleonic campaigns from 1808 until the final loss of Germany in the autumn of 1813 would be fought to an ever-increasing extent by allied and satellite troops under French command, of varying quality and questionable loyalty, especially in the event of either defeat or realignment of alliances. Furthermore, gaps in the French units came to be filled by a recurring mortgage on future annual classes of conscripts, and a continual drawing-down of the home recruitment and training base. Conscripts from 1808 onwards arrived in their combat units without the training of their predecessors and, because of their earlier call-up, when still some years short of the strength and maturity of full manhood,[h] without their predecessors' staying power. The effect on the calibre of line regiments caused by the continual expansion of elite formations has already been noted. Marbot relates[26] how, at the height of the war in Spain, after Massena's supersession following his defeat by Wellington at Fuentes d'Onoro, line regiments were still providing entrants for the Guard. There are few other factors which erode sooner the battleworthiness of a unit than to have its most experienced soldiers subjected to a continuous creaming-off process. The compensation for the reduced quality of the line infantry regiments, in terms of both technical proficiency and endurance, would be from increased artillery allocations and a growing dependence on the tactics of the mass. The latter in itself was intrinsically self-defeating in the longer term because of the greater vulnerability of densely massed infantry formations to enemy firepower. While the deterioration of the quality of cavalry and artillery took longer, the loss, when it occurred in these arms, was terminal because of the longer training time essential to mould both cavalrymen and gunners, and their total dependence on their horses. The catastrophic losses of the latter in the Russian campaign, while not quite producing a horse famine in Western Europe, were severe enough to cause Napoleon's campaign in southern Germany in 1813 to be flawed from the start, and his early victories rendered incomplete, by a chronic shortage of cavalry.

There was also a decline in the quality and performance of senior commanders and staff, caused partly by war-weariness, partly because the number of competent officers was spread too thinly over a continent-wide deployment, and partly endemic because of Napoleon's highly personalised style of command. While there was no marshal who was not a brave and competent battlefield commander when operating under the eye of the emperor, or, if out of sight, within the ambit of timely battle orders, only Massena, Davout and possibly Suchet of the twenty-six were naturally talented and trustworthy commanders fit to take on both the independent supreme command of a campaign and the military government of a province. Nor were the others encouraged or trained to develop abilities which would become

---

[h] While there were many factors in the success of the British operation to recover the Falkland Islands in 1982, not the least of them was the greater robustness of the British regular soldiers, most in their early twenties, compared with the teenage Argentinian conscripts.

essential if warfare was to be conducted and provinces governed from Portugal to Poland. Dictators have never relished the prospect of over-mighty subordinates.

The Peninsula Campaign exposed two further serious weaknesses at the level of high command. The first was the almost invariable refusal of any one marshal to either cooperate with or still less accept orders from another. In the absence of the emperor, each considered himself to be supreme. Secondly, the command structure was inadequate for its task. While Napoleon had developed the army corps system to an absolute, given the capabilities and resources of his time, for the conduct of a conventional nineteenth-century battle, the numbers of troops deployed in the peninsula and the nature of the guerrilla war required methods more sophisticated than those which could evolve from the contemporary chain of command. The circumstances needed the superimposition of a military government, which could at once provide overall direction of operations and take on the tasks of civil government and administration. Provinces as large as Aragon and Andalucia needed, in any event, the military resources of more than a single army corps. This would have allowed the purely military headquarters, corps and division, to devote their full attention to the conduct of operations. The dual function of high command to provide both civil and military government is implicit in the conduct of low-intensity warfare, which is almost invariably long-term, fought against the sympathies of a significant element of the local inhabitants, and in which the primary threat is from terrorism and irregular forces rather than the more predictable operations of a formed enemy army. In the peninsula, Napoleon's subordinates were faced by both methods of warfare. He himself served in the peninsula for a few weeks only, at the end of 1808, and never appreciated that this was a campaign entirely different from any he had conducted previously, requiring new methods of organisation and command structure. It is possible that, having placed his brother Joseph on the throne in Madrid after he had forced the Bourbon abdication, Napoleon was reluctant to trust any other subordinate commander with the vice-regal powers essential from the first. Certainly Soult, initially in Portugal and later in Andalucia, was seeking a satellite but separate kingdom for himself. The dual threat of conventional and guerrilla warfare, compounded by extreme difficulties of supply and communication, was a new problem for Napoleon but by no means a new feature in military history. The situation in Spain was a carbon copy of the difficulties suffered by the Spanish Empire itself two centuries earlier in the Netherlands, throughout the last forty years of the sixteenth century.[27] Any lessons which the French might have learned by studying this 200 year old experience were not applied.

The later Napoleonic campaigns also exposed a flaw in his method and organisation of command for conventional battle. From 1809 onwards, the numbers engaged and the consequent enlargement of the battle area introduced the need for an intermediate headquarters between Napoleon's own headquarters, which can legitimately be termed that of an army group, and those of the *corps d'armée*. The organisation of 'wing', effectively army, headquarters was never satisfactorily thought through and none of the three expedients attempted worked properly. Trusted corps commanders might be given very large corps, which often proved too cumbersome to control; or one corps commander, without any increase in staff or communication assets, might be made responsible for the operations of another corps in addition to his own; or generals were appointed as 'wing' commanders of two corps or more, who, in Field Marshal Lord Montgomery's apt phrase, had 'reached their ceiling' as commanders at a lower level. The need for good staff work increased as the overall calibre of those doing it declined. In the Waterloo campaign the combination of Soult as chief of staff and Ney and Grouchy as wing commanders, with further substantial formations retained under the direct command of the emperor in army group reserve, was a prime cause of disaster. None of the three marshals was a fool, and all had formidable combat reputations at a lower level, but they were not the best of the marshals and generals of the empire both available and willing to take part. Davout was left behind in Paris as minister of war and governor of the city, and Suchet was in independent command of a holding operation on the Upper Rhine against Schwarzenburg, advancing with typically cautious and Austrian deliberation. The presence of either Davout or Suchet in Belgium in any of the top three appointments might have tipped the scale. Soult was incapable of reproducing Berthier's expertise in transforming the emperor's expressed intentions into a proper balance of directive and explicit order to the wing commanders. Staff work at all levels was slipshod, far too many orders going astray or arriving too late to be effective. Ney's naturally impulsive temperament had been rendered even more uncertain by his exertions in Russia and the campaign of 1813 – his behaviour at Waterloo shows all the symptoms of severe shellshock amounting to death wish – and neither he nor Grouchy possessed the ability to interpret correctly the imprecise, and sometimes untimed, instructions they received. Each, at a critical point in the three days' manoeuvring and fighting which culminated on Mont St Jean on 18th June, 1815, read his immediate battle completely wrong. All too often, insufficient time allowance was made for orders prepared at army group and wing (army) headquarters to be translated into action by marching troops. The standards of expertise of staff work, tactical sense, cohesion between formations and combat capability at regimental level displayed in the campaign of 1805 had, ten years later, gone almost completely.

The Danube Valley – 1809

As 1809 opened, these terminal defects had not become apparent, but the overstretch of the armies of the empire was manifest. With three corps of the *Grande Armée*, the Imperial Guard and most of the reserve cavalry transferred to the peninsula in the previous autumn, the majority of the strength and quality of the army was in Spain. All that was left in Germany was 120,000 men under Davout, the nucleus of which was his own III Corps, but both this and the reinforcing troops provided by the states of the Confederation of the Rhine were deployed as an army of occupation in garrisons throughout Germany, and not organised as a field army. Davout had reported as early as September 1808,[28] just as the major transfers of formations to the peninsula were taking place, that Austria, by requisitioning horses, had started preparations for war. This and other intelligence indicators throughout the last three months of the year caused Napoleon to return from Spain in early January. He had chased the British army of Sir John Moore across northern Spain to Coruña, but the battle fought there after his departure for Paris was indecisive and the British gained enough time for an orderly embarkation on to their transports, to fight again in the peninsula under Wellesley.

The Austrian imperial government took the decision to resume the war as early as 8th February,[29] but kept their intent secret for the time being, with some success because, for once, the Austrian mobilisation and concentration was ahead of the French. This achievement was greatly to the credit of Archduke Charles. A younger brother of Emperor Francis II, he had first commanded an army in the field at the age of twenty-three, in the concluding phase of the campaign of 1796/7 in northern Italy, at least as competently as the geriatric generals demolished by Napoleon in the earlier stages of this one-sided contest. In 1805 he had commanded the forces detached to what became the subsidiary theatre in northern Italy, and had been worsted, though not decisively so, by Massena. The three years since Austerlitz had shown him to be a highly competent military administrator, notwithstanding fraternal imperial jealousy and the dead hand of incompetence of the Aulic Council. He had widened the basis of recruitment to the imperial armies, imposing a universal obligation for military service in defence of the Habsburg possessions, and creating the organisation to implement it. Although his territorial Landwehr were not trained soldiers, they were little different in calibre from the high proportion of young conscripts and allied troops with which Napoleon would fight the campaign of 1809, and the motivation of the Habsburg subjects in general had improved considerably on that of the Austrian imperial armies four years previously.[30] The archduke had modernised the training of the armies of the Habsburg Empire and had instituted an army corps structure copied from the French, but in the time available he could not create the effective staff organisation essential if his army were to operate with an efficiency comparable to that of Napoleon. He was also limited in his choice of subordinate commanders, and of the dismissal of those who proved incompetent. His own preference was against fighting in 1809 as delay would secure more time to perfect the training and combat capability of his army, but, in contrast to 1805, the imperial and political desire was for war. This was on the basis of perceived overcommitment of Napoleon's armies, Austrian diplomatic reports of French war-weariness and desire for revenge and restoration of the provinces lost since 1797. Following the decision of 8th February, Charles had by early April concentrated, in Lower Austria and Bohemia, either side of the Danube, a force of nearly 200,000 men, grouped as six first line and two reserve army corps, with 518 field guns in support.[31] There were further forces of 65,000 men in Italy under Archduke John, and 35,000 in Galicia under Archduke Ferdinand.

Nevertheless, and notwithstanding all this achievement, the overall strategic conduct of the continuing war against Napoleon remained flawed in that, yet again, only one nation of the potentially Europe-wide coalition opposing him would fight the land campaign and, as the critical battle approached, that nation failed to concentrate its maximum available strength at the decisive point.

In full awareness of the threat from Austria, Napoleon spent the first three months of 1809 in Paris making preparations to counter it. In order to obtain the necessary number of soldiers, he ordered the first major advance borrowing on future annual conscript classes. Already, in September 1808, there had been a combing-out of the classes of 1806 to 1809 to produce a further 80,000 recruits from those who had become liable for conscription in those years but who had not been embodied. In December 1808, 80,000 of the class of 1810 were called up, eighteen months ahead of their due date, and a further 110,000 from the same annual class in the following month.[32]

Although, at least on paper, the manpower requirements for the concurrent campaigns in Spain and Central Europe would be met, virtually a whole year's manpower had been committed ahead of its time.

For diplomatic reasons Napoleon wished to place upon Austria the onus of opening hostilities, but at the same time a concentration of forces had to be poised to take the field as soon as the Austrian hand was shown. Correctly appreciating that the main theatre of war would again be the Danube valley rather than northern Italy, Napoleon ordered two separate groupings. The first comprised 65,000 men under Davout in Thuringia, 150 miles north of the likely area of operation, but providing security for the satellite states of the Confederation of the Rhine. The second, consisting of 60,000 men under Massena and Oudinot, was placed between Augsburg and Ulm. Covering the latter on the line of the River Isar, and placed to fight a delaying action which would gain time for Davout's force to march south, was a corps of 30,000 Bavarian soldiers, commanded by Lefebvre. The distance separating these three concentrations meant that this was a preliminary deployment only; not knowing the date on which operations would start, and not wishing to give the appearance of precipitating war, Napoleon remained in Paris. From there he ordered alternative concentrations for battle. On 28th March:

> If the Austrians attack before 10th April the army will concentrate behind the Lech; the right wing [under Massena] will occupy Augsburg and the left wing [Davout] will occupy the right bank of the Rhine towards Ingolstadt and Donauworth. Donauworth must then be the centre of the army.[33]

So far, so good; the triangle of forces represented by Davout, Lefebvre and Massena would be within little more than a day's march of each other.

But two days later Napoleon ordered an alternative. If the Austrians had not moved by 15th April, the whole army was to concentrate round Ratisbon, now Regensburg, sixty miles downstream on the Danube from Donauworth. Possessed of both sets of instructions, Berthier, once again chief of staff of the *Grande Armée*, reconstituted by imperial decree on 30th March,[34] and its acting commander-in-chief pending the arrival of Napoleon, left to set up headquarters in Strasbourg, in touch with Paris by the semaphore telegraph link. Even given French standards of marching, either course, once adopted, could only be changed to the other and become effective three days after the executive order for change had reached the wing headquarters.

Austrian intentions only became clear on 9th April when Archduke Charles informed Lefebvre and the French ambassador to the king of Bavaria that he had 'orders to advance with my troops and to treat as enemies all who oppose me.'[35] There was no formal declaration of war. Berthier in Strasbourg had this intelligence on 11th April. Thus the Donauworth option should have been ordered at once and without compromise.

Unfortunately, Napoleon had continued to issue orders in detail about the Ratisbon option after Berthier had departed from Paris, and an executive summary of these was transmitted to Strasbourg by the semaphore telegraph on 10th April. In normal conditions of visibility this would have been with Berthier within hours,[36] but on this particular occasion the message was delayed by fog and took six days to travel. Meanwhile, written confirmatory and amplifying instructions were sent by hand of mounted *officier d'ordonnance* and reached Berthier on 13th April. Notwithstanding the fact that Berthier had known for two days that Austrian forces were on the move, he interpreted the written orders brought by the aide-de-camp as superseding the two options and requiring concentration of the army on Ratisbon. Davout, fully understanding the options, had, in the face of the start of hostilities on 9th April, already started his concentration on Donauworth. Berthier, on the basis of the confirmatory and misunderstood dispatches received on 13th April, ordered Davout to return to Ratisbon, which order Davout accepted against his better judgement. There followed four days of total confusion, until the emperor himself, summoned urgently by Berthier, reached Donauworth early on 17th April, having travelled the 450 miles from Paris almost non-stop in ninety-six hours, a journey which in normal circumstances might have required some ten days.

Given accurate and timely intelligence of the seventy-five mile gap which had opened up between the two wings of the *Grande Armée*, the fact that Lefebvre, supposedly covering the concentration on Donauworth, was in fact behind Davout, the disarray in the northern wing caused by order, counter-order and counter counter-order, and the advantage gained from first strike, Archduke Charles could, at least in theory, at any time up to 18th April, have brought to bear a much superior force against Davout's wing, and then, having eliminated him, turned on Massena. That he failed to do so was the fault of inferior Austrian intelligence gathering, staff work and march capability. Even had the archduke appreciated the hitherto unparalleled opportunity open to him, his army had needed six days to cover the fifty miles between the Inn and the Isar. The opportunity was thus lost before it could have been taken.

Napoleon at once ordered what amounted to a reversion to the Donauworth option, but his orders were unrealistic in that they failed to allow sufficient time for the three by now widely separated component parts of the *Grande Armée* to correct, even by forced march, the dispersion caused by the contradictory orders of the preceding four days. Davout's corps was placed at particular risk because Napoleon drastically underestimated the strength of the Austrian Army south of the Danube. Instead of a fight against equal odds, as Napoleon assumed, Davout had six corps closing in on him. Davout left a regiment to hold Ratisbon in accordance with Napoleon's order to deny the archduke the use of its bridge across the Danube. He then withdrew eastwards and, joined by Lefebvre, took up a position around the village of Abensberg with his back to the Danube but with his right flank resting on the River Ilm and so protected by it.

The three days' marching and fighting from 20th to 22nd April in the twenty miles between the villages of Abensberg and Eckmuhl became a race in time between the archduke's ability to crush Davout and Lefebvre against the Danube, and an attack by Massena and Oudinot on his own flank and rear. Summoned by the imperishable order, '*Activité, vitesse, je me recommande à vous*',[37] the marching capacity of Massena's force proved better than that of the Austrians.

Nevertheless, Napoleon was denied the victory on the scale of Jena which, on the second evening of the battle, he thought he had achieved.[38] He had continued to underestimate the size of the force opposed to Davout. He had overestimated the capability of Massena's command to execute within the time available a double envelopment of the Austrian rear; and he had assumed that his order to hold Ratisbon had been carried out. In fact, the garrison left there by Davout when he had been ordered to withdraw towards Donauworth was too small to secure the extensive fortifications of the old city, and, worse still, the key bridge over the Danube had proved too strong for the French to destroy before being forced to surrender on the evening of 19th April; the day before the start of the Abensberg/Eckmuhl battle. Forty-eight hours later, Napoleon was still issuing orders to the two wings of his army on the favourable assumption that he still held Ratisbon. Notwithstanding the loss of 30,000 out of the 210,000 with which he had opened the campaign, Archduke Charles was able to withdraw through Ratisbon towards Bohemia in good order. He left behind a garrison strong enough to ensure a tough contest for the fortress, so buying time to reorganise his army north of the river. At the same time he detached Hiller's Corps to contest the French advance on Vienna on the right bank of the Danube, by fighting a series of delaying actions on the lines of the tributaries flowing northwards from the Tyrol, in contrast to the course adopted by Kutuzov after Ulm.

Although Napoleon had restored a highly dangerous opening situation, and during the battle had demonstrated yet again his tactical mastery of any opposing commander met thus far, the engagement was indecisive, and very far from being another victorious conclusion to the campaign on the lines of Marengo, Austerlitz or Friedland. His opponent had withdrawn with a sizeable army still in the field and fit to fight. Too much had been asked of unseasoned troops, and too many deployment orders had been based on wishful thinking and assumption, rather than on properly evaluated information. Napoleon was also fortunate in that the separated wings of his army were commanded by the two marshals most competent both to read the battle in front of them and to relate it to the overall situation. The unequalled combination of Massena and Davout fighting separate but concurrent and related actions would not recur.

Napoleon's circumstances after Eckmuhl contained few of the advantages and most of the disadvantages of his broadly similar diplomatic and strategic situation after Ulm, three and a half years before. The main Austrian Army had not been eliminated and this time there would be no *coup de main* capture of a major bridge over the Danube in the vicinity of Vienna. The increasing threat from guerrillas and German embryonic nationalist aspirations forced the detachment of sizeable elements of the *Grande Armée* to secure its lines of communications while it drew eastwards in pursuit of Hiller. There was no close pursuit of the bulk of the Austrian Army north of the Danube, which left Napoleon without a clear idea of its whereabouts and intentions. Napoleon was thus forced into the course of action for which he had castigated Murat in 1805 – an advance on Vienna by the right bank of the Danube in the hope that Emperor Francis could be persuaded to abandon the war by the loss of his capital. Hiller conducted a competent delaying action but possession of the city, which then lay entirely south of the river, was not contested. Napoleon secured Vienna unopposed on 13th May, Hiller and the garrison of the city rejoining Archduke Charles, after destroying the bridges as they withdrew.

The Battles on the Marchfeldt

Environmental surgery on a massive scale has changed completely the course of the Danube around Vienna compared with its path in 1809, and the urban sprawl of the city north of the river has encroached upon the enormous plain which extends over 100 miles north and east to the mountains of

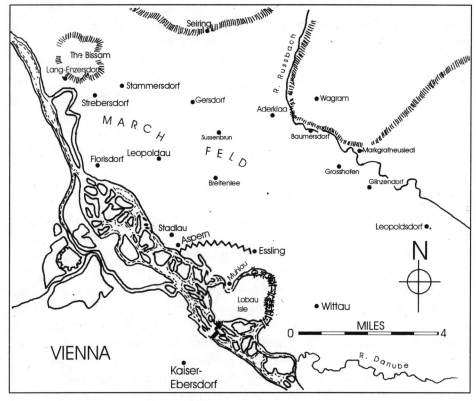

Aspern–Essling and Wagram

Moravia and Transylvania.[i] The area is natural ground for an old-fashioned battle; nowadays a soldier would describe it as 'good tank country'.

In 1278 Rudolph of Habsburg, Duke of Austria, by defeating King Ottokar of Bohemia, had established a primacy for his family in Central Europe which would endure for 600 years, and in 1683 the flood tide of Turkish land power had been turned back from its last attempt to capture Vienna by Prince Eugène of Savoy. Given the weaponry of the early nineteenth century and its influence on battlefield tactics in an area of open plain containing some villages, substantially constructed buildings could be developed into strong points, and relatively small rises in ground created possibilities for defensive works. Quite small streams and their banks constrained the movement of artillery and cavalry, particularly if the obstacle was covered by fire. Then as now, the opposed crossing of a major river produced a unique set of difficulties for the attacking force and a corresponding advantage for the defence.

In 1809 the river, as it approached Vienna, divided into a main channel, up to half a mile wide once it emerged from the gap between the Nussdorf and Bissam hills north-west of the city, and a number of subsidiary courses between islands. The largest island, Lobau, was separated from the city by the main stream and from the north bank by a semicircular branch tributary no more than 100–200 metres wide.[39] Any river crossing site must be capable of rapid development into a bridgehead compact enough for defence, but not so small as to inhibit the breakout of the crossing force. An examination of the options convinced Napoleon, correctly, that his best choice was to cross from Kaiser Ebersdorf, then a village lying outside the city limits, by way of Lobau Island. Upstream at Nussdorf the current was too swift to permit rapid bridge construction within the time likely to be afforded by an enemy known to be north of the river in strength, but not precisely where or in what numbers, the width of the main stream precluding the mounting of cavalry reconnaissance. The same lack of information also forced the rejection of the third possibility, at Fischamend, ten miles downriver from Vienna, because of the obvious exposure to the risk of flank attack before any bridgehead could be sufficiently developed. Whichever site was chosen, the impossibility of organising cavalry reconnaissance and the absence of reports from sympathisers meant that the crossing would have to be undertaken blind. By contrast, Archduke Charles would have almost real-time intelligence of French intentions. His army had secured in strength the Bisamberg feature north of the river. From its summit,

---

[i] For a description of the battlefields of Aspern–Essling and Wagram as they appear today, the reader is referred to Appendix C.

given good summer visibility, there is a commanding view of the whole course of the river past Vienna, Lobau Island (now the Lobgrund) and the south-western corner of the Marchfeldt as it extends some eight miles north of the river, to the crest of a low ridge lying between the villages of Wagram and Markgrafneusiedl. This natural rampart had (and has) its own moat. The Russbach streamlet and its steep banks are enough to throw into confusion a formed infantry assault, and, if the feature had to be attacked frontally, cavalry and artillery could cross only by existing bridges. This whole panorama is clear from the Bisamberg. If Napoleon had to embark on the battle blind, his opponent would be in the opposite position. The absence of intelligence was compounded by topographical misappreciation. Because of melting snows and sudden rainstorms in early summer, the Danube, swollen by its many tributaries upriver from Vienna, is at its most volatile in May and June. Sudden unpredicted rises in the river level are frequent,[40] which inevitably creates formidable difficulties for rapid bridging operations.

There is a wide difference, practical and psychological, both for a commander and his army, between seizure of the initiative and compulsion to attack because to do so is the least bad and dangerous of whatever options are open. The need for detachments to safeguard his flanks and ensure his lines of communication left Napoleon in mid-May with no more than 82,000 men under his hand in the neighbourhood of Vienna. If there were to be a decisive battle on the Marchfeldt, these would have to be fed over a double river crossing, first from Kaiser Ebersdorf to Lobau and from there to the north bank. Any surprise achieved could at best be no more than local and temporary. Nevertheless, it is an enduring lesson of military history that when there is only one course open it is best undertaken quickly. So ordered; on the night of 18th/19th May Molitor's division of Massena's IV Corps crossed to Lobau in boats. By the evening of 19th May, Molitor, a rising star in the *Grande Armée* firmament, destined, fourteen years later, to become a marshal of France and later minister of war under the restored monarchy, had secured the island and sited artillery to cover the proposed crossing site from Lobau to the Muhlau peninsula.

Archduke Charles had readily available 115,000 men[41] and could call in detachments larger and nearer at hand than those thrown out by Napoleon on the march to Vienna. In deciding his deployment he faced the classic dilemma of any commander seeking to contest a major obstacle crossing: whether to hold forward in strength on the waterline in order to deny any lodgement to the attacker; or, alternatively, to cover the probable crossing points by observation only, with containing and counterstrike forces held back but poised to meet any eventuality. After a period of indecision he chose the second course, rightly, given his enormous advantage of almost immediate intelligence from his observation post on the Bisamberg, and notwithstanding his unproven and inexperienced staff resources. While a screen in divisional strength held the circumference of any bridgehead likely to be thrown northwards from Lobau, his six army corps and reserve cavalry were deployed in a covering arc between the Bisamberg and Wagram.

When it is remembered that Napoleon had entered Vienna only five days previously, the inherent risks in his design for battle become readily apparent. The *Grande Armée* had to attempt to 'bounce' a crossing over a double obstacle more than half a mile wide and without tactical surprise. Molitor could not be hazarded on a crossing to the north bank until a pontoon bridge over the main stream from Kaiser Ebersdorf to Lobau had been built, and he could be joined on the island, as a minimum, by the balance of Massena's corps. The flow of troops from Kaiser Ebersdorf to Lobau was subject to frequent and sometimes prolonged interruption because of breaks in the bridge made by hulks floated down on the current by the Austrians. While by 6 p.m. on 20th May the balance of IV Corps and two divisions of the Reserve Cavalry had passed into Lobau, and a 125 yard pontoon bridge had been made ready to be swung at the crossing site to Muhlau, the main bridge was then broken again and a three foot rise in the river level overnight impeded repair work. No more troops could cross until the following day. While the French had by now lost all possibility of even local surprise, the priority given to the move of the reserve cavalry divisions to Lobau ahead of Oudinot's II Corps indicates that Napoleon was still unaware of the strength and location of the archduke's army. His remaining formation, III Corps under Davout, was placed at readiness to move from its concentration area one day's march west of Vienna.

At 4 a.m. on 21st May Napoleon took the decision to cross Massena's Corps to the north bank, and at the same time the infantry of II Corps began to cross from Kaiser Ebersdorf to Lobau, the pontoon bridge having been at last repaired. These movements were reported to the archduke by the all-seeing observers on the Bisamberg. Appreciating that this was the main thrust and not a feint, the archduke ordered a close concentration around the bridgehead. By mid-afternoon Massena and the leading elements of Oudinot's corps were heavily engaged with four Austrian corps, commanded by Hiller, Bellegarde, Hohenzollern and Rosenburg, on a perimeter no more than three miles wide and one in depth, the villages of Aspern and Essling providing vital *points d'appui* for the defence.

An initial Austrian attack on Aspern was driven off by Molitor, and the separate attacks of the four Austrian corps throughout the afternoon remained uncoordinated until, at 5 p.m., the archduke ordered a general assault. Although this was also withstood, it was apparent by evening that a French force of no more than 30,000 within the Aspern–Essling salient, whose reinforcement was slow at best and totally dependent on the continuing availability of the Kaiser Ebersdorf bridge, could do no more than hold its position with extreme difficulty against 100,000 Austrians. Massena commanding the Aspern flank and Lannes in charge at Essling had maintained local tactical superiority by making the best use of the solid stone buildings in the villages, in particular the enormous granary at Essling, while in the centre successive charges by the reserve cavalry under Bessières, to his extreme distaste under the operational command of Lannes,[42] had prevented any incursion between them. Nevertheless, without substantial reinforcement, the bridgehead could not be developed to permit a breakout, either by frontal attack or manoeuvre.

Sporadic fighting continued throughout the night and was resumed in general at dawn across the whole front. Napoleon, appreciating that the main weight of Austrian attacks thus far had fallen against the two villages, concluded that their centre might be less strongly held and ordered a counter-attack in this area, more to relieve the pressure than in expectation of a breakthrough. Indeed, nothing more can have been envisaged as, had the attack penetrated further than it did, the probability is that, given the disparity in numbers, it would have been cut off, surrounded by larger Austrian forces. Napoleon's first intention had been to use Davout's fresh III Corps, but this was still in Vienna, delayed by the constraint on movement imposed by the single bridge. A task force was cobbled together under Lannes, from the reserve cavalry, the balance of II Corps which had crossed during the night and troops withdrawn from the defence. Mounted at 7 a.m., the attack initially succeeded brilliantly, but at enormous cost to the raw French infantry advancing in mass formation. At the same time as further progress was checked by a counter-penetration force led personally by Archduke Charles, Napoleon received the intelligence that the pontoon bridge had been broken again, this time set on fire by a blazing mill. He therefore had no option but to order the recall of Lannes's task force.

By mid-morning on the second day of the battle the French position had become absolutely critical. With their retreat cut off and with no reinforcement possible until the blazing pontoon bridge could be repaired, their salient was being pressed hard at close quarters and at local odds of four against one. The defences in the villages were crumbling. Part of Aspern had been lost and the security of Essling depended upon the retention of the four-storey stone-built granary, whose walls provided protection even against artillery fire.[j] The last reserves were thrown in to stabilise the line; two battalions of the Young Guard in their first engagement. It will be realised, with the Young Guard having been formed for the first time from the pick of the 1809 class of conscripts, that these soldiers had no more than a few months' service. Their action succeeded but Napoleon, bereft of the possibility of reinforcement by Davout's corps until the bridge could be repaired, and realising that no more could be done against massive Austrian superiority of numbers and firepower, ordered a general retreat to Lobau and handed over tactical control of the battle to Lannes. Lannes, while not an independent commander of the stature of Massena or Davout, was nevertheless in their class and ahead of most of the other marshals as a battlefield tactician, and was widely recognised as such by the whole army. The withdrawal, not pressed strongly by the archduke, was completed successfully under cover of darkness but at the cost of a mortal wound to the heroic Lannes.

The side left in possession of a battlefield is generally thought to have won. Aspern–Essling was an undoubted Austrian victory, whereas Eylau, two years previously, had been no more than a check. The first clear defeat for an army commanded by Napoleon in person dealt a massive blow to his prestige and gave vast encouragement to his enemies, whether in the field, such as England and Spain, brooding and awaiting their opportunity as in Berlin and St Petersburg, or flexing their muscles in nationalist movements throughout Germany. The casualty lists on both sides were extensive and would need time to make good. The Austrians admitted a loss of 23,000 out of the 115,000 eventually engaged, but the proportionate French loss was much higher. Napoleon's declared loss of 4,100 was, for obvious reasons of propaganda, a gross understatement. The leading authority, quoted by Petre,[43] puts French casualties in excess of 20,000, out of 50,000 committed in the two days' fighting. Napoleon's gamble, albeit one forced on him, had failed. The defeat was apparent and serious enough, and would have been far worse had it not been for sluggish tactical performance by the Austrian principal subordinate commanders, particularly on the afternoon of 22nd May.

---

[j] This building still stands. See Appendix C.

If Napoleon's diplomatic and strategic choices had been limited before Aspern–Essling, they were non-existent after the battle. Historically, a battle on a comparable scale would almost invariably have been the prelude to an armistice and the conclusion of the year's campaign. Now, if Emperor Francis had not been of a mind to seek peace before the battle, he was clearly unlikely to do so after it except on terms detrimental to Napoleon. The archduke's army remained in being and could make good its losses more quickly than that of the French. Napoleon could not himself give up the war without renouncing most of his conquests. He had therefore no choice but to secure his position on Lobau, send for every available reinforcement 'from a cavalryman to a corps'[44] and, his extemporised attack having failed, organise a massive set-piece assault crossing to the north bank.

The rest of May and the whole of June passed in an uneasy and undeclared truce, with the armies in full sight of each other and separated only by the narrow strip of water between Lobau and the north bank.

Petre[45] gives the opposing strengths of the two armies, set at the beginning of July to contest the biggest battle of military history up to that time.

TABLE IV
ARCHDUKE CHARLES'S FORCES

Formation	Commander	Infantry	Cavalry	Guns
Advanced Guard				
	Nordmann	11,950	2,500	48
I Corps	Bellegarde	20,900	800	68
II Corps	Hohenzollern	25,800	560	68
III Corps	Kollowrat	17,000	740	58
IV Corps	Rosenburg	17,900	800	60
V Corps	Reuss	7,750	800	32
VI Corps	Klenau	16,200	1,400	64
Reserve Corps	Liechtenstein	11,200	8,800	48

This gives a total strength for battle of 128,700 infantry and 16,400 cavalry, supported by 446 guns. However, of this total, 1,800 men were detached from Kollowrat's corps to secure the Bisamberg, and they and the whole of V Corps were to remain uncommitted to action. Nearly one-fifth of the infantry battalions, thirty-one out of 175, were Landwehr, home defence recruits.

The significant absentee was the Habsburg Army of Italy, commanded by Archduke John. This had fought a determined delaying action against Napoleon's Army of Italy, under the nominal command of his stepson and viceroy, Prince Eugène de Beauharnais, advised by Macdonald. The latter, son of a supporter of the Young Pretender and exiled in France after the '45 rebellion, had been a senior, and sometimes successful, commander in the armies of the Republic, Directory and Consulate, but had been out of favour with Napoleon, and so unemployed, since the Peace of Amiens. The shortage of experienced commanders in relation to the demands of the concurrent Danube and peninsula theatres of war had caused his recall in March 1809, as corps commander and principal military adviser to Eugène in Italy. Archduke John had imposed a sharp check on Eugène at Sacile, north-east of Venice, but thereafter, in the absence of firm orders from his brother and commander-in-chief, had fallen not between two stools but four. His own inclination had been to attack the right rear of Napoleon's concentration round Vienna, an idea described by Petre[46] as 'the project of a madman' in view of his inferiority of numbers. Other courses open to him were to continue to delay the progress of Napoleon's Army of Italy and the corps of Marmont, the latter also marching northwards from Dalmatia to reinforce the *Grande Armée*; or he could join forces with a *levée en masse* of Hungary, which had been ordered to assemble at Pressburg, now Bratislava; or he could ignore all other possibilities and march, if not to the sound of the guns at least to the location of what was certain to be the critical battle, and join the left flank of his brother's army on the Marchfeldt. Adopting no course with determination, he was thrust aside at Raab, sixty miles south-east of Vienna, and withdrew on the Hungarians at Pressburg, who he found to be little better than an armed rabble. His remaining force of 11,000 infantry, 2,200 cavalry and thirty-four guns, though by Austrian standards of performance perhaps seven days' march distant from the army of Archduke Charles, was not too far away, if given precise orders and determined leadership, at least to influence if not to take part in the coming battle.

Table V
Napoleon's Forces

Formation	Commander	Infantry	Cavalry	Guns
Imperial Guard		7,300	3,700	60
II Corps	Oudinot	18,000	1,200	92
III Corps	Davout	30,000	4,800	98
IV Corps	Massena	24,000	3,200	90
IX Corps	Bernadotte	15,700	2,200	42
one division, Bavarian Corps	Wrede	4,800	1,000	36
Army of Italy	Eugène Macdonald	22,000	1,200	100
XI Corps	Marmont	9,000		12
Reserve Cavalry	Bessières		6,000	24

This gives a total of 130,800 infantry, 23,300 cavalry and 554 guns, all except for the commands of Marmont and Wrede, concentrated for battle at the beginning of July. However, neither of the latter, having, unlike Archduke John, received positive orders, can have been in the slightest doubt about where his presence was required, or the need to get there quickly. By calling in these two formations, the Army of Italy and Bernadotte's corps, predominantly troops of the king of Saxony, which had been covering central Germany, Napoleon accepted some risk of trouble in the eastern outposts of his empire and on his lines of communication. In resolving the perpetual option of difficulties which besets a commander-in-chief, he had yet again identified the critical point and time at which to concentrate, and in so doing had achieved a small numerical superiority over his opponent, despite the Austrian advantage of home territory.

In addition to Napoleon's field strength a further 6,000 troops provided a security force for Lobau, supported by 129 guns of position. Even when Davout's corps is included in the numbers available for battle before Aspern–Essling, Napoleon within six weeks had more than doubled his operational manpower strength, replaced the battle casualties of Aspern–Essling and achieved a fivefold increase in his field artillery. The additional cannon had been obtained from the stocks of the Vienna arsenal, which the Austrians had neglected to either destroy or remove before surrendering the city on

13th May. Napoleon's twenty-five per cent superiority in field artillery would prove highly significant.

The calibre of the troops was, nevertheless, questionable. The foundation of the ability of any army to conduct sustained operations is the strength and quality of its line infantry. The survivors of those who had benefited from the three years' depth of training achieved in the Army of the Coasts of the Ocean were by 1809 spread far and wide. The corps of Soult, Ney and Lannes had gone to Spain the previous year, and that of Augereau had been, as we have seen, virtually wiped out at Eylau. Davout's and Marmont's corps no doubt contained a nucleus of Army of the Coasts of the Ocean veterans, but the former was much attenuated by the losses of Austerlitz, Auerstadt and Eckmuhl, and the latter somewhat vitiated by three years of garrison duty in Dalmatia since that province, most of present-day Croatia, had been annexed by Napoleon after Austerlitz. The Saxons forming two-thirds of Bernadotte's corps, Eugène's Italians and Wrede's Bavarians, in all a quarter of the infantry strength, were of doubtful combat value and fair-weather loyalty. The infantry divisions of Oudinot's and Massena's corps were manned largely by the conscripts of the class of 1809 and those from the advanced call-up of later classes, as has already been mentioned. The men of II and IV Corps who had survived the campaign to date would have been well-seasoned by the experience, but up to a quarter of the battle strength of these formations at the beginning of July were no more than recruits fresh from basic training, unblooded replacements for the casualties suffered six weeks earlier. Appreciating the reduction in the quality of his line infantry, Napoleon sought to stiffen it by giving each infantry regiment a number of guns, four or six pounder, of equivalent mobility to the foot soldiers they were to accompany.[47] The captured equipment provided the necessary additional resources without inhibiting Napoleon's ability to employ artillery in mass, should this prove necessary. But, whatever the standard of the troops, the concentration achieved in the forty-three days between the Battles of Aspern–Essling and Wagram was another outstanding feat of staff work, organisation and march discipline by a Napoleonic army. Macdonald subsequently claimed in his memoirs[48] that his corps covered 'sixty leagues' in three days. In view of his probable location after the Battle of Raab this seems a slight exaggeration, but even a more probable 100 miles in the same time in the summer heat of the Austro-Hungarian plain is a considerable achievement of leadership and logistic organisation of raw troops.

When at his best, Napoleon was as much a master of deception and surprise as of concentration. His design for the Battle of Wagram was to seek to persuade Archduke Charles that the main French attack would again be mounted northwards from Lobau, on to the Muhlau peninsula. In fact something very different was intended. To this end, no attempt was made to hide the emplacement of thirty-six heavy guns of position covering the previous crossing site[49] and on 30th June, Legrand's division of Massena's corps recrossed to Muhlau, presaging another frontal attack. The need for all assaulting formations to pass through Lobau precluded an outflanking manoeuvre on the scale of Jena/Auerstadt, or even the hammer and anvil design for Austerlitz. Instead, alternative crossing sites had been reconnoitred from the eastern side of Lobau to an area on the north bank known as the Hansel Grund, according to Marbot by Napoleon and Massena personally.[50] In the hours of darkness from 30th June onwards, the corps of Oudinot and Davout, the Imperial Guard and the Army of Italy passed successively over the main branch of the Danube to join Massena on Lobau. Starting on the night of 4th/5th July, ten bridges were to be thrown over the tributary on to the Hansel Grund, for the use of a small advanced guard of Grenadier companies, to be followed by the commands of Oudinot, Davout and Eugène. Having secured the bridgehead on the Hansel Grund, II and III Corps would pivot on the village of Gross Enzersdorf to realign the axis of their advance northwards towards Markgrafneusiedl, seeking to attack the Austrian left flank, any immediate threat from the army of Archduke John being discounted, at least in this early phase of the battle. Meanwhile Massena, crossing northwards from Lobau, would secure the French left flank from Muhlau towards Aspern. The least dependable formations, Bernadotte's corps, Wrede's division and the Army of Italy, were intended to hold the centre.

The nearest present-day parallel to the traffic control and priority-of-movement problem set the staff of the Grand Quartier Général is perhaps the organisation of the departure of a very large crowd from a major ceremonial or sporting event. Berthier's march tables managed without a hitch, thanks to superb bridging operations by the *corps de génie* of the *Grande Armée*, the deployment of the 70,000 men and 300 field guns of the three right flank formations from the eastern side of Lobau on highly congested and constrained routes, notwithstanding the crossing of the lines of march of the corps of Davout and Oudinot, together with the concurrent move northwards of Massena's corps. The prevailing weather for once assisted Napoleon, a severe thunderstorm during the night helping the achievement of local surprise at all crossing sites, and by the morning of 5th July a firm lodgement had been secured on the north bank, encompassing the bend in the river north and east of Lobau.

Archduke Charles, left unaware until 5 a.m. of what was afoot, and preferring to give battle from the crescent of higher ground extending from the Bisamberg through Wagram to Markgrafneusiedl rather than on the line of the river, did not order an immediate counter-attack. Instead, he directed the immediate field fortification of the left of his position covered by the Russbach, summoned his brother John from Pressburg and moved to strengthen both his flanks at the expense of his centre. This was in preparation for a classic double envelopment of the French flanks as advocated by his chief of staff, von Wimpffen. This manoeuvre, had it been attempted, would probably have been beyond the capacity of his troops.

Massena secured the villages of Aspern and Essling, tumbling Klenau's corps back towards the Bisamberg but slightly extending his own line, and by mid-afternoon Napoleon's right wing was also well posted, the critical *point d'appui* of Gross Enzersdorf having been secured. Napoleon then sought to exploit the weakness which had developed in the Austrian centre, appreciating that the three miles between Gerarsdof and Wagram was covered only by Liechtenstein's cavalry. He ordered an attack, not solely as planned in his original design by his two right-wing corps, those of Davout and Oudinot, but by his centre as well. Davout and Oudinot could not obtain a lodgement on the Wagram–Markgrafneusiedl feature, held in strength by the corps of Hohenzollern and Rosenburg, and worse was to follow. Macdonald was on the point of breaking through west of Wagram when he was checked by Bellegarde. His Italians panicked and broke, until restrained by and reformed behind the bayonets of the Imperial Guard, in army group reserve in the rear centre. Similarly, Bernadotte, having captured as night fell the village of Aderklaa in the geographic centre of the Austrian line, withdrew from it without so informing imperial headquarters. Bernadotte considered it necessary to shorten the defence line for which he was responsible, between the positions taken up by Massena and Eugène, but Aderklaa was, as Napoleon appreciated, a valuable *point d'appui* from which to mount an attack in a future phase of the battle. Furious with Bernadotte at this unauthorised abandonment of a key point, Napoleon ordered Massena and Bernadotte to recapture Aderklaa at once after first light.

The first day of Wagram thus ended with neither side having established a clear advantage. Napoleon had broken in but had not broken through. The archduke was strongly placed to either defend or mount his double envelopment attack from the flanks of his position, and, though his centre was relatively weak, the formations at either end of his crescent-shaped deployment were still close enough for mutual support. He also had two advantages denied to Napoleon: he had visual command of the whole battlefield and the promise of substantial reinforcement if his brother's army could but march fast enough. And the *Grande Armée* still had its back to the Danube.

Both commanders-in-chief issued orders during the night for attacks as soon as the early dawn of July broke. In addition to ordering the recapture of Aderklaa, Napoleon directed Davout to mount another attack on the Markgrafneusiedl position. Archduke Charles ordered not only the execution of the double envelopment manoeuvre, but also, ignorant that Bernadotte had withdrawn from Aderklaa, set up an attack to recapture this hamlet, to be led by himself personally. For once, an Austrian formation beat a French one to the punch; on the Austrian left, Rosenburg anticipated Davout and attacked with such force as to cause Napoleon to move his centrally held reserve towards his right flank to support Davout. In the event, it proved unnecessary to commit this reserve. The battle in the centre ended for the time being with Aderklaa in French hands, but with Bernadotte's Saxons in rout. Unfortunately for Bernadotte, while galloping ahead of his troops in order to rally them, he encountered the emperor. Some ill-advised comments by Bernadotte about the conduct of the battle on the preceding day having reached the imperial eardrums, Napoleon's long pent-up fury with his brother-in-law boiled over, and Bernadotte was summarily dismissed from his command.[51] Meanwhile, the French left was also in difficulties. Massena had withdrawn troops from his defence line for the attack on Aderklaa, and came under strong pressure from the right prong of the Austrian double envelopment. Although the execution of the attacks by the corps of Kollowrat and Klenau had been dilatory, starting four hours later than that of Rosenburg, they achieved more local success. Massena's troops were driven out of Aspern and his left flank division was forced back into the Muhlau peninsula. The whole security of the French left wing, including, at least potentially, that of the line of retreat of the whole army, depended, as it had done six weeks before, on the retention of Essling. The Imperial Guard was ordered to retrace its steps from the right flank to meet this far more serious incipient crisis, but the momentum of the Austrian attack had faded, Klenau's corps on the Austrian right being taken in flank by the fire of the heavy guns on Lobau. Eugène, on his own initiative and acting correctly, had turned his command through ninety degrees to face westwards in order to maintain contact with Massena.

As a result of the second morning's fighting the concentric crescents of the overnight positions of the two armies had evolved into a French wedge, aligned broadly north-west and north, surrounded, except at its base, by an Austrian inverted U, stronger on its sides than at its foot, which extended for about three miles between the villages of Sussenbrunn and Aderklaa.

Napoleon elected not to accept any further risk to his left flank and line of retreat. Having directed Davout to maintain the pressure on Rosenburg at Markgrafneusiedl, he ordered Massena to execute a pivotal turn to bring his corps to face westwards, seeking conformity with the movement already executed by Eugène. To divert Austrian attention from a manoeuvre always complicated, and, when performed under fire, highly risky, he ordered Bessières and the Reserve Cavalry to mount spoiling attacks against the Austrian forward positions between Essling and Aderklaa. This is perfect cavalry country, and Bessières's attacks so distracted Kollowrat that Massena's realignment was completed successfully and the threat to the French left averted. Next, to regain the initiative, Napoleon mounted a counterstroke on an axis directed towards Sussenbrunn, the north-west corner of the Austrian inverted U. There could be neither surprise nor subtlety about this move. The inexperience and doubtful reliability of the infantry available, 8,000 men of the Army of Italy under Macdonald, made it necessary to send them forward in mass and close order formation, giving confidence to raw troops, but magnifying their vulnerability to enemy firepower until they could assault with bayonets.[52] The formation adopted was a hollow square on a frontage of approximately half a mile. This phalanx was supported from its left flank by a massed battery of 112 guns drawn from the artillery of the Guard and the Army of Italy, under Lauriston, like Macdonald, of Scottish descent. Casualties in infantry and artillery alike were most severe. Macdonald lost eighty per cent of his 8,000. Whole detachments of Lauriston's gunners were wiped out and had to be replaced by grenadiers of the Guard, veterans who, though infantrymen, would have learned enough about cannon to man them in this sort of emergency. Reinforced at the critical moment when Napoleon ordered forward Wrede's division, Macdonald's attack succeeded. At the end of the battle Napoleon created him marshal of France.

Elsewhere on the battlefield, what had been impending disaster was turning into an unqualified victory for Napoleon. The army of Archduke John, feebly led, had been screened effectively by light cavalry supported by a single infantry division, and had taken no part in the battle. At Markgrafneusiedl, the Iron Marshal, having had a horse killed under him for neither the first nor the last time, had broken through and the equally robust Oudinot, supported by Marmont and Eugène, had gained a lodgement at Wagram. On the French left, Massena, supported by the guns of Lobau, had regained Aspern and finally secured that flank. Archduke Charles had no option but to order a retreat north-westwards, and, as only Marmont's corps was fresh enough to mount an effective pursuit, the Austrians retired in good order with none of the disorganised chaos of the armies beaten at Austerlitz and Jena.

Nevertheless, an armistice was concluded six days after the battle and, shortly afterwards, Habsburg jealousy triumphed over common sense, and Archduke Charles was dismissed from command of the army. The peace terms produced for Napoleon a substantial financial indemnity, additions to the Dalmatian territory ceded after Austerlitz, Salzburg and part of the Tyrol for Bavaria, a small slice of Galicia for the tsar as a reward for remaining neutral and an archduchess as brood mare to produce a direct heir for the Bonaparte dynasty.

Archduke Charles had fought a more effective campaign than any general previously opposed to Napoleon. Largely because of his work over the preceding three years to modernise the armies of the Habsburg Empire, he could count on forces of a quality more nearly equal to those of his opponent than any faced by the French since 1792. He was let down by flabby subordinate leadership, an unpractised staff, march performances that, notwithstanding the similar potential of the troops, were well below the achievement of the *Grande Armée*, and which cost him opportunities throughout the whole campaign, and to a degree by his own indecision and inactivity in the six weeks between Aspern–Essling and Wagram. Napoleon by contrast had demonstrated supreme skill of generalship in twice retrieving a potentially disastrous situation, however much inevitable and of his own creation. The dangerous dispersion of his forces and confused instructions at the start of the campaign, the extreme risk in the attempt to force a crossing of the Danube in May and the operational situation on the second morning of Wagram, each of which courted defeat, were restored by a combination of strategic, tactical and organisational skills unmatched in previous military history. The deciding factors in the relative achievements of the two armies were concentration of effort at the critical point and time, and cohesion of action. Given his advantage of commanding observation of the whole battle area, the latter should have been easier for the archduke than for Napoleon at both Aspern–Essling and Wagram. In fact, the reverse happened.

Owing to the increasing size of the forces committed to battle, the expansion of the battle area and the influence of new technology, commanders-in-chief in the future would have to devise new methods of operation and work to entirely new standards.

The Political Dimension Expanded

Clausewitz, writing long enough after Waterloo to derive an objective view from prolonged study of the political, strategic and tactical events in which he had participated as staff officer and combat soldier, would put forward the parallel propositions that war is total and must, if embarked upon, be conducted with the totality of the resources of the state. The late twentieth-century perception of warfare is that the only justifications for embarking on it are a moral crusade, or for national survival when all other measures have been exhausted. This was not necessarily so in the nineteenth century after Waterloo. Bismarck would benefit from the application of the philosophy of Clausewitz and, as will be seen later, treated war as one among several possible instruments of state policy, almost as a golfer might choose to use an iron rather than a wood. The First World War would, because of its enormous and unforeseen cost, set a limit to the Bismarckian perception of warfare, but the twin pillars of the philosophy of Clausewitz would remain valid for more than a century, until the destructive power of nuclear weaponry reduced to madness the idea that total warfare could ever again be a sensible extension of the government policy of a major power. The replacement was the philosophy of deterrence. The assurance of the mutual destruction of the protagonists produced instead an uneasy peace between the superpowers, during which warfare continued by other means, through subversion, by surrogates and for limited objectives.

Napoleon was the harbinger of the doctrines of both Clausewitz and Bismarck. He contrived to generate a greater proportion of the resources of his country to the prosecution of war, and for a longer continuous period of time, than had been achieved previously by any nation state, and his method of fighting always sought the destruction of the enemy army as the primary objective, rather than the stately minuet about territory characteristic of most warfare before his time. Notwithstanding the increasing ferment of nationalism, and popular pressure for liberalisation of the reactionary governments re-established after the Congress of Vienna and maintained by alliances of ruling houses until 1848, there was no significant war involving any of the European powers for nearly forty years after Waterloo.

When war returned, it was all the more extreme. The catalyst for the unification of Germany under the leadership of Prussia was, in the event, military, not political, ethnic or economic. In 1870 France, faced with a burgeoning, expansionist and self-confident Prussia, whose growing influence she had done little to hinder and much to encourage, would attempt to mobilise her full resources in order to restrain the threat from across the Rhine, and to maintain her own position and prestige. The disastrous outcome would require, nearly half a century later, the full application of the national resources not only of France, but also of Russia, Great Britain and the United States. At the end of the First World War the lands which had been lost to France after the war of 1870 were restored to her, but at a cost in casualties which left her population lower in 1919 than it had been in 1914. The particular venom of a civil war allied to readily available technology had caused total war to engulf the United States ten years before the conflict of 1870. Japan would embrace the concept all the more readily because of the tradition of bushido.

By 1914 it appeared that warfare could be nothing other than total for any European nation involved. The Atlantic and Pacific Oceans would give the United States the benefit of a further quarter-century's isolation and limitation of commitment. But in Europe, what might have passed off as a local conflict between Serbia and the Dual Monarchy of Austria–Hungary drew in successively, because of the contemporary network of alliances, Russia, Imperial Germany and France. None could order a partial mobilisation, even supposing they had so wished. It had to be all or nothing. A moral commitment to France and a long-standing if not altogether precise guarantee to Belgium forced the United Kingdom, for the first time in her history, to devote the totality of her national effort to the direct prosecution of war; having for a century relied for her security on the prestige of the Royal Navy after Trafalgar, the world's largest fleet and a small standing army recruited wholly from volunteers, she would be compelled to order conscription and deploy a large army to the European land mass. The cost of the artillery ammunition alone to support the first trial of strength of Britain's first conscript army, at the Third Battle of Ypres in 1917, would comfortably exceed total expenditure on new ship construction for the whole Royal Navy three years previously, in the last year of peace but at the height of the Dreadnought race with Imperial Germany.[53] The entry of the United States into the conflict in 1917, however belated, was, when it occurred, total in the sense that her contribution to the war in Europe was the sum of what could be mobilised and transported across the Atlantic before the war ended. Within fifteen months of her entry into the war the United States had deployed over a million men in France, having twenty-one full-strength operational divisions ready to take the field by mid-July, 1918.[54]

Given the proposition that before 1815 only Napoleonic France had fought a total war, and that by 1914 it was inevitable that any war involving the

European Great Powers would be total, it is necessary to establish how and when the change occurred. Much of the answer lies in the events of the years between 1860 and 1870.

Notes

[1] Strengths given in Chandler, *Campaigns*, p.382.

[2] Chandler, *Campaigns*, p.385.

[3] Clausewitz, *On War*, translated Howard and Paret, Everyman's Library Edition, London, David Campbell Publishers Ltd, 1993, Chapter 14.

[4] Manceron, op.cit., pp.84 and 98; Elting, op.cit., p.560.

[5] Elting, op.cit., pp.558 and 561. It is evident that the leading company with the contract, Compagnie Breidt, cut corners at all points. Only one driver was provided for each four-horse wagon. They began the support of the march to the Danube with a mere 200 wagons, and never produced more than 540. As the company provided the horses and drivers, while the government provided the wagons, it needs little imagination to understand what would happen when conditions became difficult.

[6] Watson, op.cit., p.111.

[7] Chandler, *Campaigns*, p.397.

[8] Marbot, op.cit., vol. I, p.163.

[9] Manceron, *op.cit.*, pp.98–99.

[10] Elting, op.cit., p.561.

[11] Manceron, op.cit., p.95.

[12] Chandler, *Campaigns*, p.399.

[13] Chandler, *Campaigns*, p.402.

[14] Chandler, *Campaigns*, p.405–6.

[15] Marbot, op.cit., vol. I, pp.164–69, describes the flank guard operation of Augereau's VII Corps in the Vorarlberg and the Tyrol.

[16] Manceron, op.cit., p.27.

[17] Chandler, *Campaigns*, p.412.

[18] Strengths are given in Chandler, *Campaigns*, pp.416–20.

[19] Manceron, op.cit., p.203.

[20] Marbot, op.cit., vol. I, p.187. It might be asked how Marbot, an officer on Augereau's personal staff, came to be at Austerlitz. The answer is that it was customary, when a detached

commander was reporting a success to imperial headquarters, to send an officer who had particularly distinguished himself and merited reward at the hands of the emperor. Augereau selected Marbot to carry the news of Jellacic's capitulation. Once arrived at imperial headquarters, with a major battle clearly imminent, an officer of Marbot's proven expertise and competence would not have been allowed to depart: in any event the last thing Marbot himself would have wished!

[21] Manceron, op.cit., p.302.

[22] Chandler, *Campaigns*, p.352.

[23] Macdonnell, op.cit., p.143.

[24] For a description of Friedland, see Chandler, *Marshals*, pp.150–53. The ranges, calibres and ammunition natures of the artillery of the *Grande Armée* are tabulated in Chandler, *Campaigns*, pp.358–59.

[25] Chandler, *Campaigns*, Annex E. Anyone who has ever served as a staff officer with responsibility for either manpower or mobilisation planning knows the impossibility of arriving at figures which are 100 per cent accurate. It is, for example, all too easy to 'double count' troops in transit from one unit to another, or to omit them altogether. The practice demanded by Napoleon, of the fortnightly submission of regimental strength returns through brigade, division and corps HQ to GQG, set a standard of precision which even present-day computerised HQ might find hard to match.

[26] Marbot, op.cit., vol. II, p.179.

[27] Grierson, *The Fatal Inheritance*, London, History Book Club, 1969. This forty year struggle in the Spanish Netherlands might, with advantage, have been studied by any commander responsible for the conduct of counter insurgency operations: from the peninsula through Vietnam to Northern Ireland.

[28] Macdonnell, op.cit., p.186.

[29] Chandler, *Campaigns*, p.663.

[30] Chandler, *Campaigns*, p.667.

[31] Strengths given in Petre, *Napoleon and the Archduke Charles*, reprinted in the Napoleonic Library, London, Greenhill Books, 1993, p.31, originally published in 1909, this invaluable work of reference is based on a meticulous study of the ground and a previous detailed analysis of the Habsburg armies by Binder von Krieglstein.

[32] Chandler, *Campaigns*, p.668.

[33] Watson, op.cit., p.162.

[34] Chandler, *Campaigns*, Annex F.

[35] Chandler, *Campaigns*, p.677.

[36] Elting, op.cit., p.104.

[37] Macdonnell, op.cit., p.187.

[38] Chandler, *Campaigns*, p.685.

[39] Chandler, *Campaigns*, pp.696–97.

[40] The author had personal experience of this, and a narrow escape, when on a walking holiday in the Inn valley in 1965.

[41] Chandler, *Campaigns*, p.696.

[42] Marbot, op.cit., vol. I, pp.420–26.

[43] Petre, op.cit., p.296.

[44] Macdonnell, op.cit., p.195.

[45] Strengths given by Petre, op.cit., p.351 and p.352.

[46] Petre, op.cit., p.306.

[47] Chandler, *Campaigns*, p.708.

[48] Quoted in Chandler, *Marshals*, p.243.

[49] Chandler, *Campaigns*, pp.710–11.

[50] Marbot, op.cit., vol. II, p.7.

[51] Chandler, *Campaigns*, pp.723–24.

[52] For a description of this action, see Chandler, *Marshals*, pp.247–51.

[53] The two figures are cited respectively by Liddell Hart, *A History of the World War*, London, Faber and Faber, 1934, p.429; and Fuller, *Decisive Battles of the Western World*, Stevenage, Spa Books, 1994, vol. III, p.177.

[54] Liddell Hart, op.cit., p.479.

Chapter IV
Command, Communications and Intelligence

Government Control

The rulers of Prussia apart, it had been the exception rather than the rule throughout the seventeenth and eighteenth centuries for a monarch to take direct command of his armies in the field, though younger brothers and members of cadet branches of the royal house might do so. It follows that there existed a rudimentary system which allowed the political leadership of a nation to exercise a degree of control over the operation of its armies. But the arrangements neither needed to be nor could be anything more than basic. Because wars tended to be fought for limited objectives and almost invariably only between late spring and early autumn, the commander in the field required few guidelines beyond a directive either to defeat the enemy in front of him as soon as possible, or to avoid a major engagement pending the outcome of diplomatic negotiations. Also, one major battle tended to settle the whole issue. Once this had been fought, the army commander on the ground, because of the lengthy transition time for messages, had a very wide measure of discretion in dealing with his opposite number, to a degree inconceivable in terms of what a home government would allow once there was a system of communication faster than a man on a horse or a sailing ship. The Convention of Cintra in August 1808, negotiated on the spot and without political instructions by the commanders of the British and French armies in Portugal, returned to France 25,000 soldiers beaten decisively in the field. They had no possible source of supply, no support from the local population and were conveyed home under a flag of truce across a seaway dominated totally by the Royal Navy, without any restriction being placed on their future participation in the war. It was not so much the extreme unpopularity of a very bad deal when its terms became known in England which ensured that there would be no repetition. It was rather that the war between England and France had become total, with national war aims mutually exclusive and not susceptible to resolution by negotiation. Before the next European-scale war had ended, there was a telegraph system which allowed governments in London and Paris to intervene to an unprecedented extent in the conduct of operations more than 2,000 miles away. Wellington in the peninsula might exchange dispatches with London in three weeks if conditions of wind and weather were favourable. Even the news of Waterloo, fought no more than eighty miles from the continental terminal of a regular sailing-packet service to England, took three days to reach London because of adverse weather in the Channel. Forty years later, thanks to steamships, letters written in England reached the Crimea a fortnight later, and the electric telegraph, once installed, reduced the transit time of political direction from home and response from army headquarters in the field from weeks to a matter of hours.

If, a century after Waterloo, the political leadership of each of the Great Powers had established in the intervening time a more positive control over military strategy and the direction of operations in the field, it was the decade of the Catalytic Wars, together with their curtain-raisers in the Crimea and Italy, which provided the crucible for the philosophy and the practical proving ground for the step-advance in technology. At one end of the scale, the arrangements of the kingdom of Prussia were as simple as they could be. The king, as Supreme Warlord, assumed personal command of his armies in the wars of 1864, 1866 and 1870, and took with him into the field not only his chief of general staff and minister of war, but also his first minister and representatives from most of the civilian government departments. While in 1864 and 1866 the government of Prussia was absent from Berlin for no more than a few weeks, the country was, from August 1870, run for six months from army group headquarters in France, first in the field and thence on the move every two or three days to keep pace with the operational situation, and later during the Siege of Paris from Versailles. Co-location of all the main participants in the government of a country which subordinated everything to the military allowed both the peace terms and the future structure of Germany to be thrashed out face to face in 1866 and 1871 between the political leadership, which meant Bismarck, and the military, in which Moltke was the most important and influential but by no means the only voice. Unitary control of the total effort of the state from the supreme headquarters of the army in the field was, on the face of it, simple and basic, but it provided a precedent rather than a satisfactory blueprint for Imperial Germany in the far more complex geopolitical and social conditions of 1914. The synchrony of political and military interests needed something better.

The war of 1859 was too short to produce any useful lessons, especially as both emperors exercised direct command of their armies in the critical last phase of the campaign in Lombardy. The first-hand experience of Solferino, in which one in eight of the soldiers engaged was either killed or wounded, was a strong influence on both Franz Joseph and Napoleon III to conclude a peace whose terms fell a long way short of the initial war aims of the latter. Similarly, in 1866, while there was some discussion between the imperial cabinet in Vienna and Benedek's headquarters in Bohemia about the design for the campaign, that proposed by Vienna was unrealistic and, once the fighting started, the initiative was wholly in the hands of Prussia.

In 1870, the relationship between the civil and military government of the Second Empire was flawed from the start and collapsed within six weeks of the declaration of war. The degree of liberalisation of the empire, achieved in fits and starts from 1863 onwards, made it essential for there to be a strong civil government in Paris, capable of retaining the confidence of the Corps Legislatif and possessing both will and capability to maintain order in the capital, which was fully recognised to be the most volatile part of the whole country. This required a far more powerful civil administration than Bismarck found necessary to leave behind in Berlin. Similarly, the Bonaparte dynastic imperative required Napoleon III to take command of his army in the field. The two immediate causes of the collapse of the government of the Second Empire were the physical inability of the emperor to cope with the demands of active service because of the mind-deadening pain of a kidney ailment, and a series of disasters which nothing could explain away. An attempt to strengthen the civilian government after the first defeats, which the emperor was powerless to influence even if he had so wished, failed to improve public confidence on the streets of Paris. In the second half of August, the situation in the French capital was similar to that in St Petersburg in the third winter of the First World War or in Berlin before the wall came down: a discredited regime would be toppled as soon as the mob realised that it had the power to do so, because there were no reliable troops left behind to maintain order. Meanwhile Louis Napoleon, precluded from returning to his capital until a victory had been won, was an embarrassment in the baggage train first of one army, then of another. He was still head of state but his role as head of government had been transferred to the Council of Regency when he departed for Metz at the end of July, and his post as commander-in-chief had been abdicated a fortnight later. In the closing days of August, he felt powerless to intervene in order to prevent the imposition of a politically inspired course of action on the army with which he was in company, even though the operation as directed from Paris was clearly totally unsound in military terms.

If Prussia's system, however successful between 1864 and 1871, was over-simplistic to an extent which carried within it the seeds of defeat in the First World War, that of the Second Empire, with the overlay of the special circumstances of the Bonaparte dynasty, was proved wrong by failure. It is necessary to examine some aspects of both English and French government control of their armies in the Crimea, and of the political machinery of government of both sides in the War Between the States, to derive more precise lessons and better precedents for the future.

The Crimean War provided two such innovations. In 1853, the British Government took the first step towards the institution of a war cabinet as the supreme arbiter of national strategic policy.[1] The reason was as much political as military. The party organisations of the mid-nineteenth century were much more fluid than would be the case even fifty years afterwards; many members of both Houses of Parliament, including some of the cabinet, while disposed to support the administration of Lord Aberdeen, were not in favour of war with Russia on the side of the Ottoman Empire. Aberdeen, who had come to power in the previous year, was a compromise leader, between the prime minister who had been, Lord John Russell, and the prime minister who would be, Palmerston. The British war plan was the brainchild of Sir James Graham, first lord of the Admiralty and close political associate of Aberdeen, but without the prestige of the magnates and nationally known politicians who held the main offices in the government. Aberdeen established a cabinet committee under Palmerston, at the time Home Secretary but with much previous cabinet experience at the Foreign Office and the War Office, to have oversight of the war plans. In addition to Palmerston and Graham, the other members were the secretary at war, whose responsibility was for army administration rather than operations, the commander-in-chief and the master general of the ordnance, the two latter political appointments of cabinet status. When the war began, the committee lapsed because the size of the cabinet was still small enough for all members to exercise directly their collective responsibility. Unmodernised communications dictated that the approach to war had to be conducted along the procedures of the previous century. The British ambassador at Constantinople, Lord Stratford de Redcliffe, a diplomat with nearly half a century's experience of dealings with the Porte, had to be given very wide powers of discretion. In the period of rising tension in May and June 1853, the power to decide whether it should be peace or war was, in effect, delegated to him, because by cabinet decision of 31st May[2] he was authorised to call up the Mediterranean Fleet to Constantinople, an action which Russia was bound to regard as hostile and might well take as a *casus belli*.

It is a tenable theory that the almost unfettered discretion of ambassadors and commanders-in-chief expired shortly afterwards. Two years later, and eight months after British and French armies had established themselves in the Crimea, the headquarters in the field was connected by direct telegraph link to Paris. The doctrine of command for allied forces operating together in the field was still in its infancy. Although by the spring of 1855 the French were by far the major partner on land, having twice the number of soldiers in the Crimea as the British Army after the terrible winter, a unified command was not appropriate, for obvious political reasons. All operations had to be agreed jointly by the two commanders-in-chief; an arrangement simple enough on the face of it, but one which in reality tends to produce the lowest common denominator of decision. In May 1855, Canrobert, commanding the French Army after the death of St Arnaud, agreed after much persuasion that there should be a joint expedition to Kertch, at the entrance to the Sea of Azov. The expedition had sailed when a telegram arrived from Napoleon III, ordering a concentration of the French Army to execute a quite different design.[3] Canrobert insisted on the recall of the expedition, and resigned the army command in disgust. His successor, Pelissier, a man of rougher and stronger fibre, knew when to turn the blind eye. Notwithstanding the presence of the sapper General Niel as the personal representative of the emperor, the expedition was mounted again a fortnight later and achieved a great success. The judgement of the commander on the spot should usually be supported unless there is a compelling reason to do otherwise.

In the War Between the States, the governments of both sides appreciated that the political arm of government should exercise control of military strategy, and systems evolved in response to events. The government of the Confederacy, fighting for independent existence, had also to resolve the inherent illogicality and challenge to its authority implicit in the issue of states' rights. The member states of the Confederacy had seceded from the American Union because those with the power at the time to decide had concluded that ultimate sovereignty was an attribute of each individual state, and not of the federal union. How, then, could their own newly established federal government, given broadly the same structure and powers as the one in Washington which they had left, impose its will, even in circumstances of absolute military necessity? The answer is that it failed to do so. Even in 1864, with the cause on the point of being lost, prickly state governors would take stands on the principle of states' rights against the central government in

Richmond. This authority had done its best, its prime asset being the quality and abilities of the man elected as president. Jefferson Davis was a West Point graduate who had seen active service in the Mexican War of 1846–47,[4] and had experience of top-level military administration as secretary of war in the cabinet of President Pierce (1853–57). Departing with dignity from the United States Senate in 1861, he was at once chosen by his own state, Alabama, as the major general in command of their volunteers. Elected president of the Confederacy, against his own wish, as an acceptable compromise candidate, he furnished himself with a military adviser, first Lee, next J.E. Johnston and finally Bragg. It has to be admitted that all of these generals, while they held this post of influence rather than power, were there because at the time they could not readily be placed elsewhere, and the personal antipathy between Davis and Johnston must have eroded the impact of the latter. The Confederacy never had the resources, manpower or industrial, to defeat the Union, but, unlike the Second Empire, a flawed system of strategic direction was not a major factor in its downfall.

In Washington, neither Lincoln nor Stanton, secretary of war from January 1862 onwards, had any comparable military background, though Lincoln had held a commission as a captain of Illinois Volunteers. Stanton, an Ohio-born lawyer, who had been Attorney-General in Buchanan's administration, immediately preceding that of Lincoln, took office after allegations of corruption had caused the resignation of his predecessor. By reason of his personality, Stanton established from the first his primacy as the political head of an army which had come near to producing its own candidate for dictatorial powers. It is at first sight an anomaly that, in a totally unmilitary nation, the senior officers of the United States Army should have enjoyed the prestige which they did in 1861. Apart from the over-romanticised concept of war which permeated the whole country, there are three reasons for this. At least four of the previous fifteen presidents, together with a number of the opponents they had defeated on election day, had owed their opportunity to previous high command in the United States Army in war. Secondly, not only was the present commanding general, Winfield Scott, in the latter category he was also a hero, not just of the Mexican War but of the war of 1812 with England as well. His position as senior serving officer of the United States Army dated from 1841,[5] and this longevity in his post, combined with his majestic personality, exercised a dominating influence on more recently arrived politicians, who were generally fully conscious of their transient status. And, thirdly, there was the prestige of the West Point graduate. Few other Americans enjoyed four years' technical education in a specialist subject at the standards which West Point had achieved. Surely, therefore, those of its graduates who had risen to the top of an army in which opportunities for advancement had been limited in the extreme must be experts in their field?

Whatever Lincoln's misgivings about his own military knowledge and ability – and when it was obvious to him that the war had started badly, he drew books about military strategy from government archives[6] just like a lawyer preparing a case in an unfamiliar subject – he was never in any doubt about the supremacy of the political arm of the government, or the danger inherent in a general who appeared to be combining an agenda of his own with an unhealthy degree of adulation from the troops he commanded, which happened to be the Union Army closest to Washington and operating in the critical eastern theatre of the war. Scott was too old for active service, and was soon replaced altogether by the thirty-five year old McClellan, hero of the hour on the basis of two minor victories in West Virginia. After a mutual decline of confidence and a botched campaign, Lincoln, while retaining McClellan in command of the Army of the Potomac, reduced the status he had been given as Scott's successor by appointing Halleck over his head as commanding general. But the Illinois lawyer-turned-politician soon had to put the man considered to be the army's most erudite soldier in his place. Asked to give positive advice, Halleck evaded the issue. Lincoln, repeating the request, added the rider, 'Your military skill is useless to me if you will not do this.'[7]

If Lincoln had to wait for and partly contrive the right set of circumstances in which he could both issue his Emancipation Proclamation and dismiss McClellan altogether, his subsequent search for a general who could win the war was not inhibited by the fear of a Praetorian Guard-style palace revolution. In 1864, the Union evolved a satisfactory control system: Lincoln as *de jure* commander-in-chief and supreme political authority, Stanton as political head of the army, with very considerable logistic resources directly under his hand, Grant as supreme commander in the field and Halleck in Washington as chief of staff, in charge of army organisation and administration. Over a million men under arms and a campaign area the size of Western Europe had forced the evolution of a government machine which could harness the whole resources of the nation.

The effective direction of all levels of land warfare depends upon an efficient and reliable communication system and the acquisition of timely and reliable intelligence about the enemy. Before analysing the philosophy and exercise of command in the field in the decade of the Catalytic Wars, it is necessary first to establish the extent to which the technology of communication and the techniques of intelligence gathering and evaluation could provide the necessary support.

Communications

The developments in the transmission of information which became available in the mid-nineteenth century were on the same dramatic scale as those in the areas of firepower and mobility. They were also at least as important, because the more tangible improvements in hitting power and the ability to transport vastly increased numbers of soldiers could not have been fully utilised without them. By the same token, and as with most other innovations, what was achieved at the time was neither the end of the story nor even the best use of what was available.

The existence of a strategic communications system in the Revolutionary and Napoleonic Wars has already been noted, and its shortcomings during the hours of darkness and at other times of poor visibility discussed. By 1815, the ultimate 'state of the art' in the transmission of strategic information by semaphore had been reached. Much had been done to produce also a viable tactical system. This, however, was not appropriate for the close-quarter conditions of the land battle fought in a relatively small area. Rudimentary ship-to-ship signalling systems, to indicate either emergency or peremptory command, had existed for centuries. Between 1800 and 1803 the then Captain Home Popham of the Royal Navy devised a system based on the use of ten different coloured flags. These could be used either separately or in combination for single letters and numbers to spell out words in full, or in groups of three for the longer and most frequently used words, and as many as 3,000 standard phrases or sentences.[8] The originator hoisted his signal, which all designated recipients were expected to acknowledge and, unless ordered specifically otherwise, put into execution as soon as the signal was hauled down. The same system was still in use at Jutland a century later, but attenuated because steam-driven ships lay further apart than in Nelson's line of battle, and because visibility was impaired by smoke from funnels and gunfire. At least one authority blames a serious error in the British conduct of the battle cruiser action at Jutland on the use of flag hoists rather than signal lamp by Beatty's signals officer, from a flagship whose bunting was notoriously difficult to read because of the design of her superstructure.[9] Popham's system provided, coincidentally, the basis for an encryption code, because the use of two or three flags represented words or sentences. The core of Nelson's famous signal at Trafalgar required twenty-eight flags to be hoisted, the first eight words being covered by three-flag groups and only the last, 'duty', having to be spelled out in full. An intelligent signals officer, Lieutenant John Pascoe, had already reduced the length of the signal by advising Nelson to replace 'expects', which had a three-flag code, with 'confides', which did not.[10] But the sea system, using halyards and masts inbuilt in the ships, required also a large stock of flags and time to consult the comprehensive signal book in order to compose or interpret the messages. It was not suitable for the faster-moving circumstances of the land battle.

When the limit of development of any system has been reached, further progress is possible only through the invention and application of new technology. In the field of communications, the ability to transmit and receive a variable-length pulse of electric current provided the means. Just as Popham had reduced letters, words and phrases to a few flags, so Henry Morse translated them into combinations of long and short pulses. He was granted a US patent in 1837, and by 1844 there was a forty mile working link between Washington and Baltimore, incorporating relay stations to minimise the loss of signals through attenuation caused by uninsulated wire. Thereafter, it was wholly logical that, both in Europe and the United States, the expansion of the telegraph system proceeded in parallel with that of the railway, and along the same geographic paths. The discovery that rubber could be used to insulate wire, made and applied in the 1840s, not only expanded the distance between intervening and retransmitting relay stations, thus reducing transit time, but also allowed the installation of underwater systems. A cable linking Dover with the continental layout at Cap Griz Nez was laid in 1851, and by 1854 the European civil link extended to Bucharest. When the British and French armies deployed in May to what is now Bulgaria, a French infantry regiment laid a line from Bucharest on to Varna. In April 1855, a 340 mile under-sea link was laid from Cape Kalagria, thirty miles north-east of Varna, to Balaclava Bay.[11] Continuing dependence upon relay stations precluded 'instant' communication and normal transmission time between Paris and Balaclava was of the order of twenty-four hours. But, as we have seen, this was enough for the born meddler in the Tuileries to try to impose a detailed plan on his army commander in-theatre. The Crimean War also saw the first use of the electric telegraph in the field. A link of some twenty miles was laid from the entry point at Balaclava, connecting the administrative bases at Kadekoi and Kamiesh with British Army headquarters on the heights.[12]

The duration and scale of the War Between the States forced the deployment of a much expanded system. The links which had been installed along the railway lines were requisitioned for military use by the same act of

Congress which placed the railroads of the Union under the absolute control of the secretary of war,[a] and were expanded by an additional 15,000 miles of cable laid for operational reasons.[13] A US Military Telegraph Corps was formed and, like the railways, placed not under the control of the generals, but of Secretary Stanton. Lincoln certainly appreciated the importance of the system. Numerous contemporary accounts attest to his presence throughout the most critical events of the war in the telegraph office of the War Department: the White House did not yet have its own. When, in 1864, a state of static warfare developed during the Siege of Petersburg, Grant's headquarters at City Point was connected both to Washington and the headquarters of the principal subordinate commanders around the perimeter.[14] The Union Army also developed the system beyond the establishment of a link between formation headquarters which were likely to remain in the same place for some time. The means existed to lay cable in the field, manually or from horse-drawn cart, and there were 'battery wagons' to provide the necessary power.[13] This facility went beyond anything in any European army in the wars of 1866 and 1870. In 1914, the practice of line-laying in the field had extended to all armies but had needed little further development.

Voice transmission lay only a few years in the future.[b] Messages relied on Morse's code and both sides used simple alphanumeric or substitution encryption systems. The codes were usually easy to break, and many messages were in any event sent *en clair*. Wire-tapping techniques were also understood. For six weeks during the Siege of Petersburg, a Confederate soldier, C.A. Gaston, intercepted all messages sent over the Union Army command link.[13]

Thus we see for the first time the elements of a modern communication system, both for higher strategic direction and passage of battle orders and reports. It was a rare gap in Moltke's appreciation of the application of new technology to the battlefield that he did not provide the Prussian Army with the means of extending the telegraph system beyond its peacetime nodal points. This contributed to the dearth of vital information at royal and army group headquarters throughout critical hours in the opening phase of the campaigns of both 1866 and 1870. Moltke's omission may have derived from the absence of a Prussian observer at Union Army headquarters in the field in the War Between the States, although in its last two years most other European powers had representatives in place.[15] A valuable lesson was missed.

---

[a] See Chapter X.

[b] A prototype of the modern telephone was on display at the US Centennial Exhibition in Philadelphia in 1876.

There was too a natural tendency, almost inevitable in any army and at all levels of command, which is only to be eradicated by good staff procedures and training, for subordinate headquarters to fail to send informative and timely reports upwards in the chain of command. Unless there is a properly regulated system, with one staff officer charged specifically with the preparation and dispatch of these reports as his first duty, this requirement will be lost in the concentration of staff effort on the immediate local problem and the implicit but erroneous assumption that what can be seen on the ground is equally obvious to the higher command. In 1866, the whole Prussian plan of campaign depended upon the early capture of the vital rail link through Dresden, and in 1870 on preventing the junction of the French forces in Alsace with those in Lorraine. On both occasions Moltke had to telegraph the army commander who had been given the task to ask for the most basic information.

The Catalytic Wars saw some development of field communication systems. Both sides in the War Between the States used semaphore in the field, flags in daytime and torch flares at night, relying upon intervisible points of high ground or towers built for the purpose, similar to the fire watchtowers of today in the forests of Europe and America. The French Army arranged a similar ad hoc system on the day of the Battle of Gravelotte–St Privat.

A signal station in the latter village, on the right flank of the six mile long defensive position on the Amanvillers Ridge, could semaphore back to a church tower in Metz, from where the message was sent forward again to army headquarters at Plappeville, behind the left flank of the French line. From the Crimean War onwards, there were also sporadic attempts to direct the fire of high-trajectory mortars and longer-range guns by a simple flag-signalling system, indicating fall of shot left or right, over or short of the target. The British Army would also develop the heliograph in the conditions of perfect visibility of the north-west Frontier and on the veldt in the Boer War, but this was an offshoot of the existing semaphore system and by no means innovative technology. Apart from the telegraph, the passage of orders and information in the field continued to rely, in the Catalytic Wars and for long afterwards, upon the techniques of the era of Napoleon and Wellington, but on battlefields which had grown larger, more dangerous and less precisely defined.

Whether or not telegraph, and later telephone, links existed, the effective exercise of command continued to depend upon the liaison officer – the trained pair of eyes and trusted intelligence which could retain the confidence of both 'sending' and 'receiving' commanders and staffs, in spite of the fact that he was often the bearer of unwelcome or irrelevant orders, or bad news. Moltke's orders for the concentration of the Prussian armies on the battlefield of Sadowa were not issued until nearly midnight on the night before the battle. The result of cavalry reconnaissances had not reached army group headquarters until nearly 10 p.m., and the information made it necessary to change completely the orders for the following day, which not only had already been issued but had also been explained verbally to the chief of staff of the Prussian Second Army, visiting army group headquarters at Gitschin from his own headquarters, fifteen miles away at Koniginhof. No telephone link had been set up. It was a night of violent thunderstorms and little ambient light, and the Prussian armies were operating in hostile territory, with no certainty that the routes were clear of enemy patrols or bodies of stragglers separated from their units in the previous battles, which had forced the Habsburg army to withdraw towards Koniggratz. Moltke sent two liaison officers bearing the changed orders to Second Army headquarters by different routes, one direct and the other by way of the corps headquarters of the inside-flank corps of the Second Army, giving this formation the maximum possible warning of an early start, a forced march and deployment from the line of march at once into battle, in order to cover the flank of the Prussian First Army, likely already to be engaged against superior numbers holding a strong natural defensive position. In contrast, vital orders on 28th August, 1870, to a corps of the Army of Chalons, directing a change of route to the Meuse so as to avoid stronger Prussian forces already astride the direct roads, were sent by the hand of one aide-de-camp only. And because he was captured by a Prussian cavalry patrol, the only key participant on either side who remained in ignorance of the changed orders was the corps commander for whom they were intended.

In the fluid conditions of the battles in Belgium and north-eastern France in late August and September 1914, the liaison staff performed exactly the same functions as their predecessors, but in far more difficult circumstances. Frontages were much longer. When it became clear that the Germans had invaded neutral Belgium and Luxembourg, five French armies, containing seventy-five infantry divisions in the field, were deployed to cover a front of something over 200 miles, not all in the front line. When, three weeks later, it became apparent that the German Army was uncoiling a massive right hook directed at and beyond the open western flank of the British Expeditionary Force and the French Fifth Army, these two formations deployed the equivalent of six corps, twelve divisions in all, on a thirty mile front. The average length of line held by a division in this phase of the war was thus of the order of two and a half to three miles, four times that which the same-sized formation would have been expected to defend a century earlier. And on the Lines of Amanvillers on 18th August, 1870, for a set-piece defensive battle, the French commander-in-chief had deployed twelve infantry divisions on a six mile front, with two more in army reserve.

The limited motor transport available to commanders in 1914 tended to increase rather than reduce the problems of coordination of command. Although motor vehicles allowed commanders to travel in order to see for themselves or to galvanise subordinates,[c] the means of providing them with 'instant' communications when on the move lay some time in the future. Liaison officers sent with vital orders and information found, time and again, that formation commanders and sometimes even whole headquarters were not where they had been reported, or even where they had said they would be. The then Lieutenant (later Major General Sir Edward) Spears, senior subaltern in an elite cavalry regiment, by reason of his natural abilities, which included fluency in French, had a responsibility far in excess of his rank as the British liaison officer at the headquarters of the French Fifth Army. His description of the difficulties which he encountered, particularly during the advance from the Marne to the Aisne, echoes those of Marbot a century earlier:

> ... often seeking commanders at places they had never been at, or endeavouring to locate troops that seemed to have disappeared into thin air, and almost invariably finding the situation I had been sent to deal with completely changed by the time I had arrived on the scene. And this went on day and night. Countless cumbersome lines of transport[d] blocked the roads as usual and long columns of infantry plodded by in the mud, for the weather had broken.[16]

It is abundantly clear from every authoritative description of the opening weeks of the war in 1914 that both sides brought far more troops into concentration areas than they could subsequently deploy or control with

---

[c] Joffre, the French generalissimo, although coming to rest each evening at GHQ in good time for dinner, spent the day roaring at racing-car speed between the formation headquarters along the chord of the defensive arc across north-eastern France.

[d] Still almost entirely horse-drawn, but every bit as hard to unblock as a jammed column of trucks.

efficiency in battle. This imposed an unhealthy rigidity on previous planning, and seriously inhibited the exercise of higher command. Radio, first used experimentally in the field by the British Army in the Boer War,[17] was still in its infancy. The German command transmissions, sent in an insecure mixture of crude code and messages *en clair*, could be monitored by receivers on the Eiffel Tower, and the allies derived much useful intelligence from this source.[18] On the Eastern Front, traffic on the Russian command link between the army group headquarters of Jilinsky and those of the army commanders, Samsonov and Rennenkampf, was all in uncoded plain language.[19] French formation command links depended upon the requisitioning of the peacetime telephone and telegraph network.[20] The attempts of the nephew of the great von Moltke, unwilling and misplaced chief of the general staff of the German armies, to control from Coblenz the execution of operations on two fronts 750 miles apart, were completely frustrated by the unreliability and attenuation of the telephone links.[21] Poor communications forced the younger Moltke to abdicate control of the massive swing through Belgium by the First and Second German armies, containing nearly 600,000 men, upon which the victory of Wilhelmine Germany depended. The two army commanders, directed to coordinate their movements because army group headquarters was too far out of touch, were by nature not disposed to do so, and failed to agree a plan. With Paris in sight, a gap opened up between the two armies, creating the conditions for a defeat far beyond the ability and delegated power of Moltke's liaison officer to rectify.

In the decade of the Catalytic Wars, the contemporary 'state of the art' of communication technology had proved itself capable, just about and when deployed and used properly, of controlling armies far larger than those of half a century earlier. Between 1870 and 1914, the lethality of firepower and the organisation of mobility surged ahead, far outstripping those improvements in communications which actually reached the battlefield. Warfare provides its own impetus for technological innovation and enhancement. But in the field of communications, it needed the benefits deriving from the US space programme of the 1960s and '70s to both provide the resources necessary to meet political demand for the means of controlling the use of force, and to match the capabilities of the weaponry of the late twentieth century.

Intelligence

The first line of the Christmas carol, *I Saw Three Ships Come Sailing In*, raises many questions in the mind of the intelligence officer. What is the reliability of the source? Irrespective of the quality of the informant, is the statement likely to be correct in full, in part or not at all? Has it been corroborated? Where lies the distinction between corroboration, repetition and duplication?[e] Is the information relevant to the current or future operational situation, and has it been received and assessed in time for appropriate reaction? The process of answering these and subsidiary similar questions about every item of information gained is the task of the analyst, and it converts raw reports into the intelligence upon which a commander can base his operational plan. But if this evaluation is in any way skimped, the conclusions derived from it are no more than wishful thinking if optimistic and potentially defeatist if the reverse. There must always be a clear distinction between assumption, fact and deduction.

Until the decade of the Catalytic Wars, the priority for intelligence gathering had been to discover the political intentions of a potential enemy or unreliable ally, rather than to obtain information to forecast the operational design of an adversary already in the field, or to establish accurately the size of his army. This was because, given the limited aims of warfare and the restricted size of armies which could be maintained in the field, such information was usually obvious enough once the campaigning season opened. Obtaining immediate information of tactical value in the approach to battle, denying it to the enemy and preventing surprise was the task of light cavalry. It is also relevant that throughout previous centuries the fighting had almost invariably been for precise geographical objectives and often over the same relatively small areas of ground – the 'Cockpit of Europe' in Flanders and southern Belgium, in northern Italy, on the Marchfeldt and around the land gateway between Europe and Asia either side of the Bosporus. The topography was thus well known, from study if not experience. The geographic area of both theatres in the War Between the States was not only new campaigning ground; it was also much larger. Armies had to spend more time looking for each other. And in all the wars of the decade, because the size of armies had grown past the point at which all could march and fight within the practicable radius of operation of the commander-in-chief's trusted aides,

---

[e] During the Falklands War of 1982, the author was responsible for devising and maintaining a system to keep the war cabinet informed of the running total of Argentine combat aircraft losses. Simple addition of even the validated 'kill' claims would have implied that the Argentine air force had been shot out of the sky by day six of the start of the land battle. This was not the case.

more resources needed to be devoted to finding out where and in what strength the enemy was located, and what his intentions were.

The need for this process by and large went unrecognised until long afterwards. The techniques of intelligence gathering in the Catalytic Wars were for the most part incompetent; the practices of protective and counter-intelligence were unheard of, though the Confederate Army made good use of deception plans; and the process of evaluation of information to convert it to hard intelligence was almost non-existent, except in the war of 1870 once the German Army had learned from its previous mistakes.

ACQUISITION

Intelligence gathering in the field was the traditional and obvious task of light cavalry, but the Army of the Second Empire, despite maintaining the distinction between 'light' and 'heavy' cavalry regiments established so carefully by Napoleon I, was by no means alone in having forgotten the need for close reconnaissance. The absence of any strategic design for the war of 1870 cannot have helped. In the frontier battles, MacMahon at Froeschwiller and Frossard at Spicheren waited to be attacked in what were outstandingly good natural defensive positions which the enemy could not mask or bypass. In the attempted withdrawal of the Army of Lorraine from Metz towards the Meuse, the French light cavalry regiments failed completely in what should have been their primary task. It is hard to avoid the conclusion that the thirty-one regiments of light cavalry – lancers, chasseurs and hussars – in the order of battle of the metropolitan army of the Second Empire[22] had come to see no difference between their operational role and that of heavy cavalry, and accordingly trained for the charge and little else. This misconception was shared by their formation commanders. Although they wore no body armour, and the sabres of the chasseurs and hussars were shorter and lighter than those carried by the troopers of the cuirassier and dragoon regiments, units of light and heavy cavalry were committed indiscriminately to charges in the Battles of Froeschwiller, Mars La Tour and Sedan, usually to destruction.[f]

German and Austro-Hungarian cavalry handling was for the most part no better. In 1866, the magnificent-looking regiments of the latter performed no useful reconnaissance function but fought most gallantly in conjunction with horse artillery on the evening of Sadowa, to cover the retreat of Benedek's shattered infantry across the Elbe. In both 1866 and 1870 the cavalry of the Prussian Army found itself at the rear of the march tables of the formation for

---

[f] French cavalry took no significant part in the Battles of Spicheren and Gravelotte–St Privat.

which it should have been gathering information. It is surprising that the handling of reconnaissance at the start and for some time into the war of 1870 was no better than it had been in 1866, because Moltke's tactical instructions between the two wars, including one issued as late as 6th May, 1870,[23] envisaged the establishment of a cavalry-strong advance guard for just this purpose. But the genius of Moltke lay rather in the areas of strategic planning and mobilisation, and the intention disappeared in the detail of the move of fifteen infantry corps to railheads and their onward coordinated advance to contact, on foot on constrained routes.

The cavalry remained poorly handled for some time after the frontier battles. That of the Third Army, commanded by the Prussian crown prince, lost contact altogether with MacMahon's troops while retreating in considerable disorder from Froeschwiller, while that of the Second Army, commanded by his cousin Prince Frederick Charles, had no idea what it had hit when its supporting horse artillery batteries fired the first shots in the Battle of Mars La Tour. It was only after the Battle of Gravelotte–St Privat, with the Army of Lorraine immured in Metz and the Army of Chalons putting itself into a noose in its attempted relief march north of the Argonne, that the Uhlan regiments of the armies of the North German Confederation performed their proper function. By that time, the lessons of tasking and tactics having been learned, they carried it out to perfection. Three days before the Battle of Sedan, the chief of staff of the Prussian crown prince's army could take William Howard Russell, war correspondent of London's *The Times*, into his map room and tell him:

> These French are lost, you see. We know they are there, and there, and there – MacMahon's whole army. Where can they go? Poor foolish fellows! They must go to Belgium, or fight there (indicating the natural 'soup bowl' around Sedan), and be lost.[24]

In the War Between the States, it was two years before the Union cavalry played any useful part whatever, and thereafter its success was in the role of mounted infantry rather than that of reconnaissance. The Confederate cavalry was far more competent in the latter role, but this was not their only intelligence-gathering resource. In a war fought not only by opponents speaking the same language, but often on ground where the sympathies of the local population might be with either side, information was there for the taking. In June 1863, because Lee's cavalry commander had exceeded his instructions, the Army of Northern Virginia was advancing 'blind' not just into western Maryland, where there was some Confederate sympathy, but beyond, into totally Unionist Pennsylvania. A 'scout', said by some authorities to have been a pedlar, brought in information that there were two corps of the Army of the Potomac at Frederick, where they were poised to cut Lee's line of retreat, and more Union forces close by. Lee was not at first disposed to act on what by any definition was information rather than intelligence, saying to one of his staff officers:

> I do not know what to do. I cannot hear from General Stuart, the eye of the army. What do you think of Harrison? I have no confidence in any scout, but General Longstreet thinks a good deal of Harrison.[25]

In spite of his initial scepticism, Lee interviewed the scout, and became convinced. But this was personal reaction rather than evaluation. Because Lee's instinct was correct, the interview was a critical link in the chain of events leading to Gettysburg.

The War Between the States saw the introduction of the aerial dimension both to intelligence gathering and the direction of artillery fire. The effort, in common with most other capabilities displayed in the war, was proportionate to the resources of the combatants. The Confederates fielded one balloon only, first at Manassas in the winter of 1861–62, and then during the campaign on the James peninsula in the following summer. Made from silk dresses sacrificed for the purpose by the ladies of Virginia, the device was limited to this operational area because the only Confederate source of hydrogen gas was in Richmond. After only a very few ascents, tethered either to a railway flat-bed truck or to a steamer on the York River, the precious silk fabrication was captured when the latter vessel ran aground. The Union investment in this new resource was far greater and, for a time, more coherent. Deployed first in McClellan's campaign on the James peninsula, where because the country was flat and close the only possible commanding view was from a balloon, the US Army Balloon Corps mounted subsequent ascents before Second Manassas, and at Fredericksburg and Chancellorsville. McClellan was an enthusiast for the project and made a number of ascents himself. He evidently placed some reliance on it to provide information in the confused situation around Washington after Second Manassas.[26] But after his dismissal, the project languished for lack of funds and high-level interest, and for neither the first nor the last time with an innovative project, the reluctance of career-conscious government bureaucracy to put its weight behind a high-risk commitment.

In this as in other areas, the technology applied in the War Between the States was ahead of that used in Europe in 1866 and 1870. The balloon ascents throughout the Siege of Paris were for the purposes of coordination of national defence, passage of information and the maintenance of morale in the besieged city rather than intelligence gathering.

By 1914, the development of the aeroplane had provided a new resource and the fact of its existence assisted understanding of the importance of airborne reconnaissance. Identification both of the right wing-heavy German advance, and of the gap which had opened up between the two armies providing the blade of the scythe sweeping towards Paris, precipitating the Battle of the Marne, owed much to information brought back by aviators.[27]

General McClellan, Union Army commander in the eastern theatre from July 1861 until November 1862 was, as will be demonstrated,[g] an educated soldier who had many of the right ideas, but, whether for reasons of lack of commitment or insufficient determination and force of character, never drew full advantage from them. On his appointment to command, he was ahead of his time in appreciating the need for intelligence, but made a disastrous choice in his selection of the man to organise this function. Alan Pinkerton had been in peacetime the head of a Chicago-based private detective agency specialising in cases involving the use, or misuse, of the nationwide railway system. As a result he had operatives and contacts in every major city. Even before the start of the war, he had recruited 'stay-behind' agents in many cities of the South,[28] and the intelligence-gathering operations of his networks seem to have been effective enough. The failure, of catastrophic proportions, was in the matter of evaluation, and his appointment did not long survive the fall of McClellan. Four months later, the Union Army commander in the eastern theatre found it necessary to establish formally a 'Bureau of Military Intelligence.'[29]

PROTECTION

The era of the near-universal availability of newspapers, at least in the main centres of population, had already begun and the wide reach of the telegraph system had accelerated dramatically the speed at which information could be sent. The conduct of war, as the supreme test of human endeavour, was a natural magnet for reporters. There was, throughout the decade of the Catalytic Wars, no idea of censorship. Correspondents seem to have roamed at will and published without restriction. Moltke welcomed neutral war correspondents and, as we have seen, one of the most eminent by reason of his

---

[g] See Chapter VI.

previous achievements in the Crimea and America was given what would now be described as an 'attributable, on the record and unembargoed' briefing at army chief of staff level about developing operations. Although the French Government might state grandly during the period of rising tension in July 1870 that details of troop movements would no longer be published, this did not stop the newspapers.[30] And while the official bulletins from the higher headquarters of the armies in the field could say as much or as little as their authors chose, the war correspondent could now publish his own view of events almost as they occurred. Censorship lay in the future, but by 1914 the need for it had been understood by the governments of all the Great Powers, and army headquarters made appropriate arrangements. But it remains implicit in the competing needs of the military, for security of information about present deployment and future plans, and the civilian demand for instant information, grown to insatiable proportions by the end of the twentieth century, that the matter was never resolved in any subsequent conflict to the satisfaction of both sides. Nor is it ever likely to be.

EVALUATION

For military purposes, information can be both useless and dangerous until it has been properly assessed and then given to the man with the power to decide on the necessary counteraction. In peacetime, the information provided by military attachés accredited to foreign powers was and remains as good as the access permitted to them, their own abilities and their own inherent selectivity. In peace and war, newspapers in the decade of the Catalytic Wars and after could publish whatever they thought might interest their readers, which might or might not be true. The war of 1870 saw the first crude attempt at disinformation by planted newspaper article, and in wartime, newspapers even in non-totalitarian countries were to become increasingly bound by censorship restrictions.

In the War Between the States, Pinkerton's operatives, one of whom succeeded in penetrating the confidence of the Confederate Secretary of War, Judah Benjamin,[28] worked under the same constraints as all other agents in enemy territory in wartime. They were subject to the permanent risk of exposure and the fallibility and insecurity of communications. Some messages might not arrive at all, and others too late to be of use. With the latter, if the information they contained had been validated by intervening events, the recipient had to ask himself whether this confirmed the reliability of the source, or if it was an attempt to maintain the credibility of an agent who had been 'turned' or captured, in order to provide a background of authenticity for future disinformation. This filtering process, and the reduction of all the information received to a common time-base, is the task of the intelligence analyst, and an essential part of the process is continuous Socratic challenge to his conclusions.

It was in this matter that Pinkerton totally failed the army commander who had appointed him. The information won at great risk – at least one of Pinkerton's agents was caught and hanged – was never properly validated. Throughout the campaigns on the James peninsula and in western Maryland, which culminated in the Battle of Antietam, Pinkerton persuaded McClellan that there were more than twice as many men up against him as the Confederates actually had. Some estimates of Confederate strength were said to have been based upon the number of rations issued from depots; and similar collateral evidence was claimed to confirm others.[31] Pinkerton always presented his conclusions with a warning that the figures could be underestimates, which had a further impact on the thinking of the preternaturally cautious McClellan. Even after Pinkerton's departure, his influence lived on. In spite of the evidence of the Battle of Antietam, the commanders of the Army of the Potomac throughout the winter and spring of 1862–63 continued to credit Lee's army with twice its actual strength.

Pinkerton refined the summary of the reports of his agents by applying factors previously agreed with McClellan, to allow for enemy soldiers who, though included in strength returns, were absent from duty because of wounds, sickness, legitimate furlough or the unauthorised absence which plagued both armies. While the precision of some of the figures gave them a superficial authenticity – a Confederate division on one occasion was credited with a present-for-duty strength of 6,346 and 2/3 men – all that was proved was the folly of basing precise calculations upon false assumptions and inaccurate basic data. After the end of the Seven Days' Battle, on 1st July, 1862, Pinkerton convinced McClellan that the Confederates had brought 200,000 men into action. Despite a casualty list, similarly assessed, of 40,000, the deduction was that Lee had nearly twice as many effectives as the number fit for duty in McClellan's army, which had withdrawn to a perimeter defence around Harrison's Landing. Given McClellan's temperament, his decision to abandon the whole operation followed naturally. It seems that no one can have made an attempt to validate Pinkerton's figures against an overall assessment of the total military-age manpower available to the South, with realistic deductions for Confederate forces engaged concurrently in the western theatre and on the Atlantic and Gulf coasts, on the lines of communication and in the state militias. Any such independent check must have forced a reassessment of Pinkerton's figures.

In 1870, MacMahon, commanding the Army of Chalons, made the opposite mistake. Although in the forty-eight hours leading up to the Battle of Sedan there had been positive identification of five German corps around his line of march, and thus a manpower strength at least equal to his own, he declined the last opportunity to escape from the trap set by Moltke, but as yet not fully closed.

Moltke, from the year in which he was first appointed Chief of the Prussian general staff, produced an annual strategic appreciation of the threats facing Prussia. His work was based upon a thorough evaluation, by the historical section of the general staff, of the campaigns recently fought by Prussia's potential enemies, and also upon a continuously updated topographical assessment of their strategic movement resources. An important side effect of this was that in August 1870 the maps of France in the hands of the German armies were far more up to date than those available to the commanders and staffs of the armies of the Second Empire. Two of the French corps commanders, Frossard as an intellectual soldier and Bazaine in his capacity as commander of the Nancy military district between 1868 and the beginning of 1870, had made a thorough study of the ground on the French side of the common frontier. But the intention was that there should be an immediate invasion of Germany, and the French Ministry of War had prepared a splendid new map of the country beyond the Rhine. But their most recent edition of maps of Alsace and Lorraine had been printed in 1862.[32] This was so out of date that French officers were forced to requisition local maps from estate offices and schools, and in such short supply that a corps commander, having been issued with one map of the Department of the Moselle for himself, was forced to beg for a second for his staff.[33] In the absence of relevant and up-to-date topographical information, no correct evaluation of the effort which the enemy can exert at any given point is possible, except by chance.

A good system once started need only be updated; there was no requirement for Moltke to begin his annual strategic assessment afresh each year from first principles. He had the advantage of there being very little attempt made by any country to safeguard information, whether of strategic value or about the capabilities of new weapons. Foreign observers were freely invited to attend annual manoeuvres. Information gained from all sources during the preceding twelve months could be used to confirm or amend the assumptions, facts and conclusions of the appreciation of the previous year.

The result was that in both 1866 and 1870 Moltke had a very accurate assessment of the strength of the armies which would oppose those of the king of Prussia, extending also to the personalities and abilities of likely army and corps commanders. In each war, the main enemy in one was also a potential adversary in the other. Moltke's subsidiary assessments of French will and capacity to intervene in 1866 and that of the Dual Monarchy in 1870, and the forces which had to be laid off as a deterrent, were likewise proved correct by events. In 1870 his appreciation was refined even further by an estimate of the capacity of the railway lines serving Metz and Strasbourg, two concentration areas certain to be used by the French Army after mobilisation, but separated by the west–east grain of the Vosges.[34] This in turn allowed a deduction of the relative strengths of French forces to be deployed in Lorraine and Alsace and thus was one of the most important factors influencing Moltke's design for the campaign and distribution of force.

Command in the Field

The decade of the Catalytic Wars produced three men who, as de facto commanders-in-chief in the field of the armies of their country, stand comparison with the greatest commanders of any other era. There were also two others who, though beaten comprehensively in battle, deserved something better than to be branded by their defeated nation as scapegoats for the catastrophe. As will be seen, both Benedek in 1866 and Bazaine in 1870 were very far from faultless in their conduct of operations, but the disasters which overtook the Habsburg and French Second Empires derived at least as much from flawed national characteristics and forms of government, together with inadequate planning and preparation. High command in war has no equal for the rewards it offers for success or the penalties exacted for failure. It was an additional misfortune for both Benedek and Bazaine, both competent soldiers, that they were up against a grand master.

Much has been written about the art of command in war. The discussion points relevant to this book are, first, to establish the special characteristics and qualities which the three great commanders of the decade, Lee, Grant and Moltke, brought to the exercise of high command; secondly, to analyse how the technique of command in the field had changed since 1815 and whether this was by evolution of philosophy or application of new technology; and thirdly, to define the precedents and indicators for the future.

None of the three great commanders of the decade set out to be an extrovert motivator of troops, and even after the triumph of 1866 it is likely that Moltke was barely known by name, four years later, to the majority of the rank and file of the armies of the North German Confederation. The common characteristic in the generalship of all three men was their determination to fight to the limit and to the utmost extent of the resources available to them – in sum, the will to prosecute total war. By extension, their immediate subordinates, by a combination of leadership, example and training, were motivated to do the same. It is almost certain that only Moltke can have either formed or refined his knowledge and belief in this fundamental requirement for the conduct of war from the study of Clausewitz. For Lee and Grant, as it may have been for Moltke, this comprehension was inherent, but beyond doubt was intensified and given focus by the virulence inherent in civil war.

Lee's outstanding quality was his ability to estimate with almost total accuracy not just the intentions of his opponent, but also the flaws in the character of the opposing commander which would inhibit the execution of a good plan or the application of superior material resources. Lee combined this perception with an equally accurate understanding of the limit of effort which could be extracted from his own troops, both on the march and in combat. The former quality allowed him to establish a moral ascendancy over a succession of Union Army commanders – McClellan, Pope, McClellan again, Burnside and Hooker.

George Gordon Meade, appointed to the command of the Army of the Potomac in the last days of June 1863, was a man of different mettle. It was undoubtedly to his advantage that, unlike his predecessors, he came to army command after direct combat experience of formation command at all lower levels. He was a man of more introverted character than any of his predecessors, more phlegmatic and less easily impressed. A long war brings hard and single-minded men to the top, and perhaps Meade derived internal strength in his conduct of the Battle of Gettysburg, barely a week after his promotion to army commander, from the knowledge that he was reduced to a tactical option of one, but in far more favourable circumstances than those enjoyed by any of his predecessors. Although he had to stand and fight, he could make the best use of a good natural defensive position. The need to launch attacks over open ground at almost any cost lay for once not on the Union Army but on that of the Confederacy. Lee equally had no other option once he had accepted a general action brought on by the unexpected clash of advance guards. But the moral ascendancy which he had established over the previous Union Army commanders he had fought, combined with his ability to comprehend and exert the limit of his own army's capability, meant that the attack which he ordered Pickett to mount on the third day of the battle was not an impossible demand, with no feasible outcome other than the slaughter of the assaulting infantry.

Meade, nevertheless, was not the man to exercise supreme command in the field of all the Union armies. Lincoln's choice fell on Grant because of his successes in the western theatre. Coming to Washington in March 1864, Grant elected to make his headquarters with the Army of the Potomac, while retaining Meade in his post as army commander under him, notwithstanding the fact that 'one over one' is in principle an unsatisfactory arrangement. Given the communications capability available, it was clearly impossible for Grant to control in any more than principle the operations of Sherman in the western theatre, 500 miles in a direct line from the decisive theatre in Virginia, and more than 1,000 over the link by which messages would have to travel. But Sherman, another who understood the 'total' nature of the war, was executing the design for the campaign which Grant himself had prepared while in command in the western theatre, and could be trusted to do so to the limit. Grant had none of the deliberately contrived mass-appeal of McClellan or the flamboyance of Hooker, but on his first visit to the Army of the Potomac he impressed his determination on all the troops he encountered, and in time the word spread that the new supreme commander had brought a ruthlessness which had hitherto been missing to the direction of the war.[35] This gained him the loyalty of the veterans without the need for any of the contrivances employed by his predecessors. By 1864, an *'Il faut en finir'*[h] attitude of mind had developed in the Army of the Potomac.

Lincoln, Grant and Sherman, the chief protagonists responsible for developing the strategic design of the Union for the last year of the war, had only one meeting, at City Point in March 1865,[36] to discuss how the conflict should be brought to an end.

Grant's unshakeable determination to destroy the will of the Confederacy to fight, no matter what the cost, was matched by a flexibility of approach about the way to do it.

A month after the opening of the campaign in northern Virginia at the beginning of May 1864, the Union Army had suffered 60,000 casualties and Lee's army was still blocking the path to Richmond. A different design was essential, which Grant achieved by transferring the whole weight of the Union attack from the north and east of the Confederate capital to the application of continuous pressure from the south of the city. The two armies were

[h] A slogan much used in France in 1939 to motivate army and nation.

continuously engaged, in a precursor of First World War-style trench warfare[i] for the next ten months. Grant's role in this phase of the war was the allocation of troops to tasks, and the maintenance of the asset essential to any commander in any war, the retention of a reserve and the unfettered ability to commit it. When at length Lee was forced out of his defensive works in March 1865, Grant displayed a wholly modern approach to the grouping of the subordinate formations available to him. Groups of corps were placed under Meade, Ord and Sheridan for the respective tasks of direct pursuit and mopping up, outflanking, and an even wider right-handed swing designed to put Sheridan's cavalry across Lee's line of retreat. Grant varied the groupment in response to events. The Union Army in the eastern theatre had always enjoyed a massive superiority of numbers over the enemy opposing it, despite Pinkerton's estimates to the contrary. But it was not until Grant took command that success was achieved, by the continuous and unremitting application of stronger force.

When Moltke became chief of the general staff of the Prussian Army in 1858, the post had lost prestige and ranked in both power and influence below that of the minister of war and the head of the king's military cabinet.[j] It was 1864 before Moltke achieved even equal status and a further two years before he had established absolute control over war planning. From the start, with an area of reference little more than mobilisation planning and the resolution of matters delegated by the ministry of war, Moltke set out to achieve a consistent standard of staff training throughout the army, so that at every formation, from brigade upwards, there would be at least one officer who had been trained to think on exactly the same lines as his colleagues elsewhere. Moltke's absolute standard was that if any two of his staff officers were confronted separately with the same problem, they would produce, independently, the same solution. This requirement was met in totality in August 1914 when Ludendorff, fresh from his triumph at Liège and en route to his new appointment as chief of staff of the failing army in East Prussia, produced from the data available to him exactly the same plan as Hoffman, *en poste* as chief of the operations staff, which the latter had already set in hand to restore the situation without waiting for the arrival of the new army

[i] See Chapter IX.
[j] See Chapter VII.

commander[k] and chief of staff.[37] Far superior Russian numbers were first contained and then annihilated.

The two fundamental points in Moltke's training were that the enemy was to be engaged wherever found, and that the support of another formation already in combat was a mission overriding anything previously ordered. When the passage of orders was only achievable at the best pace and within the limit of vulnerability of a staff officer on horseback, this necessarily placed great importance on the validity of previous planning and assessment of the marching and fighting capacity of the troops responsible for its execution. The combination of basic doctrine, planning validated to the furthest degree possible in peacetime, and insistence on the highest standards of precision and accuracy in staff calculations and the preparation of orders, was founded upon comprehension to a degree greater than any of his contemporaries of the application of the new technologies – the railway and the telegraph network.

Nevertheless, Moltke's system had two drawbacks. First, the plan once laid down became too rigid. Since it was outside the authority of any subordinate commander to amend it unless actually engaged in combat, the plan became supreme. It follows that the leading authority on the history of the Prussian, and later Imperial German, general staff describes the years between 1906 and 1916 as that of 'war without generals'.[38] The master plan of Schlieffen based on the principles of Moltke had been prepared in enormous detail, and there could be no conceivable circumstance strong enough to force an alteration. When, in the event, assumptions were found to be flawed, critical assets withheld, the control mechanism discovered to be defective and considerable modification therefore essential, the means did not exist to do it. Moltke had always combined the utmost precision of planning with the view that no plan would survive contact with the enemy, but his successors lost sight of this critical rider. Over-rigidity of planning was a further ingredient in the defeat of Wilhelmine Germany. Moltke's second failing stemmed from the fact that he had never seen active service in direct command of a regiment or formation. He was a man by no means lacking in sensitivity or imagination, and if he had had first-hand experience of command in combat the formidable intellect which he applied to strategic and mobilisation planning, combined with his technological awareness, could hardly have failed to have appreciated that the development of firepower had rendered obsolete the battlefield tactics of Waterloo. In what way the king of Prussia's armies might have been

---

[k] Hindenburg, brought out of retirement as a 'safe pair of hands' to replace the excitable von Prittwitz.

retrained in a radical new approach to tactics at unit level, and how long it might have taken to achieve this fundamental redirection, are subsidiary but important questions. But Moltke's genius lay in his grasp of the geopolitical factors which affected Prussia, a state bordered by three potentially hostile Great Powers, his technological awareness, the validity of his strategic planning and his ability to devise and enforce the highest standards of staff · systems and training. A review of the nature of man-against-man combat on the battlefield was beyond his scope.

The growing geographic area of the Napoleonic battlefield had already forced some modification of a system of command solely by direct order to subordinate formations. It was implicit in the creation of permanent corps groupings of all arms introduced by Napoleon that these could fight an independent battle, and the more trusted marshals came to expect to be told what to do and when to do it, with the method of execution left to their own judgement. By the decade of the Catalytic Wars, directive from army commander to principal subordinates operating well beyond the range of the hardest and most competent galloper had become the norm. Lee in Virginia, first to Jackson and later to Early in the Shenandoah Valley; Grant to his subordinates in front of Petersburg, as well as the broad instructions which were all that could be relevant to direct Sherman in the western theatre; Moltke to the three army commanders converging on north-eastern Bohemia in 1866, both in his design for the campaign and the concentration in the face of the enemy on what became the battlefield of Sadowa; and Moltke again, particularly in his distribution of force between the besieging army for Metz and the two-army hunting pack designed to bring the Army of Chalons to a battle in which it would be pinned, with its line of retreat blocked, either against the Meuse or the frontier of neutral Belgium; the most the commander-in-chief could do in all these instances was to confirm or amend previous orders, and set a new time-frame for the attainment of objectives. It was a feature of all the orders issued to army commanders by Moltke in the war of 1870 that there was always a paragraph to indicate when and in what circumstances new orders might be expected. But until there could be direct, permanent and secure communications between formation commanders, this was the limit of the exercise of high command in battle. By 1914, it was inadequate to control events.

Notes

[1] Lambert, *The Crimean War*, Manchester University Press, 1990, p.25.

[2] Lambert, op.cit., p.21.

[3] Ffrench-Blake, *The Crimean War*, London, Leo Cooper, 1993, pp.124–25.

[4] Freeman, *Lee*, [Harwell abridgement], New York, Charles Scribner and Sons, 1935, p.132.

[5] Lanier, [ed.] *Armies and Leaders*, New York, Fairfax Press, 1983, p.164.

[6] Catton, *Mr Lincoln's Army*, New York, Doubleday and Co., 1951, p.221.

[7] Catton, *Never Call Retreat*, New York, Doubleday and Co., 1965, Centennial History of the Civil War Edition, p.65.

[8] Keegan, *The Price of Admiralty*, London, Hutchinson, 1988, pp.49–50.

[9] Barnett, *The Swordbearers*, London, Eyre and Spottiswoode, 1963, pp.141–42.

[10] Oman, *Nelson*, London, Hodder and Stoughton, 1947; Reprint Society Edition, 1950, p.545.

[11] Robins, Major Colin, 'Electric and Other Telegraphs' in *The War Correspondent*, the journal of the Crimean War Research Society, vol. XIII, no.1, pp.17–24.

[12] Above, and *A Short History of Signals in the Army*, The Royal Corps of Signals Association, London 1927, p.13.

[13] Macdonald, *Great Battles of the Civil War*, New York, Collier Books, 1992, pp.140–42.

[14] National Park Service, US Department of the Interior, City Point Unit leaflet.

[15] See in particular Lynam, *Meade's Headquarters 1863–1865*, Boston, The Atlantic Monthly Press, 1922.

[16] Spears, *Liaison 1914*, London, Eyre and Spottiswoode, 1930, p.449.

[17] *A Short History of Signals in the Army*, p.27.

[18] Spears, op.cit., p.324.

[19] Tuchman, *The Guns of August*, London, Constable and Co., 1962, Four Square edition 1964, p.304.

[20] Spears, op.cit., p.339.

[21] Barnett, op.cit., p.59.

[22] Willing, *L'Armée de Napoleon III*, Arceuil, Preal, 1994, pp.66–70.

[23] Whitton, *Moltke*, London, Constable and Co., 1921, p.213.

[24] Ascoli, *A Day of Battle*, London, Harrap, 1987, p.298.

[25] Freeman, op.cit., p.320.

[26] Coggins, *Arms and Equipment of the Civil War*, Wilmington, North Carolina, Broadfoot Publishing Co., 1962, pp.109–10.

[27] Spears, op.cit., pp.137–138 and 414.

[28] Catton, *Mr Lincoln's Army*, pp.137–38.

[29] Macdonald, op.cit., p.44.

[30] Whitton, op.cit., p.181.

[31] Catton, *Terrible Swift Sword*, New York, Washington Square Press, 1967, pp.256–57.

[32] Ascoli, op.cit., p.296.

[33] Howard, *The Franco-Prussian War*, London, Rupert Hart-Davis, 1961; St Albans, Herts, Granada Publishing, 1979, p.70.

[34] Whitton, op.cit., p.175.

[35] Catton, *A Stillness at Appomattox*, New York, Washington Square Press, 1958, pp.50–53.

[36] Catton, ibid., pp.379–82.

[37] Tuchman, op.cit., p.318.

[38] Görlitz, *The German General Staff*, London, Hollis and Carter, 1953, Chapter VII.

Chapter V
Firepower

Firepower is a compound of range, accuracy related to consistency,[a] and lethality. Its effectiveness depends in the first instance upon integrating and balancing correctly the chemistry of explosives, the construction technology of delivery means and projectile, and the ballistic properties of the missile, both imparted to it on firing and in flight. If effective weapons are to reach the battlefield, they must be generated from a powerful, up-to-date and resilient industrial base. The national economy must be strong enough to fund the development and production of capital assets which may never be used. Political will and economic strength must be willing and able to replace weapons rendered obsolete by new technology, and to sustain production under war conditions if need be. Industry must be capable of precision engineering the myriad component parts of guns and munitions, of quality control to fine tolerances and of mass production. The two essential scientific processes are the chemistry, which can design and manufacture in quantity the three quite different types of explosives needed, for initiator, propellant and bursting charge, and the metallurgy of gun and munition construction. Throughout the century after Waterloo, there was a ferment of almost continuous development in all these interrelated areas, to the point that the guns produced in the decade before the First World War were at the limit of main-line development. Thereafter, progress in this field was confined to seeking improvement of the ratio between strength, which imposes a limit on range and size of missile, and weight of delivery means, which puts a constraint on mobility. The technology of ammunition development, however, continued to break new ground throughout the twentieth century.

Given the vast number of ingredients in the recipe, an improvement to one single element, however great, is unlikely to achieve much enhancement of

---

[a] A gun is 'accurate' if the round fired hits the target; it is only 'consistent' if it can repeat this achievement without alteration to the point of aim or the data on the sights. There are some 150 causes of variation in round-to-round performance.

the overall capability. A major advance is only achieved when emerging technology allows most if not all of the main component parts to be upgraded simultaneously. The progress of the relevant scientific disciplines in the era after Waterloo created the necessary conditions, but even then the end products came to the battlefield in different wars. While Prussia's battle-winning weapon in the war of 1866 was the needle gun of the infantryman, four years later it was her artillery, the armies of the North German Confederation having been re-equipped in this interval with guns from the workshops of Friedrich Krupp of Essen, which incorporated innovations in both metallurgy and fabrication. By the end of the Franco-German War, it was apparent to any educated and objective analyst that firepower had become the dominant capability on the battlefield, and that artillery had become the primary means of delivering it.

In the light of the French strategy in 1914, of offensive at any cost, it is noteworthy that the first reaction of the defeated nation was defensive. Deprived by the peace settlement of the fortress cities of Metz and Strasbourg, and with all prospect of the natural frontier on the middle and lower Rhine gone for good, a new design of sunken fortification was being built before the end of the decade. This extended from the hills surrounding Verdun southwards to Toul, and from Epinal through Belfort to the Swiss frontier. Because Belgian territory was thought to be inviolate and the Ardennes impassable, the fortress lines were intended to canalise any future German invasion into the Trouée des Charmes, a forty mile gap left open deliberately between Toul and Epinal. This investment in deterrent capability in turn had its influence on German planning.

The armies at Waterloo had fought with weapons whose principles of construction had changed little in hundreds of years. Personal weapons, infantry muskets and cavalry carbines,[b] were smooth-bore and muzzle-loaded, fired by a spark generated by percussion – a recent advance on the original flintlock – and powder charges which, in damp weather, were unreliable in the extreme. A trained soldier with dry powder charges might fire three rounds in a minute, but it would be luck rather than skill if he hit any target at a range above 100 yards. Artillery likewise was smooth-bore and muzzle-loaded. The properties of explosives had been well known for centuries, and thus there was no theoretical limit to the quantity of propellant charge, which for a given

---

[b] The cavalryman's carbine was usually a cut-down version of the infantry musket, firing a reduced charge. The kick from the full charge meant that the standard musket could not be fired from the saddle.

weight of projectile is the governing factor in defining maximum range. However, the practical upward limit is obvious. The combustion of too much propellant bursts the gun, and the maximum pressure is sustained at the instant when primer ignites propellant charge. Hence the progressive strengthening of the chamber[c] and breech end of the gun, producing the mace-like shape characteristic of all but the lightest cannon barrels for half a millennium. But the need of the artillery supporting an army in the field for mobility imposed a top limit on the weight of the equipment. Over the centuries, a team of six horses had been found to be the optimum for traction, any larger number being counter-productive in the energy which they could bring to bear, unless it was for a very short haul over difficult country.

The twelve pounders of the *Grande Armée* Reserve Artillery Park were, in terms of eighteenth-century technology, at the absolute point of balance between the competing requirements of range and weight of munition on the one hand, and battlefield mobility on the other. The twelve pounder had a basic weight of two tons, and a maximum range for its round, solid shot of some 1,600 yards to first impact.[d] This very short reach, in terms of the fourfold increase attained little more than half a century later, meant that concentration, the sine qua non of effective artillery fire support, could be achieved only if the largest possible number of guns were deployed wheel to wheel. Such a massing of equipment had won the Battles of Friedland and Wagram, but it was highly vulnerable, for instance, to a flank attack by enemy cavalry. In any event, the concentration required was not that of guns, but of their fire on the target. Hence the need for increased range, because the further ranges could be lengthened the more fire could be brought to bear, always provided that a resolution could be found to the problem of direction of the fire of batteries engaging the same target from different positions. And the twelve pounder was a corps or army support weapon. It was too immobile to be used in the direct support of divisions and brigades. This task was performed by the eight and four pounders of the divisional artillery batteries, which were, respectively, three-quarters and half the weight of the twelve pounders, but with a corresponding reduction in range.

Gun construction material also imposed a limit of attainment. As early as the fifteenth century, bronze had been found preferable to cast iron as the best metal for fabrication, because it was more resilient to firing pressures. But this

---

[c] Basic gun construction terminology is defined in Appendix B.

[d] The range might be doubled by ricochet, especially on hard ground. The cannon ball remained lethal to life and limb for as long as it was moving.

flexibility was also a weakness, in that bronze gun barrels wore down very quickly and so lost range and consistency. The need for muzzle-loading exacerbated this failing. There had to be a small margin between the interior diameter of the barrel (calibre) and the external diameter of the cannon ball to allow the latter to be loaded down the barrel, a process requiring a powerful manual thrust. This gap, known as 'windage', not only wasted propellant energy and increased barrel wear, but, because an ill-fitting round would bounce in its progress up the barrel, it might emerge in almost any direction. Inconsistency was also compounded by the absence of precision-engineering techniques and only rudimentary standardisation. Variations in quantities and weights of propellant and projectile introduced further degradation of performance, and the round shot had very poor ballistic properties. These imperfections, combined with all the other deviations from an ideal standard, produced a spread in the fall of shot of dramatic proportions. Once a gun had fired a few times it might 'settle down', and experienced crews would be aware of the particular idiosyncrasies of the piece they served, and of the need to compensate for prevailing wind and weather conditions, which always affect a missile in flight. But the point of impact of the opening rounds was a matter for pure chance. The artillery men of Prussia had a saying, 'The first shot is for the Devil, the second for God, and only the third for the king.'[1]

Some improvements had already reached the battlefield before the end of the Napoleonic Wars, often on an experimental basis and never as a universal feature. The English in the peninsula experimented with a bursting charge for artillery solid shot, as well as for the canister and grapeshot used against infantry in the open at shorter ranges, but this innovation introduced another set of factors leading to inconsistency. The round had to burst at exactly the right moment when approaching the end of its trajectory if it were to achieve maximum lethality. Hence the need for fuses, which might or might not work efficiently. It had also been established by 1815 that the torque imparted by rifling to a projectile in its progress up the barrel had important consequences, because the increased velocity produced greater range and gave greater stability in flight, which improved consistency. The faster passage through the air also reduced the influence of prevailing weather conditions, provided that the weapon was fought at optimum rather than maximum range. Rifling also implied a better 'seat' for the round in the barrel, which, by reducing windage, gave an increase in range for the same amount of propellant charge. Small arms with rifled barrels went first to elite infantry units, but it was clear that the same advantages might be gained if artillery gun barrels could be rifled. Nevertheless, it was a long time before it became generally realised that rifling and muzzle-loading were contradictory in ergonomic terms, and thus an inefficient practice.[2]

The Development of Personal Weapons

Notwithstanding the many maxims of Napoleon about the importance of artillery and its proven battle-winning ability, combat at the end of the Napoleonic Wars was still primarily a contest between the opposing infantry. Given the shortcomings of the smooth-bore musket, it is hard to avoid the conclusion that the best protection of the soldier in battle was the inefficiency of his enemy's firearms, and it was perhaps no accident that the first important step forward came from an attempt to improve the reliability of the rifled musket. In the early 1830s a Saxon, John Nicholas Dreyse, became concerned to improve the percussion process, still undependable as an initiator. He produced an invention which ignited the propellant cartridge by a small steel rod, or 'needle', pressed through an opening in the base of the chamber by hammer action. By 1836 Dreyse had carried this development a logical stage further, to the critical point of change. He found that a screw lock process could allow the breech to be opened in order to load the round, thus disposing of the need for muzzle-loading, and that the screw lock closed the breech firmly enough to allow the weapon to be fired without danger to the user. Breech-loading produced not only a threefold increase in the rate of fire, but also, even more important, the ability to load and fire the weapon from a kneeling position behind cover, or even when lying prone.

Dreyse offered his invention not to his own monarch but to Prussia, which took up production with no great urgency. The weapon was not issued to the troops until after the convulsions of 1848 in Berlin, and then almost by accident.[3] Its first use on the battlefield was in 1851, when a Prussian corps under the future King William I was called in to assist the grand duke of Baden to put down a rebellion of his subjects, and the superiority of the new weapon over the muzzle-loader was found to be total. Infantry firepower won the war against Denmark in 1864, compensating for a weak initial performance by the Prussian high command, and in the war of 1866 it was estimated that the Prussian infantryman fired six shots to one from the antique weapon of his Austrian counterpart.[4] Given Prussian Army standards of drill and discipline, the temptation to blaze away regardless at maximum range was clearly well restrained.

Meanwhile, inventive geniuses were at work elsewhere. Krupps of Essen had traded in weaponry and other artefacts since the Thirty Years War, and in

1811 Friedrich Krupp founded a company for the manufacture of steel, a venture which dissipated, almost totally, his inherited fortune and which, in the minds of many of his contemporaries, came near to dabbling in alchemy. His son Alfred continued the project with more success, but by the 1840s such prosperity as the firm enjoyed derived from the growing demand of polite society for table cutlery. Alfred, sole proprietor of Krupp, was a self-taught metallurgist who travelled widely throughout Europe in order to learn what he could about the manufacture of steel. He was also his own chief salesman and head of business development. In 1844 he offered a sample of two steel rifled musket barrels to the Prussian Ministry of War, his selling point being the much greater durability of steel. He was turned down flat, almost by return of post:

> You are hereby informed that no use whatever can be made as regards the production of musket barrels, since the present manner of manufacturing these, and the quality of the barrels so produced, at a cost not inconsiderably less, meets all reasonable requirements and leaves hardly anything to be desired.[5]

Perhaps Alfred, who had anglicised his baptismal name after a visit to England, was not too concerned. He was already experimenting with cannon construction, and his next offer to the government in Berlin would be related to artillery and not infantry weapons.

Across the Rhine, personal weapon development was also being borne along by individual initiative in the face of official indifference. Antoine Alphonse Chassepot, superintendent of the government arsenal at Châtellerault, began experiments on breech seals in the 1850s. The end product so impressed Napoleon III that he equipped a squadron of the Guard Cavalry with the weapon for the war of 1859 in northern Italy.[6] After steady pushing against bureaucratic complacency and inertia, including the opposition of his own minister of war, the French emperor managed to have the weapon brought into full production in 1866. The main advantage of the chassepot over the needle gun was that for the first time there was a fully effective breech seal, formed by the compression of a circular rubber ring when the weapon fired, which improved safety and optimised propellant energy. The chassepot reached out to a distance of nearly a mile,[e] 1,000 yards

---

[e] It is incorrect to talk of 'range' in this particular context, because, even today, the best of marksmen, with the best of weaponry and sighting devices, does well to hit with a first-time

further than the needle gun, which, given the range capabilities of the time, covered the deployment area of artillery equipped with bronze muzzle-loaders. Both the chassepot and the needle gun were single-shot weapons, but breech-loading even of only one round at a time was a far quicker process than ramming shot down the muzzle.

At the start of the 1860s the United States was in the forefront of international small arms development, but the motivation was not so much military as the traditional right of every free citizen to bear arms, emphasised by the needs of those pioneers pressing the frontiers of the republic ever westward. These hardy individuals required guns for self-defence against the Indians, and to hunt buffalo and game in order to sustain life. The quality of weapon was higher than elsewhere, but the quantity produced before 1860 was relatively small and for home consumption only. Nevertheless, the principles of mass production were already comprehended. The US Arsenal at Springfield turned out its basic product, a muzzle-loaded rifle weighing just under ten pounds, firing a .58 calibre grooved bullet to a theoretical maximum range of 1,000 yards, by a process involving the use of over 100 different power tools.[7] In the War Between the States, the Springfield rifle became the basic infantry weapon of both sides, the Confederacy, without anything more than a rudimentary and cottage-industry level of production, relying on captured stocks. By the end of the war, nearly 1,500,000 Springfield rifles had been manufactured,[8] a rate of production over four years exceeding both in volume and time-frame anything achieved by any contemporary European power, and half as many again as the 1,000,000 chassepots produced in France between 1866 and 1870.

The Union throughout the war and the Confederacy, for as long as the blockade of its ports allowed, bought heavily overseas. The largest purchase was of over 800,000 British Enfields of 1853 vintage, comparable to the Springfield, but the purchasing agents of both sides combed the capitals and armaments factories of Europe from London to St Petersburg for whatever else was on offer. The result was a standardisation nightmare. By the end of the war, the Union had seventy-nine different types of personal weapon in service.[9] The ammunition resupply problem must have been formidable.

The specialist weapons of one era often become the standard equipment of the next, and more notice might have been taken of the variants of the

---

single shot an individual providing an opportunity target at any range above 500 yards. But the chassepot bullets remained lethal to the maximum distance imparted by their muzzle velocity.

standard rifle produced by the North, often in quite large numbers, and of their effect on the battlefield. The most important of these was the repeating rifle. A prototype, made by Colt, had been used against the Seminole Indians as early as 1838, but the revolving magazine had a tendency to produce simultaneous and spontaneous ignition of all the rounds at once, at considerable danger to the user. Nevertheless, this weapon was still in service at the start of the war, but was soon superseded by two spring-operated magazine versions, the Spencer and the Henry, named after their inventors. The Spencer had a seven-round magazine and a manual bolt action very similar to that of the standard Lee Enfield, which served the British Army well in both the world wars of the next century. The Henry's magazine held fifteen rounds of smaller calibre, but this weapon was considered to be less reliable than the Spencer. Both these 'repeaters' had a rate of fire of over twenty rounds a minute in skilled hands. There was also the single-shot breech-loaded Sharps carbine, intended primarily for cavalry, and Sharps and other manufacturers produced rifles with telescopic sights, for use by snipers. Sharps and Spencers went into major production by the standards of the time, at over 100,000 each, but only 15,000 of the more elaborate and expensive Henrys were produced. Ammunition calibres, and thus weight of individual rounds, were much greater than in successor equipment, the Spencer and the Sharp at .52 and the Henry at .44 as compared with the future Lee Enfield at .303, but this was already a dramatic reduction from the calibres of the standard weapons of the English and French infantry in the Crimean War, which exceeded 0.7".[10]

The development (by Sharps) during the war of a breech-loaded carbine for mounted men should have revolutionised cavalry tactics, but only the Americans realised this. Although the dragoons and carbineers of European armies were trained, at least in theory, to fight dismounted, the muzzle-loaded carbines of the Napoleonic era were of little ornament and less use. Every European army considered that the prime function of cavalry was the shock action of the charge. But the entry into service of the breech-loaded repeating carbine meant that the American Civil War offers no event to compare with the death ride at Balaclava in 1854, or of those yet to occur on the battlefields of 1870, at Froeschwiller, Mars La Tour, Gravelotte and Sedan. The cavalry versus cavalry actions at Brandy Station and on the third day of Gettysburg in the summer of 1863 were overshadowed by events elsewhere, but much might have been learned from those foreign observers who were in a position to evaluate the dismounted action of Buford's division of Union cavalry on the first day of Gettysburg,[f] when 3,000 dismounted horsemen armed with repeating carbines withstood for most of a morning the attack of two full-strength Confederate divisions.

While rifling and properly sealed breeches had increased maximum range by a factor of ten, and breech-loading and magazine rifles had produced the potential for a sixfold improvement in the rate of fire, these advances would have meant little unless there had been a corresponding improvement in the ballistic properties of the projectile. It was realised relatively soon after the introduction of the rifled barrel that a cylindrically-shaped bullet had far better aerodynamic performance than the round musket ball of the Napoleonic era, and the development of the gun inevitably carried along with it the development of munitions. By 1836, ammunition to match Dreyse's needle gun was in production in France as well as Prussia,[11] and by the time of the Crimean War the original cylinder-shaped bullet, which tended to 'tumble' in flight, had become tapered,[10] giving an obvious improvement to ballistic performance along the trajectory. But, until Chassepot's invention of fully effective breech sealing, propellant energy continued to be wasted, and, because rifle barrels became fouled in repeated firing by the coarse black powder used in cartridges, the advantages of rifling became eroded in any prolonged action. The critical development in this area was the invention of a bullet made of a relatively soft metal, which would expand from the heat of the ignition of the propellant charge, and so 'seat' the round firmly in its passage up the barrel. The lead bullet, invented by Captain Minié of the French Army, could be combined both with the needle ignition principle of Dreyse, the Springfield muzzle-loader and the bolt action and firing pin of the American breech-loaders. The combination of rifling and the expanding round increased the effective fighting range of the infantry personal weapon from under 100 yards to 250, just the distance on the Antietam battlefield from the Sunken Lane up the gentle slope to the crest line lying due east.

There was some experimentation during the American Civil War with explosive bullets for the Springfield, but these were not proceeded with, at least for military purposes. Lethality beyond that provided by the remaining velocity of a lead tapered bullet was unnecessary overkill. The 'minnie', as the soldiers called this standard munition for all infantry and cavalry personal weapons of the war, expanded on impact and produced some horrendous wounds, shattering bones and tearing intestines in a way quite beyond the capability of the old-fashioned musket ball. The severity of wounds,

---

[f] See Chapter VI.

exacerbated by bullets of calibres up to half as large again as today's standard 9 mm (0.35") infantry round, has caused at least one authority to conclude[12] that, in addition to those killed outright, half the wounded either died under treatment or were crippled for life. However, the natural tendency to open fire at maximum range saved at least some lives, because the Springfield round had a very low remaining velocity at the natural end of its trajectory. A pack of cards, a bundle of letters or a Bible were as effective as today's flak jacket in protecting a lucky soldier against a low-velocity impact, and there was also a safe zone within the range of the weapon because of the comparatively high curvature of its trajectory.

So, in the first instance, it was the infantry weapon rather than artillery which sounded the death knell for the battlefield tactics of the previous 500 years. The fact that the effective range of the infantryman's personal weapon had more than doubled meant that at last he had graduated beyond the 'pikeman' capability. Furthermore, it was apparent to some as early as 1864 that, whatever other uses the soldier might find for his bayonet, killing the enemy was no longer one of them. Wounds inflicted by sword or bayonet caused less than one hundredth of one per cent of the casualties suffered by Grant's command in the Wilderness Campaign in May of that year.[13] Any one of the inventions of Dreyse, Minié or Chassepot should have ended for good the era of unprotected infantry, parade ground erect and aligned, blazing away at each other over open ground less than the length of a football pitch apart, until one side or other launched a bayonet charge. Taken together, the three inventions provided the conditions for mutual slaughter, unless the defence could learn to protect itself by field fortifications and the attackers could be educated to relate the best use of ground to the coordination of fire with movement.

Infantry Support Weapons

The American Civil War saw the first appearance on the battlefield of the machine-gun,[14] which began its life as a tactical hybrid between the individual rifled musket of the infantryman and the crew-served guns and mortars of the artillery. The number of machine-guns deployed between 1862 and 1865 was too small to have any great influence on any of the battles. The rudimentary prototypes developed on alternative lines, either by hand-cranking a revolving drum magazine or by rotating a number of barrels which might be contained within a larger cylinder or cube, and could achieve a rate of fire six times that of the repeating rifle. The early versions were unreliable and unsatisfactory.

TWELVE POUNDER GUN-HOWITZER M1857 (NAPOLEON)

1. Stock
2. Cheek
3. Handspike
4. Prolonge hooks
5. Lunette
6. Cap-square

7. Part of lock chain
8. Sponge chain
9. Hand spike ring
10. Sponge hook
11. Elevating screw
12. Pointing rings

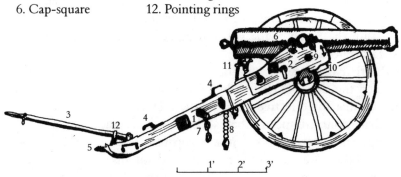

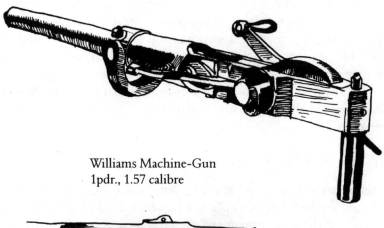

Williams Machine-Gun
1pdr., 1.57 calibre

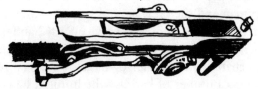

Billinghurst Requa Battery
.58 calibre

Agar Machine-Gun
Spare barrel, bullet and steel container

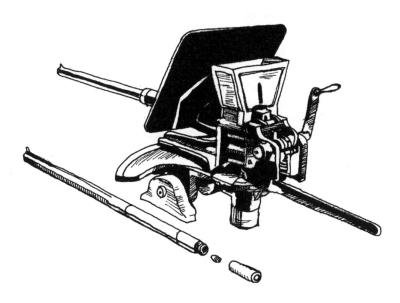

The weapon only became effective towards the end of the century when further developments resolved the related problems of cooling barrels, which became overheated by rapid fire, of utilising recoil energy to speed up and improve the reliability of ammunition feed, and of improving the propellant charge. The black powder used for this purpose by all weapons, infantry and artillery, was a compound of fifteen per cent charcoal, ten per cent sulphur and seventy-five per cent potassium nitrate. The cloud of black smoke generated by its initiation lingered round the gun after firing, blinding the crew and preventing completely the quick succession of aimed short bursts which is the optimum employment of a direct-fire automatic weapon. The first-generation systems fielded between 1862 and 1871 probably wasted much of their ammunition by firing blind at maximum range. Nor were the equipments man-portable. Constructed on mountings and wheeled carriages as though they were artillery equipments, and drawn by one or two horses, they could not accompany their infantry through untracked or wooded country.

Procurement policies were wholly informal. The first version of the Gatling gun, manufactured as early as 1862, was rejected by the US ordnance board, but the entrepreneurially minded politician-soldier, General Benjamin Butler, nevertheless acquired twelve of them for his mishandled campaign around Bermuda Hundred, on the James River, east of Petersburg, in the summer of 1864. This particular equipment had an inbuilt weakness because of a mismatch between the chamber and its six revolving barrels, and it was only after the war that an improved version entered US Army service.

The Agar machine-gun resembled a light artillery piece, in that it was carriage-mounted with a single barrel. It fired the same calibre bullets as the Springfield rifle, at a rate restricted to 120 rounds per minute in order to reduce the risk of distortion and danger from overheating the barrel. A spare barrel was carried, which could be quickly exchanged with one made too hot by prolonged firing. Bullets moved from magazine to chamber by manual hand-cranking, just like the operation of the standard-issue coffee mill, which gave this equipment its nickname.

A variant of the alternative multi-barrel concept of the Gatling was carried even further by the Billinghurst Requa Battery. Carriage-mounted like the Agar 'coffee mill', the Requa had twenty-five parallel barrels, also of .58 calibre, and looked like a collection of equal-sized organ pipes horizontally aligned. The cartridges were contained in a clip matching the barrel alignment, were loaded together and fired simultaneously, a trained crew of three being capable of firing seven volleys (175 rounds) in a minute. The characteristics of the Requa make it the forerunner of today's multiple-launch rocket system, rather than of the machine-gun.

Confederate development followed a somewhat different path. Their Williams machine-gun, a single-barrelled equipment which fired a solid shot weighing as much as a pound to a range of 2,000 yards at a rate of sixty-five rounds per minute, was likewise more the ancestor of the Second World War light anti-aircraft gun of the Oerlikon or 'pom-pom' variety.

Neither Prussia nor Austria had anything similar to field in the war of 1866. The first machine-gun-type weapon to be deployed in numbers which might have influenced a battle was the mitrailleuse of the Second Empire. Development began in 1860, on the personal initiative of Napoleon III, paid for from the imperial privy purse. The weapon entered production in 1866 in secrecy, and it reached field force formations concurrently with French mobilisation four years later, without any tactical doctrine having been evolved for its use on the battlefield. This weapon was multi-barrelled like the Gatling, but with twenty-five barrels instead of six. These were fired in turn by a rotating crank action at a rate of 150 rounds per minute. The mitrailleuse was not standardised with the chassepot, firing a slightly larger (.51"/13 mm) calibre round, which is much nearer to current dimensions than the contemporary American weapons. Chassepot's work on breech seals was incorporated to give a maximum range of 2,000 yards.[15] The multi-barrelled route of machine-gun development was rendered out of date by two inventions, by Vickers of a system of water-cooling to contain barrel overheating, and in 1887 by that of Maxim, who produced a gun which used its own reciprocating recoil energy to feed the ammunition from a belt into the chamber.

Within ten years of the introduction into service of the Maxim, at least one forward-thinking soldier had begun to appreciate the consequences. Winston Churchill, newly commissioned into the Fourth Hussars, although exhilarated by participating in the manoeuvres of the British Army's sole cavalry division in the Long Valley at Aldershot, could still find time to wonder, 'what would happen if half a dozen spoilsports got themselves into a hole with a Maxim gun and kept their heads.'[16]

Artillery

The fundamental reason artillery had, by 1870, become the dominant arm on the battlefield was the development in metallurgy which allowed guns to be made of steel. Pure steel was impervious to the shock produced by the ignition of the propellant charge, always provided that the designers had calculated correctly the firing stresses, and from it derived breech-loading and greater range for the same quantity of propellant and weight of ordnance. Breech-loading was also a far simpler and less manpower-intensive process than muzzle-loading, but its full benefits did not become clear until the emergence in 1890 of the first integral recoil systems. When a gun fires, the energy released to launch the projectile exerts an equal and opposite force on the gun, which recoils in order to absorb it. Shipboard cannon could be larger than the guns which moved with armies in the field because the ship provided the motive power. The standard twenty-four pounders of Nelson's ships of the line fired a projectile twice the weight of the heaviest viable field artillery equipments of the same era, and the thirty-two pounders of the first-rates were heavier still. But the confinement of their recoil to a limit which could be contained within the practical constraints of the gun decks required an organisation and quantity of ropes which had to be maintained always in perfect condition. Two tons of metal loose on a pitching and rolling deck were not just a hazard to life and limb; a loose gun on a lower deck could hole the ship so badly as to risk sinking it. Guns, sea and land, were loaded when in recoil, but then had to be returned to their firing position, or 'run-up', by brute force. The absorption of recoil energy within the gun became a critical improvement when the ever-increasing range capability introduced the concept of 'indirect' fire, i.e. when the gun crew cannot see the target which they are engaging. For the sake of consistency of indirect fire, it is important that the gun returns to the same flat and level platform each time after it has recoiled.

The breech-loaders made by Armstrong which formed part of the armament of HMS *Warrior*, launched in 1860, were evolutionary in that their recoil was confined to steel tracks and terminated by metal-to-metal contact stop.[17] Their 110 pound cylindrical cast-iron shot was far heavier than anything which could be brought to the support of an army in the field conducting mobile operations, though not of course any bigger than some of the siege-train or static fortress artillery which had existed for centuries. A more rapid rate of fire was a selling point for the first steel-fabricated breech-loaders on the land battlefield, This, before the invention of the integrated recoil system, spring or hydraulic, was due to the improved ergonomic characteristics, and the fact that steel produced a smaller and lighter equipment for a given calibre and weight of shell. There were thus obvious improvements in mobility and ease of handling.

Breech-loading produced, nevertheless, a whole new set of firing stresses and technical problems, because of the point of weakness introduced at the match between breech and chamber. The points of friction, contact and seal, the surfaces of moving block and static chamber, had to absorb the stresses and provide a safety factor when the gun fired. The breeches of the Armstrong and Whitworth breech-loaders deployed in small numbers in the American Civil War[18] opened and closed by continuous-threaded screw blocks in prolongation of the chamber. The screw was a natural source of strength, because the bearing surfaces of all the threads played their part in absorbing the explosive forces, but the manual operation of the screw did nothing for the rate of fire. Clearly, a sliding block would be quicker, and the first to reach the battlefield were the four pounders of Krupp, in production in 1865. This equipment had a wedge-shaped breech block, sliding on a horizontal and transverse guideway across the bore of the gun.[19] There soon followed a number of variants of sliding blocks, wedge- or cube-shaped, moving in the horizontal or vertical planes, sometimes with angled guideways and with contact points rounded rather than rectangular to improve strength for weight. But it was not until the development of the rotating cam, which allowed the transfer of a manual lever action through ninety degrees to turn an interrupted screw thread, that the optimum result was achieved. Both sliding or interrupted-screw thread breech blocks could be combined with either brass cases for the propellant charge, which expanded on firing and so sealed the chamber, or a compression pad made of rubber, or similar elastic material, on the Chassepot principle, incorporated behind the hardened steel face of the block which sealed the breech. All these construction techniques were understood by the end of the nineteenth century.

At the start of the critical decade, the bulk of the field artillery of all European armies and that of the United States was still muzzle-loaded smooth-bore. The basic artillery piece of the field armies on both sides in the War Between the States was the twelve pounder 'Napoleon', named after Napoleon III, who had sketched out the basic design during his incarceration in the Château of Ham, following the failure of his second abortive coup against the Orléans monarchy. This equipment had been in French service since 1857. Its solid shot had a range of no more than 1,680 yards, only marginally better than the guns of the *Grande Armée*'s Reserve Artillery, but the ordnance was no more than two-thirds the weight, and so was more mobile and could be served more quickly. The weight reduction had been achieved by shortening the barrel from 91" to 66", which would have caused a much greater spread of fall of shot at extreme range. A further innovation was the elevating screw, which allowed a variation between zero and five degrees in the angle of the barrel on firing. The incorporation of 'quadrant elevation', the angle between the horizontal and the line of the barrel when fired, allowed the piece itself to assist in the achievement of greater range, and led to the production of the first 'range table'. These data, increasingly comprehensive with every subsequent new equipment, provide in tabular form the adjustments to be made to the basic mathematical calculations of bearing and elevation (range) to be set on the sights of the gun[g] as part of the loading and laying process. The first example was a chart on the inside of the lid of each ammunition limber, which related the angles of the barrel from zero to five degrees to the estimated range, for a given quantity of propellant and nature of projectile. The Napoleon had three of these.[20] In addition to the traditional solid shot and canister, there was a bursting 'shell', a word derived from the German *'schale'*, meaning 'covering' or (tree) 'bark'. This early example of the replacement for solid shot contained a bursting charge and twenty-seven cast-iron balls.

It is self-evident that if the basic construction of the gun can be utilised to assist the propellant to improve the maximum range of the projectile, the best result is obtained if the gun can be fired with the barrel at an angle of forty-five degrees to the horizontal. But anything approaching such an elevation can be achieved only if the ordnance incorporates a system to absorb the recoil energy, or if a pit is dug to allow the barrel to recoil in the angle at which it is fired. This can produce a serious inhibition to the rate of fire if it is necessary to return the barrel to the horizontal in order to reload. The three related improvements of steel construction, breech-loading and integrated recoil mechanisms allowed guns to be fired at a satisfactory battlefield rate, at a quadrant elevation giving an optimum engagement range which, by the end of the century, was far beyond anything which allowed those serving the gun to observe its fall of shot.

The gridding of maps established a mathematical relationship between the relative positions of gun and target in terms of bearing, range and angle of sight to allow for altitude difference, and the two latter could be converted to a quadrant elevation for the barrel, which was laid not by direct 'pointing', as with the guns of the Napoleonic era, but by the coincidence of markers, or, for greater accuracy, centring a spirit-level bubble. Some attempts were made

---

[g] A process which introduced the need for mathematical comprehension and numeracy well above the average standard of education of most recruits to most armies. The first British Army trials of the first computerised process took place in 1962.

at indirect shooting from the map by British artillery in the Boer War, but the first serious use of indirect fire techniques, i.e. correction to the fall of shot ordered by an observer who could see the target, to the guns, who could not, was in the Russo-Japanese War of 1904–5.[21] The process had been thought through by the German Army, who passed it on to the Japanese when the empire of the Mikado opted for a German training mission. Indirect fire had, by the start of the First World War, become standard field artillery practice, introducing the need for a reliable, one-to-one system of communication between observer and gun position. The first means, by telephone link, was unsuited to the demands of a mobile battle, unreliable because of attenuation and vulnerable because the lines were subject to frequent rupture from shell bursts and foot or wheeled movement. Radio was found to be essential, but did not reach the battlefield in this role until the Second World War. The whole requirement for improved communications sprang from the greater ranges which artillery was achieving by the end of the Franco-German War.

The 'pointing' of guns by brute force was starting to be supplemented in some of the rifled artillery equipments of the American Civil War by a traversing screw, in addition to the elevating screw of the Napoleon. This allowed a small degree of fine adjustment and the ability to change to a new target. These guns were already hinting at the nature of things to come: for a comparable weight of projectile, maximum ranges were already increasing, the prized British Whitworths throwing a twelve pound shot to a maximum of 3,000 yards in the muzzle-loaded version, the limit of the breech-loader being 200 yards less. And already, all-up weights of equipments were reducing, thus improving mobility and rate of fire.

Whatever the construction material used, whether bronze or cast iron, it was always possible to produce stronger gun barrels by using more of it, but at penalty of increased weight, and thus degraded mobility. In the 1860s Armstrongs began experiments with steel wire-winding to improve the strength of barrels, but the step forward in gun construction occurred only when it became possible to use a wholly reliable new material. Steel, though giving much greater strength for weight, was only a safe metal for gun construction if it were cooled down at an absolutely even rate during the manufacturing process. In 1863, Alfred Krupp purchased the German licence for the process invented by Sir Henry Bessemer and already in use in the steel mills of Sheffield, but the initial results were disastrous. What was not appreciated at the time was that the Bessemer process depended upon ore with an absolute minimum content of phosphorous, and, while Swedish and English ores were pure enough for the construction of guns from Bessemer-process steel, the ores available on Krupp's doorstep in the Ruhr, although plentiful and cheaply obtained, were so riddled with phosphorous that 'they almost glowed in the dark'.[22]

In time, Krupp would acquire proving grounds, first at Dulmen and then at Meppen, bigger and with more advanced facilities than anything which the Prussian general staff had available at Tegel, but in the mid-1860s the need for these had not emerged. Nor were there any of the processes later to be developed by the British ordnance board to guarantee the safety of new guns and ammunition before these reached the hands of field force units. In consequence, the first steel breech-loaders to reach the battlefield, in the war of 1866, were unsafe equipments. A number burst, killing or maiming the crews. Krupp, driven almost to nervous breakdown by the news, and a past master in developing hypochondria when business was bad or decisions could with advantage be deferred, disappeared to a succession of spas. Later he was to invest heavily in sources of pure ore in Spain and Norway, but his immediate salvation came from another Ruhr firm struggling to maintain profitability on the frontiers of new technology. Siemens developed a process which burned away the phosphorous content of impure ore. The first open-hearth furnace based on the Siemens principle came into operation in England, but Krupp, making a miraculous recovery, bought the process at once. And in 1871, the new German Empire acquired the coal and iron resources of eastern Lorraine, which the French Second Empire had barely begun to develop. The rich band of geological assets which extends from South Wales through southern Belgium, Lorraine and the Ruhr to Silesia is not continuous, nor are the minerals even in quantity or quality, but at the time the 150 mile stretch of ground between Lorraine and the Ruhr probably contained more, and more easily obtainable, deposits of iron and coal than any comparable area on earth. The ores of Lorraine were similar to those of the Ruhr in their high phosphorous content, but the invention, by Gilchrist Thomas in 1875, of a process which separated out the phosphorous ingredient of ore, converting it into slag,[23] meant that the basic raw materials for the ships and guns of the Second Reich were secured in abundance. The peace settlement imposed by Bismarck left Briey, heart of the Lorraine iron basin, on the frontier between France and Germany. The assets left in French hands were indefensible and fell to the German Fifth Army by the end of August 1914. For the rest of the First World War, and in the Second, between 1940 and 1944, the whole was in the possession of Germany and under the control of Krupp.

In the early years of the nineteenth century, many others besides Alfred's father Friedrich were engaged on the quest for steel, no doubt, as is often the case when a technological revolution is in sight, without too much idea about the uses of the new medium.[h] If Friedrich's efforts seemed to his contemporaries to be nearer fantasy than practicality, those of Alfred, when, at the age of fourteen following the premature death of his father, he became sole proprietor of the rundown establishment by the side of the sluggish little Ruhr stream, were at first hardly beyond the capabilities of a modern adequately equipped school science laboratory. For twenty-five years, Alfred's infatuation with steel kept him near to bankruptcy. What brought him to prominence, and led to his business becoming by far the most important armaments manufacturer of the pre-nuclear age, was the nineteenth-century version of the trade fair. At the Great Exhibition of 1851 in London, Krupp had wanted to display a giant steel ingot, but the possibility that this might not be ready in time compelled him to arrange his wares around something else. He chose an all-steel six pounder cannon; this product stole the show.[24] Further successful displays at similar events followed, culminating in the Paris Exhibition of 1867, when he paraded an enormous 14" steel gun, the barrel of which alone weighed fifty tons. By this time he was exporting cannon worldwide, to every major power except the United States, now recovering from the Civil War, England and France.

England had her own weapons-manufacturing industry, partly in the royal arsenals and dockyards, partly in the private sector, but the Second Empire had a long internal debate about the purchase of artillery from Krupp. General Le Boeuf, the new minister of war, was much impressed by a display in Belgium in 1868, the year following the Paris Exhibition and the appointment of Alfred Krupp to the Legion of Honour, but the procurement decision went against Krupp. The reasons were the need to give national preference to Schneider Creusot, and the financing of the chassepot production programme, which left no money for artillery. Three years later, when the French war ministry file on the project was found to have been closed with the words 'Rien à faire' in Le Boeuf's own handwriting, the decision not to buy from Krupp was trumpeted as yet another instance of Second Empire frivolous incompetence; it can now be seen objectively, as a further historical example of a bad decision taken for the best of reasons.

---

[h] The author recalls a quite distinguished scientist describing, in 1968, the laser as 'a solution looking for a problem'.

Krupp's best customer until after Sadowa was Imperial Russia and not his own country.[i] This was because, shortly after his success at the Great Exhibition had made him for the first time a figure of national importance, he had offended irreconcilably von der Heydt, the Prussian minister of commerce. Further, in spite of a sustained attempt at persuasion, he had failed to convince von Roon, minister of war from 1859, of the advantages of steel over bronze in the construction of cannon. In this debate, Roon was a traditionalist, and by character far from being the easiest person in the world to convince. The controversy continued even after the crushing success attributable to the German artillery in the war of 1870, when some paladins of the general staff, including Moltke's deputy Podbielski, maintained their argument for a return to bronze muzzle-loaders. But as early as 1860 Krupp had one formidable ally. The regent, Prince William of Prussia, soon to succeed his mad brother on the throne, overrode in that year the advice of his ministers, and ordered the first steel breech-loaders. The benefit of this royal intervention to Krupp was immediate: his workforce was one of the very few categories of manpower exempted from Roon's all-embracing conscription laws.[25] As has already been mentioned, the battlefield debut of the new guns was wholly inauspicious, but, with the providential advent of the Siemens process, Krupp was able to correct the fault. To make amends, he offered in 1867 to replace, free of charge, all the breech-loaders delivered before 1866 with 400 four pounders made in the new process,[26] and by the start of the war of 1870 all the armies of the North German Confederation had been re-equipped with breech-loading four and six pounders.[27]

After the war of 1870–71, the army of the German Empire did not fire another shot in anger for twenty-nine years, until German participation in the international force which put down the Boxer Rebellion in China. In this short time-span, their field artillery benefited from no fewer than four complete re-equipment programmes. The first, in 1873, was generated by the threat of a war with France, recovering too quickly for some Prussian tastes from the débâcle of three years earlier. The other three took immediate

---

[i] Alfred Krupp was born a subject of the Grand Duchy of Berg, and so technically was a citizen of the First French Empire. Before the Revolutionary Wars, Essen had been a minor ecclesiastical state. In the division of the North German principalities between Murat's Grand Duchy of Berg and Jerome Bonaparte's Kingdom of Westphalia, Murat saw to it that the ancient city of Essen went to Berg. After 1815, the whole of the district known worldwide by the end of the century as the Ruhr became a possession of the Kingdom of Prussia, making the three year old Alfred a subject of the Hohenzollern monarchy.

advantage of major technological improvements. These were the development in 1887 of ballistite, a smokeless powder deriving from Nobel's earlier invention of dynamite, which produced a more powerful propellant charge;[28] lateral adoption of the nickel-plated steel which had emerged from the search for a better strength-to-weight ratio for protective armour for battleships, in particular their gun turrets; and the invention of the recoil system, which in turn generated the introduction of split and separated trails for gun carriages, spade-ended to assist stability of the gun platform, and protective shields for the gun detachments. On two of these occasions the German emperor intervened personally to order the new programme. All were paid for from a defence budget almost unconstrained in practical terms, because, under the constitution of the new empire, if the general staff defined a requirement which the emperor approved, the necessary expenditure became enshrined in an 'army law'. It was then up to the Reichstag to find the money. In a booming economy, and given the absolute pride of the nation in an army which had paramount status, the country could take the strain, especially with a disciplined labour force benefiting from social welfare provisions far in advance of those of any other contemporary power. The continuing development of heavy weapons and munitions matched that of field artillery.

The armaments-producing capabilities of the other Great Powers were by no means negligible. In addition to those of England and France already mentioned, the Habsburg Empire had the Skoda works in Bohemia, Imperial Russia the Putiloff–Neva factories; by the end of the century American steel production had overtaken that of Germany. But in the field of guns and munitions, Krupp led the way, both in the application of new technologies and in capacity and volume of production. Perhaps the greatest commercial triumph of Die Firma in terms of prestige was that for a short time Krupp equipped the British Army's artillery.

As we have seen, the critical development was that of the integral recoil system. As early as 1867 Siemens had suggested a concept years ahead of its time, a water- and valve-based hydraulic compression and expansion arrangement, but it was not until 1890 that the first gun incorporating a recoil system entered service. This was a fifteen pounder with a maximum range of three miles, developed and produced, needless to emphasise, by Krupp. The recoil system was spring-based, as was the French 'soixante-quinze', which entered service in 1898, and with very few modifications, remained the standard French artillery field gun throughout the First World War. The British took time to evaluate their choice. Once hardware appears, there is no such thing as a technological secret, and, inevitably, the British would opt for home production. But, until designs could be perfected, prototypes proved and main production set in hand, there was, in time for the Boer War, a British purchase for operational purposes of some of the older Krupp equipments[29] in preference to that of the French, a choice hardly surprising given the political climate and affiliations of the time.

The war of 1870 saw the introduction to the battlefield of two other first-generation weapon systems; very long-range artillery and anti-air weapons. When Paris came under siege in 1870, Moltke's lines of circumvallation extended over fifty miles, and the besieging force numbered barely a third of the 500,000 armed men they were expected to contain. The fortifications of Paris, modernised as recently as 1840,[30] had an almost circular perimeter with a diameter of some eight miles, and there were also sixteen outlying forts. But the vital ground of the Chatillon plateau, to the south of the fortifications and a bare five miles from the heart of the city, was not occupied, nor were the French able to contest Prussian possession of it. From these heights, now built over, the golden dome of the Invalides remains clearly visible. There was already some heavy artillery with the German Army, 5.9" (150 mm) guns and 8.26" (210 mm) mortars, and Krupp was rushing even heavier equipments into production. But, if specifications were observed, the Germans had nothing which could hit the centre of Paris. The maximum range of the gun was supposed to be no more than 6,000 yards. Nevertheless, the gunners experimented. Propellant charges were boosted, recoil pits dug and barrels elevated to thirty degrees for firing. This produced a twenty-five per cent increase in range capability, and brought the prestigious buildings of government and national heritage on the Left Bank into the target footprint of the weapon. Although it was starvation, rather than the steady pounding at the rate of 600 rounds a day, which forced the surrender of the city and the end of the war after a four month siege, sustained harassing fire at a range of four and a half miles was unprecedented.

The other débutante was the first ever anti-aircraft weapon. Coordination of national defence between the beleaguered capital and French armies in the field south of the Loire led to a series of balloonist departures from Paris, the first as early as 23rd September, the most famous bearing Gambetta, minister of the interior in the provisional government, a fortnight later. In the course of the siege, sixty-five balloons left Paris, the Gare du Nord having been requisitioned for use as the balloon factory. The counter weapon reached the besieging army as early as 3rd December. Looking more like a giant telescope

---

[j] See Chapter IX.

than an artillery piece, it had a six foot long barrel, rotatable on a fifteen foot high mounting. It fired a three pound solid shot to a slant range of 2,000 yards on a straight trajectory.[31] There is no evidence that the Ballongeshutz brought down a single target, but the aerial dimension had been added to combat. And even with a simple weapon, a gestation period of barely ten weeks between perception of the requirement and introduction into service was a formidable achievement.

In the nineteenth century, unlike the twentieth, it was the development of guns rather than munitions which led the advance of the technology of firepower. The four areas of importance in munition technology are the primer, the propellant charge, the material of the projectile and its bursting charge. The principle of tube ignition for propellant charges had been understood as early as the 1850s,[32] and needed little further development, and the great advance in propellant derived from the smokeless powder which followed the invention of dynamite. By 1891, the British artillery was using cordite, a mixture of fifty-eight per cent nitroglycerine, thirty-seven per cent gun cotton and five per cent mineral jelly,[33] with matching developments by the other armament-producing nations. This not only gave a far more efficient explosive compound, but also reduced barrel wear.

The need to improve artillery projectiles was, by 1860, already well understood, both to enhance range and increase the lethality of individual rounds. The ricochet effect of the cannon ball had been completely haphazard, much depending upon the nature and state of the ground at each point of impact. Rifled barrels, first used on the battlefield by France in 1859, and better power to weight ratio for propellant introduced the need for tapered cylindrical shot, and the elevation of the gun barrel to gain increased range introduced curvature to the trajectory, all of which marginalised the ricochet effect. But the search was on for improved material for projectile construction, and for a bursting charge which would produce lethal fragments. Between 1880 and 1890, the war reserve ammunition stocks of the developed nations began to consist of steel shells in place of cast iron, but the relationship between shell and bursting charge did not advance significantly until the British invention of Lyddite, in 1896.[33]

A shell which bursts on ground impact loses the greater part of its energy in creating a crater, rather than in distributing lethal fragments around the immediate area. The projectile development of the 1860s was devoted primarily to the search for a means of bursting the round at the optimum point along its trajectory before the point of impact, which for troops in the open is between ten to fifteen feet above them. The Prussian Army would have nothing to do with this process, relying totally on fuses designed to initiate a bursting charge at point of impact, on exactly the same principle as the present-day percussion fuse. The North in the American Civil War and the French Army took the opposite path, seeking to optimise projectile lethality from airburst fuses. This introduced a further set of ingredients into the pot of round-to-round variation. While fuses for mortars were still set and lit by hand, those for guns were supposed to be ignited by the flash of the propellant when the gun fired. This detonation might bypass the fuse altogether and explode the projectile in the barrel of the gun, or, at the other extreme, it might not work at all, and the round would impact without bursting. The most noteworthy development in the American Civil War was the four different standard fuses, colour-coded to show burning times of between two and five seconds, which were screwed to the shells of the 3" Parrott and twenty-four pounder Dyer as part of the loading process,[34] the fuse selected according to the range estimation of the battery, section or gun commander.

There is universal agreement among authorities that the time fuses of the French artillery in the war of 1870 were a disaster. Simple in that there were only two settings, intended to explode the shell at alternative ranges of 2,500 and 1,250 yards,[35] these had proved to be both unreliable and ineffective in the frontier battles. The provisional government ordered their replacement by percussion fuses similar to those of the Germans,[36] and in the winter battles on the Loire the French field artillery, for the first time in the war, was of some use, though still out-ranged by the Krupp breech-loaders. Mechanical time fuses, set by hand during the loading process to explode at a moment related to the time of flight of the shell, remained unreliable, adding the 'zone of the fuse' to the 'zone of the gun', in spite of efforts to improve them which continued well after the Second World War. The invention of a fuse triggered by a radar effect, with the round in flight transmitting a signal which, when reflected back at sufficient strength from the target, explodes the shell, removed this source of inconsistency, but at the penalty of a tenfold increase in unit cost. This development can be seen as the forerunner of the invention of laser guidance and detonation of shells in flight which was so spectacularly successful in the Gulf War of 1991.

The mistake of Roon and other opponents of steel guns was that, because they were lacking in imagination, they could not conceive of anything which would completely outdate the bronze gun firing a solid shot, and the fact that Waterloo had been won half a century before with such weapons provided, in the eyes of the traditionalist, the compelling reason for their retention, rather than the need to search for an improvement. And half a century later, von Schlieffen, retired at the end of 1905 from the post of chief of the general staff in Berlin, fell into the same trap: 'It seems pointless to give new tasks to the inventors. Everything conceivable has already been attained.'[37]

And yet, in 1909, the improvement of armaments based upon further developments in the technology of steel can now be seen to have barely begun. The decade of the Catalytic Wars saw the first use on the battlefield of steel-fabricated guns, and only a rash prophet would claim, a century and a quarter later, that the limit of development of steel for combat purposes has been reached.

Notes

[1] Hohenlohe Ingelfingen, *Letters on Artillery*, London, 1888, p.56, quoted in Howard, *The Franco-Prussian War*, London, Rupert Hart-Davis, 1961, p.4.

[2] The debate continued during and after the war of 1870. For the record of a contemporary discussion, see *From Sedan to Saarbrucken*, by 'An Officer of the Royal Artillery', London, Tinsley Brothers, 1870, reprinted by Helion Books, Solihull, 1992, pp.48–50 and 57.

[3] Whitton, *Moltke*, London, Constable and Co., 1921, p.98.

[4] Howard, op.cit., p.5.

[5] Manchester, *The Arms of Krupp*, Boston, Mass., Little, Brown and Co., 1964, p.64.

[6] Guedalla, *The Two Marshals*, London, Hodder and Stoughton, 1943, pp.141–42.

[7] Catton, *Terrible Swift Sword*, New York, Washington Square Press Edition, 1967, p.84.

[8] Coggins, *Arms and Equipment of the Civil War*, Wilmington, North Carolina, Broadfoot Publishing Co., 1962, pp.31–37, contains a full description of the personal weapons in the War Between the States.

[9] Macdonald, *Great Battles of the Civil War*, New York, Maxwell Macmillan International, 1988, p.54.

[10] Curtis, 'Infantry Shoulder Weapons of the Crimean War' in *The War Correspondent*, Journal of the Crimean War Research Society, April 1996, vol. XIV, no.1, p.16.

[11] Coggins, op.cit., p.31.

[12] Catton, *Mr Lincoln's Army*, New York, Doubleday and Co., 1951, p.211.

[13] Coggins, op.cit., p.29.

[14] Coggins, op.cit., pp.43–45, describes these first-generation weapons.

[15] The two weapons can be examined at the Musée de l'Armée in Paris, and at the small battlefield museum in the village of Gravelotte.

[16] Churchill, *My Early Life*, first published in 1930 by Thornton Butterworth; London, Mandarin Publishing, 1990, p.79.

[17] A visit to HM Dockyard, Portsmouth, allows direct comparison of the armaments of HMS *Victory* and HMS *Warrior*, launched a century later.

[18] Coggins, op.cit., pp.84–5.

[19] Ellacott, *Guns*, London, Macmillan and Co., 1955, p.40.

[20] Coggins, op.cit., pp.63–83, describes American Civil War field artillery.

[21] Bailey, *Field Artillery and Firepower*, Oxford Military Press, 1989, pp.119–20.

[22] Manchester, op.cit., p.93.

[23] Manchester, op.cit., p.143.

[24] Manchester, op.cit., pp.68–9.

[25] Manchester, op.cit., pp.82–3.

[26] Manchester, op.cit., p.100.

[27] Hoffbauer, *Die Deutsche Artillerie in den Schlachten und Treffen des Deutsche-Franzoschen Krieg 1870*, Berlin, Ernst Siegfried Muller und Sohn, 1876.

[28] Hogg, *Artillery: Its Origin, Heyday and Decline*, London, C. Hurst and Co., 1970, p.140.

[29] Hogg, op.cit., pp.108–9.

[30] Horne, *The Fall of Paris*, London, Macmillan and Co., 1965, reprint Society London 1967, pp.63 and 76.

[31] This weapon was still in existence in a museum in East Berlin in 1963. See Manchester, op.cit., p.128; Horne pp.82–4 and 129–31.

[32] Hogg, op.cit., pp.165–68.

[33] Hogg, op.cit., pp.140–41.

[34] Coggins, op.cit., p.82.

[35] Ascoli, *A Day of Battle*, London, Harrap, 1987, p.165.

[36] Howard, op.cit., p.298.

[37] Andreev, 'Wonder Weapons – A Means to an End?' in *History Today*, November 1996, vol. XVI, XI, p.57.

Chapter VI
Set Piece and Encounter Battle: Antietam, Fredericksburg and Gettysburg

Military Perceptions in the United States in 1860

The authors of *The Communist Manifesto* took for granted that, if their credo were ever to become the policy of an established government, it would be as a result of violent change within an industrialised nation. In the event, a combination of influences unforeseen by Marx, Engels or any of their early disciples, ensured that, when communism came to power, it was in the least industrialised of all the larger states of the early twentieth century. On the other hand, Clausewitz made no such geographic forecast about the location of the next major war, only of its inevitability and totality. When the first such conflict occurred, the nations of Europe, for a variety of reasons, could either discount or fail altogether to recognise the first practical evidence of the complete change in the nature of warfare. The fact that it was a civil war might explain the extreme virulence of its conduct, because in any such struggle one side at least is fighting for survival. The very small pre-war military establishment of the United States could allow the quarrel to be degraded in consideration to the level of a brawl between armed mobs[a] – a status which was confirmed, rather than otherwise, by the events of its first twelve months. The initial reliance, by the Union in particular, upon German drill instructors, French Army role models, and first-generation immigrant soldiers, could lead the observers, sent with varying degrees of accreditation by all the European powers, and also foreign war correspondents, to deduce that, in the conduct of war, as in so many other matters, the New World was still *in statu pupillari* to the Old. The effect of the applied technologies of the Second Industrial Revolution, already apparent in the Crimea and in the war of 1859 in northern Italy, now burst upon the battlefield with the force of a hurricane, but because

---

[a] A remark attributed to Moltke as late as 1864.

the nature of the War Between the States was misappreciated, its lessons were either ignored or misapplied. Although the four year fight to the death soon generated a mass of memorialist literature, there was no proper military–intellectual study until years afterwards. The influence of the fighting upon the thinking of those who at the time had the direction of the military destinies of the European Great Powers was, at most, minimal. While the intellectual capacity of von Moltke would independently reach many of the right conclusions, guiding the military development of Prussia accordingly, no other European country had a ruler, statesman or soldier with the necessary combination of understanding and influence.

The military tradition of the American republic, dating from the War of Independence, was the usual combination of reality and myth, complacency induced by the 3,000 mile wide moat which separated the new nation from any military challenger, and the erosion by time of those less-convenient factors and arguments which contradicted the glorious legend. Except for a short war with England between 1812 and 1814, and an even shorter conflict with Mexico for eighteen months starting in late 1846, the United States had remained at peace. The War of Independence was thought to have been won because the whole military-age manhood of the Thirteen Colonies, hardened by frontier-style existence and imbued universally with a burning desire for liberty and freedom from the British Crown, had sprung as one man to arms. Their free-spirited initiative, pioneer hardihood and countryman's natural eye for ground had been enough to defeat the rigidly drilled and over-disciplined Redcoats, pressed men and mercenaries commanded by effete aristocrats, whose battle procedures were devoid of imagination and totally unsuited to the rugged terrain of Virginia, Massachusetts and New York State, where most of the main battles had taken place. Notwithstanding the many obvious errors of fact and interpretation, this tradition was reinforced by the afterglow of the further experience of the war of 1812–1814, when the very same regiments of Redcoats, which had just driven the invincible French armies out of the Iberian peninsula, had themselves been beaten decisively at New Orleans, and their commander, brother-in-law of the great duke of Wellington himself, killed. There was, of course, some truth in part of the story, and it led to the proposition that, should the security of the fledgling republic ever again be threatened, a *levée en masse* of all the military-age manpower, organised by the component states of the somewhat imprecisely defined federal union, each in their own way, would again spring to arms with the certainty of victory, on a minimum of peacetime structure, preparation and training. This comforting theory, or fairy story, ignored some vital historical facts. General Washington's army and navy had a hard core of manpower as rigid in its drill, as much recruited by the press gang, and as much disciplined by sanction as any of King George III's regiments or line of battleships kept in hand by threat of flogging.[1] One of his principal subordinates, von Steuben, had learned his trade under Frederick the Great, and had exercised an influence, first on overall army organisation, next in command of Washington's Southern Army, and finally on the technical conduct of the Siege of Yorktown,[2] without which the war would probably have been lost. And perhaps the most important ingredient in ultimate victory was the local and temporary loss of command of the sea in the Chesapeake Bay, concurrent with the Siege of Yorktown, by the English fleet to the French allies of the embryo nation.

Whatever the numerous disagreements among the founding fathers of the new republic, and these existed in many other areas as well as the military, they were in accord on the related principles that it was the right of every free citizen to bear arms for his own defence, and that he had a duty to respond to the call of his own state if it required him to use his privately owned weapon in a common cause. Hence, every free citizen of military age, which Washington suggested in 1783 in the wake of victory as being between eighteen and fifty, had a legal obligation to appear for military training every year. Washington's proposals split this force of militia into three age groups and envisaged an annual training liability of twenty-five days for the youngest and presumably fittest group, reduced to twelve for the oldest class. For those who, by reason of circumstance, did not possess their own weapons, the states would provide, establishing arsenals or 'armouries' for the purpose.[3] None of the original thirteen component states of the new nation ever fully accepted these proposals, nor did any of the states admitted thereafter. As the memory of war receded, the training obligation reduced rapidly to the requirement to report on one nominated day in each year, subject to fine for absence but with increasingly widely drawn exempted categories. As was only to be expected, the annual muster day before long degenerated, at best, into an excuse for a good party and at worst to the level of farce. As early as 1808, there is a description of an annual muster day in South Carolina, one of the original Thirteen Colonies:

> The soldiers objected to going into these revolutions at all, in as much as the weather was extremely hot, and they had already been kept in the field upwards of three-quarters of an hour. They reminded the captain of his repeated promise to be as short as he possibly could, and it was clear that he could dispense with all this

same wheeling and flourishing if he chose. They were already very thirsty, and, if he would not dismiss them, they declared they would go off without dismission [sic] and get something to drink; and he might fine them if that would do him any good; they were able to pay their fine, but could not go without drink to please anybody; and they swore they would never vote for another captain who had to be so unreasonably strict.[4]

The point should be made in passing that the countervailing influences of American democracy were enshrined in the militia organisation from the start. The embodied men elected all ranks up to captain, i.e. company commander, but higher appointments were in the gift of the state governor, and were thus a valuable source of patronage: sinecures, conferring a gilded presence at state official functions. It might be thought that, because of the Indian threat, the state militias formed as the Union expanded west of the Alleghenies might have been more efficient than those of the former Thirteen Colonies, but such was not the case.[5]

Those who sought to do something about the matter, and all the first four presidents tried their hand at it, had to tread very carefully to avoid possible charges of creating military support for their own personal aggrandisement. Furthermore, as in any democracy in any age, if there is an important but non-urgent political problem to which there is no obvious popular solution, or, worse, no solution at all without considerable additional public expenditure, the difficulty remains unresolved unless there is a concerted and sustained attempt by the whole force of central government to find and impose an answer. The nearest approach to this state of affairs came after the end of the 1812–14 war. Although the flood of immigration from Europe had not yet begun, the population had already expanded beyond the number at which a *levée en masse* made administrative sense. President Madison's secretary of war proposed a plan which, like that of Washington thirty years before, divided the fit and eligible manpower into three classes, with annual training camps for the first two. A committee of the House of Representatives, under the chairmanship of William Henry Harrison, himself to be elected president a quarter of a century later on the basis of his victory at Tippecanoe over the Indians, agreed that something ought to be done, but, in a typical 'corridors of power' delaying tactic when unpopular expenditure is involved, referred the matter back to the secretary of war for further study. It was ten years before the subject was raised again before Congress, by which time, although organisation and obligation still existed on paper, the militia as a useful military force was defunct.

The same objections to doing anything which might improve the military efficiency of the militia extended with even greater cogency to the creation and maintenance of a standing army, and were reinforced by sensitivities over the doctrine of states' rights. The individual views of the founding fathers on the relationship between central and state government spanned all shades of the spectrum, from almost total centralisation to almost total devolution.[6] Discussion, erudite, informed and polemical, about the form which the constitution of the United States was to take continued for five years after the end of the War of Independence. What emerged was, inevitably, an imprecisely defined compromise in which, with the exception of the Supreme Court, those institutions deriving from a central government – bank, national university, armed forces – which today would be regarded as essential were authorised only by default, in that the constitution could not be said to prohibit them. The arguments against a standing army were reinforced by the geographic separation of the United States from any conceivable military threat, and by international acceptance of President Monroe's celebrated declaration in 1823 that the United States, while not proposing to overturn existing arrangements, would regard as dangerous to its peace and security any attempt by the European powers to 'extend their systems to any portion of this hemisphere'.[7] While providing cover for the newly independent former colonies in the New World of Spain and Portugal, Monroe's doctrine did not threaten continued British possession of Canada. The republic had already acquired by purchase the long-standing Spanish and French colonies of Florida and Louisiana, as she was subsequently to obtain Alaska from Russia. No European power, at the time or later, combined the wish and ability to challenge Monroe's propositions. The United States remained at peace for nearly another quarter of a century until the war with Mexico, from which she gained Texas, California and the lands between. Throughout the first half of the nineteenth century the establishment of the standing army was limited to 16,000 men, and its duties to fighting Indians in Florida and the West, and to garrisoning the fortifications of the eastern seaboard against an enemy who never existed. Even the tiny manpower and financial provisions for this force came under intermittent fire in Congress, alike from advocates of economy, anti-federalists and those who could take the view, quite legitimately after 1815, that mankind had grown out of war as a method of resolving international disputes. At the extreme, the naturally hierarchical and quasi-aristocratic organisation of any army offended pure republicanism, while its financial cost for no obvious benefit flew in the face of hard-headed business sense.

Perhaps the cradle for the military spirit of any established nation is the military academy which provides the initial training for the young men destined to officer its armies. West Point, founded in 1802,[b] for long survived on sufferance, against the hostility of all the forces opposed to the existence of a standing army, as well as the antagonism this elitist and privileged establishment attracted in its own right. The same applied to the Naval Academy at Annapolis, founded forty years after West Point. But because almost all nominations to the military academy were in the gift of members of Congress, so providing a valuable source of patronage, this privilege was also a source of strength. In addition, Washington, in his first annual message as president to Congress, expressed his desire that there should be a national university.[8] Because his wish, reiterated at intervals, for long remained unsatisfied, West Point filled at least part of the gap. The curriculum came to be modelled more on that of the *École Polytechnique* of France, which trained civil as well as military engineers for the service of the nation, rather than the Royal Military College at Sandhurst, which trained the future officers of the infantry and cavalry regiments of the British Army, but not those destined for the technical arms. The top graduates of West Point tended to opt for the corps of engineers,[9] where their employment was as likely to be on civil engineering projects as military. This at least avoided, for the pick of each graduating class, the soul-destroying effect of long service in small frontier outposts quite without any intellectual stimulus.

It remained a criticism of West Point that the drop-out rate during the four year course was very high and the retention rate after commissioning was far too low. Of 1,417 cadets admitted in the fifteen intakes between 1829 and 1843, only 610 graduated.[10] The main reason was that West Point set the highest standards of academic excellence and conformist discipline and behaviour. Those whose previous schooling had been inadequate, or who had grown up in the unrestricted environment of plantation or frontier, found it hard to adapt and so departed. Nor did an army with an establishment of no more than 16,000 need an annual average intake of 100 officers. Given that for a variety of reasons a number of officers were commissioned directly into the army from civilian life, the officer strength of the service could be sustained comfortably at no more than two-fifths of the initial West Point intake. But criticism continued that it was the most gifted who tended to leave soonest. In

---

[b] Predating both Sandhurst and St Cyr.

the 1830s the minimum term of service for a West Point graduate was set at five years, but, as he could offset his four year course against this, his required commitment of commissioned service was still only one year. By the end of the decade a minimum of four years' service after graduation had come to be expected and accepted, notwithstanding continuing discontent about the very slow promotion rate, poor pay and conditions of service, underuse of training and capacity and indifferent prospects. A captain of twenty-two years' service could demonstrate that the chief cook of the hotel in New Orleans in which he was billeted was somewhat better off than himself in terms of gross salary and considerably more so in the matter of take-home pay. A mathematical assessment in a service magazine claimed that a second lieutenant, aged twenty when he graduated, would be fifty-four before he became the most junior captain in the army, and had no prospect of promotion to major.[11] This purely academic calculation was not borne out by events; few such studies are. Brevet promotions[c] awarded quite liberally for achievement in the Mexican War, the expansion of the army in the 1850s, approved in order to secure the territories newly acquired from Mexico, and the continuing high wastage rate, all improved career prospects slightly, but there were still too many overqualified officers chasing too few top appointments. An example is Albert Sidney Johnston.[12] Graduating from West Point in 1826, he left the army in 1834 but returned to fight in the Mexican War. Rejoining the regular army in 1849, he had to serve six years as a paymaster until he was given command of the 2nd US Cavalry Regiment, raised for frontier duty. Notwithstanding Johnston's very high military abilities – he started the Civil War as the commander of all the Confederate forces in the western theatre, only to be killed at Shiloh – his appointment against the claims of many others of comparable seniority and reputation no doubt owed something to his friendship at West Point, thirty years before, with Jefferson Davis, in 1855 secretary of war in the cabinet of President Pierce. Johnston's second in command in the new regiment was

---

[c] Brevet rank was a device long used in many armies, including the British, either to reward achievement or identify starters for future high command, or both. Sometimes the award brought with it the pay of the higher rank, sometimes an appointment (usually on the staff) in the higher grade. The practice was retained in the British Army until 1967, when a widening of the age bands for promotion rendered the expedient unnecessary. Sometimes anomalies occurred; within the author's memory, a Royal Artillery field regiment in Germany in the early 1960s had four titular lieutenant colonels – the commanding officer and all three battery commanders. The system worked nevertheless; these officers, all of the highest calibre, reached at least one star rank, as did the equally talented but unbrevetted second-in-command.

Robert E. Lee. Regarded by all as the coming man in the army, Lee had earned two brevet promotions in the Mexican War as an aide to commanding General Winfield Scott, but, though aged nearly fifty, had reached no higher rank than brevet lieutenant colonel.[13]

After half a century of existence, the reputation of West Point stood high throughout the United States. This was largely the work of Sylvanus Thayer, superintendent of the academy from 1817 to 1833, and a sequence of talented successors, including Lee between 1852 and 1855. This reputation was based upon something more solid than the annual reports of the board of visitors, established as a supervisory agency by Congress, which invariably included civilian members not necessarily receptive by nature to the combination of organisation, display and hospitality which any military establishment worth its salt knows how to produce. Whatever the morality of the Mexican War, victory had given the country pride in its officer corps, which was thought to have done well. The practical achievements of the corps of engineers in driving through the ever-expanding railway network, in improving the navigability of waterways and harbours and in construction projects which included the magnificent Capitol building in Washington added much to the prestige and perceived value of West Point, even in totally business-oriented eyes. All cadets who stayed the course left with a thorough grounding in the work of all elements of the army at unit level, as good a technical education as could be obtained at any university in the world at the time, a well-taught if uncritical knowledge of military history and the indefinable patina of a high-quality military academy.

As a result, at the start of the War Between the States, West Point graduates were much sought after by the state governors to organise and train the levies of raw manpower which it became their duty to raise. McClellan and Burnside, Grant and Sherman had all in the 1850s resigned their commissions, none in any rank higher than captain, to pursue civilian careers, not always with success. All very rapidly became major generals of volunteers. Those who had stayed in the army may have been less enterprising, more prepared to put up with the discomforts and frustrations of military life, or more conformist. Their strength was that they knew the drills and minor tactics of infantry, cavalry and artillery as second nature. Their weaknesses were a lack of initiative and a long-inculcated discipline that, while all orders were to be obeyed to the letter and limit, the prudent officer did not seek to do more than those same orders enjoined: enterprise was discouraged.

It has often been suggested that those states which came to form the Confederacy predominated in providing the officer corps of the army. This was not so; because the bulk of nominations to West Point were in the hands of members of the House of Representatives, which had (as it retains today) a basis of population rather than geographic area. The ratio of entrants to West Point corresponded to the higher populations of the Northern States, and the percentage of those who graduated was, in fact, higher (fifty-four to thirty-eight)[d] among sons of the States which remained loyal to the Union.[10] If the long-term retention rate of Southern officers was higher, the reason may be that officers from the more industrial- and business-oriented Northern States were more conscious of job opportunities outside the army, and more inclined to take them. A study[14] of the officer corps, as it was in 1861 before the war began, has established that there were 491 Northern and 330 Southern officers on active duty, almost exactly the same as the graduation ratio, and that the only arm of the service which was predominantly Southern-officered was the cavalry. This confirms one legend at least, and does much to explain the Southern predominance in the cavalry arm throughout the first two years of the war. It is of course beyond dispute that a great many West Point graduates, both serving and those who had left the army to follow a career elsewhere, joined the Confederacy, but, the cavalry arm apart, there is nothing to indicate a Southern bias in West Point selection, graduation or retention rate. The influence of West Point in the military tradition of the United States in 1860 was far in excess of the number of its graduates, and it moulded the armies of both protagonists in the ensuing conflict.

By contrast, the military tradition of the country owed almost nothing to its regular soldiers. Although the enlisted man's engagement was both voluntary and for a shorter period (five years only) than in the armies of the European powers, there was no provision for commissioning from the ranks. Recruits tended to be men either brought down by misfortune or who had failed to make a living at anything else, notwithstanding the enormous opportunities open to all in the expanding nation. In both categories, first-generation immigrants predominated, often with very little understanding of the English language in which they were instructed and commanded, and many with a record of previous desertion from a European army. And when life became insupportable at a frontier post or opportunity beckoned elsewhere, as in the California gold rush of the 1840s, desertion proved almost uncontainable from the army of the United States.[15] At times as much as one-third of the paper enlisted-man strength of the army was on long-term absence without leave.

---

[d] The balance of eight per cent is unidentifiable.

When the war started in April 1861, the manpower of the regular regiments and batteries of the United States Army was not dispersed to add a leavening of experience to the state volunteer units. The consequence was that, while the artillery batteries provided a valuable steadying influence for the Union armies in every battle up to Antietam, in the eighteenth month of the war, the few infantry and cavalry regiments were lost in the hordes of volunteer units which assembled round the nation's capital in the spring and summer of 1861. It was only with the very greatest difficulty that the hierarchy of the United States Army, commanding General Winfield Scott, hero of the wars of 1812 and 1846, and his near-contemporary, Adjutant-General Lorenzo Thomas, could be brought to agree that up to 100 serving regular officers might be allowed to transfer to volunteer units.[16] The immediate rise in rank of many of these was dramatic,[e] as it was of those West Pointers who had resigned before the war and could offer their services to any state. There were also those serving regular officers who not only found themselves in the right place at the right time, but also survived the horrendous firefights which characterised all of the battles. Emory Upton, who graduated a year early from West Point in 1860, was one of over 150 officers promoted to brevet major general at the end of the war, while still in his mid-twenties.[18] Always at the forefront of the battle, particularly when in command of a picked division of storm troops attempting to break the 'Mule Shoe' at Spotsylvania Court House (May 1864), it is beyond question that Upton had earned his rapid promotion to high rank in the hardest way possible. The officers who lost out on quick advancement were those serving regulars who had neither the initiative nor the influence to take up one of the 100 transfers authorised so grudgingly by the War Department. Nevertheless, one-third of all the commissioned regular officers at the start of the war who remained loyal to the Union reached general-officer rank, as did two-thirds of those who went with the Confederacy.

It seems fair, therefore, to describe the military tradition and influence of West Point at the start of the war as extensive, but very thinly spread, across the 4,000,000 men which the two sides together would have mobilised by the time the war had come to its end. That of the United States regular army and its designated reserve, the militia, was negligible. And yet the young men who flocked on both sides to war in the spring of 1861 considered themselves to be

---

[e] The longer the war went on, the more the career-conscious Union officer used all his influence to see to it that his regular army rank did not lag behind that which he gained in command of volunteers – thus putting down his marker for higher status and employment if he survived the war.[17]

of martial stock and springing from a military tradition. There are two reasons: the military schools, often called 'academies' or 'institutes' in many of the older states, and the phenomenon of the volunteer movement.

The military academies had no counterpart elsewhere. It was of course inevitable that the standard of education across the country beyond the infant stage was uneven, depending on many factors apart from the financial circumstances of the parents, even in a nation which had not only accepted the principle of free education open to all, but was also doing more than most others in the mid-nineteenth century to achieve it. The military academies were boarding schools for the sons of relatively well-to-do parents. Most famous of them, and continuing to flourish well into the twentieth century, were the Citadel at Charleston, South Carolina, and the Virginia Military Institute at Lexington, the latter dating from 1839. Thomas Jonathan Jackson, second lieutenant at the start of the Mexican War and brevet major at the end of it, was yet another West Point graduate of high calibre who left the army in the 1850s, in his case to become professor of philosophy and artillery tactics at the Virginia Military Institute. At these and similar colleges the boys wore uniform, were drilled and disciplined much more on the lines of an officer cadet school than of a civilian educational establishment, and even, in some cases, maintained the weaponry held in the state armouries for use by the militia. And with the threat of war, the state universities of Alabama and Tennessee made military study an obligatory part of their curricula.[19] The military influence upon those individuals who had attended these places of learning would have been formidable, but, in the light of their numbers, even more thinly spread than that of West Point.

By far the largest ingredient in the American military ethos in 1860 was the volunteer movement, which had existed before the War of Independence, with inspiration and example drawn from the mother country. Perhaps the first instance of a volunteer unit is the Honourable Artillery Company. Founded in London in Tudor times, this was a voluntary association of men of standing in their community who were prepared to accept an attendance and training obligation under military discipline, and who, in time of war, would offer their services to the nation. The threat of invasion from France when the war restarted in 1803 brought about the formation of numerous similar organisations country-wide, quite apart from the quasi-compelled militia regiments raised in each county by parish quota under the authority of the lords lieutenant. In the months of England's greatest peril since the Armada, there was an explosion of patriotic and military fervour. The young Walter Scott learned cavalry exercises on the sands at Musselburgh; Pitt, in waiting to resume the premiership, became the active colonel of the Cinque Ports volunteers, in the front line of defence against any invasion force which gained a footing ashore; his long-standing political opponent, Fox, became a private in the Chertsey Association; and the pacific and liberal-minded Wordsworth attended training sessions of the Westmoreland Volunteers.[20] With the coming of peace these units survived, if at all, as little more than dining clubs, but there was a spirited resurrection of their military function in the 1840s, caused by a generalised and latent dislike of France, brought into sharp focus by the obvious growth of prosperity and military capability across the Channel under the Orléans monarchy.

It is less easy to account for the concurrent explosion of a similar sentiment in the United States, particularly when set against a half-century's lack of enthusiasm for the militia.[21] The first volunteer unit in the Americas, the Ancient and Honourable Artillery Company of Boston, had been founded in 1638. This carbon copy of the Honourable Artillery Company was followed by others, infantry, cavalry and artillery, during the next two centuries, but in the 1840s, for no obvious logical reason, the trickle became a deluge. The psychological motivation perhaps was grounded in the need of mankind, once he has gained some wealth and the leisure to enjoy it, to join a society of equals and to have something to enthuse about beyond the daily demands of home and occupation. In the era before organised team games, which a man could either take part in or support, the volunteer movement provided the only available framework. There were other contributory factors. The Romantic poets and novelists, in particular Byron, Scott and later Tennyson, enjoyed enormous popularity in lettered households throughout the United States. Their acclamation of the knightly and chivalric virtues could not only be interpreted in terms of the social graces to be expected of a modern gentleman; it also bestowed, by association, its own aura of prestige on things military. The uniforms of the numerous volunteer companies which sprang up throughout the whole country, North and South, were generally more dedicated to the proposition that 'Gold Lace hath a charm for the fair'[22] than to the hard-wearing requirements of service in the field, and further enhanced the attraction. Other causes went beyond the need to create a social concourse for the moneyed classes. Some units, in the cities in particular, derived from the volunteer firefighting companies. German immigrants tended to coalesce in rifle clubs, an obvious nucleus for a volunteer company. And some were politically motivated.

Some Irish companies were founded with the express intention of returning to Ireland at some future time in order to liberate the Land of Saints and Scholars from the British yoke. Some state governors at intervals took exception to the inappropriate political aspirations of these units, not always with success. Although a governor of Connecticut achieved the disbandment of six Irish companies, and in 1858 the governor of New York managed to terminate the existence of the state's 9th Volunteer Regiment, the personnel of the latter promptly transferred en bloc to the 69th New York, whose colonel, two years later, refused to parade his regiment in honour of a visit by the Prince of Wales.

In addition to the purely military volunteer companies, the appetite for display and entertainment, a further natural attribute of a wealthy and leisured society, found much entrancement in the spectacles offered by drill companies. These were formed as commercial 'showbusiness' enterprises, the most famous being the United States Zouave Cadets. Their founder, Elmer Ellsworth, was a young man whose wealth fell a long way short of his aspirations. After numerous vicissitudes, in which his only success was to win the heart of a Chicago heiress, Ellsworth, who was supposed to be studying law in order to provide the means necessary to persuade the young lady's father to allow the marriage, was bitten by the prevailing military fever. He founded an organisation which was a mixture of military unit, synchronised drill display and circus act. Dressed in the picturesque costume of the soldiers recruited locally by France in her North African colonies, Ellsworth's Zouaves enthralled audiences nationwide, including the wife of President-Elect Lincoln. Commissioned as a colonel at the outbreak of war, Ellsworth was killed at once in what amounted to little more than a bar-room brawl in Alexandria, across the Potomac from Washington. His body was borne back to lie in state at the White House.[23]

The states were not slow to take advantage of the volunteer movement, and soon associated its units with their militia structure, often as elite 'flank' or 'grenadier' companies. Massachusetts was the first state to go the whole way: in 1840, while retaining the statutory obligation of every fit adult male to belong to the militia, the state legislature designated its volunteers the 'active militia', with a strength of 10,000. Some of the units retained their social exclusiveness into the War Between the States. The 19th Massachusetts volunteer Infantry Regiment was by no means unique in that, even on embodiment in 1861, at the statutory war establishment of 1,000 men, it elected not only its officers and NCOs but its private soldiers as well.[24] This practice did not, and of course could not, long survive the appalling sickness and battle casualty losses, the former of which began at once to erode strengths. Regiments which had turned away volunteers because they had reached their establishment lost men immediately through physical incapacity, and because insufficient attention was given to hygiene discipline in the crowded and unprepared camps. And soon combat losses began to occur. Few of the Union regiments raised at the start of the war who went into battle at Antietam eighteen months later did so at much over one-third of their initial strength. Since recruitment, embodiment and equipment remained a state rather than a federal responsibility throughout the war, governors found it more appropriate, because of the opportunities created for patronage, to form new regiments rather than to replace the losses of those already in the field. Of the Northern States, only Wisconsin had an effective replacement system from the start of the war.[25] Regiments from other states once used up by sickness and combat losses disappeared from the order of battle, the survivors either being amalgamated with another regiment or reassigned individually, a practice followed by the British Army in both world wars.

The military capacity of the volunteer movement was thought to have been proved by the Mexican War, when, despite the fact that the cause was not universally popular, the peacetime regular establishment of the army was expanded threefold without undue difficulty, to more than 50,000. Only a minority of these saw combat. Throughout the 1850s the movement continued to flourish, the uniforms became ever-more elaborate, the Romantic writers continued to exert their thrall and some military training was done. Benjamin Butler, disappointed of gaining a nomination to West Point as a young man, had by 1860 become a successful lawyer and politician as well as a brigadier general in the Massachusetts militia. He could flatter himself, not wholly correctly, that at their annual camp he had more men under his command than General Scott had had in the field in Mexico. At the start of the War Between the States, Butler became at once (15th May, 1861) a major general of volunteers because of his political influence, a promotion which gave him seniority over all those subsequently achieving the same rank. Notwithstanding a record of military ineptitude surpassed by no other Union general, and equalled only by Banks, another political appointment, Butler remained in independent and important commands throughout the war, and was dismissed, by Grant, in December 1864,[26] only when it was too late for him to use his influence against the re-election of Lincoln.

When the war started, the total free population of the United States amounted to around 27,000,000,[f] which divided almost four to one in favour

---

[f] This population was comparable to that of metropolitan France and the states which, ten years later, would form the German Empire. While the peacetime military establishment of the

of the North. Of these, only a tiny percentage had had direct experience of combat. Many more had a faith amounting to religious fervour in the cause for which they were about to fight. In the North, some, but by no means all, believed fundamentally in either the preservation of the Union or the emancipation of the slaves. In the South, there was a much more universal but equally heartfelt belief in the inalienable nature of states' rights, and in the preservation of their way of life, which in economic terms meant the continuation of slavery. Almost endemic on both sides was an over-emotional and romanticised concept of the nature of war, caused by too much uncritical exposure to the highly-coloured literature of the time, and the gorgeous displays of picture-book, peacetime, fine-day soldiering. This fusion of inexperience and romance, when combined with passionately held convictions and complete failure to appreciate the consequences of new technologies, particularly in relation to firepower, created the conditions for mass slaughter on an unprecedented scale.

From Secession to War – the Opening Phase in the Eastern Theatre: April 1861 to August 1862

The pre-emptive strike is a twentieth-century phenomenon of warfare. Relying as it does on detailed planning and trained forces in place, ready in all respects to mount an all-out assault, this particular design for war, if it is to succeed, requires accurate intelligence, state-of-the-art and secure communications and weapon capabilities, well-stocked war reserves deployed in the right place and fully mobilised combat and support troops. Even in 1914, after nearly half a century of study, evaluation and planning, continuously updated in the wake of the experiences of 1866 and 1870 by the war ministries of all the European Great Powers, nearly three weeks elapsed after the declaration of war until the first significant contacts between the armies of the protagonists. In 1861, except perhaps in the minds of a very few officers in Prussia, both the perception of the need for this degree of planning and preparedness, and the capability to undertake and carry it through lay far in the future. In the non-military United States it was unheard of. The war had been in progress for a year before the first major battle between properly

---

United States, despite the increase during the administration of President Pierce, was still no more than 20,000, Prussia and France, as will be discussed in Chapters VII and XII, both maintained more than ten times this number of men under arms, backed in the case of Prussia by a massive trained reserve.

organised large armies occurred. Many subsequent battles would see more than 100,000 men engaged and casualty lists of killed and wounded in excess of 25,000. By its end it would become clear that the war had been fought on a titanic scale: nearly 500,000 embodied soldiers would lie dead; two-fifths killed or mortally wounded in battle and over half dying from disease.[27] More than ninety per cent of the battle casualties occurred in the three years and two days between the first major engagement of the war, at Shiloh in the western theatre on 6th and 7th April, 1862, and the surrender of the Army of Northern Virginia at Appomattox.

The number and scale of loss, related to the total population, is sufficient in itself to establish the proposition that the war was total, and therefore modern, in character, and not a war in the style of the eighteenth century, for a relatively limited objective. Three of its battles, none in themselves decisive for the outcome of the war, provide important milestones in the progress towards modern warfare. Though the first of them did not take place until the war had been in progress for nearly eighteen months, the opening phase of the conflict nevertheless provided many indications that the nature of warfare had changed. The skirmishes and clashes between what, in the first year of the war, were still little more than imperfectly organised armed mobs not only set the scene for what was to follow but also introduced new dimensions to the business of warfare.

In the glare of the hindsight which can be enjoyed more than a century later, the sequence of events leading up to the outbreak of war unfolded with the inevitability of Greek tragedy. Slavery itself was not the immediate direct cause; it was rather the determination of those states which considered it essential to retain slave labour for economic reasons, and so decided to leave a federation which was developing an overall majority but by no means a unanimous demand for emancipation, without regard for the lifestyle and livelihood of those with most to lose. The presidential election of 1860 was an extreme rarity in American history, in that four candidates put themselves forward on election day. While none sought the dissolution of the Union, Lincoln emerged with the determination to maintain it, even if the price was civil war. His predecessor, the fifteenth president, James Buchanan, from a Northern state where slavery had never become established and who had won the 1856 election against an out-and-out abolitionist, had spent his four years in office immobilised in the face of obviously rising tension from the countervailing beliefs that it was illegal for any state to secede from the Union, and, likewise, impossible legally to stop any state which so wished.

Lincoln's victory led almost at once to the secession of South Carolina, soon followed by Mississippi, Florida, Alabama, Louisiana, Georgia and Texas. Representatives of these seven states, meeting at Montgomery, Alabama, in February 1861, agreed to form the Confederate States of America, with United States Senator and former Secretary of War Jefferson Davis as president. But it was Lincoln's inauguration, which, following constitutional precedent, did not take place until four months after his election, and perhaps specifically his emphasis on that part of the presidential oath requiring him to 'preserve, protect and *defend*' the United States, which fired the starting gun for war. A number of federal arsenals, armouries and other defence installations in the seceded states had already been seized, but the act which began the fighting was taken by South Carolina. Two antiquated forts, Moultrie and Sumter, supposedly guarding the entrance to Charleston harbour, were besieged in the sense that the small Union garrison was prohibited from provisioning itself by local purchase, while the South Carolina Volunteer Artillery commanded the seaborne approaches and so prevented reinforcement and resupply by ships of the Union navy. Moultrie, whose defences had collapsed through old age, was abandoned. Sumter surrendered on 13th April when its rations had run out and after a token bombardment.

Lincoln's reaction two days later was to declare a blockade of the coastline of the seceded states and to call for 75,000 volunteers to be enlisted for three months, in order to deal with 'combinations too powerful to be suppressed' by the standing forces of the government. The implications of this presidential decree, entirely legitimate under the constitution, were to have far-reaching consequences on the course and conduct of the war. Under international law, as accepted at the time, Lincoln's declaration of a state of blockade, even though it took some months to become fully effective, conferred belligerent status on the Confederacy, giving notice that any ship bound for a Southern port was liable to be stopped, searched and stripped of any warlike cargo. But this policy risked the hostile reaction of any nation whose ships were coerced in this way. Once the blockade was in place, it destroyed both the overseas trade and credit of the Confederacy, including of course the crucial ability to purchase and import weaponry from abroad.

The blockade also ruined the livelihood of the cotton mills of northern England, there being total mutual reliance on the single-crop economy of the Southern states. The hardship thus created produced a trend of opinion in

The United States in 1861

Legend:
- Territory controlled by Federal Govt
- Northern States
- Secession States

Labels on map: Me., Vt., N.H., Mass., N.Y., Conn., R.I., Pa., N.J., Del., Md., Ohio, Ind., Ill., Va., Ky., N.C., S.C., Ga., Tenn., Ala., Miss., Fla., Mich., Wis., Minn., Iowa, Mo., Ark., La., Texas, Kansas, Indian Terr. controlled by the Confederacy, Neb. Terr., Colorado Terr., New Mexico Terr., Utah Terr., Nev. Terr., Wash. Terr., Oregon, California

England favouring full recognition of the Confederacy and securing the resumption of the supply of cotton, by force of arms if need be. France was also sympathetic towards the South because of the concurrent intervention of the Second Empire in Mexico.[g] This tide ran in England for about a year, turning only when Lincoln – by no means himself a convinced hardline abolitionist, total, immediate and unconditional, who nevertheless fully grasped the importance of the emancipation issue in both domestic and foreign policy – succeeded after Antietam in linking it to his own war aim, the preservation of the Union.

The military effects of Lincoln's decree were of greater and more immediate significance. The volunteer companies, what remained of the State militias, and individuals all rushed to enlist, with the result that the 75,000 total was soon oversubscribed. Most of this manpower, at best barely trained, converged on Washington, not only expecting a short war – was not the term of service to be for three months only? – but creating its own pressure for immediate action. Washington was entirely appropriate as the main point of concentration for the eastern theatre, because the nation's capital, as it remained until as late as the summer of 1864, was at considerable risk from a raid in force, if not actual capture, by the Confederate Army. Washington at the start of the war was in the front line. South of the Potomac, Virginia had declared her secession immediately after the fall of Fort Sumter on the issue of states' rights, so ensuring a prolonged conflict because of the manpower and material assets of the Old Dominion. Surrounding Washington, north of the river, was Maryland, whose adherence to the Union was doubtful in the extreme, especially in Baltimore and the eastern half of the state. For a time the direct rail link into Washington from the Northern and Eastern States was severed, and even after it was restored Union troops in transit through Baltimore, where it was necessary for them to march between railway termini, remained targets of serious rioting throughout the summer of 1861.[28]

The defence of Washington was to exercise a powerful and sometimes disproportionate influence upon Union strategic thinking for the whole of the war. Not wholly unreasonably; in the spring of 1861, Confederate outposts were deployed on Arlington Heights in full view of the Capitol and Alexandria, which was a stronghold of Confederate sympathy. While the capture of Washington would have had no effect upon the material ability of the Union to wage war, its loss in terms of both international and domestic prestige would have been catastrophic and probably terminal. The

[g] See Chapter XI.

preoccupation of Lincoln and his closest advisers with the security of their capital was thus well justified, but after the immediate crisis had passed, over-insurance would deny troops to Union commanders in the field when their availability might have turned the scale.

After the secession of Virginia, Richmond, lying less than 100 direct miles from Washington, became the capital of the Confederacy. Equally important as a status symbol, Richmond had far greater consequence in the South's war effort because the city was the largest industrial centre in a national capacity barely a tenth the size of that of the Union.[29] It followed that any Confederate army operating in the eastern theatre had always to remain capable of covering Richmond. The difference between the two sides in their conduct of the war was that the South had a soldier of genius, coming to command early, who appreciated that aggressive action at the right moment by the whole of his army created its own security for the capital of the Confederacy. What really mattered was the destruction of the enemy's army. For the North, by contrast, the city of Richmond remained for too long the main objective in its own right.

The troops arriving in Washington were in no way ready for war, nor were there any proper reception arrangements. Initially both the executive mansion and the Capitol building had to be taken into use to billet the troops. Among the soldiers there was a degree of holiday atmosphere and old-style militia non-discipline. An Illinois volunteer could write home that his regiment '... was leading an awful lazy life...' and that... 'soldiering beats clerking ever so much.' The soldiers elected their own company officers and NCOs, whom, in all probability, they knew well from civilian life. A recruit in a New York company, tiring early of drill on a hot day, could call out to his captain, 'Say, Tom, let's quit this darn fooling and go over to the sutler's.'[30]

A considerable proportion of the more senior regimental officers, all owing their appointments to political or civilian influence and status, were completely unfit for the work. In fairness, there were enough men at all levels conscious of their military ignorance, but in no doubt about what was to follow, who made great efforts to educate themselves in the minor tactics of warfare so that they could train their commands.[31] The best of these, provided they survived, attained very high rank in both armies. The level of equipment was uneven. While some state governors had already bought muskets and ammunition from England, others had not. Western volunteers, accustomed to the best that the market could provide in terms of breech-loaded rifles, both for hunting and in extremis for defence against the Indians, were aghast when given smooth-bore muzzle-loaded muskets.[32] Though these would soon be replaced by the rifled variety, the single-shot muzzle-loader remained the basic infantry weapon throughout the war.

The gaudy uniforms of the volunteer companies, chosen for parade-ground and guest-night soldiering, proved, at best, unsuitable for the rigours of camp life and, at worst, dangerous, because some Northern units mustered in the grey selected in peacetime, which soon became associated with the Confederate armies. But more serious was that very few of the volunteers had ever drilled above company level. Although volunteer regiments existed, these, even in areas of high population density, had come together at most only for the occasional ceremonial parade. Before the Union Army could take the field with any prospect of success in an attack – and attack it had to if the Confederacy were to be defeated – the mechanics of turning the marching column into the assaulting line had to be learned so thoroughly that the manoeuvre could be carried out as second nature, at all levels, from the 100-strong company to the division of 10,000, in all weathers and conditions of visibility, over any terrain and in the confusion of battle; and, as yet, field formations above regimental level did not exist.

It was the search for men able to transform large numbers of untrained soldiers into formed military units, in camps providing the rudiments of satisfactory daily administration and sanitation, and able to teach the basic drill movements, which placed such a premium on the West Point graduates available, and a great many personal futures depended upon who happened to be where in April and May 1861.

The search for a potential commander for the Union Army in the field had started some time previously. Robert E. Lee, after a prolonged furlough, granted to enable him to settle the estate of his late father-in-law, which included the Arlington property, had returned to Texas in February 1860. An aristocrat of refined intellect, he had watched with increasing dismay a conflict developing beyond the point at which it could be resolved within the existing political process. In March 1861 he was ordered to report in person to the general-in-chief in Washington, a summons involving something more than the routine administration of his promotion to colonel and appointment to command the 1st US Cavalry. There were no witnesses to what transpired, and neither man subsequently divulged the conversation, but it is impossible to reasonably challenge the proposition of the definitive biographer of Lee, that Scott, knowing himself to be too old and infirm for active service, offered his long-hand-picked successor the command of the field army.[33] Lee had already received, and ignored, the offer of a commission as brigadier general from the government of the Confederacy. There then followed in rapid succession the fall of Fort Sumter, Lincoln's appeal for three-month volunteers, and the secession of Virginia. At this point Lee received a further offer; that of command of all the volunteers converging on Washington, conveyed by a Lincoln intimate, the brother of the postmaster general in the new president's cabinet. After much heart-searching, Lee concluded that his primary loyalty lay with the state of Virginia, and after sad farewells in Washington travelled to Richmond, where the state legislature appointed him to command the troops to be raised by his native state. Lee never saw his beloved Arlington again. Within a month the Confederate patrols had been cleared from the south bank of the Potomac immediately opposite the capital; and Lee's family home became the headquarters of the commander of the Union forces charged with the conduct of an immediate advance on Richmond, which every authority and pressure group in the North was demanding.

This luckless officer was Irvin P. McDowell, before the war no more than a major in the department of the adjutant general. No one would show patience with McDowell, a competent staff officer thrown into a situation in which he was completely out of his depth, or give him the time essential to organise and train the volunteers. He received his high appointment because no officer senior to him was fit, available and willing to serve. After Lee, the next choice for Union Army field commander had fallen on Albert Sidney Johnston, who, after his tour in command of the 2nd US Cavalry Regiment, had been appointed to command the Pacific Department[h] from the San Francisco Presidio.[34] Johnston was from Kentucky. His native state, after a vain attempt to remain neutral, was soon, by a combination of political and military *coup de main*, brought on to the side of the Union. A.S. Johnston chose to offer his services to the Confederacy. After meticulously turning over his Pacific Department responsibilities to a pro-Union officer, he was appointed by his old friend and West Point classmate, Jefferson Davis, to the command of all Confederate forces west of the Mississippi. Another possibility for the Union field command had been his unrelated namesake, Joseph E. Johnston. A Virginian and contemporary of Lee's at West Point, J.E. Johnston, at the outbreak of war, resigned his appointments as quartermaster general and president of the ordnance board of the United States Army, and offered his services direct to the government of the Confederacy rather than to his native state,[34] which explains why it was he and not Lee who was responsible

---

[h] 'Department' remained the term for a United States military area command for long into the twentieth century.

throughout the first year of the war for the defence of northern Virginia and the approaches to Richmond.

The onus having been placed on the individual states to raise and equip the volunteers, there was at once much competition among the governors to obtain the services of the talented West Pointers who had left the army to make their fortunes elsewhere, and there were more of them available than the 100 serving officers released so grudgingly by Adjutant General Lorenzo Thomas. A few days in April 1861 in the life of former captain George Brinton McClellan were to have far-reaching consequences, both on the conduct of the war and the destinies of many of his contemporaries. McClellan seemed at the time to be a man who had excelled in everything he had undertaken. Second in his class (1845) at West Point, and choosing, inevitably, to serve in the corps of engineers, McClellan emerged from the Mexican War a brevet captain. He was one of three officers sent as official observers to the war in the Crimea, and to report in depth on the organisation and training methods of the armies of the European powers. His report, entitled with typical mid-nineteenth-century literary prolixity, 'The Armies of Europe: Comprising Descriptions in Detail of the Military System of England, France, Russia, Prussia, Austria and Sardinia, adapting their Advantages to All Arms of the United States Service, and Embodying the Report of Observations in Europe During the Crimean War, as Military Commissioner from the United States in 1855–56,'[35] attracted Congressional notice, and marked him as an educated soldier and strong candidate for future high advancement. His appointment as an instructor at his country's military academy, always a mark of distinction in any army, followed inevitably. Nevertheless, with his military career set for the heights, McClellan chose in 1857 to leave the army in order to enter the burgeoning railroad construction industry, first as vice-president of the Illinois Central, and then as president of the Eastern Division of the Ohio and Missouri.[36] In 1860 he found time to marry well, winning the hand of the beautiful and well-connected Ellen Marcy, triumphing over the suit of his junior at West Point, A.P. Hill.[i]

---

[i] Hill, two years behind McClellan at West Point, was commissioned too late to earn distinction in the Mexican War, and by 1861 his career had advanced no further than first lieutenant of artillery. A Virginian, Hill's loyalties went with his state, and he became at once colonel of the 13th Virginia Infantry Regiment. Army of the Potomac gossip would always credit Hill with bearing an undying grudge against his successful rival, because their units were so often on the receiving end of his notably aggressive conduct of operations.[37]

Immediately following Lincoln's call for volunteers, McClellan received a telegram from Governor Curtin of Pennsylvania, offering him command of the levies of his native state. En route from Cincinnati to Harrisburg, McClellan's journey took him through Columbus, state capital of Ohio, where he was intercepted by Governor Dennison, from whom he accepted instead the command of Ohio's troops, in the rank of major general of volunteers. This created two interesting might-have-beens. Command of Pennsylvania's men went instead to George Gordon Meade, an officer of the elite topographical engineers. By the time of Gettysburg, twenty-six months later, Meade had risen to command the Army of the Potomac. Instead of being thrust to the top at once, as happened to McClellan, Meade graduated through the hardest school of all – battlefield experience, successively in command of brigade, division and corps. And on an April day, when McClellan happened not to be at the headquarters of his new command, he received a visit from a West Point and Mexican War contemporary, Ulysses Simpson Grant. Although Grant had gained much distinction in Mexico as an infantry officer, his career thereafter had achieved nothing but seedy drink-related failure. After leaving the service, the future general of the armies of the United States and eighteenth president had been reduced to the status of accounts clerk in his brother's store, and now was seeking an appointment on McClellan's staff. Denied an answer in the major general's absence, Grant at once mobilised a political contact, and instead went west to take up an appointment as Colonel of the 21st Illinois Volunteers.[38]

It so happened that, of all the Union forces, McClellan's troops were first into action. There was abundant evidence that the part of Virginia lying west of the Blue Ridge, having no dependence on slavery and resenting the superiority of the tidewater plantation aristocracy of the Old Dominion, wished to secede from the secession, that is, to remain part of the Union. In a short and well-conducted operation, but with no more than 10,000 troops involved in total, one which was miniscule by later standards, McClellan secured the new state of West Virginia for the Union. His dispatches contrived to present this success as a victory of Napoleonic dimensions, and, when received in Washington, contrasted tangibly with the earnest, well-meaning but ineffectual efforts of McDowell to organise more than 50,000 men, under the direct scrutiny of government and press, into a fit state to take the field. When, in mid-July, McDowell advanced, mainly so that something might be achieved by the three-month volunteers before their term of service expired, the result, predictably, was a disaster. Joseph Johnston had some 30,000 troops spread over sixty miles between the Shenandoah Valley and Manassas, the latter only thirty-five miles south-west of Washington and the junction point of the Manassas Gap and Orange and Alexandria railways. These were vital to the Confederacy if northern Virginia were to be held and the supply of food and forage from the valley secured. Johnston, although outnumbered, also barred the direct route to Richmond. McDowell launched his army on an operation designed to hold Johnston in front and outflank him right-handed; a good plan in theory, but one which at this stage of the war was well beyond the capacity of his staff to organise or his troops to execute.[39] Both sides would soon learn much by experience, but in this first significant battle poor staff work brought only 35,000 troops south of the Potomac and the planned flank march fell apart because the route, through broken and wooded country, was not reconnoitred, guided or controlled at the critical points. Only half the Union forces committed to the operation were actually engaged. Staff work in Johnston's more dispersed army was no better. Similarly, no more than half the troops available were brought to battle, and the Confederate Army was saved only by the hard centre of its defensive position, on Henry House Hill,[j] held by the brigade of the recent professor of artillery tactics and philosophy at the Virginia Military Institute.[k] Jackson refused to accept impending defeat and was reinforced not a moment too soon. The disorganised Federal troops tumbled back across the Bull Run and Cub Run streams towards their camps on the Potomac. The bridge over the Cub Run broke, stranding some hundreds of the wealth and beauty of Washington who had come out in their carriages to witness the battle, further contributing to the general air of panic and chaos. This was more apparent than real, because Johnston's army was in no condition to exploit its defensive success. The losses on both sides, at around 2,000 killed and wounded, were much the same, but the Confederates remained in possession of the disputed ground and the result was an evident defeat for the Union.

---

[j] Today the site of the battlefield visitor centre. This battle, and one near the same ground thirteen months later, are known impartially as the First and Second Battles of Bull Run, or Manassas.

[k] Thus gaining Jackson his nickname of 'Stonewall', conferred by the commander of his supporting brigade, General Barnard E. Bee, who did not survive the battle. The nickname was not wholly appropriate, because Jackson had already proved to be a hard-driving commander of troops on mobile operations. He had demonstrated his Cromwellian characteristics by cashiering a subordinate who had retreated without orders for no better reason than that his unit had run out of ammunition.

McDowell was clearly not the man to command the army in the field. Lincoln had already recognised, tacitly, that the war would not be over in three months, having made a further demand in early May, ten weeks before First Manassas, for 300,000 volunteers to serve for three years,[40] a term of service which had been determined from the start by the Confederacy.

On the day after the battle McClellan was summoned to Washington, to be greeted by all from the president down as the potential saviour of the nation. The immediate situation was one which brought out the best of McClellan's good qualities. He was a military organiser and administrator of the highest calibre and he captured at once the absolute loyalty of his volunteer soldiers to an extent and by methods which seem incomprehensible in a more cynical age. Old General Scott, having delivered himself of the design for war by which the North would ultimately win – don't lose in Virginia, blockade the coast and split the land mass of the Confederacy by clearing the Mississippi down to the Gulf of Mexico – was soon packed off into retirement, and McClellan combined the appointments of general-in-chief of all the armies of the Union, and commander of the Army of the Potomac. At once his shortcomings as both supreme and field army commander became evident. He did not understand that a political dimension had emerged which would influence strongly, if not totally govern, the employment of his army in the field; and, for whatever combination of reasons which have since been adduced, he could never bring himself to commit totally the full force of his whole army to battle. Everything had to be in perfect place before McClellan would move, and there would always be in his mind some critical detail which was not quite right, so requiring the postponement of action. Although initially he would be granted the time denied to McDowell to organise and train the Army of the Potomac, this would never, in the mind of the perfectionist military engineer, be enough. The absence of any positive action by the army in front of Washington as summer drew into autumn began to erode the political, public and press confidence which had marked McClellan's arrival in Washington, and the knowledge that the general was by no means a convinced and vocal abolitionist soon had those politicians who were of this persuasion doubting not only his competence as army commander, but also his loyalty to the cause. McClellan was never, as would soon be whispered, a traitor to the Union or the North; but equally he never had the will to win at any cost which must be fundamental to the make-up of any national leader, politician or soldier, who has to fight a modern war.

Both aspects of the impending crisis of confidence came into focus before the end of the winter of 1861–2. As a result of demands for action from politicians and the press, an ill-conceived operation with no clear aim was mounted across the Potomac at Ball's Bluff, thirty miles upriver from Washington. There was no reconnaissance in force and no attempt was made to secure a bridgehead from which future operations might be developed. Five Union regiments supported by no more than three guns were ferried across the river, roughly handled and forced into ignominious and costly withdrawal, compounded by the fact that the number and capacity of the boats assembled ad hoc was totally inadequate, and no staff planner had thought of the necessity for a pontoon bridge which might have allowed the assaulting troops to be either reinforced and supported, or withdrawn in good order after a demonstration of force. The bungle, while bad enough in itself, had serious political overtones. In command of the troops committed had been Colonel and Senator Edward Baker, of Oregon. Directly commissioned in command of the 71st Pennsylvania volunteer Infantry at the start of the war, the colonel was without previous military experience or knowledge beyond that derived from copious reading of the works of Sir Walter Scott.[41] His uselessly gallant death in this pointless little action, with the words of Scott on his lips, meant more than just the loss of a Lincoln political confidant and close family friend.[1] Baker was a hardline and articulate abolitionist. Worse, most of the casualties had been taken by two Massachusetts volunteer regiments, whose state governor, Andrew, was of the same persuasion and who had already quarrelled with the divisional commander in overall charge, Brigadier General Charles P. Stone, because during the quiet lull in August the general had ordered some escaped slaves to be returned to their owners.

In these circumstances, a full-scale political inquest was inevitable, and its consequences went far beyond the immediate supersession and disgrace of General Stone. The Congressional Joint Committee on the Conduct of the War, established initially to enquire into the circumstances of the Ball's Bluff fiasco, remained in being for the rest of the war, and was always strongly representative of the extreme abolitionist element in the uneasy coalition of interests which made up Lincoln's Republican Party. Any Union general who failed to take account of this committee's views was courting serious trouble. In their eyes, McClellan already had the stigma of potential disloyalty. In the twelve months left to him in command of the Army of the Potomac, McClellan never understood why all of his own actions and proposed plans for the army would be weighed in the balance by men who did not wholly trust him. In spite of his considerable study of Napoleon's campaigns and

---

[1] Lincoln had named his second son for him.

direct experience of the business of war in the Crimea, he never comprehended the existence, let alone the power, of the political factor which, henceforth, would dominate the conduct of any war.

Thus the gloss which had first distinguished the relationship between the army commander and the political leadership was soon tarnished by mutual mistrust. McClellan refused to divulge his plans. Lincoln, snubbed deliberately on more than one occasion, went so far as to describe the Army of the Potomac as 'General McClellan's bodyguard', and to say that if the general were not going to use the army, he himself would like to borrow it for a time.[42] Lincoln took a step, fully justified, which not only diminished McClellan's standing and reduced his confidence in the political leadership, but also intervened directly in the internal organisation of the Army of the Potomac. It was the president and not the army commander who, in March, appointed the four senior generals of division as corps commanders.[43] McClellan had sought to defer this step, even though he must, both from study and experience, have understood fully that his army headquarters could not exercise direct command in battle of all twelve divisions of the army. On military grounds alone, the establishment of this intermediate level of formation command, so well proven in the armies of Napoleon, was an absolute necessity. The fact that it was Lincoln who had to order this step and who chose the men is further evidence of McClellan's political *naïveté*. If the president, in his capacity as commander-in-chief, said that there were to be corps commanders, corps commanders there would be, whether the army commander liked it or not, and if he did not get the people he wanted in these appointments he had no one but himself to blame.

For all the criticism of McClellan, both at the time and later, his work in the second half of 1861 was an essential ingredient in the ultimate victory of the Union. He created order out of the muddle of raw regiments severely shaken by the defeat at Bull Run. He structured and trained the brigades and divisions, and, above all, inculcated the self-confidence essential to the success of any large organisation, which the Army of the Potomac retained throughout the war in spite of a series of near disasters. His work was appreciated afterwards even by the acerbic George Gordon Meade, who commanded the Army of the Potomac from the week before Gettysburg until Lee's surrender at Appomattox: 'Had there been no McClellan there could have been no Grant.'[44]

Gettysburg, seventeen months to the day after the formal establishment of the first four corps of the Army of the Potomac, terminated any remaining chance that the Confederacy might force a negotiated peace which would recognise its independent nationhood. In this time the army achieved the transition from novice to veteran status, through five separate campaigns including seven major battles[m] and a host of lesser engagements.

None of the battles was an unqualified victory for the North, but, taken together, they achieved the strategic success which had been the foundation of General Scott's design, albeit at a cost of 120,000 casualties, killed or wounded. One reason for this unprecedented cost was that the higher command structure of the army never settled down. In this short time-span the Army of the Potomac fought under five different army commanders and there was a fifty per cent turnover at the corps commander level. Given the further erosion of battle casualties among the subordinate formation and regimental commanders, this continual change placed an enormous demand on the spirit of the army McClellan had done so much to create. While this book does not seek to present a full description of all these actions, a table listing the corps, their commanders and main engagements may assist the reader in following the course of the three battles which heralded a fundamental change in the conduct of warfare.

TABLE VI

CORPS ORGANISATION IN THE ARMY OF THE POTOMAC, MARCH 1862 TO JULY 1863[45]

Corps	Formed/ Reformed	Commanders	Principal Battles	Merged (M) Disbanded (D)	Date
I	3 Mar. '62	McDowell (S)		To Dept of Rappahannock	4 Apr. '62
				(M) III Corps	26 Jun. '62
	12 Sept. '62	Hooker (W)(P) Reynolds (K) Doubleday (S) Newton	Antietam Fredericksburg Gettysburg	(M) V Corps	24 Mar. '64
II	3 Mar. '62	Sumner (W)	Peninsular Second Manassas Antietam Fredericksburg		
		Couch	Chancellorsville Gettysburg	(D)	28 Jun. '65

[m] The peninsula phase – Fair Oaks, the Seven Days' Battle and Second Manassas; Antietam; Fredericksburg; Chancellorsville; Gettysburg.

Corps	Formed/ Reformed	Commanders	Principal Battles	Merged (M) Disbanded (D)	Date
III	3 Mar. '62	Heintzelman	Peninsular Second Manassas		
		Stoneman	Fredericksburg		
		Sickles (W)	Chancellorsville		
			Gettysburg	(M) II Corps	24 Mar. '64
IV	3 Mar. '62	Keyes	Peninsular	(D)	1 Aug. '63
V	3 Mar. '62	Banks		To Dept of Shenandoah XII Corps	4 Apr. '62 then
	18 May '62	Porter (S)	Peninsular Second Manassas Antietam		
		Butterfield	Fredericksburg		
		Meade (P)	Chancellorsville		
		Sykes	Gettysburg	(D)	28 Jun. '65
VI	18 May '62	Franklin (S)	Peninsular Second Manassas Antietam		
		Smith	Fredericksburg		
		Sedgwick (K)	Chancellorsvillle		
			Gettysburg		28 Jun. '65
VII	22 Jul. '62	Dix	Garrison troops Fort Monroe	(M) XVIII Corps	1 Aug. '63
VIII	22 Jul. '62	Wool	West Virginia	(D)	1 Aug. '63
IX	22 Jul. '62	Burnside (P) Reno (K)	Second Manassas		
		Cox	Antietam		
		Wilcox	Fredericksburg	To Western Dept (D)	Mar. '63
					1 Aug. '65
XI	12 Sept. '62	Sigel (W)	Chancellorsville		
		Howard	Gerrysburg	To Western Dept (M) XX Corps	Apr. '64
XII	12 Sept. '62	Mansfield (K)	Antietam		
		Slocum	Chancellorsville		
			Gettysburg	To Western Dept (M) XX Corps	Apr. '64
Cavalry	Feb. '63	Stoneman	Fredericksburg Chancellorsville		
		Pleasonton			
				(D)	May '65

Corps Commanders: P: Promoted to Army Command;
K/W: Killed/Wounded when in command; S: Superseded.

Although McClellan's manoeuvring and minor skirmishes throughout the winter of 1861–2 had gained the Union some elbow room south of the Potomac, he remained unwilling to force the issue with Johnston, who had strongly entrenched the Army of Northern Virginia in defence of the critical railway junction at Manassas. McClellan decided instead to move his army downriver to Urbanna, at the tip of the peninsula bounded by the Potomac and Rappahannock. With a substantial force on and behind his right flank, Johnston would be forced to withdraw from northern Virginia, the immediate threat to Washington would be removed and, correspondingly, McClellan would be well placed to threaten Richmond from the east. On a large-scale map, the proposition appears feasible, given accomplishment of the formidable logistic tasks of collecting the necessary shipping, embarking the troops, horses, guns and ammunition and disembarking them on hostile territory in a condition fit to fight. At a conference of the newly appointed corps commanders called by Lincoln, from which McClellan himself was absent through illness, three out of four spoke against this plan, and when at last everything was in place to the army commander's satisfaction, his design was overtaken by events. Johnston abandoned the lines of Manassas, withdrawing towards Richmond, and McClellan's prestige suffered further damage in the eyes of the politicians when it was discovered that a substantial number of the 'cannon' protruding from the supposedly impregnable earthworks were no more than painted tree trunks. No army of the Potomac cavalry reconnaissance had penetrated close enough to verify the strength of the defences.

McClellan still would not attempt a direct advance on Richmond. His revised plan required McDowell's corps to advance to the line of the Rappahannock, while he himself would take the rest of the army one step further than in his original plan; to the Virginia peninsula. Bounded by the York and James rivers, its eastern tip, Fort Monroe, had remained in federal possession after Virginia had seceded. Once McClellan was ready to advance up the peninsula, threatening Richmond from the south-east, Johnston would be caught in a pincer movement.

Once again, a plan good on paper came to grief, this time because of topographical fact, military failure and political timidity. The first inhibition was imposed by Jackson. Left behind in the Shenandoah Valley when Johnston withdrew, Jackson, with no more than 4,000 men, had little object beyond creating what nuisance he could. Although defeated in his first encounter, at Kernstown on 23rd March, for the next three months Jackson kept 30,000 Union soldiers pinned in the valley and thus unavailable for deployment elsewhere. After their initial success, these troops, ineptly commanded by the politician–general Banks, suffered a series of gadfly defeats, the effect of which was to persuade the civilian leadership to detach McDowell's corps from McClellan's direct command, because of the perceived need to provide for the security of Washington. Thus, the proposed pincer movement was rendered abortive until this decision should be reversed. The detachment of McDowell's corps is a classic instance of political interference in a military plan, and it caused a further deterioration in the relationship between McClellan and the government. While the general felt that he was being deprived, for no valid military reason, of the troops he needed, the extreme abolitionists were taking out what they considered to be a necessary insurance against possible disaffection, or worse, on the part of their field commander.[n]

McClellan's operation on the Virginia peninsula failed for three reasons. The first was his own excessive and perfectionist caution, compounded by a massive overestimate[o] of the forces opposed to him; secondly, misappreciation of the terrain, in that it had not been foreseen that, in the hot, wet summer of tidewater Virginia, the unsurfaced roads turned to liquid mud, seriously inhibiting all foot and horse movement; and, thirdly, his inability to concentrate his army at the decisive point. By the end of May, a deliberate advance had brought the Army of the Potomac to within ten miles of Richmond, but the corps were advancing on both sides of the River Chickahominy, tributary of the James, and could not provide mutual support. While leaving no more than a holding force in front of the eastern approach to Richmond, Johnston concentrated the bulk of his army against the weaker part of the Army of the Potomac, the corps of Porter and Franklin, deployed north and east of the Chickahominy. McClellan made no attempt to probe what was no more than a screen force in front of Richmond, and, although the Confederate Army had failed to coordinate its attacks, the defeat in the mind

---

[n] In the opinion of the author, the effect of Jackson's Shenandoah Valley campaign was disproportionate also on the British Army. The professor of military history at the British Staff College, Camberley, in the 1890s, Colonel G.F.R. Henderson, published a two-volume history of this campaign which became required study for those attending the two year course. While the lessons of Jackson's operations in terms of concentrated hitting power and mobility to be achieved by a small force are entirely valid, the students, of the age group which was to provide the senior commanders of the British armies in the First World War, can have gained little of future relevance to them.

[o] See Chapter IV.

of the Union Army commander was decisive. Johnston, wounded late in the battle, was replaced by Lee. Much the same pattern of events recurred a month later. In seven days of almost continuous fighting, Lee, reinforced by Jackson arriving by forced march from the valley, could coordinate his attacks no better than Johnston had managed. Nevertheless, McClellan was again morally beaten, and fell back despite the urgings of some of his divisional commanders that Richmond and victory were there for the taking. A holding action at Malvern Hill on 1st July brought to an end seven days of intense fighting in conditions of extreme heat and humidity in wooded swampland. McClellan established a defensive cantonment round Harrison's Landing, on the north bank of the James, still only twenty miles from the Confederate capital, where, a week after Malvern Hill, he received a visit from the president. McClellan urged abandonment of the enterprise and a phased withdrawal from the peninsula, a course to which Lincoln agreed with great reluctance. The process began as soon as the necessary shipping could be assembled, unimpeded by the Army of Northern Virginia. Lee's men were equally fought out by the Seven Days' Battle, and soon had to take fresh stock of a developing threat from the area of Manassas.

On his return to Washington, Lincoln set in hand two changes which were designed to remove the immediate conduct of the war from the hands of the commander of the Army of the Potomac. He summoned to Washington Major General Henry Wager Halleck, of high reputation in the peacetime army as an earnest student of his profession, and who had been in nominal charge of the far more successful operations conducted by the Union armies in the western theatre. Halleck superseded McClellan as general-in-chief. And Major General of Volunteers John Pope, until the outbreak of war a captain in the topographical engineers, who was likewise thought to have done well in command of troops in Missouri, was appointed to command the newly designated Army of Virginia, consisting initially of McDowell's corps, and the troops still in the Shenandoah, licking their wounds from Jackson's treatment. Pope's task was to advance on Richmond by the direct route McClellan had discarded. Lincoln's common-sense reasoning at this stage of the war was some way ahead of that of his generals; if the bulk of the Confederate forces in the eastern theatre were defending Richmond against an attack from the east on the axis of the Virginia peninsula, there could not be too many on the Rappahannock barring the approach from the north, and if Pope could but move fast enough...

Pope could not. He concluded that he needed reinforcements, and additions to his command could come only from the troops withdrawn from the peninsula. McClellan was not replaced formally in command of the Army of the Potomac as he had been as general-in-chief, but as his formations returned they were moved to join Pope's concentration, in the area of the Manassas battlefield of the previous year. The corps, first of Porter, then of Heintzelman, were disembarked in mid-August, at Aquia Creek and Alexandria respectively, and put under Pope's command. By the end of the month the corps of Sumner and Franklin were following. Only Keyes was left on the peninsula: McClellan had become a general without an army. But while Pope was massing the numerical superiority which he considered essential, the combination of Lee and Jackson moved too fast for him.

Jackson, brought down from the Shenandoah in time to take part in the Seven Days' Battle, had been rushed back north again, this time with nearly a third of the 55,000 troops under Lee's command. Having inflicted yet another defeat on the unfortunate Banks, at Cedar Mountain on 9th August, he destroyed the logistic stockpile which McDowell had built up at Manassas, and then disappeared into the wooded foothills of the Blue Ridge Mountains, west of the Bull Run. Lee, appreciating that he had no need to worry further about any offensive action on the peninsula, followed with the rest of the Army of Northern Virginia. On the evening of 29th August, Jackson unmasked only part of his position against Pope's advance guard. The following morning, Pope, thinking that he had to deal only with a Jackson en route to his old haunts in the Shenandoah Valley, launched the corps of Heintzelman and Porter in a series of frontal attacks on a westerly axis against a defensive position which Jackson had based on an unfinished railway cutting, in closely wooded ground. For neither the first nor the last time, Jackson's troops, many out of ammunition, held on in circumstances in which most other armies would have broken. It was not until 4 p.m. that Lee could send in the rest of his army, under Longstreet, in a surprise attack against Pope's southern flank. Each side had brought to battle three times the numbers which had fought on almost the same ground thirteen months earlier, but the training and battlefield experience gained in the meantime produced five times as many casualties, approximately 10,000 killed or wounded on each side. The complete surprise achieved by Longstreet's flank attack caused even worse disorder in Pope's army than after First Manassas, with over 4,000 men surrendering, unwounded, to become prisoners of war.[46]
Once again, a Union Army withdrew towards Washington in conditions of near rout, to be met on the road by McClellan. His presence had an immediate and dramatic effect in restoring the army's morale and self-belief.[47]
Pope and McDowell, who in a very short time had earned the detestation of

their troops, were removed from command, the civilian leadership realising that, for the time being at least, there was no option but McClellan, whatever the reservations might be about his commitment to the cause of emancipation or his willingness to risk his troops. McClellan's administrative flair and ability to motivate his soldiers, together with the logistic resilience deriving from the vast manpower and material resources of the Union, were proved amply by the fact that within a fortnight the Army of the Potomac was ready to take the field again.

The Plans that Went Wrong – the Antietam Campaign, September 1862

By any military criteria in any age, Harper's Ferry is indefensible. The small town lies at the bottom of a deep, horizontally aligned T-shaped valley, where the broad Shenandoah flows from the south to join the more turbulent Potomac, imparting its more placid characteristics to the combined river. This then flows eastwards from the tail of the T, passing Washington, fifty miles downstream, before reaching tidal waters at the Chesapeake. For up to twenty miles below Harper's Ferry the Potomac, though in places up to a quarter of a mile broad, is often fordable, particularly in the late summer.

Before the outbreak of the war, Harper's Ferry had been of both military consequence and emotional significance in the emancipation issue. A river bridge carried the Baltimore and Ohio railroad, which provided the most direct link between Washington and the Midwest, and the town was also the northern terminus of the Winchester and Shenandoah branch line, serving the granary of the valley. There was an armoury, holding more than 10,000 stand of arms for the use of the Virginia militia, and a small but important federal weapons foundry, manufacturing small arms. In October 1859 the armoury had been the target of the raid which conferred martyr status on John Brown. Brown had attempted to seize the armoury in order to arm the slaves and provoke a full-scale insurrection throughout Virginia and the border states. Cornered with seven surviving followers in the engine house of the foundry, Brown had surrendered to a mixed force of US Marines and militia from both Virginia and Maryland, the whole under the command of Colonel Robert E. Lee.[48] Unbalanced to the point of insanity, Brown is an early and archetypal example of a personality too familiar in the twentieth century; the single-issue violent protester, prepared to go to any lengths. Three years previously, he had gone unpunished for the particularly gruesome murder of five supposedly

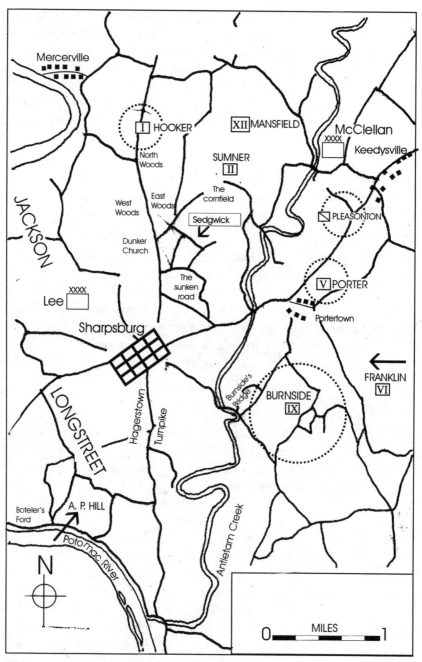

Antietam, 17th September, 1862

pro-slavery inhabitants of Pottawotomie Creek, Kansas.[49] This time Brown did not get away with it. He was hanged a week later, at Charlestown, Virginia.

At the start of the war, Harper's Ferry was one of the federal military installations and key points which had fallen at once into Southern hands. A half-company of regular infantry, commanded by a cousin of Lee's, could not hold the town against 1,000 Virginia volunteers. The weapons were secured for the South, and everything movable from the foundry sent down to Richmond.[50] In time, the railway bridges were blown up and the track of the Winchester and Shenandoah torn up. Jackson, taking command of a tiny force of Confederate troops in the valley in the summer of 1861, could not defend its northern half against much stronger federal forces. But, even without regard to any Confederate presence in the valley, the Union felt it essential to maintain strong garrisons both at Harper's Ferry and Martinsburg, the next station to the west on the Baltimore and Ohio. Quite apart from its importance as a source of food and forage to whichever side held it, the lie of the valley was of far greater strategic significance to the South, because from it Washington could be directly threatened. For the North, the valley led nowhere.[P] It followed that, at the end of the summer of 1862, there were some 14,000 Federal troops at Harper's Ferry; quite inadequate to secure the heights dominating the town and the confluence of the rivers and so bolt the door to Washington, but too many to extricate themselves in a hurry if threatened from more than one direction by a superior force. Any perimeter which a garrison of this size might hold would be at the mercy of an enemy on the Maryland, Lowdon and Bolivar Heights, dominating ground north-east, south-east and west of the river junction.

Second Manassas, and an attempt two days later at Chantilly to outflank and bring to battle Franklin's corps as it withdrew towards Washington, had gained the military initiative for the Army of Northern Virginia. But the Union Army had retreated into fortifications round the capital which were too strong to attack, and the tactical successes achieved, although considerable, fell short of the scale of victory prerequisite if the Confederacy were to obtain recognition as an independent nation. Lee could adduce a number of valid

---

[P] There is an unmistakable parallel between the strategic significance of the Shenandoah Valley to the armies of the Confederacy and the valleys of the Moselle and the Meuse to armies seeking to invade France from Germany. To the attackers, these natural thoroughfares offer a direct route to the enemy heartland, with a degree of flank protection. For the defence, there is not only a corresponding strategic debit, but a counter-offensive leads to nothing of comparable importance. See Chapters XII and XV.

reasons for invading the North at a time when the Army of the Potomac was in a state of considerable confusion. Any invasion would take the war away from ravaged Virginia, and would threaten Washington. Lee's army could live off the fertile farmlands of western Maryland and Pennsylvania, and so gain some much needed respite for the strained logistic resources of the South. The population of Maryland was thought to favour secession;[q] at least the Army of Northern Virginia might pick up some recruits, and at best might bring about the transfer of the allegiance of the whole state, leaving the Union capital isolated and completely cut off. An advance deep into Maryland could be developed to break the best remaining railway link between the Union's eastern states and those of the Midwest. The garrison at Harper's Ferry would be a sizeable if non-decisive prize; too big to be masked, this force would have to be eliminated because it could not be left at the rear of the proposed line of advance. And, above all, the invasion might bring on the decisive battle which the Confederacy had to win. After the events of the next fortnight had disappointed nearly all his other hopes, Lee chose to risk this terminal contest while his army was still widely dispersed, to fight it with his back to the Potomac against odds of more than two to one, despite having concentrated everything available by forced march, and to offer to renew the battle on the following day, in spite of having suffered nearly thirty per cent casualties. Lee's enormous gamble is both explained and justified by the absolute necessity for the Army of the Potomac to be defeated so comprehensively as to destroy the will of the North to continue the war.

So the decision to invade the North was made, and the Army of Northern Virginia splashed across the Potomac fords west of Leesburg. Although the administrative machinery of the Confederacy had made great efforts to replace the casualties of Second Manassas, Lee still had no more than 45,000 men to take into Maryland. The reasons were that many of his soldiers took the view that their enlistments required them to do no more than to defend the territory of the South, and that the majority of the army had long worn out its boots and was marching barefoot. While this was possible on the unsurfaced roads and mud tracks of the Virginia peninsula, some soldiers could not cope with the metalled highways of Maryland. At least 10,000 men left, for the time being, the Army of Northern Virginia. Those that remained were the hardest, fittest and most committed to their cause. Between 7th and 9th September, the Army of Northern Virginia was concentrated round Frederick, twenty-five

---

[q] Maryland volunteer regiments fought on both sides in the war – and clashed at Culp's Hill on the second day of Gettysburg.

miles north-east of Harper's Ferry and forty north-west of Washington. Lee's declared objective was the line of the Susquehanna. An advance north-eastwards on the axis of the Cumberland valley, objective Harrisburg, no more than seventy miles from Frederick, would isolate both Washington and Baltimore and cut both the Pennsylvania and Northern Central railroads, leaving the roundabout route by way of the Great Lakes the only remaining link between the eastern and western halves of the Union. Lee expected to have between three and four weeks before the Army of the Potomac had recovered from its withdrawal from the James and the defeat at Second Manassas.[51] But the first task was to capture Harper's Ferry.

Lee had grouped his 45,000 men into one cavalry and nine infantry divisions, none of which was more than 6,000 strong. Retaining the cavalry (led by J.E.B. Stuart) under his own command, the infantry was grouped into two corps:

TABLE VII

	Longstreet	Jackson
Divisions	Hood	Lawton
	D.R. Jones	A.P. Hill
	McLaws	J.R. Jones
	Anderson	D.H. Hill
	Walker	

In Lee's Special Order No. 191, issued on 9th September, Longstreet, with no more than two divisions (those of Hood and D.R. Jones), was sent northwards on the intended line of advance, towards Hagerstown and Chambersburg. The cavalry was to operate as a screen for the right flank of the army on the Catoctin Hills, with a more substantial flank guard provided by two more of Longstreet's divisions (Anderson and McLaws). McLaws was tasked with the capture of Maryland Heights, while Anderson covered the passes across Elk Ridge and South Mountain, which prolong the line of the Blue Ridge north-eastwards through Maryland. Longstreet's remaining division (Walker) was detached temporarily to Jackson, and tasked with the capture of Lowdon Heights. With Harper's Ferry cut off on its eastern side, the attack would be launched by three divisions of Jackson's corps (Lawton, A.P. Hill and J.R.

Jones) with Jackson's remaining division (D.H. Hill) in army reserve east of the Shenandoah, poised to reinforce either Longstreet's forward divisions, Anderson on South Mountain, or the Harper's Ferry assault divisions, and ten to twelve miles from each of them. Lee expected to have captured Harper's Ferry by 12th September, and his intentions thereafter were to re-concentrate the army on either Boonsboro or Hagerstown in order to follow the advance north-eastwards in the wake of Longstreet. The effect of this order was, within forty-eight hours of its issue, to disperse the Army of Northern Virginia over an area thirty miles by twenty, with its corps groupings temporarily disrupted, and its divisions deployed on both sides of two major rivers. Any delay or amendment to the plan would demand the utmost of the army's staff and communications systems, and a very clear understanding, in the mind of the army commander and his principal subordinates, of the lapse of time between the issue of an order and the earliest moment at which it could first be complied with and later become effective.

Meanwhile, in Washington, the main reason a government which abhorred military dictatorship should dismiss its army commander was also the reason he had to be retained in post; the events leading to Second Manassas had shown that the Army of the Potomac would fight for no one but McClellan. On 1st September a presidential order placed him in command of the defences round Washington. With the extent of the defeat at Second Manassas becoming hourly more apparent, and the northern wing of Pope's army hard pressed as it withdrew, McClellan signalled to Pope: 'I am in charge of the defences of Washington and am doing all I can to render your retreat safe, should that become necessary.'[52]

This at once displayed McClellan's ineradicable conviction that the Union Army was vastly outnumbered, his contempt for Pope and his opinion of Pope's chances. Never having been dismissed from command of the Army of the Potomac, McClellan was never formally reinstated, but he might well have concluded that his present remit to take charge of the defences of Washington hardly extended to countering an invasion of western Maryland forty miles away, unless his directive were to be considerably expanded. In an age in which generals might still be condemned to death for acting outside the authority they had been given, this was a further inhibition to a naturally cautious character, and McClellan would state long afterwards that he had fought at South Mountain and Antietam with a noose around his neck. Nevertheless, even with a majority of Lincoln's cabinet advising formally that McClellan should be dismissed, the president retained him in command, in spite of his own reservations, on hearing that McClellan proposed to attack the invading army. Lincoln had already shown that he would forgive anything of a general who would fight.

There was an immediate falling out between McClellan and Halleck over the orders to be sent to the garrison at Harper's Ferry. McClellan pressed for its withdrawal at once, while there was still time. The place had no current military significance in its own right, and would return to Union hands once Lee had been driven off. Halleck demurred. His appointment had been recommended by Scott, perhaps on assessment of merit, perhaps as a pay-off by the older man for McClellan's treatment of him, and Halleck had gained much credit for the successes won by the Union armies in the western theatre, of which he had been in overall charge. But, in the two months since his summons to Washington and appointment as general-in-chief, he had proven that, while it was difficult to get him to state an unequivocal opinion or to come to a decision, to make him take responsibility was impossible. He had already evaded, without actually declining, a suggestion from the president that he should take command of the army in the field. The one thing absolutely clear to Halleck in his own mind was that he was not going to be set directly against Robert E. Lee. Faced with the need to come to a decision for which he might ultimately be held accountable, this prime example of *Parasitus bureaucraticus*,[r] a type far too prevalent in any structured governmental organisation, hedged. No orders were sent, but some days later, when it was well known in Washington that Lee was north of the Potomac in strength and between the capital and Harper's Ferry, Halleck placed the garrison under McClellan's command, provided that he could relieve it.

It was on this basis that the Army of the Potomac advanced to the north-west, with its left flank on the line of the river. McClellan had grouped 90,000

---

[r] Halleck continued to run true to form throughout the war, remaining as chief of staff in Washington after the appointment (in March 1864) of Grant as general-in-chief of the Union armies. In July of that year, Washington came under greater threat than at any time since April 1861. Fifteen thousand hard-bitten Confederate veterans under the command of Jubal Early, yet another of the Confederacy's fighting generals, had developed an attack from the Shenandoah Valley which was probing the western defences of the Union capital, on the arc of high ground upon which now stand the national cathedral and the observatory. These men were all Lee could spare from countering the stranglehold which Grant was tightening around Richmond. With Grant fully occupied in the reduction of Petersburg, southern gateway to the Confederate capital and nearly 150 miles in a direct line from Washington, Halleck, from his office in the War Department, would argue that it was for Grant rather than himself to provide for the defence of the Union capital.[53]

men into six infantry corps, and the speed at which he had achieved their reorganisation and re-equipment did more than furnish further proof of his quality as a military administrator. It also invalidated the most important assumption underlying Lee's plan – that he would have between three and four weeks before he could be opposed by any appreciable Union strength. McClellan introduced, informally and incompletely, an intermediate level of command between his army headquarters and those of the corps. Sumner (II Corps) was given operational direction also of that of Mansfield (XII), as was Franklin (VI) of Porter (V). Major General Ambrose Burnside, long-standing friend of McClellan and, like him a West Point man who had gone into the railway construction business, was given a slightly different position. He had commanded satisfactorily an expedition to the Carolina coast, which had captured Roanoake Island. His troops, having returned from this duty, formed the basis of the new IX Corps, command of which was given to former captain of ordnance Jesse Reno, now major general of volunteers. Burnside, without a corps command, was given overall charge of IX Corps and also of that of Hooker (I).[s]

First contact between McClellan's advance guards and Stuart's cavalry patrols on the Catoctin Hills occurred on 12th September, and on the basis of Stuart's reports Lee moved D.H. Hill's division twelve miles eastwards, to strengthen his covering force on South Mountain. This feature is misnamed. It is a long, broad ridge, running north-eastwards from Harper's Ferry into Pennsylvania. If its main passes at Crampton's Gap and Turner's Gap were not secured, Longstreet's two forward divisions would be cut off, the division of McLaws on Maryland Heights caught between two fires, and the line of retreat of the Army of Northern Virginia compromised. Lee's plan was already disrupted. He had expected the surrender of Harper's Ferry by 12th September, but not only was the garrison still holding out, there was also evidence from Stuart that the Army of the Potomac had made a far quicker recovery than had been expected. Worse was to follow.

On 13th September, a regiment (27th Indiana) of Mansfield's corps, at the left centre of McClellan's advance, paused for a routine on-the-march rest halt in a field vacated the day before by Confederate troops. Two NCOs came

---

[s] There were elements of two further corps in Washington, not committed during the Antietam campaign: III (Heintzelman), which had been roughly handled in the peninsula, and had borne the brunt of Second Manassas, and XI (Sigel) still forming, with a nucleus of units from the original I Corps which had been transferred to McDowell's command as the 'Department of the Rappahannock' before the peninsula expedition. See pp.195–98 above.

upon a package of three cigars wrapped in a paper which curiosity led them to read. Not that the men recognised it as such, but the document turned out to be a copy of Lee's Special Order 191. The soldiers had the wit to take the paper at once to their company commander. The best information in the world is useless unless it reaches as speedily as possible the command level at which it can be validated and acted upon. On this occasion, the intermediate headquarters did the needful, and the paper was very soon in front of McClellan, who had established his headquarters in Frederick. The signature on the order was identified to be that of Colonel R.H. Chisholm, a pre-war officer in the Union Army, and now assistant adjutant general in the Army of Northern Virginia. McClellan, disposed initially to suspect a 'plant', accepted the intelligence as genuine on the basis of this identification.[54]

This stroke of luck delivered the Army of Northern Virginia into McClellan's hands, provided he could move fast enough. Had he acted quickly, the War Between the States would have been over within the month. The situation was even more favourable to him than the order disclosed, although it was ninety-six hours old by the time it had been evaluated at army headquarters. By his indecision, Halleck had baited, quite unintentionally, a

---

[t] The responsibility for this appalling breach of security in the staff work of the Army of Northern Virginia has never been established. As we have seen, Lee's corps organisation had been temporarily suspended, and army headquarters was issuing orders direct to some divisions. It is beyond question too that D.H. Hill received a copy of the order. Not only had he carried it out, but when, months later, the facts emerged he could produce his action copy from his headquarters files. The copy found by Corporal Barton W. Mitchell, killed four days later at Antietam, therefore may have been either a duplicate prepared at army headquarters, which had been located at Frederick when the order was issued, or a repeat copy prepared and dispatched by Hill's normal immediate superior headquarters in the chain of command, that of Jackson; legitimate enough, even if Hill were, for the time being, operating directly under army headquarters. At some point a surplus copy of Special Order No. 191 *was* discarded, by someone. But if this person was on Hill's headquarters staff, how did the paper come to be found at Frederick, ten miles *east* of Hill's division even after the relocation deployment ordered by Lee on 12th September? And if it were indeed a copy made at Jackson's headquarters, how is the signature of Lee's senior staff officer to be explained? The signature was critical in convincing McClellan that the intelligence was genuine. The most likely possibility seems to be that army headquarters prepared more copies of Special Order No. 191 than were needed for dispatch to subordinate headquarters, internal working copies and filing, even though this mistake is more easily made in the era of the photocopier than when everything had to be copied out in longhand.

trap at Harper's Ferry. Not only, as McClellan knew, was the garrison still holding out, but Jackson's three divisions west of the town were not yet ready to assault, and Longstreet's two forward divisions were already at Hagerstown, twelve miles beyond Turner's Gap. Even after realising that his design for the campaign was now totally flawed, Lee would need at least a further twenty-four hours to re-concentrate his army, and until Harper's Ferry fell, there was no secure area for him to achieve this north or east of the confluence of the rivers. Something should have been done at once. Franklin's corps (VI), on the left of the advance, was only twelve miles short of Crampton's Gap, between Elk Ridge and South Mountain, when the corps commander received information and orders from McClellan. In themselves a model of clarity, and entirely correct in their deduction that McLaws' division was unsupported and could be pinned between the advance of VI Corps and Harper's Ferry, McClellan's directions ordered Franklin to move, not at once, but 'at daybreak in the morning'. Franklin, a typical product of the peacetime army, in that he would carry out his orders to the letter but not one jot more, saw no need to impart any more urgency than his army commander had enjoined. Nor could he blame the condition of his troops. Although they were just going into bivouac in the late afternoon, they had had no more than three days' routine marching, following ten days' rest and re-equipment, and could have made an extra effort. It was not until the following morning, 14th September, that VI Corps began a somewhat ponderous advance to contact against a force they outnumbered by more than three to one. Similarly, it was not until late on the same afternoon that any appreciable pressure was exerted, by IX Corps supported by I, against Lee's two understrength divisions on South Mountain. If these could not hold, the Army of Northern Virginia would be not so much defeated in detail as swept up.

It was not, of course, until long afterwards that Lee learned the story of the lost order, but, even so, his biographer assesses it was as early as 13th September[55] that he appreciated he was now opposed by a general quite different from the McClellan of the peninsula; cautious to the point of timidity. Longstreet was ordered to return at once, and his first troops to arrive were thrown in on the afternoon of 14th September to reinforce D.H. Hill's defence of South Mountain. Meanwhile, Lee learned from Jackson that the fall of Harper's Ferry could be expected the following morning, but by the evening of 14th September it was apparent that South Mountain could not be held and that Crampton's Gap had been lost. Lee ordered a concentration of the army at Sharpsburg. The problem was McLaws. If Harper's Ferry had fallen, he could move directly; if not, he would have to extricate himself southwards across the Potomac fords, in order to escape.

In the event, Harper's Ferry surrendered as Jackson had advised, without having put up much resistance, and with Franklin's corps barely five miles away. McLaws had melted away during the night, and VI Corps had no Confederate troops between them and Harper's Ferry. Leaving A.P. Hill to organise the surrender and disposal of 11,000 prisoners of war (the initiative of a subordinate had managed to extricate 2,000 Union troops, mostly cavalry but some infantry), 13,000 stand of small arms and seventy-three guns,[56] Jackson at once set the remainder of his troops on a forced march to the position selected by Lee, seventeen miles to the north, east of the little town of Sharpsburg at the base of a small peninsula formed by a loop in the Potomac, and with its front demarcated but in no way protected by the sluggish little Antietam Creek.

As 15th September drew on, Lee, with nothing on the ground at the start of the day except the divisions withdrawn in the hours of darkness from South Mountain, saw his force build up to seven infantry divisions, all except those of McLaws and A.P. Hill, but all seriously eroded by straggling. Had McClellan attacked with the superior numbers under his hand at any time on 15th or 16th September, Lee's concentration would have been blown apart. South Mountain, which had cost both armies around 2,000 casualties, including on the Union side the newly appointed commander of IX Corps, Reno, had been reported to Washington by McClellan as a victory." But the Army of Northern Virginia had been patted rather than punched, and, instead of pressing on with everything he had, the cautious engineer, true to form, waited until five of his six corps, all but that of Franklin, were on the ground, a process which took the whole of 16th September. McClellan spent the day perfecting his plan for a set-piece attack on the Confederate position at first light on the following morning.

Throughout the afternoon of 15th September and for the whole of the next day, Lee could see the numbers against him building up on the other side of the Antietam Creek. He had picked a good position on gently rising but not dominating ground, running north–south along the line of the Hagerstown turnpike. The country was typical arable small-farm land, tilled largely by descendants of German immigrants of the austere Amish sect. At the left

" McClellan's report had included the somewhat ill-advised statement, 'General Lee admits they are badly whipped', prompting Lincoln's down-to-earth Secretary of the Navy, Gideon Wells, to speculate aloud about the source and speed of McClellan's information.[57]

centre of the Confederate line stood a small white church, at the base of a diamond no more than a mile square, with woods at its west, north and east points, enclosing a cornfield. The area was crossed by lanes deepened by years of usage. By the end of 17th September the Dunker Church, East, North and West Woods, the cornfield and the sunken road would have secured their undying place in American legend.[v]

16th September passed with the armies in presence but not contact until evening, when Hooker's corps, en route to its forming-up points, clashed with Confederate patrols. This provoked an exchange of artillery fire of sufficient violence to concern the iron-nerved Longstreet, but the Army of the Potomac intended no more than a framework operation and the firing died away. Lee had at most 25,000 men on the ground, supported by 200 guns.[58] Although many stragglers came in during the night, as well as the division of McLaws towards morning, even if the whole of A.P. Hill's division was to arrive, Lee would have a maximum of 40,000 men to hold five miles of front, a dangerously light dispersion given the range coverage of the infantry and artillery weapons of the time. He would be fighting against odds of at least two to one, with the Potomac at his back and the consequent near-certainty of annihilation if the ground could not be held, at least to the point of securing a clean break. On the other hand, the chance for a decisive victory was there, and might never recur.

McClellan's plan for the battle set aside the command structure he had established at the start of the campaign, partly because of the disposition of his formations on the ground after the battle for South Mountain, and partly because of the importunity of Major General Joseph Hooker. Flamboyant and ambitious, Hooker had supported his fellow divisional commander, Kearny ten weeks earlier, when, towards the end of the Seven Days' Battle, the latter had told McClellan that the eastern approaches to Richmond had been stripped of defending troops and the Union Army could walk into the Confederate capital at once without opposition. When the army commander had rejected this advice, Kearny had been insubordinate to the point of mutiny.[59] He now lay dead, shot out of his saddle in the concluding moments of the Battle of Chantilly, thereby depriving the Union of a hard-driving and inspirational divisional commander, but Hooker had been promoted to command the reconstituted I Corps. The campaign on the peninsula had left him with no opinion of McClellan's abilities, and, with command of the Army of the Potomac as his goal, he was already doing his utmost to curry favour

---

[v] The reader is referred to Appendix C for a description of the battlefield today.

with extreme abolitionist politicians. For the time being, however, he was not averse to using McClellan for his own ends. Hooker had no intention of fighting a major battle in a subordinate position to Burnside, and, in any event, after his flanking movement at South Mountain, he was on the right flank of the advance towards the Antietam. McClellan's plan envisaged the launching of three simultaneous attacks, but not in the groupings previously laid down. Now, Hooker would attack on the right, supported by Mansfield (XII Corps), until now subordinated to Sumner (II). Sumner's corps was to support this attack, but Hooker was not empowered to give orders to the senior corps commander. In the centre, Porter (V) was to attack on his own until joined by his designated superior, Franklin. The VI Corps was expected to reach the battlefield during the morning.[w] This left only IX Corps to mount the southern prong of the simultaneous attack. Here the command arrangements were even more strange. Although these were the troops Burnside had commanded on the expedition to the Carolina coast, and Reno, his successor in command of the corps, had been killed on South Mountain, Burnside chose not to resume direct command, although under the new grouping IX Corps constituted his sole responsibility. Appointing instead the senior divisional commander, Cox, and consumed with resentment over the prominence given to Hooker, throughout the day Burnside, with all the dignity of a senior higher formation commander, passed majestically on to Cox the increasingly imperative messages from McClellan directing him to get IX Corps into the battle. Beyond this, Burnside took no further part.

The muddled chain of command also served to confuse the structure and emphasis of the attack. Instead of the equal and simultaneous thrusts intended by McClellan, the assault was right-wing heavy, and within the right wing successive attacks were launched without coordination or mutual support. Discounting Franklin, McClellan had left himself without any reserve with which to exploit success, and a commander without additional resources to commit becomes little more than an interested spectator of events. Such was the situation of the Commander of the Army of the Potomac on 17th September. Once he had begun the battle he was unable to influence it. Although his personal bravery was unquestioned, he spent the day at his headquarters, the farm house of one Pry, behind the right centre of his line

---

[w] Which VI Corps did, some twelve hours later than McLaws's division, their erstwhile opponents on Elk Ridge. McLaws, having broken contact, had a longer and more difficult route than Franklin, but nevertheless reached the battlefield half a day sooner. The comparison between powers of leadership, commitment and endurance need not be laboured.

and two miles away from the action. In fairness to him, no one had yet worked out a satisfactory method of commanding more than 80,000 men attacking simultaneously on a five mile front.

Lee, as Commander of the Army of Northern Virginia, had hitherto fought only offensive battles, in the peninsula and at Second Manassas. In these, his method of command had been to define tasks and objectives, make the best possible distribution of resources always fewer than those of his opponent and thereafter to leave the tactical conduct of the engagement to his trusted subordinates, Longstreet and Jackson. Now he had to fight a defensive battle. Although his corps commanders were given responsibility for part of the line, Jackson northwards from the Dunker Church and Longstreet to the south of it, Lee himself on this occasion retained tactical control, at times from his static headquarters in Sharpsburg, but in the main from the saddle. The length of the line to be held precluded the creation of an uncommitted reserve at the army commander's disposal. As the battle developed, Lee's only means of bolstering the most threatened parts of his line was to transfer brigades and regiments from other sectors under less immediate pressure – a tactic which could not have worked had the Army of the Potomac ever concurrently exercised its full muscle. Thus the battle, once joined, was never in McClellan's control, but never altogether beyond that of Lee.

There are three reasons the Army of Northern Virginia stood at the end of the day on the ground it had occupied at the beginning, in spite of having sustained over 11,000 casualties. The first is Lee's masterly overall conduct of the defence; the second is the ferocity of the local counter-attacks, launched with perfect timing as opportunities arose throughout the day from Lee himself, Jackson and Longstreet; and the third is the arrival of A.P. Hill, with no more than 3,000 men, at the end of a seven hour forced march, during which the divisional commander had urged stragglers on at sword point. Hill arrived just in time to strike the open flank of a Union attack in two-division strength, which was on the point of achieving the critical breakthrough.

At the start of the day, Stuart's cavalry provided a flank guard between the northern bend of the Potomac and the North Wood, which was held by the division of J.R. Jones. Southwards on the line of the turnpike were, successively, the divisions of Lawton, whose position was marked by the West Wood, and Hood, on the rising ground upon which stood the Dunker Church, where Jackson, skilled gunner, had concentrated all his available artillery. McLaws' division was deployed behind the small ridge between the Dunker Church and West Wood, giving some depth to the position. South of the church the divisions of Walker and Richard H. Anderson[x] were placed on the gently rising ground between the turnpike and Sharpsburg, as was part of D.H. Hill's division. Two brigades of the latter, commanded by Rodes and George B. Anderson,[x] were positioned 400 yards east of the road, in a sunken farm track, of perfect depth to protect a standing infantryman, and angled to form a natural ravelin.[y] The remaining division, that of D.R. Jones, continued the line southwards, but with one brigade, three regiments of Georgia troops under the command of Brigadier General Robert Toombs, holding half a mile forward on the line of the Antietam. A cavalry brigade guarded the flank towards the southern loop of the Potomac, covering also Bottelers Ford, on the vital approach route of A.P. Hill's division.

It was around 6 a.m. and the light was breaking when Hooker's corps opened its attack, striking due south against the division of J.R. Jones in North Wood. They ran into a firestorm from Stuart's horse artillery, from the batteries concentrated by Jackson in the area of the Dunker Church, and from the Confederate infantry. In spite of the most appalling losses – the 12th Massachusetts went into battle at a strength of 334 and lost 220 of them,[60] Hooker's men penetrated as far as the critical ridge between the Dunker Church and West Wood, but were at once driven off by a counter-attack by Early's brigade of Lawton's division, picked up and thrown into the fight by Jackson. Advancing too far, they were counter-attacked in their turn, suffered similar losses and were forced back. The battle developed into a slogging match for the forty acre cornfield, in the area bounded by the Dunker Church and the three woods. By 8 a.m., Hooker's corps had made no further progress. From an opening strength of around 9,000, it had lost some 2,500 killed or wounded and perhaps as many more had left the firing line. There were all sorts of good reasons why a man might do so, the most legitimate being as a stretcher-bearer or escort to walking wounded; but few sought to come back, and I Corps, having attacked in isolation, was destroyed as a fighting force.

At the height of the Confederate counter-attack, Hooker had committed Mansfield's corps. Attacking south-westwards towards the Dunker Church, XII Corps was stopped only when Jackson threw in McLaws's division, to be followed up by Lee ordering in the divisions of Hood and Walker. The Confederate line held by the barest of margins, but the position taken up at the start of the battle could not be retained. This sector of the defence was

---

[x] By the end of the war, the Confederacy had commissioned five generals surnamed Anderson, hence the need for initials.

[y] See the glossary of military terms at Appendix B.

now bent back westwards along a subsidiary crest line. Lee had been forced to commit more than half his army on the northern quarter of his front; the divisions of Lawton and J.R. Jones were wrecked and the Army of Northern Virginia could not afford to give any more ground in this sector because there was no further suitable defence line east of the Potomac. Having committed so far no more than a third of its strength, the Union Army was on the point of victory, but the success had been won at enormous cost. The less experienced XII Corps had suffered casualties proportionately higher even than I Corps; Mansfield himself had been killed and Hooker wounded. In the first three hours of the battle, two corps of the Army of the Potomac had been fought out.

McClellan nevertheless had more troops available and to spare, and Sumner now received orders to attack. Sumner was another product of the pre-war army, grown old in long service in frontier outposts fighting the Indians. He was incapable of adjustment to changed circumstances and had there been scope for tactical subtlety he would not have known how to display it, but he was brave and he knew his duty. His corps advanced in column of divisions, each division following the next, on a westerly axis headed through East Wood. Their first view of the action was unnerving. The burning and broken woodland was packed with wounded and an excess of Good Samaritans not anxious to return to the battle lines of the shattered I and XII Corps. Sumner's leading division, that of Sedgwick, struck the centre of the Confederate line south of the Dunker Church, and once again the breakthrough was nearly achieved. But Sumner's second division was too far behind to exploit the opportunity.

Jackson launched a local counter-attack with troops of McLaws's and Walker's divisions, and Lee, taking an enormous tactical risk on his right, detached a brigade from the division of D.R. Jones to strengthen his threatened centre. Sedgwick himself was wounded and his division stranded in the open, able to move neither forward nor back. Although the situation was stabilised for the time being, Lee realised that something had to be done to try to restore the initiative to his side, because at the present rate of exchange, McClellan's superior numbers should eventually tell. He directed Jackson to mount a flanking attack around the Union right, with whatever could be cobbled together. Lee had the essential attribute of a great commander: he could always assess the limit of capability of his own troops, while having at the same time a complete understanding of the state of mind and reaction of his opponent. A counter-attack on the northern flank of the Army of the

Potomac, even if delivered by no more than a cavalry regiment, might well be enough to make the cautious McClellan stop and think.

Sumner still had two divisions to commit. With the East Wood and the cornfield now impassable because of the dead and dying on the ground and the fired crops and vegetation, he launched them on a westerly axis, half a mile to the south of Sedgwick's wrecked division. They struck the strongest part of the Confederate line. Coming over a small crest, they found themselves on a bare slope leading down to the sunken road, at a range at which even muskets could hardly miss. Possession of the sunken road, also known as the Bloody Lane, was contested for four hours. By early afternoon the lane itself and the 200 yard glacis leading down to it were choked with 4,000 dead and wounded. Lee and Longstreet threw in every available soldier; Longstreet's staff had to take over the working of some guns after their crews had all been killed or wounded. But the Confederate position was precarious in the extreme. In later years Longstreet would state that one more attack in mid-morning by 10,000 fresh federal troops would have destroyed Lee's army.

McClellan had the men available. Porter's corps was as yet uncommitted, having done no more than secure the ground east of the Antietam while waiting for Franklin. The VI Corps was now arriving on the battlefield. Because of the carnage in front of the sunken road, these were deployed on the Union right, with the intention of attacking over the ground already attempted by Hooker, Mansfield and Sedgwick. Following the death in action of the commander of Sumner's third division, Richardson, McClellan had already appointed a replacement divisional commander, Hancock, with orders to continue the attack, and now sent a suggestion rather than an order to Sumner that the remnants of his corps should mount a joint effort with that of Franklin. Sumner countermanded the order to Hancock and told McClellan's staff officer:

> Go back, young man, and tell General McClellan I have no command. Tell him my command, Banks's command [sic][z] and Hooker's command are all cut up and demoralised. Tell him General Franklin has the only organised command on this part of the field.[61]

---

[z] He meant that of Mansfield, whose corps was made up of troops previously commanded by Banks, but in the heat of battle...

Although the counterstroke round the Union right desired by Lee had not been launched because Jackson could find no troops to spare, this advice from the senior corps commander was enough to deter McClellan. The fighting died down to sporadic skirmishing and artillery fire in the centre as well as the north of the battlefield. D.H. Hill's men were forced to abandon the sunken road. This half-mile of farm track was running with blood and so full of dead, wounded and torn flesh that it could no longer be used as a trench.

Meanwhile, what of the somewhat over-commanded IX Corps of the Army of the Potomac? At the southern end of the battlefield, Union left and Confederate right, the Union Army's immediate tactical problem was to get across the Antietam, which, on the IX Corps front, broadens to a width of about twenty-five yards before joining the Potomac two miles south of Sharpsburg. The current is barely perceptible and the stream itself nowhere more than three feet deep, and thus fordable at almost any point by infantry and cavalry. It was the banks, sheer, about fifteen feet high and set back by a few yards either side of the river course, which caused the problem, rather than the sluggish little creek. Nevertheless, in the eyes of the Union commanders in this part of the field, everything was thought to depend upon the capture of the one stone bridge, though earnest efforts were made by IX Corps staff officers to find a ford.[aa]

By mid-morning, with the attacks of Hooker, Mansfield and Sedgwick already ground to a halt and the attack on the sunken road making no progress, the Union left, which had been supposed to attack at first light, had achieved nothing. Thus Lee was able to transfer troops from the division of D.R. Jones to reinforce his hard-pressed line in front and north of Sharpsburg.

At last, after a series of increasingly urgent orders from McClellan, IX Corps made its attack on the bridge. As we have seen, the nature of the ground had caused Lee to deploy one brigade of his right flank division forward, on the line of the little escarpment on the west bank of the stream and commanding the bridge. These three understrength regiments, no more than

---

[aa] Their difficulties would have been resolved had any of them thought to emulate the action of the young Lieutenant George A. Custer on the Chickahominy four months earlier. Similar tooth-sucking and jaw-pulling about this river's depth in the presence of McClellan was terminated at a stroke by the dashing subaltern of cavalry, who had recently graduated to the staff of the army commander from that of Kearny. Custer simply rode his horse into and through the river,[62] the first of a series of exploits leading to his promotion by the end of the war to brevet major general – and later still to his death and the massacre of his command by the Indians at the Battle of Little Big Horn.

1,200 men, were commanded by Robert Toombs, formerly secretary of state in the first carefully balanced cabinet of Jefferson Davis. Toombs, a hardline secessionist, had soon resigned over differences about the emphasis rather than nature of policy and had gone to the army in the rank of brigadier general. With no thought before the war of soldiering, and contemptuous of the elitist culture of West Point, Toombs had proved to be yet another Confederate formation commander who relished battle, and the afternoon was well advanced before the fourth of a series of piecemeal attacks drove the survivors of his command from the bridge and back on to D.R. Jones's much depleted division south of Sharpsburg.

Although the battle for the sunken road had by this time ended in mutual exhaustion, Lee had nothing left on the ground to meet the threat of two advancing fresh IX Corps divisions, those of Rodman and Willcox. The Army of Northern Virginia was fought out. Eleven of its regiments[bb] had taken casualties of forty per cent or more of their entry-into-battle strengths, the 1st Texas, of Hood's Division, suffering, at 82.3%, the highest percentage loss of any regiment of either side in any battle of the entire war;[63] when, after the battle, the losses came to be totalled it would be found that the Army of Northern Virginia had lost some thirty per cent of its entry-into-battle strength. With 12,000 fresh Union troops on and nearly behind the Confederate right, disaster impended until, at about 4 p.m., A.P. Hill's leading troops reached the battlefield. There were no more than 3,000 of them, as many again having fallen out through exhaustion on the forced march from Harper's Ferry.[64] The surprise, perhaps increased because Hill's men had replaced their ragged uniforms from the abundant booty stocks of Union dark blue, and the vulnerability of any formation to a flank attack, threw back the Union divisions. Neither Cox nor Burnside did anything to mount another attack, the initiative in this part of the field returning entirely to the Confederates, and between them A.P. Hill and D.R. Jones pushed IX Corps back across the Antietam. The fire-eating Toombs was, with difficulty, restrained from continuing the pursuit over the creek.

Although the corps of Hooker, Mansfield and Sumner had been fought out and that of Cox defeated and disorganised, McClellan still had two corps,

---

[bb] From a table[63] listing fifty Confederate regiments which suffered at least forty per cent casualties in a single action. The Confederate records were, inevitably, less accurate and complete than those of the Union, but it seems indisputable that Antietam produced not only the highest losses on any single day of the war, but also by far the largest number of regiments to incur a casualty rate of more than two men for every five engaged.

those of Porter and Franklin, which had hardly been engaged, and which, together, were equivalent in numbers to the Confederate strength on the battlefield. But McClellan himself was morally beaten, and the wounded Hooker rejected the impassioned request of a subordinate that he should put himself at the head of another attack, from an ambulance if need be.

By the end of the day both sides had returned to the ground which they had occupied at the start of the battle, to gather their wounded, bury their dead and regroup their shattered units and formations. The losses in terms of killed, wounded and missing amounted to over 11,000 Confederate and 12,000 Union troops; nearly one in four of the total numbers engaged, and the highest of any day of the war.

As night fell the Army of Northern Virginia began to evacuate its wounded, but Lee, against the advice of his generals, chose to remain on the ground. Drawing in his lines, he invited a resumption of the battle on the following day, but McClellan chose not to attack. Lee dared wait no longer; on the night of 18th September the Army of Northern Virginia slipped away across the Potomac fords, but it was not until two days later that McClellan pushed Porter's corps across the river after them. They received a rough reception from Lee's covering force, inevitably the division of A.P. Hill, and the attack was not pressed.

Both armies settled down to recover their strength, initially regaining the stragglers, those who had left the battlefield and, in the case of Lee's army, the men who had chosen not to take part in the invasion of Maryland. But while McClellan's reorganisation was totally passive, Lee's was not. In order to gain time and to disrupt his opponent, Lee launched Stuart's cavalry on a ride right round the Union Army, repeating a feat already achieved on the peninsula. In each case the confusion and destruction of logistic assets served to confirm Lee's domination of his opponent.

Lee's gamble against enormous odds had failed, but his strategy had been the only one possible if the Confederacy were to achieve its war aim. His tactical conduct of the battle had been a model of its kind when any mistake would have led to disaster, his subordinate commanders and troops had fought to the limit of their capability and endurance and he had retained an army in being. But, in spite of everything, the political and strategic initiative had passed to the North.

Since Lee's invasion had clearly been repulsed, Lincoln was enabled to do two things. First, he could issue his long-withheld proclamation decreeing the emancipation of the slaves. For both foreign and domestic consumption this major change of policy was essential, but its announcement had to be founded upon victory. Once issued, it would inhibit any European power which had itself renounced slavery from recognising or even supporting the Confederacy. And, while domestically, the proclamation was no more than a sop to the extreme abolitionists in that it decreed freedom only for slaves in areas 'in rebellion' – exactly the places where the measure could not be enforced – the action linked inextricably the issue of abolition to Lincoln's own war aim; the preservation of the Union. Too many domestic considerations remained to be balanced for Lincoln to be able to do more, for the time being. Secondly, the result of the battle allowed Lincoln to dismiss McClellan – a further encouragement for the abolitionists, and one which they had long sought. The victory at Antietam, such as it was, had obvious limitations. Lee's army had not been destroyed, and the attempt to follow up and bring the withdrawing enemy to a conclusive battle had been at best half-hearted. Nurturing suspicions that either general or army might act unconstitutionally if the news of McClellan's intended supersession became known beforehand, the Administration exercised some subterfuge to convey the news to him. The various schemes worked; on a snowy evening on 7th November, seven weeks after the battle, the president's emissary first apprised the chosen successor, Burnside, of his elevation. The two men then went on to McClellan's headquarters tent. The fears of a military *coup d'état*, whether inspired by the general or spontaneous on the part of the army, proved groundless. Three days later, McClellan departed without incident. He was never again employed in the field, emerging instead as the candidate of the Democrat Party to contest the re-election of Lincoln in 1864.

The Winter of Discontent – Fredericksburg, December 1862

It is just possible that if McClellan had, after Antietam, shown any sign of determination to take the offensive, Lincoln might have retained him in command. After all, though he had become anathema to the radical Republicans, his support among Northern Democrats was at least as strong, and he clearly retained the full confidence of the Army of the Potomac. But he showed no such intention. Ten days after the battle, he telegraphed to Halleck that he proposed to concentrate his forces:

> somewhere near Harper's Ferry and then [to act] according to circumstances, viz., moving on Winchester, if from the position and attitude of the enemy we are likely to gain a great advantage by doing so, or else devoting a reasonable time to the organisation

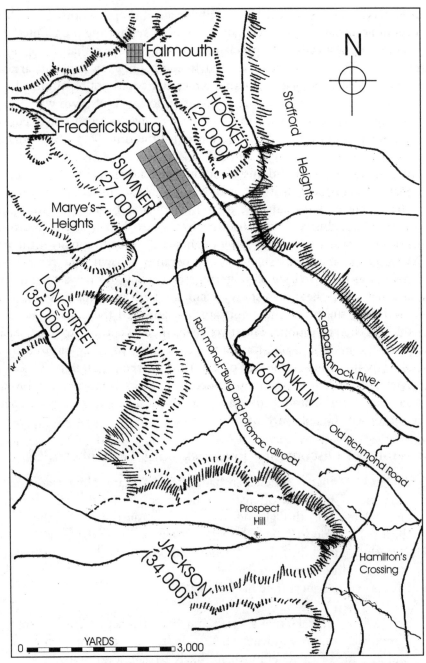

Fredericksburg, 13th December, 1862

of the army and instruction of the new troops, preparatory to an advance on whatever line may be determined.[65]

This was the statement of a politician anxious to keep all his options open, rather than that of a general determined to unleash a killer punch on an enemy in disarray.

There followed the concentration of the army east of Harper's Ferry, Stuart's epic ride and the consequent Union dislocation, a leisurely move to a new concentration area around Warrenton and an even vaguer statement of intent to advance southwards at some time in the future in order to cut the Confederacy's east–west lifeline; the Virginia Central railroad. Concurrently, McClellan placed a series of demands on Washington for reinforcements of men and all types of matériel. His last, for horses, on the grounds that those of the Army of the Potomac were 'absolutely broken down from fatigue and want of flesh', and the evident surrender of the initiative so hard-won at Antietam, finally wore out Lincoln's patience. The specific demand for horses prompted the presidential enquiry: 'Will you pardon me for asking what the horses of your army have done since the Battle of Antietam which fatigues anything?'[66]

During the transfer of command on 8th and 9th November, Burnside formed the view that he would not, as had seemed to be McClellan's intention, court battle with the Army of Northern Virginia in or around the Shenandoah Valley and the Blue Ridge. Instead, he would move south-eastwards, seeking to cross the Rappahannock at Fredericksburg. Thereafter he would advance on Richmond on the axis of the Richmond, Fredericksburg and Potomac railroad. Although the line out of Aquia Creek was in poor shape and the bridge at Fredericksburg destroyed, the line south of the Rappahannock was too valuable an asset to the Confederacy to have been torn up, and the North had a railway engineer of genius, Colonel Haupt, who had already worked miracles and would prove capable of restoring the link between Aquia Creek and Fredericksburg in short order. Burnside's proposed line of advance, while guaranteeing his main supply route, would nevertheless require at least four more river-crossing operations after he had passed the Rappahannock before he could assault the Confederate capital, depending upon the exact route of advance which he chose across the grain of the Virginia peninsula. But the movement down to Fredericksburg would inevitably draw Lee's army after it, and the conditions for a decisive battle might emerge at some point on the advance between Fredericksburg and Richmond. On 12th November, Burnside presented his proposed plan to

Lincoln, through Halleck. Halleck, true to form, produced Delphic advice, but Lincoln, on 14th November, telegraphed his approval, remarking nevertheless that the plan would succeed only if Burnside moved fast.

Notwithstanding the detachment of two corps, XII (Slocum) to Harper's Ferry and XI (Sigel) at Gainesville, to cover the western approaches to Washington, Burnside moved with a strength of nearly 120,000 men, a third as many again as McClellan had had for the Antietam campaign, but the quality of the troops had begun to deteriorate.

Just as the battles of 1915 in France were to destroy the flower of the manpower of England, who had rushed to volunteer at the outbreak of war in the preceding year, so the ecstatic volunteers of 1861 had been wasted by battle and disease. The North by now had to find its manpower by compulsion – draft quota and bounty.[cc] The increased risk of desertion, by either compelled and unwilling recruits or 'bounty jumpers', produced the need for more rigid discipline and thus an erosion of the mutual confidence between officers and their men which had been the best feature of the volunteer regiments. Unit discipline soon deteriorated further once the advance was underway because the commissariat arrangements broke down. The tragedy of Burnside, as well as that of a good many of his soldiers, was that he was ever promoted above regimental command. Unlike McClellan, he did not himself have the ability to administer an army, nor to direct a competent staff to do it for him. The collapse of the supply chain produced the inevitable increase in looting and indiscriminate foraging, which in turn created a state of mutual hatred between the soldiers of the two armies. And at the top level, neither side could achieve what had become its declared war aim unless there was total surrender by the other. As a result, there emerged a perception of all-out and total war. Individual romantic notions of picture-book soldiering had not survived the first engagement, but, after eighteen months of conflict, chivalric ideas of confining the fighting to the armies were also going for good. Both sides had become almost totally directionist in the management of their own manpower, free as well as slave. Both governments suspended the right of habeas corpus.

[cc] Each state, city and county was given a draft quota, met in theory by drawing lots among all the men of military age. But such was the increase of wealth in the North generated by the war that the authorities at all levels preferred to offer bounties of up to a year's wages for an unskilled worker to induce men to volunteer in order to fill their quota. Similarly, substitutes could be purchased. These practices produced the 'bounty jumper' who would attest, receive his lump sum and desert, to re-enlist elsewhere. Such an individual would be likely to be the first to find an excuse to leave the firing line if he actually got into combat.

And the civilian caught in the path of the march of the armies had nothing better to expect than ruin.

Burnside had carried one step further the higher structuring of the army initiated by McClellan. His six corps were grouped into three 'grand divisions', Right, comprising II Corps (Couch) and V (Butterfield), commanded by Sumner, Centre, III Corps (Stoneman) and IX (Willcox) under Hooker, and Left, I Corps (Reynolds) and VI (W.F. Smith), led by Franklin, each corps having three divisions of a strength varying between 5,000 and 10,000 men. None of the grand division commanders can be said to have earned his promotion on merit, and the five corps which had fought at Antietam were all under new leaders. The promotions to corps command and the battle casualties at Antietam had produced a very high turnover among the generals of divisions. The higher command of the Army of the Potomac was at best unproven; Hooker was already intriguing as fiercely against Burnside as he had against McClellan, and other generals would soon follow. On the other hand, some good soldiers, proven in combat, were beginning to come to the front in command of divisions.

Meanwhile, on the other side of the hill, Lee fully understood that he had to stand on the strategic defensive. Although his army had doubled in size since the withdrawal after Antietam, he had barely half the full strength of the Army of the Potomac, and his movements would depend entirely on whether Burnside chose to attack in West Virginia, overland towards Richmond, or by repeating McClellan's Peninsula Campaign of the previous summer. For the time being, Lee retained Jackson in the upper half of the Shenandoah Valley, and sent Longstreet down to the peninsula, south of the Rappahannock. Of the waters which rise in the 600 mile sweep of the Appalachian Chain extending from Georgia to Pennsylvania to flow towards the Atlantic, this river is inferior in size only to the Potomac and the James and was an ideal obstacle upon which Lee could base the defence of central Virginia. His cavalry, operating under army command and far ahead in battlefield technique of that of the Army of the Potomac, brought him increasing intelligence as November drew on that the blow would fall in the centre, and on 18th November, on receiving reports that a substantial federal force had reached Falmouth on the left bank of the Rappahannock,[dd] Lee ordered Longstreet to concentrate on the heights opposite, above the small post-colonial town and

---

[dd] The general flow of the Rappahannock is a little south of east, and parallel with the Potomac fifty miles to the north, but the course of the river is south-eastwards between Falmouth and Fredericksburg.

trading centre of Fredericksburg, in order to deny the crossing to the enemy. Fredericksburg had at the time some 6,000 inhabitants, and extended something over a mile along the right bank of the river and about five blocks westwards from it.

On 19th November, the mayor of Fredericksburg brought to Lee a demand for the surrender of the town, signed by Major General E.V. Sumner, Commander of the Right Grand Division of the Army of the Potomac. Further reports from his excellent cavalry soon confirmed that Lee had estimated Burnside's intentions as accurately as he always had those of McClellan and Pope. Jackson was ordered down from the valley at once. If the Army of the Potomac wanted to cross the Rappahannock at Fredericksburg, they would have to fight for it.

A set battle may be defined as one which is fought on ground chosen by either or both army commanders, and with an objective essential to the achievement of their campaign or war aim. Lee, though on the defensive, constantly sought a battle in which the Army of the Potomac would be so damaged as to destroy the will of the North to continue the war, and if Burnside wanted to fight at Fredericksburg, the Army of Northern Virginia was unlikely ever to find a better tactical defensive position. To do him justice in the light of later events, such had never been Burnside's intention. In the construction technology of the time, Fredericksburg was the last suitable crossing point before the river flowed into the Chesapeake. The climate at the time of year is also relevant. While often remaining perfect throughout the fall and early winter, the deterioration in the weather, when it occurs, is sudden. A rise of six feet within twenty-four hours in the river level at Fredericksburg is not unusual even today, and the unsurfaced roads of the mid-nineteenth century turned to liquid mud after heavy rain at any time of year, as McClellan had already discovered on the peninsula. In such circumstances the coordinated and timed programme essential for the movement of large bodies of troops becomes unachievable. Thus, once the Army of the Potomac was concentrated around Falmouth and the heavy rains had begun, it could not manoeuvre to seek an unopposed crossing point elsewhere.

Lee delayed his orders to Jackson until the last minute and the best obtainable confirmation of the movements of Burnside's troops. Once these orders had been received, Jackson's four divisions, total strength some 35,000 men, embarked upon yet another epic march in deteriorating weather. Covering 175 miles in twelve days,[67] they arrived at Fredericksburg on 1st December. Lee deployed three divisions in prolongation of the position taken up by Longstreet, but sent D.H. Hill's division a further twenty miles to the south-east, to Port Royal, in order to guard his open flank on the Chesapeake.[cc] Once Lee had both his corps in position south of the Rappahannock, time was on his side. The winter rains had started and no further grand manoeuvres would be possible until the roads hardened again under the late spring sunshine. The Confederacy, hard-pressed by superior numbers and overwhelming weight of *matériel* in the western theatre, on the Atlantic and Gulf coasts as well as in Virginia, had gained a breathing space, always provided that the Army of Northern Virginia could hold on to its ideal defensive position.

When Sumner first arrived at Falmouth, he could have crossed the river by fording. But in the absence of positive orders to this effect from the army commander, and anticipating the possibility that the rapid rise in the river level to be expected once the rains started would leave him isolated on the far bank against superior numbers, the cautious old frontier campaigner would risk nothing. His ultimatum, surrender or bombardment of Fredericksburg on 22nd November, allowed the evacuation of the civilian population but was not followed up. The Right Grand Division consolidated a strong defensive position on the Stafford Heights south-east of Falmouth, and settled down to await the arrival of the rest of the Army of the Potomac.

Burnside had envisaged Fredericksburg not as the site for a decisive battle starting with the most difficult of all offensive operations, an assault river-crossing against a warned and prepared defence, but as the jumping-off point for his further advance into Virginia. Therefore, the permanent bridges over the Rappahannock would need to be repaired, and the crossing capacity enhanced by additional pontoon bridges. The bridging train of the Army of the Potomac was provided by the 50th New York Volunteer Engineer Regiment, which had been deployed in support of the concentration round Harper's Ferry after Antietam to provide additional bridging across the Shenandoah and Potomac. After the further deployment of the army around Warrenton, some of these bridges had become redundant and as early as 6th November army headquarters ordered them to be taken up. These orders were given no priority and, instead of being sent by telegraph or courier, were consigned to the army's routine mailing system. In consequence, they did not reach the headquarters of the regiment until 12th November. What had been a routine matter under McClellan became, once Lincoln had approved

---

[cc] Possibly over-insurance by Lee. There had been nothing in the performance of the Army of the Potomac to date to suggest that it had either the skill or flexibility of mind to mount a simultaneous water-borne flanking operation.

Burnside's design for the campaign, absolutely vital to its success. The new army commander and his staff were seriously at fault, in that they neither sought to instil some sense of urgency nor even saw to it that this relatively small cog in the machine was given an updated explanation of its new and critical task. Nor was the engineering headquarters of the army in Washington informed of the new plan or priorities. Even after the engineer-in-chief, Brigadier General Woodbury, had called on Halleck on 14th November specifically to discuss the tasking of the bridging train, the general-in-chief allowed him to depart none the wiser. In consequence, the unfortunate regimental commander, Major Spaulding, never had any idea that the speed of his unit's redeployment was of the essence until he himself reached Burnside's headquarters on 24th November.

Meanwhile, he and his men had made Herculean efforts to surmount the difficulties which arose in every single element of the movement plan, including the need to introduce to draught harness 200 unbroken horses from the Washington remount depot. The heavy and cumbersome pontoons moved in increasingly vile weather, which mired their transporter wagons down to the axles. On the day upon which Spaulding reached Burnside's headquarters, the essential equipment had reached no further than Belle Plain, east of Aquia Creek and still ten miles from the intended bridging sites across the Rappahannock, a distance which took another three days to cover in the appalling road and weather conditions.[68]

Had even some of the pontoons been under Sumner's hand eight days earlier, when the Right Grand Division closed up to the Rappahannock, they might have been emplaced to sustain his 40,000 men south of the river, against what, at the time, was an approximately equal strength. In such circumstances it is unlikely in the extreme that Lee would have contested passage of the Rappahannock. He would have been forced to withdraw Longstreet's corps at least to the Mattapony and perhaps as far as the South Anna River, in order to await the arrival of Jackson. Neither compares with the Rappahannock as an obstacle upon which to base the conduct of a defensive battle in which the whole future of the Confederacy could be at stake. Instead, in the light of the situation which did emerge, Burnside's pontoons would now have to be laid under the guns of Lee's army. The archetypal set-piece battle of Fredericksburg developed partly because once the weather had broken Burnside could not manoeuvre, and partly because, after the arrival of Jackson, Lee, with the necessary force to hold a near-perfect defensive position, did not need to.

The first ten days of December brought no activity beyond outpost contacts. Burnside consolidated his position, deploying 147 heavy guns on Stafford Heights to provide covering fire for the engineers laying the pontoon bridges at his three chosen crossing sites, two on the Fredericksburg waterfront, about three-quarters of a mile apart, and the third a further mile and a half downstream, below the point at which the small Deep Run creek joins the river on its right bank.

To the west of Fredericksburg there was a stretch of waste ground half a mile wide, bisected by a drainage ditch deep enough on the one hand to present an obstacle to movement, but on the other providing a line of dead ground where an attacking force could form up to assault Marye's Heights, dominating the town. There was a sunken road at the base of this feature, which rose quite steeply, but for no more than 100 feet, to a stone wall on the visible crestline. Both the ditch and the wall afforded natural protection for the defence. From Marye's Heights the high ground leads south to Telegraph Hill, overlooking the Deep Run re-entrant, at which point the crest line is some two and a half miles from the river, before looping back eastwards to Prospect Hill, within half a mile of the right bank. If Lee's defensive position had a weakness, it was that the southernmost of Burnside's three chosen crossing points could not, given the weapon technology of the time, be dominated by fire, either from the infantry at the centre and right of the Confederate position, or by any but the heaviest guns on Marye's Heights. But a frontal attack on the left of Lee's line would be in trouble at once. The two northernmost bridging sites were in point-blank range of any skirmishing line deployed in the cover of the brick buildings along the waterfront. The axis of advance would be constrained by the town streets and when the assault troops fanned out to cross the open ground they would be in full view, and range, of the Confederate position on Marye's Heights. And, inevitably, troops would bunch when crossing the drainage ditch. The Confederate artillery commander, Lieutenant Colonel E. Porter Alexander, assured both Lee and Longstreet, 'A chicken could not live on that field when we open on it.'[69]

Longstreet's five divisions held the left of the Confederate position, with successively from the north R.H. Anderson, McLaws (with one brigade forward in Fredericksburg on the river line), Pickett and Hood, the latter on Telegraph Hill, with Ransom's Division and the army and corps artillery in depth behind McLaws on Marye's Heights. Jackson's corps on the right followed the grain of Prospect Hill to face north-eastwards. His artillery had a good field of fire down to the Deep Run, and was protected by Taliaferro's division on the refused left flank of the corps layout, with A.P. Hill forward and Early's division on a refused right. Stuart's cavalry and horse artillery covered the southern flank of the army's deployment, in all some five miles long, down to the line of the river. There was a tactical weakness in that a small ravine between the positions of Taliaferro and A.P. Hill was left uncovered, and Jackson's position had neither depth nor reserve until D.H. Hill was summoned back from Port Royal.[ff]

But the initiative lay with Burnside. At 4.30 a.m. on 11th December, his engineers began the attempt to lay the three sets of bridges. The sites in Fredericksburg came at once under heavy fire from Barksdale's Brigade of Mississippi troops, deployed for that very purpose and protected by the brick buildings on the river bank. When this defence came under the full weight of the artillery on Stafford Heights, there was a further foretaste of the events of the First World War. Despite a bombardment of over 5,000 rounds in two hours, from an allocation of fifty rounds per gun built up on the gun line for this task, Barksdale's infantry, though sometimes neutralised, was not destroyed. They could still bring down enough weight of small arms fire to deny work on the two sites leading into Fredericksburg. Although the bridges at the Deep Run site were in place by mid-morning, Burnside chose not to order an all-out assault until those at the Fredericksburg sites were also established. This did not happen until the December day was far advanced, after some of the pontoons had been utilised as assault boats and enough Union troops ferried across the river to winkle out the survivors of Barksdale's three understrength regiments. For all the military history learned, no doubt so painstakingly, at West Point, it seems not to have occurred to Burnside or to any of his officers that lessons might have been learned from Napoleon's forcing of the Danube before Wagram in 1809.[gg]

So far for Burnside, so good, except that there could be no possibility of surprise and no manoeuvre except frontal attack. Yet another day elapsed without a general assault. All that happened in the Army of the Potomac on 12th December was that the town of Fredericksburg was occupied and a small bridgehead secured on the right bank at the Deep Run site. Meanwhile, Lee ordered up D.H. Hill's Division from Port Royal. Arriving during the night, this formation deployed as planned to give depth to Jackson's position on Prospect Hill.

[ff] The infinitely better continuity in command in the Army of Northern Virginia will have been noted. The Confederates would fight under the same army and corps commanders as at Antietam, and with five of the nine divisional commanders.

[gg] See Chapter III.

When the orders issued by Burnside on 12th December for an attack on the following morning are compared with his allocation of troops to tasks and his own conduct of a battle fought under his direct view, a discrepancy emerges. From his allotment of resources, it would seem that his intention was to attack left-wing heavy, because Franklin was reinforced to a strength of 60,000 men by the attachment of three divisions from Hooker's command. And after the battle, Burnside would claim that his design had been for Franklin to outflank and attack Jackson, so that the Left Grand Division could roll up the Confederate position from its southern flank. Meanwhile Sumner, reinforced similarly by another of Hooker's divisions, should mount no more than a holding operation until it was evident that Franklin's attack was succeeding. Only then was the Right Grand Division to assault Marye's Heights. This pincer movement should force Lee to withdraw, and the assault divisions of the two formations would meet on Telegraph Hill, cutting off those Confederate troops who had been too slow to pull out. Hooker, his command reduced to half by these detachments, was to be prepared to reinforce either Franklin or Sumner. Burnside also issued restraining orders – to Sumner, forbidding the fiery old warrior from crossing the river himself, and to both grand division commanders that their leading units were to take care not to fire into each other as the pincers closed.[70]

Both Franklin and Sumner interpreted their orders in exactly the opposite sense. The early morning of 13th December broke in thick fog. When this had partially lifted, Franklin embarked on what he considered to be no more than a reconnaissance in force. His orders required him to secure Hamilton's Crossing, a road and railway junction of no tactical significance on the extreme southern limit of Jackson's position, to send 'a division at least' to seize 'the rising ground north of this feature' and then to await further orders. Finding his advance from the Deep Run bridgehead impeded by Stuart's cavalry and brilliantly handled horse artillery, Franklin threw out Doubleday's division of I Corps to mask them, while the other two divisions of Reynolds' corps sought to seize the high ground as ordered. Franklin became, in a way, the victim of his own success, because Meade's battle-hardened Pennsylvanian division struck the gap between Taliaferro and A.P. Hill. One of Hill's brigadiers was killed and Meade's veterans threatened to roll up his division but Franklin, established, as he had been ordered, on the rising ground above Hamilton's Crossing, considered that he had done all he had been told, and, as we have seen, he was not the man to go beyond the letter of his orders. Although the irascible Meade, both at the time and later, could claim that victory was in his grasp, Franklin would not send him any support. The inevitable counter-attack by D.H. Hill's depth division restored the integrity of Jackson's defensive position. Burnside sent no further orders to Franklin and, as darkness fell, the Confederate line was back where it had been at the start of the day but with the gap closed, and Franklin's reinforced grand division, half the battle strength of the Army of the Potomac, was drawn up in a convex arc on the right bank of the river, on low ground dominated by Prospect Hill, awaiting orders which never came.

Sumner also misinterpreted what Burnside claimed afterwards to have been his intentions, behaving throughout as though he had been directed to capture Marye's Heights at any cost. His first attack did not go in until about 11 a.m., after the fog had lifted. The first assault, by a division of his own former II Corps, was mown down by Alexander's guns as soon as it emerged on to the flat ground beyond the town. In all, fourteen separate assaults were mounted, to be met by the artillery firing from Marye's Heights at a range of no more than three-quarters of a mile, and by coordinated volleys of musketry from infantry in the sunken road and behind the stone wall on the crest. In spite of a series of acts of desperate gallantry by infantry and artillery, thrown forward to try to blast a way through, no Union soldier came any closer to Marye's Heights than 30 yards short of the sunken road. Successive assaults in division and brigade strength by formations of II, III, V and IX Corps were massacred in First World War proportions. One veteran brigade of II Corps went into action 1,400 strong and had no more than 250 men present with the colours at the end of the day. The experience of another brigade also foreshadowed things to come; moved up in order to be in a position to exploit any success gained, the soldiers did not fire a shot from their own weapons but nevertheless sustained 140 casualties from artillery fire.[71]

As darkness fell, the ground between the limits of the town and the sunken road appeared to be a gently swaying mass of dark blue – wounded Union soldiers seeking to crawl away, stretching out hands for help or trying to restrain comrades committed to yet another hopeless assault. The carnage continued in full view of army, grand division, corps and divisional commanders; none thought to stop successive attempts to reinforce failure. Sumner's Corps Group suffered over 9,000 casualties, nearly all in front of Mary's Heights, and with a further 3,000 in Franklin's formations the Union loss on the day was some ten per cent of the battle strength of the whole army, half of which never got into action. After the battle Stuart wrote to Lee's eldest son:

> Englishmen here who surveyed Solferino and all the battlefields
> of Italy say that the pile of dead on the plains of Fredericksburg
> exceeds anything of the sort seen by them. [72]

By contrast, Lee's army, fighting rested, warned, prepared and protected, suffered a bare forty per cent of the Union loss, two-thirds of this in Jackson's corps. And none of the desperate expedients of Antietam had been needed.

It was not so much that Sumner had learned nothing from the failure of the piecemeal attacks put in at Antietam. Given the limitations of the route capacity over the bridges and through the ruined town, it was never possible to attack with more than one division at a time from a bridgehead dominated by direct fire from the enemy's main defensive position. Yet again, the Army of the Potomac failed to bring to bear its superior strength.

Burnside, a decent man out of his depth and appalled by the slaughter, resolved to make one more attempt on the following day by putting himself at the head of his own former IX Corps, but was talked out of it by his generals.

On 15th December, a flag of truce allowed the collection from the ground in front of Marye's Heights of those Union wounded who had survived the initial shock and two cold December nights in the open. The Army of the Potomac withdrew to the left bank, the pontoons were taken up and the troops on both sides of the river settled down to an uncomfortable Christmas.

But Lee, always with the next battle in mind, had fortifications built all along the river line from Port Royal to Banks's Ford, next crossing point upriver from Fredericksburg, to guard against any attempt by Burnside to turn his flank. Predictably, Burnside attempted this manoeuvre a month later. Equally predictably, it floundered in a sea of mud and after two days, with nothing achieved, the Army of the Potomac withdrew into its ad hoc winter quarters around Falmouth. Although the soldiers had built hutments, largely by self-help and with materials looted from the countryside, the army was in very poor shape. Its logistic support had collapsed, in spite of the open supply line by way of Aquia Creek and the Potomac to the north. There was a quite unnecessary death toll from malnutrition, pneumonia and hypothermia, which Burnside's mud march exacerbated. After the mud march, army morale plummeted to rock bottom, and a strength return on 31st January indicated that 85,123 soldiers of the Army of the Potomac were absent from their place of duty. [73]

By that date, Burnside had been relieved of his command. The whisper of intrigue against him before Fredericksburg became a breeze after the battle and a hurricane after the mud march. Over the New Year, two of W.F.

Smith's brigadiers took leave in Washington, with the full concurrence of their corps commander, to 'complain to their congressman'. Whistled up the line within the day, they were interviewed first by Secretary of State Seward and then by the president. Lincoln was already aware that there was no mutual confidence between Stanton, his secretary of war, and Halleck on the one hand and Burnside on the other and here was evidence, obtained however contrary to discipline, that Burnside did not have the confidence of his generals.

In response to presidential queries, Burnside produced a paper stating that he was unwilling to remain in command of the army unless Franklin, Smith and a number of other pro-McClellan officers were dismissed, and combined this with the publication of an army order which attributed the blame for the disloyalty within the army to Hooker. This, however justified, was hardly appropriate reading for all ranks down to private. It is beyond question that by now Hooker was intriguing with anybody who might help him to the command of the army, but, while he was after promotion for no one but himself, most of the senior officer-discontent in the Army of the Potomac sought the reinstatement of McClellan. This was naïve in the extreme as, for political reasons, McClellan's reappointment was impossible.

Five days after the army stumbled back into the shanty-town camps at Falmouth following the futility of the 'mud march', Lincoln relieved Burnside of his command 'at his own request', replacing him with Hooker. But the president's reservations were made known forcibly to that officer, for with the order appointing him there came also a private letter from Lincoln:

> ... during General Burnside's command of the army you have taken counsel of your ambition and thwarted him as much as you could... I have heard, in such a way as to believe it, of your recently saying that the army and government needed a dictator. Of course it was not for this, but in spite of it, that I have given you the command... What I ask of you now is military success and I will risk the dictatorship... I much fear that the spirit which you have aided to infuse into the army, of criticising their commander and withholding confidence from him, will now turn on you. I shall assist you as far as I can to put it down. Neither you nor Napoleon, if he were alive again, could get any good of an army while such a spirit prevails in it. And now, beware of rashness. Beware of rashness, but with energy and sleepless vigilance go forward and give us victories.[74]

Part at least of the reasoning behind Lincoln's promotion of a man in whom he clearly had something less than total confidence was political. Hooker was not a McClellan man, and was therefore acceptable to the radical wing of Lincoln's cabinet and party. But the president's letter put Hooker on notice. His disloyalty to McClellan, to Burnside and even to the constitution had been registered and the tolerance granted to his predecessors in command would not be extended to him.

And yet Lincoln would forgive anything of a general who seemed to promise the elusive victory. As the miserable winter drew to an end, and if self-confidence was anything to go by, it began to appear that Hooker might be the man. Whatever his faults, he had in him something of McClellan in his ability to administer his army, to see that it was properly rationed and lived in hygienic camps, to train the recruits arriving to replace the appalling wastage of Fredericksburg and the winter, and above all, to inspire the soldiers. With the approach of spring, the Army of the Potomac began to recover its spirits.

Encounter in Pennsylvania – Gettysburg, July 1863

FALTER IN THE WILDERNESS

Fortunate in that he was not expected to take the offensive until the winter had ended, Hooker used his time well. He decided to dispense with the experiment of intermediate headquarters between army and corps. Burnside himself was sent to command the Department of the Ohio, at the start of 1863 a quiet sector of the war, and IX Corps was also detached to the western theatre. Of Hooker's former co-equals as grand division commanders, Sumner refused to serve under him but died on the way to take up a new appointment, and Franklin, too much a McClellan man for the temper of the time, was dismissed, not to be re-employed until eight months later. Hooker put the cavalry of the Army of the Potomac under centralised command (Stoneman) for the first time in the war. For long it had been a favourite taunt of the long-suffering infantry that the one thing they never saw was a dead cavalryman, and this was the first step towards bringing the cavalry of the Union armies up to a standard to enable it to compete with that of the Confederacy. Although Stoneman's first effort, a raid south of the Rapidan crossings, fell far short of the aims set at the start of the operation, this was nevertheless one of a series of limited actions and reconnaissances in force throughout the approach to spring which were designed to keep Lee's army overstretched and on constant alert.

Worse for the Confederacy was the necessity in February of detaching Longstreet and two divisions to counter an amphibious operation mounted from Washington against Newport News, on the James peninsula. Although, as with so many Union efforts during the war, a good strategic design was negated by lack of energy and feeble performance on the ground, this experienced commander and two good battle-hardened divisions would be unavailable to Lee at the start of a campaign when he would again be on the strategic defensive.

At the end of the winter, Lee had no more than 60,000 men on the heights above Fredericksburg. The reason was that, once the threat on the peninsula had been contained, Longstreet's force had to be sent into North Carolina so that its wagons could bring back rations and forage to sustain the army in central Virginia. Not only were there insufficient resources locally to allow the army to live off the country, but the transport system was unable to transport anything. The railway system of the Confederacy after two years of war was in a state of collapse. Rolling stock and track alike were worn out, and the Confederacy had no foundries or workshops to manufacture more. Imports were denied by the blockade and the enlistment into the armies, usually as riflemen, of craftsmen, mechanics and platemen, without any consideration of balancing the competing needs for this skilled manpower, was playing havoc with basic routine maintenance.

For the opening of the campaign, Hooker had more than double Lee's numbers, grouped in one cavalry and seven infantry corps. But for the fourth time in a year, the troops would be going into battle with a new command structure and under new leaders. Only I and II Corps were under the same commanders (Reynolds and Couch) as at Fredericksburg. Of the other corps which had fought in that battle, V and VI would be led by Meade and Sedgwick, both of whom had beyond question proved their competence as generals of division in combat, but III was under Sickles, a politician–general of as yet unproven quality. The two corps, which, throughout the winter, had been left to safeguard the approaches to Washington, were in the main newly recruited and short of battle experience. The XI Corps (Howard) was predominantly made up of German immigrants, and XII Corps (Slocum) had had to be almost entirely reconstituted after its losses at Antietam.

It is beyond the scope of this book to do more than to describe in outline the course of the campaign and battle of Chancellorsville, from 27th April to 5th May, 1863, which set the scene for Lee's second invasion of the North. Yet again, masterly tactical conduct of the battle by Lee out-generalled and morally defeated yet one more Union Army commander, and yet again the Army of

Northern Virginia won a victory against odds of more than two to one in terms of troops available.

Hooker produced a good and imaginative design for the battle. He allocated VI and I Corps, under the direction of Sedgwick, to threaten a series of feint attacks across the river at Fredericksburg, which were intended to persuade Lee that the main assault would be made over the same ground as in December. Meanwhile, V, XI and XII Corps, with Slocum in overall charge, were to march twenty miles upriver to cross the Rappahannock at Kelly's Ford. Then, screened by Pleasanton's cavalry division while the rest of the Cavalry Corps embarked upon a raid in force towards the James, these three corps would return south-eastwards on two parallel axes, Meade on the inner and Slocum and Howard on the outer, crossing the Rapidan at Ely's Ford and Germanna Ford respectively. They would then be joined by the two remaining corps, those of Couch and Sickles, to be brought over the Rappahannock by Hooker himself at the US Ford, a mile downstream from the confluence of the Rappahannock and the Rapidan. All five corps were then to continue the march south-eastwards, behind Lee's prepared positions on the right bank of the Rappahannock, either forcing him out into open country or surrounding him if he chose not to move.

The drawback of Hooker's plan was that it would require the five flanking corps to concentrate within and to cross the Wilderness as one coordinated entity. This area of about thirty square miles south of the Rapidan and west of Banks's Ford was at the time, as it remains today, very thickly wooded, swamp-bound and with vegetation of second-growth jungle density. There were a very few poorly surfaced roads, leading either from the fords or eastwards towards Fredericksburg, and all horse and wheeled vehicle movement was confined to them. Some of these tracks met in a clearing slightly east of centre of the area, where stood the abandoned plantation house of one Chancellor. Six miles further east, beyond a map line drawn due south from Banks's Ford, the country opens out, to become rolling and wooded farmland. It follows that the movement of nearly 80,000 men through the Wilderness would be severely constrained, that no coordinated battle could be fought within the area and that the whole success of Hooker's plan depended upon the unimpeded passage of his assault divisions to the open country to the south of Banks's Ford. Equally, if Lee were to prevent this, he had first to realise that the attacks at Fredericksburg were no more than diversionary. Then, if he were prepared to take the high risk of dividing his army in the face of far superior numbers, he could leave a holding force at Fredericksburg, and move the bulk of his troops some ten miles westwards, to strike Hooker's enveloping force at its most vulnerable, as it emerged from the Wilderness and before Hooker could bring his whole strength to bear. But whether or not Lee guessed Hooker's intentions, he could not remain where he was. He had either to fight, having divided his army, on the tactical offensive against superior numbers, or abandon the line of the Rappahannock and withdraw south, always covering Richmond, to await the return of Longstreet.

On 27th April the Army of the Potomac abandoned its winter quarters, burning the camp structures. The smoke was enough to alert the Army of Northern Virginia to the fact that Hooker was opening his offensive. Slocum's group of corps passed the Rappahannock at Kelly's Ford as planned two days later, but in the move down to the Rapidan crossings the contest between Stuart's cavalry to obtain information and that of Pleasanton to deny it was won by the former. Prisoners were taken from V, XI and XII Corps, their identification simplified by the shoulder badges which Hooker had instituted to enhance corps spirit.

Lee moved at once. Leaving no more than 10,000 men, Early's division plus Barksdale's brigade detached from that of McLaws, to hold the heights above Fredericksburg, the rest of the Army of Northern Virginia marched to deploy facing north-westwards, covering the eastern exits from the Wilderness, on a position about three miles in length.

The battle began on the morning of 1st May, and by early afternoon Meade's leading division had penetrated the Confederate centre, with Couch on his left and Slocum on the outside flank, the latter having nothing but Stuart's cavalry in front of him. The roads to the Rappahannock below Fredericksburg were all but open, and Lee's army faced destruction, but the confused nature of the fighting in and around the thick forestation and undergrowth prevented Hooker from obtaining a clear impression of the battle. This was further obscured by the success of local counter-attacks launched by McLaws and Anderson, which checked the advance. At this point, the self-confident Hooker lost his nerve. To the disgust of Meade and Couch, the corps commanders in contact, he ordered a withdrawal to a giant hedgehog of a defensive position east and south of the Chancellorsville clearing, the perimeter held successively by V, II, XII and XI Corps, and with III Corps in reserve. Hooker had perhaps 75,000 troops in the Wilderness, with more available from Sedgwick's group should they be needed, but the close country prevented proper control, organisation or mutual support.

Facing him, Lee had perhaps two-thirds the numbers and no reserve. The situation had been contained for the time being only, and as darkness fell Lee understood that, if he were to continue to conduct a conventional defence against an attack which Hooker was almost bound to resume the next morning, the superior strength of the Army of the Potomac must tell. Perhaps the idea for the masterstroke of the following day came from a combination of reports from Stuart, to the effect that the western end of the Union position, held by Howard's inexperienced troops, was unguarded, and a chaplain in Jackson's corps who claimed to know the area well and could point out a road which could be used to outflank the Union position from the west.[75] Army and corps commanders refined the detailed plan.

Jackson moved at 4 a.m. on 2nd May with his whole corps, leaving Lee with no more than 17,000 to contain Hooker's exits from the Wilderness. The Confederate Army was now divided into three parts, all of which were faced by a larger number of Union troops, and incapable of concentrating to support each other if attacked. The game was placed even more firmly in Hooker's hands, first by the sight of Jackson's westward march and secondly by the misunderstanding of an order to Early to detach one brigade to reinforce Lee's tenuous blocking position. Early ordered the whole of his force to move, abandoning the heights above Fredericksburg, but Sedgwick was slow to seize his opportunity. The mistake was rectified in the nick of time to allow the vital ground of the December battles, Marye's Heights, Telegraph Hill and Prospect Hill, to be retained.

Having first assessed correctly Jackson's movement for what it was, by wishful thinking, Hooker soon convinced himself that the Confederates had concluded that his position in the Wilderness was too strong to be attacked, and that the Army of Northern Virginia was withdrawing. Nevertheless, he did not order an immediate pursuit, but brought up I Corps from Fredericksburg, with a view to attacking the next day. At 6 p.m. heavy gunfire was heard from the west. Jackson had struck Howard's open flank, catching the unfortunate Germans as they were cooking their evening meal. The whole of XI Corps was routed, losing 2,000 men. Jackson drove on his Corps, and was only stopped by a division of III Corps holding a rare piece of commanding ground, Hazel Grove, no more than a mile from the centre of gravity of the position of the Army of the Potomac, at the Chancellorsville crossroads.

When Jackson's guns opened on XI Corps, Lee ordered a concurrent attack on the eastern half of the Union position, to deny the movement of reinforcements. As night fell, the Army of the Potomac was pressed back into a wedge-shaped position around Chancellorsville. Still the Cromwellian Jackson was not done. He rode forward to reconnoitre a new line of attack, with the intention of cutting off the whole of Hooker's striking force from the

Rapidan crossings, but on returning into his own lines he was shot, his party having been mistaken in the darkness for a Union cavalry patrol. Jackson died of his wounds eight days later. The command on the Confederate left passed to A.P. Hill, who was himself wounded by artillery fire shortly afterwards. The morning of 3rd May broke with Lee having no thought other than to maintain the pressure, while Hooker's eyes were over his shoulder at the Rappahannock crossing site at US Ford, because Confederate cavalry under Fitzhugh Lee had already reached Ely's Ford on the Rapidan. Stuart, succeeding Hill in temporary command of Jackson's corps, started the day well. A blunder by Sickles caused the knoll at Hazel Grove to change hands. Alexander massed a battery of thirty guns which maintained continuous fire into what had become a salient little more than a mile across, centred on Chancellorsville and overcrowded with disorganised elements of five Union corps. The bursting shells set the undergrowth alight, burning to death many of the unevacuated wounded from the fighting of the previous day.

In mid-morning a shell struck the Chancellorsville plantation house, where Hooker had established his headquarters. The army commander was stunned by falling masonry. Evacuated out of the salient, he turned the command over to Couch,[hh] directing that there should be a withdrawal to a perimeter in an arc of approximately four miles south of the Rappahannock crossing at US Ford, with its front on two small streams, Hunting Run and Mineral Spring Run. Even with Howard's corps routed and with over 15,000 men lost on this part of the field, the Army of the Potomac still had far superior numbers, and Meade had expected to be told to resume the attack. The Confederate pressure faltered, partly because of the exhaustion of the troops, and partly because Stuart, cavalry subaltern until two years previously, did not quite have the knack of Jackson or A.P. Hill in driving on his infantry.

But as the right wing of the Army of the Potomac was pulling back into its giant redoubt covering US Ford, there came the news that Sedgwick had attacked across the river at Fredericksburg, and that Early's troops were in flight. Leaving Stuart in charge of the western end of the battle, Lee hurried east with McLaws's division, and by the end of the day had contained Sedgwick's advance in the area of Salem Church, three miles west of Marye's Heights.

On 4th May, the difference in quality of generalship between Hooker and Lee was again demonstrated. Hooker, besought by Sedgwick to send him

---

[hh] Opinions differ about the severity of Hooker's wound. He resumed command on the following morning.

troops to reinforce a major success, sent nothing. Lee, appreciating that for the time being nothing would be achieved if the 25,000 men under Stuart were to attack the 75,000 men of the Union Army covering US Ford, moved Anderson's division to join in an attack which Early had planned on Sedgwick's southern (and open) flank. As night fell on 4th May, Sedgwick had been driven back, and, in response to orders from Hooker withdrew over the Rappahannock during the night. Lee,[ii] returned the following day to the Chancellorsville flank, issued orders for an attack all along the line on 6th May, but during the night Hooker withdrew into an even tighter perimeter round US Ford.

The Confederacy had once again avoided disaster by the narrowest of margins. But in the west, their hold on the Mississippi and the vital link to the states beyond that river was being reduced to the few square miles of the fortifications around Vicksburg, where Grant was poised to open a siege which could have only one end.

In spite of this impending triumph, which by splitting the Confederacy in half would mark the beginning of the end of secession, the news of Chancellorsville brought Lincoln nearer to despair than at any other time in the war. On hearing that Hooker was again north of the Rappahannock, with nothing to show for the loss of another 17,000 men, Lincoln's reaction encapsulated the total dejection of official Washington: 'My God, what will the country say?'[76]

THE SECOND INVASION OF THE NORTH

Chancellorsville had restored the initiative in the eastern theatre to the Army of Northern Virginia, but the overall situation of the Confederacy remained perilous and Lee needed time to reorganise after the losses of the battle. This task was set in train at once. The return of Longstreet gave Lee one of his proven corps commanders, but the death of Jackson at Guiney's Station on 10th May meant that a replacement had to be found for him immediately, and, in order to achieve greater flexibility in the handling of the army, Lee decided to form a third corps. He filled the two vacancies by promoting Ewell, who had commanded a division under Jackson at Second Manassas and who since that battle had been regarded as the latter's alter ego, and A.P. Hill. But the loss of Jackson was irreparable. Longstreet, though a master of the defensive

---

[ii] Between 1st and 5th May Lee covered a greater distance on horseback than Wellington over the three days of Ligny, Quatre Bras and Waterloo, which says much for the fifty-six year-old's stamina.

battle, would never, as Second Manassas had shown, launch an attack until absolutely satisfied that everything was in place, and neither of the two newly promoted lieutenant generals of the Confederacy proved to have the knack of interpreting Lee's intentions, expressed invariably in terms of directive rather than order, relating these to a correct perception of the situation on their own front and combining them into rapid and pulverising attack. The promotions, detachments to other theatres and the heavy casualties of Chancellorsville meant that the Army of Northern Virginia forfeited at least some of the advantage in continuity of higher command it had enjoyed hitherto. For the new campaign, Lee decided upon the following structure:

TABLE VIII

Corps	Commander	Divisional Commanders
I	Longstreet	McLaws, Pickett, Hood
II	Ewell	Johnson, Rodes, Early
III	A.P. Hill	Heth, Pender, R.H. Anderson
Cavalry		Stuart

Lee also had to resist demands from the government in Richmond that some part of his army should be transferred to the western theatre. These were fully justified in that the Confederacy was too weak at all points to resist strong Union pressure wherever it was applied. There was no central reserve, and one threatened front could be strengthened only at the expense of another. But president and general held to their view that, whatever happened elsewhere, the security of Richmond was paramount. Lee was reinforced accordingly, and the return of Longstreet's divisions and the replacement of the 12,000 battle casualties of Chancellorsville gave him slightly over 75,000 men for the coming campaign. But an army of this size could not subsist where it was. After two years of warfare, central Virginia was devastated and could not support the army defending it. There was also the evident increase in war-weariness in the North, and reports of a growing peace party. For all these reasons, and despite the fact that the Army of the Potomac had returned to encamp around Falmouth, Lee determined upon a second invasion of western Maryland. He convinced his government that such a move was the best way of defending the Confederate capital, appreciating, correctly as it proved, that the authorities in Washington would insist that Hooker should also move north-west to keep his army between that of Lee and the Union capital, even though Richmond would be unmasked almost as soon as Lee left Fredericksburg. Lee also assessed correctly that the threat of invasion might draw off some of the forces operating on the Atlantic and Gulf coasts to reinforce the Army of the Potomac. Although unaware of the full extent of the Union losses at Chancellorsville, Lee knew that Hooker's army had been reduced by 20,000 men because of the expiry of their short-term enlistments. His strategic objectives were the same as in the previous year. An advance to the line of the Susquehanna by way of the Cumberland Valley might provoke a decisive battle either in western Maryland or Pennsylvania. One more Union defeat might bind together all the forces in the North which wanted an end to the war, rendering irresistible their demand for a peace which would confer recognition on the Confederacy. Lee proposed to vary his design for the first invasion, in that this time he would enter Maryland west of the Blue Ridge. And if he failed, the overall situation of the Confederacy would be no worse.

The Army of the Potomac returned to its camp sites at Falmouth, aware that it had been defeated but not knowing why, confused and sceptical of the ability of its high command. Nearly half the soldiers had never got into battle at all, and there was a near-universal tendency to blame the 'cowardly Dutchmen' of XI Corps, a sentiment which the solid citizens in command of its divisions and brigades believed was fomented by press leaks from Hooker's staff.[77] Hooker himself first vented his rage on the cavalry. As soon as they returned to Falmouth, he relieved of their commands Stoneman, the corps commander, and Averell, the divisional commander who had had charge of the raid to the James. Not altogether unreasonably; the raid, though it had caused some fluttering in Richmond, had not required Lee to detach one single soldier from his army.

More important, however, was the total collapse of confidence at the top of the Army of the Potomac. Exactly as Lincoln had forecast in his private letter to Hooker less than four months previously, a cabal formed against him which included all the corps commanders. Couch went so far as to refuse to serve under Hooker any longer, and a delegation from the Congressional Joint Committee on the Conduct of the War visited the army, making somewhat heavy-handed attempts to find a general prepared to take Hooker's place. Hooker's staff produced a number of outline plans for consideration by the War Department, but Stanton and Halleck, though by now with as little confidence in Hooker as they had had in Burnside, were reluctant to leave him in command of the army for another major battle. Nevertheless, they could not summon the moral courage needed to recommend his dismissal. The strategic problem for the Union remained the same as it had been for the previous two years. Although on any cold calculation of resources and probabilities, all the North had to do in Virginia was not to lose, the perceived importance of the Confederate capital magnified this into the requirement for a victory in the field, for reasons of prestige and credibility. Every success gained by Lee was a further humiliation for the Union and enhanced the need for the Army of the Potomac to win an undisputed victory. But for the moment, the parallel disagreements between the administration and Hooker and between Hooker and his principal subordinates meant that the army was in a strategic vacuum, waiting for some manifestation of Lee's intentions.

On 3rd June, Lee began the advance upon which the whole fate of the Confederacy depended. Throughout the following week the corps of Ewell and Longstreet moved towards the upper Shenandoah, with Hill retained at Fredericksburg until Lee could be certain that all of the Army of the Potomac had marched to his tune. There was an attempt to disrupt the move by the Union cavalry, now under Pleasanton, and in a sharp cavalry-against-cavalry combat at Brandy Station on 9th June, the Confederates, although ultimately victorious, for the first time in the war did not have a mounted action wholly their own way. There was further cautious manoeuvring throughout the middle of June, culminating in a battle at Winchester on the 15th between Ewell's corps and the perennial Union covering force in the valley. This was won by Ewell and cost the Union Army 4,000 prisoners. On the same day as the action at Winchester, the infantry of the Army of the Potomac began its move. Although forestalled by Lee, they were on an inner arc between the advance of the Army of Northern Virginia and Washington, and, whatever the hiatus in the high command, the soldiers had by now learned how to march. In the heat of midsummer Virginia, the troops achieved distances of which Napoleon's veterans would have approved. On one day, XII Corps covered thirty-three miles,[78] and on 24th June, though the whole of the Army of Northern Virginia was west of the Blue Ridge, Hooker was poised to cross the Potomac, in order to cover Washington from the north-west.

There then followed a rare mistake of control by Lee. While the Army of Northern Virginia was still east of the Blue Ridge, the mission of the cavalry had been to protect its flank. This part of the march accomplished, Lee gave Stuart discretionary orders, further qualified by Longstreet on the right of the advance, to do what damage he could in the rear of the Union Army. Stuart's assumption that Hooker was already north of the Potomac was incorrect.

Although in an action on 28th June at Rockville, a mere ten miles north-west of the defensive perimeter of Washington, Stuart captured 125 supply wagons destined for the Army of the Potomac, he could not return by the way he had come because the whole of the Union Army was now between him and the infantry of the Army of Northern Virginia. Stuart was thus forced to continue on a circuit of the enemy army, as far north as Carlisle in the Cumberland Valley, but his third achievement of this feat not only failed to inflict any further damage but deprived Lee of the eyes and ears vital to him if he were to have choice of time and place of action. Stuart did not return to the main body of the army until the evening of 2nd July; far too late to be of any use and with the horses worn out. For five critical days at the end of June, Lee was without his essential reconnaissance assets.

On the day of the action at Rockville, Lee's army was advancing blind, spread over fifty miles of the Cumberland Valley. Ewell's leading elements were approaching the Susquehanna, with Hill's corps at Cashtown and Longstreet's at Chambersburg following on parallel axes.

Early on the same morning, the Army of the Potomac acquired yet another new commander. The crisis of confidence between Hooker and the War Department boiled over, for much the same reasons as before Antietam. Hooker, having shed stragglers in his rapid march northwards from the Rappahannock, requested reinforcements from the Washington garrison, which were denied him. There then ensued a repetition of the squabble about responsibility for the garrison at Harper's Ferry. Failing to obtain the decision he wanted, Hooker, impetuous on every occasion except at the critical moment of Chancellorsville, dashed off a letter resigning the army command, which Stanton and Halleck accepted at once, no doubt with a very great sigh of relief. Hurried top-level consultations in Washington resulted in the commander of V Corps, Meade, being woken up to be told that he was now the army commander. By no means the senior corps commander, and a man with none of the charisma of McClellan, the flamboyance of Pope or Hooker or the fatherly qualities which IX Corps at least had discerned in Burnside, Meade was unknown in the army as a whole. His own troops knew him as a man of snapping temper, quite unable to suffer fools. He had won the command because of his hard-hitting eagerness to fight, first as a general of division at Antietam and Fredericksburg and then in command of a corps at Chancellorsville. And it is at least probable that Lee, knowing Meade as he had his predecessors in the close fraternity of the pre-war officer corps, respected him more than any of the others.

On the night of 28th/29th June, Lee received the information brought in by Longstreet's 'scout.'[jj] This man said that he had seen two army corps at Frederick, and had heard that two more were around South Mountain. During the morning of 29th June, Lee recalled Ewell, directing him to return either towards Cashtown, the current location of A.P. Hill's Corps, or Gettysburg, ten miles to the west, at his discretion. Gettysburg was at the centre of prosperous Pennsylvania farmland. Served by a branch of the Northern and Central railroad, which connected Baltimore with Harrisburg and the Northern States of the Union, a community of some 2,000 people had grown up at the natural junction of ten roads. These led north and east into Pennsylvania, south-east towards Washington, south into Maryland and south-west and west into West Virginia and Ohio.

Deprived of the information Stuart's cavalry might have provided, Lee delayed further decisions about his concentration until the afternoon. Then, having made up his mind, he said to his staff, 'Tomorrow, gentlemen, we will not move to Harrisburg as we expected, but will go over to Gettysburg to see what General Meade is after.' And shortly afterwards, he added, 'General Meade will commit no blunder on my front, and if I make one he will make haste to take advantage of it.'[79]

Longstreet was directed to leave one division, that of Pickett, to guard the rear of the army, and with the rest of his corps to follow up A.P. Hill's advance towards Gettysburg. These movements were intended to bring the three corps of the Army of Northern Virginia within mutually supporting distance, in an area particularly well served by roads and where for some time they could live off the country.[kk] On the following day, 30th June, Hill reported that he was in place between Cashtown and Gettysburg. A brigade had been sent forward into the little town, seeking to obtain boots from a shoe factory there, to replace those worn out on the march from the Rappahannock. They had encountered parties of Union cavalry, and had heard drums beating beyond the town.

[jj] See Chapter IV.

[kk] Lee had issued stringent orders about behaviour towards the civilian population, which were enforced. Goods were formally requisitioned, and if Confederate money in payment was refused, a receipt given for fair value. There seems to have been very little indiscriminate looting, at least by Lee's troops. The same was not true of stragglers from the Army of the Potomac.

THREE DAYS OF BATTLE

Gettysburg was the prototype of the 'encounter' battle. Neither army commander wanted to fight a major engagement at that place or time, as there was no critical asset to be captured or defended, and yet, once the battle began, it was continued until the strength and resources of one of the protagonists were exhausted. Meade, barely seventy-two hours in command of the Army of the Potomac when the battle opened, might well have wanted more time to impose his own ideas on the organisation and tactical doctrine of his new command, and to make himself more widely known to the troops.

During the last days of June, the march northwards into Maryland had continued almost under residual momentum, until, on 30th June, six of Meade's seven corps, the same as had fought at Chancellorsville but with two new corps commanders,[ll] had reached the line of the Monocacy and its tributary, Pipe Creek. There was a screen and covering force to the north-west, Buford's cavalry division watching the roads leading to Gettysburg, with I Corps (Reynolds) in support, eight miles behind Buford at Emmitsburg. Meade was thus well placed to block any approach which Lee might make towards Washington[mm] or Baltimore, and poised to either take in flank a continued march towards the Susquehanna or cut off Lee's retreat towards the Potomac fords.

Lee was moving blind in enemy country. Deprived by Stuart's impetuosity of his main source of information about the enemy's whereabouts, he had had to allocate the only brigade of cavalry remaining with the Army of Northern Virginia to screen Ewell's advance towards Harrisburg. It follows that the Confederate Army was not only vulnerable to surprise but also, bereft of intelligence, would have difficulty in bringing its opponent to battle at a time and place of Lee's choosing. Although his strength, around 77,500, was more nearly equal to the 93,500 under Meade than in any other battle fought between the two armies throughout the entire war, Lee's least desirable option for battle was a tactical offensive, even on ground which Meade's troops would have had little or no time to prepare. Far preferable choices would be either tactical defence of a position which the North had to attack, as at Antietam or Fredericksburg, or, having concentrated his own army, to fall upon an isolated wing of the Army of the Potomac, as he had done in the peninsula and at Second Manassas. For him to have to attack Meade on

---

[ll] Hancock for Couch in command of II Corps, and Sykes taking over V Corps from Meade.

[mm] Halleck nevertheless found it necessary to send a nagging telegram to Meade, to the effect that he had strayed too far west of the capital.

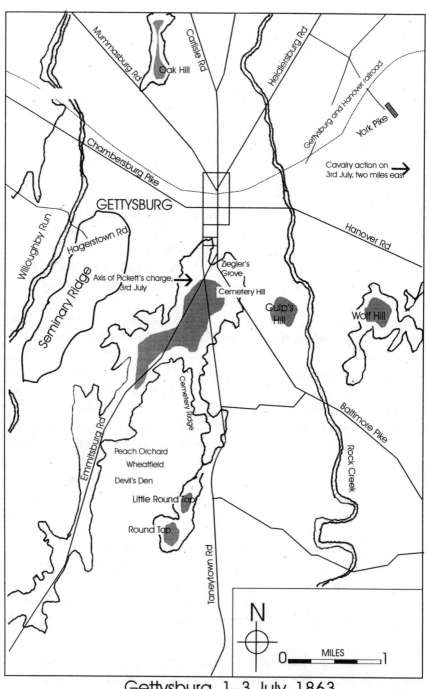

Gettysburg, 1–3 July, 1863

ground not of his own choosing would leave the South relying for victory upon the moral domination Lee had established over every previous Union commander he had fought, and on the greater staying power and hardihood of his troops.

The skirmish on the afternoon of 30th June indicated to Buford that he had caught something, but also that he needed to remain on the ground until the following morning to find out what it might be. Buford was one of the more competent Union cavalry commanders coming to the fore at last after two years of war. He deployed his division over a three mile arc on the high ground, Seminary Ridge, west of Gettysburg and Oak Hill to the north. Warning his troopers to remain alert for 'campfires at night and dust in the morning',[80] he sent off a contact report to Meade and Reynolds. Meade directed Reynolds to move up to Gettysburg, and gave similar orders to XI Corps (Howard) to follow in support.

Day One:
The battle started at daybreak. Heth's division of A.P. Hill's corps, moving to secure the south-eastern limit of Lee's desired concentration area, bumped into Buford's men, who were fighting, dismounted, in a prolonged skirmish line. The rolling ground was all in favour of a defence armed with breech-loaded repeating carbines and Buford, although supported by only one artillery battery, held off Heth and the second division of Hill's corps to be committed, that of Pender, without much difficulty. Reynolds, arriving on the ground ahead of his corps, deployed the first brigades which came up on Seminary Ridge to reinforce Buford, but found his right flank under attack from the area of Oak Hill by the leading division of Ewell's corps, under Rodes. Not a moment too soon, the first division of Howard's corps arrived at Gettysburg. While Reynolds was deploying these troops in prolongation of his own line, he was shot dead by a Confederate sniper.[nn]

At much the same time, Lee arrived on the battlefield at Seminary Ridge, having directed that priority for routes should be given to Ewell's corps ahead of that of Longstreet. The situation as presented to him was that Rodes was heavily engaged on Oak Hill, and that the other two divisions of Hill's corps were poised to support a resumption of the attack by Heth. Lee's immediate reaction was not to bring on a general engagement without Longstreet's corps,

---

[nn] Reynolds was a fine officer, and a gentleman. As Meade's corps commander from after Antietam until Meade himself received a corps command after Fredericksburg, Reynolds had shown no resentment at the promotion of his former subordinate over his head, and indeed had gone out of his way to show his loyalty to the new army commander.[81]

or before the whole of Ewell's corps had come up. But the decision was taken from him almost at once. Early had marched his division to the sound of the guns, and was attacking on the left of Rodes. The opportunity was not to be lost. Lee ordered a general attack with the five divisions immediately available; and I Corps, now under Doubleday, and the unfortunate Germans of XI Corps broke against superior numbers.[oo]

Driven off Seminary Ridge and Oak Hill and back through Gettysburg, they began to improvise a defensive position along Cemetery Ridge, which extends south from the town parallel to and about three-quarters of a mile east of Seminary Ridge, and along the shank of high ground running at a right angle east of the town, to the small eminence of Culp's Hill.[pp] On hearing the news of the death in action of Reynolds, Meade had sent the newly promoted II corps commander, Hancock, to take charge of the battle until he could arrive himself; and XII and III Corps had also been set on the route for Gettysburg. Nevertheless, for perhaps an hour in the late afternoon of 1st July, the opportunity existed for the Army of Northern Virginia to convert the tactical success already gained into the annihilation of two corps of the Army of the Potomac, which might possibly have led to the defeat in detail of the rest on the following day.

Lee sent to Ewell the sort of order which would have been enough for Jackson, to take the high ground in front of him, i.e. Culp's Hill, 'if practicable'.[82] Ewell demurred. Rodes's division had lost heavily during the day, one of Early's newly promoted brigadiers had been unduly alarmist about what was on his front, and, all in all, Ewell felt that if he himself were to attack there should be a simultaneous attack on Cemetery Ridge. It is beyond question that Ewell allowed himself to be intimidated by difficulties which would not have deterred Jackson, and it is likewise beyond question that if Culp's Hill had been taken that evening, Cemetery Ridge could not have been held on 2nd July. But Hill's corps was in no shape to mount another attack: the corps commander himself, incapacitated by illness, had not shown to advantage during the day[qq] and his divisions, having been in battle since early morning, needed a pause for rest and replenishment. Longstreet's troops were

---

[oo] For a variety of reasons, including the different manning and organisation policies, and relative losses through straggling, the Confederate infantry corps at Gettysburg were double the size of those of the Union.

[pp] For a description of the ground, see Appendix C.

[qq] Although without equal as a hard-driving general of division, future events would demonstrate that A.P. Hill had been promoted above his ceiling.

not yet on the battlefield, but Longstreet himself was. He did not like the concept of a frontal attack and suggested, not for the first time, that Lee should seek to manoeuvre the army round Meade's southern flank. Lee overruled him, with the words, 'If the enemy is there we must attack him,'[83] but the stubborn Longstreet continued to hanker after his own design, and on both the next two days was excessively slow to carry out the orders given to him by Lee.

Against his better judgement, Lee had to defer to this unanimous view. No further attack would be mounted that night, but the assault would be resumed on the following morning. After the events of the day, this would be in the circumstances least favourable to the Army of Northern Virginia – a tactical offensive against a position which the Army of the Potomac had been given the precious night-hours to reinforce and prepare.

On the other side of the hill, Hancock, reputation established ever since the peninsula as a thrusting formation commander, had taken over the control of the battle despite the protests of his senior, the brave but somewhat uninspired and uninspiring Howard. Hancock's remit from Meade had been to stabilise the situation, return and report. With the leading divisions of XII and III Corps approaching Cemetery Ridge, the immediate circumstances were secure enough. But I and XI Corps had been hard hit. The 24th Michigan, which had joined the army after Antietam at the full established strength of 1,000, had brought 496 men to battle at Gettysburg,[r] and was by this time the largest regiment in the celebrated 'Iron Brigade', the First Brigade of the First Division of the First Army Corps of the Army of the Potomac. On the evening of 1st July, only ninety-seven men were left with the colours, a loss rate of eighty per cent during the day, and the whole brigade was reduced to a strength of 600. The combined entry-into-battle strength of I and XI Corps, approximately 20,000, was down to no more than 5,000 effectives at nightfall.[84] Nevertheless, Hancock could estimate the potential strength of the fish-hook-shaped ridge east and south of the little country town. Disregarding the complaints of Doubleday, acting commander of I Corps, about the exhaustion of his troops, Hancock forcefully directed him to strengthen the position on Culp's Hill with one division and returned to recommend to Meade that the battle should be continued. Let the Army of Northern Virginia batter itself to pieces in trying to force as good a tactical-defensive position as the Army of the Potomac was likely ever to find.

---

[r] Fredericksburg, the winter at Falmouth, Chancellorsville and straggling had cost this regiment half its original strength.

Day Two:

Hancock's appreciation was correct. By any normal standards, the Army of Northern Virginia had lost its opportunity, and if it were now to win the battle there would have to be some disastrous mistake or collapse of confidence at the top level of the Army of the Potomac.

The morning of 2nd July was similar to the previous day – hot, sultry and oppressive – but before the worst of the noon heat Meade had all but one of his corps on the ground. Culp's Hill had been transformed into a giant bastion during the night, the New England lumbermen in Slocum's Corps having cut down trees to form breastworks. The XII Corps held the eastern face of Culp's Hill, with its front on Rock Creek, running southwards to join the Monocacy. Wadsworth's division of I Corps, sent to Culp's Hill the previous evening at Hancock's insistence, faced north and Howard's XI Corps held the shank in the ridge as far as the town cemetery of Gettysburg. Cemetery Ridge itself was held for two miles from the north by the balance of I Corps, in command of which Newton had replaced Doubleday, and III Corps, under politician-general Sickles. Meade's former command, V Corps, now led by Sykes, was in reserve and placed to reinforce any part of the front. By midday, leading elements of Sedgwick's VI Corps were also approaching Cemetery Ridge, having covered thirty-five miles non-stop throughout the night and morning to reach the battlefield, but the corps as a whole would not be operational on the ground until evening. Nevertheless, Meade had passed his first test, though it was perhaps less stringent than that faced by some of his predecessors. Lee's intentions had been evaluated correctly, and the whole of the Army of the Potomac was on hand to counter them.

If Meade's position had a weakness, it was that the left (southern) end of the fish-hook was in the air. A two mile walk southwards along Cemetery Ridge affords progressively less commanding views to the west, until the ground again rises steeply, to two hills, Little Round Top and Round Top, which dominate the shallow valley between Seminary Ridge and Cemetery Ridge. Meade concluded that his line would be too far stretched if he took in these features. Little Round Top was occupied only by a signal detachment and there were no troops at all on the larger hill. To this extent, Longstreet's argument for a flanking manoeuvre round the south of the Army of the Potomac was valid, but, without any cavalry to screen the advance and provide timely information, the security of such a move would have been highly questionable.

The more Sickles looked at the ground which he had been told to take up, the less he liked it. Extrovert lawyer and politician, he had, before the war, as a wronged husband, killed a man in a duel, evading conviction for murder with a plea of temporary insanity. On the morning of 2nd July he again took the law into his own hands. He brought III Corps about a third of a mile forward from Cemetery Ridge, but on to a position where its command of the ground to the west was no better.[ss] As at Antietam, commonplace country features known to generations of local inhabitants as the 'wheatfield' and the 'peach orchard' would gain for all time the dignity of capital letters, and on the southern flank of the position chosen by Sickles for himself, at the western foot of the steep rise leading to Little Round Top, there was an area of broken ground, rocks and twisted vegetation called 'Devil's Den'. In justice to Sickles, he attempted to obtain authority for his unilateral decision. He went to army headquarters, established in a two-room cottage on the south-eastern edge of Gettysburg, and sought to persuade Meade that III Corps should deploy on the ground chosen by himself. Meade, disliking Sickles in any event, perhaps having the contempt of the professional soldier for the unproven amateur, directed Sickles to carry out the orders he had been given, but relented sufficiently to send back with him the commander of the army artillery, Hunt, to observe and report.

Returned to his corps area, Sickles was further disconcerted to find that Buford's cavalry, supposed to be guarding his open flank, had been withdrawn through a misunderstanding on the part of Pleasanton, the Cavalry Corps commander. Sickles received at the same time a report from his skirmish line that Confederate troops were moving in strength across his front. Jumping to the conclusion that he was being outflanked again, as he had been at Chancellorsville, Sickles asked Hunt to authorise a further move westward by III Corps. Hunt told him that this decision was a matter for the army commander, and rode off to inform Meade. Sickles advanced nonetheless, further isolating his corps from the rest of the army. The unsupported move was so obviously ill-advised that the experienced General Gibbon, veteran artillery man before the war and commander of the Iron Brigade until elevated to command of a division, now commanding the left flank division of II Corps' defensive position, wondered whether he had failed to receive a general order to advance. News of the disobedience of Sickles brought Meade himself to the ground. He was directing Sickles to return to the position which III Corps had originally been told to occupy when the full fury of a Confederate attack broke. Meade, fully realising the danger implicit in an unplanned withdrawal when in contact, particularly if this difficult manoeuvre

---

[ss] A typical mistake by an inexperienced soldier without a natural eye for the ground.

were to be conducted by the incompetent Sickles, told the latter to remain where he was, and ordered Hunt to bring up all the army reserve artillery in order to prevent the annihilation of III Corps.

The Confederate attack, not launched until the afternoon was well advanced, went in much later than Lee would have wished and the delay was caused entirely by the recalcitrant Longstreet. With Pickett's division still detached as rearguard, and still pushing his preference for a flank move, Longstreet had made no effort to hasten the attack which Lee wished him to make, on the axis of the Emmitsburg Pike. Having, as early as 9 a.m., expressed his firm wish to Longstreet that this attack should be mounted as soon as possible, Lee had ridden round to his left flank to direct Ewell to be ready to attack Culp's Hill as soon as it was evident from the sound of the guns that Longstreet was engaged. Lee also ordered Hill to join the assault, by a converging attack on the angle of the Union position on Cemetery Hill once it was apparent that Longstreet's attack had begun. Thus Ewell and Hill were both expected to wait for Longstreet, but because of the latter's reluctance to carry out his orders, the whole morning and most of the afternoon of 2nd July went by with no more than skirmishes between outposts and occasional bursts of artillery fire. It is beyond question that the further loss of time was to the advantage of the Union Army because it allowed more time for the improvement of their defensive positions and gave a pause to the troops rushed up by forced march. And when Longstreet's attack at last went in on Sickles' isolated corps, Ewell and Hill did no more than provide artillery support. Both corps commanders would attack later in the day with enormous gallantry, but without coordination. Each of the three Confederate attacks, delivered separately, nearly achieved success, but because the blows were not simultaneous the Army of the Potomac, though swaying with each punch, did not break. The systematic control which had saved Antietam and won Chancellorsville for the South was no longer evident, partly because of the irreparable loss of Jackson, partly because of the inexperience of newly-promoted formation commanders, but, most of all, because of the reluctance of Longstreet.

If Longstreet had been dilatory in coming into action, his troops more than made up for it by the ferocity of their attack. The left flank of Sickles's position, in the Devil's Den, was driven in by Hood's Division, led by two Georgia regiments, the 9th and 15th, which between them lost 360 men out of 677.[63] The way to the summit of Little Round Top was open. Had the Confederates been able to consolidate on this feature to the point at which they could have deployed artillery, the whole of Cemetery Ridge would have been enfiladed and the battle won.

The situation was saved for the Union by Meade's chief engineer, Brigadier General Gouverneur Warren. Meade had wanted Warren as his chief of staff instead of Butterfield, whom he had inherited from Hooker, but Warren himself had dissuaded him, on the grounds that a change of both army commander and chief of staff with a battle imminent would be too disruptive. It is possible that Warren found himself at the critical point at the right time because he was acting as a second pair of eyes for Meade on the southern half of the battlefield. Evaluating the situation at once, Warren persuaded Sykes, moving on Meade's orders to fill the gap opened by Sickles, to send a brigade of infantry to the summit of Little Round Top. This vital ground was held by the barest of margins; the left flank regiment of the whole army, 20th Maine under professor-of-theology-turned-soldier Joshua Chamberlain, settling the matter with a bayonet charge when their ammunition had run out. A further Confederate attack on the weak link on the northern ridge leading up to Little Round Top was also beaten off by the initiative of Warren, who took responsibility for detaching another regiment of V Corps to plug the opening gap. A battery of Union artillery, manhandled up a slope too steep and broken for the gun teams, finally secured the critical *point d'appui* at the southern end of the Army of the Potomac's defence line.

The battle round Devil's Den, the peach orchard and the wheatfield between Longstreet's troops and those of Sickles and Sykes continued to rage until dark and the exhaustion of the soldiers on a day of boiling midsummer heat. Sickles had a leg shot off and III Corps was driven beyond the ridge into the Rock Creek valley, except for one division kept firmly in hand by its commander, Humphreys. This corps took no further part in the battle and was never reconstituted. The V Corps, thrown in piecemeal to hold the line, was also in some disorder and for an hour the integrity of the defence of Cemetery Ridge depended upon the last guns of the artillery reserve, firing at point-blank range. Meade placed Hancock in charge of the southern half of the battlefield, and the slackening of the Confederate attack allowed V Corps to be gathered and deployed at last on the ground which Sickles should never have left. As the leading elements of VI Corps came up, they prolonged the defence line south and east of the Round Tops, and the position became too strong for Longstreet's two divisions to break. McLaws on the left and Hood on the right continued to press nevertheless. As evening was falling, Hancock saw the opportunity for a local counter-attack. The 1st Minnesota took 262 men into this action and lost all but forty-seven.[85] By the end of the day, 4,000 men lay dead or wounded in the square mile of ground for which Longstreet and Sickles had contended.

But the battle in the south had slackened by the time that Ewell first and then A.P. Hill launched their belated attacks. Ewell's assault was not only late but badly coordinated, in that only Johnson's division got into action. But yet again, the total commitment of the Confederate soldiers who did engage nearly managed to atone for the lapses of command and staff work in a corps headquarters sadly missing the single-minded direction of Jackson. Johnson penetrated to the saddle between Culp's Hill and Cemetery Hill, hitting the weak junction point between Wadsworth and Howard, and also lapped southwards round Slocum's position. The fighting on Culp's Hill continued long after dark, and it was perhaps here that the Civil War reached its most poignant and tragic moment. Johnson's division included a regiment recruited from Maryland, and it came up against a regiment from the same state in the service of the Union. The Confederate Marylanders, attacking at all hazards a defence which had had twenty-four hours to prepare its position, lost fifty-two men killed, and 140 wounded from an entry-into-battle strength of 400. The percentage loss of a sister regiment in Johnson's division, the 3rd North Carolina, was even higher; twenty-nine killed and 127 wounded out of 312.[86]

But Ewell's attack had been held by a defence which had not needed to call for reinforcements, and much the same happened to A.P. Hill's assault, which went in as darkness was falling. It will be remembered that the divisions of Heth and Pender had borne the brunt of the first day's fighting on Seminary Ridge. Both generals had been wounded, and the divisions had needed the whole of 2nd July to reorganise. Thus, only Anderson's division was available, and, like Johnson's on Culp's Hill, this formation fought to the limit. Its assault carried it to Ziegler's Grove, a small wood on Cemetery Ridge, directly south of Gettysburg and at the junction between the left of Howard's corps and two divisions of I Corps, under Newton. Hancock was forced to detach a brigade to bolster Howard, but the shallow re-entrant running north-east from the main valley towards the copse was enfiladed by Gibbon's division, moved over to the right of Hancock's corps. A local counter-attack as night was falling by the remnant of the Iron Brigade, reduced to less than half a regiment in numbers, forced Anderson's men to withdraw.

Throughout the night, with the armies in close contact and sentries with perceptions dulled by exhaustion, there were sporadic outbursts of fire, and hand-to-hand skirmishes between parties looking for water in the little streams which provided a natural demarcation line between the opposing forces. Towards midnight, Meade called a conference of his corps commanders. At similar critical moments in the past, McClellan had drawn back and Hooker had lost his nerve. The Army of the Potomac had been hit at least as hard as in any previous battle, having taken some 20,000 casualties, and, if precedent were any guide, with a further half as many again lost from the combat strength which would be available the next morning. Meade turned the meeting into a formal council of war, asking each of his principal subordinate commanders in turn for his opinion, which Butterfield recorded. None spoke in favour of an attack, but none advocated withdrawal either. Meade laconically summed up the meeting thus: 'Such then is the decision.'[87]

This time, the Army of the Potomac would remain on the ground it had held at such enormous cost. And, because of the strength afforded to a prepared defence against infantry attacking unprotected up open and rolling slopes, it was the onus rather than the initiative which this collective decision had handed to Lee. As the generals left the meeting, Meade warned Gibbon to expect the full weight of the Confederate attack on the following day to fall upon the centre of the Union defence.

Day Three:
Perhaps Lee could have broken off the battle at this point and withdrawn over the Potomac fords. There is no evidence that he gave this course any consideration whatever. If the Confederacy were to survive, his army had to defeat the Army of the Potomac. However unfavourable the present tactical situation, in which Lee was compelled to attack, over open ground, a warned and prepared defence with numbers superior to his own, it might never be possible for him to create a better set of circumstances. If his subordinates on the first evening of the battle had allowed their own difficulties to obscure those of the enemy on the other side of the hill, Lee had not, and perhaps he was already regretting the fact that he had allowed himself to be over-persuaded. More serious was the reduction of his conduct-of-battle options to one. There would have to be a frontal assault against some part of the centre of the Union line, without any possibility of surprise, which could succeed only if an overwhelming superiority of strength, manpower and firepower were brought to bear on a single point.

Meade's army now occupied a position resembling a reversed question mark, with its base on the Round Tops, the stem along Cemetery Ridge and the arc around Culp's Hill. The critical *point d'appui* of the Round Tops had been consolidated, to the point at which Sedgwick's corps and Kilpatrick's cavalry division were deployed facing southwards, ideally placed to take in flank the right-handed manoeuvre by Lee's army which Longstreet was still continuing to advocate. But had this option existed on 2nd July, the arrival of

Sedgwick's corps had unquestionably foreclosed it by the next morning. The final piece of Meade's jigsaw was in place.

Thus, the southern end of the Union position was clearly too strong to attack with any prospect of success. Similarly, the arc from Cemetery Hill, around Culp's Hill to Slocum's corps, now deployed to face eastwards along Rock Creek, was also too strong for anything but a diversion. The main attack would therefore have to go in against Cemetery Ridge. And if Sickles on the previous day had doubted the westward command of the ground for the mile or so along the ridge north of the steep slope up to Little Round Top, the same possible weakness was evident to Lee. From the point at which Lee made his reconnaissance, where the Virginia Memorial now stands, the proposition does not look wholly impossible. But it would be necessary for the axis of the attack to be set north of the debris of the battle fought on the previous day for the peach orchard, wheatfield and Devil's Den. No plan makes itself. But, on this occasion, Lee's one option was to order feint attacks against the extremities of the Union line, Ewell's corps against Culp's Hill and the divisions of McLaws and Hood from Longstreet's corps against the Round Tops, to try and divert Union reserves, while his one fresh division, and whatever could be cobbled together from A.P. Hill's corps, attacked in the centre.

It will be recalled that Pickett's division of Longstreet's corps had not been committed thus far to the battle, because it was guarding the rear of the Army of Northern Virginia against a Union thrust from the direction of Harper's Ferry. Pickett would be joined in the attack by the two divisions of A.P. Hill's corps, uncommitted on 2nd July but much reduced by their casualties on the previous day, Heth's division, now under Pettigrew, and Pender's division commanded by Trimble. Stuart's cavalry had returned at last to the army on the previous evening. Since the action at Rockville on 28th June their anticlockwise circuit round the Army of the Potomac had taken them over 100 miles in four days and men and horses were worn out. Nevertheless, a flanking move on a narrow arc north of Gettysburg would bring Stuart's troopers east of Rock Creek, in a position to perform a terrible execution if the Union defence on Cemetery Ridge did not hold, and, even failing this, there might be rich pickings from the Union logistic trains. Given the strategic imperative to attack, Lee had no other tactical option.

There can never be too much time for the preparation of a defensive position. Entrenchments and abbatis can be strengthened, alternative and depth positions prepared, fields of fire improved, ammunition stockpiled on gun lines to supplement ready-use holdings and artillery dug in. It follows that any delay in mounting an attack is justified only if the increments to the assaulting force substantially exceed the improvements the defence can make in the extra time afforded to them. The matter cannot be reduced to a mathematical formula because every one of the numerous quantities in the equation varies with each situation, but the historic rule of thumb, that the attacking force should have a three to one superiority at the decisive point, was already proving inadequate. At the Siege of Petersburg a year later, the required ratio would be found to be nearer six to one. The situation on the third morning of Gettysburg demanded that the Army of Northern Virginia should attack as soon as possible, desirably with the diversionary attacks on the flanks going in slightly ahead of the main assault. But even the timing had gone from Lee's control.

It was perhaps inevitable that, with the armies in such close contact, one of the clashes between the outposts or watering parties would escalate into a full-scale fight. On Ewell's front, soon after daybreak on 3rd July, just such a skirmish developed into an artillery duel involving all the guns in range on both sides. Ewell attacked with his infantry, but, with coordination impeded by superior Union firepower, his divisions attacked separately and by mid-morning were fought out. During this scrappy phase of the battle Ewell had received a message to the effect that Longstreet would not be ready to attack before 10 a.m., but by the time he received this the battle was out of his hands. Similarly, on the right, the divisions of Hood and McLaws attacked too soon and achieved nothing against a Union defence now anchored securely south of the peach orchard. The assault in the centre would go in unsupported.

The delay in mounting this attack was caused entirely by the obstinacy of Longstreet. He did nothing to hasten Pickett's move to his forming-up point behind Seminary Ridge, and made a final attempt to persuade Lee to manoeuvre round to the south of the Round Tops. Again Lee overruled him. Elements of three divisions, the whole of Pickett's and what was left of Heth's and Pender's, were to be committed to the last hope for the Confederacy. Pickett's division was on the right of the assault, attacking in two echelons, with the brigades of Kemper and Garnett forward, and that of Armistead in support. All of Pettigrew's four reduced brigades were in the first line, three of them under temporary commanders, Pettigrew himself having succeeded to the division, Archer captured and Brockenborough wounded on the first day of the battle. The division now commanded by Trimble had two brigades in the first line of the assault, under Lowrance, another who had risen to command during the battle, and Lane, with Willcox in support. The one remaining division, that of Anderson, much reduced, like the rest of Hill's corps, by battle casualties, was in reserve.[88] Supporting the attack was the whole of the artillery of the Army of Northern Virginia except for the guns of Ewell's corps, 130 guns under the commander of the artillery reserve, Alexander.

Sources differ about the time at which the Confederate bombardment started and for how long it lasted. At some time between 1 and 2 p.m., Alexander's guns opened fire, seeking to drive the Union batteries off Cemetery Ridge, and paying particular attention to a concentration of eighteen guns firing from Ziegler's Grove, focal point of the attack. Estimates of the duration of the bombardment vary from half an hour to two hours, but, given that the normal deliberate rate of fire of one round per gun per minute was probably exceeded, and having regard to the limited time available to stockpile ammunition on the gun positions, the shorter estimate seems the more likely. Alexander had already expressed his concern to Longstreet that he would run out of ammunition before the infantry could assault, and stocks were running low when at last, at around 2.30, the guns at Ziegler's Grove were seen to be coming out of action. Alexander sent a report to Longstreet, and Pickett, standing with his corps commander, asked for confirmation of the order to attack. Longstreet, according to Lee's biographer, slowly nodded his head, 'as if the effort cost him his heart's blood.'[89]

The assault divisions came over the crest of Seminary Ridge, and, in the fashion of the time and as though it were a ceremonial parade, dressed their ranks[tt] around the colours of the forty-four regiments committed to the attack. Field officers were ordered to attack dismounted, to avoid drawing fire. For perhaps 200 yards, the lines advanced in silence. Then the Union artillery opened fire. Notwithstanding the weight of Alexander's preliminary bombardment, Hunt still had some eighty guns in action along Cemetery Ridge, too many for 15,000 infantrymen advancing over half a mile of open ground in full daylight. As the first assault echelon crossed the Gettysburg–Emmitsburg road, it came within range of the Union infantry. A split-rail fence disorganised the pace and cohesion of the attack, and as the brave men climbed over it they made perfect targets for Hunt's artillery and Hancock's infantry. Pickett and his subordinate commanders pressed the attack to the limit, as far as the stone wall along the crest of Cemetery Ridge. Armistead and

---

[tt] Tactical doctrine then and for the next fifty years required attacks to be made in continuous unbroken lines, to reduce the risk of enfilade fire by 'stay-behind' defenders cut off from their main position.

perhaps 150 men of his brigade fought their way over this in hand-to-hand combat, but not one returned. Armistead fell mortally wounded.

It so happened that Armistead and Hancock had, immediately before the war, been serving together under Albert Sidney Johnston in the Western Department, and the two men had become friends. At the outbreak of war, Johnston and Armistead had gone with the Confederacy, Hancock with the Union. With his dying breath, Armistead requested a Union soldier to take the few personal belongings with him to Hancock, who, when he received the watch, spurs and other small possessions, was himself lying wounded a bare 200 yards from where his friend of pre-war days had fallen.[90]

From his vantage point Lee could see that the attack had failed, and there were no more troops left to commit. Of the 15,000 who had gone over Seminary Ridge that afternoon, 7,000 failed to return. Neither then nor at any time afterwards did Lee seek to blame anyone but himself for the defeat. Pickett returned distraught. Garnett's brigade had lost 941 out of its entry-into-battle strength of 1,400, the division under Pettigrew was reduced to 1,600 men, and one infantry company, which had crossed the Potomac less than three weeks earlier at its full strength of 100 was down to one officer and eight men.[91] Perhaps the worst loss of all was in the 26th North Carolina, of Heth's division. Taking part in the fighting throughout 1st July on Seminary Ridge and in Pickett's charge, this regiment lost 588 men out of 820.[63]

Lee met Pickett's reproaches with the words:

Come, General Pickett, this has been my fight and upon my shoulders rests the blame. The men and officers of your command have written the name of Virginia as high today as it has ever been written before.[92]

The phlegmatic Meade, imperturbable as ever under fire, had watched the attack being beaten off. At much the same time as Lee was trying to console Pickett, his one comment was, 'Thank God.'

The armies drew off, exhausted. Concurrently with Pickett's charge, the cavalry had met in an encounter two miles east of Rock Creek, where, for the first time in the war, the Union cavalry had the better of the action. But in all the Army of the Potomac, there was neither infantry regiment nor cavalry squadron with the energy left to follow up the repulse of Pickett's assault. The day ended, as after Antietam, in uneasy calm with the armies still in presence.

THE AFTERMATH

On 4th July, Lee began the evacuation of his wounded. Under the escort of Imboden's cavalry brigade, the column of ambulances, farm carts, and any other conveyance for which horse and harness could be found, stretched for seventeen miles. At around midday the weather broke. The battle throughout had been fought in extreme heat and the troops on both sides had suffered agonies of thirst, but now at least this pain passed from them. For nearly a week afterwards there was continuous heavy rain. The Union Army had established temporary field hospitals on the low ground between the Baltimore Pike and Rock Creek, where the wounded, under canvas and lying on straw if they were lucky, awaited evacuation, a process delayed because Stuart's troopers had torn up the spur railway link to Hanover and the main line to Baltimore. The meadows flooded and many of the wounded were drowned. Movement off the paved roads became an impossibility, as the farmland turned into a quagmire.[uuu]

The following day, Lee began his withdrawal. Of the 77,500 men brought across the Potomac in mid-June, over a third, 28,000 in all, had been killed, wounded or taken prisoner. The Army of the Potomac was in no better shape. Meade's strength returns the morning after the battle showed that there were no more than 51,000 men present with their units. The Army of the Potomac had suffered 23,000 casualties and a further 15,000 men had been 'blown loose' from their regiments. Between 5th and 7th July the Army of Northern Virginia was ushered rather than pursued out of Maryland, by way of Williamsport, some ten miles upriver from the Sharpsburg peninsula.

The failure to mount an energetic pursuit irritated Lincoln, who felt that the Army of the Potomac had again missed its opportunity to destroy the Union's most serious opponent, and Meade's initial report, to the effect that the enemy had 'been driven from our soil'[93] did him no good with a president who was fighting the war to 'preserve, protect and defend' the Union, and who never at any time admitted that any part of the soil of the United States belonged to an enemy. Meade was nevertheless retained in command and by August the two armies were again facing each other along the line of the Rapidan and lower Rappahannock.

Lee tendered his resignation to Davis, who declined it in a letter:

[uuu] The author can vouch for this, from personal experience of just one day's rain on the good solid Pennsylvania farmland when attending the annual re-enactment on the anniversary of the battle in 1995. This also followed a few days of oppressive summer heat.

To ask me to substitute you by someone in my judgement more
fit to command, or who would possess more of the confidence of
the army or of the reflecting men of the country, is to demand an
impossibility.[94]

The nearest Lee ever came to an excuse for the defeat was years later, after the
war: 'If I had had Stonewall Jackson with me, so far as man can see, I should
have won the battle of Gettysburg.'[94]

This judgement, by one of the greatest commanders of all time, may well
have been right. The enormous gamble had failed, but as the only course
which might have won independence for the Confederate States, the attempt
had to be made. It had come breathtakingly close to success.

The War Between the States – Civil, Total and Modern

Any civil war is by definition total, in that there can be no compromise
solution. Either the breakaway movement succeeds and another new nation is
formed, or it fails and the original entity is re-established, though perhaps set
on a different course. In the War Between the States there could be no
compromise between the war aims of the two leaders. Lincoln never wavered
from his goal; the preservation of the Union. Similarly, Davis could never
moderate his aim, that the seceding states had the right and should be allowed
to depart in peace. Although, even after Gettysburg, some would try to find a
solution on middle ground, there was none. Strictly speaking, the War
Between the States was outside the definition of total war as established by
Clausewitz and executed by Bismarck, in that it was not the continuation of
policy by other means, but rather the consequence of the failure of policy. The
war derived from circumstances which could not be contained within the
normal political processes of the nation, and was all the more violent in
consequence. It is beyond question, therefore, that the War Between the States
was total. The proposition that it was also modern, and the prototype for the
wars of the twentieth century, rests upon four arguments: the political element
in the relationship between the government in Washington and its
commanders in the field, the nature of the three battles which this chapter has
sought to analyse; the conduct of the war after Gettysburg and the degree to
which both sides succeeded in mobilising the totality of their resources, both
human and material.

It was of course no new thing for a commander in the field, if he was not
also the supreme authority in the State, to have to retain the confidence of his

home government, but the further the theatre of war was from the seat of government, the more that had to be left to the discretion of the army commander. In the War Between the States, with the headquarters of the army conducting what was throughout considered to be the most important campaign never more than 100 miles from the national capital, and with the added advantage of the telegraph, the surprise and novelty is not that Lincoln and his cabinet interfered so much with the conduct of operations, but that they interfered so relatively little. The novelty lay rather in the fact that, for the first time, the political views of the army commander became second only to military success as the key factor which first gained him the command and then maintained him in it. An influential body of policy makers and opinion formers in the North were prosecuting the war with an aim, the emancipation of the slaves, quite different from that of the president. That the two were not incompatible was proved, because within a year of the first shot Lincoln realised that they would have to be combined if the North were to generate the will to fight to a finish. But it was the more radical aim which the successive Commanders of the Army of the Potomac ignored at their peril. The lukewarm views of McClellan about the emancipation of the slaves explain why, after the initial euphoria of his appointment, he soon ceased to be trusted, and the declared abolitionist convictions of both Pope and Hooker were undoubtedly a factor in their promotion to army command. The Joint Committee on the Conduct of the War, when it visited the army after the defeat at Chancellorsville, was seeking reassurance more about political reliability than military genius in trying to find a successor to Hooker. The fact that Meade, like McClellan and President Buchanan before him, was from Pennsylvania, a northern industrial and arable farmland state which had never had any dependence upon slavery, might excuse his lack of strongly expressed views. The victory of Gettysburg, however limited, was enough to mute any immediate doubt about him, and his views became less relevant to the politicians in the campaign of 1864 because of his subordination to Grant.

In terms of eighteenth-century warfare, the casualty rates of any one of the battles of Antietam, Fredericksburg or Gettysburg, as well as those of the peninsula battles and Second Manassas, would have been enough to persuade most governments in the era before modern war that the time had come for an armistice and the discussion of peace terms. Fifty years previously, notwithstanding the stated intention of all the partners in the Coalition of 1813 to remove Napoleon from power, there was a four month armistice during that summer, during which he was offered peace terms which would have left him on the throne of a France with natural frontiers exceeding anything achieved by Louis XIV. Throughout the War Between the States, Lincoln would not negotiate with Davis on any terms which recognised the Confederacy as an independent nation; thus, after Antietam, Fredericksburg and Gettysburg, there was no truce for negotiations.

But it was something more than the politically indecisive results of these three battles, and something in addition to their scale, which brought a new intensity to the conduct of land warfare. Beyond doubt, the most important factor was the increase beyond computation in the effectiveness of firepower. It was the application of improved firepower which caused the total casualty list of Gettysburg, over 50,000, to be higher than in any previous battle except Borodino and Leipzig, and half as many again as at Solferino, four years previously, although at Solferino the numbers engaged were fifty per cent greater than at Gettysburg. The great leap forward in the technology of firepower totally outdated the basic tactics of the battlefield which had stood for the previous 500 years, though it took another half century for this to be realised. Only then were new technologies harnessed, to try to counter the improvements in firepower by similar improvements in protection and mobility.

It was also a characteristic of modern warfare when Lee embarked upon all these battles with his primary aim; the destruction of the enemy army, and thus the destruction of the political will of the enemy to fight, which Clausewitz had established as the basic objective of warfare. Lee's overriding aim was the same, whether the battle was being fought to secure a line of retreat, as at Antietam, or in the old-fashioned battle for position, as at Fredericksburg, or in the new-style 'encounter' battle at Gettysburg. The 'encounter' battle was new to warfare, but it would soon be seen again at Mars La Tour in 1870, and in the opening battles of the First World War, on the Western Front at Mons and First Ypres, and in East Prussia. In each case, the leading elements of the opposing armies collided on ground and at times which were not of the army commanders' choosing. Whereas before Gettysburg major battles had invariably been 'set piece', in that one side at least had chosen the ground upon which they would fight, the 'encounter' battle became increasingly frequent thereafter.

The War Between the States continued for another twenty-one months after Gettysburg and the concurrent fall of Vicksburg, which capitulated to Grant the day after Lee's army had recoiled from Cemetery Ridge. This gave the Union control of the Mississippi from source to mouth, as Scott's 'anaconda' design had suggested. With the Confederacy split in half, the Virginia theatre assumed greater importance than ever in the eyes of both governments. Grant, brought east by Lincoln, promoted to lieutenant general (for which a special act of Congress was required), and appointed commander-in-chief under the president of all the armies of the United States, made his headquarters with the Army of the Potomac.

When the campaigning season opened in the spring of 1864, Grant used Meade's army in a continuous campaign of attrition, unprecedented in warfare. On 4th May the Army of the Potomac crossed the Rapidan for the last time. There was serious fighting every day for the next thirty, including four major battles, in the Wilderness, around Spotsylvania Court House, for the North Anna crossing and at Cold Harbour. When this last battle ended, on 3rd June, the Army of the Potomac had suffered another 60,000 battle casualties,[95] an average of 2,000 a day. None of Grant's bludgeon-like operations was conducted for ground of the slightest strategic or logistic importance, and none was decisive. On each occasion Grant was seeking to turn Lee's eastward flank, and each time he failed because the Confederates, however outnumbered, when fighting behind breastworks and from entrenchments could always bring superior firepower to bear on Union soldiers advancing in lines over open ground. Attempts by subordinate commanders to devise alternative tactics enjoyed at best only temporary success. However, every battle, though indecisive, brought Grant's army closer to Richmond, whose capture would, it was thought, end the war. President and general, both sensitive men deeply concerned at the shocking loss of life, steeled themselves to accept a sustained rate of loss from enemy action without previous parallel in military history.[vv]

If Grant used Meade's army as a bludgeon, Sheridan in the Shenandoah Valley and Sherman, advancing eastwards from Atlanta on Savannah, were pillars of fire, destroying by direction everything in front of them. The Confederate Army of Tennessee, formed by combining the previously separate armies of the Mississippi and Kentucky and commanded first by J.E. Johnston and then by Hood, evacuated Atlanta on 3rd September. Over the next ten weeks Sherman, Grant's chosen successor in chief command of the Union armies in the western theatre, cleared Georgia and Tennessee. Leaving holding forces to secure the territory gained, he left Atlanta on 15th November with 60,000 troops, to march to the coast 250 miles away. There was no supply line; the army lived off the country, and the aim was not victory

---

[vv] Napoleon's *Grande Armée*, on the retreat from Moscow and the furthest points eastward reached by October 1812, lost more men than Grant, but the main cause was the cold rather than combat.

in the field but devastation of the Confederacy's resources. Everything of value on a forty mile front was either requisitioned without compensation, looted or destroyed, and when Savannah fell to Sherman's troops on 21st December, the general estimated that his army had caused $100,000,000's worth of damage, one-fifth of which 'inured to our advantage' while 'the remainder is simple waste and destruction.'[96] It was estimated that 10,000 slaves had declared their own independence in the wake of Sherman's march, abandoning the plantations where they had lived and worked all their lives as the buildings and crops were destroyed, to follow the Union Army. They suffered a terrible loss from hunger and privation. The days were long gone in which a Union commander might return escaped slaves to their owners, an action which had contributed greatly to the disgrace of General Stone after Ball's Bluff, or, as McClellan had on the peninsula, issued and enforced the strongest instructions about the sanctity of property of civilians, even when these were undoubtedly sympathetic to the enemy. The majority of inhabitants of the Shenandoah Valley were probably more in sympathy with the Union than with the Confederacy, but nevertheless Sheridan devastated the area in the fall of 1864. Total war implies wanton destruction.

The final argument in the contention that the War Between the States was modern rests upon the attempts made by both sides to mobilise their total resources, and the growing perception of the need to forsake everything, including dearly held principles and all other priorities, to the prosecution of the war. Lee saw the point sooner than most: in the first winter of the war, before either side had learned how to bring the whole striking force of an army to bear, he had written that there was no way to hold short-term regiments in service when their enlistments expired, except by a compulsory service law which would bind them for the duration, and had continued:

> The great object of the Confederate States is to bring the war to a successful issue. Every consideration should yield to that; for without it we can hope to enjoy nothing that we possess, and nothing that we do possess will be adequate without it.[97]

By 'everything we possess', Lee included the principle of states' rights, which had decided his own attitude to the war and caused him to reject a glittering future as general-in-chief of the Union Army. Other fundamental beliefs to go by the board included the individual right to habeus corpus, and the absolute right of possession of property, including slaves. Lee had been convinced as early as 1856 that slavery was 'a moral and political evil',[98] and at the start of the war owned no slaves except for the few living out their old age on the Arlington estate.

But there were many in the South who would not wish to go so far. These, before long, would see their slaves requisitioned by the government, to build defence works such as those protecting the approaches to Richmond in the summer of 1862 or along the lower Rappahannock in the winter after Fredericksburg. By the last few months of the war the South had had to accept not only that there should be Negro combat soldiers, but also that any slaves so drafted would have earned their freedom if they survived.

That neither side succeeded fully in mobilising the whole of its potential is explained by the lack of a modern pervasive bureaucracy with a competent information-recording, retrieval and transmission system. Perhaps only the United Kingdom in the Second World War achieved the optimum total direction of its manpower, and approached a correct balance between the competing requirements of soldiers and industries vital to the war effort. The techniques and technologies essential to this aim were, if they existed at all in 1860, embryonic. It would have been, as we have seen, far more beneficial to the South if all foundry workers, mechanics and railway maintenance men had been exempted from military service and continued their artisan skills under overall national direction. Later in the war, Lee would put a strong case for total government control of a critical national asset. In the winter after Gettysburg, unable to move his cavalry or artillery for want of forage, he suggested in a letter to General Braxton Bragg, military adviser to President Davis, that all civilian rail movement should be prohibited until sufficient stocks of forage had been built up.[99]

Both armies were plagued not so much by long-term desertion, for which the Union executed over 200 offenders, as by an abundance of shirkers. Presidents and commanding generals on both sides found it almost impossible to return a recovered wounded or sick soldier from hospital to his unit in the field, unless the man himself was so minded. And on both sides there developed, inevitably, an excess of individuals in uniform but not in combat units. Too many found jobs doing too little for the war effort in recruiting, drafting, training militias composed of men too old, too young or too infirm to fight in the field, and in the remount and supply services. By the time Lee was stating the need for total direction of the railways, the South had a conscription law, but this was evaded by many, much as the old militia service liability had been. Governor Brown of Georgia was among those who did not support Lee's propositions with action. A states' rights hardliner, in the winter after Gettysburg, Brown had exempted from military service 1,350 justices of the peace and the same number of special constables, and had commissioned 2,751 officers in the state militia,[100] for local service only. While some will have been over the age for active service, and many no doubt fought in the gruelling battles around Atlanta the following summer, the figures suggest that some at least preferred to give assistance rather than all-out commitment to the cause, rejecting the concept of total war.

Nevertheless, simple arithmetic establishes that the majority on both sides gave all they had. The free white population of the South at the start of the war was around 5,500,000. Assuming that half were women, and half the males were outside the ages normally regarded as appropriate for service in a combat unit (say eighteen to forty), there remains a total of 1.38 million men available for mobilisation. This matches, within a very small tolerance, the total of 1.3 million Confederate enlistments during the war, given by Catton.[101] The Union, with four times the population and an industrial capacity perhaps ten times that of the South, did not need quite so careful an allocation of resources to optimise its war effort, but still it mobilised more than twice as many men as the Confederacy. And of the 4,000,000 mobilised, one in ten died, on the battlefield, from wounds or from disease.[101] The percentage of adult males mobilised exceeded that achieved by the French *levée en masse* or the annual conscriptions of the Napoleonic Wars. Brigadier General John Preston, director of the Confederate War Department's Bureau of Conscription, an office undreamed of at the start of the war, wrote during the last winter of the conflict about the sort of war which the Confederacy had tried to fight, and which all developed nations would seek to attain when they went to war in future:

> The whole population and the whole production of a country (the soldiers and the subsistence of armies) are to be put on to a war footing, where every institution is to be made auxiliary to war, where every citizen and every industry is to have for the time but one attribute – that of contributing to the public defence.[97]

In the years to come, successive chiefs of the general staff in Berlin would build plans on just such a foundation, and in 1940, with the survival of the United Kingdom at stake, Prime Minister Winston Churchill would clothe the same aim in more rhetorical and inspirational terms. But the War Between the States established the pattern, and this had come about in the nation which had been, of all the major powers of the mid-nineteenth century, the least militaristic in character.

Notes

The War Between the States generated, very quickly, so much memorialist literature in the shape of letters, diaries and regimental histories that the course of each battle and the units and formations taking part can be established with almost total precision. The one doubtful quantity is timing: we are still dealing with an era before watches were an almost universal possession and before the instant availability of synchronised time. Hence, sources differ about the time at which individual events occurred and how long they lasted, although there is little dispute about the events themselves.

Bruce Catton's three-volume centennial history of the American Civil War, *The Coming Fury*, *Terrible Swift Sword*, and *Never Call Retreat*, provides both political and military bases for an understanding of the conflict, and his further three-volume history of the Army of the Potomac, *Mr Lincoln's Army*, *The Glory Road* and *A Stillness at Appomattox*, is the invaluable work of reference for the operations of that army throughout the war. Similarly, Richard Southall Freeman's epic biography of Lee remains the standard work, and is an essential guide to the operations of the Army of Northern Virginia.

The author walked the three battles analysed in this chapter, together with others in the eastern theatre of the war, in the summer of 1995, using the authoritative *West Point Military History Series Atlas for the American Civil War* [Avery Publishing Group, Wayne NJ, 1986]. The highly knowledgeable guides at the centres run by the National Park Service of the US Department of the Interior are a mine of information and the configuration of much of the ground remains apparent, in spite of urban development at Fredericksburg and the National Memorial aspect of Gettysburg.

[1] Tuchman, *The First Salute*, London, Michael Joseph, 1989, p.46.

[2] Fuller, *Decisive Battles of the Western World*, Stevenage, Spa Books Ltd, 1994 [first published 1955], vol. II, pp.310–13.

[3] Cunliffe, *Soldiers and Civilians: The Martial Spirit in America 1775–1865*, London, Eyre and Spottiswoode, 1969, p.181.

[4] Evidently originating in John *Lambert's Travels Through Lower Canada and the United States of America*, published in London in 1810 and quoted by Cunliffe, op.cit., pp.187–88.

[5] Cunliffe, op.cit., pp.189–90.

[6] See for a résumé, *The Basic History of the United States*, Charles A. and Mary R. Beard, New York, The New House Library, 1944, Chapters IX to XI.

[7] Beards, op.cit., p.177.

[8] Beards, op.cit., pp.154–55.

[9] Freeman, *Lee*, [Howard Abridgement], New York, Charles Scribner's Sons, 1961, p.19.

[10] Cunliffe, op.cit., p.363.

[11] Cunliffe, op.cit., p.131.

[12] For a summary of the career of Albert Sidney Johnston, see Macdonald, *Great Battles of the American Civil War*, New York, Maxwell Macmillan International, 1992, p.24.

[13] Freeman, op.cit., p.88.

[14] Cunliffe, op.cit., pp.366–69.

[15] Cunliffe, op.cit., pp.111–26.

[16] Cunliffe, op.cit., p.280.

[17] Catton, *The Glory Road*, New York, Doubleday, 1952, Pocket Cardinal edition 1964, p.19.

[18] Lanier [ed.] *Armies and Leaders*, New York, Fairfax Press, 1983, p.304.

[19] Cunliffe, op.cit., pp.75–80.

[20] Bryant, *Years of Victory*, London, Wm Collins, 1944, Reprint Society 1945, pp.70–85.

[21] For a comprehensive description of the volunteer movement in the United States, see Cunliffe, op.cit., Chapter 7.

[22] Gilbert, W.S., *Patience*, Act I.

[23] Cunliffe, op.cit., pp.243–47.

[24] Catton, *Mr Lincoln's Army*, New York, Doubleday, 1951, p.307.

[25] Catton, op.cit., p.207.

[26] Lanier, op.cit., p.180.

[27] Lanier, op.cit., p.148.

[28] Catton, *Mr Lincoln's Army*, p.192.

[29] Catton, *Picture History of the Civil War*, New York, American Heritage, 1982, p.79.

[30] Catton, *This Hallowed Ground*, London, Gollancz, 1957, p.23.

[31] See, in particular, Sears, *For Country, Cause and Leader: The Civil War Journal of Charles B. Haydon*, New York, Ticknor and Field, 1993, Chapters 1–7.

[32] Catton, *This Hallowed Ground*, p.37.

[33] Freeman, op.cit., pp.100–10, covers in detail the choices offered to Lee in the spring of 1861.

[34] Catton, *The Coming Fury*, New York, Doubleday, 1961; Washington, Square Press Edition, 1967, pp.431–32.

[35] Cunliffe, op.cit., p.391.

[36] Lanier, op.cit., p.164.

[37] Macdonald, op.cit., p.57 and Catton, *Mr Lincoln's Army*, p.337.

[38] Catton, op.cit., p.68–69.

[39] For a detailed description of the First Battle of Manassas, see Macdonald, op.cit., p.12–23.

[40] Catton, *This Hallowed Ground*, p.25.

[41] Catton, *Mr Lincoln's Army*, pp.88–91.

[42] Catton, op.cit., p.109.

[43] Cunliffe, op.cit., p.323.

[44] Lanier, op.cit., p.167.

[45] Lanier, op.cit., pp.164–68, 186–215 and 238.

[46] Macdonald, op.cit., pp.48–55.

[47] Catton has a vivid description of what was effectively the resumption of command of the Army of the Potomac by McClellan after Second Manassas, in *Mr Lincoln's Army*, pp.55–56.

[48] Freeman, op.cit., pp.99–103.

[49] Catton, *This Hallowed Ground*, pp.8–10.

[50] Catton, *The Coming Fury*, p.336.

[51] Freeman, op.cit., pp.250–51.

[52] Quoted by Catton, *Terrible Swift Sword*, New York, Doubleday and Co., 1963; Washington Square Press Edition, 1967, p.422.

[53] Catton, *A Stillness at Appomattox*, New York, Doubleday and Co., 1953; Washington Square Press Edition, 1958, p.289.

[54] Catton, *Mr Lincoln's Army*, pp.234–36.

[55] Freeman, op.cit., p.251.

[56] Macdonald, op.cit., p.59.

[57] Catton, *Mr Lincoln's Army*, p.268.

[58] Freeman, op.cit., p.255.

[59] Catton, *Mr Lincoln's Army*, p.155.

[60] The author's descriptions of Antietam, Fredericksburg and Gettysburg are based on study on the ground in 1995, related to the works cited of Catton, Freeman and Macdonald. While there are some minor discrepancies between sources, any errors of interpretation are the author's own.

[61] Catton, *Mr Lincoln's Army*, p.323.

[62] Catton, op.cit., p.132.

[63] Lanier, op.cit., p.158.

[64] Catton, op.cit., p.336, Freeman, op.cit., p.261 and Macdonald, op.cit., p.66.

[65] Catton, *Terrible Swift Sword*, p.450.

[66] Catton, op.cit., p.452.

[67] Freeman, op.cit., p.270.

[68] Catton, *The Glory Road*, p.25–29, 'For want of a nail...'

[69] Macdonald, op.cit., p.68.

[70] Catton, *The Glory Road*, p.43.

[71] Catton, op.cit., pp.57–66.

[72] Catton, *Never Call Retreat*, New York, Doubleday and Co., 1965, p.24.

[73] Catton, *The Glory Road*, p.108.

[74] Catton, *Never Call Retreat*, pp.67–68.

[75] Macdonald, op.cit., p.92.

[76] Catton, *The Glory Road*, p.224.

[77] Catton, op.cit., p.226.

[78] Catton, op.cit., p.263.

[79] Freeman, op.cit., pp.320–21.

[80] Catton, op.cit., p.282.

[81] Catton, op.cit., p.291.

[82] Macdonald, op.cit., p.105.

[83] Freeman, op.cit., p.325.

[84] Catton, op.cit., p.300.

[85] Catton, op.cit., p.319.

[86] Lanier, op.cit., p.158. A memorial on Culp's Hill tells the story of the Confederate Maryland Regiment.

[87] Catton, op.cit., p.325.

[88] Freeman, op.cit., pp.335–36.

[89] Freeman, op. cit., p.337.

[90] Catton, op.cit., p.341.

[91] Freeman, op.cit., pp.340–41.

[92] Catton, op.cit., p.346.

[93] Catton, op.cit., p.349.

[94] Freeman, op.cit., pp.346–47.

[95] Catton, *A Stillness at Appomattox*, p.199.

[96] Catton, *Never Call Retreat*, p.416.

[97] Catton, *Terrible Swift Sword*, p.114.

[98] Freeman, op.cit., pp.92–93.

[99] Catton, *Never Call Retreat*, pp.315.

[100] Catton, op.cit., p.404.

[101] Catton, *Picture History* p.359, and Lanier, op.cit., p.148, produce slightly different total casualty figures for the war.

Chapter VII
The Simmering Cauldron: Central Europe 1815–1866

The Rise and Nature of Prussia

The Congress of Vienna imposed successfully upon Europe much of the status quo ante 1792, and the policy of Metternich, in spite of his own fall from power in 1848, contrived to perpetuate this for nearly the next half century. Nevertheless, the peace of Europe remained under continual threat and was eventually terminated by four main related influences. Nationalism in Italy challenged the Habsburg rule re-established after 1815, whether exercised directly from Vienna or through cadet branches of the family in Naples and the duchies. Nationalism in Germany produced a unifying force in direct contradistinction to the patchwork of sovereign states which the settlement of Vienna had restored, though much reduced in number from the era before 1789. A fragmented Germany was fundamental to the policies of both Austria and Russia. Thirdly, as the nineteenth century progressed, there grew within the Habsburg realms a crisis both of government identity and direction of policy. This could not be contained by the concept of the 'unitary state' of Maria Theresa and her Chancellor Kaunitz, upon which they had based the administration of the empire in the previous century. The nineteenth century posed new questions: to what extent could, or should, Austria seek to take the leadership of Germany? And, as a parallel and in no way subsidiary issue, to what degree might any position taken by Vienna on this key issue come into conflict with the measure of federalism, intended to be dominated in perpetuity by German–Austrians, which might have to be granted in order to contain the aspirations to self-rule and enhancement of status of its non-German subjects within the empire? Such aspirations were by no means confined to the Italians; they were shared in equal or greater measure by Magyars, Czechs, Croats, Poles and Slavs. Finally, there was the particular position of Prussia in these vital issues, tempered by her own geopolitical imperatives, especially the fragmented nature of her territories, and compounded by their lack of defensible frontiers.

The length of time for which the alliance of autocracies could maintain a common view was not unlimited. Neither was the extent thereafter to which diplomacy could secure acceptable compromises when the inevitable differences occurred. It follows that, given the nineteenth-century perception of warfare as an instrument of state policy, war in some form, deriving from at least two sets of diametrically opposed philosophies and perceptions of national interest, was bound in due course to break the pattern of the continent of Europe set in 1815 and to establish another.

In all these questions, dormant for some years after the defeat of Napoleon but never extinct, the common factor was the view of Prussia and her will and power to make this felt. At no time was Prussia ever a homogeneous state within well-defined borders. The ruling house of Hohenzollern had originated in southern Germany, and it was a Hohenzollern who, in 1283, brought to Archduke Rudolph of Habsburg the news of his election as Holy Roman Emperor. In 1417 a Hohenzollern prince was established as margrave of Brandenburg, the territories around Berlin. As such, the family became one of the more important among the rulers of the 400 princely and ecclesiastical states into which the land mass of present-day Germany remained divided up to the end of the eighteenth century. All of these were sovereign in their own right but owed allegiance to the Holy Roman Emperor. The ruler of Brandenburg became one of the six lay and three episcopal authorities who chose the new Holy Roman Emperor on the death of the incumbent. The military significance of Brandenburg derived from the fact that this state had replaced the Teutonic Order of Knights as the first line of defence against the heathen and barbarian hordes to the east. In 1618, at the start of the Thirty Years War, the hitherto separate duchy of Prussia, East Prussia in terms of modern history, was added to the possessions of the margrave of Brandenburg. Later in the century, a soldier and administrator of genius brought the state of Prussia out of the ruck of minor German principalities. The great elector, Frederick William, defeated the Swedes, at the time probably the leading military power in Europe, at the Battle of Fehrbellin (1675). His son, Frederick I, in return for services rendered and promised, gained from the emperor the title of king, and in 1701 crowned himself, not in Berlin but in the fortress city of Konigsberg, capital of East Prussia. No other ruling house within the Holy Roman Empire held this title, though some, such as Augustus the Strong, elector of Saxony and king of Poland, derived it from lands held outside the empire. The great elector had already acquired territories in the Rhineland, widely separated in terms of eighteenth-century travel from the ancestral lands of his house. His son's espousal of the winning side in the War of the Spanish Succession (1701–13), which included positive support in the form of substantial contingents at all of the four great battles won by the duke of Marlborough, consolidated the new kingdom of Prussia, if not quite as a European power of the first rank, certainly as one which could not be ignored. Austria, France and England would all be glad of an alliance with Prussia in any future conflict, the latter particularly because of the accession in 1714 of the elector of Hanover to the crown of England.

The quarter century of peace between the Wars of the Spanish and Austrian Successions produced for Prussia her third consecutive outstanding ruler, King Frederick William I, grandson of the great elector. Driven by the geographic facts, the widely separated elements of his kingdom and the lack of a defensible frontier against any likely opponent, he subordinated everything to the creation of an army intended to be unmatched in Europe.

A state education system was established to produce soldiers. Compulsory service combined with rigorous economy in every other area of government expenditure allowed the expansion of the Prussian standing army from 50,000, already large by the standards of the time, to 80,000. Frederick William I died in 1740. His last words were the murmuring of, when hearing the Lutheran hymn, *Naked I Came into This World, and Naked I Shall Go*, 'No, not quite naked: I shall have my uniform on.'[1] His son, Frederick II, might be thought lucky to have survived his father's tyrannies. He soon found an opportunity to apply his inherited violent tendencies, unparalleled military machine and hitherto unsuspected military genius.

The Holy Roman Emperor, Charles VI of Habsburg, also died in 1740 but without male issue. By assiduous diplomacy over the previous ten years he had secured the guarantees of all the European powers, including Prussia, of the succession of his daughter Maria Theresa to the ancestral lands of the Habsburgs, though she remained debarred from succession in her own right to the imperial crown by Salic law.[a] The imperial title was intended for her husband, Francis of Lorraine, which was itself disputed territory between the empire and the France of Louis XV. Charles VI put forward his daughter's claim notwithstanding the existence of what might be thought to be the superior right of the daughter of his elder brother and predecessor as emperor. As if these causes for friction were not enough, there was the growing colonial rivalry between England and France, with a powerful element at the French

---

[a] i.e. succession could not descend to or through the female line.

court determined to seek revenge for the humiliations inflicted by the duke of Marlborough, the decline in the power of Spain and the Dutch republic and, on all sides, the feeling that something could be gained by war. Warfare was by no means seen at the time as:

> the devastating curse which science and conscription have now contrived to make it. It was waged by small mercenary armies, hibernating for half the year, and during the short campaigning season, no longer as in the Thirty Years War living upon the country, but supplied by a regular commissariat service.[2]

There was also a boredom factor. Compelled by public opinion to go to war with Spain in the preceding year, because of an assault on a merchant captain, the English Prime Minister, Sir Robert Walpole, remarked, 'They now ring their bells, but they will soon wring their hands'.[3] A desultory war between England and Spain was already in progress when, without interest either in principle or previous commitment, Frederick II seized the opportunity to annex Silesia, part of the Habsburg dominions which his father had promised to respect.

There followed two wars, those of the Austrian Succession (1740–48) and the Seven Years' War (1756–63), in which there were no constant alliances, only constant enmities between Prussia and Austria, and England and France. The detailed course of these two wars is not relevant to this book.[4] It is sufficient to say that, though sometimes beaten badly in the field and more than once threatened with extinction, Frederick II brought his country through to Great Power status. By his conduct of successive campaigns, always against the odds, he established himself as one of the greatest military commanders in history. In particular, his campaign in the winter of 1757 was a masterpiece, and its study a great influence on Napoleon. Leaving subordinate commanders to conduct holding operations on two other fronts, on 5th November, he defeated a French army twice the size of his own at Rossbach, west of Leipzig. He then turned east, and exactly one month later, after an approach march of 240 miles, beat an Austro-Russian army, also at odds of two to one, at Leuthen, west of Breslau.[5] At the end of the Seven Years' War, Prussia's possession of Silesia and her status as a Great Power were alike unquestioned. Further substantial territorial acquisitions followed, some from the successive partitions of Poland, in which the spoils were shared with Russia and Austria, others in central and southern Germany.

Frederick the Great lived on until 1786. He never had to fight another war, but maintained nevertheless his army at full strength and as the foundation stone of the state. The soldiers of Prussia continued to be disciplined under the conditions of extreme severity established by his father, in which the dangers of active service were thought to be preferable to the rigours of life in barracks.[6]

We have already met Augereau as a marshal of the First Empire and corps commander in the *Grande Armée*. His early military career had been unstable in the extreme. Already in flight from the royal French Army for killing an officer who had struck him with his cane, he had subsequently enlisted in, and soon after deserted from, the army of the tsar. Nevertheless, he was accepted readily into the Prussian Royal Guard because of his height and soldierly appearance. Finding yet again the discipline more than he could bear, he deserted for the third time, this time in grand style at the head of sixty comrades. Twenty years later, in the pursuit which followed Jena, he captured, lock, stock and barrel, his old regiment. It is a telling illustration of the atrophy which often follows great military achievement that he found the colonel, second in command and regimental sergeant major to be the same as in his own time.[7] Let no one think that this episode is either purely anecdotal or unique.

Twenty years after the death of Frederick the Great, his army had become superannuated. The average age of the twenty-one general officers who surrendered when the fortress of Magdeburg capitulated was over sixty. Of 540 infantry officers of the rank of major and above, over a quarter were also more than sixty, and of 945 captains, the 'centurions', who in any army of any age need to be able to match the physical agility of the rank and file, one-eighth (119 out of 945) were over fifty, eighteen had passed sixty and there was one septuagenarian. The combined ages of the three senior officers of one regiment amounted to over 250. The twenty five senior cavalry officers were all over sixty, and the garrison artillery possessed a major who was a mere stripling of seventy-seven.[8]

As we have seen, Prussian diplomatic performance as a member of the Third Coalition was hesitant and indecisive, and her military achievement abysmal. In the Prussian Army after Frederick the Great, as in the nineteenth-century Royal Navy after Trafalgar, an excessive reliance on seniority, meaningless traditions, stereotyped procedures and outdated practices had taken the place of the continuous rigorous analysis of threat, national geopolitical priorities and resources, likely battlefield conditions and emerging technology, which is essential if armed forces are to be kept up to date and at a peak throughout a long period of peace. This process, essential for any state unless it is prepared to eschew totally the use of force, was doubly the case for Prussia. As it was, feeble battlefield leadership of an ageing army antiquated in its techniques, by the great-nephew of the Great Frederick, not necessarily assisted by the advice of octogenarian subordinate commanders who had actually served under the genius himself nearly half a century before, proved no match for the *Grande Armée* at the height of its capability. At Tilsit, Prussia lost virtually all her territory except for the historic Hohenzollern possessions of Brandenburg and East Prussia, and the size of her army was restricted to 42,000 men.[9]

Defeat is more often the parent of root and branch reform than victory. In July 1807 a military committee was established to investigate the causes of the cataclysmic defeat just suffered, and the civil structure of the state underwent similar fundamental review and modernisation. The military reforms of Scharnhorst, chief of the General War Department of the Prussian Ministry of War from 1807 until mortally wounded in the early part of the campaign of 1813, and as such de facto chief of the general staff, enabled Prussia to field 80,000 soldiers against Napoleon in the latter year, notwithstanding the limitation imposed at Tilsit six years previously.[10] For the campaign in the Low Countries, ended by the Battle of Waterloo, the Prussian Army under Blucher numbered 117,000, nearly four times the strength of Wellington's British Army.[11] Prussia's reward at the Congress of Vienna was restoration of the territories lost at Tilsit, but Metternich's principle of the status quo and practical reluctance to strengthen further Prussia's position ensured that she continued to suffer the strategic disadvantages of separated enclaves of territory and indefensible frontiers.

Scharnhorst's reforms founded the superb military machine which in 1871 took Prussia to the leadership of a united Germany and the house of Hohenzollern to an imperial crown. His work was based upon three principles, none new but all of an emphasis wholly relevant to the circumstances of Prussia, both current and future. The army of Frederick the Great had had a general staff, of sorts. Scharnhorst ensured that this body would select its members from the ablest officers and that its tasks would include the continuous evaluation of the threats facing Prussia on all her frontiers and the preparation of coordinated contingency plans related to resources which could be adopted or adapted in the light of circumstances. As will be seen, there is a clear line of descent from the ideas of Scharnhorst through those of Moltke to Schlieffen, and Manstein. His second principle was that of universal service. While both Frederick the Great and Napoleon had, in law, required this of their subjects, the effect of an annual quota system related to a lengthy if not indefinite period of service had been to produce large numbers of recruits. Those that survived formed a long service army, but were not backed by much in the way of trained reserves. Scharnhorst took further the liability to universal military service. Because the size of the standing army had been limited at Tilsit, he saw that the means of evading the restriction on numbers was to decree a relatively short period of service 'with the colours', to be followed by a compulsory longer period of service in a reserve with a training commitment and liability to recall to active duty. The lesson was not lost on future generations of officers of the German general staff. The Weimar Republic of the 1920s would similarly evade the restrictions imposed by the Treaty of Versailles, with further refinements superimposed by another military organiser of genius, Hans von Seeckt. Scharnhorst's third principle derived from the first two. Not merely regiments but also larger formations would mobilise from defined geographic areas of the kingdom of Prussia. In broad terms, each province produced an army corps complete with cavalry division and artillery regiment; the principle was extended to include the states of southern Germany after 1866 and applied to the whole empire after 1871. Formations and units, when not required elsewhere for training or operations, would remain stationed in their home province, which of course suited well the circumstances of Prussia. In peacetime, units were at peace establishment, and some at no more than training cadre strength. On mobilisation, recruits would report to depots near their homes, draw their equipment and flesh out units and formations up to army corps level, to their war establishment.

The Habsburg monarchy by contrast, because of the doubtful loyalty of at least some of its subjects, was forced into the opposite solution. During the approach to war in 1866, Bohemia was garrisoned by Italian-recruited regiments, and Venetia by the empire's Hungarian units. All were at a peace establishment which, for economy reasons, had reduced infantry company strengths to fifty-four men; less than half their war strength.[12] The relative advantages on mobilisation need no emphasis. Successive forms of government in France in the century up to 1914 also contrived to combine the worst of all three worlds: a long service army larger than necessary for peacetime requirements but too small for the needs of a continental war; reserves of dubious quality and, until after the reforms which followed the defeats of 1870–71, inadequate numbers; and, in order to minimise the risk of local political contamination, units invariably stationed away from their recruitment and reservist catchment areas. Although the Prussian Army fell again into neglect in the long years of peace after 1815, the principles of the Scharnhorst reforms endured for a century and longer.

In what has become a cosmopolitan age it could be argued that different distinct national or racial 'types' no longer exist, and in a society which has sought to outlaw racial discrimination and prejudice it is a short step to pretend that they never did. This proposition would have been strange to historians of earlier and perhaps more discriminating generations.

> The Prussian is a distinctive European type. Goethe, who lived in Weimar and may be taken to represent the mid-German view of the Prussians, speaks of them as barbarians. There was an uncouth vigour and asperity about this remarkable people which jarred on the more refined susceptibilities of the Saxon, Franconian and the Rhinelander. To what causes the special characteristics of the Prussian race are to be attributed, whether to the Slavonic blood which flows through their veins, or to the harsh North German climate, or to the stern military tradition which nature imposes on a state undefended by geographical frontiers or, if to all these causes, in what proportion: these are questions which admit of no precise answer. Let it suffice that before the eighteenth century had half run its course the world was aware that this vivid and masterful people, so sparingly furnished with the graces of life, presented by reason of their frugality, their discipline, their skill at arms and heroic capacity for sacrifice a new and formidable problem for the statesmen of Europe.
>
> In contradistinction to other Germans, the Prussians had a strict sense of service to the state. Their rulers could count, not upon their judgement, for the sturdy population of Prussia had no mind for politics, but upon a blind, ungrudging obedience to the word of command and upon a technical probity which ensured that every task would be faithfully discharged...[13]

Thus H.A.L. Fisher, author of the historian's base document on European history from the earliest times to the 1930s, and member of the pre-First World War Liberal administration of Asquith, perhaps the most intellectually distinguished cabinet ever to hold office in the United Kingdom. A.J.P. Taylor, likewise a historian of impeccable liberal conviction, writes in the same terms.

The junkers of East Prussia, who were what might be termed a peasant–aristocrat caste, provided a natural officer class. Their lands, which they worked themselves, were mostly poverty stricken and service to the state was almost invariably not just a duty but the only way to secure a bare livelihood. By the nineteenth century, many junker families had in any event lost their lands. Hindenburg, the family estate at Neudeck long passed into other hands, retired corps commander, was living very simply in Hanover when called upon to assume command of Imperial Germany's armies on her eastern frontier in August 1914, replacing a commander whose abilities had proved inadequate for events.[14] Von der Goltz, architect of the alliance between Wilhelmine Germany and the Ottoman Empire, warrior–philosopher whose works commanded wide attention in his own country before 1914 (and which might with advantage have been studied elsewhere) was nearly lost to the army altogether. He writes:

> of Fabiansfelde, the East Prussian estate on which he was born [in 1843] and describes the typical seat of an impoverished junker family. He shows us a square farmyard, around which are white-painted office and workshop buildings with thatched roofs. There is a pond, and the chief pride of the family home (also thatched) was the possession of stone fireplaces. Add to this the steward's house and a wretched little garden with a few oaks and wild pear trees, and you have the picture. Von der Goltz's mother could not even keep this poor habitation together, and it had to be sold. There was so little money that she considered having her son trained as a cooper.[15]

Von Moltke, the greatest of them all, came from a similar background and, as a bright young officer on the general staff in the 1820s was forced to eke out a miserable salary by translating Gibbon's *Decline and Fall of the Roman Empire* into German, and whose reasons for going, in 1835 'on secondment', as it would now be termed in the British Army, for four years to the Turkish Army were as much financial as professional.

The bare and simple lifestyle, allied to an unbreakable sense of duty, created an iron-hard race and this as well as the absence of other career choices, ensured that military dynasties proliferated, even more than in the nineteenth-century English or Anglo-Irish landed classes, or the French families '*de particule*' between 1871 and 1914. In the staff lists of Prussian and Imperial German armies from 1806 to 1940, the same names recur in generation after generation: von Moltke, von Manstein, von Manteuffel, von der Marwitz, von Stulpnagel, von Kleist, von Hutier, von Falkenstein, even von Francois, and many others. Whatever degree of political naïveté or culpability attaches to the abject acceptance of Hitler by nearly all of the 1930s generation of the junker military hierarchy, there can be no question of their love of the fatherland, their sense of duty or their military fitness and competence.

To the canvas of geopolitical imperative and military capability there was added an intellectual and philosophical dimension. Unrestricted by the class division of the nineteenth-century structure of education in England, or by the conflict between clerical and anti-clerical prejudices which undermined the French system, 'German universities were at this time the best in Europe'.[16] A succession of philosophers of worldwide renown preached a series of messages very comforting to the susceptibilities of a state whose very existence depended upon the proficiency of its army: there is no propaganda so effective as that which its target audience wants to hear and longs to believe. Kant taught the doctrine of duty for duty's sake. Hegel considered that the state was 'God walking upon earth' and that individual well-being or happiness were of no account when they conflicted with the greatness of the state.[17] Nietzsche preached the philosophy of the superman (*Übermensch*) whose most important characteristic was his will to achieve power. In the closing years of the century Treitschke, professor of philosophy in Berlin, would draw together these threads in the doctrine that Germany under the house of Hohenzollern had a supranational ruling destiny. The historical process had achieved its ultimate attainment in the Prussian state of his time. Nothing was impossible to German heroism, and Germany was far more fitted to be the governing race of the world than the frivolous and decadent French or the amateur Anglo-Saxons.[18] It is small wonder that A.J.P. Taylor summarises the governing strand of thought in Prussia in the wake of her experience at the hands of Napoleon as: 'Unless we grow greater we shall become less.'[19] This is put forward as the guiding principle for the actions of Bismarck, who for forty years, from 1851 onwards, following his appointment as a virtual 'unknown', even within Prussia, to be the delegate of his country to the recently established German Federal Diet at Frankfurt, was master of Prussia's foreign policy.

Twenty years later, when the unification of Germany under the unquestioned leadership of Prussia had been achieved, this policy might perhaps be relaxed to ensuring that everything possible was done to secure what had been gained. This relaxation did not long survive the dismissal of

Bismarck in 1890. Given Prussia's strategic circumstances, and what can justifiably be described as her national characteristics, state of mind and intellectual beliefs, a head-on conflict with the Habsburg Empire was inevitable.

The Habsburg Dilemma

In contrast to the imperative for expansion which drove the energies of Prussia, Austria after the Congress of Vienna sought no more than to hold on to what she had and to govern her multi-racial empire by a continuation of the benevolent despotism of Maria Theresa and her son, Emperor Joseph II. If the forces of liberalism and nationalism were to render this course impossible, notwithstanding the numerous attempts made throughout the nineteenth century to produce a governmental structure acceptable to all and to placate the non-German races of the empire, it is possible nevertheless to argue that the nineteenth-century realms of the Habsburgs, administered as they were with some degree of competence from Vienna, provided a far better guarantee of the peace of Europe and a state structure more likely to achieve the greatest good for the greatest number than any system in the twentieth century.

The Peace of Versailles which concluded the First World War was an attempt to produce nation states in Central Europe which would be strategically and economically viable, and at the same time to put into practice the tenth and eleventh of President Wilson's Fourteen Points. These required, *inter alia*, that the peoples of Austria–Hungary should be accorded an opportunity for 'autonomous development' and that Serbia should be given access to the sea. Writing in the concluding years of the twentieth century and after sufficient lapse of time to allow an objective view to be taken of the pattern of Europe established at Versailles, it is self-evident that this particular design has proved to be an unmitigated disaster. The unnatural marriages of mutually inimical peoples which produced the states of Yugoslavia and Czechoslovakia have failed totally. Well-meaning but dogmatic liberalism could do no more than paper over the cracks of centuries-old antagonisms. The fourteen points, combined with a perception that Austria had to be punished for her part in initiating the First World War, fathered a structure of weak states, mutually mistrustful, which when threatened fell victim almost at once to 'the first plausible rabble-rouser'.[20] These owed their re-establishment entirely to the enormous cost of the Second World War. Only post-Versailles Austria, comprising the lands of the ancient archduchy of Austria and the Tyrol, escaped engulfment in the glacis of buffer states designed to protect the western frontiers of the Soviet Union. Once the dead hand of totalitarian despotism had been removed for the second time inside half a century, the composite creations of Versailles disintegrated as soon as the incompatible ethnic strains within them had gained the freedom to make their views felt.

It is tempting to conclude that, for all its faults, the Habsburg Empire provided a better form of government for its peoples than any of its heirs. Things might have been better ordered had an attempt been made to support an evolutionary development of the status quo ante 1914 in Central Europe, instead of adopting wholesale the guileless designs of a professor from Princeton with an inadequate understanding of European history. Of course it may well be that, had this course been chosen, the forces of nationalism would have been too strong for any federal structure.

Whatever groundswell of belief or perception of wrong and deprivation causes a revolution, the event which precipitates violence in the streets is, more often than not, trivial. As with the smashing of a baker's shop window in St Petersburg in March 1917, so it was throughout Europe in February 1848. By the end of that month, after no more than a few days' rioting in Paris, Vienna and Berlin, the bourgeois monarchy of France was at an end and its king fled to England. Metternich, the stabiliser of Europe since the fall of Napoleon, was in flight and King Frederick William IV of Prussia and Emperor Ferdinand of Austria had been forced to abandon their capitals. It must be recorded that neither monarch was personally at risk from the demonstrators. The emperor was faced with three concurrent crises, any of which could have been terminal for the empire there and then. The king of Sardinia, which since 1815 had included Piedmont, assisted by the forces working towards Italian unity, seized the opportunity to invade the empire's possessions in northern Italy east of the River Ticino, which formed the boundary between Piedmont and Lombardy. Hungary was in total revolution. Although its nobility, a peasant–aristocracy, not dissimilar in lifestyle and attitude to the junkers of Prussia, maintained a degree of loyalty to the emperor as king of Hungary, their fundamental aim was independence from the German-dominated rule of Vienna – an independence which, once achieved, they continued strenuously to deny to the minority races within the lands of the Crown of St Stephen. Their obduracy and its psychological and practical consequences was a prime cause of the ultimate collapse of the Habsburg Empire. Thirdly, liberal forces in Germany, had combined to offer the crown of a united Germany, excluding Austria, to King Frederick William IV, who had accepted under duress a liberal constitution for Prussia. Subsidiary difficulties for the Habsburg monarch included a revolt in Prague inspired by Czech nationalist aspirations and the rioting in Vienna already alluded to, which had forced the fall from power of Metternich and the hurried departure of court and government, first to Innsbruck and later to Olmutz. The emperor, Ferdinand, feeble-minded, epileptic and rickety, was not the ruler to set things right. His abdication was engineered and he was succeeded by his nephew Franz Joseph, destined for a reign of sixty-eight years and a series of personal tragedies and public disasters, any one of which might have been regarded as enough for one lifetime or reign. The empire lasted Franz Joseph's lifetime, but for only two years thereafter.

Nevertheless, it is a measure of the strength rather than the weakness of the Habsburg government in 1848 that most of these impending disasters were averted by the internal resources of the empire. Marshal Radetzky had 75,000 soldiers in the quadrilateral of fortresses south of Lake Garda – Peschiera, Mantua, Legnano and Verona. As a young general he had emerged with more credit than most from the campaign of 1809. Now, he defeated the forces of Italian nationalism at the Battles of Custozza and Novara. A second paladin of the empire, Prince Windischgraetz, restored order in Prague and Vienna and a third, Prince Schwarzenburg, effectively first minister of the empire for the first four years of the new reign, re-established a central government as firmly as was possible in the circumstances of the empire at the time. But it took two years, the mobilisation of four Austrian Army corps and a final ultimatum to expire within three days to force Frederick William into rejecting the pan-German crown; a surrender as humiliating as his soldiers had found the original offer at the hands of liberalism. Within twenty years, international disagreement about the offer of another crown would see Prussia handing out the humiliation.

The revolt in Hungary could not be suppressed by the resources of the empire, and the tsar had to be called in to help. Not only was this intervention the first cause of endless subsequent friction between the two empires, but Hungary and its Magyar ruling caste imposed a total inhibition on any form of satisfactory political evolution for the other races of the empire. By demanding self-government within the historic lands of the Crown of St Stephen and parity of standing with the Germans within the rest of the empire, they enforced second class status on all the other nationalities. The most authoritative and sympathetic study of the last seventy years of the life of the empire assesses the Magyar contribution as 'some dashing regiments of cavalry, a large number of surpassingly beautiful women and an infinity of woe'.[21] The practical effects of Magyar arrogance are perhaps best illustrated by the fact that even as late as 1914 there was no direct rail link between Vienna and Agram (now Zagreb), the capital of the imperial province of Croatia. Since Croatia was part of Transleithnia, as the Hungarian sphere of influence came to be called after the foundation of the Dual Monarchy in 1867, all rail traffic had to be routed through Buda Pesth. This had already seriously hampered the mobilisations for the wars of 1859 and 1866 and would do so again in 1914.

The ambition of Prussia, the negative influence of the Magyars and Italian nationalism remained fundamental problems of extreme difficulty for the Habsburg Empire for the remainder of its life.

The last was compounded by the course of events in France. Two forms of monarchy having failed and the Republic of 1848 likewise failing to gain the confidence of any element of the population outside Paris, France turned again to the Bonapartes. The nephew of Napoleon I was elected first as prince president but soon established himself as emperor of the French. This brought to power an intellectual believer in the rights of nationalities, who had in his youth fought for the cause of Italian nationalism, to which he was still bound by oath.

Louis Napoleon proved more than willing to commit France to war in this cause, victory in which, as an issue of equal importance to him, would regain some of the prestige of his country lost by the defeat of his uncle. The probability of war between France and Austria was obvious. Some in Prussia saw further. In a letter to his brother, written in January 1853, Moltke, soon to become what would now be termed the military secretary to Prince Frederick William of Prussia, nephew of the king and ultimate heir-presumptive to the throne, said, 'He can scarcely hold his place without some victories.'[22]

Forging the Weapon

That Prussia regained at Vienna the territories which she had lost at Tilsit was due entirely to the contribution made by her armies in the campaigns from 1813 in southern Germany up to Waterloo. However, with the lapse of time, the fundamental quality which had made this success possible came to be misappreciated, except by a very few brains within the general staff. Political and popular imagination formed the view that the key factor had been the *levée en masse*, inspired by a universal determination to throw off the French yoke and a growing belief in German nationalism. A white heat of patriotic fervour, combined with a necessary minimum of training, equipment and organisation, was thought to have been enough to inflict a series of defeats on the armies of Napoleon, however much these had been hardened by almost continuous campaigning over the preceding twenty years. What was not widely grasped was that the most important ingredient in the victory had been the availability of the continuous *roulement* of trained manpower as organised by Scharnhorst, within the ceiling strength of 42,000 imposed at Tilsit. This had made the most of nationalist and patriotic enthusiasm at a time when the recalled conscripts had still been of an age to reacquire very quickly their battlefield skills and fitness. Nor, as the years went by, was the attenuation of the *Grande Armée*, which had been brought about by the campaigns in the peninsula and Russia sufficiently appreciated.

The mobilisation laws enacted by the kingdom of Prussia in 1814 and 1815 were intended to meet the two fundamental requirements of the nation. First, the large standing army essential, as we have seen, because of Prussia's geopolitical situation; secondly, the availability of all fit manpower for the army in emergency. All fit adult males were compelled, starting at age twenty, to serve for three years with the colours followed by two in the army reserve. After completing this five year obligation, they then had a liability to serve for a further fourteen years in the Landwehr. This was an organisation of territorial units, administered separately from the standing army, and structured in two divisions, each of seven annual intakes of conscripts. Thus, in theory at least, every male subject of the king of Prussia between the ages of twenty and forty was available for the army. On mobilisation, the units of the standing army were brought up to their war establishments by the recalled reservists, and the formations, brigade, division and corps, made up of a mix of standing army and first-division Landwehr units. Second-division Landwehr units were intended to provide fortress garrisons, lines of communication security detachments and the raw material for the circumvallation[b] force in sieges.

The 1815 laws also established the relationship between the army corps organisation and the provinces of the kingdom which was to remain the foundation of the structure of the army of Prussia, and later that of Germany, for the next century. Each province of the realm provided an army corps on a common organisation of two infantry divisions and one cavalry division, with supporting artillery batteries. After mobilisation, which was expected to take no longer than three weeks, even before the availability of railways, the total war strength of the corps was about 30,000. Each corps drew its manpower from a single province: I East Prussia, II Pomerania, III Brandenburg, IV Lower Saxony, V Polish Prussia, VI Silesia, VII Westphalia, VIII Rhine

---

[b] See Appendix B.

provinces. Only the Guard Corps recruited nationwide. This framework was to prove itself fully capable of expansion and extension. By 1870, the armies of Hanover, Saxony, Hesse and Bavaria, all but the last of which had fought *against* Prussia in the war of 1866, had been readily assimilated on the same organisation. The two army corps furnished by Bavaria were numbered I and II in deference to the continuing independence of the Wittelsbachs, but the manpower of Schleswig–Holstein formed IX Corps, X Corps came from Hanover, XI from Hesse and XII from Saxony. As we shall see, X Corps played a critical role in the first, and strategically decisive, battle in Lorraine in 1870. It speaks volumes for the competence of the Prussian military machine that it proved able to pick up, equip, train and motivate manpower from a state which had been hostile four years previously and bring it to a point at which this formation could undertake a battlefield task which went well beyond a stolid and static defence.

The strengths of Prussia's military organisation were, first, its ability to form a cohesive grouping of all arms strong enough to conduct at least a holding action on any threatened frontier until it could be reinforced. Secondly, unlike those in the French Army, the brigade, division and corps formations and their headquarters were permanent and not formed ad hoc on mobilisation. Commanders and staffs knew their units and vice versa. Thirdly, and perhaps most important, the liability to universal service provided the strongest of unifying influences in a disparate and fragmented nation. After 1815, the majority of the subjects of the king of Prussia were not Prussians at all. But however dissimilar the Prussian and the Rhinelander, the Silesian and the man from Westphalia, their common experience of the Prussian Army, and continuing liability to recall in its service, was perhaps the strongest practical factor in the creation of a single national entity. Nor did the voice of liberalism in Prussia dissent. When the military leadership of Prussia decided that reform of the national service laws required a major expansion of the army, liberal opinion, which had its adherents even among the general staff, did not disagree with the principle of universal service. What it baulked at, to the point which almost brought down the monarchy, was the abolition of the separate status of the Landwehr.[23]

Nevertheless, the Prussian Army had its inherent weaknesses. The standard corps organisation presupposed an equal number of recruits from each province, the populations of which were, inevitably, unequal. More importantly, as the years went by, the induction system could not cope with the larger number of conscripts deriving from the growing population of Prussia. In 1815, this had been around 10,000,000, which had generated 40,000 recruits annually, and thus a rank and file strength of 120,000 for the peacetime standing army. The reservists and the first-division Landwehr units aggregated with the peacetime strength gave a theoretical first-line war establishment of 480,000 rank and file, or the product of twelve annual classes of conscripts, with a further 280,000 supposedly available from the remaining seven classes who formed the second division of the Landwehr. Of course, the notional baseline figure of 40,000 was progressively eroded by such natural causes as early mortality and emigration. Other shortcomings became apparent. There was an obvious inbuilt disparity between the units of the standing army and those of the Landwehr which together were expected to constitute a homogeneous army corps. The officers of the Landwehr were not only far less well trained than their long-service counterparts in the units of the standing army, receiving their commissions on the basis of no more than a single year's preparatory training, but also, drawn as they were from outside the junker caste, could no longer be regarded as politically reliable, as the events of 1848 were to prove. And although the revolt in Berlin in that year was brought to an end by the timely intervention of the standing army, successive mobilisations from 1849 onwards were to show that machinery and procedures had grown rusty. First, in a curtain raiser for the later conflicts over the ownership of Schleswig–Holstein, the Prussian Army was defeated by the Danes. Moltke, in a detailed study of this war, not completed until 1862, summed up the root cause, not so much as defective mobilisation procedures, which by then had become fully apparent through other events, but because: 'Die Danen kämpften eben mit zwei Waffen, zu Lande und zur See, die Deutschen nur mit einem.'[c24]

This mistake would not be repeated in 1864. Nevertheless, the humiliation for a military state was emphatic.

Worse was to happen. The great lateral road which traverses the North German plain, equally important to Napoleon and Hitler, and which provided Prussia with her military and administrative link between Brandenburg and her Rhineland provinces, runs though Hesse. In a dispute with his subjects, the elector of Hesse had asked for, and received, military support from Austria and Bavaria, thus disregarding a long-standing but unformalised convention that, in disputes within states of the empire north of the River Main, Prussia had the primary interest and should be the power of first resort. Intervention by south German states not only threatened Prussia's immediate practical interests, but also provided Schwarzenburg with the necessary vehicle to

---

[c] 'The Danes fought with two armies, on land and sea, the Germans [sic] only with one.'

enable him to force Frederick William IV into rejecting the crown of a united Germany, as has already been described. Although Prussia had mobilised, and shots had been exchanged between Austrian and Prussian troops, Prussia preferred not to risk war. Mobilisation was ordered again in 1859, so that Prussia could offer support to Emperor Franz Joseph, currently losing his war in Lombardy against the renascent French Second Empire and the forces of Italian nationalism. The threat of Prussian intervention at a time when the French eastern frontier was virtually undefended was the determining factor in the decision of Napoleon III to settle for peace without having obtained Venetia as well as Lombardy for the new kingdom of Italy.[25] The military leadership of Prussia was once again glad enough not to have been put to the test of war. Nevertheless, Moltke in 1860, two years after his confirmation in post as chief of the general staff, in an appreciation of his country's geopolitical interests in relation to those of the other European powers, foresaw as inevitable war with both Austria and France, if necessary concurrently but, if so, not without allies.[26]

Matters had drifted throughout the 1850s because of the increasing incapacity of King Fredrick William IV.[27] In 1858 he was declared incurably insane and his brother William became regent, succeeding to the throne three years later. King William I had been a soldier all his life, starting his direct military experience as a boy of sixteen in the Prussian Army at the Battle of Arcis sur Aube in 1814.[28] He loved the army as an end in itself, with a passion akin to that of Frederick William I. The new Supreme Warlord was convinced by the shortcomings of the mobilisation of 1859 that something had to be done.

The chief cause of the decay was that, though the population of Prussia had almost doubled by the middle of the century to 18,000,000, the capacity of the army to accept recruits had not grown beyond the 40,000 a year generated by the 1815 population.[29] The consequence was that, while an estimated 25,000 fit twenty year olds were escaping conscription altogether, breadwinners and fathers of families into their thirties remained liable for front-line combat service by reason of their commitment to serve in the first-division units of the Landwehr. The existing minister of war, the liberal-minded von Bonin, did not feel equal to the task of a reconstruction, which all appreciated would involve some diminution of the status of the Landwehr. Late in 1859 he was succeeded by the third member of the triumvirate (we have already encountered Bismarck and Moltke), who within twelve years had carried Prussia to the summit and made an emperor of their somewhat reluctant king. Albrecht von Roon had none of the charm of appearance and manner so highly prized before the advent of the era of the common man. Indeed, he resembled a more than usually brutish drill sergeant and liked to refer to himself as 'the king's sergeant'.[30] As major general commanding the 14th Division of VII Corps, based in Dusseldorf, he had already, at the request of the regent, produced a blueprint for reform. As war minister, he now had to carry this through the Prussian parliament. Prussia since 1850 had had a constitution of sorts, which vested the raising of taxes within the constitution itself rather than by annual vote of parliament, but there had been an earlier promise by the monarch that no new loan would be raised without the consent of a national assembly.[31] And it was beyond question that Roon's reforms would need a great deal of money.

These required an expansion of one-third in the size of the standing army. Service with the colours was to remain at three years, but the annual intake of manpower would increase from 40,000 to 63,000, thus ensuring that all available manpower was conscripted, and the term of service in the reserve would double from two years to four. Men would then pass to the Landwehr, but would remain liable to recall on mobilisation to first-line units for their initial year in this organisation.[32] Thus the army at war strength would draw upon eight conscript classes much larger than the previous five. The theoretical rank and file strength of 504,000 on mobilisation was, on paper at least, not much larger than before, but it was far more efficient by reason of the increased number of men in their physical prime, the higher proportion of soldiers with the colours and reservists with recent service, and, above all, because of the abolition of the separate administration of Landwehr and field army. As has already been noted, it was the degradation of status of the Landwehr which caused the Prussian parliament to refuse to vote the necessary finance. For three years, various expedients and compromises were tried. Roon, but not the king, was prepared to reduce the period of full-time service to two years. Parliament voted finance for single years only, and only on condition that there would be no change to the status of the Landwehr, something manifestly incompatible with the principle of the Roon restructuring.

An increasing number of people in Berlin began to see Bismarck as the 'homme necessaire' to resolve a constitutional crisis which had already caused King William I to threaten to abdicate. He would not give up the proposed reforms, forbade Roon to offer the reduction in the period of full-time service (on which the liberal-minded crown prince supported his father) and, while still regent, had already presented colours to the thirty-nine new regiments of infantry and ten of cavalry raised to accept the increased manpower.[33] But

Bismarck, who, following seven years' service as Prussian delegate to the Assembly of the Federal Diet in Frankfurt, had been his country's ambassador in St Petersburg and Paris, was very far from being the natural choice of the king. When the appointment had first been mooted in 1860, Bismarck had demanded full control of Prussia's foreign policy. It was not until two and a half years later, when all other options had been exhausted, that William conceded this vital point and Bismarck became prime minister of Prussia.

It was very nearly one of the shortest-lived ministries in history. On his first appearance in the Prussian parliament, within a week of taking office, Bismarck made what has become celebrated as his 'blood and iron' speech:

> Germany does not look to Prussia's liberalism, but to her strength... The great questions of the day will not be decided by speeches and the resolutions of majorities... but by iron and blood.

King William, who had gone to Baden-Baden to take the cure, was appalled by this confrontational approach and entrained for Berlin to dismiss his new first minister. Bismarck travelled to meet him. The argument ended, as so many between the two men were to do in the future, with the capitulation of the sovereign. William forecast the same fate for himself and Bismarck as had befallen King Charles I of England and his minister Strafford. Bismarck's reply, 'Better that than surrender', restored the nerve of the simple soldier–king, and Europe was set on course for all that followed.

Bismarck set out to resolve the constitutional struggle in a way his country, and later Europe, would soon come to recognise as characteristic. First, he offered to withdraw the budget for reconsideration; when this was refused Bismarck succeeded in having the budget passed in the upper house.

> There was now, he said, 'a hole' in the constitution. Money could be spent only with the agreement of the king and the two houses. They had failed to agree. Therefore the king must spend the money until they reached agreement.'[34]

On 13th October, three weeks after Bismarck had come to power, parliament was adjourned and, in September of the following year, dissolved altogether. It was not until 1866, in the wake of the triumph in the war with Austria, that the expansion of the Prussian Army and its cost were regularised retrospectively by the Prussian parliament.[35]

Before examining the part played by Bismarck in precipitating the Wars of Prussian Supremacy it is necessary to look at the organisation within Prussia for the administration of the army, and for the planning and control of operations. Under the king, part of whose title was Supreme Warlord, there were, between 1815 and 1866 three foci of power: the chief of the general staff, the minister of war and the chief of the king's military cabinet. The first of these posts had existed effectively since 1801, and had included the right of *Immediatvortrag*, that is, direct access to, and thus unimpeded ability to influence, the Supreme Warlord. From the time of Scharnhorst's appointment up to the end of the war in 1815, it is beyond question that the chief of the general staff had primacy. However, more heads of state, including even Prussian and German monarchs, enjoy playing soldiers than are out-and-out warmongers, and in the prolonged period of peace after 1815 the chief of the military cabinet increasingly assumed a preponderant influence, which by the 1850s was decisive. The post had also assumed most of the functions of a present-day adjutant general's department, thus dealing with the minutiae of ceremonial parades and uniforms so dear to the heart of so many rulers. The minister of war was always a general; his function with regard to parliament was to explain rather than to justify the administration of the army, and still less to seek approval by gaining a majority vote, at least until the head-on clash brought about by Roon's proposals. When von Moltke was appointed provisional chief of the general staff in 1857, the office was subordinate to that of the minister of war and undoubtedly lying third in the pecking order, the *Immediatvortrag* having long since lapsed. Moltke was not consulted about the Roon proposals for the expansion of the army, and in 1861 his office was bypassed completely in a scheme designed to resolve the dispute over the army budget by force of arms. Instructions emanating from von Manteuffel, the head of the military cabinet, and the minister of war directed the commander of one of the two Guard infantry divisions, Hiller von Gaertringen, to prepare plans for the occupation of Berlin by a force of 35,000 men and 100 guns.[36] This plan was never implemented.

The responsibility of the general staff as inherited by Moltke was to prepare strategic appreciations and operational plans, including those for mobilisation, and to superintend all major formation training exercises, but the functions were in essence those of a think-tank rather than an executive. The office, however much it might appear to be operating *in vacuo*, nevertheless had two strengths. The first was the high quality of its officers, even before the rigorous processes of selection and training instituted by Moltke. The second was the personality and attributes of the man himself.

Many authorities have stated that when Moltke was appointed he was virtually unknown in the army. Certainly his appointment was a surprise. He himself, in a letter years earlier to one of his brothers, had envisaged the summit of his career as chief of staff of a corps, and retirement thereafter.[37] However, after a successful tour of duty in just such an appointment with IV Corps, throughout the excitements of 1849–50, at a time when the Lower Saxony formation would have been in the forefront of the battle had there been war with Austria, he was appointed, as has already been noted, military secretary and aide-de-camp to Prince Frederick William of Prussia. In attendance on the ultimate heir presumptive to the throne he visited the courts at Balmoral and Paris, and witnessed manoeuvres by the English and French armies. His perspicacious assessment of the weakness of the Second Empire has been mentioned previously. After successfully controlling the manoeuvres of the two Polish-recruited corps (V and VI) in Silesia in the summer of 1858, he was confirmed in his appointment in September of that year. His early appreciation of the strategic effects of railways and the electric telegraph are analysed elsewhere in this book. Fundamental as was Moltke's application of these major technological advances in the successes shortly to be gained by the Prussian Army, his most important contribution lay in his long-term education programme for the officers of the general staff.

Although the Kriegs Akademie came under the inspector general of military education and would so remain until 1872, when it was placed under Moltke's direct control,[38] the career development of its graduates was in the hands of the chief of the general staff. Entry to the Kriegs Akademie was by competitive examination, from the best of the officers in their late twenties, i.e. those who had already proved their competence as regimental officers. An annual intake of forty emerged from a field of about 120. Moltke took no more than twelve of these at the end of each course and set out to prepare them to be the nervous system for the command and control of the Prussian Army in the field. By a combination of supervised desk work and practical instruction on the 'staff rides' which have since become a training medium in all staff colleges and developed armies, he set out to ensure that his pupils, when confronted with a given operational set of circumstances, would all react in the same way. As officers throughout their service alternated in each rank between staff and regimental duty, as has been the practice in the British Army since the end of World War I, Moltke's concepts would, in the fullness of time, percolate through all arms and most regiments, but the primary aim of his training was to guarantee that formations in the face of the enemy would base their action on common principles predictable alike to higher headquarters and other combat groupings ordered up in support. Moreover Moltke combined a thorough study of Clausewitz with a comprehension of the military effects of emerging technology. He could relate a detailed knowledge of the campaigns of Frederick the Great and Napoleon both to the Clausewitzian doctrine of the total nature of warfare, and appreciate also that warfare based on the sum of the resources of a contemporary modern state would generate battles far larger than any single commander could control on the basis of his own direct observation. Since in these circumstances no detailed plan would survive contact with the enemy, it followed that a new technique of high command was required. But it was not enough for subordinate commanders to learn to operate within a framework of broad directive rather than precise order. It was essential that they be trained to act, and react in the same way. Nevertheless, the senior generals of the Prussian Army already *en poste* and suspicious of new ideas might prove unreceptive and untrainable. Old dogs, especially those of princely birth, might be reluctant to learn new tricks. It was essential, therefore, to place at their side an officer who had been trained and proven in the new methods as far as was possible in conditions short of battle.

At the start of the war of 1866, the general staff numbered no more than eighty-three officers, eight at royal headquarters, seven at each of the three army HQ, three with each of nine corps HQ, and one with the headquarters of each infantry and cavalry division; twenty-seven in all. Although by the war of 1870 this figure had more than doubled, to 190,[39] the critical fact remained the influence of the officers of the general staff, rather than their numbers. Moltke remained as chief of the general staff until after the accession of the young emperor, Wilhelm II. By the end of his thirty-year term of duty he had inculcated the principle that all orders emanating from a formation headquarters were the dual responsibility of both the chief of staff and the commander. The latter might or might not be general staff-trained, or otherwise unamenable to discipline. But his alter ego, the chief of staff, had not only passed through this training but had been chosen specifically for his present appointment, with a view to ensuring that his commander conformed to the general staff intention.

However, in 1858 the practical evolution of Moltke's command technique, necessarily and diametrically different from that of Napoleon and geared totally both to the conditions of mid-nineteenth-century warfare and the human material with which he had to deal, was some way short of attainment. Nevertheless, within the limits allowed to him, Moltke's influence began to make itself felt. The year 1858 saw the publication of the first of his annual summaries, not only of the lessons derived from his own staff rides but also those emerging from the exercises conducted by all formations of the Prussian Army. Thus, a common concept of the conduct of battle began to emerge. The long drawn-out study of the 1849 war with Denmark was at last completed, and its lessons disseminated. More immediately, there was a meticulous analysis undertaken at a far more urgent pace of all aspects of the operations of both sides in the war of 1859 between France and Austria, including critical evaluations of formation commanders. At the same time the general staff was reorganised into three geographic planning divisions, together with a historical section given improved status and impetus, and an entirely new department, with responsibility for railways. The first major rail transport exercise was held in 1862, and dealt, prophetically, with the mobilisation of the army to the area north-east of Hamburg, the 'general idea' of the exercise being the build-up to a war with Denmark.[40]

The genesis of the war for Schleswig–Holstein, when it occurred in 1864, was political and will be examined in the next section of this chapter. Suffice it to say for the present that it was this war which began the restoration of the office of chief of the general staff to its primary position. At the formal request of the minister of war, Moltke had made a number of suggestions for the conduct of the campaign, but initially these were disregarded. Operational directives emanated from the king, which meant the military cabinet under Manteuffel, through the war minister, Roon, to the appointed field commander, von Wrangel, a general of fossilised intellect, who saw no need for a general staff and stated that it was a shame and a disgrace for a field marshal of the Prussian Army to have to submit to a lot of 'damned clerking'.[41] It was the incompetence of von Wrangel, and the concurrent need to replace his chief of staff, Vogel von Falckenstein, which gave Moltke a post of executive responsibility. He had gone to the war in attendance on the king as no more than an observer, but when the army was regrouped into separate components, one to pursue the Danes into the Jutland peninsula and the other to undertake amphibious operations across the Bight of Kiel towards Zeeland, Moltke was made chief of staff of the whole field army.[42] Concurrently, Manteuffel was replaced as the head of the king's military cabinet, as a result of a political manoeuvre by Roon, by the less ambitious and more cerebral von Tresckow. The latter persuaded the king that Moltke should attend meetings of the ministerial council whenever military matters were likely to come under discussion.[43] Moltke's influence grew to the point that, on 2nd June, 1866, with war against Austria imminent, a cabinet order decreed that the chief of the general staff could issue orders on his own authority, subject

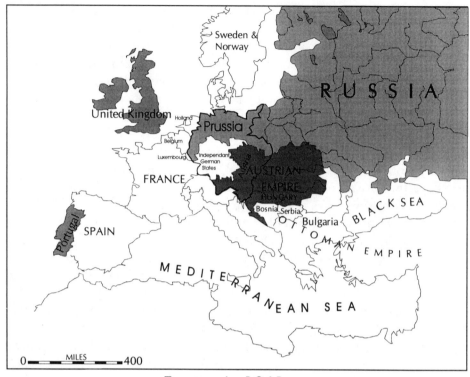

Europe in 1861

to his keeping the war minister informed.[44] Nevertheless, for a little while longer, Moltke's authority would remain open to question. Both Goerlitz and Howard[45] quote the celebrated incident at the critical moment of the Battle of Sadowa. Moltke despatched an order to Manstein, commanding the reserve division of the Prussian 1st Army, to restrain him from joining in the attack until the 2nd Army had reached the battlefield after a difficult approach march. Manstein's reaction: 'This seems to be all in order. But who is General von Moltke?'

It is impossible to credit that Manstein, commanding a division in the Brandenburg Corps, did not know Moltke, already eight years in post as chief of the general staff. But here was royal, or army group, headquarters, interfering directly 'two down'[d] in the tactical conduct of a battle in progress. To that extent, Manstein's question was justified. But after Sadowa it would not be asked again.

The Road to Sadowa

Since the conduct of politics is a matter of expediency rather than principle, few politicians can lay claim to total consistency, Bismarck perhaps less than any. If, throughout his whole life, his twin detestations were the forces of liberalism and any exercise of Austrian power in Germany, he was never reluctant to manipulate one against the other, or both against a third party. Hindsight may give events an aura of inevitability, and although at the end of his career, a politician may claim that all his actions were geared to the attainment of a goal which he had set himself from the outset, it is the responsibility of the analytical historian to test any such contentions. The tactics of Bismarck's foreign policy were never consistent. Regarding the other three continental Great Powers, he would in turn provoke wars with Austria and France, and very nearly come to blows with Russia, but, while opposing any one of them, he would find means to conciliate, or at least to neutralise, the others. Nor can Bismarck have foreseen for any great length of time before it actually happened the ceremony in the Galerie des Glaces at Versailles on 18th January, 1871, which inaugurated the German Empire while the Siege of Paris was still in progress. Even less can Bismarck have predicted far ahead his role in 1878 as the arbiter of Europe, when the Congress of Berlin, under his chairmanship, resolved for the time being the competing involvements of

---

[d] On the face of it, three down. But the 1st Army had abandoned temporarily their corps organisation, and orders were going direct from first army HQ to divisions.

Austria, Russia and Turkey in the Balkans, while at the same time satisfying the maritime interest of England in the region.

What it is possible to claim for Bismarck is that the success of each of the steps he took towards a relatively limited objective led inexorably to the next. He went in 1851 as the delegate of Prussia to the Federal Diet at Frankfurt in a position of extreme weakness, not only because of his own minimal experience of diplomacy and public affairs, but also because of the recent double humiliation of his country, in the war of 1849 with Denmark and the enforced acceptance of Schwarzenburg's terms at Olmutz the following year. Nevertheless, his personal aim from the start was to secure acknowledged parity for Prussia with Austria within Germany. He had no instructions to this effect from either his king or his government. He evolved his own, and, notwithstanding his subordinate position, the policy of Prussia's representative at Frankfurt became almost inevitably the foreign policy of his country. Perhaps he saw sooner than most that Austria neither would nor could concede equality of status without a war. Unlike a twentieth-century statesman, who will seek to avoid war at almost any price because his whole thinking has been conditioned by the horrors of two world wars, it is beyond question that Bismarck considered war not merely as a threat, but to engage in it as legitimate in the interests of his country. It followed that the diplomatic ground had to be thoroughly prepared in order to ensure that Prussia embarked upon war on the most favourable terms possible, to compensate for her strategic weakness; hence the shifting tactics. Although Moltke would remind him that nothing in war is certain, Bismarck would court it nevertheless, whenever he considered that Prussia's immediate aim could not be achieved in any other way.

Four strands of events led to the war of 1866: the exclusion of Austria from the German customs union (*Zollverein*) established in 1818; the claim of Prussia to supremacy of status in Germany north of the River Main, which originated with William I rather than with Bismarck; the failure of Emperor Franz Joseph to achieve by negotiation a federation of the states of Germany under Austrian leadership; and the actual *casus belli*, the dispute over the sovereignty of the twin duchies of Schleswig and Holstein. Bismarck's attitude to all these points of conflict was totally pragmatic: each was exploited without regard to any principle other than the immediate advantage of Prussia. Either, as with admission to the *Zollverein*, Austria wanted something within the gift of Prussia which could be alternatively conceded if the price were right, or rejected if to do so would enhance Prussia's international prestige; or, as with formal acknowledgement of 'lead power' status for Prussia north of the Main,

Prussia could gain something from Austria without having to make an equivalent concession.

Throughout all his twenty-eight years as prime minister of Prussia, Bismarck's interest in commercial affairs was minimal. It might also be argued in retrospect that the exclusion of Austria from the *Zollverein* was inevitable, in view of the massive development of primary resources and heavy industry in the Ruhr, Prussian territory after 1815, and the influential body of opinion within Austria–Hungary which envisaged the Danube rather than the Rhine as the main axis of development for the empire. Nevertheless, a practical obstacle to the inclusion of Austria within the *Zollverein* had been removed by the abolition of a tariff barrier between Austria and Hungary in 1850. But when Austria applied to join, Bismarck, without any regard for commercial considerations, managed, from his position of little apparent influence and less power, to force deferment of consideration of the application for ten years. In 1865, when Austria duly sought a decision, Bismarck was in a position to make it himself. Predictably, the Austrian request was rejected outright.

Similarly, formal acknowledgement of Prussian primacy north of the Main was treated by both sides as a matter of prestige. It was the price demanded by the regent for positive Prussian support for Austria in the war of 1859. The concession would have conferred little practical benefit on Prussia, and would have cost Franz Joseph nothing to make.[46] Nevertheless, he would not do so. When Prussia mobilised, it was in her own interests rather than those of Austria, and the Prussian threat was enough to persuade Napoleon III to bring the war to a close. The Habsburg Empire lost Lombardy to the new kingdom of Italy, but, as future events were to prove, had failed to restrain the march towards Prussian hegemony in northern Germany.

The initiative of Franz Joseph and his advisers in the quest for a more positive German union than had stemmed from the Frankfurt Diet sprang from a variety of motives, some contradictory. In discussions monarch-to-monarch, Franz Joseph suggested to William I that his proposal was the only way to buttress the sovereign princes of Germany before they were engulfed by the tide of liberalism. Conversely, because the motive power towards German unification was liberal and not conservative, liberal thinkers were encouraged by the prospect of an all-German parliament with more power to act than the Diet. There was the obvious need to restore Habsburg prestige after the disastrous war of 1859. There was the German–Austrian view in Vienna that the proposed federation would secure the primacy of German influence within the empire, thus containing the aspirations of Magyars, Czechs and others; and, perhaps above all, there was the view of Franz

Joseph's principal adviser throughout this diplomatic passage of arms, von Biegeleben, that this was the way to ensure Prussia would remain subordinate in status to Austria.[47] It was intended that the federation should be under Austrian presidency, with an executive consisting in the main of Austria and Prussia, a parliament of delegates from all the states of Germany and all the armies under unified control, nominally that of the parliament, but in practice of Austria.[48] While King William's simple soul rejoiced at his invitation to attend a conference of all the princes, to be held at Frankfurt in August 1863, which would discuss the imperial design for the future, Bismarck forced him to see the flaws in the proposal from the Prussian standpoint. The argument with the Prussian parliament over the Roon reforms was at its height; how could the king coerce or circumvent his own parliament but admit that a federal assembly had the right to operational control over the Prussian Army? What was to become of the Prussian claim to primacy in Germany north of the Main? And was the Prussian Army really to fight for continued Habsburg possession of Venetia and the Trentino? Or against the Magyars in the not unlikely event of a repeat performance of 1848? Or against Russia on the side of Austria, in a quarrel over the Balkans? The king was persuaded not to attend the conference, which without Prussia could achieve nothing. The gathering ended with a face-saving formula to the effect that the princes of Germany would submit their individual sovereignties to a federal assembly if Prussia also agreed to do so.[48]

It is against this background – failure to achieve a greater measure of German unity by consent, a succession of Prussian diplomatic victories over Austria and the massive strengthening of the Prussian Army – which by late 1863 was well in hand – that there then occurred the death of King Frederick VII of Denmark, the last in the line of direct succession to the throne. His approaching demise had already precipitated a European crisis over Schleswig–Holstein. Opinions differ about the complexity of this problem. Lord Palmerston, in his second term of office as prime minister of England, declared that only three people had ever understood it: Albert, the Prince Consort, who was dead; a professor, who had been driven mad by it; and he himself, who had forgotten all about the matter. On the other hand, it has been suggested that the question could have been resolved without fuss by any competent property solicitor.[49] What is certain is that Bismarck used the crisis to destroy, for all time, any possibility of Austrian leadership of Germany.

To the late twentieth-century mind, aware of the agonies of indecision and conflicting interests which preceded the entry of both England and the United States to both world wars, the pretexts for the wars of 1864, 1866 and 1870 seem trivial in the extreme. It has to be remembered that this was an age in which men were still prepared to risk their lives in duels over 'affairs of honour' (whereas today they would more probably initiate legal action), and national leaders, Bismarck more than any, who felt justified in using war as an instrument of policy. National prestige was still sufficient excuse for fighting.

Schleswig and Holstein had been adjuncts of the Danish crown since 1460, but unlike the crown itself were subject to the provisions of the Salic law: '*In terram Salicam mulieres non succedant.*'[50] Holstein, but not Schleswig, had been a fief of the Holy Roman Empire and so after 1815 was a state of the German Confederation, which meant that Austria would have an interest in any question of its sovereignty. By the middle of the nineteenth century, the population of Holstein and the southern half of Schleswig was predominantly German. Affected by the general spirit of unrest of 1848, and with a pretender, the duke of Augustenburg, laying claim to independent sovereignty over the duchies, the indigenous Germans rebelled against the Danish crown. They were supported by the armies of Prussia and Hanover, which, as we have seen, were defeated, and the Treaty of London of 1852 confirmed the duchies as Danish possessions, broadly on the previous terms. The pretender was bought off[51] but his son would claim twelve years later that this renunciation by the father did not affect the rights of his heir.

Thus matters rested until 1863, when, in the closing months of his life, King Frederick VII decreed the incorporation of the duchies within the sovereign territory of Denmark, partly in order to forestall the claim under the Salic law of the son of the 1849 pretender. While the German Diet directed that the forces of Saxony and Hanover should be used to restore the status quo, Bismarck decided that Prussia should take a hand in defence of the sanctity of the 1852 treaty. There were more practical influences shaping his policy. The need for possession of the Kiel Canal, to provide transit for a German fleet between the Baltic and the North Sea, thus avoiding the need to circumnavigate the Jutland peninsula, was an emerging issue. More importantly at the time, Bismarck was concerned to prevent the accession of a prince of reputed liberal and pro-Austrian sympathies and the foundation of yet another petty state in northern Germany. He wished above all else to prevent any permanent Austrian influence so near Prussia's borders. But while his own preference was for incorporation of the duchies within Prussia, he had to take account of the scruples of his king. William would accept the duchies if they were offered to him, but did not feel morally justified in taking them by force. Nor could Bismarck himself make such a move unilaterally in defiance of the 1852 treaty. Palmerston, as the voice of England, had spoken movingly about the independence of Denmark, but was not prepared to intervene. Russia was preoccupied with the assimilation of yet more Polish territory, and in any event Bismarck, while always grateful for Russian diplomatic support, was consistent in preferring never to have her practical help as this would always arrive too late and in too great a strength. Napoleon III, while favourable to the Prussian aspirations to incorporate the duchies on the basis of the rights of nationalities, was disinclined to take part because of the increasingly apparent open-ended nature of the French commitment in Mexico. There remained Austria. In a reversal of all previous positions and attitudes, Bismarck concluded an alliance with Austria in which no mention was made of either a Prussian guarantee of Venetia or Austrian concessions north of the Main. The alliance covered only an agreement to take joint action against Denmark because of her abrogation of the Treaty of London. The question of the ultimate sovereignty of the duchies was left for later decision.[52]

The course of the campaign of 1864 is of significance only as a proving ground for the restructured Prussian Army and the emergence of Moltke. A combination of the Prussian Army and the Austrian fleet reversed the result of 1849. Although neither England nor France was wholly sympathetic to the outcome, there was nothing practical which either nation was prepared to do about it. By the Treaty of Gastein, signed on 14th August, 1865, Austria received the administration of Holstein, Prussia that of Schleswig, while a small sliver of territory south-east of Hamburg, the duchy of Lauenburg, was ceded to Prussia outright.[e53]

It remained to extract Austria from Holstein. The triumvirate of Bismarck, Moltke and Roon all saw war with Austria as inevitable, and the reservations of the king were subdued by an unduly arrogant attitude taken by Austria over minor difficulties concerning the administration of Holstein. On 28th February, 1866, a council of war was held in Berlin, with the king presiding. He declared that Austria's conduct 'must finally be checked, even at the risk of war. We will not provoke a war, but we must go forward on our way and not shrink from war should it come.'[54] Moltke emphasised the importance of an alliance with Italy, because of the limitation this would impose on the number

---

[e] It was not, surely, coincidental that this title was among the mass of honours conferred on Bismarck when he finally left office in 1890. As he was already a prince of the German Empire it can have meant little to him and nothing, in any event, would have seemed sufficient compensation for the loss of the power which he felt himself uniquely equipped to exercise. His gratitude for this *douceur* is perhaps best assessed in the light of his stated determination to use the title 'only when travelling incognito'.

of soldiers which Austria could deploy on the northern frontiers of the empire. The bait for Italy was Venetia, and on 8th April Prussia and Italy concluded a treaty, to be valid for three months only, which obliged Italy to support Prussia in any war with Austria starting within that time limit. The promise of Venetia to Italy was sufficient to purchase the neutrality of France, because Napoleon III could feel that his long-standing promise was redeemed without the need for any positive contribution at a time when the Second Empire was heavily committed elsewhere. In a strategic appreciation prepared in the previous year at the request of Roon, Moltke had calculated that, while France could mobilise perhaps 270,000 men to fight in a European war, she had 'in Algeria, Mexico, Rome and on the way to Cochin-China at least 84,600,[55] and was therefore seriously overextended.

Bismarck got his war within three months partly because of the fact that Austria needed twice as long to mobilise as Prussia. Put at a disadvantage by the pincer threat posed by the Prussian–Italian alliance, Vienna ordered preparatory steps to be taken towards mobilisation on 13th April, in response to which Italy mobilised. Bismarck thereupon offered Austria a settlement on terms which would give Prussia her long-sought after command of all German forces north of the Main, thus disposing of the Austrian presence in Holstein, while command of the armies of the south German states would be conceded to Austria. The Austrian counter was a demand for a Prussian guarantee of Venetia, which Bismarck was unable to give because of his three month alliance with Italy. On 1st June, Austria referred the question of the sovereignty of the duchies to the Frankfurt Diet. Prussia claimed that this was in violation of the Gastein agreement ten months earlier, and proceeded to occupy Holstein. Although this operation took longer than either Bismarck or Moltke would have wished, it was nevertheless complete on 7th June, the small Austrian garrison being permitted to entrain at Hamburg for southern Germany.[56] A further appeal by Austria caused the Diet to agree on 14th June that the armies of Germany should be mobilised against Prussia. Thereafter, a state of war can be said to have been in existence between Prussia and Italy on the one hand, and the Austrian Empire on the other. The degree of involvement of the other states of the confederation, the most important of which were the kingdoms of Bavaria, Saxony and Hanover, remained in doubt for a few days longer.

Thus the pattern established by the Congress of Vienna and maintained thereafter by Metternich was broken. An Austrian victory in the ensuing war might have been the prelude for the evolutionary development of a federation of Central European states. Prussia's victory not only extinguished this possibility but also, by producing an immediate and obvious challenge to the security of France, made war in the near future between the two a virtual certainty, and in the longer term ensured that the European Great Powers would divide into two separate camps.

Notes

Seven principal sources have provided the background for the arguments put forward in Chapters VII and VIII, and for the military detail of the Sadowa campaign:

Fisher, *A History of Europe*, London, Edward Arnold and Co., 1936. This classic work remains the historian's best guide to the evolution of Europe, from the earliest times until the immediate aftermath of the Treaty of Versailles.

Fuller, *Decisive Battles of the Western World*, Stevenage, Spa Books, 1994, originally 1953, vol. II. Read in conjunction with Fisher, this comprehensive study of warfare gives the background to the military development of Prussia, and in particular the campaigns of Frederick the Great, which influenced so strongly the military education of Napoleon and the thinking of Clausewitz.

Crankshaw, *The Fall of the House of Habsburg*, London, Sphere Books, 1970, originally Longmans, 1963. A most comprehensive and sensitive analysis of the last seventy years of the Habsburg Empire. The author was prophetic at the time of writing, when Soviet power over Central Europe appeared to be both monolithic and permanent, about the fundamental non-viability of the states manufactured from the Habsburg domains by the Treaty of Versailles.

Goerlitz, *The German General Staff 1657–1945*, London, Hollis and Carter, 1953. This is an essential work of reference in any attempt to analyse the symbiotic relationship between the Prussian, and later German, army and nation.

Taylor, *Bismarck, the Man and the Statesman*, London, Penguin Books, 1995, originally Hamish Hamilton, 1955. This study, by the most authoritative British historian of nineteenth-century Europe, covers the key role of Bismarck as the originator and driving force of the foreign policy of Prussia from 1851 until 1890.

Bonnal, *Sadowa: Étude de Stratégie et de Tactique Générale*, Paris, Librarie Militaire, R. Chapelot et Cie, 1901. General Bonnal conducted detailed studies of the campaigns of 1866 and 1870 at a time when the French Army was concerned to establish the causes of the German victories in these two wars, in order to be prepared for the war of revenge which would gain the return of Alsace and Lorraine. Bonnal, a 'thinking soldier' and a meticulous analyst, when an instructor at the *École Supérieure de Guerre* in 1890, had as one of his students a tall, reserved and impressive-looking captain of chasseurs called Philippe Pétain, who was already developing an obsessive and at the time unfashionable belief in the primacy of firepower.

Whitton, *Moltke*, London, Constable and Co. Ltd, 1921. This book, long out of print, has been the author's primary source for the early career of Moltke and his decisive influence on the training of the general staff of the Prussian Army from 1857 onwards, and, in conjunction with Bonnal, for the campaign of 1866. Colonel Whitton himself relied upon Bonnal, and also on a study of the campaign in northern Bohemia made in the early years of the present century by a British officer, the then Lieutenant Colonel Niall Malcolm. Malcolm and Bonnal had the advantage of being able to walk the ground at a time when there would still have been local inhabitants with adult memories of the events of 1866, and before twentieth-century urban, industrial and communications developments had altered the perspective of the terrain over which the battle was fought; though the effect in northern Bohemia is less than elsewhere, see Appendix C. The fact that Malcolm undertook this work before the First World War indicates that he was a highly professional and thoughtful soldier, concerned to analyse the most recent campaigns in Europe at a time when Teutonic sabre-rattling was rising to a crescendo, and after nearly a century had passed since the British Army had last fought in a European war, apart from the Crimea. In the First World War Malcolm became a major general, CB and DSO. He had command of a division on the Western Front in the later stages of the war, having been previously chief of staff to Gough's Fifth Army. Colonel Whitton describes Malcolm's study, unfortunately not available to the author of this book, as 'an admirable critical survey and a model of what a campaign text book should be'; a description which might equally be applied to Whitton's own book, and also to David Ascoli's study of the battles of August 1870. See the notes and references to Chapter XI.

[1] Fuller, op.cit., p.189.

[2] Fisher, op.cit., pp.684–85.

[3] *The Everyman Dictionary of Quotations and Proverbs*, London, Chancellor Press, 1988, originally published in 1982 by J.M. Dent and Sons, p.307.

[4] See Fisher, op.cit., pp.742–46 and Fuller, op.cit., Chronicle 6 for the political and strategic background.

[5] The course of this campaign is described in absorbing detail by Fuller, op.cit., Chapter 6.

[6] Fuller, op.cit., p.189. The expression to fight [or work] *'pour le roi de Prusse'* became proverbial for doing something for nothing, and is so used by Tolstoy.

[7] Macdonnell, *Napoleon and his Marshals*, London, Macmillan, 1934, pp.6 and 132.

[8] Whitton op.cit., p.11.

[9] Fuller, op.cit., p.456.

[10] Goerlitz, op.cit., pp.17–40.

[11] Ascoli, *A Day of Battle*, London, Harrap Ltd, 1987, p.22.

[12] Crankshaw, op.cit., p.222.

[13] Fisher, op.cit., p.744.

[14] Tuchman, *The Guns of August*, London, New English Library, 1964; originally Constable and Co., London, 1962, pp.318–20.

[15] Goerlitz, op.cit., p.56.

[16] Taylor, op.cit., p.17.

[17] Fisher, op.cit., p.931.

[18] Fisher, op.cit., pp.996–97.

[19] Taylor, op.cit., p.10.

[20] Crankshaw, op.cit., p.432. For a caricature of a Czech working-class view of the Dual Monarchy in Prague in the approach to World War I and at the front thereafter, see *The Good Soldier Svejk*, by Jaroslav Hasek. Many editions are available in English, Everyman's Library in print at the time of writing.

[21] Crankshaw, op.cit., p.311.

[22] Whitton, op.cit., p.63.

[23] Taylor, op.cit., P.59 For the liberal view within the Prussian general staff, see Goerlitz, op.cit., Chapters 1 to 3.

[24] Whitton, op.cit., p.62.

[25] Crankshaw, op.cit., p.173.

[26] Whitton, op.cit., pp.85–87.

[27] Taylor, op.cit., p.42. It is hard not to feel some sympathy for Frederick William IV, who appears to have liked argument for its own sake and would therefore have been more at home as a permanent protester rather than an upholder of the status quo His own opinion of his capabilities and those of his brothers was not high: 'If we had been born as sons of a petty official, I should have become an architect, William an NCO, Charles would have gone to prison and Albert become a drunkard.'

[28] Fuller, op.cit., p.95.

[29] Whitton, op.cit., p.78.

[30] Goerlitz, op.cit., p.79.

[31] Taylor, op.cit., p.17.

[32] Howard, *The Franco Prussian War*, St Albans, Granada, 1961, p.21.

[33] Whitton, op.cit., p.80.

[34] Taylor, op.cit., pp.56–58. Taylor establishes that Bismarck spoke the words in the sequence 'iron and blood', not in the more generally quoted order.

[35] Howard, op.cit., p.21.

[36] Goerlitz, op.cit., p.86. The first four chapters of this book analyse the three–way struggle, sometimes dormant, for primacy of place between 1801 and 1866. Also of interest is Moltke's own view of his position at the start of the mobilisation process in 1866. This is given in an essay

309

entitled 'Memorandum of the Pretended Council of War in the Wars of King William I', included as an appendix to his book, *The Franco German War of 1870–71*, first published in English in 1907, and reprinted in 1992 by Greenhill Books, London.

[37] Whitton p.55.

[38] Whitton, op.cit., p.69.

[39] Whitton, op.cit., p.75.

[40] Goerlitz, op.cit., p.77.

[41] Goerlitz, op.cit., pp.83–4.

[42] Whitton, op.cit., p.84.

[43] Goerlitz, op.cit., p.85.

[44] Goerlitz, op.cit., p.86.

[45] Goerlitz, op.cit., p.87, and Howard, who attributes the remark to Manstein, op.cit., p.29.

[46] Taylor, op.cit., p.46.

[47] Crankshaw, op.cit., p.203.

[48] Taylor, op.cit., p.68.

[49] Guedalla, *The Second Empire*, London, Constable and Co., 1922, p.348.

[50] Shakespeare, *Henry V*, Act 1, Scene 2.

[51] Guedalla, op.cit., pp.348–9.

[52] Taylor, op.cit., p.73.

[53] Taylor, op.cit., pp.78–79. For the story of Bismarck's dismissal and his reaction to it, see also *Massie – Dreadnought*, London, Pimlico Press, 1993; originally Jonathan Cape, London 1992.

[54] Whitton, op.cit., p.90.

[55] Whitton, op.cit., p.88.

[56] Whitton, op.cit., p.84.

Chapter VIII
The Strategy of Encirclement: Sadowa 1866

Philosophy

It fell of course to Moltke to prepare the plan of campaign, and his proposed concept for the operation met with considerable criticism, both at the time and subsequently. To understand why, it is necessary to penetrate the mind of conventional mid-nineteenth-century generalship. It is a fallacy to suppose that this was completely uninformed; on the contrary, the military leaders of all the Great Powers would have acquired a good detailed knowledge of the campaigns of Napoleon, and also of the pre-eminent commanders of the previous century, in particular Frederick the Great and Marshal Saxe. But in so far as this learning had been applied to contemporary conditions of international warfare, their guide would have been Jomini and not Clausewitz, and Jomini was of the eighteenth rather than the nineteenth century. Of Swiss origin, Jomini, general and baron of the First Empire and, like Marbot, surviving to see the dawn of the Second, had been Ney's chief of staff from Boulogne onwards, and so had a ringside seat at many of the more important Napoleonic battles. His subsequent studies of the art of war, the campaigns of Napoleon and the wars of the Revolution were at the time far more widely renowned than the monumental work of Clausewitz, which was then barely known outside Prussia. Jomini taught that operations should be developed perpendicularly from a secure starting point, that the war aim should be the capture of the enemy's capital and that both strategic and tactical success depended upon the advantage gained from the possession of 'interior lines'. This theory was a military–philosophical rationalisation of the fact that Napoleon I had gained many of his victories by interposing successfully his own army between two opposing forces which, given good intelligence and superior marching and fighting qualities, he could then engage consecutively and defeat in detail.

The educated soldier should understand, apply and teach that there is no such thing as a standard blueprint for success in battle. Wavell, one of the finest trainers of troops the British Army has ever had, made the point for all time in words which should be engraved in the main lecture hall of every military academy in the world. In a series of lectures to staff college candidates of the Aldershot Command in the 1930s, that is, to the officers who were the seed corn for the formation commanders and senior staff officers of the British Army in the Second World War ten years later, Wavell said:

> Military history... is not a series of cold-blooded formulas or diagrams, or nursery book principles, such as:
>
> Be good and you will be happy.
> Be mobile and you will be victorious.
> Interior lines at night are the general's delight.
> Exterior lines in the morning are the general's warning, and so on.
>
> To learn that Napoleon in 1796 with 20,000 men beat the combined forces of 30,000 by something called 'economy of force' or 'operating on interior lines' is a waste of time. If you can understand how a young, unknown man inspired a half-starved, ragged, rather bolshie crowd; how he filled their bellies; how he outmarched, outwitted, outbluffed and defeated men who had studied war all their lives and waged it according to the textbooks of the time, you will have learned something worth knowing.[1]

Most mid-nineteenth-century generals, though not Moltke, would have benefited from this compelling warning against the stereotypical. And the sanctity of 'interior lines' bedevilled much of what has, by courtesy, to be called military strategic thinking for a century and longer. The theory is questionable in any case. No one has ever contended that the geopolitical position of Prussia, and later Germany, was anything other than one of weakness if France and Russia concluded any sort of defensive alliance; the three week campaign which followed the outbreak of war on 15th June, 1866, produced what should have been compelling proof for all time that mere possession of tactical interior lines was no guarantee of victory, especially in default of the willpower and ability to make use of them.

Intellectual criticism of Moltke's plan derived from the fact that it contravened all the basic principles of Jomini, but Moltke was the essential

Prussian Concentration, 1866

and decisive exception in applying his study of the teaching of Clausewitz rather than the doctrines of Jomini. Any operational plan produced by Moltke would be based on the fundamental principle of Clausewitz: that the aim of war should be the destruction of the enemy will and capability to resist, and thus the destruction of the main enemy army. This would, in Moltke's analysis of contemporary conditions, be accomplished by keeping his forces dispersed for as long as possible throughout the advance to contact, always retaining the ability to unite on the field of battle; by inculcating in subordinate commanders the overriding requirement to move at once to support another formation which had made contact; and by ensuring, so far as he could, that the tactical design of one subordinate commander would be instantly comprehensible to any other. However, Clausewitz, writing between 1818 and 1830, had not foreseen the additional influence capital cities had acquired by no more than a quarter century later as centres of radial networks of modern roads, railways and the electric telegraph. Moltke's intellectual grasp of the military importance of railways and real-time communication being far in advance of any of his contemporaries, Clausewitzian principle would be refined by these technological capabilities, and the more widely known but out-of-date recipe books of Jomini discarded.

Planning and Mobilisation

Moltke's plan relied on three assumptions. First, that Italy would play a timely and effective part; secondly that Russia would be a sympathetic non-belligerent; and thirdly that France, notwithstanding the fact that her long-term security would be significantly threatened by a Prussian victory over Austria, would be neutralised, partly because of overcommitment elsewhere and partly because of the retention of the Rhineland and Westphalian army corps, VII and VIII, to watch the Rhine frontier. In the event, however, Moltke assessed the risk of French intervention as so slight that all but one division of these two corps was directed against Austria. All these propositions stemmed from Moltke's strategic appreciation of 1860, already quoted (Chapter VII, p.291 and note 26). His plan also had to take into account the lack of enthusiasm for the war on the home front. Not only were both the king and crown prince reluctant participants, because the struggle was seen as one between brothers and not against a hated and hereditary enemy, but the war was unpopular with all in the country except the junker class. Nor in practical terms could Prussia count upon the inevitability of success in a prolonged conflict, as the Union side had been able to do in the American

Civil War, recently concluded. Interested foreign powers, France in particular, must not be given time to intervene. And, perhaps most important of all, as Prussia and her army were a single entity, there would be a shattering collapse of confidence if the opening phase of the war were seen to go badly; no Prussian territory could be forfeited at the outset, even as a temporary measure for tactical reasons, and important centres of population must be protected. The cities most at risk from a rapid Austrian advance were Breslau (now Wroclaw), no more than forty miles from the frontier with Bohemia, and Berlin itself. It followed that the plan must be based upon the completion of mobilisation certainly no later than and preferably ahead of the opposition, to be followed by an early invasion of and prosecution of the war on enemy territory. This proposed concept was in obvious conflict with the reservations of king and crown prince. Above all, the plan must achieve a quick and decisive victory over the largest imperial army in the principal theatre of war, which might be either Bohemia or Moravia. But before the main enemy army could be brought to battle, three preliminary framework operations were necessary. Possession being nine points of the law, the Austrian presence in Holstein had to be eliminated at once. Two of the Northern German states, Hanover, separated from the British crown since 1837, and Hesse, saw their only hope of a continued independent existence in an Austrian victory. Although the military capability of neither was formidable, they could not be left to create disruption in the rear of the main deployment. Saxony was an even more important factor. Moltke assessed as certain a future Saxon alliance with Austria. The consequence of this lay not so much with the Saxon Army, which at the time was perhaps equivalent in combat value to a single Prussian corps, but in the east–west rail link through Dresden. After mobilisation, the Prussian Army would be spread facing southwards on a front of nearly 300 miles, and considerable lateral eastward relocation would be needed almost at once, for which the railway Erfurt–Leipzig–Dresden–Breslau was essential. Without it, all Prussian Army rail traffic from west to east would have to be routed roundabout, through Berlin and Posen. The need for the capture of Dresden dictated a preliminary thrust from Lower Saxony along the axis of the River Elbe, but this movement would be risky until after the threat posed by Hanover had been eliminated.

Faced with these major constraints and limitations, Moltke had four advantages. The first of these was the superior quality of the Prussian Army, at all levels. The Roon restructuring, which had produced universal service for three years backed by reserves of good combat value because of their annually invoked training commitment, was in full working order by 1866. By contrast, the Habsburg army was in poor shape, notwithstanding its gorgeous uniforms and a pretty parade-ground appearance to impress foreign visitors to Vienna. An emperor never seen out of uniform, and an opera house whose seats were so constructed that officers attending performances were not encumbered by their swords, were no substitute for combat capability. Although throughout the realms of the Habsburgs there was a theoretical liability to universal military service, the numbers called up in practice were limited by quota from each province, largely because of the chronic financial problems of the empire. The quota system allowed the purchase of substitutes, which meant that the recruits who were actually enrolled came from the most disadvantaged, worst motivated and least trainable element of the population. The same financial stringencies ensured that many recruits spent no more than one year's service with the colours,[2] after which they were sent home on indefinite and unpaid leave, but with liability to recall. The consequences were that the conscripts reverted very rapidly to the status of untrained levies, and there was an additional time and numbers penalty on mobilisation. No attempt was made to make a virtue of necessity, by using the long-service element which the empire could afford to maintain, to train annual classes of recruits on a cadre system. Such a concept might have been within the ability of a Scharnhorst or a Seeckt to carry through, but lay completely outside the comprehension of Grunne and Crenneville, successively head of the emperor's military cabinet and de facto Adjutant General of the army before and after Solferino. Unlike in the Prussian Army, the structure of field formations, brigade, division and corps did not exist in peacetime. And, as has already been noted, the latent political instability of the empire required regiments to serve elsewhere, and not in the provinces producing their rank and file, which further complicated and lengthened the process of mobilisation. Nor was there anything to compare with the long-standing staff system in the Prussian Army, developed further by Moltke. This meant that not only would Austrian routine staff work always be inferior to Prussian, but that, in the science of deploying formed bodies of troops to their intended battle position and maintaining them once there, the Prussian Army would always be in the ascendant. Additionally, Vienna had nothing to match Moltke's development of a common concept of how to bring troops into battle and develop a decisive encounter. Without this ability, the Austrian Army would either have to fight as a single entity under the eye of its commander-in-chief, as though military-related technological development had stood still for a century, or hope that dispersed formation commanders would, by luck, achieve a common design for battle. In the Prussian Army, this process derived from the more reliable base of teaching and practice. The attitude of Viennese '*Schlamperei*' to the imperial army would endure for the remaining life of the empire; at the end of August 1914 it would be said, sadly, 'We had the prettiest cavalry in the world. What a pity to have wasted it on a war!'[3]

Moltke's second advantage was that he comprehended better than any other general of his time the military potential of the railway and the electric telegraph. More than a quarter of a century before, he had invested all the money he had saved during his four years in Turkey in the new Berlin–Hamburg rail link, and in 1843 he had produced a prescient study of the principles which should govern railway layout and operation for military purposes, at a time when Prussia had no more than 300 miles of track layout with a further 200 in construction. In the same paper he advocated state expenditure on railways rather than on fortresses,[4] in which suggestion he was years ahead of his time. After his appointment as chief of the general staff he had an ever-growing influence in all subsequent development of Prussia's railway system, not merely in line direction and track capacity, but also in important matters of detail such as bridge loadings, tunnels and junction points. The result by the mid 1860s was a rail network far better suited to military use than that of either the Austrian or French empires. These had been laid out more with regard to commercial considerations, and the former was also bound by Magyar susceptibility, which caused all rail links within the lands of the Crown of St Stephen to be routed through Buda Pesth and not Vienna. The result was that, on the critical frontier, Prussia in 1866 mobilised approximately the same number of men as Austria, but in half the time, and in 1870 four times as many as the French Army in much the same time. Moltke's understanding of the power of control offered by the electric telegraph allowed him to contemplate with equanimity the concurrent supervision from his office in Berlin of the mobilisation process and the preliminary operations in the duchies, against Hanover and Hesse and towards Dresden. In Prussia, development of railway and telegraph networks had proceeded in parallel. But though Moltke had taken note of the successful use of the telegraph in the American Civil War, he had not yet made provision for its continued availability once the field armies had debouched from concentration areas and main centres of population served by the railway links. In this capability the Prussian Army was less well-equipped than the Union Army three years earlier. As a result, operational command of separated formations would still rely on much toing and froing by mounted officers, and headquarters would often be left in ignorance about whether orders given had been carried out or not.

Prussia's third advantage was in firepower, though not yet in Krupp steel breech-loaded rifled artillery pieces. Those making their debut at Sadowa on a land battlefield were not a significant success and contributed nothing to Prussia's victory. What produced the overwhelming superiority in firepower was the Dreyse 'needle gun'.[a] The development of this breech-loaded and rifled infantry personal weapon had been completed as early as 1836, but the Prussian Army had not been fully equipped with it until 1848. Although Dreyse's invention was not markedly better in either range or accuracy than the muzzle-loader which it replaced, the needle gun produced two enormous improvements. It had a rate of fire of five to one compared with the muzzle-loader and, even more importantly, breech-loading allowed it to be operated from a prone position. The layman needs little imagination to comprehend the advantage of a five to one superiority in rate of fire when troops in mass formation are engaged in line of sight combat without much attempt at tactical subtlety. It needs even less to understand the benefits of protection and concealment given to infantry able to develop their firepower lying flat on the ground against a standing enemy. If the latter is committed to the charge, the defence has even greater benefit because the assaulting troops, if equipped with muzzle-loaders, have to stop to reload, in which case they lose momentum, or they must charge with the bayonet. In this case, however great their élan, their fighting value against a defence equipped with breech-loaders is no more than that of an equivalent number of mediaeval pikemen. It is relevant that Moltke had, on an official visit to Vienna in January 1865, noted the existence of Austrian breech-loading rifles in the Vienna arsenal,[5] but there is no evidence that his vote for war in the Prussian Crown Council thirteen months later[6] was in any way influenced by the need for a pre-emptive strike before the Austrians introduced this weapon into service and so cancelled the Prussian advantage.

The fourth factor working in Prussia's favour was the relative abilities of the command-in-chief. History is invariably unkinder to defeated generals than to almost any other failures, even more so to those who are made the

[a] See Chapter V. Notwithstanding the decisive advantage in this particular war which Prussia gained from the needle gun, it was still inferior to the magazine rifles introduced in the American Civil War, and to the chassepot, which entered service in the French Army in 1866. Not surprisingly, the two latter weapons were twenty years later in development.

scapegoats for national catastrophe and most of all if the military disaster is treated as no more than a parenthesis to more detailed consideration of the subsequent political upheaval generated by the defeat. The fate meted out to Field Marshal Alexander von Benedek was a foretaste of the ignominy visited on Marshal François-Achille Bazaine, half a decade later by a humiliated French nation desperate for a whipping boy. Neither man was a fool or a coward; both embarked upon their allotted tasks with highly justifiable reservations in the light of most disadvantageous start conditions over which they had had no control, and both were appointed with the full confidence of their sovereign, their nation and the troops they were given to command. After their defeats, both stood alone in the dock to be declared guilty, but both, with justice, should have been accompanied by most of their subordinate commanders and indeed by the political leadership which had given them their impossible tasks.

Benedek was the same age as Moltke and the century. His high military reputation had been gained throughout a long and distinguished career, culminating in a considerable local success at Solferino seven years before. In a war marked by blinding incompetence on both sides, and in marked contrast to all the other Austrian commanders, Emperor Franz Joseph not excepted, Benedek had held the right flank of the Austrian position all day throughout a thoroughly confused battle. At the end of the day, after launching a spoiling attack to discourage too close pursuit, Benedek had brought his corps back across the River Mincio in an orderly retreat into the Quadrilateral. Nevertheless, the Prussian general staff's detailed study of the war had caused Moltke to sum him up as: 'No commander in chief or strategist; will want a great deal of assistance in running an army'.[7]

While such assistance might have been forthcoming in the Prussian Army because of the system of higher staff training developed by Moltke, the Austrians had no such resource.

The Austrian Empire needed commanders-in-chief in two theatres of war, in Italy as well as against Prussia. This consideration has tended to further obscure the issue by suggesting that Benedek had of necessity to be appointed to command against Prussia. The other contender, Archduke Albrecht, son of Archduke Charles, had to be given the softer option, on the ground that the imperial family could not afford to lose prestige by having one of its members defeated on the battlefield. The leading authority has refuted this view conclusively.[8] It is beyond debate that Benedek was, at the time the appointments had to be made, considered to be the leading soldier of the empire, had the greater measure of confidence of both army and nation and that the command against Prussia was by far the more important. Nevertheless, if the first requisite of a general is his own belief in his ability to win, Benedek, like Bazaine four years later, was beaten before he began. His objection to commanding in Bohemia or Moravia because all his previous service had been in Italy, and that therefore he should command there, was not a valid argument for a general of his experience, and is evidence of a disastrous lack of self-confidence. But as a thoroughly professional soldier with nearly half a century of service, he knew that the Austrian war machine was inferior by far to the Prussian. It is also possible that, as a non-aristocrat Protestant Hungarian, he felt himself at a social disadvantage when dealing with his princely, Catholic and German–Austrian subordinate commanders.

Notwithstanding the importance of early mobilisation to Prussia, it was not until 3rd May, nearly three weeks after the Austrian process had started, that Moltke was allowed to issue the necessary orders. Even then these applied only to the four corps raised from the provinces nearest to the frontiers with the empire, and to the Rhine Provinces Corps.[9] Full mobilisation was not decreed until 16th May. In allotting the troops available to tasks, Moltke grouped the bulk of his available formations into three separate armies, with a total strength of approximately 280,000 men,[b] to take the field against Austria, Saxony and, if need be, Bavaria. Three smaller task forces were formed to undertake the preliminary operations north of Hamburg, and the occupation of Hanover and Hesse. Manteuffel and Falckenstein had 14,000 men each at Hamburg and Minden for the first two of these tasks, while Beyer was poised with a force of 20,000 at Wetzlar for the third.

The three army groupings were:[10]

---

[b] This total has been calculated from first principles, and differs only marginally from the 278,000 given by Bonnal.

TABLE IX
ARMY OF THE ELBE

Commander: General Herwarth von Bittenfeld (Elder)
Chief of Staff: Colonel von Schlotheim
Combat Strength: 50,000

Corps and Commander	Division and Commander	Infantry Battalions	Cavalry Squadrons	Guns	Concentration Areas
VII	14–Munster Meinhovel	12	4	24	Schildau
VIII	15–Canstein	12	5	24	Belgern
	16–Etzel	12		12	Liebenwerde
	reserve cavalry		17		Liebenwerde
	artillery			84	Torgau
TOTAL		36	26	144	

TABLE X
FIRST ARMY

Commander: Prince Frederick Charles of Prussia
Chief of Staff: Lieutenant General von Voigts-Rhetz
Combat Strength: 100,000

Corps and Commander	Division and Commander	Infantry Battalions	Cavalry Squadrons	Guns	Concentration Areas
III	5–Tumpling	12	4	24	Gorlitz
	6– Manstein	12	5	24	
IV	7–Fransecky	12	4	24	Hoyerswerde
	8–Horn	9	4	24	
II–Schmidt	3–Werder	12	4	24	Senftenberg
	4–Herwarth (jr)	12	4	24	
	corps troops		8	30	
Cavalry Corps Prince Albert of Prussia	1–Alvensleben (elder) 2–Weghorn		41	30	
	reserve artillery			96	
TOTAL		69	74	300	

The mitrailleuse

General Lee

General Jackson

General Grant

General McClellan, with his wife

Napoleon III

Count von Schlieffen

Marshal MacMahon

General von Manstein

Von Moltke the Younger

Von Moltke the Elder

Marshal Bazaine

King William I of Prussia

Gettysburg Cemetery Ridge
Guns in Barbette

Gettysburg
Napoleon twelve pounder and Little Round Top

Chlum Ridge
Memorial to General Hiller von Gaertringen

Mars la Tour
Route of von Bredow's charge

Aspern Essling
The Granary

Woerth
Memorial to second regiment of Algerian tirailleurs

The bridge over the Antietam Creek

Marye's Heights, Fredericksburg

TABLE XI
SECOND ARMY

Commander: Crown Prince Frederick William of Prussia
Chief of Staff: Major General von Blumenthal
Combat Strength: 130,000

Corps and Commander	Division and Commander	Infantry Battalions	Cavalry Squadrons	Guns	Concentration Areas
Guard	1–Hiller von	12	4	24	
Prince Augustus of Wurtemburg	Gaertringen		5	24	
	2–Plonski	12	4	24	
	Cav–Alvensleven (jr) artillery		4	24	
1–Bonin	1–Grossman	12	4	24	Hirschberg
	2–Clausewitz	9	4	24	
			8	30	
V–Steinmetz	9–Lowenfeld	12	4	30	Landshut
	10–Kirchbach corps troops	12	4	24	
VI–Mutius	11–Zastrow	12	4	24	Waldenburg
	12–Prondzynski	6	4	12	
	corps troops		4	24	
Army Troops		9	32	16	Streigau
TOTAL		96	94	352	

A corps on a standard organisation of one cavalry division, two infantry divisions (these being composed each of two brigades, two regiments and three battalions) and supporting artillery – and most varied slightly from this norm – had a mobilised strength of about 30,000. The approximate strength of an infantry battalion was 1,000 and a cavalry squadron fielded about 150 sabres. Guns were most usually fought in batteries of six, which, allowing for ammunition trains, had a strength of about 200. In addition, each division had a skirmishing (*feldjäger*) battalion, and a pioneer battalion for simple field engineering tasks. The proportion of infantry combat soldiers to the rest, perhaps five out of six, was much higher than in armies of the twentieth century. Allowing for the holding force on the Rhine frontier, Prussia mobilised for first-line operations approximately 350,000 men and no fewer than 80,000 horses. This total excludes garrisons, supply trains, and a secondary mobilisation of reserve formations. In 1866 the latter were embryonic; reserve corps formed from provinces on the same basis as the first line formations. British Army intelligence failed to identify this development until some time after battle was joined in August 1914, notwithstanding the presence of observers in both 1866 and 1870.

'Has There Been a Battle?'

Since the campaign of 1866 has, of necessity, been treated in shorthand by most military historians in the last sixty years,[c] Moltke's mobilisation and relocation deployments, which were complete in the concentration areas listed in the tables above by 8th June, have been represented as a massive right hook round the Austro-Saxon armies. This proposition tends to be reinforced if related only superficially to a post-World War I map, which depicts Bohemia as a vast salient projecting into twentieth-century Germany. That such is not the case is proved by joining, by a line on a map, the corps concentration areas. This shows that on 8th June, Prussia's formations were aligned almost straight on the northern frontiers of Saxony and Bavaria, a point which in no way minimises the quality either of the plan or its execution. The lateral relocation deployments had reduced by nearly half the distance between the corps mobilisation areas, to about 150 miles. There then followed a somewhat double-edged stroke of luck. On 11th June, the order of battle of Benedek's concentration in the area between Brunn and Olmutz became known in Berlin, which seemed to indicate the likelihood of an Austrian thrust towards Breslau. The crown prince asked for, and received, permission to extend the Second Army's front forty miles to the east to cover this important psycho-political asset and industrial centre, thus re-expanding the spread between formations which Moltke had been at pains to reduce.[11]

Notwithstanding the fact that in the light of hindsight Bismarck's policy can be said to have led inevitably to war, it is fair to record that, in the week after the completion of the Prussian relocation deployments, King William did all he could to avert it. In the event Austria precipitated the war much as she had done in 1859, by sending emissaries to Turin to say to the king of Sardinia, in effect, 'Demobilise, or else...' The day after Austria had formally referred the matter of the duchies to the Federal Diet, on the morning of 15th June, Moltke sent orders to the army and task force commanders, for execution the following day. Hanover and Hesse were to be occupied as soon

---

[c] For the reason, see Appendix C.

as possible, and the Army of the Elbe was ordered to invade Saxony and to capture Dresden, likewise without delay. The commanders of the First and Second Armies were directed to secure their routes forward to the frontier, but were forbidden to invade Austrian territory without further orders.

In spite of the fact that the kingdom of Sardinia had mobilised ahead of either of the other two main belligerents, the early active participation of an Italian Army proved, not for the last time in history, to be more than their allies could expect. However, the importance of the alliance with Italy, for which Moltke had argued so cogently, lay in the fact that it tied down 100,000 Habsburg troops to the defence of the Quadrilateral and the approaches to Venice. And although Custozza, fought a week before Sadowa on the same ground as the 1848 battle, was a decisive Austrian victory, there was insufficient time for any part of Archduke Albrecht's army to be moved through the passes of the Dolomites and Vienna, or by the railway link through Agram (Zagreb) and Buda Pesth, to reinforce Benedek in Bohemia.

The dilatory Italian performance was counterbalanced by the fact that Bavaria, in spite of the close family ties between Habsburgs and Wittelsbachs and community of interest with the empire, elected to remain neutral, thus removing a threat worth perhaps two army corps from the right flank of any Prussian advance beyond Dresden. Although the king of Saxony had loyally agreed that his army should join the main Austrian concentration, thus leaving his country wide open to the Prussian invasion, his brother monarch in Munich declined to make an equivalent sacrifice. Bavaria had no asset comparable with the Dresden railway link to tempt Prussian notice. Neither did any right-flanking encirclement manoeuvre need to violate Bavarian territory. As a result, Bavaria sat out the war and retained her status as an independent kingdom, but within the German Empire, until 1918.

By mid-June, the Austrians and Saxons were mobilised on the Prussian front in the following formations:[10]

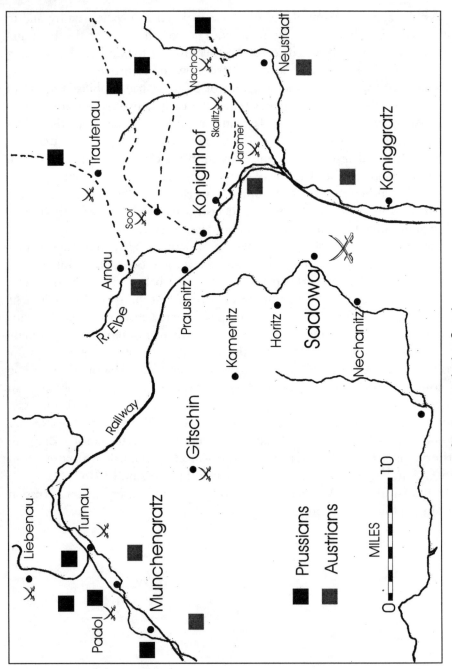

Approach to Sadowa

TABLE XII
AUSTRO-SAXON ARMY

Commander: Field Marshal von Benedek
Chief of Staff: General von Henickstein
Chief of Operations: General Krismanic

Formation	Commander	Infantry Battalions	Cavalry Squadrons	Guns
I corps	Clam Gallas	35	5	88
II corps	Thun-Hohenstadt	28	5	72
III corps	Archduke Ernest	28	5	80
IV corps	Festetics–Molinary	28	5	72
VI corps	Ramming	28	5	72
VIII corps	Archduke Leopold	27	5	72
X corps	Gablentz	28	–	72
Divisions				
I light cavalry	Edelsheim		30	
II light cavalry	Tour und Taxis		20	
I reserve cavalry	Schleswig–Holstein		26	
II reserve cavalry	Zaissek		26	
III reserve cavalry	Coudenhove		26	
army artillery				128
Saxon corps	Crown Prince Albert of Saxony	20	16	18
Brigade Trentemiglia		4	1	
TOTAL		226	175	674

Using the same unit strength figures as for the Prussian Army, and they will not have been markedly different, the total mobilised strength of Benedek's army was around 275,000, almost identical to the combined strength of the three Prussian armies, but much larger than any one of them. In theory, therefore, Benedek could create the opportunity to defeat the Prussians in detail.

The Austrian organisation had a serious weakness. The army corps were no more than 'grand divisions', too large for one commander to control without intermediate headquarters between corps and regiment. Although formations were made up ad hoc within corps, all the orders were prepared at corps headquarters. The need to prepare separate and detailed conduct of battle orders to as many as twenty units would have taxed the resources of the most competent staff and communications system.

The corps commanded by Clam Gallas, magnate of Bohemia as well as career soldier, was directed to advance north-westwards to Jung Bunzlau (now Mlada Boleslav), on the River Iser, a southwards-flowing tributary of the Elbe, and there to link up with the Saxon army. The combined force was then to fall back on the main concentration. The whole of the rest of Benedek's army, with the exception of a single cavalry division screening the approaches from Silesia, was in a broad parallelogram approximately eighty miles by forty, the geographic centre of which was, almost exactly, the 1805 Austerlitz battlefield. The significant asset was the railway; running northwards from Vienna, the lines divided at Lundenburg (now Břeclav), one route going through Brunn and the other through Olmutz, to join up again at Zwittau (now Svitavy) before continuing on to Prague, the third city of the empire after Vienna and Buda Pesth. A lesser line ran northwards from Zwittau to the fortress towns of Koniggratz (now Hradec Králové) and Josefstadt (now merged in the modern town of Jaroměř). The railway layout of the Czech Republic today is little altered. Benedek, who had, from intercepted telegrams, by 20th June a fairly clear idea about the Prussian deployment, but no comparable understanding of what was really happening, had three choices. He could either remain where he was, forcing the Prussians into a long approach march and battle on ground of his own choice; this was his own preferred option based on a plan by his chief of operations, Krismanic. Alternatively, he could move north-westwards towards Prague to join Clam Gallas and the Saxons, or northwards to threaten Silesia (already assessed by the Prussians as his most likely course), which would put him on the direct axis to Berlin. On 16th June, Benedek put the problem to the emperor. He reported that in any event he needed four more days to complete the concentration and equipment of his army – some of his reservists were still without boots – after which he would need a further eleven days to move his concentration to Josefstadt, a bare sixty miles north of Olmutz. On 17th June he issued preparatory orders to set this movement in hand, which were endorsed four days later by a not particularly helpful 'hurry up' directive from the emperor. Franz Joseph, his mind no doubt beset both by his obligations to the king of Saxony and also by the squandered opportunities in Lombardy seven years previously, directed Benedek to move northwards as soon as possible; objective Berlin.[12] This is a classic example of the folly of conducting strategy with big fingers on small-scale maps; if it were going to take until the end of June to move the army the relatively short distance to Josefstadt, a breakthrough into Silesia followed by a 200 mile approach march to Berlin would succeed only if the Prussians remained absolutely static. This proposition flew in the face of all the evidence, both available and accumulating.

Meanwhile, Prussian operations were proceeding according to Moltke's plan, but with something less than total fluency. It was an irritating distraction for the chief of staff, when occupied in hour-to-hour control of the main operation, to learn that the occupation of Hanover had been bungled. Falckenstein, employed notwithstanding his incompetent performance in the 1864 war, took until 27th June to bring the army of the kingdom of Hanover to battle, and the fact that this force capitulated two days later is due more to ammunition shortages and supply deficiencies than to a defeat in the field.[13] An even greater cause for concern was that the fog of war was even more dense than usual. The information reaching Moltke (or not) was even more than usually inaccurate and incomplete. The invasion of Saxony had begun on 16th June as planned, and Dresden, the key objective, was no more than a day's march from the concentration areas of the Army of the Elbe. But forty-eight hours into the operation Moltke was telegraphing to von Schlotheim, chief of staff of the Elbe Army: 'No report received. Has General Herwarth entered Dresden? Where are the Saxons? Have any Austrians joined them?'[14] Reassured belatedly on these points, and on the basis of the information available, Moltke concluded that the main Austrian concentration was in north-eastern Bohemia. On 22nd June he issued orders which placed the Army of the Elbe, minus a division retained to occupy Saxony, under the operational control of First Army. Moltke's order continued: 'His Majesty orders both armies to enter Bohemia and to endeavour to unite about Gitschin [now Jičín]. The VIth Corps is to remain available at Neisse.'[d][14]

Moltke's strategic design was always to keep his formations dispersed during the approach to contact and to unite them only on the intended battlefield. But on 22nd June he was mistaken about the location of the main Austrian Army, and, in spite of the fact that his order removed the prohibition on entering Austrian territory, the Prussian cavalry proved almost totally ineffective throughout the campaign in finding and reporting accurately the Austrian deployment. The reason was that in both First and Second Army march tables, the cavalry was left to follow behind the infantry formations when it should have been searching ahead of them.

Moltke's plan presented Benedek, at least in theory, with the opportunity to mask one of the two Prussian armies while concentrating a superior force

---

[d] Now Nyasa, in southern Poland. The effect of this order was to cover Breslau and to retain VI Corps in army group reserve.

against the other. The severe criticism at the time within the Prussian Army, and later, from Bonnal in particular,[e] was not wholly removed by its success. For all the euphoria in the aftermath of victory, the Prussian post-action report, published a year later and drafted in all probability by Moltke himself, is almost disarming:

> The timely junction of the Prussian armies in the war of 1866 has never been represented – at least by our general staff – as a stroke of genius or a brilliant idea. It was merely an expedient and a remedy chosen skilfully and applied with vigour for a situation inherently defective, but unavoidable.[15]

If victory failed to dispel the strictures on Moltke's design for the campaign, the condemnation of Benedek for failing to take up his advantage was virulent following his defeat and endures to this day. Not wholly justifiably; the vital words in the quotation above may be 'applied with vigour'. The concept might have been within the comprehension of Napoleon I or Lee, but was outside that of the conventionally-minded Benedek, for all his soldierly qualities. And the staff work and marching capacity might have been within the ability of the *Grande Armée* or the Army of Northern Virginia once hardened by two years' campaigning, but was well beyond that of a newly mobilised Austrian Army, consisting in the main of poorly trained conscripts, and with commanders and staff practised in neither working together nor managing the operation of large formations.

Benedek has been further criticised for having failed to make the best use of the ground in an 'interior lines' design for battle; again, not wholly fairly. The area of northern Bohemia of particular interest to the student of this campaign is bounded on three sides by the River Elbe. Rising in the Riesengebirge (Giant Mountains, on Czech maps the Krkonose Hory), the crest of which is the present-day frontier between the Czech Republic and Poland, the river flows initially south-east and then south through Josefstadt and Koniggratz before turning sharply in a right angle westwards at Pardubitz (now Pardubice), twelve miles south of Koniggratz. The course is then west and north-west to the junction with the Iser, fifteen miles north-east of Prague, and thereafter more northward to the German frontier at Ustin, thirty miles south-east of Dresden. In its course through Bohemia the Elbe forms three sides of a rectangle, the east–west base between Pardubitz and the Iser

---

[e] See the introduction to the notes and references to Chapter VII.

some eighty miles long, the north–south sides about a third of that distance. From the point at which the river emerges from the Riesengebirge, it is a major obstacle to military movement, to be crossed only by existing bridges or after extensive bridging operations by a properly constituted military bridging train. It follows that an army which has crossed the Elbe northward fights under the severe disadvantage, in the event of defeat, of a major river at its back, and so incurs a risk comparable to that run by Lee at both Antietam and Gettysburg.[f] The Iser is similarly a major obstacle requiring formal bridging. The hollow rectangle is closed by a flat cone formed by two mountain ranges, the Erzgebirge (Metal Mountains, Krušné Hory in Czech) to the north-west on the frontier with Saxony, and the Riesengebirge to the north-east. Thus, armies invading from either Saxony or Silesia and seeking to give battle in the area bounded by the Elbe are each faced with two substantial topographical obstacles: on the western face of the cone the Erzgebirge and the Iser, and on the eastern the Riesengebirge and the Upper Elbe. The mountain ranges are not, nevertheless, the impenetrable barriers implied by commentators concerned to exaggerate either the Prussian achievement or the Austrian failure. The Riesengebirge is the more formidable. It is now a national park and pleasant summer walking country, similar to Northumberland and the border region in Britain, or the Catoctin Hills in Maryland. However, an army on an approach march as a formed body would be constrained to road movement only, and in mid-nineteenth-century road conditions heavy rainfall would impede its progress severely. In 1866 the three passes over the Riesengebirge, Parschnitz, Braunau and Nachod, were of vital importance to the Prussian Second Army. They give access to a U-shaped re-entrant aligned north-east to south-west, some twenty miles broad at the mouth. Parschnitz and Nachod lie respectively at the northern and southern points of the arms of this natural salient, and Braunau at its north-western corner. No lateral movement is possible between the passes by any body of troops above patrol strength, and because the passes all lead to the *east* bank of the Upper Elbe, an army has to force a crossing of the river in order to reach the broad, open, sometimes wooded but rolling country, not unlike Sussex downland or the country round Gettysburg, towards the angle of the river south of Koniggratz.

In so far as Benedek had a plan beyond moving up to Josefstadt and waiting then to see what happened next, it was to block the Riesengebirge passes while engaging First Army with the greater part of his force along the line of the Iser. In theory, his alternative choice – to conduct a holding operation against First

---

[f] See Chapter VI.

Army while engaging Second Army as it emerged from the Riesengebirge passes – was still open. Neither course was adopted and pursued with decision. On 20th June Benedek wrote: 'So soon as I am established at Josefstadt, and after a few days of rest, which is absolutely indispensable, I propose to resume the offensive.'[16]

And Benedek had already told the emperor that he would need until the end of the month to organise his army for a further advance beyond Josefstadt. Yet, with two armies converging on him, time was of the essence. Clam Gallas and the crown prince of Saxony achieved their desired junction on the Iser, sixty miles west of Josefstadt, on 24th June, but with a total strength of 60,000 they were too many and too immobile to act as a screen or a delaying force, and not enough to withstand concentrated pressure by the combined First Army and Army of the Elbe.

Critics writing without personal knowledge of the ground have heavily censured Benedek for failing to seal the Riesengebirge passes against the approach of the Prussian Second Army, in order to give himself a decisive superiority against Prince Frederick Charles. However, the passes were not 'strait paths in which 1,000 may well be stopped by three'.[17] None is more than 1,200 feet above the valley of the Upper Elbe, and all would have had to be barred to enable such a plan to work. This would have required either separate but well coordinated blocking positions covering each pass, or a continuous defence line across the twenty mile mouth of the salient. Even supposing that other critical factors, such as the quality of staff work and individual firepower capability, had been equal, an allocation of troops powerful enough to hold off the crown prince might well have left Benedek with insufficient force to seek a decisive victory on the Iser. This contention is borne out by what in fact happened in and around the salient in the last five days of June. Five Austrian corps, admittedly operating without any satisfactory coordination, were insufficient to withstand a break-in operation by the four corps of the Prussian Second Army. But Benedek's initial deployment fell between two stools and was flawed from the start. Apart from the force on the Iser, at least four days' march away by Austrian standards of march discipline, he had six corps available. One was tasked to reinforce the single cavalry division which had hitherto screened the passes. Four were deployed in an arc Josefstadt–Schurz–Miletin–Horitz, from where, at least theoretically, they could move in either direction, and the sixth was left in army reserve. A reconstruction of the Austrian deployment as it stood on 26th June, for a lecture about the campaign given in London in December 1866, places these six corps concentration areas as II at Josefstadt, III at Miletin, IV at Koniginhof, VI at Neustadt, VIII at Jaroměř and X at Arnau.[18]

Moltke was at this point still of the opinion that Benedek was moving up to the Iser, but he retained the critical detachment to realise the deficiency of the reports he was receiving. On 24th June he admitted, 'the intelligence is in a bad way' and in later memoirs Caprivi, at the time a captain in the intelligence division of the general staff, wrote:

> Everything had to be created in 1866. Although two years earlier we might have had to contend with the Austrians, we had very little information as to the dislocation [sic] of their various corps when war broke out.'[19]

And the poor tasking and handling of the Prussian cavalry has already been noted.

Nevertheless, Moltke retained as his tactical objective a junction of the two armies around Gitschin. The orders issued on 22nd June had continued:

> As the weaker Second Army has the more difficult task of issuing from the mountains, it is the more incumbent on the First Army, so soon as ever its junction with the force of General von Herwarth has been effected, to shorten the crisis by its swift advance.[14]

Not for the last time, one of Moltke's concepts would be frustrated almost to the point of total compromise by an army commander. In an age in which royal birth was still an almost automatic passport to high military command, Prince Frederick Charles, the thirty-eight year old nephew of the king, could not be denied employment at a very senior level. He had done well enough under the tutelage of Moltke in the later stages of the 1864 war. However, his soubriquet, 'The Red Prince', derived from the glory of his hussar uniform rather than from any qualities of dash or, worse, impetuosity. Both in 1866 and, as we shall see later, in 1870, his performance as an army commander was mostly stodgy and unimaginative. Moltke was said to have the gift of silence in seven languages and his written prose style is a model of economy and avoidance of the use of hyperbolic adjectives and adverbs. Nevertheless, as time went by, he found it increasingly difficult to restrain professorial sarcasm when dealing with a particularly heavy-witted student. By 1870 the antipathy between the two was mutual. On receipt of the orders of 22nd June, his royal highness baulked. Even with the addition of the Army of the Elbe, he considered himself too weak to take on the enemy on the Iser, and asked if I Corps could therefore be reassigned from Second Army to his own, in order to çover his left flank. When told it could not, his advance began at a crawl, and it was only on 26th June, having advanced unopposed a bare thirty miles in four days, that he made contact with the Saxons. While his combat achievement in the campaign was by no means negligible, his rate of advance continued to be much slower than the situation required, or than was enjoined by the spirit of his orders. After successful preliminary skirmishes which had secured a crossing over the Iser, he telegraphed Berlin on 28th June for permission to halt and rest on the following day. In a return signal, Moltke gave him a summary of the position of the crown prince, at the time by no means satisfactory, and ended with a polite but barbed reminder that, 'the complete debouchment of the Second Army will be materially facilitated by the advance of the First Army.'

The following morning, the stalwart and soldierly monarch, feeling no doubt that his chief of staff deserved support, added a crusty avuncular reproof:

> His Majesty expects that the First Army, by a more rapid advance, will disengage the Second Army, which, in spite of a series of victorious actions, is still for the moment in a difficult situation.[20]

These were strong words in the formal and polite context of the time, and were strongly needed. It was, after all, only five days after Custozza, and the possibility could not be excluded that in the wake of his defeat King Victor Emmanuel might seek an armistice, which would free at least part of the army of Archduke Albrecht to move north to reinforce Benedek.

The royal rebuke, nevertheless, was ineffective. First Army had already (and inexcusably) lost contact with the enemy on its front, and did not resume its march until after midday on 29th June. The army commander had contributed to his own difficulties by the sort of decision which, though taken for the best of good reasons, produces a result directly opposite from the one intended. No doubt with the concurrence of his chief of staff, Prince Frederick Charles had concluded that, because routes forward were limited, they should, as a scarce and vital resource, be controlled at the highest level, that is, by his own army headquarters. The corps organisation was suspended, and army headquarters found itself under the necessity of issuing precise march orders daily to twelve subordinate formations: six divisions of First

Army, three of the Army of the Elbe, the cavalry of both armies and the artillery park. Of course, none of this paperwork created any more material assets, and its volume strained the capacity of army headquarters, which found itself involved in far too much comparatively low-level detail. Preparation and transmission of orders took considerably longer than if the work had been delegated to the corps headquarters accustomed to the task. On the ground, divisions were forced to follow each other on such routes as were available, with a corresponding time penalty when it became necessary to change from column of march into battle configuration.

In order to enable the reader to follow the confused events of the last five days of June, in which the concurrent, concerted but separate actions of the two Prussian armies forced twelve separate battles on the Austrians, a chronology related to an outline map may help.

TABLE XIII

| Date | First Army Front | Second Army Front | Corps Engaged | |
			Prussian	Austrian
26th June	Padol, Turnau, Liebenau			
27th June	Huhnerwasser	Trautenau	I	X
		Nachod	V	VI
28th June	Munchengratz	Soor	Guard	X, IV
		Skalitz	V	VIII, II
29th June	Gitschin	Jaroměř	V	IV
30th June	Gitschin	Koniginhof	VI	IV

Some of these combats, particularly those at the beginning on First Army front, were no more than skirmishes, but most were fought at corps level and so in terms of numbers engaged were equivalent in size to any but the very largest battles fought before Austerlitz.

OPERATIONS ON FIRST ARMY FRONT

The skirmishes on 26th June not only shepherded most of the Saxons and the Austrian I Corps east of the Iser, but also captured the important bridge at Turnau. No sooner had this been lost than a signal was received from Benedek directing that Turnau and Munchengratz should be held at all costs. The crown prince of Saxony, who throughout the campaign did conspicuously well as a corps commander, and who now had operational command of the corps of Clam Gallas as well as his own, organised a night attack towards Liebenau to regain the Turnau crossing. Had this succeeded, the flank of First Army would have been turned. In the event, the attack failed, with the loss of over 1,000 killed, wounded or taken prisoner.

Apart from a skirmish at Huhnerwasser between the Prussian 16th Division and the Saxons, 27th June was a day of inactivity, with the Prussian advance at a dead stop. In the words of Bonnal, Prince Frederick Charles 'prend son temps'[21] in taking the day to organise a set-piece attack on Munchengratz. This action was unnecessary. Because the Prussians had secured the crossing over the Iser at Turnau, Crown Prince Albert could not have maintained his position at Munchengratz. It would have been more in the spirit of Moltke's directive if the Red Prince had masked Munchengratz and pressed on with the bulk of his army to the intended junction point with Second Army at Gitschin.

The crown prince of Saxony did not wait for First Army to develop its attack. Leaving a rearguard to impose some delay, he withdrew his two corps towards Gitschin, expecting to be joined there by Benedek. However, because Benedek's northern front was crumbling in the face of unremitting pressure from Second Army, the Austrian commander-in-chief changed his plan. Belatedly, as we have seen, First Army got itself on the move on the afternoon of 29th June, and at 6 p.m., as the bulk of Crown Prince Albert's force was preparing its evening meal in and around Gitschin, it was attacked by the leading Prussian division, 5th, commanded by von Tumpling. For a time Tumpling was isolated and in danger of being overwhelmed, but, in accordance with Moltke's teaching, the two flanking divisions, 3rd (von Werder) and 4th, (the younger Herwarth von Bittenfeld) marched towards the sound of the guns, and were poised to support Tumpling when, at 7.30 p.m., the Austro-Saxon force ceased offensive action. A staff officer from Benedek had arrived at Gitschin, with orders to the crown prince of Saxony to avoid battle against an enemy in superior numbers, and to withdraw by way of Horitz and Miletin towards a general concentration of the whole army north and west of Koniggratz. By 9 p.m. orders for the retreat were issued, but with unpractised staff and untrained troops the essential clean break was not achieved. Confused fighting continued throughout the night and into the early morning of 30th June. At the end of the withdrawal, the Saxon corps, which had got away first, was in relatively good order, but the corps of Clam Gallas was wrecked. First Army, having secured Gitschin, again lost contact with the enemy, which says little for the offensive spirit of its commander and less for both the tasking and operation of his large body of cavalry.

OPERATIONS ON SECOND ARMY FRONT

As Moltke had assessed, rightly, the Prussian Second Army had the harder task because it had to traverse the more difficult country and, not at all as expected, because it was opposed by the larger element of Benedek's army. The Second Army plan for the break-in operation involved simultaneous advances to contact over all the three passes of the Riesengebirge. On the evening of 27th June, Moltke, still controlling events from his office in Berlin, had just cause for serious concern. His Italian allies had been beaten decisively three days previously, First Army was making unnecessarily heavy weather of the Iser crossing, Falckenstein was bungling the operation against the despised Hanoverian Army, and reports received from Second Army indicated that their attempt to force the Riesengebirge passes had failed. The I Corps, commanded by von Bonin, the minister of war replaced seven years before by Roon, and a convinced sceptic about both the need for the war and Moltke's plan of campaign, had been beaten decisively at Trautenau on emerging from the north-western pass at Parschnitz. The initial clash between his advance guard and the Austrian X Corps appeared to be going well, and Bonin declined assistance from the First Infantry Division of the Guard Corps, which had debouched unopposed from the centre pass at Braunau. However, the Austrian corps commander, von Gablentz, contrived to reinforce his position more quickly than Bonin, with the result that, by 2 a.m. on 28th June, the latter had been forced back across the frontier to his original starting point. The X Corps had paid a heavy price for its success, losing 196 officers and over 5,500 men; more than twenty per cent of its strength. Although the Prussian I Corps' loss of sixty-three officers and 1,200 men was much smaller, their operation had failed completely.

Not so that of the Prussian V Corps at the south-eastern pass, Nachod; here the course of the battle was the exact opposite from that at Trautenau. Nachod lies at the end of a five mile long defile, and the Austrian VI Corps under von Ramming initially held off without much difficulty the attack of the infantry advance guard of V Corps. At 11 a.m. the Prussian commander, von

Steinmetz, a veteran of the war of 1813, ordered the cavalry division of his corps to attack. Ramming responded by forming his troops into squares, a manoeuvre which had worked well enough for Wellington at Waterloo, but which now was an invitation to disaster against troops armed with a breech-loading rifle. At 4 p.m. the Austrians were forced into a retreat to Skalitz, but in the absence of telegraphic communications in the field it was not until the following morning that the crown prince knew that this part of his plan had succeeded. Again the Austrians had paid a heavy price; the losses on both sides at Nachod were almost the same as those at Trautenau, but there the Austrians had managed to hold their ground.

During 28th June the Austrians met with further disaster at the hands of converging attacks by the Guard Corps and Steinmetz. Gablentz, although now supported by IV Corps (Festetics), was decisively beaten when withdrawing towards Koniginhof, and the Guard Corps secured Soor, thus freeing the route of I Corps through Parschnitz and Trautenau. The Austrian VI Corps, so roughly handled at Nachod, had withdrawn through a defensive position taken up at Skalitz by VIII Corps (Archduke Leopold), supported by II Corps (Thun-Hohenstadt). Thanks to the needle gun, which more than compensated for an Austrian superiority in numbers of nearly two to one, they were beaten decisively by Steinmetz, advancing westwards from Nachod. In the two actions on Second Army front on 28th June, the Austrians suffered a further 11,000 casualties. On the following day Steinmetz bundled IV Corps out of Jaroměř, closing up to the left bank of the Upper Elbe. Having fought and won three battles in three days, the V Corps was withdrawn into army reserve, to the disgust of its fiery commander. It was replaced by VI Corps, whose task covering Breslau had been made redundant by this series of victories. The VI Corps, hitherto unblooded, secured the Elbe crossing at Koniginhof on 30th June.

THE PRELUDE TO SADOWA

Thus, on the evening of 30th June, the Prussian Second Army was fully established on the Upper Elbe and in a position to cross uncontested. No more than twenty miles now separated the right flank corps of the crown prince's army from the left flank formation of the First Army, and the two had made contact by mounted patrol. On the same day, King William and Moltke left Berlin for the front. They were accompanied by War Minister von Roon and Prime Minister von Bismarck, the latter hurriedly commissioned and garbed as a major of reserve cavalry.[22] Army group headquarters, and effectively that of the government of Prussia, was established initially on the evening of 30th June at Reichenberg, ironically the country estate of the unfortunate Clam Gallas. Having received, shortly after arriving there, the welcome news of First Army's victory at Gitschin, royal and army group headquarters moved on to that town the following day. It is notable that, at a conference held at Gitschin on 2nd July, attended by the commander of First Army and fortuitously by the chief of staff of Second Army, neither could provide Moltke with any worthwhile information about the whereabouts of the main body of the Austrians. Notwithstanding their victories, both armies had been out of contact with the enemy for at least the preceding thirty-six hours.

Meanwhile, on the other side of the hill, the events of the concluding days of June had completed the destruction of the morale of the Austrian commander-in-chief, who had already sought, and been denied, permission to withdraw on Olmutz. Of the eight army corps under his command, all but one had been engaged and all but one of the battles had ended in defeat. Three corps, I, VI and X, had suffered at least twenty per cent casualties. Five days of diffused fighting had cost Benedek's army more than 30,000 men, with nothing but disaster to show for it. Benedek was a soldiers' general and was devastated by the losses. Worse, he felt that he had failed in his promise to the troops given when he had taken up command. Then, his order of the day had declared:

> The enemy have for some time vaunted the excellence of their firearms, but, soldiers, I do not think that will be of much avail to them. We shall give them no time, but we will attack them with the bayonet and with crossed muskets.[23]

While the king of Prussia and his chief of staff were moving to join their armies for the *coup de grâce*, the spirit of Austrian Army Headquarters in Koniggratz was broken utterly. The segment of country within the triangle Koniggratz–Nechanitz–Koniginhof contained a disorganised mass of men separated from their companies, companies separated from their regiments, and regiments separated from their formations. The original attempt to concentrate around Josefstadt meant that supporting elements of the army had continued to be moved northwards, where they were colliding on the routes with the logistic support trains and broken elements of the formations driven south-west across the Upper Elbe by the victories of Second Army. And all this before the Austrian Army as a whole had fought a battle. On the evening of 30th June, Benedek had reported the defeat on the Iser:

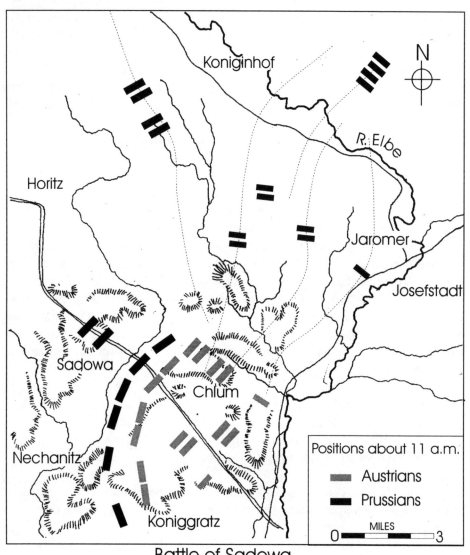

Battle of Sadowa

Débâcle of the 1st and Saxon Corps forces me to retreat in the direction of Koniggratz. Headquarters tomorrow in that neighbourhood.'[24]

Benedek was joined there the following afternoon by a visitor who had come the 200 miles from Vienna, not for the first time, to convey the special wishes of Franz Joseph. The thirty-six year old Lieutenant Colonel Beck was on the personal staff of the emperor, but was much more than the gilded equerry this description implies. He was, rather, the experienced and trusted aide-de-camp in the style of Napoleon's army, expected to have the ability to relate his master's wishes to the situation as he found it. In the present instance, Beck assessed this as chaotic. He drafted a telegram which the shaken Benedek signed: 'Your Majesty most urgently requested to make peace at any price. Catastrophe inevitable.'

This he supplemented with a telegram of his own, to Crenneville: 'Armistice or peace imperative because withdrawal scarcely possible. My heart is breaking, but I must report the truth.'

In Vienna it was the usual glorious high summer of late June, with the perennial gaiety of the lovely city on the Danube reinforced by the unexpected good news about Custozza. There had been no previous indication of the extent and rapidity of the disaster in Bohemia. In the circumstances it is hardly surprising that the reply emanating from a conventionally minded nineteenth-century character which, for all its many excellent qualities, lacked totally that of imagination, was: 'Impossible to conclude a peace. I order – if imperative – retreat in best order. Has there been a battle?'[25]

Sadowa

The answer to this pathetic cry was that there had not, but, in default of an immediate armistice, there was certainly going to be. Big-finger-on-small-scale-map appreciation suggests that Benedek might have withdrawn his army south of the Elbe, giving battle on a defensive position of his own choice based on the east–west course of this enormous river, and attacking the bridgeheads which the Prussians would be forced to develop. In view of the disastrous state of affairs around Koniggratz on 1st July, it is hardly surprising that this course, if indeed it were even considered at the time, was rejected. Having regard to Austrian standards of staff work and march discipline, Benedek would have needed at least ten days to implement any plan on these lines; ten days which Moltke would not allow him.

Benedek chose therefore to stand and fight on the rolling country north and west of Koniggratz. His front was marked by the Bistritz stream which joins the Elbe ten miles to the south, but which was an obstacle only to cavalry and artillery. The important feature of the Austrian position was the excellent command of the ground, which was afforded by the broad ridge running north-west from the hamlet of Chlum towards the rather larger village of Sadowa. As the ground drops through the hamlet of Lipa towards the Bistritz, which runs through Sadowa, it becomes more wooded. Benedek deployed his army in a sixty degree arc with its centre on Chlum, facing west and north on a frontage of about six miles.[g] To counter the image of superiority established by the Prussian needle gun, the numerous Austrian artillery was deployed in front of the static lines of infantry. Accepting, in the fashion of the time, the consequent risk to gun detachments, and, indeed of the total loss of the guns if the position had to be abandoned in a hurry, the gunners could not have wished for a better field of fire; out to the maximum range of equipment little changed in capability since Wagram. The terrain, and the position Benedek took up, is very similar to that of the Union Army on the second day of Gettysburg, but without the commanding *points d'appui* provided at the extremities of the Union line by Culps Hill and the Round Tops. Six of Benedek's corps formed the outer arc, the Saxons in the south covering the approach to Koniggratz from due west, then successively VIII – X – III – IV – II, the latter two facing north-west and north respectively. This was a classic Austrian defensive posture to guard against an outflanking manoeuvre. The two remaining corps, I and VI, were positioned in a second line south of Chlum, in the rear of X and III Corps and on the crest of the ridge. This deployment gave greatest protection to those corps which had suffered most in the frontier battles, in that X, in the first line, was effectively flanked, and I and VI were in the second line. The cavalry divisions were retained in reserve, off the ridge and south-east of Chlum. Benedek's deployment resembles nothing so much as a hedgehog, and it was about as mobile, with the very serious further drawback that, in the event of a forced and hurried retreat, there was only a very limited number of bridges across the Elbe. Nevertheless, the position was too strong even for the united Prussian armies to mask or bypass, and it was the best available against an enemy who had won the priceless

---

[g] A translation of Benedek's operation order, taken from, and heavily criticised by, Bonnal, is in Appendix 1 to this chapter.[26]

advantage of being able to force battle at a time of his own choosing. Benedek went down to complete defeat and subsequent disgrace. This has tended to obscure the enormous efforts of his formation commanders and regimental officers in creating the measure of order which they did inside the thirty-six hours before the Battle of Sadowa started. It also ignores the fact that Benedek's design for battle, option of one as it may have been, very nearly succeeded.

As the king and Moltke travelled south on 30th June for the former to assume direct command of his armies in the field, most of the concerns uppermost in the mind of the chief of staff three days previously had been resolved, and the last was removed shortly after midnight on 1st July with the report of the victory at Gitschin. The 300 mile long dispersion of the armies on mobilisation had now been reduced to the twenty miles between the inside flanks of First and Second Armies. Either could concentrate on the other in a day's forced march. But Moltke did not wish to effect the junction of the two armies while he was still without any information about the whereabouts of the Austrian field army. If the armies were to converge completely before Benedek had been found and fixed, Moltke would forfeit the flexibility which was the foundation of his design for the decisive battle – to bring the maximum possible concentration of force to bear only when the location of the battlefield had been established by defining precisely the position of the main enemy army. The point bears repeating that neither Prussian army commander should have allowed the Austrians on his front simply to disappear after the successful engagements of 30th June, and a competent cavalry leader in either army would have seen to it that this serious mistake was avoided.

During the journey south, Moltke had sent orders to First and Second Armies to stand fast on 1st July in order to allow the Army of the Elbe, echelonned in the rear and a day's march to the south-east of First Army, to continue to wheel left-handed until it was in a position to advance due east on Nechanitz and Koniggratz, thus covering the southern (right) flank of First Army. In default of information, still less intelligence, about the present whereabouts of the Austrian Army, Moltke made his own appreciation of Benedek's most likely course of action. He concluded that the enemy would withdraw eastwards across the Upper Elbe with a view to establishing a defensive position covering the river line between the fortified garrison towns of Koniggratz and Josefstadt, with his right flank further protected by the rivers Aupa and Mettau. These flow westwards to join the Upper Elbe at

Josefstadt. This would have been intrinsically a very strong position indeed. But the first necessity was to find the enemy.

After royal and army group headquarters had opened at Gitschin, orders for 2nd July were sent to the armies. The Army of the Elbe was to continue its approach march, the cavalry of First Army was to seek the enemy between Gitschin and Koniggratz, while Second Army was to conduct a reconnaissance in force simultaneously on both banks of the Upper Elbe. In this way, all options remained open: either Benedek could be manoeuvred out of his putative position on the Upper Elbe or he could be 'fixed' while the bulk of the Prussian Army embarked on a flank march south-eastwards which would have turned his position. This proposed repeat version of the events – though not the plan – of the twin battles of Jena and Auerstadt was a highly dangerous course, and as such has been criticised strongly by Bonnal. The postulated manoeuvre would have required a march across the front of the presumed Austrian position and around its southern flank while within range of its operations.

Second Army's part in the initial execution of this operation met with the total disapproval of its chief of staff:

> On the 2nd we received orders for an extraordinary disposition of the troops, according to which both armies were to reconnoitre in force on both banks of the Elbe. That was a little too strong, and I felt sure that they did not know quite what they were doing at headquarters.

Blumenthal rode the fifteen miles from his own headquarters at Koniginhof to deliver his protest in person. Once at Gitschin he displayed all the disdain of the warrior just emerged from hard-won victory when dealing with the braves of the base who had not heard a shot fired in anger.

> Headquarters to me was not an impressive experience. A crowd of long-faced loafers is always an odious sight, especially when they greet one in a sort of condescending manner, fancying themselves omniscient, and apportioning blame freely, in some cases neither understanding nor wishing to know the circumstances.

Blumenthal went on to say to the king, 'Your Majesty should just lay your ruler on the map between Gitschin and Vienna, draw your pencil along the ruler and march straight along that line,'[27] a proposal which Moltke appears to have treated with silent contempt.

The very fact of Blumenthal's protest might have delayed Second Army for a day, because he did not return to Koniginhof until three o'clock next morning, having presumably secured some modification and clarification.[28] As has already been noted, now that the armies were in enemy territory there was no telegraphic communication. Orders and reports were being transmitted at no better than the best speed of a horseman, after nightfall in the total darkness of the pre-industrial age, and, on the night of 2nd/3rd July, in vile weather caused by a succession of summer storms. Towards evening, the Red Prince began to receive the reports of the cavalry reconnaissances ordered so belatedly. These soon showed that Moltke's basic assumption was incorrect; there were substantial Austrian forces west of the Upper Elbe.

Reversing completely his previous ponderous approach to the conduct of operations, Prince Frederick Charles issued, at 9 p.m., orders to the six divisions of his army to attack at daybreak the following morning along the axis of the road Horitz–Sadowa–Chlum–Koniggratz,[h] and for the Army of the Elbe, still half a day's march to his right rear, to engage the Austrian left flank through Nechanitz. At the same time he sent a letter direct to the crown prince at Koniginhof, asking his cousin for the support of the right flank corps of Second Army. Immediately after these orders and requests had been prepared and dispatched, the chief of staff of First Army, von Voigts-Rhetz, an ambitious soldier with fingers in many pies including the one being baked by Krupp of Essen, rode the short distance to army group headquarters, to seek the approval of the king as commander-in-chief.[i]

His majesty was retiring to bed; he was, after all, sixty-nine. He directed his visitor to consult his chief of general staff, who had found a billet in a house on the other side of the town square. 'If General von Moltke is of opinion that any new steps ought to be taken, you can apply to me tonight for the necessary orders. You will find me ready at any hour.'[30] The sixty-six year old Moltke was asleep. On being woken, he at once understood not only that here was an entirely new situation, but also that the plan of First Army was inadequate to secure a decisive victory. More force was needed; not just the possibility of

---

[h] The route of the present road E442.

[i] It is worth remarking that in many subsequent 'shorthand' accounts both of this war and that of 1870, the king of Prussia is treated as a cypher, with all the decisions emanating from Moltke. The action of Voigts–Rhetz in going to the king first on the evening of 2nd July shows that this is not so. The sequence of events is described in detail in Moltke's own account.[29]

help from one corps of Second Army, but all the effort the crown prince could bring to bear.[j]

Yet it would be at least half a day before Second Army could come down in sufficient force to affect the outcome of the battle. Their advance guards had a march of at least ten miles, and the overnight storms would seriously degrade the routes. It might have seemed sensible to order First Army to postpone its attack for twenty-four hours in order to allow Second Army, and, for that matter, the Army of the Elbe, time to come up in order to achieve the long-contemplated junction on the decisive field of battle. But to delay would give the Austrians further time to recover from the pounding which they had taken in the frontier battles. It was also known that a special ambassador from Napoleon III was on his way, no doubt with yet another scheme generated by that fertile brain. While a suggestion from that quarter might serve Prussia well enough, any interference by Napoleon III would certainly seek advantages for France she had done nothing to earn, but which Prussia might be unable to deny in any circumstances short of total victory. The fact that First Army orders had already gone out for an attack was also a factor, though not a decisive one.

It speaks volumes for Moltke's ability to grasp a new and unexpected situation and for the working efficiency of the officers and staff clerks of his headquarters that by midnight orders were on their way to the three army headquarters. The plan of First Army was endorsed; the Army of the Elbe,[k] still under operational control of First Army, was also directed to proceed as ordered. But the orders to Second Army were altered completely and are worth quoting in full:

---

[j] 'The best laid plans...' The letter of Prince Frederick Charles, from one army commander to another, remained unopened at Koniginhof until Blumenthal returned from his visit to Gitschin. He just had time to send off a message rejecting the request of First Army commander before receiving orders from army group headquarters which altered completely those he had protested so violently on the previous day.

[k] The system under which the commander of the Army of the Elbe might receive operational orders from two superior headquarters, army group and First Army, would be comprehensible in late twentieth-century terms of command techniques and communications assets. In the mid-nineteenth century, it might have caused endless confusion, and often did. See Chapter XI. Herwarth appears to have been a competent, unfussy, principal subordinate commander who understood what was required and did it.

Gitschin, July 2, 11 p.m.

According to reports received by the First Army, the enemy, strength [of] about three corps, which may, however, still further be reinforced, has advanced to and beyond the line formed by the Bistritz at Sadowa, and an encounter there with the First Army is to be expected very early tomorrow morning. The First Army will be tomorrow morning with two divisions at Horitz, one at Milowitz, one at Cerekwitz, two at Pschansk and Bristau, and the Cavalry Corps at Gutwasser.

Your royal highness will be good enough immediately to make the necessary arrangements to be able to advance with all your forces in support of the First Army against the right flank of the enemy's probable advance, and in doing so to come into action as soon as possible. The orders issued from here this afternoon in other conditions are no longer valid.[31]

There are some obvious mistakes. 'Three corps'? Probably all the cavalry reconnaissance of First Army had been able to identify, but the order leaves open the likelihood of others. 'Enemy's probable advance?' With hindsight, we know that Benedek's tactical intention was entirely defensive; any Austrian advance west of the Bistritz would be patrol action only. These are minor criticisms of an order which can have left no doubt in the mind of its recipient about what he was expected to do, the urgency of the situation and the supersession of the previous orders. The simple inclusion of date and time would show Blumenthal that these orders derived from a completely new state of affairs arising since his own departure from army group headquarters late the previous evening. Nor was the crown prince to be fettered by the inclusion of any particular geographic objective or precise boundary with the left flank division of First Army. While normally essential, in this particular instance such definition could only cause confusion. Since battle would have been joined long before Second Army could possibly reach the scene, it would be absolutely clear to them when they did arrive exactly where 'the enemy's right flank' was situated. In all, Moltke's order is a model of its kind – given a like-minded and trained recipient.

For added security, duplicate copies were carried by officers directed to take different routes to Koniginhof. By Moltke's express order,[29] one of these couriers, Lieutenant Colonel Count von Finckenstein, travelled the more roundabout route by way of I Corps, the right flank formation of Second

Army, in order to give its commander advance warning of the orders which he might expect shortly to receive from his own army headquarters. The aide travelling by the direct route, whose name Moltke does not give, arrived at Second Army headquarters at 4 a.m.

It all now depended on the troops, their regimental officers and their formation commanders. First Army was required to attack an enemy at least twice as strong in infantry and artillery. Miller[18] assesses the relative strengths on the battlefield at the start of the day as Benedek; 180,000, Prince Frederick Charles; 75,000, and Benedek had the advantage of a naturally formidable defensive position. First Army could be seriously mauled before the Army of the Elbe, or, more importantly, Second Army, could deploy in support, and both were needed to give the Prussians a significant superiority in numbers. If Prince Frederick Charles were defeated decisively before the supports had arrived, the most likely outcome would be renewal of the battle on the same ground one or two days later, a slogging match between two forces of roughly equal size in which the defence would have a valuable advantage. It follows that First Army was required to fight a 'holding' engagement, rather than seeking to win on its own.

As dawn broke, the divisions of First Army fanned out left and right of the Horitz–Sadowa road, and at 7.30 a.m. battle was joined on the line of the Bistritz. The Prussian 7th Division (von Fransecky) was on the left (east) bank of the stream, attacking southwards. the 8th, 4th and 3rd Divisions successively in first line attacking south-eastwards, and 5th and 6th Divisions in reserve. The Cavalry Corps was covering the gap between First Army and the Army of the Elbe, whose leading elements were at this time still some six miles west of Nechanitz. This village was held by a covering force of the Saxon Corps.

It is at this point that impetuosity took over on the Prussian side, and so risked the whole campaign. Prince Frederick Charles had been directed to mount no more than a holding action until the arrival of the other two armies, but when his army artillery, on the command of the king , opened rapid fire at around 8 a.m., Fransecky took it as the signal for all-out assault. He proceeded to entangle his division in a general attack on the shank of the hook-shaped Austrian position, held in strength by III Corps in and either side of the Cistowes hamlet, covering Cistowes and Maslowed woods to their front. The rashness of 7th Division's commander drew in all the other assault divisions of First Army. One of the reserve divisions also became committed, and only the direct order from Moltke, already quoted, restrained the last reserve division, the 6th, from joining in. Contrary to army group intentions, fighting became general on the left (eastern) bank of the Bistritz, and until late morning the Austrians had very much the better of the battle.

Rashness was not unique to the Prussian Army, and on the Austrian side it was compounded by downright disobedience. At around nine o'clock, General Count Festetics, commanding the Austrian IV Corps, discerned what he thought was a great tactical opportunity. Influenced perhaps by the need to redeem the poor showing of his command in the battles on the Upper Elbe in the preceding week, and also perhaps by patrician contempt for the battle orders of the parvenu Benedek, he launched an attack on the luckless Fransecky. Festetics sought subsequently to justify his disobedience of orders, which had enjoined him to secure the crest line of the Chlum Ridge against an approach from the north, by explaining that he thought the troops in Maslowed Wood formed the extreme left of the Prussian Army. Evidently there was no thought in his mind about the whereabouts of Second Army, from whom he had disengaged only sixty hours earlier.

The abandonment of vital ground by Festetics was bad enough, but worse was to follow in that he drew in after him the Austrian II Corps, commanded by Count Thun-Hohenstadt. The latter was doubly disobedient in that Benedek had directed him not only to hold the Chlum position to the right of IV Corps, but also to prepare and secure routes of withdrawal eastwards across the Upper Elbe north of Koniggratz. The headlong assault of these two corps did not quite lay bare the Chlum feature to an attack from the north, i.e. towards and behind the Austrian right flank, because I Corps was positioned in reserve south of Chlum village. This formation, however, reduced as it was from the Iser and Gitschin battles, could not be expected to withstand for long anything much above corps strength.

Benedek's concern, manifest in his battle orders, had been for his left flank. Reassured that there was as yet no action on the Saxon Corps front, he and his staff directed their horses to the sound of the battle. Arriving at Chlum at around 10 a.m., he was at once informed of the misplaced initiative of IV and II Corps. Appreciating at once the appalling potential risk to his right flank, he immediately sent a staff officer with the most positive and definite orders to Festetics and Thun-Hohenstadt to disengage and return to their assigned positions astride the Chlum Ridge. His first order was ignored, as was a second an hour later. A third, sent at around midday, brought IV Corps commander back to Chlum to protest in person. At 1.15 p.m. a chastened Festetics returned to his corps and gave the orders to withdraw, but such orders are always more easily and quickly given than they can be executed by troops in contact.

Meanwhile the hierarchies of the military and civil government of Prussia, expanded by a number of foreign observers, among whom was the future father-in-law of a stormy petrel of a politician called Winston Churchill, were watching events from the Hill of Dub overlooking Sadowa village. Although by mid-morning the Army of the Elbe had made contact with the Saxon covering force, it would be some time before their weight would be fully felt. At around eleven o'clock, an Austrian battery was seen to be firing ranging shots from Chlum Ridge, not north-westwards into the carnage in the Cistowes and Maslowed woods, but northwards towards Horenowes. Their target[1] could only be the leading elements of Second Army, who had, as we have seen, received their orders only seven hours earlier, but whose advance to contact had been much delayed by the poor condition of the roads after the storms of the night before.

Although it was becoming evident that the design for battle was working and that the flank armies were converging on the battlefield as intended, the immediate situation was bad. First Army was in poor shape, all its assault divisions having suffered heavy casualties from the well-sited and served Austrian artillery, and fighting at close quarters in the woods and hamlets had to some degree neutralised the advantage of the needle gun. Commissariat arrangements in First Army had broken down: the infantry divisions had gone into the battle on empty stomachs after a miserable night in the open, and were nearing the end of their endurance. The casualty rate had been horrendous, especially in Fransecky's division. One regiment of 7th Division, having taken its three battalions into the battle at their full strength of 1,000 men each, emerged at the end of the day with a total effective strength of only two officers and 400 men; a loss rate approaching ninety per cent. The Red Prince was contemplating the withdrawal of all his infantry, and sent a warning order to his cavalry corps to be prepared to mount a covering action. Bismarck, always a prey to nerves, was at the end of his tether: were all his efforts of the last fifteen years to be wrecked by the generals? Even the soldier–king was affected by the general air of unease. Addressing an earnest question to his principal military adviser, he was reassured, 'Your majesty today will not only win the battle, but decide the war.'[29]

---

[1] This was in all probability patrols from the guard cavalry division, commanded by Major General Konstantin von Alvensleben, whom we will meet again in a critical role in the Battle of Mars La Tour in 1870 (Chapter XIII). At last, the Prussian cavalry was being used properly.

In later years Bismarck would claim that it was he who first discerned[m32] at about 2 p.m. the approach of soldiers of Second Army, and at about that time the battle, which had died down around Sadowa, flared up again on the northern approaches to Chlum. The crown prince's army brushed aside the units of Austria's IV and II Corps, returning at last to the positions they should never have left. These two corps were reduced to complete disorder. With Bonin's I Corps securing the left bank of the Bistritz, the Prussian Guard Corps, commanded by Prince Augustus of Wurtemburg, penetrated to Chlum village. There the weakened Austrian I Corps advanced to meet them. This formation died with great bravery, with drums beating, colours flying and the loss of half its residual strength in twenty minutes of carnage. Hiller von Gaertringen, commanding the First Prussian Guard infantry division, was killed in the hand-to-hand fight when leading from the front. His memorial still stands at the point of contact between these two equally brave bodies of men.

Benedek, soldiers' general to the end, had allowed himself to be drawn forward into the thick of the fighting around Lipa at the north-western end of the Chlum Ridge. He did not at first credit the reports of substantial Prussian forces on and behind his right flank, and would afterwards claim that the smoke of the battle and the damp haze of the day after the previous night's rain had prevented him from discerning the approach of Second Army. At 3.30 p.m. the king of Prussia ordered a general advance by all three armies. With the Austrian position in a stranglehold, and, as Benedek was forced to realise, with VI Corps of Second Army almost across his line of withdrawal towards Koniggratz and the precious bridges over the Elbe, there was no option but to order a retreat. This was accomplished thanks to heroic rearguard actions by the Austrian cavalry and artillery, and the exhaustion of most of the victors.

By an order from army group headquarters timed at 6.30 p.m. Moltke brought the battle to a close and ordered that the next day (4th July) should be a day of rest to unscramble the units of all three armies which had achieved their junction, not simply on the field of battle, as Moltke's design had intended, but on the vital ground which formed the heart of the defensive position of the main enemy army. Steinmetz, whose V Corps had, to his

---

[m] This claim is unlikely. It is five miles as the crow flies from the summit of the Hill of Dub to that of Horenowes, and it was a day of poor visibility. For further discussion, see Appendix C. A staff officer sent by the crown prince appears to have reached the Hill of Dub at about half past two.

extreme displeasure, been in reserve all day, continued to pester army group headquarters until darkness fell for permission to harry the Austrian retreat. Moltke forbade him, with consequences which would make themselves felt four years later. The Austrian Army made good its retreat towards Olmutz.

Of previous battles on the European continent, only Wagram, Borodino, Leipzig and Solferino had been fought by comparable numbers and the result of none was as emphatic as the colossal political impact of Prussia's victory at Sadowa. In purely military terms, the losses were unprecedented. On the day of Sadowa, Prussia lost 359 officers and nearly 9,000 rank and file, largely from First Army, but the allied Austro-Saxon loss amounted to over 14,000 killed or wounded, and nearly 20,000 prisoners, half of whom were unwounded. They also left behind on the field 160 guns. The total loss to the Austrian Army in eight days of battle from 26th June to 3rd July was assessed as 10,407 killed, 27,805 wounded and 43,264 prisoners, including 32,000 unwounded;[33] over thirty per cent of the strength mobilised around Olmutz three weeks before.

The Last Act

The war was not yet over. On the day following the battle Austria sought an armistice, which Prussia rejected on the ground that her Italian ally had to be consulted. Archduke Albrecht, summoned to the command-in-chief to replace the unfortunate Benedek, conducted a competent retreat and achieved a local success at Blumenau against a Prussian pursuit which was not being pressed with any great vigour or urgency.

When preliminaries of peace were eventually signed on 26th July, the demarcation line, pending a final settlement was the Russbach stream south of the village of Wagram, a bare ten miles from Vienna.

Before this, however, there had been one further battle which, within its sphere, would exercise a surprising degree of influence for the rest of the century. As has already been established, the performance of the Italian Army was dilatory in spite of the fact that the kingdom of Sardinia had been the first of the major protagonists to mobilise. That of the Italian Navy was even more so. Nevertheless, in the wake of both Custozza and Sadowa, the fleet of the king of Sardinia found itself at sea on 20th July, halfway up the Adriatic, prepared to give battle to the Austrian fleet, which had emerged from its base at Pola. Contact was made within sight of the island of Lissa, which lies forty sea miles due west of Ragusa (now Dubrovnik).

Nelson's ships of the line under full sail had an awe-inspiring beauty, and in the twentieth-century warships would for a time become beautiful again.

'The mighty *Hood*' had a unique place in the affections of the whole British Empire between the two world wars.[34] However, in this critical decade, warships were ugly hybrids. To the horror of conservatively minded admirals, steam power had begun to be introduced, little by little, into the ships of the world's leading navy as many as thirty years before, and where the Royal Navy led, the others followed, for good or ill. Five years before Sadowa, the battle in the mouth of the Chesapeake Bay between the *Monitor* and the *Merrimac* had demonstrated that the day of the wooden-walled warship had gone for good, to the extent that the naval constructors of all nations had to return to their drawing boards. By the mid-1860s, to add to the contradictions of sail and steam, oak and armour, there were the new developments in gunnery. With the vessel rather than the horse providing the motive power, larger guns for use in a mobile battle (as opposed to fortress or siege guns) were developed initially for warships. Parallel developments were occurring in most aspects of gun and projectile design: improved materials for gun and ammunition; breech-loading; better propellant charges; more effective shells. Thus a warship of the 1860s was a mass of contradictions in three areas of combat capability – firepower, protection and mobility.[n]

The Austrian and Italian navies were as modern as they could be in contemporary terms, and the former had benefited from a series of reforms introduced by Archduke Maximilian, brother to the emperor himself. Otherwise engaged in Mexico, Maximilian was not among those present at Lissa and so missed the unusual phenomenon for the nineteenth century of a decisive Austrian victory; this notwithstanding an Italian advantage in all areas. They had more ships, forty-two to thirty-seven. More of their ships were steam-powered, thirty-three to twenty-eight, and twelve Italian ships were armoured (eight part only), as against only seven Austrian. The Italian ships mounted a total of 680 guns, the Austrian only 550.[35] What should have given the Italians a decisive advantage was the superior steam- and gunpower of the largest units of their fleet. Naval warfare in the twentieth century was to prove time and again that one significantly more powerful ship had a decisive advantage in an engagement, threatened or actual, against a number of smaller and weaker opponents. The two largest and most modern Italian ships, *Re d'Italia and Re di Portugallo*, not only generated twenty-five per cent as much horsepower again as their Austrian counterparts, *Archduke Ferdinand Maximilian* and *Habsburg*, but also mounted more guns, thirty-six to sixteen

---

[n] A visit to the superbly presented and maintained HMS *Warrior*, in Portsmouth dockyard, establishes this proposition beyond all doubt.

each. In total broadside power of the largest calibres, the Italian fleet had an advantage of almost two to one:

TABLE XIV

Austria Heavy Guns			Italy Heavy Guns		
Ships	Number	Shells (lbs)	Ships	Number	Shell (lbs)
14	118	48	15	250	40
23	115	24	14	20	80
			3	6	300
			2	4	150

The latter two gun types in the Italian fleet were current state-of–the-art Armstrong Whitworths. On a coarse calculation of weight of broadside (number of guns multiplied by pound weight of shell) the Italian advantage was 14,000 to 8,424.[o]

Whether or not the Austrian admiral, Tegethof, appreciated the Italian superiority, his reaction was that of a cavalry subaltern rather than an admiral. His more powerful steamships were equipped with rams. These he ordered to charge straight for the more powerful units of the Italian fleet, some of which were sunk, some damaged; the rest turned tail. Tegethof's feat is commemorated to this day by a statue in a square named after him in Vienna.

In terms of naval construction, his achievement set a precedent until the advent of the *Dreadnought* battleship forty years later. In spite of the continually increasing range and proven improved lethality of naval ordnance, battleships for the rest of the nineteenth century continued to be built with rams.[p] The

---

[o] 'Coarse calculation' because in no circumstances could all the guns of all the ships be fired simultaneously. But the method was not disdained by Churchill in computing the relative strengths of the British and German battle fleets in World War I.

[p] There is only one recorded instance of the Royal Navy sinking a ship by ramming; unfortunately, one of their own. On 23rd June, 1893, off the Lebanese Coast, a somewhat over-ambitious evolution ordered by the commander-in-chief of the Mediterranean Fleet, Vice-Admiral Sir Hugh Tryon, caused his flagship, HMS *Victoria*, to be rammed and sunk by that of his second in command, Rear Admiral A.H. Markham (HMS *Camperdown*). Three hundred and fifty-eight out of 700 souls on board *Victoria* were lost, including the gallant but headstrong Tryon.[37]

availability of this 'weapon' had a negative effect on the development of thought about fleet tactics in a naval battle. Most maritime strategic intellects could grasp the key principle of the American Admiral Mahan – the continuing and undefined threat posed by the 'fleet in being'.[36] But its tactical corollary, the stand-off advantage possessed by fleet or individual ship with heavier or longer range guns (usually synonymous) was virtually ignored in terms of the need to develop techniques of target acquisition and fire direction. The 'line of sight over the bore of the gun' mentality imbued in the Royal Navy since the Armada endured until Jutland – and longer. And the Royal Navy sailed to Jutland with a target acquisition capability unaltered since Trafalgar, and fire direction techniques inadequate for the capabilities of the guns of the battleships.

The Aftermath

Napoleonic victories had invariably ended with massive transfers of provinces and population to swell the French Empire, but few of these outlasted Waterloo. In 1866, by contrast, Prussia took nothing tangible from Austria for herself, but the direct consequences of Sadowa endured until at least 1918, and debatably until the present day. Austria's lesser allies, Hanover and Hesse, were, together with the duchies, incorporated without delay or qualification within the lands of the Hohenzollerns. Prussia accordingly gained a continuous sweep of territory within one unbroken frontier for the first time in her history, and an increase of population of 4,000,000, enough to generate another three first line army corps. This expansion of the army was achieved without any administrative difficulty by 1870. Franz Joseph negotiated successfully for the continued independence of his only loyal and effective ally, Saxony, but Saxony was constrained, nevertheless, to adhere to the North German Confederation and in the war of 1870, her army fought as XII Corps of the German army, under the continued leadership of Crown Prince Albert. The issue of military command of all German forces north of the Main was now decided for all time. The reward for Italian incompetence was Habsburg cession of Venetia, but not the Trentino. This Austrian province was destined to be the reward for a similar level of Italian performance in World War I.

Bismarck gained his point against the initial wish of the king and most of the generals, though not Moltke,[q] for a punitive settlement against Austria, or at the very least a triumphal march through Vienna. With his next move

---

[q] See Appendix 2 to this chapter.

already in view, Bismarck saw, from the moment the last shots of Sadowa had been fired, the absolute necessity of regaining the friendship of Austria.

Sadowa ended 600 years of Habsburg predominance in Germany, hitherto interrupted only briefly by Napoleon. This in turn was the culminating act in compelling the attention of Vienna away from Germany and towards the Balkans. In a position of extreme political and economic weakness after his defeat, Franz Joseph was forced into an agreement with the Magyars which enshrined their position as co-equal with the Austro-Germans and superior to all the other races within what for the next half century would be known as the Dual Monarchy – with such disastrous consequences. Furthermore, the diversion of Austrian interest towards the Balkans and the second-class status of the Slav population of the Dual Monarchy inevitably came to cause conflict with Russia. Already on the worst of terms because of Austria's refusal to support Russia in the Crimean War, the latent ill-feeling between the two empires would be held in check only for so long as Bismarck could maintain a balancing act, by Dreikaiserbund and Reinsurance Treaty. After his departure from the stage, the historic role of protector of the Slavs assumed by Russia, which was maintained throughout the twentieth century, was bound to clash with the Austro-Magyar dynamic of the government of the Dual Monarchy, once this was focused on the Balkans.

Quite apart from Prussia's material gains, her increase in international prestige and national self-confidence was dramatic. There could be no doubt that the Prussian system of universal service for a relatively short period, retention of military skills after full-time service and a continuing universal liability on the part of those of military age to mobilisation in emergency had produced the finest army in Europe, and the one best adapted to any probable task which might arise under a government philosophy that treated war as an instrument of policy. The upsurge in national confidence was immediately a cause of concern to some. Colonel Sir Henry Hozier, whose presence as an observer at Sadowa we have already noted, was also present at the triumphant return of the army to Berlin, on 21st September. He wrote a prophetic warning for the future:

> In many places words of welcome to the returning soldiers, or mottoes recording victory, were traced in lamps which burnt with coloured flames. But nowhere was to be seen a single congratulation for peace. Every fiery inscription, every device of flame, told of the fierce joy of the people for victory and conquest, and to the minds of many men foreboded that thirst

for further war and for military glory was taking a strong hold of the heart of Prussia'.[38]

It is worth emphasising that Colonel Hozier published his account of what became known as the Seven Weeks War in 1867, and in the light of subsequent events it may be wondered whether he ever discussed the matter with the man who became his son-in-law forty-one years later. The latter was destined to play some considerable part in curtailing the ambitions of both Second and Third Reich.

A further contemporary account by another British observer drew a purely military lesson which should have been fastened upon at once by every general staff:

> Of all the improvements that have been made in military weapons I should think none ever fulfilled its mission with such brilliant results as the breech-loading needle gun.[39]

No one in any position of authority and able to make his views felt stopped to think through the consequence of this dramatic improvement in infantry firepower on the conduct of battle. The lesson would be repeated four years later on the bare uplands of Lorraine, once more to be ignored; hence the casualty rates of the First World War.

Not even Moltke learned this lesson. Perhaps because the master strategic planner never commanded so much as a battalion, his transcendent military intellect was never applied to battlefield tactics. For all his skill and training of others in getting troops on to the battlefield, the tactics of the field commanders once there, both in 1866 and 1870, were those of the bludgeon, with casualty rates which only blind belief in the cause would induce troops to suffer, and which could be justified, if at all, only by total victory.

The worst loser in an era when national prestige was important both internationally and domestically was the European power that had not fired a shot. This was at once widely comprehended throughout Europe, by authorities as diverse as the papal secretary of state and the French minister of war. The latter's comment, 'It is France that has lost at Sadowa,'[40] indicated the need for massive reform of the French Army, but will, ability and resources to achieve anything worthwhile in such time as might be allowed were all questionable. The public efforts of Napoleon III to obtain some reward for good offices, which might enhance the fading prestige of his dynasty at home, were dismissed contemptuously by Bismarck as the efforts of a waiter to obtain a tip – '*trinkgeld*'. His secret negotiations to obtain the forced annexation of Belgium were to have a disastrous international effect four years later on the moral standing of the cause of the Second Empire in the war of 1870, when Bismarck, with exquisite timing, made them known to the world. It was a further blow to French prestige that Italy received Venetia as a result of Prussian, and not French, lifeblood and exertion. The most Napoleon III could secure was an agreement between his plenipotentiaries and those of the municipality of Venice that the city might join the kingdom of Italy.[41] The First War of Prussian Supremacy left the Second Empire with seriously diminished prestige both at home and abroad, a manifestly inferior army and a rampant, predatory and historically hostile neighbour much increased in strength.

Appendix 1
The Austrian Army Operation Order for Sadowa

Koniggratz, Prague Square, 2nd July, 1866

Information which has reached us today makes us aware that great masses of enemy troops are gathered in the area of Neu Bidsow, Smidar and near Horitz. Our advanced posts have already engaged in some skirmishes with the enemy, at Kobilitz and Sucha.

Because of his situation, it is probable that the enemy will attack tomorrow. Following all probability, our most exposed formation is the Saxon army corps. In case of an isolated attack on the Saxons, all are to conform to the following orders:

The Saxon army corps is to occupy the heights around Popowitz, withdrawing slightly its left flank in a defensive posture, and covering its position by some squadrons of cavalry. Only advanced posts are to deploy forward of this position. The 1st light cavalry division is to establish itself in a good position to the left and a little behind that of the Saxons, at Problus and at Prim, and will form the extreme left. X Corps will take up a position to the right of the Saxon Corps; next, III Corps will occupy the heights of Lipa and Chlum, to the right of X Corps. VIII Corps will act as a reserve to the Saxon Corps and will establish itself in rear of the latter.[r]

If the attack is restricted to our left wing, the formations not designated in the preceding paragraph have no more to do than to hold themselves in readiness to march. But if the enemy mounts a full assault, extending it at the same time to our centre and right,

---

[r] In fact VIII Corps deployed to the right rear of the Saxons.

the whole army is to take up battle positions and will deploy as follows:

The IV Corps will deploy on the right of III Corps, on the heights of Chlum and Nedelist.[5] The II Corps will deploy by its side and form our extreme right. The 2nd light cavalry division is to take up a position behind Nedelist, and is to be ready to march.

The VI Corps will regroup on the heights of Wsestar. The I Corps will take up position at Rosnitz, and both these formations are to form up on these points in close order. The 1st and the 3rd Divisions of the reserve cavalry are to take up position at Sweti, the 2nd reserve cavalry division at Briza.

In the second case, that of a general assault, I and VI Corps, the five cavalry divisions and the army artillery reserve will form the general reserve and will remain exclusively at my disposal. The army artillery reserve is to establish itself behind I and VI Corps.

The whole army is to be ready to give battle early. The corps which is attacked first is to make this known without delay to those which, in accordance with these orders, are to take up positions either side of it. These in their turn are to pass on the message which they will have received.

The VIII Corps is to leave at once the bivouac area which it is occupying at present. It is to send a staff officer to the Saxon Corps headquarters; according to the state of affairs, and if the battle is already engaged or on the point of becoming so, this officer is to return at the gallop to VIII Corps and to act as their guide in taking it to the position it is to occupy in rear of the Saxon Corps. If there is no sign that the enemy is going to attack, VIII Corps is to establish itself at Charbusitz, and encamp there.

If the left wing of the army is the only one to be attacked, I will place myself near it; in the case of a general attack, I will be on the heights of Chlum.

If the army is obliged to make a fighting withdrawal, this movement will be executed along the road through Horitz, through Hohenmauth, passing through Koniggratz.

As soon as the order is given to conduct a fighting withdrawal, II and IV Corps are to throw pontoon bridges across the Elbe: II

---

[5] That is, facing northwards.

Corps two bridges between Lochenitz and Predmeritz; IV Corps, likewise two bridges, at Placka.

If they have not sufficient material they are to draw on the resources of the VI [Corps] pioneer battalion. If it is necessary to make approach roads in order to reach the points where the bridges are to be set up, they are to undertake the necessary work.

The I Corps Pioneers are immediately to construct a bridge across the Adler [stream], at Swinar. Officers will be sent to report either verbally or in writing that this order has been carried out, and are to make clear precisely the locations chosen for the emplacement of the bridges.

A special order will be issued tomorrow in the event of a retreat.

Benedek

Bonnal's comment:

> This order is lamentable both in background and form. It reveals infantile preoccupations and does not set out any plan.
>
> For the Austrian commander-in-chief, the main body of the enemy is around Smirdar and Horitz. There is no mention of the army of the crown prince of Prussia which could and should have been identified during the preceding days, in its positions on the left bank of the Elbe, at Koniginhof and downstream.

One feels from a reading of this document that General Benedek only accepted battle to save appearances. And in order to finish with it as soon as possible.

Bonnal goes on to say:

> In accumulating the 200,000 [sic] men of his army in a triangle whose base did not measure more than 10 kilometres, Benedek was playing completely into the hands of[t] the Prussian double-envelopment manoeuvre.
>
> Except at Ulm and Sedan, an army has never been worse deployed when expecting to receive battle.[26]

---

[t] *'favorisait singulièrement'*.

Appendix 2
The Terms of Peace between Prussia and Austria

In a bitter argument between Bismarck and the generals, it is worth recording Moltke's view:

> Were the war to be carried on in the hope of yet greater results? Our army stood before Vienna, and Preszburg [sic] was all but in our grasp. The outcome of a second battle gave us but small concern, and an entry into Vienna might have been made without serious loss. With so much in our favour from a military point of view, it was only natural that we should wish to follow up our triumph to its farthest limit and give full scope to the energies of our forces. A goal which the First Napoleon had never omitted to reach, the enemy's capital, lay temptingly at hand with its spires already in sight. On the other hand it must be remembered that Austria, even after the loss of Vienna, would not be compelled to make peace. She could make her way into Hungary, and there await further European complications. Again, if no peace arrangements on the Napoleonic basis were come to, the interests no less than the honour of France would suffer. Our great end had not been reached, and for a yet greater one were fresh sacrifices, fresh efforts to be asked of the Prussian nation, jeopardising anew the results already gained? A wise policy measures its aims by its needs rather than its wishes. By this contemplated peace the national development of Germany, under the guidance of Prussia, was now secured, and further schemes of conquest formed no part of the plan of her government. Both king and people could say that they had discharged to the full the duties laid upon them by the state; and they were bound to acknowledge that to the security and development of the national

existence of both Prussia and Germany there was absolutely nothing wanting. What Prussia now expected to gain in territory and power might subsequently be hers by a later peaceful development. The conditions offered by Austria did not preclude the possibility of a reconciliation between herself and her former confederates. Her honour and might had not suffered to such an extent as to make such enmity irreconcilable. To demand more, even if a successful continuation of hostilities admitted of it, would leave a thorn behind which time would not be able to remove; to perpetuate such a rupture would not be in the interest of either Germany or Prussia.[42]

Notes

[1] Connell, *Wavell, Scholar and Soldier*, London, Collins, 1964, pp. 161–62.

[2] Whitton, op.cit., pp. 96–97 and Crankshaw, op.cit., pp. 221–22.

[3] Ascoli, op.cit., p. 314.

[4] Whitton, op.cit., p. 53.

[5] Whitton, op.cit., p. 98.

[6] Whitton, op.cit., p. 90.

[7] Whitton, op.cit., p. 100.

[8] Crankshaw, op.cit., p. 229.

[9] Bonnal, op.cit., p. 11.

[10] Lecomte, *Guerre de la Prusse et de l'Italie et la Confédération Germanique en 1866*, Colonel Fédéral Suisse, Paris, Librarie pour l'art militaire, les sciences et les arts, vol. II, 1868; pièces annexes, vol. II, pp. 1–45. Not, so far as this author is aware, translated into English. Lecomte was a disciple of Jomini, and therefore his strategic analysis was no sooner written than outdated.

[11] Whitton, op.cit., p. 100.

[12] Whitton, op.cit., p. 107 and Crankshaw p. 230.

[13] Whitton, op.cit., p. 127.

[14] Whitton, op.cit., pp. 110–11.

[15] Whitton, op.cit., p. 120.

[16] Whitton, op.cit., p. 118.

[17] Macaulay's Lays of Ancient Rome, Horatius, Stanza XXIX.

[18] Miller, Lieutenant Colonel F., VC, Royal Artillery, 'A lecture on the Campaigns of 1866 in Germany, paper presented to the London Institution in *Minutes of Proceedings of the Royal Artillery Institution*, Woolwich, vol. V, 1867, pp.355–85. Miller had earlier published one of the very few accounts which is both coherent and detailed of the campaign in Lombardy in 1859, published in vol. II of the RAI Proceedings. He won his Victoria Cross as a major, at Inkerman.

[19] Whitton, op.cit., p.121.

[20] Whitton, op.cit., pp.129–30.

[21] Bonnal, op.cit., p.47.

[22] Taylor, *op.cit.*, p.84, and Crankshaw, *op.cit.*, p.231. There is a discrepancy between these two sources about what rank Bismarck was actually given. He had undergone his compulsory military service as a subaltern in the Potsdam Garrison in 1838, earning a medal for life-saving when he rescued an NCO from drowning in a ditch. Crankshaw states that he was commissioned as a major in 1866, Taylor believes he was made a major general for the occasion. His part in the battle was confined to attempting to prevent the king from coming too close to the firefight on the Bistritz, without complete success.

[23] Miller, *op.cit.*

[24] Whitton, op.cit., p.154.

[25] Crankshaw, op.cit., p.234.

[26] Quoted in full, and heavily criticised, by Bonnal, op.cit., pp.121–23.

[27] From *The Journal of 1866 of General Count von Blumenthal*, not published until 1903, quoted by Whitton, op.cit., pp.144–45.

[28] Whitton, op.cit., p.151.

[29] Moltke, op.cit., p.415.

[30] Whitton, op.cit., p.148.

[31] Whitton, op.cit., p.151.

[32] Whitton, op.cit., p.158

[33] Casualty figures from Miller, op.cit.

[34] Kennedy, *Pursuit: The Sinking of the Bismarck*, London, Fontana, 1975, first published William Collins, London, 1974, p.59.

[35] Lecomte, op.cit., Annex 3, pp.46–47.

[36] Mahan, *The Influence of Seapower on History 1660–1783*, and other works.

[37] Massie, *op.cit.*, pp.393–95.

[38] Hozier, *The Seven Weeks War 1867*, p.465, quoted Whitton, op.cit., p.168.

[39] Miller, *op.cit.*

[40] Fisher, op.cit., p.979.

[41] Lecomte, op.cit., Annex 3.

[42] Whitton, op.cit., pp.161–62.

Chapter IX
Protection

Fortifications are as old as organised warfare. Whenever the Roman legion halted for any length of time, it threw up an earthwork on a standard pattern – ditch, wall, rampart and keep – and for permanent strong points and fortified cities the walls and secure buildings were built from the best stone available locally. Labour was cheap. In time, an understanding of the basic principles of geometry led to fortifications which went beyond the simplest and most basic square or circular shape. As early as the mid-sixteenth century, the Knights of Malta, among others, had comprehended that the angled walls of a star construction[1] provided a degree of mutual support for the defence, because an enemy attacking one wall could be fired upon from another, and from the star shape derived the whole configuration of outworks, strong points and recessed walls which reached the zenith of its achievement a century and a half later. Vauban, master of fortification for King Louis XIV, combined the precision of a mathematician with the eye for ground of a natural soldier. The critical invasion route into France by way of the Low Countries was first secured, as far as the other European powers would tolerate, by the armies of the Grand Monarque, and then fortified by an engineer of such recognised genius that he was made a marshal of France, a distinction hitherto reserved almost exclusively for generals who had exercised successful independent command of an army in the field.[2] Fortified cities and towns, provided that they were properly garrisoned, dominated their local area, and with magazines well-stocked with food, forage and ammunition, could support an army operating beyond their walls. Fortresses were not only important strategic objectives in their own right. By the mid-eighteenth century, the stronger and more important had become status symbols to the same degree as the battleships of the first half of the twentieth century, and deterrents similar to the nuclear armouries of the Cold War. After the failure of the '45 rebellion, the English ensured that there would be no similar rebellion in future by building an enormous fortress on the Ardeseir peninsula, on the Moray Firth, east of Inverness. Fort George, which never fired a shot in anger and is still in use as a military installation, was not only impregnable in relation to anything which might be brought against it. The garrison could never be starved out while an English fleet retained command of the sea, and the fortress itself was an imposing base for a network of smaller strong points throughout the Scottish Highlands, linked by roads built for the purpose. These outposts could give early warning of an incipient insurrection and, if necessary, could be reinforced rapidly to nip it in the bud. Fortress systems such as that built by Vauban across Flanders and north-eastern France, and the Quadrilateral of the army of the Habsburg Empire in northern Italy, had similar prestige status and deterrent value – and in building made the same proportionate demands on defence expenditure as would the 'flagship of the fleet' weapon systems of the future.

Every weapon system has its counter, and the fortress had three potential areas of vulnerability. The garrison might be inadequate to secure a defence perimeter of walls, strong points and outworks which sometimes extended for several miles. The quantity of ammunition, food and water within the walls was finite, and, if the besieging army could not be drawn away, the fortress was bound to fall; walls of brick or stone could not withstand indefinitely the constant battering of solid shot fired at short range with the same point of impact. Conversely, time was not necessarily on the side of besieging armies. They might be compelled to raise the siege, either by external forces, political or military, or because they had become weakened by privation or disease, to which, given the almost non-existent contemporary understanding of military hygiene, they were as vulnerable as the garrison. In addition, few armies could keep the field after the onset of a European winter. Since the besieging army could not usually afford to sit back and wait for a capitulation, there developed the precise techniques of siege warfare, which in a more structured era than that of today produced its own set of rules and usages.

Guns much heavier than those of field artillery were used to batter a selected section of the wall. These equipments, usually too heavy to be moved as a single unit, were brought to the site in separate components, ordnance and carriage, and assembled *in situ*. They then had to be dug in, in order to protect gun, ammunition and detachment from the fire of the defenders, within effective range of the main wall. Thereafter, the achievement of a breach was a contest between the intrinsic strength of the wall and the gunpower and ammunition resupply rate of the siege train. In addition to the excavations for the battering artillery, other trenches would be dug, known as 'parallels', to provide protected forming-up points for storming parties. From these, trenches, or 'saps', were usually dug forward, oblique to the line of fire from the ramparts, so as to offer the smallest possible target. These provided a covered way to 'second parallels' closer to the walls, and the process might be repeated to provide a third parallel. Parallels and saps might be punctuated by 'gabions', tightly bonded bundles of wood and impacted earth placed pillar-like in zigzag patterns along the trench path, or 'traverse', to minimise the effect of enfilading fire. Parallels and saps were invulnerable to any firepower except a direct hit landing within the excavated ground, but might be interrupted or even destroyed altogether by a sortie. This was a highly risky enterprise when mounted, as often it had to be, in sight and range of the supporting artillery of the besieging army.

The progress of a siege was predictable to both sides and the structured manners of the age led to conventions which the armies of all civilised powers observed. Negotiations might be conducted under flag of truce. The commander of a besieged fortress might surrender without dishonour as soon as an effective breach had been made in the main defensive wall. If he did so, the garrison was allowed to march out 'with the honours of war', retaining their personal weapons and not necessarily precluded from taking further part in the war. The civilian population, and also their property, was, at least in theory, inviolate and entitled to the protection of the discipline of the army which had taken the city. But if, on the other hand, the defending commander refused to surrender once there was an effective breach, the garrison might be slaughtered indiscriminately and the town sacked. Such were the basic ground rules until the start of the wars of the French Revolution.

The extent to which one fortress could support another was nevertheless already debatable. Throughout the twenty years of war between the France of Louis XIV on the one hand and England and the Netherlands on the other around the turn of the seventeenth and eighteenth centuries, the Low Countries were both a permanent and the most important theatre of the war. Within a stretch of country 150 miles by 100, bounded by Dunkirk, Nijmegen, Venlo, Maastricht and Namur, there were over thirty fortified cities and towns, mostly the work of Vauban and his disciples. The status of many varied as the war continued through phases of total combat, truce de facto for the winter months and short-term negotiated settlement. Some were garrisoned throughout, by one side or other depending on the progress of the war or the outcome of negotiations; others were from time to time 'neutralised' by agreement, in that they were left without fortress artillery and stocked magazines, and had only a token garrison. But it was only when a field army was capable of moving to the support of a threatened fortress that its security could be assured. In the closing stages of the war, with France already decisively worsted and war-weary as a result, the relationship between fortification and army in the field received further definition. Louis XIV, in the hope of a change of government in England which might produce an administration less dedicated to the continuation of hostilities, directed Marshal Villars, his commander on the critical Flanders frontier, to conduct a wholly defensive campaign. Villars was forbidden to risk a battle in the open, and ordered to fight only behind parapets.[3] The immediate result was the construction of the 'Ne Plus Ultra' lines, a continuous belt of fieldworks connecting all the fortified places on a line from the Channel coast to Namur. Anchored at its western end by the fortified town of Montreuil, near the mouth of the River Canche, the line proceeded by way of Hesdin and Frevent to Bouchain and Valenciennes on the Scheldt, thence to Quesnoy and along the line of the Sambre through Maubeuge to Namur, at the confluence of the Sambre and Meuse rivers.[4] The breaching of the Ne Plus Ultra lines, when Bouchain fell on 12th September, 1711, should have ranked with Marlborough's four more celebrated great victories. It was the linking of the fortified towns and cities by field fortifications, and the additional defensive potential and freedom of movement thus gained, which enabled Villars to stave off defeat almost until the end of the campaigning season of 1711. A century later, the construction of the lines of Torres Vedras above Lisbon gave the British Army under Wellington a secure base in Europe from which to develop further operations, for the first time in nearly twenty years of war.

The refusal of the tatterdemolian French Army of Italy in 1796 to accept physical constraints hitherto regarded as absolute, combined with the genius of their commander, manoeuvred the Habsburg armies out of their well-prepared and numerous fortified cities across northern Italy. Forced to give battle in open country at Lodi, Arcola and Rivoli, the Austrians derived little benefit from the fortifications of Milan and the Quadrilateral. They could not comprehend an enemy commander who was prepared to risk long marches with unprotected flanks in order to place his own army between two or more of their own, in time to defeat each in detail. A combination of Napoleonic genius and unprecedented feats of marching altered the eighteenth-century balance between protection and mobility in favour of the latter, but throughout the Napoleonic Wars fortresses still retained prestige, strategic importance and tactical value. Stone walls and solid ramparts would still be effective counters on the board for as long as masonry walls could be breached only by the impact of solid shot fired at close range but relatively low velocity, or tumbled by mines based on low-intensity explosive. And earthworks needed even more battering, because solid shot tended to impact with minimal effect. But the structured format of the siege was ended by the refusal of Napoleon to accept that the conduct of warfare could be limited by any rules. With the security of the western approaches into Spain from Portugal dependent upon the fortresses of Ciudad Rodrigo and Badajoz, the French emperor directed that any military commander who surrendered a fortified place before it had been stormed would be shot,[5] thus ending the convention of centuries which had accepted that no disgrace attached to a surrender after a practicable breach had been achieved. The result was the sacking of Badajoz by a British army, at a level of violence towards the potentially friendly civilian population which took three days to contain.[6]

If the advent of total war in the Napoleonic era meant that siege warfare would no longer be conducted according to a mutually accepted set of rules, sieges as a form of land warfare were by no means at an end. In 1840 Thiers, historian of Consulate and First Empire and de facto First Minister of the Orléans monarchy, carried through a total re-fortification of the city of Paris. The perceived threat was of war with England,[a] the most likely *casus belli* being the conflicting aims and aspirations of the two nations in the Middle East. There was as yet no perception of the strategic relationship between protection and mobility, and so no attempt at an analysis of balance of investment. It was another three years after the completion of the new fortifications of Paris before an intellectual soldier on the other side of the Rhine suggested that national funding might be better directed towards building railways rather than fortifications.[b] Paris was given a system of walls, bastions, moat and outlying defence works in which any general of the armies of the *Grand Monarque* would have found himself at home. The only innovation was a light railway within the walls to allow the rapid redeployment of troops. The wall was thirty feet high, the moat ten feet wide and there were sixteen outlying forts, each intended to be self-sufficient with garrison, artillery and magazines, but capable of providing fire support for its neighbours.[8] The nineteenth century built for permanence, and some of the Paris forts are still in use, as

---

[a] Until the reversal of alliances some ten years later, shortly before the Crimean War, it was always more probable that England and France would be enemies rather than allies in a future war. As late as 1846, while the Duc d'Aumale, soldier–son of King Louis Philippe, was winning glory for the dynasty in Algeria, his sailor–brother, the Prince de Joinville, published a pamphlet urging the need for the construction of a steam-powered battle fleet, in order to contest command of the sea with England[7] - a policy which gained contemporary notice in Thackeray's *Vanity Fair*, published in 1847–48.

[b] See Chapter X.

defence or internal security force installations, but the wall, moat and bastions have long been engulfed in the expansion of the city. Even at the time, the perimeter wall had a circumference of nearly forty miles, far more than the enceinte of any fortress–city of the previous century. The measures needed to sustain a population living within such a large area were not thought through, though effective work was done in September 1870 to both build additional earthworks and to provision the city in the bare fortnight between news of the capitulation at Sedan and the establishment of encirclement by the German armies.

Fortified places in the style of Vauban became obsolete only when the development of more powerful explosives, combined with longer-range artillery capable of precise adjustment of fall of shot, enabled even the most solid masonry construction to be pulverised within a day's firing. But even the rudimentary capabilities of personal weapons and field artillery had rendered out of date any form of personal protection long before the decade of the Catalytic Wars. The plumed and burnished helmets and cuirasses of the elite cavalry regiments of the European Great Powers were for little more than show; the cuirass might perhaps protect its wearer against a pistol bullet. Nevertheless, many of the horsemen of the armies of 1914 still went to war equipped with them. By contrast, the cavalry on either side in the War Between the States wore no protective armour whatsoever. The helmet was restored to the battlefield in the First World War, to provide protection against the fragmentation pattern of bursting shells, but the idea of reintroducing body armour for soldiers, if ever contemplated, was rightly discarded because it would have reduced the mobility of the infantryman to nothing; hence the emergence of the armoured crew-served weapon, dependent upon the internal combustion engine for its mobility and capable of launching much heavier firepower, but introducing a whole new scale and set of requirements for sustainability.

With masonry fortification verging on the obsolescent and personal protective armour in abeyance, the development of protective techniques in the wars of the decade after 1860 was confined to earthworks and field fortification systems. The United States had no fortified cities in the European style. Moreover, throughout the half century between the war of 1812 and the start of the War Between the States, there was, for much of the time, a substantial body of influential opinion which questioned any need for a standing army. As a result, the fortifications of the ports and harbours on the Atlantic coast, mostly dating from the years following the War of Independence, were only partially equipped and in a very poor state of repair.

Fort Sumter was a symbol, and in no way significant either as a military asset or as a strategic objective. When the war began, earthwork fortifications soon ringed both capitals. Those round Washington had a perimeter of nearly forty miles, which throughout the war swallowed up a garrison of up to 40,000 men, though not necessarily troops of the highest combat value. Nevertheless, as we have seen,[c] the refusal of the government to reduce this allocation caused a complete collapse of confidence between one commander of the Army of the Potomac and the political leadership, and led directly to the resignation of another.

Both Union and Confederate armies soon came to understand the value of field entrenchments. The Confederacy in particular, in the search for a way in which it might redress the superiority of the Union in numbers and firepower, began the process. Joseph E. Johnston proved a master of the coordination of the natural lie of the ground with trench line, earthwork and timber abbatis. For example, when he was in northern Virginia after First Manassas, on the peninsula, until his wound at Seven Pines forced him to relinquish command of the Army of Northern Virginia in favour of Lee, and in his conduct of a delaying action in 1864 against Sherman when in command of the Confederate Army of the Tennessee, until his ill-advised replacement by Hood. The War Between the States was the first in which troops began automatically to entrench, or to build breastworks from the timber usually readily available, whenever they halted for any length of time. Sometimes the process was carried too far. The victory of the Union Army in the Battle of Shiloh (6th–7th April, 1862) depended upon the retention of a sunken road, lying by chance on the right line in depth in a position in which they had been surprised. Grant, although he won the battle, incurred much criticism for having failed to entrench his camp around Pittsburgh Landing on the Tennessee River beforehand, and directly after the battle was superseded in command of the army in the field by Halleck, at the time in overall charge of the Union armies in the western theatre. Halleck made every effort to avoid criticism for the mistake imputed to Grant. Although speed was of the essence if he were to complete the destruction of the Confederate Army, decisively worsted at Shiloh, Halleck's advance on their position covering the important railway junction at Corinth, twenty-two distant, was conducted at the pace of the snail and by the techniques of the mole. Believing himself to be greatly outnumbered despite the relative battle casualties at Shiloh, it took three weeks before Halleck had assembled what he felt to be a sufficient force.

---

[c] See Chapter VI.

When at last the advance began, the Union Army, 120,000 strong, entrenched at the end of each day's march, spending two hours every evening digging trenches in which they stood to arms the following morning from 3 a.m. until daybreak.[9] On a good day the advance covered two miles, and Halleck took four more weeks to cover what should have been a day's march to Corinth. Inevitably, a Confederate Army less than half the size of the force Halleck had so painstakingly accumulated had not waited to be attacked, but had completed without hindrance a strategic withdrawal to Tupelo, fifty miles further south. Halleck considered that he did not have the necessary strength to continue the advance, and compounded his timidity by dispersing his army to hold the ground gained. The initiative thus surrendered, it took another year for the Union Army to clear the valley of the Mississippi.

Lee's defence of central Virginia on the line of the Rappahannock after Fredericksburg depended, as we have seen, on the field fortifications which he had caused to be built along the twenty-five mile stretch of river between Port Royal and Banks's Ford. The Army of the Potomac, after the failure of its frontal attack across the river in December 1862, was not disposed to make another similar attempt against any part of this line; hence Hooker's flanking manoeuvre, the poor execution of which gave Lee and Jackson the opportunity which they seized so ably around Chancellorsville. A year later, the construction of field defences had reached standards approaching those of the Western Front in the First World War. After Gettysburg and Vicksburg, all hope of a Confederate victory in the field had long gone, and the best that could be hoped for was a peace through Northern war-weariness and refusal to accept further enormous casualty lists. When the campaigning season of 1864 opened, Grant took 120,000 men across the Rapidan, and committed a further 25,000 from Fort Monroe to a landing at Bermuda Hundred. Command of the latter operation, intended to threaten Richmond from an approach to the rear of the position of the Army of Northern Virginia, went to Butler. Against these troops, Lee had a bare 60,000, there were no more than the usual headquarters details in the Confederate capital, and, given the limits of a manpower policy which fell some way short of total direction, the Confederacy was at the end of its resources. Grant, on the other hand, was not constrained by a limit on battle casualty replacement. The spade had to make up the difference.

Some of the outlines of the trench systems of the 1864 battles, in particular those at the 'Mule Shoe' on the Spotsylvania battlefield and to the south of Petersburg, are still visible in outline. At the former, the troops were deep-entrenched with timber-reinforced parapets, and there was a system of communication trenches and protective timber walls which enabled 3,000 Confederate soldiers, supported by twenty-two guns, also dug in, in a semicircular salient barely half a mile in diameter but with good all-round natural fields of fire, to hold off, for two days, a series of determined attacks launched from the total resources of two full-strength Union army corps. The position was lost to a combined attack by 18,000 Union troops, but a local counter-attack, before the survivors of the assault had been allowed to reorganise for exploitation, gained sufficient time for another defence line to be built across the mouth of the salient. A holding action allowed the Army of Northern Virginia to withdraw in good order to another prepared defensive position, at Cold Harbour, the ingenuity of which amazed a war correspondent:

> The lines are intricate, zigzagged lines within lines, lines protecting flanks of lines, lines built to enfilade an opposing line, lines within which lies a battery... a maze and labyrinth of works within works and works without works, each laid out with some definite design of defence or offence.[10]

The age of the fortified city was coming to an end, but the principles and techniques of Vauban had passed on to the battlefield in open country, always provided that the necessary time, will and manual effort were available.

All the Confederate defensive positions in the campaign of May 1864 were to some degree extemporised, but, in the assessment of a Union Army staff officer at the time, the Army of Northern Virginia needed no more than three days to dig a fully integrated defensive position, with fire and communication trenches, support lines and gun pits for artillery.[11] Whenever Grant's army achieved, at enormous cost, the capture of one position, they could not prevent the withdrawal of the Army of Northern Virginia to the next tactically suitable piece of ground, always covering Richmond, and the whole process had to be gone through all over again. After a month, four major battles, 60,000 Union casualties and the stagnation of Butler's attempts to break out from Bermuda Hundred, Grant initiated a new design. Making the best use of unimpeded strategic mobility deriving from absolute Union command of the sea, Grant moved his whole army south, not only of the James peninsula but the Appomattox River as well, to envelop the critical railway meeting point at Petersburg, southern gateway to Richmond. Lee's army would have to sacrifice itself in the defence of Petersburg, because once that town fell Richmond could not survive.

There followed, from mid-June until the beginning of the following April, the 'Siege' of Petersburg; not, strictly speaking, a siege as understood hitherto, because the town was never fully surrounded. The vital rail link to the west remained open, and it was in order to protect it that Lee was at length forced out of his fortifications. From the beginning of June, largely by the use of slave labour, the Confederacy built a continuous defence line extending for thirty-five miles in a shallow arc, from the Appomattox east of Petersburg, covering the town and the vital railway lines from the south and west, to a road junction known as Five Forks. Lee's army, reduced to 40,000 effectives, was never strong enough to hold the whole line and the open western flank was vulnerable throughout, but given the strength of the entrenchments, his army could always beat back a frontal attack on any threatened sector.

The entrenchments had been prepared on the same principles as the construction of a fortress. The approaches which an assault would have to take were cleared to produce a glacis half a mile in depth, removing all obstructions to fields of fire. A ditch fifteen feet wide and ten feet deep produced the spoil for an earthwork twenty feet thick at its base and six feet high, with redoubts and mini-forts at mutually supporting intervals. Forward of the ditch, felled trees were interlocked to provide an initial obstacle which was covered by trenches for skirmishers. On and behind the earthwork, there were successive lines of trenches for the infantry in the main defensive position, and dug-in positions for the artillery.[12] The whole was built by manual labour, without any of the modern advantages of mechanical excavators or power tools.

To protect themselves, the Union Army excavated a similar defensive system: obstacles, earthworks, strong points and trenches, including substantial dugouts intended to give cover against cannon and mortar fire. The armies settled down to a First World War Western Front-style existence. There was a degree of 'live and let live', but more generally continuous harassing fire. Some of the more aggressively inclined regimental commanders required a minimum ammunition expenditure per man per day.[13] The day-to-day routine was punctuated by attempts by the Union Army, forced on to the tactical as well as the strategic offensive, to end the business with a breakthrough.

These failed at considerable loss, for much the same reasons as similar operations on the Western Front half a century later. The entrenchments were a significant 'force multiplier' for the defence, enabling it first to withstand the heaviest preparatory bombardment the Union logistic train could support, and then to absorb an initial assault mounted at odds of six to one or more. If a lodgement or 'break-in' was achieved, staff work and communications were never good enough to bring up a second assault wave to complete the breakthrough. The contest, one-sided from the start in terms of availability of both troops and firepower, ended only when Lee was forced to give battle in open country, beyond the western limit of the earthworks.

There was no comparable battle in either of the major European wars of the decade. In 1866, Benedek's tactical instructions on assuming command of the army in Bohemia were, as we have seen,[d] to close as soon as possible in order to fight with the bayonet, and there was no Prussian impetus towards entrenchment, though the forces caught in the firestorm in Maslowed Wood during the Battle of Sadowa no doubt made what use they could of local cover. In 1870, the senior commanders of the armies of the Second Empire were forced into considering field entrenchments by the superior firepower of the German artillery. Before the battle for the Gravelotte–St Privat feature west of Metz, the commander of the Army of Lorraine, who by reason of his involvement in the Second Empire's campaign in Mexico had been closer than most to the War Between the States, ordered his corps commanders to establish their positions, '*le plus solidement possible.*'[14] The two corps deployed on the southern half of the strongest of natural defensive positions, one commanded by a sapper and the other by a gunner, did so, with the result that every German assault thrown at them throughout the afternoon of 18th August failed at enormous cost. But failure to pay any more than lip-service to the army commander's direction contributed substantially to the crumbling of the northern end of the line, and the loss of a battle which, if won, would have left the German Army in open country with the French across their line of retreat. A fortnight later, following the experience of two comprehensive defeats in the field, a corps commander in the Army of Chalons, who coincidentally had also served in Mexico, ordered his troops to entrench on the bare hills north of Sedan. His army commander deprecated the process: 'What, entrenching! But I do not mean to shut myself up as in Metz, I mean to manoeuvre.'[15]

By this time, the situation of the Army of Chalons was so bad that a decision on whether or not to entrench could have made no difference to the result, though it might have saved some French lives the following day. The reluctance of the French Army to entrench, and its lack of peacetime training in what had become an essential ingredient of land warfare, remained apparent in 1914.[16]

---

[d] See Chapter VIII.

After Sedan, the emphasis returned to siege warfare, but at neither Metz nor Paris was it necessary for the German armies to mount an assault on the fortifications. Both cities were starved out, as was Strasbourg. There was a pointer to the future at Paris, the only one of the besieged fortress-cities where attempts were made to break out. While indiscipline and lack of cohesion contributed to the failure of these sorties, they were foredoomed by the absence of surprise. With all possible axes of advance dominated by observation and covered by fire, the besiegers always had sufficient warning to enable them to assemble sufficient force to contain the thrust. In the face of improving firepower, the telegraphed punch was bound to fail. Also, in any garrison running short of food and forage, the hitting power of successive sorties was subject to the law of diminishing returns, because the horses of the artillery and cavalry had either to be slaughtered for food, or slaughtered because there was no fodder for them.

The era of the siege was still not done. In the Boer War, British garrisons held out for months at Ladysmith and Mafeking, but against an enemy who had neither siege artillery nor the surplus manpower to risk in an assault. In the Russo-Japanese War of 1904–5, a Russian garrison of between 80,000–90,000 men, not all combat effectives and provisioned ahead for an anticipated strength of only half the actual number, held Port Arthur for eight months. They surrendered only after a relieving army had been driven off, a series of bombardments and a successful assault following the undermining of a critical *point d'appui*. Starvation was also a factor in the decision to capitulate. A month before the surrender, the daily individual ration had been reduced to half a pound of biscuit, four ounces of horseflesh, a mouthful of vodka and an unspecified quantity of bread.[17] But the enduring impression was of the power of artillery, now firing high-explosive bursting shells. In the words of a British official observer:

> The greatest impression made on me by all I saw is that artillery is now the dominant arm and that all other arms are auxiliary to it. The importance of artillery cannot be too strongly insisted upon, for, other things being equal, the side which has the better artillery will always win.[18]

What was not foreseen was that, within little more than a decade, mechanical power would be harnessed to move a weight of armour which would confer protection against ordinary high explosive.

It was not the German artillery, devastating in the field though it had been, which forced the surrender of Paris at the end of January 1871. In consequence, investment in fortified systems was still considered to be worthwhile; hence Séré de Rivière's constructions on the bare slopes between the Meuse and the Moselle to safeguard the Franco-German frontier contrived after Bismarck's imposed peace and defined by no significant natural feature. Similarly, the revenues of Belgium from her African colonies funded the work of Brialmont in the 1880s. Despite a guarantee of neutrality which had stood for half a century, King Leopold II ordered the construction of modern fortifications on the high ground above Liège and Namur, intended to deter invasion by Germany and France respectively. Namur was given a system of nine mutually supporting forts and Liège twelve; six on either side of the Meuse. Most of the construction was underground, with only the gun cupolas and observation towers above the surface. Against the destructive power of artillery at the time these forts were built, they might well have survived.

But by 1914, the development of firepower had moved on. Because the bridges across the Meuse at Liège were vital to the success of the German war plan, Krupp artillery had been developed specially to destroy the forts. In the event, those east of the river fell on 6th August within seventy-two hours of the violation of Belgian territory, to a combination of *coup de main* and overwhelming odds, but those on the western side held out until the arrival of the German super-heavy artillery – guns weighing nearly 100 tons firing high-explosive shells weighing nearly a ton each. The arrival of the guns was delayed by successful Belgian sabotage of the railway tunnel at Herbesthal, which prevented fire being opened on the forts west of the Meuse until 12th August. Four days later the last of them fell, destroyed by a shell which penetrated to and exploded the underground magazine. The enormous Belgian investment of the 1880s in resources had set back the German timetable by no more than two days.[19]

The emergence of a weapon which provided a degree of protection against firepower, and which also restored mobility to a battlefield evidently set rigid by trenches, barbed wire, machine-guns and indirect-fire artillery, initiated the need for the trade-off between capabilities which has been fundamental to the design of every land warfare weapon system ever since. In terms of strategy and the peacetime resource allocation, which is the basis of national defence policy, the debate has also been continuous, and resolved more usually by external considerations and the prejudices of those with the power to decide, rather than by rational analysis of all the factors. The fact that only the very heaviest artillery was capable of penetrating underground defence systems constructed in steel and reinforced concrete, combined with an absolute determination to avoid a repetition of the casualties of the First World War, led France into the construction of the Maginot Line. Costing more than half as much again as its original estimate, and laying an excessive burden on the French economy, the fortified system also made a disproportionate demand on national defence appropriations at a time when the capabilities of tanks and ground-attack aircraft cried out for thorough evaluation and investment. The annual expenditure on the Maginot fortifications in the five main years of construction after 1930 matched the total expenditure on all army and army airforce weaponry.[20] Resting upon assumptions which proved to be invalid and without the support of the mobile forces which its progenitor, Pétain, had always considered to be the essential partner of the fortress system, the Maginot Line failed totally as a system of national defence. The troops tied to the fortifications fired hardly a shot in anger before France capitulated in June 1940, thus avoiding the losses of the First World War but hardly in the way intended.

Later still, it was the politicians in power who decided that Israel's gains in the war of 1967, and, above all, the attainment of a defensible frontier for the first time in the history of the state, would be best secured by the construction of a continuous earthwork along the east bank of the Suez Canal, rather than by a network of roads in depth in Sinai, which would allow the rapid deployment of counter-penetration forces.[21] The Bar Lev Line was also intended to be garrisoned adequately at all times, and, like the Maginot, supported by mobile forces. The debate was political and personal rather than focused on the strategic issues, and factors not wholly within military control caused a default on the essential preconditions. As a result, when Egypt attacked in October 1973, the Israeli defences based on the earthwork along the canal were taken by surprise and failed to hold. It might be deduced that, if the balance between firepower, mobility and protection swings unduly in favour of the last, the risks of surprise, obsolescence, dependence on previous assumptions and preconditions, and the inhibition of any viable alternative strategy are all increased.

Notes

[1] Bradford, *The Great Siege: Malta 1565*, London, Hodder and Stoughton Ltd, 1961; The Reprint Society, 1962, p.40, for the construction of Fort St Elmo.

[2] Lynn, John A., 'Vauban' in *Military History Quarterly*, winter, vol. I, no.2, pp.51–61.

[3] Churchill, *Marlborough: His Life and Times*, London, George G. Harrap and Co. Ltd, 1933; Folio Society, 1991, vol. II, p.65.

[4] Churchill, op.cit., vol. IV, pp.320–21.

[5] Bryant, *The Age of Elegance*; London, Reprint Society, 1954, p.21.

[6] Bryant, op.cit., p.25.

[7] Lambert, *The Crimean War*, Manchester University Press, 1990, p.25. See also Thackeray, *Vanity Fair*, Chapter XXII.

[8] Horne, *The Siege of Paris*, London, Macmillan and Co., 1965; Reprint Society, 1967, p.63.

[9] Catton, *This Hallowed Ground*, London, Victor Gollancz Ltd, 1957, p.125.

[10] Page, *Letters of a War Correspondent*, Boston, 1899. Quoted in Catton, *A Stillness at Appomattox*, Washington Square Press Pocket Books, 1958 p.180.

[11] Macdonald, *Great Battles of the Civil War*, New York, Collier Books, Macmillan Publishing Co., 1992, p.153.

[12] Catton, *A Stillness at Appomattox*, pp.211–12.

[13] Catton, ibid., p.231.

[14] Guedalla, *The Two Marshals*, London, Hodder and Stoughton Ltd, 1943, p.191.

[15] Fuller, *Decisive Battles of the Western World*, originally published 1956 by Eyre and Spottiswoode; Spa Books Ltd, Stevenage, 1994, vol. III, p.122.

[16] Spears, *Liaison 1914*, London, Eyre and Spottiswoode, 1930, p.107.

[17] Fuller, op.cit., pp.155–63.

[18] Fuller, op.cit., pp.167–68.

[19] Tuchman, *The Guns of August*, London, Constable and Co. Ltd, 1962; Four Square Edition, 1964, pp.189–90, 199–201 and 218–20.

[20] Horne, op.cit., pp.70–75.

[21] The Insight Team of *The Sunday Times*, *The Yom Kippur War*, London, André Deutsch, 1975, pp.166–67.

Chapter X
Mobility

Until the middle of the nineteenth century, strategic mobility in-theatre, logistic support and all tactical mobility depended upon the marching power of the infantry and the availability and fitness for work of a sufficient number of horses. The only additional asset which might be available, more often by chance than design, was a usable waterway, coincident with the line of supply or the route of approach to battle. The staying power of infantry remains relevant to this day. Even though for some part of the time on the modern battlefield, the soldiers may move in armoured vehicles, in the last resort there is no substitute for infantry on foot if it is necessary to clear or occupy ground, or to protect vital fire support or logistic assets. The horse also continued to exercise a considerable influence on combat capability until the Second World War. Much of the German artillery in the blitzkreig campaigns in Poland and on the Western Front in 1939 and 1940, in the invasion of Russia and in the battle for Normandy in 1944 was still horse-drawn, as was nearly all the logistic support of the Wehrmacht in the latter battle. The priority for the few motor logistic vehicles available went to the replenishment of the tanks, the self-propelled anti-tank guns and the versatile dual-purpose 88 mm guns. Everything else depended upon the horse and cart,[1] and the dead carcasses strewn on the ground in the Falaise Pocket in August 1944 were by no means all cattle.

A fit young man, carrying a personal weapon, ammunition and immediate sustainability, to a total weight of up to sixty pounds if the load is properly distributed, can maintain an average march of twenty miles a day for a virtually unlimited span of time in a temperate climate, subject to four conditions. He must have been made physically fit by a working-up process. He must be resupplied and, when necessary, reshod, because of the limitation on what he can carry and on the durability of his boots. If there are a great many men going in the same direction on the same or converging routes, the march must be in formed parties to a strict timetable, because of the constraints of intersections and choke points. Finally, he must be motivated. These principles should have been clear to any student of warfare from an analysis of the march of the *Grande Armée* from the Channel coast to the Danube in the autumn of 1805,[a] a combination of planning and endurance never afterwards surpassed, and perhaps equalled only by those formations of the German Army which, in August 1914, were on the flank of the enormous right hook required by the Schlieffen Plan. And in emergency, Davout's march to the battlefield of Austerlitz,[a] that of Slocum's corps of the Army of the Potomac from the Lower Rappahannock towards Gettysburg,[a] numerous exploits by the Army of Northern Virginia and the approach march of the German X Corps throughout a burning August day to fight at Mars La Tour[a] showed what could be done by trained, well-organised and motivated troops. But if on the other hand the ability to produce coherent march tables, route control and the essential minimum of logistic support at the right time was not there, as in the Army of the Potomac before McClellan took command, and if motivation and leadership within the unit were absent as well, as in the march to destruction of the armies of the Second Empire in August 1870, the result was always immediate chaos and imminent defeat. Nothing blunts the cutting edge of the foot soldier more quickly than to have to stand, with pack and weapon, for some hours before starting on a march. In 1870, when the German troops, two-thirds of them recalled reservists, could achieve twenty miles a day without difficulty and more in emergency, the French formations managed a bare ten. As far as the mobility of the foot soldier is concerned, the only developments in the decade of the Catalytic Wars were those of scale and the emergence of the need for more positive leadership and motivation of a rank and file which was beginning to show signs of political consciousness.

The love affair between horse and rider had existed for centuries, and it might be thought that by 1860 everything possible was known about horses. In addition to their civilian uses; social, transportation and agricultural, they were essential to every single aspect of the life of an army in the field. Thanks to a combination of years of peace and an over-romanticised concept of war, the paramount place was given to the near-sacred event of the charge. The thinking soldier might add reconnaissance, the transmission of all orders and reports beyond voice range, the distribution of the daily miracle of the resupply of ammunition, food and forage, and casualty evacuation. Everything depended upon the horse, and in enormous numbers. The *Grande Armée*, as we have seen, left its camps in August 1805 with a theoretical establishment of nearly 50,000 horses, but as more than twenty-five per cent of these were

---

[a] See respectively Chapters III, VI and XIII.

supposed to be provided for the logistic train by a civilian contractor of proven unreliability, it is doubtful whether more than eighty per cent of the required total actually took part in the campaign. The increasing number of troops engaged produced the inevitable requirement for a greater number of horses. Government purchase of a larger number of horses than usual became an intelligence indicator. Davout, left in command of what amounted to an army of occupation in central Germany after the division of Europe at Tilsit, with a perspicacity and flair for intelligence well ahead of his time, picked up and reported to Paris as early as September 1808 the fact that Austrian Government agents were buying large numbers of horses in Galicia.[2] Five months later, the Habsburg Empire resumed the war.

In the age of the motor vehicle and mechanised agriculture it is hard to visualise the sheer number of horses mobilised for the campaigns of the Catalytic Wars. Simple calculation tends to confirm the rule of thumb established by study of previous campaigns that the ratio of horses and mules required for an army in the field was somewhere between one to three and one to four of its manpower strength. During the War Between the States, the Union Government disbursed a total $124 million for the purchase of horses, which at an average price of $150 each[3] indicates that the number of horses employed on the Union side throughout the four years of the war was of the order of 820,000. If the Confederacy, whose mounts remained the property of their soldiers, mobilised only half as many, the total number of horses in the United States called up for war work between 1861 and 1865 would have been approximately 1,250,000, compared with a total mobilised manpower strength of around 4,000,000. The pre-war horse establishment of a Union Army which never had a manpower strength greater than 22,000 cannot have been more than one per cent of the number mobilised for the war. The prime user was artillery as much as cavalry. A battery of six 'Napoleon' twelve pounders at full strength had a minimum of twenty six-horse teams;[4] one for each gun and another for its ammunition limber; six more teams for the wagons carrying the balance of the first-line ammunition, and one more each for camp stores and the travelling forge. In addition, officers and sergeants were mounted, and if, as often happened, extra ammunition wagons and reserve gun teams were attached, a single battery might require as many as 150 horses. The numbers multiply to tens of thousands very readily indeed.

While there is an element of 'coarse calculation' in assessing the number of horses used in the War Between the States, there is, as might be expected, a greater degree of precision about the figure for the German Army on mobilisation in July 1870. Moltke states that there were 'over 200,000 horses on the ration strength.'[5] From the strength figures of the three German Armies which participated in the battles in the first six weeks of the war up to the capitulation at Sedan, and making due allowance for artillery replenishment ammunition and logistic trains, it is likely that three-quarters of these accompanied the first-line manpower strength of 484,000; a ratio of approximately one to three. Moltke also found it significant to mention that among the spoils of war which fell to the German Army after Sedan there were '6,000 serviceable horses'.[6] There was no similar dividend from the subsequent surrenders of Metz and Paris, after sieges lasting two and four months respectively. By the time of the surrenders all the horses had long since been eaten; Horne[7] quotes a contemporary but unsubstantiated figure of 65,000 horses eaten during the Siege of Paris.

The horse resembles the human being in that he has both limitations of physical capacity and a capability for enormous additional exertion when a special effort is demanded. Until he has reached full physical maturity at around four years of age, the horse is unlikely to have the endurance necessary to cope with the demands of war service, and his energies decline after a working life of no more than ten to twelve years.[8] Nor is every horse suitable for every task. There is a very great difference between the big, strong animal necessary to mount the heavy cavalryman, who with his equipment had a total weight estimated at the time as eighteen stone,[9] and the small, wiry steeds of the reconnaissance units, particularly the Uhlans who 'fixed' the Army of Chalons throughout its approach march from Rheims across Champagne to disaster at Sedan. The load borne by these horses was some four stone less. And a quite different type of animal was needed to draw the guns of the artillery and the wagons of the ammunition and logistic trains. For draught horses, extremes of size must be avoided: the best results are obtained when teams of four or six are matched carefully to maintain the optimum line of draught; the shortest pair nearest the load. If this is not done, the horses are apt to 'nick' each other's legs, especially in the concertina-type movement inevitable in a long column,[b] and even a small injury, if not seen and attended to at once, can soon render the animal unfit for service.

The impeccable grooming of the horses of the ceremonial units of the British and French Armies of today, seen on state occasions in London and Paris, displays an absolute but by no means an exaggerated standard of what had to be done to ensure that horses remained fit for work on the battlefield. The better the condition of the coat, the less likely is the sore back which

---

[b] The stop-go movement on a crowded or partially blocked autoroute is an exact parallel.

renders the animal unfit for duty. An hour's grooming a day is needed to prevent mange or infestation by parasites, and constant attention must be paid on the march to the correct fitting of harness and equipment. A combination of a sweating horse and a loose girth creates a soreness as quickly as a badly fitted pack on an infantry soldier. The horse cannot be worked until the contusion is cured, with a consequent loss to unit strength. The plethora of equipment and the demands of active service created additional risks to the well-being of the animal. Much of the equipment the cavalryman was expected to carry might have been designed to chafe, quite apart from the extras with which he provided himself. In the American Civil War at least, the experienced squadron and troop officers and NCOs soon saw to it that much of this was jettisoned.[10] A further fact of life was that a long day in the saddle tired the rider, and there are few quicker causes of a sore back than the slovenly seat of a trooper almost asleep in the saddle.

Clearly, the enormous number of horses existed. There is no evidence of any prolonged shortage of horses, cavalry or artillery, in any French Army in the Napoleonic Wars until 1813. Thereafter, for the next two years, because of the losses in Russia, Napoleon was handicapped severely by want of cavalry horses. In the War Between the States, the almost limitless potential of the country, the extent of the land mass and the fact that the horse in itself was a measure of wealth ensured that the numbers needed were available, albeit at an overall penalty to agricultural production, especially in the South. Sometimes the armies resorted to total local impressment. At a critical moment in the campaign in Georgia in 1864, with the Union remount service desperate both for cavalry and draught horses, even a pair belonging to Vice President-Elect Andrew Johnson were not exempted.[10] In the War Between the States, four years' worth of breeding came to maturity, but the wars of 1866 and 1870 were so short that there can have been little further conscription of horses after the initial mobilisation.

All the armies engaged in the wars of the decade, efficient or not, had an organisation capable of acquiring horses, preparing them at least to some degree for service in the field, and retaining them until they were needed to replace losses or to reinforce a cavalry, artillery or logistic unit. This made necessary efficient arrangements for the bulk supply of forage and water, and an infrastructure of farriers, blacksmiths, grooms, saddlers and associated trades, all with the necessary facilities and support. The largest recorded remount depot was that of the Union Army, at Giesboro, near Washington. This was capable of holding up to 30,000 horses at a time, and the Union Army had five similar depots elsewhere.[3]

Given the enormous number of horses on the strength of the armies, Union and Confederate, Austrian, German and French, the demand for forage was commensurate. As an approximate guide, a horse must have a daily food intake of two and a half pounds for every 100 pounds of its live weight, which produces a rule of thumb average of ten pounds per horse per day, ten times as much as the needs of a man. The fodder should be a combination of oats and barley for energy and hay for bulk, never administered all at once and desirably between three and five times during the day. The animal requires this intake of food whether it is working or not. Left to himself, a horse will graze freely, and on a new and suitable picket line find for himself much of the bulk requirement, also drawing part of his need for liquid from the moisture in the grass. But if an army in the field maintained its position for any length of time, the grass on the picket lines would soon be worn down to nothing, and with every individual cavalry squadron and artillery battery requiring at least half a ton of forage per day, it is easy to see how an army might soon become immobilised. If local resources became used up and if the logistic train, which had its own cumulative demand for forage, could not bring forward the volume required, the combat capability of cavalry and artillery soon became eroded. In such circumstances, the army could neither sustain its position where it was nor move elsewhere to new grazing grounds, irrespective of the tactical situation. However, methods of stockpiling of grain and hay were well known, because the same need to prevent deterioration of stocks existed in peacetime, between one harvest and the next. If crops existed and could be moved to where they were needed, the mobility of the army could be maintained. Water discipline was also essential. Watering the horses was a process which could not be hurried. At the beginning of the day, and at the end of it, once the animals had been given time to cool down, every horse had to be allowed to drink its fill, but to permit a horse to drink when still overheated killed it, and if the time for watering was skimped, the horses coming last to water would receive less than they needed. If the trumpet call for the end of watering were sounded too soon, all the animals would obey the herd instinct and stop drinking. The availability of sources of drinking water for the number of horses involved was perhaps less of a problem than it would be today, because in a temperate climate and a less structured society there were more ponds and standing water. But the horse was as vulnerable as his rider to waterborne disease.

Given time, organisation and resources, the natural bond between horse and rider or teamster would ensure that the animals were as well cared for as possible. In optimum circumstances, the trained unit of cavalry or artillery could manage a day's march of twenty miles without difficulty, at a combination of walk and trot and with frequent halts to check horseshoes, hooves and abrasions to fetlocks. But failing any of the basic requirements for grooming, feeding or watering, and irrespective of exposure to enemy fire, there would soon be a worrying casualty rate among the horses and consequent degradation of the army's mobility and hitting power.

Once exposed to action, the need for care of the horse did not disappear, and the experienced and prudent cavalry commander saw to it that his horses always had a reserve of energy left for emergency. In battle, the horse was at least as vulnerable as his rider and probably less likely to survive anything but a minor wound. The sacred charge would always go into the gallop at the last possible moment, because after anything more than half a mile over any but the best ground, the horses would be blown and incapable of rallying for further effort. Casualty rates to men and horses were cumulative until surviving troopers could be matched with remounts, and were often enough to write a whole formation out of the order of battle, at least for some time. At Balaclava, the five regiments of the light brigade, already much reduced by disease and previous losses, charged at a strength of 670 over no more than a mile and a quarter of ground. At the end of the action, the mounted strength of the brigade was down to 195.[11] Sixteen years later, at Mars La Tour, von Bredow's 12th Cavalry Brigade 'charged' over a distance of two miles, the first half of which was on dead ground and conducted by the prudent commander at a walk. Achieving total surprise and with energy in hand, this brigade nevertheless lost more than half of the 804 men committed.[12]

Horse management remained an integral part of the life of most armies for long afterwards. A training manual published in 1923[13] of nearly 1,000 pages, for the guidance of reserve officers of the United States Army artillery, devotes ten per cent of its content to the basic principles of horse management. Nor did the role of the horse in war end completely in 1945. As late as the 1980s, the resupply of the Mujaheddin guerrillas fighting the Russians in Afghanistan depended totally on the packhorse. The whole of the animal's load was devoted to the resupply of weaponry. The 'safe areas' under guerrilla control provided, night by night, the fodder and water to maintain the viability of the only means of resupply.[14]

Road Routes – Maintenance and Denial

It was not the increased weight of the weaponry of the Catalytic Wars which inflated the loading on road routes. The heaviest equipments, still the guns of the field artillery until the advent of the tank half a century later, were, if anything, slightly lighter than their counterparts of the Napoleonic era, and the design and capacity, and thus ground-bearing pressures, of ammunition limbers and logistic vehicles were hardly altered. What made the difference was the numbers. On the predominantly unsurfaced roads in all the Confederate states, and in the Union beyond the Appalachian Chain, a single squadron of cavalry or battery of artillery might negotiate a stretch of highway made glutinous by heavy rain, but every transit made the bad patches worse. Where timber was readily available, as often it was in all the theatres of the American Civil War, bad stretches of track could be 'corduroyed'. In this process, the trunks of tall trees were laid side by side as close together as possible along the axis of the route, and traversed latitudinally by planks cut to size, the gaps being filled in by smaller logs and impacted mud. No particular engineering skill was required, the infantry provided an instant labour force and those soldiers who were country-bred were well used to the process in peacetime anyway. In the wars of 1866 and 1870, the greater extent of surfaced roads in the theatres of war produced problems of congestion caused by poor planning, rather than of deterioration from excessive use in bad conditions.

As we have seen, the *Corps de Genie* of the *Grande Armée* had reached a very high standard of river bridge construction. The Danube crossings north of Vienna in the summer of 1809 were a feat of which any engineer unit might justifiably be proud. In the wars between 1860 and 1870, the presence or absence of a bridging train in the enemy army, and its operational proficiency, were critical factors in the estimate of its mobility, and thus of its commander's intentions. When Hooker handed over the command of the Army of the Potomac to Meade on the eve of Gettysburg, he passed on the intelligence that the Army of Northern Virginia had invaded Maryland without a bridging train,[15] which defined the limit of Lee's advance as the west bank of the Susquehanna. Meade could therefore safely concentrate in western Maryland, and ignore the nagging telegrams from Washington suggesting that he had strayed too far west of the capital. But by the same token, the lack of a bridging train placed no great inhibition on Lee's withdrawal route, because in the height of summer the upper reaches of the Potomac were fordable in many places. Similarly, the advance of the Army of Chalons to the relief of Metz in the last ten days of August 1870 was severely constrained, because without a bridging train MacMahon's approach march was channelled to the permanent bridges successively across the Marne, the Aisne and the Meuse, and also the Moselle if the German forces of circumvallation were to be struck at their weakest point, east of the fortress city. The engineers of the German armies had, by contrast, thoroughly efficient bridging trains, used to good purpose before Mars La Tour to supplement the permanent bridges upriver from Metz, and later across the Meuse to support the encircling movement of the army of the Prussian crown prince. Bridging trains remained invariably an army resource, for commitment by the army commander. In the American Civil War they were essential in all theatres except Maryland and Pennsylvania, because there were too many waterways, large rivers and smaller streams, which were not readily fordable.

The principles of operational bridge construction were well understood. The materials and skilled manpower had to be ready to hand in a secure area near the chosen crossing site, so that work could start as soon as a lodgement had been gained on the far bank. The essential first step if construction were to proceed unimpeded by small arms fire, and preferably out of range of artillery as well, was achieved by infiltrating an attacking force, not necessarily always specialist or hand-picked troops, across the river in whatever boats happened to be available, to secure a bridgehead. Then flat-bottomed pontoons, standardised at least in the Union Army to a size twenty-six feet long and five foot six inches in beam, were moored across the river, bow to stern on the line of the current, the centre-to-centre distance being set at twenty feet. If the current were particularly strong, a cable would be stretched across the river upstream from the bridge, and the pontoons lashed to it. The pontoons were then linked by timber baulks, and the trackway was provided by planking, standard-sized 'chesses' giving a track width of thirteen feet. Side rails would also be added. In appropriate operational and weather conditions, complete sections of pontoon and trackway might be prefabricated, and floated into position. Wherever possible, bridges were duplicated to provide 'up' and 'down' routes, and traffic control established. In 1864 the Union Army matched the performance of Napoleon's engineers by building a 750 yard long bridge across the James in five and a half hours.[16]

A typical bridging train produced an even greater demand for horses and route space than an artillery battery or cavalry squadron. To build a one way section of bridge 400 feet long (or a two-way bridge of 200 feet), the bridging train would need twenty wagons for pontoons, between seven and ten for the planking which formed the trackway, three or four more for linking timbers and side rails, four for tools and two travelling forges, the whole needing at least 200 horses.

The American Civil War saw also the first venture into the technology of minefields and booby traps. In the retreat up the James peninsula after the holding action at Williamsburg, the Confederate Brigadier General Rains left mortar shells with fuses primed to explode on contact around watering places and other likely troop concentration areas, and booby-trapped the doors of some abandoned buildings. His immediate superior, Longstreet, ordered him to discontinue the practice:

> It is the desire of the major general commanding that you put no shells or torpedoes behind you, as he does not recognise it as a proper or effective method of war.[17]

The navies of both sides experimented with what were still called 'torpedoes' – in modern parlance mines – which were either moored in navigable rivers and inlets or floated down on tide or current towards an identified target, in both cases designed to explode on impact. But it needed the further development of explosives, which derived from the invention of dynamite a quarter of a century later to produce an effective anti-personnel mine. What was required was a combination of sensitive primer and concentrated bursting charge beyond the capacity of black powder. With land mines, anti-personnel or anti-tank, it is the shock of the bursting charge rather than fragmentation which has to inflict the damage.

The Coming of the Railway

The first regular scheduled passenger service was instituted in England in 1830 between Liverpool and Manchester,[18] and in the same year a regiment of infantry was moved eastwards[19] on this thirty-four mile stretch of line, covering in two hours a distance which would have taken them two days to march. The first military operational use of a railway occurred in the following year, in the United States. A strike of railway workers degenerated into a riot at Ellicott's Mills, fourteen miles from Baltimore. A brigadier general and 100 volunteers of the Maryland militia were moved up the line to quell the riot, which terminated when they arrested the more vociferous strikers.[18]

This revolution in transport converted a journey hitherto lasting a day to one of no more than an hour.[c] The strain on the traveller was much less, but there were considerable requirements for investment, provision of the necessary infrastructure and logistic support. It was inevitable that the railway would be seen both to have a military use and, conversely, to increase the

---

[c] The regular airline services introduced in the mid-twentieth century produced the same step increase, converting a day's journey by train or car into one of an hour by aeroplane, but at similar penalties.

threat of invasion. But the strategic movement of troops was not, at least initially, a major factor in the route selection and development of any national railway network, nor did it become so except in Prussia, and even then not for another quarter of a century. The railway tracks radiated from capital cities and major industrial centres, and in Western Europe tended to follow the historic trade and pilgrim routes established in the Middle Ages. Like them, the track paths were greatly constrained by topography. It was the grain of the country rather than any strategic imperative which caused the main thrust of development to be east–west in Germany. In France, the same reasons caused most of the layout to run north–south. Financing the construction process was haphazard. Only in Belgium was the necessary planning and investment considered from the start to be the responsibility of the state. Every other national system was founded upon a combination of private enterprise and the benevolent neutrality of government, which sometimes extended to sleeping partnership. Government goodwill was always essential if the necessary land rights were to be obtained. There was no attempt at standardisation. Even in Germany, where the measures between 1819 and 1834 establishing the *Zollverein* (customs union) and the first impact of the railway were concurrent, there developed a multiplicity of systems. By 1870, the states of Germany had between them fifty-one different railway companies, owned variously by the state, state-commercial partnerships or privately,[20] each with its own operating methods and standards, and still on a variety of different gauges.

In the United States, the commercial impetus was given a massive boost by the continuing westward extension of the frontier. In 1830, the republic had no more than forty-one miles of track, which by 1840 had expanded to 2,818 miles. Up to this point the mileage of the network in the United States was comparable with that of France and Germany. In 1844 Germany had some 3,300 miles of track and France just over 1,000. Thereafter, the length of railway in the United States took off. By 1850 there were over 10,000 miles of line, but the great leap forward occurred in the eleven years between 1850 and the start of the War Between the States. A link to Canada was opened in 1851, and ten years later there were, in all, 30,635 miles of track,[21] nearly all east of the Mississippi, and two-thirds of it traversing those states which would elect to remain in the Union.[22] A projected link beyond Kansas City to California, which had achieved statehood in 1850, had always foundered upon the inability of Northern and Southern members of Congress to agree on a route. Land acquisition for the line in itself was by no means a minor factor in the Senate debate on the Kansas Nebraska Act in 1854, which was a significant milestone in the descent towards civil war. It was only when the representatives of the Southern states vacated their seats in Washington at the outbreak of war that the necessary legislation was passed. The coast-to-coast link was eventually completed in 1869.[23]

If the enormous expanse of the United States provided its own impetus for continuing railway expansion, it emphasised the constraints of topography and the plethora of operating companies and different gauges of the European systems. Across the country, there were six different main gauges and a whole host of smaller ones. A gauge of four foot eight and a half inches was beginning to be accepted as the standard, but there were others as wide as six feet, together with many smaller variations for local lines.[24] The continental land mass between the Atlantic seaboard and the Mississippi is equivalent to that of Europe within the bounds of the Atlantic, Mediterranean and Baltic coasts and the western frontier of the former Soviet Union. Within this area, across which in due course would be spread all the main campaigns of the War Between the States, there were in 1861 a number of continuous east–west links. The most northerly, on the modern gauge, ran from New York, through Philadelphia, Harrisburg, Pittsburgh and Springfield to Kansas City, nearly 200 miles beyond the Mississippi, where the line terminated. There were branch lines, also on the four foot eight and a half inches gauge, diverging at Pittsburgh to Cincinnati, and through Columbus and Indianapolis to St Louis. In the states which were to secede, there was a similar east–west link, but on the obsolescent five foot gauge. This ran from Norfolk by way of Lynchburg, through a pass in the Appalachians to Knoxville, following thereafter the line of the northern borders of Georgia, Alabama and the state of Mississippi before terminating at Memphis, where it was joined by a line of the same gauge to New Orleans and the Gulf Coast. There were also north–south lines in the Confederate states either side of the Appalachians. That to the west, on the old gauge, ran from Dalton, Georgia, to Atlanta, which was the junction point for three lines, one running south-east to the Atlantic coast at Charleston and Savannah, a second southwards into Georgia and the third south-west to the Chattahoochee River, where recent building on the new gauge provided a double link, diamond-shaped on the map, to Montgomery, Alabama. To the east of the Appalachians there was a modernised system, running northwards for 300 miles from Wilmington through Richmond to Fredericksburg. This crossed the non-compatible east–west line at an otherwise unremarkable town and trading post called Petersburg, thirty miles south of Richmond. A spur line on the modern gauge ran westwards from Richmond to Gordonsville, which was the junction point for three more lines, north to Alexandria, west to the head of the Shenandoah Valley and south-west to Lynchburg, providing there a second but likewise non-compatible meeting point with the southern east–west line from Norfolk.[25] This description of the more important lines on the network and their appearance on the map create a false illusion of coherence. Where the termini of lines run by different companies were in the same city, it must not be assumed that there was a continuous link. Typical was Baltimore. Meeting point of two lines, the Northern and Central and the Baltimore and Ohio, the latter with a spur line to Washington at a distance of two hours by train or two days' march, there was no connection for complete trains between the two depots. Individual freight cars could be manhandled along tramways, but troops had to be marched, putting Union soldiers at risk from rioters in a city strongly pro-Confederate in its sympathies, and at a strain on discipline, especially in the early months of the war, with newly mustered untrained volunteers being rushed to Washington by way of the only rail link between the national capital and the Northern States. Nor, at any point of the layout, was the quality of even the best track comparable with what is to be expected on any trunk route today. The majority of the network was single-line, and track beds were frequently poorly ballasted, having been laid in a great hurry to meet a commercial need. The sleepers ('ties' in American parlance) were often of unseasoned wood, bridges were also made of wood and the rails themselves were of cast iron. The first steel track was laid in 1864.[26]

A system quickly laid could be destroyed as readily, and was vulnerable to disruption from natural causes. But with everything working to plan and capacity, the limit to the number of troops which could be moved in a shuttle system at a planning rate of up to 250 miles in a day was the availability of rolling stock.

These limitations applied to both sides in the War Between the States. But, as will have been comprehended from the description of the networks in the Northern and Southern states, the former was the more modern, with fewer incompatible track penalties, at least on the main routes, than that in the South. In addition, although the land areas of North and South were comparable, the North was served by twice the length of track mileage, and, unlike the Confederacy, the Union had the facilities both to extend and replace its system.[23] In the Confederacy, not a single mile of new rail could be manufactured once the war started. To put down new track or to replace that destroyed by the Union Army, the South was forced to take up rails from existing but lower priority routes.[27] As a result, while the rail network of the Northern States continued to expand throughout the war, that of the South declined. Construction of a critical forty mile link between Greensboro,

North Carolina, and Danville, Virginia, vital for the movement of forage for the Army of Northern Virginia, though approved by the Confederate Congress in February 1862, was not completed until May 1864.[23]

Meanwhile, in Western Europe, the debate about the role of railways in the improvement of strategic mobility followed the by no means unique cycle for a major technological development: the enthusiastic advocacy of innovative intelligence, derision from authorities set in their ways, shrill alarmist warnings, better-structured forward thinking, trials in training exercises and, finally, operational use. First into the argument was a Westphalian, a man of some substance, Friedrich William Harkort. Harkort as early as 1833, proposed the construction of a railway link for military purposes between the Lippe and the Weser rivers, and also one on the right bank of the Rhine from Mainz to Wesel, only to have his ideas condemned as 'nonsensical fantasy' by officialdom and laughed to scorn in the press.[28] But at much the same time in France, an aide-de-camp general to King Louis Philippe, Rumigny, was drawing attention to the threat to France implicit in Harkort's ideas, and was supported in the chamber by another general, Lamarque.[29] Development in both France and Germany continued apace, but, as we have seen, with more than three miles of track built in Germany to one in France during the life of the Orléans monarchy. In 1842 another German, Carl Eduard Pönitz, published a book entitled *Die Eisenbahnen als militarische Operations – linien betrachtet und durch Beispiele erlautert*, which was an analytical discussion of the uses of railways in war, and a survey of the experience up to that date of the conveyance of troops on manoeuvres by the railways. Pönitz was already concerned by the danger to Germany of concurrent hostilities with France and Russia:

> We have to look to these two fronts; and if we want to avoid the risk of heavy losses at the outset, we needs must – also at the outset – be prepared to meet the enemy there with an overwhelming force. Everyone knows that the strength of an army is multiplied by movements which are rapid in themselves and allow of the troops arriving at the end of their journey without fatigue.[30]

Pönitz, a Saxon like Dreyse, the inventor of the needle gun, was also, like Dreyse, directing his work towards the king of Prussia rather than his own monarch. Whether by coincidence or not, it was the railway which brought 12,000 men of the Silesian-recruited VI Corps to Cracow to put down a riot in

1846, and even the derided Austrians took up the new resource. In the winter of 1850–51, at a time of extreme tension between Austria and Prussia, an Austrian army of 75,000 men, 8,000 horses and 1,000 guns and wagons was moved from Vienna to the border between Bohemia and Silesia, almost producing a foretaste of 1866. This movement over no more than 150 miles took twenty-six days to complete, but the troops arrived fresh and the general staff in Vienna clearly learned from the experience, because in the following summer a division, 14,500 strong, with 2,000 horses, forty-eight guns and 464 other road vehicles was moved 187 miles in only two days.[31]

At the same time as Pönitz, another observer, who at the time was considered, if it all, to be as much a theoretician, was watching and analysing. Helmuth von Moltke had returned from four years on seconded duty in Turkey in 1839. Posted to the general staff in Berlin, he was promoted to major three years later, aged forty-two. In the following year, he published a study of the use of railways in war, in an unclassified magazine article. He had already backed his convictions in the most positive way open to him, by investing all his savings from his time in Turkey in the company running the newly established railway line between Berlin and Hamburg.[32] Some of his ideas might have seemed at the time to verge on the futuristic. In 1840, as we have seen, the Orléans monarchy had invested millions of francs on fortifying Paris. Moltke's view was radically different:

> Every new development of railways is a military advantage; and for the national defence a few million on the completion of our railways is far more profitably employed than on our fortresses.[33]

There is no evidence whatsoever that this study of itself exercised any influence on German railway development. Although Moltke had good connections with the court and was known to a narrow circle in the army as an intellectual soldier who, notwithstanding his reserved and academic manner, had done well as a combat staff officer in Turkey, he was by no means young for his rank and appointment. He was not an obvious contender for the highest military appointments, and his career might have been considered to have been effectively sidelined when, in 1846, he was appointed as personal military staff officer to a Hohenzollern prince who, having converted to Roman Catholicism, had long been resident in Rome. At the time, Moltke saw his own 'ceiling' as chief of staff of a corps. For at least the next fifteen years after the appearance of his magazine article, he can have had no more than a minimal influence on the railway layout in Germany. What is certain is that his own views did not change, and that from 1864 onwards he was in a position of increasing power in matters affecting the network, until 1871 for the lines north of the Main, and thereafter over the whole of the Second Reich. In addition, he could fashion a control staff and a plan for the use of the railways on mobilisation and in war to his own blueprint.

Military Uses of the Railway from the Crimea to the Fall of Paris

THE CRIMEA AND ITALY

The first consistent use of the railway in war which went beyond a one-off operational, training or administrative move was of a track built specially for the task. In the middle of the winter of 1854–5 the grim conditions in which the British Army was living while conducting the Siege of Sebastopol had become a national scandal, mainly because there were, for the first time, war correspondents with the armies whose reports, for the most part uncensored, would reach home almost within hours. In December 1854 the duke of Newcastle, Secretary of State for War in Lord Aberdeen's administration, authorised a contract for the construction of a railway from the entry port of Balaclava to the British lines on the Saboun Hills six miles away and 1,200 feet above sea level. A labour force of 1,000 men, consisting of British workers engaged at home for the task by the contractor Sir Morton Peto and Turks recruited en route, went to work in mid-January. Within a month the first two and a half miles of the line had been built, over level ground from the port to the main supply depot at Kadekoi. This was brought into use at once, with five locomotives providing a shuttle service. The next two mile section, climbing the steep gradient to the Crimean uplands, was in service a month later and was operated by a stationary locomotive at the top of the hill hauling up the supply wagons. By May the track was complete as far as the camps in which the troops lived between spells of duty in the trenches before the fortifications of Sebastopol. Horses were positioned to draw wagons in pairs up the steeper undulations, the wagons rolling downhill and up the shorter slopes under their own inertia. The link, which was operated by the newly formed Land Transport Corps, reached a total daily capacity of 200 tons, and was estimated to have saved the work of 2,000 horses or mules.[d34] The bulk of the tonnage moved was gun ammunition. In the six bombardments of Sebastopol, between 17th October, 1854 and 7th September, 1855, the British artillery, including naval guns operating ashore, fired over 250,000 rounds.[35]

---

[d] And in all probability the lives of many of these animals.

Both sides in the war of 1859 in northern Italy made extensive use of their national railway networks to bring their troops to the theatre of war. In eleven days between 20th and 30th April, the French railways moved 75,966 men and 4,469 horses[e] from Paris, either to the Mediterranean ports or to St Jean de Maurienne in Haute Savoie, and for the eighty-six days of the war up to 16th July, the participating companies presented a bill for the movement of a total of 604,000 men[f] and 129,000 horses.[36] But the movement plan was not thought through. Ammunition and supplies were moved separately from the units which needed them. There was no coordination of a sea-movement plan across the Gulf of Genoa, which transported the men in steamships and the horses and artillery under sail, and the forty mile distance from St Jean de Maurienne over the Mont Cenis Pass into the Aosta Valley had to be covered on foot ahead of the spring thaw. Nevertheless, the volume of operational movement achieved by France was unprecedented, and it is beyond question that the Prussian general staff learned from it. In contrast, as was to be proved in 1870, the French did not.

The Austrian general staff made the same mistake as the French, and some of their soldiers suffered at least equal hardships. There was a cumulative deficiency of rolling stock in Vienna because there was no plan to return empty wagons. At Laibach, railhead for troops arriving from Hungary and Croatia, there was no transit organisation or movement plan to take them onward into Venetia and the Quadrilateral. The line through the Dolomites between Innsbruck and Bolzano was incomplete and the Austrian I Corps, in transit from Prague to Verona, had the same experience traversing the Brenner Pass as the French Army over the Mont Cenis. Nevertheless, the 40,000 men and 10,000 horses of this formation completed in fourteen days a move which would have taken them two months if they had had to march all the way.[36] This war also saw the first extensive use of railways to evacuate the wounded. Efforts were made by both sides, but the results can hardly be described as 'ambulance trains'. While the walking wounded could sit like ordinary passengers, stretcher cases had to lie on straw, in conditions of terrible discomfort. Again, it was the Germans who took most notice. A Doctor Gurlt suggested that special ambulance coaches should be fitted with hammocks, but a trial in 1861 established, mercifully, that this expedient was impractical

---

[e] A dangerously low proportion of horses to manpower if the army were to embark upon active operations at once.

[f] Considerable double counting, because many of the soldiers will have been moved more than once. The French strength in Italy did not exceed 150,000.

because the motion of the train swung the hammocks against either the carriage walls or each other. The Prussian general staff had made little further progress in this matter by 1866, when it was stated that the wounded evacuated by rail after Sadowa suffered 'unheard-of tortures.'[37] But by 1870 the German Army had specially fitted ambulance trains, which evacuated a total of 89,000 wounded during the war.[38]

THE WAR BETWEEN THE STATES

The War Between the States fully established the proposition that the railway had become the primary means for volume overland strategic movement of troops. Neither side could have mobilised the numbers they did in the summer of 1861 had it not been for the extensive railway network, or been able to sustain them thereafter. Also, we see for the first time the existence and capacity of the railways exercising a direct influence on the course of campaigns. The railways, in particular their most vulnerable points, became in their own right not only significant tactical targets for raids in force, but strategic objectives for a whole campaign as well. It soon became understood on the Union side that the underlying requirement was control of the system, and in an act of Congress of 31st January, 1862 the president was authorised

> ... when in his judgement the public safety required it... to take possession of any or all of the railroad lines[g] in the United States, their rolling stock, their offices, shops, buildings and all their appendages and appurtenances; to prescribe rules and regulations for the holding, using and maintaining of the aforesaid telegraph and railroad lines and to extend, repair and complete the same in the manner most conducive to the safety and interest of the Government; to place under military control all the officers, agents and employees belonging to the telegraph and railroad lines thus taken possession of by the President, so that they shall be considered as... a part of the military establishment of the United States.

The act went on to lay down that the transportation of troops, munitions of war, equipments, military property and stores throughout the United States should be under the immediate control of the secretary of war 'and such

---

[g] The same act conferred upon the president exactly the same powers and rights over the telegraph lines, the natural development of which coincided with that of the railways.

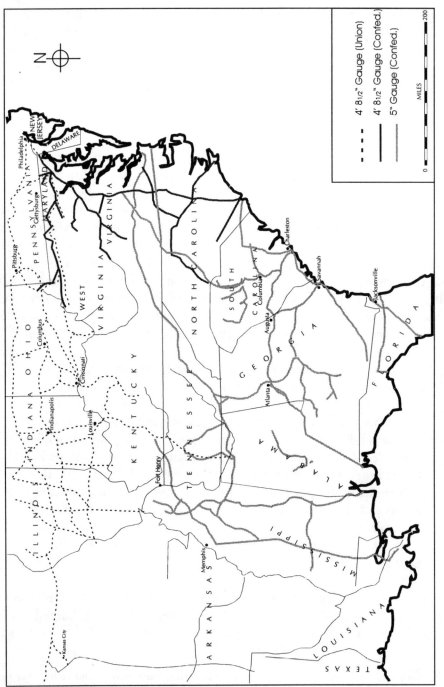

United States Railway Network, 1861

agents as he might appoint.'[h][39]

No government legal draughtsman can have improved on this subsequently as an instrument for the total state control of a national railway system in war, and it will have been noted that control was vested in the political and not the military authority. The principal 'agents' appointed by Secretary Stanton had a power far in excess of their rank. While maintenance, repair and new construction throughout the whole of the United States came eventually under the control of Herman Haupt, a railway engineer by profession, who was commissioned directly as a colonel, the overall management of the system was the responsibility of another railwayman taken from civil life. Daniel Craig McCallum, Superintendent of the Erie Railroad, was also commissioned as a colonel, and later promoted brevet brigadier general. However much *beaux sabreurs* in command of corps and divisions, ignorant of railway management, might fulminate, they could not discipline two men who were absolute masters of their craft, and who retained throughout the total confidence and immediate support of both president and secretary of war.

The achievements of McCallum and Haupt were unprecedented, and as a contribution to victory stand comparison with anything accomplished by any Union commander in the field. In September 1863, with the initiative in the eastern theatre firmly in the hands of the Union after Gettysburg, and the Mississippi also restored to Union control from source to mouth as a result of Vicksburg, the Union position in the central area of operations was imperilled by the defeat of Rosecrans at Chickamauga. This defeat was thought to pose a potential long-term threat to Washington, and one option open was the immediate reinforcement of Rosecrans, by troops who, as a result of Gettysburg, could be spared from the eastern theatre. Halleck gave a typical display of indecisiveness and reluctance to be associated with any decision which might prove afterwards to have been wrong. He advised the president that nothing could be done to send sufficient troops to Rosecrans in time. Stanton tasked McCallum to prove the contrary. Lincoln accepted McCallum's staff check in preference to the opinion of his chief military adviser, and the upshot was that Hooker, unemployed since his supersession by Meade three months earlier, was sent west in command of a force consisting of XI and XII Corps of the Army of the Potomac, reconstituted after their losses at Gettysburg. Within seven days McCallum had moved

---

[h] The railways were restored to their peacetime owners four months after the end of the war, in August 1865.

23,000 men, together with their supporting artillery, logistic vehicles and horses, a distance of 1,200 miles to the nearest suitable railhead, at Bridgeport, Alabama.[40] Rosecrans was relieved of his command. His Army of the Cumberland and Hooker's reinforcements were combined under Grant, who restored the situation and opened the way into Georgia by his decisive victory at Chattanooga at the end of November. Without the reinforcements conveyed by McCallum's railways, Grant would have had only a marginal numerical superiority over the Confederate Army of the Tennessee, and could not have fought any battle based upon the bold tactical offensive design of his plan for Chattanooga.

With Grant's promotion in March 1864 to the overall command of all the Union armies, it was left to Sherman to capitalise on this victory. In his advance on Atlanta, Sherman's whole logistic support depended upon the Western and Atlantic railroad; 120 miles of single track between the Union Army's point of departure at Ringgold, Georgia, fifteen miles south of Chattanooga, and Atlanta. This campaign lasted four months, ending when Hood evacuated Atlanta on the night of 1st September. Throughout the summer, all the supplies for an army of 100,000 men and 23,000 horses and mules[41] were conveyed along a rail link highly vulnerable to disruption by Confederate cavalry.

The achievements of McCallum in the area of organisation were matched by those of Haupt in the fields of construction and repair. Haupt, a wealthy man from his peacetime profession as a railway construction engineer, agreed to serve without pay when he was appointed, on 28th May, 1862, as 'Chief of Construction and Transportation in the Department of the Rappahannock'. The railroads of northern Virginia had been for the previous year a significant tactical objective for Confederate cavalry raids, but the appointment of Haupt had an immediate effect. Working initially with unskilled soldiers detached from infantry regiments, no doubt including the usual proportion of sick, lame and lazy who had exhausted the patience of their regimental officers, his immediate achievement was the repair of five bridges with spans of between 60–120 feet in a single day.[42] But the blustering and opinionated Pope was unable to appreciate the genius of his railway engineer. Haupt resigned in disgust and went home, to be recalled ten days later by a despairing telegram from the assistant secretary of war: 'Come back immediately. Cannot get on without you. Not a wheel moving.'[43] No doubt suitable direction was given also to the egregious Pope. When successive corps of McClellan's army were returned from the peninsula to the disembarkation points on the right bank of the Potomac below Washington, it was Haupt's previous repair work and ability to deploy gangs at once to restore breaks in the line which moved four corps from their disembarkation points in time to reach the concentration for Second Manassas. Haupt's men built a bridge over the Potomac Creek 414 feet long and eighty-two feet above the water level inside nine days, using a quantity of timber which it was estimated would have extended for six and a half miles had the planks and joists been placed end to end.[44] The route had a capacity of twenty trains a day, and the achievement evoked the unstinted admiration of President Lincoln:

> That man Haupt has built a bridge over the Potomac Creek...
> over which trains are running every hour... There is nothing in it
> but bean poles and corn stalks.'[45]

Haupt was subsequently appointed chief of the Construction Corps, which by the end of the war had expanded to a strength of 24,000 skilled workers, train operators and track construction and maintenance men. His relations with McClellan and Burnside were much better than with Pope, perhaps partly because of the railway background of both generals after they had resigned from the peacetime army.

To support Burnside's campaign on the Lower Rappahannock in the winter of 1862–3, Haupt repaired the line between Aquia Creek and Fredericksburg, and also improvised a train ferry down the Potomac from Washington. He acquired a number of coal barges from the Pittsburgh coal fields. These were linked in pairs and fitted with plank decks and trackway, each pair of barges with a capacity of sixteen loaded freight wagons. Trains arriving at Alexandria from the granaries and munitions factories of the north and west were loaded on to the barges, moved down on the current to Aquia Creek, disembarked and re-coupled to locomotives waiting for them, for onward movement to the camps round Falmouth. The whole movement beyond Washington was accomplished in less than a day.[46] As we have seen, in the following summer, Stuart's troopers destroyed the country spur line between Hanover and Gettysburg in their anticlockwise swing round to the north of the Army of the Potomac. In peacetime, this single-track link had had a capacity of no more than four trains a day, the limiting factors being passing places, sidings, turntables and the water towers essential to refuel the steam boilers of the locomotives. Within a week after the battle, Haupt had the line back in service and expanded its capacity fivefold, for the evacuation of the wounded and the replenishment of the Union Army at the rate of 1,500 tons a day, to replace the enormous ammunition expenditure during the three days of combat.[47] Perhaps the most spectacular feat of all was the restoration of the bridge over the Chattahoochee west of Atlanta, in 1864. This viaduct, 780 feet long and ninety-two feet high, was rebuilt by the Construction Corps in four and a half days.[48]

Although the tracks were flimsy by today's construction standards, and so easily destroyed and rebuilt, this takes nothing from the achievements of McCallum and Haupt in providing the means of volume transport essential to the conduct of a war fought by hundreds of thousands of men over an area comparable in size to Western Europe. For all that the action in what both sides considered to be the critical theatre of the war was confined to an area barely 150 miles square in northern Virginia, Maryland and Pennsylvania, the war had to be won in the western theatre. Owing to the unprecedented distances, this could not have been done without the railways. Attempts were made to protect the critical points most easily sabotaged, in particular bridges and junction points, usually by block houses with a small static garrison, but the determined cavalry leader on either side needed no more than to take his opportunity. It was impossible to protect every mile of track. Sometimes the destruction was deliberate; to deny the asset to the enemy. Sherman, having lived off the Western and Atlantic railroad throughout the summer of 1864, stockpiled enough supplies in Atlanta to sustain the forces left behind to secure Georgia while he marched with the rest of the army on Savannah, without a supply line, since he intended to live off the country. Before his departure he ordered the destruction of sixty miles of track which had outlived its usefulness to him.[49]

The War Between the States also saw the first combat use of the railway gun and the armoured train. The two concepts are quite separate, and should never have been confused. The railway gun operated within the lines of the army it was supporting, while the armoured train was supposed to be capable of fighting its way out of trouble. During the Siege of Petersburg, the Union Army had a 13" mortar mounted on a flat-bed wagon, which operated on the track built initially for the logistic support of Grant's army. Also, in the later part of the war, especially in the western theatre where the areas under Union control were never totally contiguous with each other, some benefit, perhaps mostly psychological, was derived by the provision of bulletproofing for the most vulnerable points of locomotives. But Haupt at least saw the fallacy inherent in the armoured train. This engine of war, however impressive it might appear to the superficial observer, was no more secure than the most vulnerable portion of the track over which it ran. In August 1862 the assistant secretary of war somewhat disingenuously informed Haupt that, 'an armour-clad car, bulletproof and mounting a cannon,[i] has arrived here and will be sent down to Alexandria,' and asked for a report on its potential use. Although the machine continued to be described enthusiastically as much as twenty-five years later, Haupt's reaction was negative at the time and scathing afterwards:

> The kindness was appreciated but the present was an elephant. I could not use it, and, being in the way, it was finally sidetracked on an old siding in Alexandria.[50]

While railway guns had a future which extended into the Second World War, the same should not have applied to armoured trains, as a cavalry subaltern-turned-war correspondent found to his cost early in the Boer War.[51] The subject nevertheless continued to be canvassed in military journals and studies on both sides of the Atlantic.

In the War Between the States, the railways themselves became for the first time strategic as well as tactical objectives, and important factors in influencing the designs of commanders for the conduct of campaigns. The fact that the first two Union Army commanders to see the wider military implications of the railway both failed to capitalise on their ideas does nothing to invalidate the argument. McClellan was at best half-hearted after Antietam in putting forward any future plan of intentions, and his indication that the possible objective for the next campaign of the Army of the Potomac might be the rupture of the Confederate rail link westwards from Virginia did not survive his dismissal. Likewise, Burnside was unable to break through at Fredericksburg and so was prevented from embarking upon an advance on Richmond along the axis of the Richmond, Fredericksburg and Potomac railroad. In contrast, Grant, forced to accept the strategic failure of his campaign in the Wilderness of May 1864, notwithstanding its success in attritional terms, comprehended fully the importance of Petersburg as the focal point of those lines remaining open in the Confederacy, vital both to the support of Lee's army and the survival of Richmond. It was the need to secure the Confederate rail link which drew Lee's dwindling army continually to the west, out of the massive field fortifications which, throughout the second half of 1864, had enabled him to withstand Grant's enormous superiority in numbers and firepower. No strategic planning after 1865 could afford to ignore the significance of the railways.

---

[i] The device looked like a garden lean-to on a flat-bed truck. It was pushed by the locomotive when in the advance, and the armoured sloping front had a gun port.

IN EUROPE

In the War Between the States, the enormous land mass of the campaign areas, combined with the high level both of the will towards war and response to the call of both governments to arms, had forced maximum use to be made of the railway system. But the organisation for its control, management and repair had evolved as the need arose, and the strategic importance of the railway in its own right emerged only during the course of the conflict. In contrast, the Prussian plan for war against Austria in 1866 was based not merely on a highly detailed mobilisation plan dependent entirely for its success on the use of the railway system north of the Main, to precise timetables and loading allocations: the railway network of Germany as a whole defined Prussia's first strategic objective.

As a result of lessons learned in the war against Denmark in 1864, Moltke had formed a railway section of the general staff,[52] which for the next half century had first call on the pick of the graduates of the Kriegsakademie. Moltke's annual geopolitical appreciations had long foreseen the inevitability of war against the Habsburg Empire, in which it had to be assumed that the kingdoms of Bavaria and Saxony would support Austria. But unless the war were to be conducted initially on the strategic defensive on Prussian territory, the difficulty lay in bringing to battle what would be the main enemy army – a matter fundamental to the philosophy of Clausewitz and so of his disciple Moltke. Whatever the design for the campaign, the first action which had to be completed successfully was the mobilisation and movement to initial concentration areas of some 300,000 men, two-thirds of them reservists, from peacetime barracks and homes spread right across the whole of present-day northern Germany, western Poland and East Prussia, the historic lands of the electors of Brandenburg high on the Baltic coast. While concentrating the bulk of the army against Austria and her putative allies, Moltke also had to provide a sufficient force on the Rhine, as a deterrent to possible French intervention. In the event, only the equivalent of one of the eight corps of the line was committed to this task. The remaining seven, the Guard Corps and the Cavalry Corps of the Prussian Second Army, a total of 280,000 men and at least 70,000 horses, having been mobilised on 16th May, were by 8th June in initial deployment areas along a shallow arc some 280 miles long between Erfurt and Neisse (now Nyasa in southern Poland). All were within a day's march of the frontier between Prussian possessions and those of the Habsburg Empire and Saxony. Then, for reasons which were more political than military, this deployment, concentrated neither for attack nor defence, was extended a further forty miles to the east, in order to cover Breslau.[53]

An outstanding feat of planning and execution though this was, it still remained to concentrate a force large enough to bring to battle and defeat the main enemy army, which had a numerical strength at least equivalent to that which Prussia could bring to bear. A glance at the map is sufficient to establish that the deployment of the three Prussian armies on 8th June was at most a containing line, and in no sense a concentration of equal or superior force for a decisive battle. Worse, the western half of Prussia's forces was not facing Habsburg territory at all but that of Saxony, and an advance by the main Austrian Army into Saxony was not to be expected. Thus the decisive battle would be fought elsewhere, by definition on the eastern end of the Prussian deployment, which defined further the geographic area in which Moltke had to achieve his concentration. As we have seen, the main thrust of the railway layout in Germany was from east to west. The southernmost of the lines of importance to Moltke was that which ran from Frankfurt on the Main through Erfurt, thence via the Saxon cities of Leipzig and Dresden, to Breslau. If the central section of this line was not available, any troops relocated from the western half of the deployment would have to be moved on a long detour, round three sides of a near-rectangle, by way of Berlin.[54] It followed that the campaign plan required the weaker enemy to be eliminated first, not for any political objective but in order to secure the vital rail link through Leipzig and Dresden.

So it was achieved;[j] but by no means without flaw. While the plan for the initial mobilisation and concentration had worked well enough, subsequent arrangements had not. Although everyone had worked with total dedication to move troops and combat supplies to the front, there had been no effective organisation for the return of railway wagons. Many of these had been appropriated, in the time-honoured fashion of quartermasters in every army the world over, as mobile storage units. The multiplicity of railway companies caused the existence of too many authorities in a position to give orders, and no one to ensure that efforts were coordinated and directives carried out effectively. Choke points and railheads became blocked. The war was won too quickly for these failures to affect the performance of the army in the field, but when it was over Moltke ordered a combined study by staff officers and railway officials, which he supervised personally. The result was a 'Route Service Regulation', approved by the king on 2nd May, 1867. This established an authority for the control of the German railway system in war by the general staff, and provided the foundation for more detailed planning. The

---

[j] See Chapter VIII.

ordinance placed too much emphasis upon mobilisation and the replacement of battle casualties, in that each army corps was allotted its own line of communication and railhead,[55] and not enough on resupply, because munitions factories and, to a lesser extent, sources of fodder for the horses, were not evenly distributed throughout the country. The replenishment of combat supplies cut across the dedicated corps lines, with consequent confusion in the war of 1870.

Nevertheless, the Route Service Regulation of 1867 was the first attempt by any country at forward planning to take the national railway network from peace to war. The regulation had three objectives: first, to provide for effective planning and liaison in peacetime among military, civil government and railway authorities; secondly, to achieve a smooth transition through the 'peace to war' measures implemented during the mobilisation and deployment phases; and thirdly, after the start of fighting, to put into effect pre-planned procedures for reinforcement and replenishment, the evacuation of battle casualties, the sick and prisoners of war, and maintenance and repair of the vital railway links, both on home soil and any taken into use on occupied enemy territory. A central commission, consisting of representatives at the highest level of the general staff and the Ministry of War, the Ministries of Commerce, Industry, Public Works (responsible until 1871 for the supervision of the railways, succeeded thereafter by the Imperial Railways Bureau), and the Ministry of the Interior, gave authority to the day-to-day work of an executive commission. This permanent body, located in Berlin, validated the plans prepared by the general staff for all phases of transition to war and combat, and directed the work of line commissions, consisting of military staff and railway managers, which were established at every major traffic centre.

In 1870 the system worked well for as long as Moltke and the general staff remained in Berlin, but when, on the fifteenth day of mobilisation, the chief and most of the officers left to establish royal (and army group) headquarters at Mainz, those left behind had insufficient authority. There was a recurrence of the mistakes and failings of 1866, particularly in the unloading and return of supply wagons. After the war, there was a further fundamental review of the system, leading to a new regulation in 1872. This established, on a permanent basis, the appointment of an inspector general of railways and lines of communication. The creation of this senior post on the general staff had become essential, not only to avoid the mistakes of the war of 1870, but also because the imperial general staff now had to deal with fifty-one railway companies, the sequestered lines in the 'Reichsland' of Alsace–Lorraine and the ministries of commerce of nine kingdoms and principalities in the federation which made up the German Empire. The control system established in 1872 underwent very little change, except in its last major revision six years before the First World War. The 1908 Regulation, while retaining the dedicated corps lines for the movement of reinforcements and battle casualty replacements, placed the links for logistic replenishment under army control.[56] The plan which had emerged in 1905, from the work of Alfred, Count von Schlieffen, over fourteen years as chief of the general staff, placed nearly 1,500,000 men grouped in seven armies on the Western Front. The 1908 regulation provided the executive machinery for a design for war which was even more dependent upon the railways than those of 1866 and 1870, and, like the former, relied upon the early capture of critical lines and junction points on non-German territory.

There was never any single law which established the Prussian, or later the Imperial German, general staff as the absolute authority over peacetime railway development. But the standing of the army fundamental to the make-up of the nation, much enhanced by the success of the lightning campaign in Bohemia, gave this organisation such prestige and paramountcy of position in state and government that it had a de facto dominating influence. New construction between 1867 and 1870 of lateral routes between the existing lines, which tended to run north-east to south-west, was related entirely to the future war with France, now seen as inevitable, and particular emphasis was placed on the need to support the critical convergence on the stretch of common frontier between Saarbrucken and Strasbourg. But at the time, and afterwards right up to the outbreak of war in 1914, it was the detail of construction which was of equal importance. The expansion from single to double track, the lengthening of platforms, particularly in the early years of the twentieth century, of the stations which served the tiny villages in the Eifel Mountains near the junction point of the frontiers of Germany, Belgium and Luxembourg, the reduction of gradients and curves to improve route timings and the positioning of water towers, all came under the scrutiny of Moltke and his successors. Plans which included the detailed deployment of locomotives, rolling stock for troops and horses and transportation for supplies were continuously updated by the picked officers of the prestigious general staff railway section.

On the other side of the Rhine, railway construction, in spite of massive encouragement in the first decade of the Second Empire,[57] had fallen behind that in Germany, and the north–south grain of the country and the commercial rather than military impetus for development meant that the critical length of joint frontier was unevenly served. There was a good modernised link from Paris through Chalons – the two largest peacetime concentrations of troops – to Nancy, and then on to Strasbourg. But troops and, more critically, supplies from the centre of the country destined for the equally important initial deployment area east of Metz had also to use this line for the first sixty miles from Paris. Then they could either turn off at Epernay for a long 'north-about' detour by way of Mezières, Sedan and Thionville; or they could continue beyond Chalons, on the line towards Nancy through Bar-le-Duc and Toul, before turning north towards Metz at a T-junction at Frouard on the left bank of the Moselle. Construction of a direct route between Chalons and Metz had not progressed far beyond the Aire, petering out ten miles short of the Meuse crossing at Verdun. The capacity of the lines from the Mediterranean ports, vital for the timely arrival of troops from North Africa, was adequate, but the most direct route to Strasbourg lay east of the Vosges, via Dole, Besançon and Colmar, and was vulnerable to any German penetration west of the fortress city.[58]

When the Second Empire went to war in July 1870, it was not the railway system which failed, but the use made of it. Dormant powers of direction had been taken during Marshal Niel's short tenure at the Ministry of War after 1866, and a commission similar to that in Prussia worked throughout 1869 to produce a provisional plan. On 15th July, 1870, the day following that upon which mobilisation was ordered, the Est, Nord and Paris–Lyon companies were directed to put all their resources at the disposal of the Ministry of War, and the rolling stock of the Ouest and Orléans companies was similarly placed on call to supplement the assets of the three companies who would bear the brunt of the task.[59] But the French attempt to gain time by combining the quite separate processes of mobilisation and movement to concentration areas produced chaos. The 1869 plan existed in framework only, and was too rigid in that it laid down specific train compositions and timetables without regard to the readiness of units or the number of troops to be moved. When units were moved, the regimental officers abdicated all responsibility for discipline, and there was no transit organisation to hold mobilised reservists, who were allowed to roam free round the major traffic centres while waiting for a train which might, or might not, take them in the right direction. Nevertheless, by the end of August the railway companies had moved to the armies something approaching the total projected mobilisation strength. Notwithstanding the casualties incurred in three major battles, the French armies in Lorraine and Champagne had more men with the Colours at the end of August than they had had on 28th July, the day on which mobilisation was supposed to have been completed.[k] And a fortnight later, there were 500,000 under arms in Paris, by no means all of them Parisians.

On the German side, in spite of the lessons of 1866 and the work since to establish an effective control system for the return of rolling stock, the resupply of the armies did not work according to plan. It was apparent to royal headquarters as early as 11th August that congestion was already building up on the routes into France, because on that date an order was issued prohibiting any further movement of supplies unless specifically authorised by the commissary general or his deputies at the three army headquarters. Nevertheless, on 5th September there were nearly 2,500 loaded wagons blocking five of the nine routes into the combat zone. Arrangements for the onward movement of supplies from railheads also broke down. The logistic staff of First Army, having started with 2,000 horse-drawn wagons, could, on 17th October, lay their hands on no more than twenty.[60] For much of the autumn, the German armies in France were living off stocks captured when the French abandoned the field depot at Forbach after the Battle of Spicheren, and from those captured later at Dole, Verdun and elsewhere.

On 10th August, 1869, there had been established in the Prussian Army a battalion of railway troops, including both train operators and track men, which was intended to be no more than a cadre for expansion in war. In the event, this was achieved most effectively. By the end of January 1871, 3,500 railwaymen had been brought from Germany to run the 2,500 miles of the French railway system in occupied territory, supporting the armies both besieging Paris and on the Loire. They used rolling stock which the French had omitted to remove or destroy, 16,000 wagons having been included in the booty when Metz capitulated. The main feat of construction was miniscule by the standards of the American Civil War – a twenty-two mile link between Remilly, on the line between Metz and Saarbrucken, and Pont à Mousson, on the Metz–Frouard line. This was intended to support the army besieging Metz, and was necessary because the terminus itself was in French hands. A survey was undertaken on 14th August, almost as soon as the ground had been secured, and 3,000 miners from Saarbrucken, deprived of their normal employment because of the war, were brought in to do the construction work. This was much impeded by an abnormally wet autumn, and a line of poor quality operated at low capacity for only twenty-six days before being made superfluous by the surrender of Metz.[61]

---

[k] See Chapter III, Appendix 1, for the computation of French battlefield strengths throughout August 1970.

Not everything had worked, even for the Union armies in the War Between the States, who were the least constrained by resources, or for the Prussians, who more than any other power had thought through, planned for and applied the military use of the railway. But what had emerged out of necessity in the American Civil War by 1866 had become both the critical mobilisation asset and the defining factor in determining Prussia's first strategic objective. In 1870, the benefit derived from detailed planning and a control system which could take the network from peace to war was an important factor in the German victory. Thereafter, the national railway network and capacity became the baseline for the war contingency planning of every European power.

Notes

[1] Keegan, *The Second World War*, London, Arrow Books Ltd, 1989, p.373.

[2] Macdonnell, *Napoleon and his Marshals*, London, Macmillan and Co., 1934, p.186.

[3] Coggins, *Arms and Equipment of the Civil War*, Wilmington, North Carolina, Broadfoot Publishing Co., 1990, p.52.

[4] Coggins, op.cit., p.63.

[5] Moltke, *The Franco-German War of 1870–71*, first published in England, 1907, Greenhill Books, London 1992, p.7.

[6] Moltke, op.cit., p.100.

[7] Horne, *The Fall of Paris*, London, Macmillan and Co., 1965; The Reprint Society, 1967, p.178.

[8] The author is most indebted to Captain David Harrington, RHA, and the officers of the King's Troop, Royal Horse Artillery, for reminding him of the basic principles of the care of military horses, on a visit to St John's Wood in April 1995.

[9] 'An Officer of the Royal Artillery', *From Sedan to Saarbrucken*; first published in 1870, Helion Books, Solihull, 1992, p.60.

[10] Coggins, op.cit., p.53.

[11] Affidavits in the libel action brought by Lord Cardigan against Lieutenant Colonel the Honourable Somerset Calthorpe in 1863, quoted in *The War Correspondent*, the journal of the Crimean War Research Society, October 1996, vol. XIV, no.3, pp.24–27, article by Tony Lucking.

[12] Ascoli, *A Day of Battle*, London, Harrap Ltd, 1987, pp.168–70.

[13] Babcock, *Elements of Field Artillery*, Princeton University Press, 1923.

[14] A point established in discussion between the author and a war correspondent who had witnessed the process.

[15] Catton, *Glory Road*, New York, Doubleday, 1952; Pocket Cardinal Edition, 1964, p.273.

[16] Coggins, op.cit., p.105.

[17] Macdonald, *Great Battles of the Civil War*, New York, Collier Books, 1992, p.36

[18] Carter, *Railways in Wartime*, London, Frederick Muller Ltd, 1964, p.11.

[19] Pratt, *Rise of Rail Power in War and Conquest 1833–1914*, London, P.S. King and Son, 1915, p.1.

[20] Pratt, op.cit., p.51.

[21] Carter, op.cit., pp.14 and 23.

[22] Catton, *Pictorial History of the American Civil War*, New York, American Heritage Publishing Co., 1960, 1982 edition, p.79.

[23] Catton, *Pictorial History*, pp.11 and 414.

[24] Carter, op.cit., p.30.

[25] *Atlas for the American Civil War*, Wayne, New Jersey, Avery Publishing Group, 1986, in particular p.2.

[26] Carter, op.cit., p.37.

[27] Catton, *Pictorial History*, pp.396–97.

[28] Pratt, op.cit., pp.2–3.

[29] Carter, op.cit., pp.13–14.

[30] Pratt, op.cit., pp.4–5.

[31] Pratt, op.cit., pp.14–15.

[32] Whitton, *Moltke*, London, Constable and Co., 1921, p.53.

[33] Moltke, *Deutsche Vierteljahresschrift Magazine* article, 1843; quoted Howard, *The Franco-Prussian War*, London, Rupert Hart-Davis Ltd, 1961, p.2.

[34] Carter, op.cit., pp.16–18.

[35] Cooke, Brian, 'An Assessment of the Artillery Bombardment of Sevastopol' in *The War Correspondent*, April, 1996, vol. XIV, no.1, p.27.

[36] Pratt, op.cit., pp.10–11.

[37] Pratt, op.cit., pp.84–85 and 92.

[38] Pratt, op.cit., pp.95.

[39] Pratt, op.cit., pp.16–17.

[40] Pratt, op.cit., pp.23–24.

[41] Macdonald, op.cit., p.156.

[42] Pratt, op.cit., p.31.

[43] Pratt, op.cit., p.43.

[44] Pratt, op.cit., p.30.

[45] Coggins, op.cit., p.112.

[46] Catton, *Glory Road*, p.30.

[47] Catton, *Glory Road*, p.317.

410

[48] Carter, op.cit., p.37.

[49] Pratt, op.cit., p.35–36.

[50] Pratt, op.cit., p.73.

[51] Churchill, *My Early Life*, [London?], Thornton Butterworth in 1930, Chapter 19.

[52] Pratt, op.cit., p.104.

[53] Whitton, op.cit., pp.94–95.

[54] Whitton, op.cit., end papers, 'Map of 1866 War'.

[55] Pratt, op.cit., p.107.

[56] Pratt, op.cit., p.104–21.

[57] Brogan, *The French Nation*, New York, Harper & Brothers, 1957, pp.125–28.

[58] Whitton, op.cit., end papers, 'Map of the War of 1870–71'.

[59] Pratt, op.cit., pp.138–39.

[60] Pratt, op.cit., pp.112–13.

[61] Pratt, op.cit., pp.127, 130–31, 215 and 216.

Chapter XI

The Legacy of Defeat: France and her Army 1815–1870

Les Vaincus de l'Europe

Although comprehensive defeat is almost invariably the precursor of large-scale military reform, the Bourbons, when they were restored for the second time after the One Hundred Days, were driven by a quite different imperative. Their highest priority was to eradicate from the new royal army all traces of Napoleonic association.[1] The *Grande Armée* organisation was broken up and abandoned. Conscription was abolished. The regiments lost the tricolour, their eagles and numbers. *Ésprit de corps* was destroyed by dissolving the units and re-forming the retained manpower on an entirely different basis. An attempt was made to associate units with departments. Each department was expected to furnish a 'legion', consisting of two battalions of line and one of light infantry, with supporting cavalry and artillery. Some departments were also required to raise a cavalry regiment. The Imperial Guard, part of which had survived the first restoration, albeit reduced to the status of garrison troops for Metz and Nancy, was abolished altogether. The absurd attempt made during the first restoration to recreate the household troops of the *ancien régime* was not repeated, and the new royal guard was a division-sized groupment of all arms, similar in size and structure to the Imperial Guard in the Army of the Coasts of the Ocean,[a] with some companies of Swiss Guards, which were a resurrection from earlier times. But recruitment of new volunteers languished and enthusiasm was lacking. This was partly because of war weariness and partly because of the total absence of attraction of the Bourbons in the eyes of those long-serving officers and soldiers of the *Grande Armée* who knew no livelihood other than soldiering, and who, notwithstanding their doubtful loyalty, managed to retain employment in the

---

[a] See Chapter II.

new royal army. Many more of the *'grognards'* were on half pay and more still had their services terminated without further reward or pension. The whole army simmered with discontent. Worst of all in relation to readiness for war, the permanent formation structure of the *Grande Armée* was jettisoned. Until after 1870, brigades, divisions and *corps d'armée* were formed only on mobilisation, as had been the practice under the *ancien régime*. Appointments to formation command therefore depended on political reliability,[b] seniority and favouritism. The point has to be made in fairness that only the Prussian Army retained a permanent formation structure.

This organisation was the work of Clarke, Duc de Feltre, who had succeeded Berthier in the post of minister of war in 1807. A competent bureaucrat, he was one of the rare band who achieved the 'double' of turning his coat at the right time in 1814 and picking the winning side a year later. This select company included Marmont and Bourmont, who, by reason of their treachery to Napoleon in 1814 and 1815 respectively, were the two most detested senior officers in the whole army, a fact which did not prevent their retaining employment throughout the duration of the second Bourbon restoration. Clarke was one of four new marshals promoted in 1816.[2] The others, aged eighty-two, seventy-nine and sixty-four, were aristocratic veterans of the wars of Louis XV, and any service they had seen since 1792 had been against France. These appointments were symptomatic of the initial attitude of the restored monarchy to the institutions of the empire, the army in particular.

Among the failings of Louis XVIII was a complete absence of any military qualities, but he has to be excepted from the Bourbon stereotype – incapable of learning anything and forgetting nothing. Having told his totally reactionary brother and heir-presumptive, the comte d'Artois, that he did not wish to be the king of two nations, he replaced Clarke with Gouvion St Cyr. One of the ablest of the First Empire marshals, St Cyr might well have been on the first promotion list in 1804 had he not refused to sign the 'round robin' message from the senior officers of the army of the Consulate congratulating Napoleon on the establishment of the empire. Although his success in command of one of the flanking corps during the campaign in Russia eventually gained him his baton, he remained persistently under-employed in the First Empire in relation to his talents both as a military administrator and as a commander in the field. His reforms of 1818 set the pattern for the French Army for the next half century. The attempt to man the army by voluntary recruitment having

---

[b] Between 1815 and 1870 France was to have three revolutions, one *coup d'état* and five quite different forms of government.

failed, St Cyr reintroduced Berthier's quota system of conscription which had produced the recruits for the armies of the First Empire, but the annual intake was set at no more than 40,000. By coincidence this figure was the same as that of Prussia, but from a population dependency nearly three times the size.[c] It was possible for high physical standards to be set. Some recruits had to be rejected because their teeth were so bad they could not bite off the ends of their cartridges, an essential part of the drill when loading a musket. In general, the hardier children of the peasantry proved to be better material than those who were town-bred. However, universal registration in conjunction with a relatively low percentage actually enlisted enshrined the principle and practice of substitution.[3] As the century wore on, and in contrast to the motivation, organisation and practice on the other side of the Rhine, it became apparent that all classes of French society preferred to run the risk of a *'mauvais numéro'* for sons of military age, against which contingency it was possible to buy insurance to pay the going rate for a substitute, rather than accept the principle of universal service for a shorter period, followed by reserve liability. The period of initial enlistment varied between six and eight years under the Bourbons, before being set at seven in 1832. There was no part-time training commitment for those who had escaped or who could afford to buy their way out of the draft. After their long period of first enlistment, most soldiers had lost all contact with civilian life and preferred to re-enlist. It follows that there were only a very small number of reservists who could be recalled in the event of full-scale war.

St Cyr's reforms also included a provision, wholly desirable in principle, that one-third of all officer commissions should be from the ranks, and he set minimum standards of literacy for NCOs. However, with time these became eroded. General the Marquis de Castellane, commanding the Perpignan military district in 1841, noted that out of ten new captains posted in to his command in that year, only two could spell.[4] Because few of the commissioned rankers had the educational background necessary to support any promotion beyond major, there was a very high proportion of elderly *'troupier'* officers, of whom Zola's Lieutenant Rochas is typical.[5] Adventurous young men who had failed the entrance examination to the military academy

---

[c] The *British Almanac and Companion for 1829* [publisher Charles Knight, London], a forerunner of *Whitaker's* and the *Statesman's Year Book*, gives the population of France in 1828 as 32.5 million and that of Prussia as 12.5 million. At the same time the population of the other states who would in time form the German Empire was a further 13,000,000, of which nearly half came from Bavaria, Saxony and Hanover.

founded by St Cyr, or to the *École Polytechnique* which trained officers for the technical arms and engineers for the state service, or whose families could not afford the very high fees of these centres of learning, might enlist in the ranks. One such was François Achille Bazaine. St Cyr's reforms, like those secured by Niel fifty years later, though some way short of ideal, were the best the market would bear. The main reason they proved inadequate to cope with the demands made by events was the poor standard of education in the elementary schools of the countryside.

A combination of recruitment pattern and political feasibility committed France to a long-service army bereft of fit and trained reserves, which was dissociated from the mainstream of the life of the nation. The chronic political instability of two forms of monarchy, Second Republic and Second Empire required units in the garrison towns of metropolitan France to be stationed as far as possible from the departments which provided their recruits. This deliberate policy was intended both to minimise the risk of the garrisons sympathising with any local disaffection and to provide a security force without inhibitions about dealing with any eruption into disorder. Ambitious or well-connected officers would seek appointments in and around Paris, where they might attract the attention of one of the paladins of the military hierarchy, most important of whom was the minister of war. Those stifled by the garrison round would volunteer for service in Algeria, where a reputation might be made in battle. These considerations enlarged the proportion of '*troupier*' officers in the regiments of the provincial garrisons. For the vast majority of the army, poor pay and different regional origin exacerbated isolation from the local community. An elderly and inadequately educated officer corps imposing a rigid discipline bred conformism and stifled initiative. Originality of thought was not encouraged. The result was an army drawn in on itself, over-respectful of seniority, hidebound in its attitudes and stereotyped in its routine and training. These conditions remained fundamental to the state of the French Army right up to 1870 and to a great extent continued to apply to the army of the Third Republic.[6]

With the lapse of time, and especially after the death of Napoleon in 1821, even the Bourbon monarchy began to make use of the Napoleonic legend. The first promotions to marshal since 1816 were made in 1823. Those honoured were Molitor and Lauriston,[2] both of whom, as we have seen, had distinguished themselves greatly at Wagram fourteen years before. Even under the ultra-reactionary government of Charles X, who succeeded his brother in 1824, Beranger could publish his view that, in fifty years' time, France would know no history other than that of the triumphs of Napoleon.[7] The establishment of the Napoleonic legend gathered pace in the 1830s under the Orléans monarchy, which could see the benefits of associating itself with the glories of the First Empire. This impetus accelerated to full speed in the next decade. The Arc de Triomphe was completed, and in 1841 the remains of Napoleon were returned from St Helena to lie at the Invalides. Those surviving marshals of the empire who had either preferred to live in retirement or, by reason of their support for Napoleon during the One Hundred Days, had been in disgrace throughout the Bourbon restoration, regained their full honours and sometimes more than that. Soult and Mortier were successively figurehead prime ministers in the 1830s, and it was Soult who, from 1831 onwards, as minister of war and marshal general of France, restored the regimental organisation of the army of the First Empire. It is beyond question that the biggest single asset of the emperor's nephew and step-grandson, initially in his attempts to seize power and later of the Second Empire after he had succeeded, was the prestige of the First.

The army of the restored Bourbons was not unduly extended by its promenade into Spain in 1823 to support the likewise restored King Ferdinand VII against the revolt of some of his subjects. Its worst handicaps were its commander-in-chief, the Duc d'Angoulême, nephew of Louis XVIII, and inadequate logistic provision. The first real test was provided by the start of the colonisation of Algeria, which was to continue for the next century and a quarter. This began in 1830, more as a punitive expedition than as an attempt to build an empire beyond Europe. Commanding the French invading force was the detested Bourmont, who as a general of division had deserted to the Prussians in June 1815 with the battle plans of the Armée du Nord in his pocket. His tenure of command did not survive the July Revolution. His successor was D'Erlon, corps commander in the Waterloo campaign, who, as the recipient of contradictory orders from Napoleon's army group and Ney's 'wing' headquarters, had spent the day of the simultaneous battles of Ligny and Quatre Bras marching his 21,000 men to and fro in the eight miles of soggy farmland between the two battlefields, reaching neither in time to fight and so ensuring that both were indecisive.

Algeria

The early years of the French involvement in Algeria were marked by confusion of policy both in the home government and in-theatre. A strong body of opinion in metropolitan France disapproved of the operation altogether, on grounds of priority and practicality. On the spot, D'Erlon at first attempted to conciliate Abd-el-Kader, the most important of the tribal leaders and the only one whose authority transcended, at least in part, tribal loyalties. It was only after Abd-el-Kader had received substantial gifts of French weaponry and munitions that it became apparent that he sought independent supreme power rather than vassal status. Initially, French progress was slow and difficult. The army could secure only what were little more than bridgeheads around Oran, Algiers and Bone. Constantine, inland between the two latter, did not fall until 1837. Agriculture to support the fledgling colony had to have military protection and many of the attempts made to expand into the hinterland met with disaster. Typical was the rout in 1835 of a Foreign Legion[d] battle group 2,000 strong in the marshes of the Macta south of Oran. The bulk of Abd-el-Kader's forces were mounted; 6,000 riders flung an ambush at the head of a defile round the legion column of march, inflicting over twenty-five per cent casualties and capturing all but one of the legion's guns and all of its transport. Five years later, Miliana, an important strongpoint sixty miles west of Algiers, safeguarding the vital road to Oran, underwent a four-month siege. Of the initial garrison of 1,200, only sixty were alive by the end of 1840.[8]

In spite of these and other setbacks, the bridgeheads became connected, the land area of the colony grew and the first settlers arrived from France, the ancestors of the Pieds Noirs of a century later.[e] But it was soon apparent that tactics appropriate to European warfare, and applied by commanders described disrespectfully by their juniors as the *'Reliques de l'Empire'*, could not contain the hit-and-run methods of Abd-el-Kader. In the late 1830s the French developed a like response. The design was that of Bugeaud, who had fought as a junior officer in the wars of the First Empire in Spain. He relied on a chain of strong points, each of which was capable of very rapidly mounting 'sweeping' operations in their area of tactical responsibility. Often acting on information gathered from an increasingly effective intelligence network, in which French fomentation of intertribal rivalries played its part, the strong

---

[d] The Foreign Legion had been formed in 1831 to make use of the Swiss Guard of the deposed Charles X, which was thought inappropriate to the style of the bourgeois monarchy, and to provide employment mutually acceptable to the government and to the thugs of all nations who had been attracted to Paris by the July Revolution.

[e] It is a remarkable example of the transient nature of human affairs that the liberal humanist historian, H.A.L. Fisher, writing in the 1930s, could praise the French conquest of Algeria for 'inaugurating by that notable feat of arms the recovery of the North African littoral for the Latin races.'[9]

points could, at very short notice, deploy columns self-sufficient for a few days' operation, consisting of three or four battalions of infantry supported by some squadrons of native-recruited cavalry, and artillery which was pack-transported rather than horse-drawn. By 1840 Bugeaud, successively area commander, commander-in-chief and governor-general, had cleared the coastal belt of present-day Algeria. In 1843 the 'Smala' (mobile headquarters and capital) of Abd-el-Kader, was captured by a column commanded by the Duc d'Aumale, youngest son of King Louis Philippe, sent out in search of glory for the Orléans dynasty. In the following year, Bugeaud, in a pitched battle at Isly on the border between present-day Algeria and Morocco, defeated a force of 45,000 tribesmen. After fifteen years' continuous campaigning the French had conquered Algeria and eastern Morocco as far as the northern limit of the Sahara. Although dangerous surprises continued to occur – a company of the elite *chasseurs à pied* was annihilated at Sidi Brahim, no more than forty miles west of supposedly safe Tlemcen – Abd-el-Kader was forced to surrender at the end of 1847, two months before the revolution which ended the Orléans monarchy.

Notwithstanding the long drawn-out campaign and all the mishaps, ultimate success had restored the confidence of the nation in the army, and of the army in itself. The war in Algeria had also established a new generation of French commanders: Bugeaud's younger subordinates, such as Canrobert and MacMahon, founded their reputations in Algeria. Others, such as St Arnaud, had reputations manufactured for them. Good combat achievement in Algeria was a powerful assistance to advancement for the many junior officers who had become adept in the organisation and tactics of the *'razzia'*, as Bugeaud's flying columns were known. But effective as these had proved in what were, Isly apart, the small-change operations of counter-insurgency warfare, their total relevance to the probable conditions of a mid-nineteenth-century war between the Great Powers of Europe was doubtful. France had no higher staff college or military think-tank which could relate the lessons of Algeria to general war, or to keep under review and teach the principles which should govern the organisation, operation and sustainability of a large army in the field. It is as if the British Army of the late twentieth century, having concentrated totally for twenty-five years, in terms of its equipment, training and tactics, on internal security operations in Northern Ireland, had been plunged without any other preparation into the Gulf War. It became fashionable to blame all the shortcomings the French Army was to display in 1870 on false lessons drawn from Algeria, but it can be argued, at least as cogently, that valuable and significant experience gained there was ignored, with disastrous consequences. The first requirement in counter-insurgency operations, whether for firm base or mobile combat grouping, is to maintain an absolute guard against local surprise. This applies also to operations in general war. Time and again in 1870, French units and formations came under heavy attack without warning because they had neglected this principle, which Algerian experience should have ingrained as second nature.

The Wars of the Second Empire

The French Army went to war in 1870 bereft neither of intelligence about Prussian motivation and capability nor experience of large-scale contemporary general warfare. For the former, the reports of the French military attaché in Berlin in the late 1860s, Lieutenant Colonel Baron Stoffel, were and remain a model of their kind.[10] For the latter, the wars of 1854 and 1859 required France to make a war plan in conjunction with allies and to cooperate with them in the field, to organise the formation, command and support of large armies, to integrate all arms on the battlefield and to harness new and developing technologies relevant to warfare, particularly those relating to firepower, communication and transportation. And although the five year involvement in Mexico called for battlefield techniques more akin to the continuing war in Algeria than to general war, nevertheless Mexico, as did the battlefields in the Crimea and Italy, brought into prominence the men who would hold high command in 1870, with all their individual qualities, failings, prejudices and operating methods, all derived from their personal experience. But in the French Army these were unrefined by the common doctrines which von Moltke sought to inculcate in the thinking and so the tactical operations of Prussian senior commanders. While the detail of these three wars is superfluous to this book, an appreciation of the events and the main personalities which emerged from them is essential if the nature of France and her army at the start of the Second War of Prussian Supremacy is to be understood.

The judgement made by A.J.P. Taylor of the Prussian motive for expansion in the post-Napoleonic era – 'Unless we grow greater we shall become less' – has already been quoted.[f] The driving force of the Second Empire was not markedly different, and if both nations were to seek enlargement of territory or predominant influence in Europe, conflict between them was inevitable. But, unlike Prussia, France suffered from an internal confusion of purpose. A majority of Frenchmen had in turn despised the restored Bourbons, become

---

[f] Chapter VII, note 19.

bored with the bourgeois monarchy and been frightened by the extremists who had threatened to impose pure communism on the Second Republic. Although each of these factions would retain, at least until the end of the century, a hard core of loyal, lifelong and irreconcilable supporters, France at the end of 1848 was willing to give the Bonaparte dynasty a second chance, but within limits. A majority of 4,000,000 within an electorate of 7,000,000 made Prince Louis Napoleon Bonaparte the 'representative' but not 'executive' head of state. But the dichotomy within France was more fundamental than about which form of government the nation should have. While one part of the national psyche craved glamour, expansion, excitement and adventure, in short 'La Gloire', the other wanted security, low taxes and the avoidance of military service. That the two propositions are mutually incompatible is obvious, and at no point until well into the twentieth century was any form of government able permanently to contain them, the Second Empire perhaps least of all; this combination of Offenbach operetta and accumulator gamble was an attempt to resolve this insoluble difference. A fuller quotation[g] from the evaluation of the newly established Emperor Napoleon III made by Moltke in January 1853 becomes relevant:

> The French must grow weary of this adventurer, who will find it harder to remain an emperor than to become one. He can hardly hold his place without some victories; and whether he is a general, and a general on the lines of his uncle, remains to be proved. But he must fight and win his own battles, or his general will be emperor.

The imperative underlying all the policies and actions of Napoleon III was to enhance the prestige and security of his dynasty, but the methods adopted were often contradictory and came increasingly to emphasise rather than to soothe the inherent conflicts in French society.

THE COUP D'ÉTAT AND THE CRIMEA

The quest for prestige for the Second Empire began almost at once, and with it early validation of part of Moltke's forecast. The stated casus belli for what history has termed the Crimean War[h] was right of access for Roman Catholic

---

[g] Chapter VII, note 22.

[h] 'Crimean' is a misnomer because there were substantial operations in the Baltic and in the Caucasus.

monks to the Church of the Nativity in Bethlehem, which was thought to encroach on the rights of Greek Orthodox priests under the protection of the tsar. The real cause was the incipient collapse of the Ottoman Empire. For the first time since the Stuart Restoration, England and France had a common interest because neither wished to see Russian power and influence penetrating the Mediterranean. Prussia and the Habsburg Empire remained neutral. Tsar Nicholas I had expected a quid pro quo for crushing the Magyar revolt in Hungary on behalf of Emperor Franz Joseph and Schwarzenburg five years previously, and Tsarist Russia never forgave this ingratitude. The surprise participant was the king of Sardinia, who sent a division to the Crimea in time to form part of the Army of Observation along the River Chernaya, and thus was not involved in the attempts to storm Sebastopol. The Piedmontese suffered more casualties from disease than from enemy action, but their presence earned the kingdom of Sardinia a seat at the peace conference in Paris at the end of the war. Once there, Count Cavour ensured that the related issues of Italian nationalism and Italian unification could no longer be considered merely as internal problems for the Habsburg Empire, but would escalate to international level.

Commands in the French Army of the Crimea, initially of four divisions but expanded to eight at the beginning of 1855, were rewards for successful service in North Africa and political reliability. The two top appointments acknowledged effective participation in the coup of December 1851, which converted the Second Republic into the prince-presidency. If President Prince Louis Napoleon Bonaparte were ever to be more than, in his own phrase, 'the Prince Albert of the constitution', he needed a general, as much as had Barras when seeking to change the form of government of the First Republic, or Sieyes, when intriguing to replace the Directory with the Consulate. A presidential emissary, talent-seeking in Algeria on borrowed money, found a general willing to undertake the task. St Arnaud, at the time commanding the Constantine military district, was by no means the most senior general on the active list (Cavaignac and Changarnier, both his superiors, were convinced republicans) nor had he any particular military achievement to his credit. This was rectified by a successful campaign contrived for him against the Kabylie tribesmen of eastern Algeria, and in the summer of 1851 he was brought to Paris and appointed minister of war in September. The key military commands in and around Paris went to officers of known Bonapartist sympathies – Espinasse, Forey and Canrobert.[11] The coup was well managed; someone saw to it that the drums of the Paris National Guard were stove in so that this pro-republican force could not be summoned to arms. The prince-presidency was transmuted into the Second Empire in December 1852, on the anniversary of the coup, and of Austerlitz and the coronation of Napoleon I. St Arnaud was made a marshal, and although he was a man dying of stomach cancer, was appointed commander-in-chief of the Army of the Crimea when France went to war fifteen months later. Canrobert, one of the four original divisional commanders, sailed with a 'dormant commission' as commander-in-chief should anything happen to St Arnaud.

François de Certain-Canrobert's Bonapartist credentials were impeccable and provide the reason why, throughout the duration of the Second Empire, he continued to be appointed to commands demonstrably above his ceiling. He was of *ancien régime* nobility, '*de particule*', and had done well in Algeria. Equally importantly, he was a cousin of Baron de Marbot.[12] With the rehabilitation of all things Napoleonic under the Orléans monarchy, this hero of the First Empire had become inspector general of cavalry and military aide to the Duc d'Orléans, eldest son and heir apparent of King Louis Philippe. Marbot, who survived to see the Second Empire, deservedly enjoyed prestige as great as that of any surviving marshal of the First, and the connection can have done no harm to the rising Canrobert. However, his tenure of command of the French Army, which included the Battles of Balaclava and Inkerman and the first attempts to capture Sebastopol, was marred by his extreme caution and reluctance to commit his forces. The promise (or threat) that Napoleon III would arrive to assume personal command of the army was always present, and it was with some difficulty that the emperor was at length, in the summer of 1855, dissuaded from this step by his ministers and his allies.[13] The Imperial Guard was already en route. Canrobert had, since January 1855, been subject to the intervention of the special representative in-theatre of the emperor; the sapper General Niel. And when the submarine cable link from Varna to Balaclava had been completed in April,[14] there were 'instant' messages by electric telegraph from Paris. This new facility precipitated Canrobert's resignation in favour of Pelissier. The latter had arrived in January to command one of the two corps[15] formed when the French Army was expanded to eight divisions, which in contrast to those of the British were maintained at full strength. After considerable inter-allied wrangling, Canrobert had agreed to the dispatch of a force to capture the Kertch Isthmus, with the object of opening the Sea of Azov to allied gunboats. This would develop a threat to the Perekop Isthmus, which links the Crimea to mainland Russia, and deny the Russian Army supplies from the grainlands of the Don basin. Two hours after the expedition had sailed, a telegram from the emperor required its recall because it did not conform to an entirely new design for the campaign conceived in the Tuileries.[16] Pelissier, on taking over from Canrobert, ignored the imperial directive. The expedition sailed again and did enormous damage. Canrobert spent the rest of the war as he had begun it, in command of a division.

The establishment of the allied bases at Kamiesh and Balaclava south of Sebastopol in September 1854 meant that the city was never fully invested by the allied armies. The Russians were always able to bring in fresh troops by way of the Perekop Isthmus and roads leading through the north of the city to the fortifications south of the River Chernaya. Sebastopol was not, therefore, formally besieged, but unlike the sieges of the war of 1870 (Metz, Paris, Strasbourg, Toul and Belfort) the fortifications were assaulted by formal siege operations – the digging of successive 'parallels', mining and counter-mining, with six separate major assaults over eleven months, each preceded by a bombardment. The Russians evacuated the city south of the river on 9th September, 1855, the day following the sixth bombardment and (only partially successful) assault. Peace talks were already in the air, but it was another five months before an armistice was concluded.

The last significant operation was the capture of Kinburn, at the mouth of the Dnieper estuary, in October. Commanding the French component of the task force was a *général de brigade* called Bazaine. Not entirely the obvious selection for this independent command – he had earned the disapproval of Forey, his divisional commander, on a matter of discipline – his appointment may have owed something to Pelissier's[i] partiality for the attractive and musically talented young Madame Bazaine, who had accompanied her husband to the theatre of war. The success of the expedition established this former ranker as a future contender for high command, along with another *général de brigade*, Bourbaki, who had distinguished himself at Inkerman. Others more senior stood ahead of them and all had previously earned reputations in Algeria. In addition to Canrobert, who was made a marshal at the end of the war, Niel and Forey, there was MacMahon, first general officer to set foot on the hotly contested Malakoff redoubt, the only success gained in the sixth assault on the fortress. If Algeria bred the paladins of the Second Empire, the Crimea provided them with their schooling.

---

[i] Pelissier, sixty years old at the end of the war, was created Duc de Malakoff and appointed governor-general of Algeria, where he died *en poste* in 1864.

ITALY

In the next venture of the Second Empire, principle and expediency coincided. Prince Louis Napoleon had fought for the cause of Italian unity in his youth, and had sworn an oath binding him for life to a secret society dedicated to the achievement of that goal. The summer of 1858 saw an early version of shuttle diplomacy, with secret visits by Cavour to Napoleon III at the newly fashionable resort of Plombières in the southern Vosges, and so conveniently near the border with Piedmont. In a treaty which remained secret until after the war began in April of the following year, Napoleon drove a hard bargain. In return for Nice and Savoy, which although on the French side of the Alpes Maritimes were long-standing possessions of the crown of Sardinia,[j] France would assist the latter to acquire the whole of northern Italy, in the words of Napoleon III, 'from the Alps to the Adriatic'. The future sovereignty of central Italy, Naples and the Papal States was left open for the time being. Napoleon III favoured federation rather than unification of Italy. For central Italy he had waiting in the wings his cousin, Prince Napoleon, son of ex-king Jerome of Westphalia, who since the birth of the prince imperial in 1856 was no longer the heir presumptive to the empire. To cement the treaty, this thirty-seven year old of somewhat shop-soiled reputation was married off to the fifteen year old Princess Clothilde, daughter of King Victor Emmanuel of Sardinia. For Naples, the schemer in the Tuileries had available the grandson of King Joachim Murat, currently enjoying the usual pursuits of a cavalry subaltern of good family on the imperial staff.

Had the provisions of the treaty, and still more Napoleonic aspirations, become known, the package would not have suited the doctrinaire leaders of the Risorgimento. They would have baulked at the loss of Nice and Savoy, the former in particular as the birthplace of Garibaldi. And in the light of hindsight it cannot be doubted that, throughout the round of diplomacy and the moulding of public opinion before the start of the war, Napoleon either preferred to ignore or else underestimated the strength of feeling of French Roman Catholicism about the temporal possessions of the Papacy. In the general unrest of 1848, Pius IX had had to flee Rome; he was re-established there, in March 1849, by the bayonets of a French Army commanded by General Oudinot, son of the marshal of the First Empire. A French garrison had remained in Rome throughout the 1850s, and was to stay for the following decade, until the troops were required for the war of 1870.

---

[j] Except between 1797 and 1815, when these states belonged to France, first as the Cisalpine Republic and later when absorbed under the First Empire.

Here was another dichotomy in Second Empire policy. Growing Italian resentment of the French presence in Rome, and thus denial of the natural capital, alienated the forces of Italian nationalism from Napoleon, and was a major factor in deciding Italian neutrality in 1870. But the inadequacy of the garrison and its ultimate withdrawal played their part in further alienating from the dynasty French Roman Catholic opinion, likely in any case to be legitimist.

Even to achieve the limited objective of freeing northern Italy from Habsburg rule, it would be necessary for the allies to isolate Austria from the other Great Powers. It was certain that Russia would in no circumstances support Austria, but, while English liberal opinion was broadly favourable to the aim of Italian unification, the English Government would not tolerate an unprovoked war to attain it. And as we have seen, the Prussian price for an alliance with Austria was concession by the latter of the command of the armies of all the German states north of the River Main, a price Emperor Franz Joseph was not prepared to pay. The best efforts of mid-nineteenth-century diplomacy combined to try to prevent the war. From a variety of motives the governments of Queen Victoria, the tsar and King Leopold of the Belgians all proposed mediation. Napoleon III was so impressed that, on 5th March, 1859, he caused to be published in the *Moniteur*, in the fashion of the time, a semi-official guide to the policies of his government:[17]

> The emperor has promised the king of Sardinia to defend him
> against every aggressive act on the part of Austria; he has promised
> nothing more and we know that he will keep his word.

And there were those who relied upon the imperial promise of 1852, notwithstanding the Crimea: *'L'Empire, c'est la paix.'*

The *Moniteur démarche* grievously fluttered the government dovecots in Turin. Sardinia had already mobilised her army. King Victor Emmanuel wrote to Napoleon that if France revoked on her commitments in the secret treaty, he (King Victor Emmanuel) would be forced to abdicate exactly as his father had been ten years earlier, following the defeats inflicted by Marshal Radetzky. Cavour, less diplomatically, threatened to publish the secret treaty. Thus Napoleon III was faced with the alternatives of being shown up either as a liar or as a sovereign whose pledged word could not be trusted.

Napoleon was saved by a combination of Austrian Government arrogance and '*Schlamperei*',[k] not unlike that in the weeks immediately preceding the outbreak of war in 1914. Franz Joseph was not a bad man, and by the standards of the time the administration of the Italian provinces of his empire was well conducted. Faced with increasing unrest in the 1850s, his government had followed the classic pattern of any well-meaning colonial power when threatened with the end of its rule. The day-to-day conduct of affairs was relaxed, and the most distinguished personage available was appointed viceroy, in the hope of both conciliating and flattering local opinion. In this case, the appointment went to Archduke Ferdinand Maximilian, brother of the emperor, liberal in his beliefs and newly married to Princess Charlotte, daughter of King Leopold of the Belgians, who had become by the 1850s what might today be described as chief consultant to the crowned heads of Europe. When Maximilian replaced the veteran Radetzky in 1857, the Milanese failed to be impressed. The entry of the viceregal couple into their capital was received with little enthusiasm,[18] and the Italian attitude overall is best summed up by the remark of an Italian nationalist quoted by Crankshaw: 'We don't want the Austrians to turn humanitarian; we want them to get out.'[19]

On 19th April, the Austrians, not for the last time, delivered an ultimatum in Turin: 'Demobilise, or else.' A week later the king and Cavour rejected it. But while circumstances had finally ensured that Austria would fight without allies, and that France could fulfil her obligations under the secret treaty without incurring the wrath of England, the French Army was completely unprepared for a war which had been foreseen ever since the Paris Conference at the end of the Crimean War.

Conclusive evidence of the lack both of inter-allied planning and of the organisation and preparation of the French Army for war is provided by the instructions received by Canrobert as he left Paris to take command of a corps. Marshal Randon, the minister of war, had to admit that there was as yet no joint plan of campaign and noted with regret that, 'the troops under your command are not organised for active service. You will remedy this situation.'[20] While the logistic support provided for the French Army in the Crimea had been less bad than that of the British, the mistakes made then were repeated in 1859, with interest. While, thanks to railways and steamships, the manpower of some units arrived in Genoa only five days after leaving

---

[k] This word is untranslatable. It is intended to convey a combination of frivolous and irresponsible leadership, supported by letter-perfect bureaucracy.

Paris, their guns, horses and logistic backing followed more slowly, by sail. Even boots had to be borrowed from the Italians. A further imaginative use of the railways envisaged the movement of another part of the French Army through Haute Savoie into the Aosta Valley, but when it was discovered, rather late in the day, that the line terminated at St Jean de Maurienne,[21] the troops were committed to a forty mile hike over the Mont Cenis Pass, still encrusted with the winter snow, as though it had been the approach march of the first consul to Marengo, nearly sixty years earlier. These troops entered the theatre of war without blankets, tents, artillery, or fodder for the horses. In a country divided by waterways there was no bridging equipment, and the army had no siege train to assault the fortress cities of the Quadrilateral, an operation essential to the achievement of the stated war aim. The emperor, arriving in Genoa to take command of the army in the field, telegraphed despairingly back to Paris:

> We have sent an army of 120,000 men into Italy before having stocked up any supplies there. This is the opposite of what we should have done.[22]

Had the Austrian preparation for war been even moderately competent, and had there been even average generalship when it began, the army of the king of Sardinia should have been comprehensively defeated during the month needed to bring the French Army to a battleworthy state. The Austrians had maintained a peacetime garrison of 100,000 men in the fortresses of the Quadrilateral south of Lake Garda, but no effort had been made to put these on to a war footing in the period of tension before the delivery of the ultimatum in Turin. The Austrian commander-in-chief, Field Marshal Gyulai, was not the best selection for the job. He was entirely defence-minded, mesmerised by the security of the Quadrilateral, and incapable of appreciating that the logistic chaos of the allied armies was at least as great as that of his own. Nevertheless, he contrived, at the end of April, to invade Piedmont with 50,000 men and briefly threatened Turin. Then, in late May, after a clash with the first elements of the French Army to take the field, he decided to withdraw to the line of the River Ticino, which marked the frontier between Piedmont and Lombardy.

Napoleon III took personal command of the French Army, which was formed into five line corps and the Imperial Guard. All the principal subordinate commanders had seen active service in the war of 1854, and most, together with many of the divisional and brigade commanders, would play significant parts throughout the remaining life of the Second Empire and its aftermath. Baraguey d'Hilliers, I Corps, son of a First Empire general, divisional commanders Forey, Ladmirault and Bazaine, had commanded the allied expedition in 1854 against Bomarsund at the confluence of the Gulfs of Bothnia and Finland, and had been promoted marshal for the success of this enterprise. MacMahon (II Corps), Canrobert (III), Prince Napoleon (V) and Regnault de St Jean d'Angely (Imperial Guard) had all had formation commands in the Crimea, while IV Corps went to Niel. The appointment of a sapper to this important combat command caused considerable jealousy. Early evidence of imperial misgiving about the capacity and Algeria-based reputations of some of his infantry and cavalry generals emerges from Napoleon's response:

> When one wants anything done, only the officers of the technical services are capable of doing it; but if one gives one of them an important command, all the others start complaining.[23]

The two armies collided in an old-fashioned set-piece engagement at Magenta on 4th June. Gyulai and the allies each had about 100,000 men within a day's march of the battlefield, but neither commander succeeded in bringing more than half the number available to him into action. MacMahon's II Corps made the first contact. A frontal attack across the Ticino at Buffalora failed to capture the essential bridge. MacMahon withdrew to think again but neglected, both at the time and later, to send any report to his emperor and commander-in-chief. In the flat, featureless and close-cultivated country of the Po and Ticino river courses, no allied commander had a good view of the whole battle area, but the belfry in the village of Magenta provided a reference point. Napoleon, thinking he was reinforcing success, sent in his next formation to hand, the guard under Regnault. The bridge at Buffalora changed hands seven times in a day's hard-fought close combat, but was at last secured by the French. Meanwhile MacMahon had moved northwards up the west bank of the Ticino, and had crossed unopposed at Bernate, three miles north of Magenta. He then embarked on a flank march across the front of the refused right of Gyulai's position in and around Magenta. This highly risky operation, though within sight and musket range of the Austrians, was not seriously interfered with. However, when MacMahon turned into line to attack, he was again repulsed. Niel brought his corps promptly into action to support Regnault, and later MacMahon, but Canrobert was dilatory and his III Corps was hardly engaged. Meanwhile Gyulai, having held his ground and almost won the battle, decided that he had lost it. Snatching defeat from the jaws of victory he ordered a withdrawal, abandoning Milan in the process. Napoleon III and King Victor Emmanuel entered the city in triumph three days later.

MacMahon was promoted to marshal and created Duc de Magenta. The battle established him as the leading soldier of the empire on the active list and in 1864 he succeeded Pelissier as governor-general of Algeria, where he remained until taking up his mobilisation appointment in Alsace in July 1870.

Prince Napoleon's corps had been detached to secure Tuscany and Modena. Baraguey's corps, which had not been engaged at Magenta, now took up the lead. As the bells were ringing in Milan to celebrate the end of Habsburg rule, there was a battle at Melegnano, ten miles south-east of the city, at the end of a day's forced march in driving rain. The leading division, commanded by Bazaine, bumped the Austrian rearguard under Benedek. Bazaine personally led the attack which captured the village, and the Austrians continued a controlled withdrawal towards the Quadrilateral. Ten days later, Gyulai was superseded. Emperor Franz Joseph arrived to take personal command of his army, with the seventy-two year old Field Marshal Hess as his chief of staff, as this veteran had been under Radetzky ten years before.

There followed, on 24th June, in a day of torrid heat, the pounding match of Solferino. Notwithstanding the fact that the allied armies were stricken with malaria and cholera, and the Austrians had more than 50,000 sick in the hospitals of the Quadrilateral and so unavailable for action, a total of 250,000 men were engaged in roughly equal numbers on either side, making Solferino the largest battle in history up to that time except for Wagram and Leipzig. Nearly all the soldiers on both sides fought with muzzle-loading personal weapons, though a squadron of the chasseurs of the guard had just received the first production of the new breech-loading chassepot. The French had the advantage in artillery. Guns were still bronze-fabricated and muzzle-loaded, but the new French rifled nine pounders outranged Austrian smooth-bores, hardly changed in capability since Wagram. The superior French artillery and the dogged tenacity of the fighting men on both sides produced a casualty rate of one in eight of the numbers engaged.

Both sides fought under a misapprehension. Napoleon thought that he had to deal only with a covering force protecting the withdrawal of the main body of the Austrian Army, while Hess advised Franz Joseph that the two leading allied corps had drawn too far ahead of the others and so could be defeated in detail. The allied armies had been on the march for five hours when first contact was made at 9 a.m. against an extemporised but strong Austrian defensive position making good use of hills and ridges along an eight mile front, at the centre of which the stone-built village of Solferino formed a natural strong point. By mid-morning, the army of the king of Sardinia and the corps of Baraguey, MacMahon and Niel were all heavily engaged, from north to south respectively, in poorly coordinated attacks on the Austrian position, but Canrobert was again late in bringing his corps into action. An account of the campaign published two years after the battle (and nine years before the war of 1870) considers that Canrobert 'nearly lost a battle by moving up too late at Magenta, and showed a caution amounting almost to timidity at Solferino.'[24]

In the late afternoon Baraguey's corps captured Solferino village, driving a wedge into the centre of the Austrian position which rendered the whole untenable. The Austrian Army was able to withdraw into the Quadrilateral unmolested because of a rapid counter-attack launched by Benedek, who had held the north of the Austrian line without difficulty all day, a violent thunderstorm which brought to an end a day of oppressive heat, and the exhaustion of the allied armies.

Both emperors were sickened by the bloodshed, and neither could risk a continuation of the war. Prussia was threatening mobilisation; but against whom? Napoleon knew that the eastern frontier of France was undefended, that an army barely capable, on the evidence of the last two months, of winning a war on one front certainly could not risk having to fight on two, that he had no siege-train for a direct assault on the Quadrilateral and, at the end of a highly tenuous line of communication, he could not manoeuvre to outflank this massive fortified zone. For Franz Joseph, the threat posed by Prussia was already implicit, the empire was in chronic financial difficulty, the Magyars, as usual, were simmering and the army which was his pride had been outclassed.

Eighteen days after the battle the two emperors met to agree peace terms which gave Lombardy, but not Venetia, to what, two years later, would be proclaimed as the kingdom of Italy. Although only half the promised job had been done, France received the full payment of Nice and Savoy. The people of Paris could be reminded daily that the dynasty was matching the achievements of the First Empire, with the Pont de Solferino and the Boulevard de Sebastopol joining the Rue de Rivoli in Baron Haussmann's controversial redevelopment of the city. And because Austria had been humiliated, Prussia could be content. The personalities fighting for Italian nationalism were less so, and Italy would soon seek an ally other than France to assist her in obtaining Venetia, to the ultimate disadvantage of the Second Empire. Italian displeasure was compounded by the continuing presence of the French garrison in Rome. The kingdom of Italy proclaimed in 1861 excluded not only Venetia, over which Napoleon III was considered to have reneged on his commitment, but also the 800 square miles of territory around Rome, since the thirteenth century the 'Patrimony of St Peter'. Two attempts made to capture this enclave by Garibaldi, without the overt support of the government of the new kingdom, failed. The second, in 1867, was defeated wholly thanks to the French garrison, whose commander, General de Failly, in reporting his success, could claim, '*Les fusils Chassepot ont fait merveilles.*'[25]

However, in 1870 this force was required to complete the order of battle of the French VII Corps in Alsace. After its withdrawal from Rome, to the disgust of French Catholics, the kingdom of Italy had only token opposition in completing the acquisition of all of the former Papal States, except the present-day Vatican City.

MEXICO

Throughout the 1860s until the thunderclap of Sadowa, the main preoccupation of the external policy of the Second Empire lay outside Europe. The North African colonies were extended into the Sahara. In 1859, a century of French missionary involvement in South-East Asia led to the occupation of Saigon by French marines, and within ten years the southern half of present-day Vietnam was a French colony and Cambodia a protectorate. A short expedition to Syria in 1860 was terminated because of English disapproval, but the two nations cooperated in the same year in a punitive expedition against the Chinese Empire. The forts at Taku fell to General Cousin de Montauban, who was rewarded by the title of Comte de Palikao, and the allies penetrated to Peking. While the colonisation of North Africa and South-East Asia continued to be major influences on French policy for the next century, by far the largest involvement in the first half of the 1860s, and the one with the most serious immediate consequences, was the intervention in Mexico. This was brought about by a ragbag of otherwise unconnected considerations. A Swiss banker named Jecker, seeking French citizenship, among whose investors was the Duc de Morny, half-brother of Napoleon III, had lost heavily when the incoming Mexican government of President Juarez repudiated the foreign loans taken out by its predecessor. English and Spanish interests were also involved, and in 1861 all three countries sent small expeditionary forces to Mexico. But by the following year, while English and Spanish interest had cooled, that of Napoleon III had increased beyond all reason. His thought process was a triumph of what would in late twentieth-century jargon be styled 'lateral thinking'. It would redound to the credit of the dynasty if the Second Empire, like the First, could have its own satellite kingdoms. French Roman Catholic opinion might be pleased if the anti-clerical Juarez could be replaced; and it might also be possible to improve relations with Vienna in the wake of the war of 1859 by providing a throne ready made for Archduke Maximilian. No longer his brother's heir since the birth of Crown Prince Rudolph, deprived of his employment as viceroy following the cession of Lombardy, and with the Austrian Navy having absorbed all the modernisation[1] it could take (or the empire could afford), Maximilian's presence in the Habsburg domains, in gilded inactivity at the castle of Miramar, near Trieste, was an embarrassment to his brother because of his potential as a focus for discontent. It was also an affront to his wife, who, as a member of the House of Saxe–Coburg–Gotha, felt herself underemployed without a throne.

Napoleon III underestimated the difficulty of conquering Mexico as grievously as his uncle had underestimated the difficulty of conquering the Iberian peninsula. The initial French intervention force of 6,000 men under General Lorencez could hold on only with difficulty to a strip of territory in the fever-ridden coastal belt around Vera Cruz, and proved quite incapable of capturing the fortified town of Puebla, 100 miles inland on the route to Mexico City. Substantial reinforcement became necessary, and in July 1862 Napoleon sent out a corps of two infantry divisions, which increased the strength of the French Army in Mexico to 40,000. The corps commander was Forey, and the divisional commanders Bazaine and Felix Douay. Meanwhile, Maximilian, who would have won few intelligence contests but was reluctant to relinquish his status as an Austrian archduke, a step insisted upon by his elder brother if he were to accept the offer of the throne of Mexico, had his reservations overborne by the ambitions of his wife. Even the canny King Leopold I of the Belgians advised in favour of the venture. Nevertheless, it was apparent long before the couple sailed from Miramar, in April 1864, that Maximilian would have to be installed by force of European arms. The only Mexican enthusiasm for an imported emperor came from the Catholic Church and those dispossessed by Juarez; and European arms meant French, because neither Maximilian's brother nor his father-in-law had any troops to spare in view of higher priorities nearer home.

In the circumstances, the military achievement of a French intervention force which never exceeded 40,000 men was highly creditable, rather than

---

[1] See Chapter VIII.

contemptible, as would be claimed later in attempts to discredit everything undertaken by the Second Empire. But this was not the work of the conventionally minded Forey. After a ten week siege, Puebla surrendered to the French commander-in-chief in May 1863. But it was Bazaine, in command of small task forces organised and operating on the same principles as the 'razzia' of Algeria, who had held off attempts by Juarez to raise the siege, and who, after the fall of Puebla, had opened the road to Mexico City and cleared central Mexico. The French entered the capital in June.

Four months later, Forey was promoted marshal and superseded in command by Bazaine. For the next eight months, pending the arrival of Maximilian and his empress, Carlota as she now styled herself, this former ranker and warrant officer in the Foreign Legion was the de facto viceroy of Mexico. The fact that Bazaine was a fluent Spanish speaker, having served for four years in Spain with the Foreign Legion in the First Carlist Civil War, and that, before going to the Crimea as colonel commanding the first regiment of the Foreign Legion, he had spent ten years in civil–military government in Algeria, made him better qualified for the task than the rigid and unimaginative Forey.[26]

The continuing success of Bazaine's military operations forced Juarez to withdraw to a nomadic existence near the border with Texas, but he and his supporters retained the capability to mount hit-and-run raids at any time and in any part of the country not physically held by French troops. Even the road between Vera Cruz and Mexico City was never fully secured. On 30th April, 1863, a company of the Foreign Legion, at only half strength because of disease, was annihilated at Camerone by a force of 2,000 Mexicans. The heroic self-sacrifice[m] of these sixty-two men succeeded in diverting Mexican attention from a convoy containing the treasure chests of the army en route from Vera Cruz to the besieging force round Puebla.[27] And three years later a formal embassy, sent to announce the accession of the Empress Carlota's brother as King Leopold II of the Belgians, was ambushed on the essential artery between the port and the capital, and an aide-de-camp of the count of Flanders killed.[28] The number of French troops in Mexico was simply inadequate for the task. If the First Empire had been unable, even with over 300,000 troops in-theatre, to subdue Spain and Portugal, Mexico, with a land area half as large again, was unlikely to submit to a force one-eighth the size.

---

[m] Commemorated annually to this day by every unit of the Foreign Legion, no matter where stationed or in what circumstances.

The new regime had rapidly to secure the support of a majority of the indigenous inhabitants.

Maximilian was amiable and well-meaning but lacking in brains and drive. His Empress possessed both of these qualities but was quite without a sense of proportion or common sense. Neither realised at all what they had taken on. The voyage from Europe, in an Austrian warship, had been spent preparing a handbook of court etiquette more suited to the Hofburg of Maria Theresa than to providing a blueprint for the day-to day-life of the head of state of a country whose forty years of independence had been marked by chronic turbulence and instability. French bayonets secured a loyal reception for the imperial couple, when at length they reached Mexico City, in June 1864. Bazaine was promoted to marshal in October, and early in the following year commanded a highly successful operation which cleared the south of the country round Oaxaca, capturing 8,000 prisoners and sixty guns.

Nevertheless, the new regime was flawed from the start. While Maximilian wished to govern on liberal principles, his supporters wanted an authoritarian regime, and liberal-minded and nationalist Mexicans did not want him at all. When Maximilian agreed that Church property sequestrated by Juarez should remain in lay hands, the newly appointed papal nuncio saw to it that the Church withdrew its support for the empire. Relations with the French became soured because of the continuing role of the latter as debt collectors. Very little revenue could be raised internally, and the failure to attract foreign loans forced the abandonment of an attempt to raise a native-recruited Mexican army, because there was no money to pay it. And with the end of the American Civil War, the European-imposed empire had an unfriendly neighbour on its northern border in the shape of the re-established United States of President Andrew Johnson and Mr Secretary Seward, instead of the acquiescent Confederacy of President Jefferson Davis. While initially relations between Maximilian and Bazaine had been most friendly, each was soon writing letters of complaint about the other to Napoleon III. Maximilian could not understand why Bazaine could not bring the forces of Juarez to a decisive battle which would pacify the country once and for all. No one sought to remind him that the only major battle in the prolonged campaign to conquer Algeria had been fought fourteen years after the initial landing, and still had not settled the issue. For his part, Bazaine drew attention, justifiably, to the lack of decision on major matters of policy.

Napoleon III had begun to have second thoughts about the venture as early as 1863. The Mexican involvement became progressively more unpopular in France, to an extent which began to threaten the dynasty. Even before the outbreak of the war between Prussia and Austria, it was evident that the French troops committed in Mexico were more likely to be needed on the Rhine. French troop withdrawals began in 1866. A distraught Carlota rushed to Europe, and was driven to dementia by her failure to obtain help from any quarter. After Sadowa, Bazaine was ordered to withdraw the whole intervention force. The operation did not go quite fast enough for Napoleon. Perhaps influenced by malicious gossip which imputed to Bazaine charges of feathering his own nest[n] (after the sudden death of his first wife, Bazaine had married again, into an aristocratic but impoverished Hispano-Mexican family), the emperor sent out a personal aide-de-camp to maintain a watching brief, much as he had sent Niel to oversee Canrobert and Pelissier in the Crimea. In the event, it was greatly to Bazaine's credit that, in the face of ever-increasing enthusiasm for Juarez and the consequent threat to the security of his force, he brought off the remaining 28,000 French troops without any significant loss. By June 1867 the withdrawal was complete.

A month later, Paris was host to Europe in the Exhibition of 1867. One of the principal features of this event was a review of the pride and pick of the French Army at Longchamps racecourse. The troops were commanded by Canrobert and showed off their paces in front of Napoleon III, Tsar Alexander II and King William I of Prussia, the latter accompanied by his chief of general staff. Emperor Franz Joseph was neither present nor represented. In the previous week the new transatlantic submarine telegraph cable had brought the news of the execution of Maximilian, by firing squad, at Queretaro.

Criticism by the Orléanist and Republican politicians opposed to the empire had made the utmost of a good case in decrying the Mexican adventure from the start. But this criticism had invariably exempted Bazaine; Thiers, even after the débâcle of 1870, would continue to refer to him as '*notre glorieux Bazaine*'. The marshal, without doing anything to encourage it, acquired the status of 'most favourite soldier' of the opposition politicians. Nor, evidently, had he lost the confidence of the emperor. Early in 1868 he was appointed to command the important Nancy military district, again taking over from Forey, and two years later his next command was the Imperial Guard. It was becoming evident to all that sooner rather than later there would be war with Prussia. When it came, the three marshals still of an age for

---

[n] One of the sources was the unrewarded General Felix Douay, in letters to his brother Abel, also a general. The most serious imputation was that Bazaine was seeking to install himself in place of Maximilian – a charge dismissed rightly by Guedalla, the leading authority, as nonsense.

active service who would be certain to hold high commands were, in order of seniority of promotion, Canrobert (1856), MacMahon (1859) and Bazaine (1864). In 1870, their respective ages were sixty-one, sixty-two and fifty-nine.

Re-Equipment and the Niel Reforms

If after the war of 1859 there had been some misgivings about the ability of the French Army to cope with the demands of a European war, by 1866 its serious deficiencies vis-à-vis its most likely opponent were self-evident. The three obvious areas of concern were command and staff capacity, weaponry and manpower, both trained and serving with the colours, and reserve strength. Among the features of the Paris Exhibition of 1867 had been the premiere of Offenbach's *Grande Duchesse de Gerolstein*. Having seen this delightful work, some, including the emperor, might wonder whether the full-blooded marshals and generals of the empire would be outmatched by the disciples of the ascetic and professorial von Moltke. Napoleon III comprehended the advantages the Prussians had drawn from their system of staff training and organisation. But in the second half of the 1860s his greater preoccupation was with the liberalisation of the empire, and his energies were increasingly impaired by poor health. As a result, he failed to impose his views on the conservatively minded hierarchy of the army, in particular his long-serving minister of war, Marshal Randon.

The training standards of the army were inadequate. Although there were annual manoeuvres every summer in the great plain around Chalons, the units taking part were grouped into formations solely for the event, and there was no continuity. Some of the training had no relevance to battlefield conditions. Attending the manoeuvres as an invited observer, General Sir James Hope Grant, co-commander with Cousin de Montauban of the expedition to Peking, watched an equestrian ballet performed by 2,000 immaculately groomed horsemen. Enquiring of his hosts in what circumstance in war the intricate evolution he was watching might be performed, he was told there was none. The graceful arabesques, though evidence of fine horsemanship, were merely for display.[29] A cardinal principle, which should be axiomatic in any age and any army, had been ignored: all drill movements should be related either to safe and effective weapon-handling, or to altering the configuration of troops in order to meet a changed situation.

A commission set up by the emperor to examine and report on the state of the army recorded the view in February 1867 that there were serious deficiencies in all fields: discipline, training, mobilisation procedures and war reserves were all inadequate. In a wholly modern manner the main conclusions were at once leaked to the press by one of the members of the commission, General Trochu. Trochu had been the senior aide-de-camp to the commander-in-chief in the Crimea and had commanded a division in Italy. This highly promising ascent towards the upper echelons of the army had been blighted because Trochu was a committed and verbose Orléanist. He had therefore both a personal and a political point to make. His subsequent book ran to twenty editions by 1870. The inevitable result, apart from providing ammunition for use by the political opponents of the empire, was the formation of a bureaucratic hedgehog by military officialdom for mutual protection.

The point has already been made that the empire did not go to its doom in a state of blind ignorance. Baron Stoffel was not alone, either in forecasting[10] the inevitability of war with Prussia, or in setting out the many ways, practical and moral, in which the French Army was inferior to the Prussian. Bourbaki, who had done well in command of a brigade in the Crimea and a division in Italy, went as an official observer to the Prussian Army manoeuvres in 1864. At the beginning of the First War of Prussian Supremacy two years later he warned: 'Be as rude as you like about this army of lawyers and oculists, but it will get to Vienna just as soon as it likes.'[30] Rich, handsome, always impeccably turned out and with an outstanding combat record, Bourbaki was high in court and public favour. Before the era of national competitive sport, the military paladins of the nineteenth-century Great Powers often enjoyed public adulation equivalent to that of today's football stars.

Inevitably, France drew no more than superficial lessons from the war of 1866. It was comforting to think that the Prussians had won only because their needle gun was a better infantry personal weapon than the Austrian flintlock muzzle-loaded musket, and by 1867 the French Army had been re-equipped completely with the chassepot. This weapon had two advantages over the needle gun. The ammunition was lighter, therefore the foot soldier could carry more of it; and a more effective breech seal gave greater range. The chassepot had an interdiction capability out to nearly one mile. This might discourage too close deployment by artillery which had not yet discovered the techniques of indirect fire, and which the Prussians used as a weapon of shock action. Also, in time for the 1870 war, the French Army would have the mitrailleuse, the first effective machine-gun to reach the battlefield. Faced by bureaucratic inertia and obstruction, the emperor had paid for the development of this weapon out of his own private funds, and by July 1870 there were about 150 of them with the army in the field.[o] But no thought was given to their tactical organisation and employment, because there was no general staff either to formulate provisional doctrine or refine it in the light of field trials. The mitrailleuses were grouped in batteries of six, one battery to each infantry division, and fought as a divisional artillery fire unit. They might more profitably have been employed, singly or in pairs, in close support of infantry regiments. Owing to their hurried introduction into service, at least some of the weapons arrived in units with no one knowing how they worked.[33] There is also evidence that the unprecedented range capability of chassepot and mitrailleuse tempted poorly disciplined troops to open unaimed fire at maximum range, firing their chassepots from the hip. On the evidence of a contemporary observer,[34] Prussian fire discipline was far better than that of the French, who eroded their potential advantage in infantry weaponry by wasting ammunition.

The Prussians had an undoubted superiority in artillery. The French field batteries had been re-equipped with the nine pounder in time for the 1859 war, firing a fused shell intended to airburst, but there were only two fuse settings and too many of the fuses were to prove defective. The French equipment was overtaken between 1866 and 1870 because the armies of the North German Confederation re-equipped after Sadowa with a steel, breech-loading, gun firing a percussion-fused shell,[p] which outranged its French counterpart by some 600 yards; little enough in late twentieth-century terms, but a formidable stand-off capability for a direct fire weapon engaging troops for the most part unprotected. In the battles of August 1870 the Prussian superiority in this arm would prove to be the decisive factor, apart from the advantages gained from twelve years' consistent formation command and staff training and practice.

The French, had they so chosen, could have matched the Prussian improvement in artillery. They were offered, but in March 1868 declined, the products of Krupp of Essen.[35] They could have gone equally well to their own Le Creusot works, or to Armstrong–Whitworth of England. One reason they did not was financial: rearming the infantry regiments with the chassepot had cost FF 113,000,000.[36] The concurrent manpower reforms were also likely to be expensive and there was no more money for artillery, which, as the financiers would argue, had been given new guns a bare ten years previously.

---

[o] Guedalla gives the number with Bazaine's army at Mars La Tour as sixty-six,[31] and the Army of Chalons surrendered another seventy after Sedan.[32]

[p] For development and comparisons of gun and munition construction, see Chapter V.

438

More fundamentally, the predominant school of opinion in the French Army felt that their best course in action was to come to close quarters as soon as possible, for which range and lethality improvements in artillery were unnecessary. This was a further assumption which there was no general staff to study or validate, and one directly contrary to the experience of Benedek's army in 1866.

The most obvious and serious problem, however, was the question of manpower and in particular the strength of the army on mobilisation. In November 1866, the emperor convened a conference at Compiègne to discuss the matter. The problem was not then insoluble, given time. The French birth rate did not fall significantly below the German until after 1870, and the 'military age dependencies' of metropolitan France and the North German Confederation were broadly similar. The Second Empire had, in addition, the advantage of the highly proficient fighting units recruited in her North African colonies. Many regiments of *chasseurs d'Afrique* and *tirailleurs Algerienne* were to render outstanding and self-sacrificial service to France in 1870. Nevertheless, it was apparent to anyone who had bothered to do the arithmetic that Prussia had mobilised no fewer than 350,000 men for first line combat operations in the war of 1866, and that these were backed by reserve formations and individual reinforcements to give Prussia on mobilisation an army of at least 1,000,000 men. On coarse figuring, multiplying the known quantities of the annual call-up of 60,000 and the total length of service, line and reserve, of twenty years, their maximum strength in 1866 could have been 1,200,000.

It was also a known fact that, as a result of Sadowa, Prussia had annexed Hanover, Hesse and the duchies, furnishing the manpower potential for another three *corps d'armée*, while the forced adherence of the kingdom of Saxony to the North German Confederation would provide a fourth. Thus, with the Guard Corps and the eight province-linked corps of the original Scharnhorst organisation,[q] Prussia would field thirteen first line corps on mobilisation, backed by a formidable trained reserve strength.

Against this mass of manpower, a study previously prepared for the emperor by General de Castelnau, the imperial aide who had been sent to hasten Bazaine's withdrawal from Mexico, indicated that France could oppose no more than 288,000, a figure remarkably similar, had Castelnau but known it, to the estimate of 270,000 made by Moltke in his strategic appreciation which had preceded the 1866 war.[37] Napoleon III set a mobilisation target figure of 1,000,000 men.[38] An expansion of this order could be brought about

---

[q] See Chapter VII.

only by a complete volte-face of manning policy. For the previous fifty years, although every Frenchman had had a theoretical liability for military service, the nation had relied in practice on a long-service army because there was no training obligation imposed on the majority of twenty year old men who were not conscripted. Notwithstanding the Prussian triumph in 1866, the received military wisdom of the time considered that the only effective manpower was that present with the colours – that is, long-service regulars. Prominent in this line of thinking was the minister of war. Although Marshal Randon could make a case for Castelnau's figures being unduly pessimistic, his proposed solution, an increase alike in the quota and in the period of conscript service from seven years to nine, even had it been acceptable politically, was insufficient to meet the goal set by the emperor. In January 1867 Napoleon replaced him with Niel.

In a tenure of the Ministry of War cut all too short by terminal illness (he was to die after only two years *en poste*), Niel was to show that he was both a competent military administrator and a skilful political operator. With the liberalisation of the empire, Niel had a far more difficult task than that of any Prussian minister of war. He had not merely to explain the army money and manpower budget to the civilian legislature, but he had to gain their approval for it. Given the radical changes and expansion necessary if the mobilisation target strength of 1,000,000 were to be met, Niel's task was as great as that of von Roon, and he had none of Roon's advantages.

Niel's solution to match the reserve strength of the Prussian Army was to resurrect the national guard. In France this organisation, historically territorial and usually volunteer, had been raised successively under the Revolution, the First Empire and the Orléans monarchy as the force of first resort against local disorder. However, in the large cities, Paris in particular, the prospect of arms in the hands of civilians, unamenable to military discipline and potentially hostile to the government of the day, had had no attraction for Napoleon III, and he had abolished it soon after the coup of December 1851. Niel's original proposals reduced the period of service for those conscripted into the regular army, still by lot, to five years, but required that all young men in every annual class, including those who had purchased exemption, should receive training in the first section of the national guard, the *Garde Mobile*, which would be embodied on mobilisation without restriction on place of service. Regular soldiers would also revert to the *Garde Mobile* on completion of their service with the colours. All former regulars, those who had purchased exemption and those lucky in the conscription lottery would serve in the *Garde Mobile* for four years. Afterwards, all would revert to the second section of the national guard, the *Garde Sédentaire*, which was intended for local defence. On Niel's calculations, this would produce, by 1875, a first line strength on mobilisation of 824,000, backed by a manpower reserve of 400,000. It should be self-evident that any new category of military reserve based on the age factor requires years to build up. The most important policy deduction the emperor and his advisers might have drawn was the need to avoid war with Prussia for the next eight years, until after Niel's reforms had worked through.

Although these proposals fell some way short of the universal obligation to serve with the colours which were imposed on every fit male twenty year old subject of the king of Prussia, they nevertheless met with virulent opposition in the legislature. Under the newly liberal empire, this body had bite as well as bark, and, following a series of political amnesties, had become representative of all shades of French opinion. Extreme republicans saw no need for a standing army at all. If the state were in danger, it would be saved by a *levée en masse*, as was thought to have happened in 1793. The representatives of the solid bourgeoisie objected to the erosion of the principle sacred to them of substitution. The liberals saw the proposal for universal service in the *Garde Mobile* as an attempt to militarise France. Jules Favre, ornament of republican opposition to the empire, enquired of the minister of war: 'Do you want to turn France into a fortress?'

Both at the time and later,[r] the not-so-simple soldier had the last word: 'Take care that you do not turn her into a cemetery.'[39]

Debate and political compromise watered down Niel's proposals. The period of service was set at five years with the colours and four with the first section of the reserve. While all had a theoretical obligation for first line service, the call-up was split into two sections, of whom the majority would serve for five months only. Thereafter, the training commitment in the *Garde Mobile* was limited to fourteen days a year. By law, the pampered reservist could only attend this training for one day at a time, for no longer than twelve hours in the day, and had to be home by evening because he was not to be contaminated by even one night spent in barracks. While this would have produced by the mid-1870s a paper strength comparable to that of the forces of the North German Confederation, the quality and depth of training clearly

---

[r] Even for a politician, Favre's utterances remained accident-prone. As the representative of the provisional government which replaced the empire after Sedan, he had, in 1871, to negotiate peace terms with Bismarck. Going into the discussions with the ringing statement that not an inch of French territory would be ceded and not a stone of her fortresses given up, he had to surrender Alsace, including Strasbourg, and Lorraine, including Metz.

would be far inferior and in the event France was not to be allowed the time essential if the numbers were to build up as planned.

The calculations should have made clear the fact that in any war embarked upon before 1875 French strength would be less than Prussian, and that France could not expect either superiority of weaponry or better quality of generalship to redress the balance. This in turn should have dictated a quiescent international stance. Instead the opposite course was followed: the external policy of the Second Empire remained adventurist and became suicidal.

Notes

The Second War of Prussian Supremacy generated a quantity of written coverage greater than that of any previous war, comparable in volume and scope to the mass of material produced during and after the major wars of the twentieth century. The war of 1870 was the first to originate a complete spectrum of coverage, both in range and time-frame, before, during and for long afterwards. The Crimean War had been the first from which the eyewitness reports of qualified observers had appeared in print for public consumption almost at once. In the war of 1870, the reports of journalists with the armies were not censored; the intelligence implications are obvious. The American Civil War led very quickly to numerous unit histories and personal memoirs, and in time to the scholarly and detailed analysis and biography which continues to this day. While including these aspects, the reportage of the Franco-German War of 1870 added all the others which the late twentieth century has come to expect. The spate of material began even before the war, with Trochu's book, *L'Armée Française en 1867*.[s] By mid-1871 there was a politically slanted version of events intended to mould French opinion. There followed the official histories, the memoirs of the commanders-in-chief and other key protagonists, and, in time, objective evaluation and biographies. The war continued to be the best and most recent source for contemporary professional study for long afterwards, overtaking very quickly the war of 1866, and so remained until the Russo-Japanese War of 1905. Thus the written works continued to flow and a bibliography produced in 1898 contained over 7,000 entries.[40]

---

[s] A copy of the twentieth edition, published in 1870, is in the library of the Royal United Service Institute for Defence Studies.

Inevitably, this massive output was of varying quality. First into the field was the highly tendentious *Metz; Campagne et Négotiations*. Published in Paris initially under the soubriquet of an '*Officier Superieur de l'Armée du Rhin*', this was an attempt by an Orléanist sympathiser, the comte d'Andlau, to prove not only that everything had been Bazaine's fault but also that he had been a traitor to France. Bazaine's riposte, *L'Armée du Rhin*, published in 1872, did him more harm than good. Like his defence at his court martial in 1873, the record of which runs to 800 close-printed pages, it was flawed because of his efforts to protect the possibility of a Bonapartist restoration. In 1883, with Napoleon III and the prince impérial both dead, Bazaine's *Episodes de la Guerre de 1870 et le Blocus de Metz* was a better account, but by then the damage was irretrievable. As far as French political history is concerned, Bazaine, the scapegoat at the time, remains to this day the culprit.

Imperial Germany and France both published official histories, complete editions of which still gather dust on the shelves of underfunded military libraries which have so far contrived to escape vandalised modernisation. The historical section of the German general staff produced a weighty five-volume chronology, with numerous supporting studies in a sixth. The French twenty-two-volume equivalent is very hard to follow, because the volumes are unrelated to each other, each dealing with a separate aspect or campaign area. The work is not sequential and seems designed to confuse rather than to clarify. The quality of more recent work is such that the official histories need be consulted only to provide corroboration of detail or to resolve discrepancies.

Moltke took longer than Bazaine to publish. His *Franco-German War of 1871* did not appear until 1887, and was not translated into English until twenty years later. His spare, restrained and detailed narrative is totally factual, saying little but disclosing much about the nature of the man. The personal accounts of many other participants at all levels were published either in their lifetimes or shortly afterwards. Most interesting of these are the memoirs of the acerbic von Blumenthal, chief of staff of the army commanded by the crown prince of Prussia as he had been in 1866, and of von Verdy du Vernois, head of the intelligence section of Moltke's army group headquarters staff, but also employed in much the same way as Napoleon I had used his general-officer level aides-de-camp.

Around the turn of the century there began to appear biographies and histories written by the next generation of authors, who had taken part in the war, if at all, only at a subordinate level. These accounts are therefore less subjective. Bonnal followed his meticulous study of the war of 1866 with two volumes about MacMahon's operations in Alsace and three more on those of the French Army in Lorraine from the outbreak of war to the retreat into Metz. In the latter, Bonnal establishes beyond reasonable doubt that even had Bazaine managed to brush aside the forces blocking his retreat at Mars la Tour, inevitably he would have been trapped shortly afterwards between the Meuse and the Argonne. Bonnal's work, published between 1899 and 1914, came too late to alter the French received view of the war. Appearing concurrently was Bapst's six-volume biography of Canrobert. More perhaps than the achievement of the latter deserved, but Bapst's monumental study is invaluable as a commentary on the state of the French Army throughout Canrobert's forty years of active service.

Given this plethora of material, any historian's sources are of necessity highly selective, and perhaps after the lapse of a century in which passions have died and objectivity has been enabled to emerge, the best sources are the most recent. Those upon which this author has relied most are:

Howard, *The Franco Prussian War*, London, Rupert Hart-Davis Ltd, 1961; reprinted by Granada Publishing Ltd, St Albans in 1979. This is treated as the definitive work about the war as a whole.

Horne, *The Fall of Paris*, London, Macmillan and Co., 1965; The Reprint Society, 1967, is likewise authoritative about the Siege of Paris and the defeat of the Commune.

Whitton, op.cit.,[t] is as important a source for the war of 1870 as it is for that of 1866.

Brogan, *The French Nation: From Napoleon to Pétain, 1814 to 1940*, New York, Harper and Brothers, 1957, provides essential background about the political, intellectual and cultural influences in France under its successive governments from the restored Bourbons to the end of the Third Republic.

Ascoli, *A Day of Battle*, London, Harrap, 1987, is a superb 'conduct of battle' account of the war, from the frontier battles to the capitulation after Sedan.

Finally, every author should declare a prejudice and preference. Two works which in terms of time of writing fall between the first post-war generation studies and the fully objective modern sources provide much material faithfully attributed in the latter. They also, together with A.G. Macdonnell's *Napoleon and His Marshals*, founded this author's interest in military history and in nineteenth-century France. Philip Guedalla's *The Two Marshals*, published by Hodder and Stoughton in 1943, fulfils many roles. The most important of these at the time was to expose, with the Second World War still in the balance, the absence of moral standing of the Vichy regime. For the historian, this work is authoritative about Bazaine's early military career and on the French involvement in Mexico. Similarly, Guedalla's *The Second Empire*, first published by Constable and Co. in 1922, has not since been surpassed as the definitive work about the second edition of Bonapartism in power, and about the French Army and nation under Napoleon III.

[1] Elting, op.cit., pp.668–70.

[2] Chandler, *Marshals*, Appendix A.

[3] Brogan, op.cit., pp.24–26.

[4] Howard, op.cit., p.16.

---

[t] See Notes to Chapter VII.

[5] The work of novelists of enduring reputation is of course invaluable as a guide to contemporary living conditions. Thackeray's *Vanity Fair* has much to say about the lifestyle of Wellington's army in the approach to Waterloo as does Tolstoy in *War and Peace* about the Russian Army and nation in the campaigns of 1805, 1807 and 1812. Tolstoy himself saw combat service in the Crimean War at Sebastopol. A guide of compelling importance about the degraded state of the line regiments of the French Army in 1870 is Zola's *La Débâcle*, first published in 1892. Zola, born in 1840, did not serve in the war but was writing from within his own experience. *La Débâcle* is written at the infantry soldier level, and encompasses the French withdrawal on Chalons after the Battle of Froeschwiller, the approach to Sedan and the battle, and later what amounted to civil war in Paris in May 1871 between the forces of the provisional government and those of the Commune.

[6] De la Gorce, *The French Army*, translated Kenneth Douglas, London, Weidenfeld and Nicholson, 1963. Chapters 1 to 5 cover the period between the end of the Franco-German War and the start of the First World War.

[7] Guedalla, *Second Empire*, p.28.

[8] Guedalla, *Two Marshals*, pp.47–48, in particular on the Siege of Miliana.

[9] Fisher, op.cit., p.889.

[10] Fuller, op.cit., vol. II, pp.102–3.

[11] Guedalla, *Second Empire*, pp.208–9.

[12] Marbot, op.cit., vol. I, p.2.

[13] Brogan, op.cit., p.116.

[14] Robins, 'The Electric and Other Telegraphs' in *The War Correspondent*, the journal of The Crimean War Research Society, vol. XIII, no.1, April 1995, p.22.

[15] Ffrench-Blake, *The Crimean War*, London, Leo Cooper Ltd, 1971, reprinted 1993, p.114.

[16] Ffrench-Blake, op.cit., p.124.

[17] Crankshaw, op.cit., p.153.

[18] Aronson, *The Coburgs of Belgium*, London, Cassell, 1969, p.42.

[19] Crankshaw, op.cit., p.147.

[20] Guedalla, *Two Marshals*, p.83.

[21] A contemporary, comprehensive, well-mapped and uniquely clear account of the campaign in northern Italy in 1859, by Major, later Lieutenant Colonel, F. Miller VC, is contained in the *Minutes of Proceedings of the Royal Artillery Institution*, Woolwich, 1861, vol. II, pp.205–78. The author is greatly indebted to Brigadier K.A. Timbers, historical secretary of the Royal Artillery Historical Society, for drawing his attention to this work, which contains the order of battle of the French Army.

[22] Howard, op.cit., p.17.

[23] Bapst, quoted Howard, op.cit., p.16.

[24] Miller, op.cit.

[25] Fisher, op.cit., p.961.

[26] Guedalla, *Two Marshals*, Chapter 3.

[27] Perrett, *Last Stand: Famous Battles Against the Odds*, London, Arms and Armour, 1991, Chapter 3.

[28] Aronson, op.cit., p.73.

[29] Guedalla, *Two Marshals*, pp.142–43.

[30] Bapst, quoted Howard, op.cit., p.29.

[31] Guedalla, *Two Marshals*, p.187.

[32] 'An Officer of the Royal Artillery' in *From Sedan to Saarbrucken*, first published in 1870; reprinted Helion Books, Solihull, 1992.

[33] Guedalla, *Two Marshals*, p.158, and Ascoli, op.cit., p.73.

[34] *From Sedan to Saarbrucken*, p.66.

[35] Manchester, *The Arms of Krupp 1587–1968*, Boston and Toronto, Little, Brown and Co., 1964, p.101.

[36] Howard, op.cit., p.36.

[37] Whitton, op.cit., p.88.

[38] Howard, op.cit., p.30.

[39] Howard, op.cit., p.51.

[40] Howard, op.cit., preface.

Chapter XII
The Triumph of Planning: Alsace–Lorraine 1870

Storm Clouds and a Clear Sky

Sadowa indirectly and Mexico directly had cost the Second Empire dearly in prestige both at home and abroad. The revelations of Trochu had shaken public confidence in the one national institution in which all Frenchmen could take some pride, irrespective of their political belief. At the same time, Napoleon III was attempting that most difficult of all political manoeuvres, the liberalisation of a dictatorship. This is hard enough to accomplish from a position of strength, but when attempted from one of weakness the necessary concessions of authority do nothing to win over the opponents of the regime. All they do to dishearten and confuse the supporters of the government which is relinquishing its power. So it was with the Second Empire, which was shaken by domestic scandal and whose propagandists were unable to match the intellect, wit and appeal of their opponents.

Victor Hugo, disdaining all amnesties, continued to fulminate from Jersey. Rochefort's *La Lanterne*, a weekly broadsheet exploiting to the limit the weapons of satire and ridicule, reached at once a circulation of 100,000 copies when no more than 4,000 had been anticipated. The first sentence of the first issue set the tone for what followed: '*La France contient, dit* L'Almanach Impériale, *trente-six millions de sujets, sans compter les sujets de mécontentement.*'[1] The author/editor exiled and the magazine suppressed, Rochefort continued to publish from Brussels and elsewhere. The copies smuggled back into France by a variety of ingenious means acquired the appeal of contraband. But a riot in Paris stemming from the funeral of a republican sympathiser, shot dead in questionable circumstances by a cousin of the emperor, was put down without difficulty. The disturbance was nevertheless symptomatic of the fact that the empire was failing to convince its political opponents and had no attraction either on the streets of Paris or among the younger elements of society in the country as a whole.

In the circumstances, and even though Louis Napoleon's first concern by the late 1860s was to pass the empire on to his son, a cautious external policy was perhaps impossible. The dynasty needed to be able to set some achievement against growing internal discontent. The offer of the emperor, directly after Sadowa, to mediate between Prussia and Austria was rejected by Bismarck, and was in any event unnecessary because Prussia, as we have seen, gave Austria terms which were very lenient in relation to the scale of the Habsburg defeat. But concurrently with the peace negotiations and the establishment of the North German Confederation, Bismarck had also secured within four weeks of Sàdowa, by the Treaty of Nikolsberg, the agreement of the independent states of southern Germany to accept the leadership of Prussia in the event of war. The military unification of Germany was now a fait accompli, at least on paper.

Napoleon's diplomatic counter-move was to seek return from Prussia for some good French offices during the 1866 war and after. This started with a claim to the left bank of the Rhine northwards from Strasbourg as far as, and including, the fortress city of Mainz. This latter was a most unlikely concession by a victorious Prussia, not only because of the strategic importance of the city at the junction of the Rhine and Main rivers and as a nodal point in the new railway system, but also for reasons of prestige. Only during the First Empire had Mainz been under French rule. Historically it was the seat of one of the three episcopal electors of the Holy Roman Emperor. Nevertheless, within a month the French demand had expanded in secret to include the annexation of Luxembourg and Belgium, which would have regained for France the north-eastern frontier allowed to her in 1814 after the first Bourbon restoration. Bismarck's reaction was at best ambivalent, and France, a signatory to the treaty of 1839 which had established the independence and perpetual neutrality of Belgium,[2] did not care to press the matter, especially given the certain opposition of England. The bipartite Franco-Prussian negotiations over Belgium remained secret until 1870, when Bismarck chose to make their content public at the worst possible moment for the Second Empire. By 1867 the French demand for something, anything, which could be used to impress domestic opinion had been reduced to seeking Prussian agreement that the Second Empire might acquire Luxembourg by purchase if the king of Holland were prepared to sell this part of his patrimony.

The ownership of Luxembourg was a nineteenth-century anomaly not dissimilar to those of Schleswig and Holstein. The Grand Duchy was an appanage of the king but not the crown of Holland. As a minor state of the former Holy Roman Empire, Luxembourg had become part of the post-1815 German Confederation, and as such had a Prussian garrison. Moltke, on record fifteen years previously about the inevitability of war between Prussia and France,[3] was quite prepared to go to war over Luxembourg, on the basis that sooner was better than later.[4] It was Bismarck who stayed the Prussian hand, for reasons which were as much military as diplomatic. Militarily, time was needed to incorporate the armies of the other states of the North German Confederation within that of Prussia, and to improve the quality of those of the kingdoms and lesser principalities of southern Germany. On the diplomatic front, the alliance forged with Italy for the war of 1866 needed to be strengthened, in order to prevent any Italian backsliding towards France. Additionally for the longer term, when war came, Bismarck's aim was that France should enter it isolated and if at all possible should be seen as the aggressor by the international community. The problem was allowed to evaporate with Prussian agreement to demilitarise Luxembourg, and with a degree of Franco-Belgian customs union and railway integration. Napoleon III had gained little beyond Prussian contempt, internal ridicule and the risk of being a hostage to fortune if his attempt to annex Belgium became known.

Nevertheless, there then followed eighteen months of relative peace and quiet. The 'Liberal Empire' was inaugurated at the beginning of 1870 and confirmed later by plebiscite. In the light of international calm and to gratify domestic opinion, the conscription for 1870 was reduced by 10,000 men. At the end of June, Emile Ollivier, the new young president of the council of ministers, could claim that European peace had never seemed more certain,[5] and concurrently the permanent head of the Foreign Office in London could brief Earl Granville, incoming foreign secretary in Mr Gladstone's first administration, that he had never in his experience known such a lull in foreign affairs.[6] The fuse which within a fortnight was to set off the explosion sputtered more than once, and even given the precedents of the previous sixteen years it remains incredible to late twentieth-century eyes that the two leading European continental powers went to war with each other for the trivial reason they did, or that the forces of international diplomacy could not have combined to prevent the outbreak.

Ostensibly, the *casus belli* originated with the proposed succession to the throne of Spain. Since the enforced abdication of Queen Isabella II in 1868, power had lain in the hands of a military dictatorship under Marshal Prim, with the remit to find a new ruling house. Prim's choice fell upon Prince Leopold of Hohenzollern, heir to the principality of Sigmaringen. His family, though Catholic, was a cadet branch of the Hohenzollerns of Brandenburg and Prussia. In the light of subsequent events it is worth recording that the Spaniards expected this candidate to be acceptable to the French Government. Napoleon III had encouraged a younger brother to accept the throne of Romania, and the two families were related, although distantly, through Beauharnais and Murat connections.

The Sigmaringens, father and son, were reluctant. In February 1870 the ruling Prince Charles Antony sought the advice of the head of the family, on the basis that his eldest son would accept the Spanish offer only out of duty to the house of Hohenzollern. King William, from beginning to end, viewed the Sigmaringen candidacy as a family matter. He saw little point in a Hohenzollern assuming the throne of a country which was ravaged by long-standing inter-racial hatred and beset for the previous sixty years by instability, whose power was in decline and where the house of Hohenzollern had no more natural support than a Habsburg younger son in Mexico. Bismarck had a different perspective. As the master of Prussia's foreign policy, he considered that the question went far beyond a family issue for the Hohenzollerns. As the culmination of at least six months' exercise of his influence he wrote, on 28th May, 1870, a letter to Prince Charles Antony urging strongly that Prince Leopold should accept the Spanish offer. Bismarck's reasons were as much negative, in that such acceptance would pre-empt the possibility of the Spanish crown falling into the hands of interests hostile to Prussia, as from any perception of military or commercial gain. Deferring to this pressure, the Sigmaringen princes did as they were told and accepted. King William, not pleased that his advice as head of the family had been overruled by his prime minister, nevertheless acquiesced. It is at this point that Spanish incompetence and French overreaction combined to escalate the matter into a European crisis.

Prim's offer required the approval of the Cortes of Spain. Don Eusebio de Salazar, the principal promoter of the Sigmaringen candidacy, was in Germany throughout June conducting the final negotiations with the intended monarch and his father. Due to a decoding error in a telegram from Salazar to Prim in Madrid, the latter allowed the Cortes to adjourn for a fortnight without informing them of the proposal so that they could vote on it. Before the members could be recalled the news leaked out. The result was fury in Paris. It was evident that for some considerable time the Prussian Government had been conniving in a clandestine manoeuvre to outflank France. After the lapse of a century and a quarter, the question has to be posed whether the French outrage had any basis other than emotion and wounded pride. The military threat to France in 1870 across the Pyrenees from a Spain shorn of most of her possessions in the Americas and torn by internal strife was negligible,[a] and the maritime threat to the sea lines of communication between metropolitan France and her colonies in North Africa non-existent. At the time France had the most modern and powerful navy in the world.[b]

In the face of strong diplomatic pressure and protest by France both to Berlin and Madrid, the Sigmaringen princes on 7th July withdrew their acceptance. It appeared that the matter was closed. Napoleon III, increasingly troubled by an agonising kidney complaint, had not left St Cloud. King William I was taking the waters at Bad Ems. Bismarck was on his estates at Varzin and Moltke similarly at Kreisau. In Paris, Ollivier could say to Thiers, elder statesman of the Orléans monarchy, historian of the Consulate and First Empire, and perpetual chief critic-in-residence of the Second: 'Nous tenons la paix, nous ne la laisserons pas échapper.'[8]

It was at this point that the most extreme anti-Prussian and chauvinist viewpoint in French Government circles gained the upper hand. The Prussian Government had not made itself party to the Sigmaringen renunciation of the Spanish throne. The Duc de Gramont, newly appointed foreign minister, was given a general permission to send instructions to the French ambassador to Prussia, Count Benedetti, to seek the personal assurance of King William that the Sigmaringen candidacy would never be put forward again. Similarly Gramont required the Prussian ambassador in Paris to ask his monarch to write a personal letter of explanation to Napoleon III. On 13th July, Benedetti met the king in the public gardens at Bad Ems. King William greeted the Frenchman courteously. Adhering to his view that the Sigmaringen candidacy was a domestic matter for his family, and no doubt feeling that the cause was a bad one, the king congratulated Benedetti on Prince Leopold's renunciation of the Spanish crown. Benedetti, bound by his instructions, sought against his better judgement the assurance of the king, as Gramont had directed, which William declined to give. Common sense and goodwill should at that point have concluded the matter. But when Benedetti reported the outcome to

---

[a] Understood even at the time. When France mobilised in mid-July only a single division was allocated to the Pyrenees frontier.

[b] The French La Gloire was the first all-weather ocean-going ironclad, predating HMS Warrior. By 1870 the Second Empire had fourteen similar warships, nine other steam-powered and armoured heavy gunships, and a total of forty-nine ironclads.[7]

Gramont by telegram, the latter directed him to seek a further audience with the king and to press the issue with the utmost firmness. Benedetti's thrice-repeated requests for another audience were declined, on the ground that there was nothing further to discuss.

Warned of the possibility of a crisis, both Bismarck and Moltke had, on the afternoon of 12th July, returned to Berlin. On the following evening, accompanied by Roon, they were dining in Bismarck's domestic apartments at the Prussian Foreign Ministry. The mood of the triumvirate was gloomy; with the Sigmaringen withdrawal now public, it appeared that France had gained a significant diplomatic victory and a golden opportunity to create a permanent embarrassment for her on the Pyrenees frontier had been lost. Bismarck, seeing his policy in ruins, was openly contemplating resignation. However, during dinner, he received a routine report of the events of the day from Abeken, the Foreign Office official in attendance on the king at Bad Ems. Abeken's factual report ended with the words:

> His Majesty leaves it to your excellency whether Benedetti's fresh demand and its rejection should at once be communicated to our ambassadors, to foreign nations and to the press.[9]

The mood of the dinner party improved at once. The triumvirate was by now united in the view that war with France was not only inevitable, but also that the sooner it came the better, before the Niel reforms had had time to take significant effect. By nineteenth-century standards, the demand that the king should underwrite the Sigmaringen retraction was an insult to Prussian national pride and a sufficient *casus belli*. It remained to present the case in the way best suited to Prussian interests. Shorthand reportage of history for long had it that, in exercising the discretion he had been given, Bismarck 'forged' the Bad Ems telegram. He did nothing of the kind.[10] In a way totally comprehensible in terms of late twentieth-century media selective reporting, Bismarck's communiqué was a version of Abeken's report, edited to fit his own policy and calculated to inflame French opinion. For the outcome of events it is tragic that, earlier on the same day, when they were informed of the full text of the instructions sent to Benedetti by Gramont, the French council of ministers had approved them *ex post facto* only reluctantly, and had added a rider: 'The demand for guarantees was susceptible of mitigation, and any honourable transaction would be welcome.'[11]

Too late. When Bismarck's version of events reached diplomatic and press outlets in Paris, on Bastille Day, this moderated approach was submerged in a torrent of wounded national susceptibility. The mood of the more extreme anti-Germans in the government and on the streets of Paris demanded war,[c] but it was with considerable reluctance that the emperor bowed to this pressure and authorised mobilisation late on the evening of 14th July. The following day, after a passionate debate in which Ollivier declared that he accepted the possibility of war *'d'un coeur leger'*,[d] Le Boeuf, minister of war since the death of Niel, claimed that the army was ready 'to the last gaiter button' and Gramont hinted archly at impending alliances with Austria and Italy,[12] the Corps Legislatif voted the necessary financial measures by 267 votes to ten. The formal declaration of war by the Second Empire on Prussia followed four days later.

Planning and Mobilisation

Since the war had long been foreseen by both belligerents, it might have been expected that they would have thought through, to the ultimate extent possible, what they were going to do and how they were going to do it. In military terms the contingency planning should have encompassed and related to each other the strategic design for operations and the mechanistic processes of mobilisation, concentration, deployment to battle positions and logistic support. As the options were so limited, the planning should have been completed in very considerable detail. As always, and increasingly so with the mutually dependent expansion of numbers, firepower potential and battlefield areas, both armies were constrained by topography. Geographically, the least obstructed invasion route from Germany into France, and the one best suited to the railway network upon which the mobilisation and concentration of the armies of the North German Confederation depended, lies north of the Ardennes and east of the Meuse, on an axis Aachen–Liège–Sedan. Some of Moltke's previous annual appreciations had envisaged a major thrust over this well-fought piece of ground, but on the assumption that France would be the first to violate Belgian neutrality. In July 1870 the enormous diplomatic advantage Bismarck had gained for Prussia, by making public the secret French attempt to annex Belgium two years previously, could not be thrown away. The nature of the terrain ruled out a major effort by either army on the eighty miles of what was, to all intents and purposes by 1870, the common

---

[c] A demand perhaps not echoed in France as a whole. On 15th July, the departmental prefects, who although government appointees might be expected to reflect the views of the majority outside Paris, voted by two to one in favour of peace.

[d] And spent the next forty years trying to explain away this remark.

frontier between Strasbourg and Basle. The same geographic factors denied to both sides the means of concentration and exploitation. A Prussian invasion of France was not well served by the railways necessary for the concentration of sufficient force, and after crossing the Rhine a German army would have to traverse the north–south massif of the southern Vosges, across the grain of mountainous and difficult country. Similarly, a French invasion of southern Germany would be seriously constrained by the difficulties of assembling a large army in this area west of the river, by the limited number of bridges between Strasbourg and the Swiss frontier, and by the shortage of routes west to east through the Black Forest. Even without regard to the restraints imposed by the ground, either side committing the bulk of its army to an invasion in this sector risked being taken in flank by the other. The attention of the planners in both Paris and Berlin was focused perforce on the 150 miles of frontier between Mezières and Strasbourg. Here, the grain of the routes, rivers and valleys is south to north, or south-west to north-east, which, though not favouring a French advance eastwards into the palatinate, imposes no similar inhibition on a German invasion once this has closed up to the line of the Moselle south of Metz. The coordination of a French defence to cover the area most at risk, from Thionville to Strasbourg, was made more difficult by the west–east spur of the Vosges which separates the Lorraine plateau from the hilly, wooded and broken country of eastern Alsace.

THE SECOND EMPIRE

France was bound to take the offensive, not merely because the Second Empire saw itself as the aggrieved party. In practical terms, with the massive potential superiority of the armies of the North German Confederation, fully comprehended by both Napoleon III and his minister of war, France had either to join forces with allies or mount a rapid pre-emptive strike which would so disrupt German mobilisation as to render any subsequent concentration impossible. The latter purely military design predicated an attack north-eastwards from Lorraine, but the diplomatic considerations compelled Napoleon III to consider and provide for a quite different strategy. An alliance between the Second Empire and the newly restructured Dual Monarchy of Austria–Hungary[e] had been under discussion at the highest levels since 1867 and the emperor also had the prospect of both Italy and Bavaria. Although the latter was bound to Prussia by the Treaty of Nikolsberg, some influences in Munich saw the only hope of continued Bavarian

[e] See Appendix A.

independence in an alliance with France, much as the kings of Hanover and Saxony had chosen to throw in their lot with the Habsburgs in 1866. In the event, any expectation from Bavaria was dashed at once. The Wittelsbach monarchy abided by its treaty obligations and provided two more army corps for the king of Prussia. The kingdom of Italy was bankrupt, beset by internal tensions between north and south, and inhibited politically from an alliance with France by the continuing presence of the French garrison in Rome. Although these troops were removed when France ordered their mobilisation to complete the order of battle of their army corps forming in Alsace, their withdrawal came too late to influence Italy but soon enough to alienate even further French Catholic and legitimist opinion from the empire. Napoleon's best prospect, which was in his view to remain a possibility for at least another month, was the Dual Monarchy. The Saxon Count Beust, Foreign Minister of Austria–Hungary and as such the only civil power apart from Franz Joseph himself with authority in both countries, had been a strong influence in Vienna for an alliance with France. But now he was appalled by the feckless irresponsibility of French diplomacy, which had brought on a war with insufficient justification and long before his master's armies had had time to recover from the catastrophe of 1866. It followed that active Austrian participation depended upon early French military success leading to the junction of the armies of the two empires in southern Germany. These diverging military and political considerations pulled the deployment of the French Army in opposite directions. The only common denominator was the need to take the offensive and invade Germany at once, a course for which the streets of Paris were also clamouring.

Neither of these incompatible aims was supported by a military concept of operations, much less a plan. In so far as the army had a design for the campaign, it was defensive, based upon an appreciation by the sapper General Frossard, military tutor to the prince imperial, of the fortress-like potential of the many 'positions magnifiques' along the critical stretch of frontier. And although the staff of the Ministry of War in Paris had busied itself with a masterly production of a map of Germany beyond the Rhine, Bazaine, when commanding the military district of Nancy for two years up to the beginning of 1870, had been at pains to familiarise himself with the defensive attributes of the ground on the French side of the frontier.[13]

The absence of any plan of campaign, offensive or defensive, was compounded as late as 11th July by the first of a series of major changes in the command structure of the army in the field. From 1868 onwards Niel, and Le Boeuf after him, had been working on the assumption that the eight corps into which the French Army would be formed after mobilisation would be grouped in three armies, one in Lorraine under Bazaine, one in Alsace under MacMahon and the third in reserve under Canrobert at Chalons, the whole under the emperor as army group commander. At the eleventh hour the emperor, acting on the advice of Archduke Albrecht, victor of Custozza, ordered an entirely different organisation. He would personally command all eight corps, seven line and the Imperial Guard, with Le Boeuf as chief of staff. The direct command of eight major formations on a front of over 100 miles would have taxed the genius of the first Napoleon and the communications resources of an army a century later. The expectation that Le Boeuf could carry out the combined functions undertaken by Roon and Moltke in the Prussian Army was likewise wholly unrealistic.

In the event, the departure of Le Boeuf for the front on 24th July left a vacuum in Paris. Many tasks vital for the support of the army in the field, ranging from organisation of the lines of communication to the arrangement of medical services either remained unperformed, were progressed with insufficient authority, or had to be extemporised.

From 2nd July, the day upon which the crisis broke in Paris, the action lay with Le Boeuf and his staff at the Ministry of War to bring the mobilised army at full strength to its battle positions. Thereafter, his task as army group chief of staff was to translate the intentions of his commander-in-chief into a coherent and comprehensive battle plan. A gunner by background, Le Boeuf had the essential Second Empire qualifications of loyalty to the emperor and outstanding service in the field, in his case in the Crimea and Italy. He had been promoted marshal earlier in the year in order to reinforce his authority as minister of war, the last to be so honoured until the elevation of Joffre in 1916. While as minister of war for the previous eighteen months he must bear his share of the blame for a plan which was incomplete and not thought through, the scant respect given after the débâcle to his efforts should not obscure the fact that his task was impossible against a far better organised and practised opponent, and that he did the best he could. Transports were assembled at the Mediterranean ports to bring the troops from Algeria and Rome; officers were recalled from leave; the railway companies were placed on alert and made subject to military direction and contracts for forage were placed in the United States. And, as in any war ministry in a period of rising tension, the existing contingency plans were dusted off, detail added and, ahead of mobilisation, 'no cost' and 'reversible' measures set in hand. But the key political and financial decisions were not made until 14th and 15th July. The call-up of the reservists was ordered late on 14th July, after a threat earlier in the day by Le

Boeuf to resign, and only one day ahead of Prussia. Le Boeuf tried to gain time by directing that what should be the sequential processes of mobilisation and concentration were to be implemented concurrently. This decision, taken for the best of reasons – to attempt to gain time for the only French strategy which had any chance of succeeding – achieved the worst of results.

The first internal decisions, simple enough in themselves, were the structuring of the regiments into brigades, the composition of these into divisions, the organisation of the latter into corps, and the appointment of the formation commanders.[14] The three marshals hitherto designated for army command would now, in consequence of the decision of 11th July, be relegated to corps, but each of these corps would have four infantry divisions instead of the French standard three, with a larger staff both to exercise this wider span of command and to enable further formations to be taken under command if and when appropriate.

The four infantry division corps verged on the unwieldy, in particular for route organisation in both advance and withdrawal, and also for logistic support. Each infantry division had thirteen infantry battalions (twelve line, one light), each around 1,000 strong at war establishment, and three artillery batteries, two four pounder, one mitrailleuse. In addition, each corps had a cavalry division of 3,000 sabres and an artillery group of up to eight batteries, of various calibres. The total envisaged strength of a four division corps would therefore have been in excess of 55,000 men, but because of the failure of the mobilisation process no French formation ever approached its designated war strength.

The organisation and concentration plan which emerged for what would be styled 'The Army of the Rhine', and intended to cater for both the strategic options, was:[15]

TABLE XV

Corps	Commander	Division	Concentration Area
Lorraine:			
II	Frossard	Vergé Bataille Laveaucoupet (cav.) Valabregue	St Avold
III	Bazaine then Decaen then Le Boeuf	Montaudon Castagny, later Nayral Metman Decaen, later Aymard (cav.) Clerambault	Metz
IV	Ladmirault	Cissey Grenier Lorencez (cav.) Le Grand	Thionville
Alsace:			

I	MacMahon
	then Ducrot
		Ducrot, later Wolff
		Abel Douay, later
		    Pellé
		Raoult, later
		    L'Herillier
		Lartigue
		(cav.) Michel
			Strasbourg

V	Failly	Goze L'Abadie d'Aydrein Guyot de Lespart (cav.) Brahaut	Bitsch
VII	Félix Douay	Conseil-Dumesnil Liébert Dumont (cav.) Amiel	Belfort
Reserve:			
VI	Canrobert	Tixier Bisson La Font de Villiers Levassor-Sorval (cav.) Salignac- Fénélon	Chalons

Corps	Commander	Division	Concentration Area
Guard:	Bourbaki	Deligny Picard (cav.) Desvaux	Initially Nancy, at Metz by 24th July
Reserve Cavalry:		Du Barrail	Lunéville, later brigades to Metz and Chalons Pont à Mousson
		Forton Bonnemain	Strasbourg

Note: French divisions and brigades were not numbered. They took the name of their commander – a further ingredient for confusion.

Le Boeuf expected the whole army to be in these positions and at its complete war establishment strength of 385,000 on 28th July, the fourteenth day of mobilisation.[16] But even then, the Army of the Rhine would not be concentrated for action. It would be covering some 120 miles of frontier, neither poised for an offensive, nor in positions of mutual support for defence; as Napoleon I is alleged to have said of a similar deployment by a formation commander, more suited to prevent smuggling than to fight a battle.

It was, of course, a drawback of massive proportions in terms of preparation for war, and even more so for operations unless there was time for a prolonged period of combined training, that formation commanders, staffs and units had no experience of working with each other. Only the guard and the reserve cavalry divisions had a formation structure in peacetime. The potential for disaster is encapsulated by the plaintive telegram sent by a brigade commander (designate) in VII Corps to the Ministry of War. Arrived at Belfort, he reported: 'Cannot find my brigade. Cannot find my divisional commander. Do not know where my regiments are. What shall I do?'[17]

While the concentration of VII Corps perhaps presented more difficulties than that of the others because the units had to come from Algiers and Rome, this episode highlights the criminal lack of planning for a war long seen as inevitable. Timed movement tables, concentration areas and a logistic support plan should have been prepared in advance down to regimental level, and made known to the designated formation commanders, units, and movement and logistic agencies. The need for anything approaching an annual senior commanders' conference, with the aim of updating all formation commanders and their staff officers on the mobilisation and concentration plans had occurred to no one in the French Army. Such a gathering would undoubtedly have exposed the more glaring planning deficiencies. Napoleon III and his successive ministers of war must bear the blame for a most damaging omission. As late as 27th July, Le Boeuf, now in Metz in his dual role as army group chief of staff and minister of war, was telegraphing to the commander of VII Corps, whom he supposed to be in Belfort, 'How far have you progressed with your formations? Where are your divisions?'[18] when in point of fact Douay was still in Paris, winding up his peacetime function as duty imperial aide-de-camp general.

And perhaps the most serious handicap of all lay in the abilities, physical and professional, of the commander-in-chief. Napoleon III was devoid neither of military experience nor understanding. Without his impetus, the French Army in 1870 would have had neither the chassepot nor the mitrailleuse, and his physical courage was undoubted. Because of the non-existence of higher command and staff training in the French Army, he was probably alone in its top echelon in being able to see all aspects of the war in European terms, and of comprehending the difficulties of commanding over 100,000 men in the field. Also, it was almost certainly unquestionable, as Moltke had long foreseen, that the head of the Bonaparte dynasty had to command his army in person. Even his age, sixty-two at the outbreak of war and some years younger than both the king of Prussia and Moltke, was not necessarily a handicap. But his military talents were academic rather than practical and he was without at least two of the essential attributes of a higher commander; physical stamina, and the ability to impose his will on his subordinates. Napoleon I, in 1815 no longer the lean and hungry commander of Austerlitz or Wagram, not in the best of health and softened by a year's exile on Elba, had nevertheless spent fifteen hours in the saddle[19] on the day before the twin battles of Quatre Bras and Ligny, coordinating the advance to contact of the two wings of the Armée du Nord. In 1870, his nephew was so ill as to be barely capable of mounting a horse. Whatever its many other failings, the French mobilisation plan had not omitted to include one significant detail. In a memorandum from the imperial household:

> *L'empereur a une retention d'urine intermittente; alors il eprouve des angoisses inexprimables. Vous emporterez avec vous les instruments de sondage et même d'opération.*[20]

The emperor left Paris for Metz on 28th July and never saw his capital again. The government of the country, and by default the support of the army in the field, was left in the hands of a council of regency under the empress. This body was destined to make its own contribution to the disaster. On 2nd August, present as a spectator at the first skirmish of the campaign, Napoleon III collapsed in agony after having ridden only a few paces, and a specialist had to be summoned from Paris. Thereafter, Napoleon's presence with his armies was an embarrassment. Although the debilitating effect of excruciating pain further weakened his ability to command, he was debarred for reasons of prestige from returning to Paris without a victory and was forced to remain with the army in the field even after relinquishing the command-in-chief.

The attempt by Le Boeuf to combine the processes of mobilisation and concentration produced chaos. On the face of it, it is a simple enough matter to order an individual reservist to report to his regimental depot, fit him out and send him on to his regiment. But the units were all on a peacetime basis. With men on permanent leave as an economy measure, some were as much as two-thirds below their war establishment. Perhaps forty per cent of the postulated war strength of the Army of the Rhine had first to be moved as reinforcement drafts. No more than a third of the regiments happened to be stationed in the same department as the depots to which their reservists had to report. What, because of Le Boeuf's decision, became the concurrent processes of concentration of the units on the eastern frontier and movement of bodies of reservists to join them choked the system.

Nevertheless, too much should not be made of the problem of unit movement. The regiments stationed in peacetime in the frontier military districts, Lille, Metz and Nancy, were in or near the right place already. The concentration plan was also logical in being based on a radial convergence. The garrison units of northern France concentrated on Thionville or Metz, those from the centre of the country on Chalons or Nancy and those from the Midi or overseas on Strasbourg or Belfort. Railway timetables had been prepared and rolling stock laid off. But train composition and running times were inflexible, and an over-optimistic assessment had been made of the reporting rate of recalled reservists. The consequence was that in the early days of mobilisation, train capacities were either too small for units or too great for the drafts of individuals ready to move. As the latter built up, movement capacity became insufficient for both. Before long, hordes of undisciplined individuals, liberally plied with wine, were clogging the focal points of the railway network. The district commander at Marseilles, having tried and failed to obtain movement orders for 9,000 men for whom no one seemed to have a use, threatened to pack the lot off to Algeria.[21]

The principle that returning reservists should report first to regimental depots was fine in theory, but in a country as large as France was lacking in common sense. All authorities have quoted favourite examples of wasted time and resources. The depots of the North African-oriented units, recruited from French volunteers as well as locally, were all in Algeria. One reservist in a Zouave regiment, living in Alsace, reported first to Strasbourg, from where he was sent, via Marseilles, Oran and a two day march, to his regimental depot. Kitted out for war, he was then returned over the same route to join his regiment, part of MacMahon's I Corps forming up at Strasbourg.[f22] The depot of the 98th infantry regiment was at Lyon, the peacetime station of the unit Dunkirk and its war concentration area Thionville, to join Ladmirault's IV Corps.[23] While some degree of muddle is inevitable in military movement on the scale of the French Army in 1870, particularly if a paper plan has never been validated by practice of even a sample, there are too many similar examples for these to be written off as isolated cases. Between 16th July and 4th August the French railway companies claimed to have moved 300,000 men, 64,700 horses, 6,600 guns and wagons and 4,400 wagon loads of ammunition and supplies.[22] But some at least of the men were 'double counted'; home to depot, depot to unit. On 6th August, when battle was joined in both Lorraine and Alsace, neither VI nor VII Corps was operational, and the Army of the Rhine as a whole was still some twenty-five per cent under war establishment.[24] Substantial numbers of reservists continued to reach the army throughout August. Notwithstanding battle casualties, the strength return of those surrendered at Sedan and Metz was fifty per cent as many again as that of Le Boeuf on 31st July.[g]

In the mobilisation debate in the chamber on 15th July, Le Boeuf's claim was something more than an empty boast in the sense that the equipment existed – somewhere in the country. By 1870 1,000,000 chassepots had been manufactured,[25] and until the *levée en masse* in the winter no French infantryman went into battle without one. However, by the mid-nineteenth century, combat units already required a plethora of equipment that was not on individual issue, but which nevertheless had to be immediately available to the troops if the unit were to become and remain combat effective. Perhaps

---

[f] MacMahon, governor-general of Algeria, did not reach Strasbourg until the eleventh day of mobilisation.

[g] See Appendix 1 to Chapter XIII.

the most obvious example is cooking pots, essential in the French Army of 1870 which, in the field, issued and cooked its rations, fresh or preserved, on a ten man section basis. Items such as this may be held in peacetime at the regimental depot and issued on the appropriate scale to drafts when leaving to join the field-force unit; they may be kept as 'mobilisation stores' by the unit, inviolate in peacetime and issued during the expansion from peace to war strength; or stored at mobilisation depots in concentration areas, and drawn by units as they arrive. It does not matter in general terms which system is adopted and a combination is possible because the methods are not mutually exclusive. But one or other must be laid down for every item required by the individual, or on a unit scale, a plan made and fully understood, and stores maintained in the appropriate place and quantity. However, because, in spite of the lessons of the Crimea and Italy, no such arrangements had been made, too many units and soldiers embarked on the campaign without essential items of equipment. Furthermore, while plans had catered for initial movement of stores by rail, nothing had been done to arrange their onward movement from railheads. The main army mobilisation wagon park was at Chalons, surrounded by a high stone wall with a single gate. Days were needed to extricate the vehicles.[17] Railway sidings became choked with unloaded railway trucks, uninventoried stores, and deteriorating rations. Before long all the corps commanders were badgering Le Boeuf, and rightly so, about critical deficiencies. An insufficient peacetime build-up and the blockage in the supply chain at railheads contributed alike to shortages of essential ammunition, rations and forage stocks at all the frontier logistic depots – Mezières, Metz, Sedan, Strasbourg and Belfort. Belfort, the base not merely for VII Corps, but for any advance eastwards into southern Germany, had no ammunition stocks whatsoever. In some corps, there was no money either to pay the troops or procure services and supplies from the inhabitants, whose initial goodwill was soon exhausted by looting.

The morale of compulsorily re-enlisted reservists is always likely to be questionable. The men must be motivated by total acceptance of the necessity for their recall in a cause which commands their full support, or, in the case of long-term first enlistments, by the regimental family spirit and tradition engendered by their previous service. In any case, firm discipline and impeccable unit administration are essential. Few of the Second Empire's returning warriors were imbued with the necessary spirit, discipline in units was poor and on the lines of communication worse, and without pay and rations the morale of the army deteriorated almost at once to a level which would not sustain the soldiers in withdrawal, and which only immediate victory might restore. Bazaine, taking a train at the Gare de l'Est for Metz on the first day of mobilisation, was heard to say, '*Nous marchons à un désastre.*'[26]

THE NORTH GERMAN CONFEDERATION

In contrast to the pervasive chaos in Paris, Moltke, on the day following the order for the mobilisation of the units of the North German Confederation,[h] was found with his feet up on a sofa reading a novel, and would claim afterwards that, in the fourteen days which preceded his journey with the king to the operational headquarters at Mainz, he had never had so little to do.[27] His design for operations, which unlike either of the French alternatives was supported by detailed and coordinated planning, derived from an appreciation two years earlier. He had two related objectives:

> ... from the first, the capture of the enemy's capital, the possession of which is of more importance in France than in other countries. On the way thither the hostile forces were to be driven as persistently as possible back from the fertile southern provinces into the more confined background to the north. But beyond everything the plan of campaign was based on the resolve to attack the enemy at once, wherever found, and keep the German forces always so compact that this could be done with the advantage of superior numbers.[28]

It is worth noting that, despite the related concepts of encirclement and junction of superior forces on the battlefield, which had been achieved so successfully at Sadowa, there is no suggestion that this had provided a unique elixir for victory. Moltke goes on to say:

> It is a delusion that a plan of campaign can be laid down far ahead and fulfilled with exactitude. The first collision with the enemy creates a new situation in accordance with its result.

Moltke had divined correctly the dispersion of the two forward elements of the French Army forced on the Second Empire by its alternative policy options, the topography and also from his own evaluation of French railway capacity. Moltke appreciated that in the first three weeks of mobilisation, no

---

[h] The mobilisation of the south German states was 'requested' under the terms of the Treaty of Nikolsburg, for a day later.

more than 150,000 men could be moved to Metz and 100,000 to Strasbourg. In the same time, and notwithstanding the far more 'linear' nature of the movement, the German railways could carry more than 300,000 men to concentration areas near the frontier west of the Rhine, with a further 60,000 in reserve forward of Mainz.

Moltke's intention was to attack the northern element of the French Army across the line of the River Saar, while maintaining a holding operation against the forces in Alsace. However, in 1869 he modified the concentration for this design to safeguard against the possibility of a large-scale raid across the frontier immediately on the outbreak of war by the forces already in place in Lorraine, which would have put the proposed detrainment and concentration areas near the frontier at undue risk. In the light of hindsight it can be realised that an attack on a scale large enough to succeed would have had to be planned in advance in total secrecy. Its execution would have required the *coup d'oeil* of a Rommel or a Dayan and a planning capability perhaps within the capacity of the Prussian general staff, but well beyond the collective military ability of Napoleon III and his generals. Moltke withdrew the detrainment areas to the right bank of the Rhine to provide the necessary security. He provided a screen in no more than divisional strength for the whole of the Lorraine frontier to cover the German mobilisation, relying upon an assessment that the French march capability would require six days to close the line of the Saar from Metz. There was a further advantage in placing the detrainment areas east of or on the Rhine: the march to the Saar would harden the reservists.

Moltke had a total of fifteen *corps d'armée*, eight and the guard from the original Scharnhorst structure, three from the states incorporated in Prussia after Sadowa, the Saxon Corps, now numbered XII in the Army of the North German Confederation, and two from the kingdom of Bavaria. There were also independent divisions from the principalities of Baden and Wurtemburg. While all corps for peacetime training and administration conformed to the standard Prussian organisation of one cavalry and two infantry divisions, Moltke had ordered an operational regrouping. Appreciating that the cavalry arm had been poorly handled in the war of 1866, until the very last hours before Sadowa, his original intention had been to combine as many of the cavalry divisions as movement resources would allow into a single formation under the direct command of army group headquarters. This would, at least in theory, allow better coordination of reconnaissance and, if the formation were to be provided also with an infantry division, it could be used as a strong covering force behind which the infantry corps could deploy from line of march to assault. But in a memorandum dated 6th May, 1870,[29] he amended this design. One or two cavalry divisions, detached as in the previous reorganisation from their provincial corps, would operate directly under the headquarters of each army. As will be seen, this change also failed to have the desired effect, at least in the early stages of the campaign. German infantry advance guards frequently bumped French defensive positions to the mutual surprise of both, and it is hard to avoid the conclusion that the four commanders of the 'army' cavalry divisions were somewhat too stolid and slow-thinking to control and coordinate reconnaissances across an army front. As will be seen, their junior commanders soon learned to be more enterprising, and, by the second half of August, probing and intelligence gathering by small mounted patrols had been developed to a very high standard.

Moltke's plan initially committed all but three of the corps, and one division of IX Corps, to the front against France. The excluded formations, I, II and VI Corps, were retained in strategic reserve and to guard the German North Sea and Baltic coasts against the French maritime capability (which Prussia had nothing to match) and against a possible invasion of Silesia or Thuringia by the armies of the Dual Monarchy. There was in any case insufficient rail capacity until after the twentieth day of mobilisation to move the East Prussian-, Pomeranian- and Silesian-recruited corps to the Rhine. But on 7th August, the day after the frontier battles, Moltke appreciated that these threats could be ignored and the three formations were added to the concentration against France. In all, Moltke had over 1,000,000 men including fortress, garrison and lines of communication troops, and 200,000 horses 'on the ration list.'[30] This total mobilised manpower was nearly double the French maximum of 567,000,[31] out of which had to come the residual security force for Algeria, a division for the Pyrenees frontier and garrison and lines of communication troops.

Notwithstanding the experience gained in 1866, the German concentration did not proceed with total smoothness. Some troop trains were up to two days late, and, as on the French side, insufficient planning had been devoted to the onward movement of stores from railheads. By 5th September, twenty-six days' worth of rations for Second Army, 16,830 tons of supplies, were stuck on the lines of communication.[32] But these blemishes were negligible compared with the chaos behind the French front.

Furthermore, Moltke had none of the organisational problems of the French Army as the formations up to and including corps level were well established, with commanders and staff in place. The territorial basis of the *corps d'armée* meant that reservists seldom had any great distance to travel when reporting to their depots, or subsequently when joining their units. The war had far more popular support than the '*Bruderkrieg*' of 1866. As Bismarck would later claim, France had invaded Germany thirty times within the previous two centuries.[133] The war was against a hated and hereditary enemy and morale was far higher in consequence than in the regiments of the Second Empire. All Moltke had to confirm was the grouping of the corps and detached cavalry divisions into armies, and the selection of the army commanders. The following structure emerged:[14]

TABLE XVI
FIRST ARMY

Commander: von Steinmetz
Chief of Staff: von Sperling

Corps	Commander	Division	Commander	Concentration Area
VI	von Zastrow	13	von Glumer	Trier-Wadern
		14	von Kamecke	
VIII	von Goeben	15	von Weltzien	
		16	von Barnekow	
3rd cavalry division			von der Groben	
I (after 7th August)	von Manteuffel	1	von Bentheim	
		2	von Pritzelwitz	
		1st cav.	von Hartmann	

---

[i] An exaggeration. Fuller[33] puts it at fourteen occasions between 1675 and 1813.

SECOND ARMY

Commander: HRH Prince Frederick Charles of Prussia
Chief of Staff: von Stiehle

Corps	Commander	Division	Commander	Concentration Area
Guard	Prince Augustus of Wurtemburg	1 gd. inf.	von Kessel	Kaiserslautern– Neuenkirchen
		2 gd. inf.	von Bruditzki	
		Gd. Cav	von der Goltz	
III	von Alvensleben (younger)	5	von Stulpnagel	
		6	von Buddenbrock	
IV	von Alvensleben (elder)	7	von Grosz von Schwarzhoff	
		8	von Scholer	
IX	von Manstein	18	von Wrangel	
		25	Prince Louis of Hesse	
X	von Voigts- Rhetz	19	von Schwarzkoppen	
		20	von Kraatz-Koschlau	
XII	Crown Prince Albert of Saxony	23	HRH Prince George of Saxony	
		24	von Holderburg	
		12 cav.	Count Lippa	
5 cavalry division			von Rheinbaben	
6 cavalry division			HRH Duke William of Mecklenburgh-Schwerin	
II (after 7th August)	von Fransecky	3	von Hartmann	
		4	von Weyhern	

THIRD ARMY

Commander: HRH Crown Prince Frederick William of Prussia
Chief of Staff: von Blumenthal

Corps	Commander	Division	Commander	Concentration Area
I	von Kirchbach	9	von Sandrat	Rastatt–Landau
		10	von Schmidt	
XI	von Bose	21	von Schachtmayer	
		22	von Gersdorff	
I Bav.	von der Tann	1 Bav.	von Stephan	
		2 Bav.	Count Pappenheim	
II Bav.	von Hartman	3 Bav.	von Schleich	
		4 Bav	von Bothmer	
Wurtenburg Division			von Obernitz	
Baden Division			von Beyer	
4 cavalry division			HRH Prince Albert of Prussia	
VI (after 7th August)	von Tumpling	11	von Gordon	
		12	von Hoffman	
		2 cav. div.	Count Stolberg-Werigerode	

A corps at full strength numbered about 29,000, or 26,000, if its cavalry division had been detached. The standard artillery organisation was four six-gun batteries to each infantry division, and one or two batteries of horse artillery per cavalry division. Every corps had an artillery group of a further six batteries, sometimes more, and a field engineer unit. The 'national' formations from Bavaria, Wurtemburg and Baden also included a cavalry component.

The organisations of Second and Third Armies, which after 7th August had respectively under command seven and five corps as well as additional divisions, were too large to be controlled by a single commander. Perhaps fortunately, they never had to fight a battle in the field as a single entity all at once, thanks to the German superiority in numbers and in artillery firepower. It is beyond question that the Second Army commander spent the critical day of 16th August in the wrong place, more preoccupied with getting the main body of his army across the upper Moselle than with the encounter battle involving his leading elements which was developing on the Lorraine plateau. Also, the quality of at least some of the non-Prussian troops, placed out of courtesy to their ruling princes in the army commanded by the crown prince of Prussia, was questionable. In a letter not made public until 1928, the crown princess wrote to her mother:

> It is a dreadful position for him, as the Bavarian and Swabian troops are so ill-disciplined that they are of very little use – their leaders are more of a hindrance than otherwise.[34]

In confirmation there is a mordant note by Moltke against the staff table of the Baden Division: 'Subsequently many changes in the commands.'[35] The remedy lay in the allocation of some of Moltke's personally selected and trained general staff officers to the non-Prussian formations on the same scale as in the Prussian Army, three at each corps headquarters and one for each division. In any circumstances, these officers would follow what by now was accepted doctrine in the Prussian Army and one of the pillars of Moltke's philosophy of command. If any conflict should arise, they would act as the representative of the chief of the general staff, and only secondarily as the alter ego and executive of their own commander.

Moltke's influence on the choice of senior commanders lay far more in the selections made for corps commands in the years since Sadowa than in those appointments which required confirmation on mobilisation. He had to accept whoever the kingdoms of Saxony and Bavaria provided to command their corps, but at least one of the latter, Crown Prince Albert of Saxony, was well up to the exacting Prussian standard. He had done well as a corps commander on the opposing side in 1866 and before long would be promoted on merit to an army command. Some of the choices made to command Prussian corps had depended on seniority and the hierarchical nature of the army. Voigts-Rhetz, for example, Second Army chief of staff in 1866, was due for a corps command as an essential 'career move'. But some at least of the promotions between the two wars were evidence of assimilation of and obedience to Moltke's teaching. The von Alvensleben brothers, Manstein, Zastrow and Tumpling had all done well commanding divisions in the Sadowa campaign, and Fransecky had to be rewarded for bearing the brunt of the hard fighting east of the Bistritz during the first half of that battle. Only two of the corps commanders were aged under sixty, the crown prince of Saxony, forty-two, and Prince Augustus of Wurtemburg, fifty-seven, a career officer in the Prussian Army despite the Roman Catholic and long-standing pro-French sympathies of his principality. The junior appointment, and the only corps commander who was not a full general, was the younger of the von Alvensleben brothers, Konstantin. Although the ages of the formation commanders were comparable with those of their opposite numbers in the French Army, it is beyond doubt that the Prussians were the harder men and by far the better fitted for the rigours of campaigning.

The area in which Moltke had no choice at all was in the selection of the three army commanders. Two chose themselves. The two royal princes, Frederick William and his cousin Frederick Charles, could not be denied, notwithstanding the antipathy between Moltke and the latter. There was a compelling claimant for the third post. Von Steinmetz, on the basis of seniority, reputation as the 'Lion of Nachod', and his standing as almost the last in the army to share King William's experience of combat service in the Wars of Liberation over fifty years before, was the obvious choice. Moltke's book about the war is silent on the fact that before long Steinmetz proved to be impetuous to the point of rashness, disobedient and totally unamenable to control. He was dismissed a month later, after the Battle of Gravelotte–St Privat. Neither of the other army commanders was any more than competent. The strength of the German army lay in the planning which brought it into battle, the coordination of its greater strength, its immeasurably superior artillery and twelve years' selection on merit and training on common principles for the staff who provided its nervous system.

The Frontier Battles

The second half of July drew on in uneasy calm. To the surprise of many, not a shot was fired. Most Prussians, from the king downwards, had expected an immediate invasion of German territory and Moltke's surprise was tinged with relief that France had declared war evidently some time before her army was ready for active operations. The crown prince, an educated soldier and an open-minded man, confided to his diary:

> It may well be that, for all the French sabre-rattling and all our age-long preparations against a sudden onslaught, we shall be the aggressors. Whoever could have thought it?[36]

The less cerebral hawks in the French Government echoed the Paris mob in clamouring for an invasion of Germany. But Bazaine, first of the senior commanders to take up his appointment in the probable theatre of operations, and placed in temporary command of all the four corps forming in Lorraine pending the arrival of the emperor and Le Boeuf, was given no directive when he took leave of Louis Napoleon apart from an imprecise indication of the importance of Saarbrucken to the enemy as a railway junction. This was not so: the town lay, then as now, on the common frontier and Moltke's 1869 revision of the German concentration plan had cancelled its use in this role in the first stage of the war. When Le Boeuf arrived at Metz on 24th July, he directed the preparation of an offensive, and the formations in Lorraine were drawn in towards Metz. The project was countermanded by Napoleon III when he in turn reached the city four days later. It was apparent that the army was in a condition of what has since been described as 'administrative bedlam'[37] and would not be ready for active operations for some time. Nevertheless, for political reasons something had to be done.

At a conference of the available corps commanders on 29th July, the emperor rejected both Le Boeuf's plan and a variant put forward by Bazaine as being beyond the scope of the current capability of the army, but authorised Frossard to mount an operation which the latter had planned for the capture of Saarbrucken. The corps of Ladmirault and Failly were moved inwards to support the striking force, and Bazaine's corps was echelonned behind that of Frossard at St Avold. Frossard's limited operation was undertaken on 2nd August, with total success; hardly surprisingly, as the whole of II Corps was launched in a set-piece attack against the outskirts of the town, held by no more than a battle group of Moltke's covering force. But even this simple operation was flawed by poor staff work, unsatisfactory march discipline and inadequate marching performance, no division contriving to cover more than ten miles in a day. It remained a feature of the campaign for the next month that, although the French were campaigning in their own country, the standing procedures of operations in Algeria were followed, in that columns closed up tightly at the end of each day's march, and thus needed additional time the next morning to unravel. All the operation proved, as has been noted, was the physical incapacity of the emperor to command the army in the field. Nevertheless, Frossard's minor success was exaggerated progressively as it was reported rearwards, and by the time the news reached Paris, three Prussian divisions had been overwhelmed and a vital railway junction destroyed. In point of fact, no more than 1,200 German soldiers had been engaged, they had withdrawn at the cost of eight casualties and, on the evidence of a neutral observer two months later,[38] the town was hardly damaged. Saarbrucken lies deep in the river valley. Frossard rightly left it unoccupied, but wrongly allowed the telegraph office to remain undisturbed. The operators continued to send reports back to Mainz.

Moltke's design for the campaign, once the threat of invasion could be discounted, was for First and Second Armies to hold the stronger component of the French Army on the Saar, while Third Army neutralised the weaker in Alsace. Once protection of the southern flank of Second Army was assured, the Red Prince was to swing right-handed behind the flank of the French Army in Lorraine, pinning it against the Saar. Thus a static role only was enjoined on First Army.[j] This scheme was at once contorted, for two reasons. The first was a typical planner's overestimate, from which even Moltke was not immune, of the intelligence and unquestioning obedience of executants and the working efficiency of resources. Moltke had expected the crown prince's Third Army to be ready to launch the covering operation on 30th July, but the orders and timetable drew, as before Sadowa, a snarl of protest from von Blumenthal, Third Army chief of staff. His army could not be ready for at least another four days, and for the task envisaged would need the projected reinforcement of VI Corps. As Blumenthal knew full well, this formation was required to watch the Silesian frontier for as long as Habsburg intentions remained unclear and could not be moved to the Rhine for at least another week for want of rail capacity. There are more ways than one of saying 'no'. It required a visit to third army headquarters by Verdy du Vernois, one of

---

[j] Where the relevant authorities described in the notes to chapters XI to XIII are in agreement, no reference is given in this text.

the three staff colonels in charge of the sections of Moltke's staff, known collectively throughout the army, in spite of their relatively low rank, as the 'Demigods', to secure mutual agreement that Third Army's advance to contact would cross the frontier on 4th August, for the time being without VI Corps. The second reason lay in the personality of the veteran First Army Commander, von Steinmetz. He acknowledged no authority other than that of the king, and in the wake of Saarbrucken *his* army at least was ready to move. Unrestrainable by his chief of staff, and in all probability still resenting the refusal of the pen-pusher Moltke to unleash him on the retreating Austrians on the evening of Sadowa, the Lion of Nachod resolved to attack on his own. Disregarding the carefully calculated route allocations of army group headquarters, his first move on 3rd August was south-*east*wards, across the routes reserved for the advance of the right flank corps of Second Army. This incurred the first but by no means last of a series of rebukes from von Moltke, but the damage had been done. Nevertheless, the concept of operations remained unchanged, and Third Army was instructed to speed up its advance. It is worthy of note that, despite the lessons of the campaign of 1866, the march tables of both First and Third Armies consigned their cavalry divisions to the rear of the infantry, except for one division sent by Steinmetz to watch the Luxembourg frontier, for no obvious purpose. Inevitably therefore, both Steinmetz and the crown prince advanced 'blind', the former persisting with his movement west of the Saar in continued contravention of Moltke's orders.

WISSEMBOURG

The first clash nevertheless came in Alsace, as Moltke had intended. MacMahon had sent forward Abel Douay's division to watch the frontier crossings over the Lauter at Wissembourg, twelve miles north of his main position at Woerth on the Sauer and twenty miles east of the nearest division of Failly's corps, at Bitche. Failly, notwithstanding the grouping of corps proposed up to 11th July, was not at this point under the operational control of MacMahon. Given contemporary standards of French march performance, Abel Douay was a day or more distant from any support, and with the wrong force for the purpose; unnecessarily strong to watch and report, but inadequate to fend for itself and too immobile to withdraw quickly out of trouble. Douay had at least sent cavalry patrols forward of the Lauter but these returned on the evening of 3rd August having found nothing to report, in spite of the presence of three German corps, six infantry divisions, closing the river line and within three miles of it by the end of the day. The following morning, II Bavarian Corps made the first tentative contact, soon supported more forcefully by V and XI Corps. The ensuing battle was typical of those fought during the next month. Douay's understrength division was outnumbered at odds of eight to one by the German troops committed to action, and became the first French formation to experience the greater range and lethality of the German artillery. In their turn, the firepower of the chassepot, against infantry using no tactics other than massed frontal assault, cost the crown prince's army over 1,500 killed and wounded. Douay himself was killed, and his division reduced to no more than a brigade in fighting value. This was a serious erosion of MacMahon's strength, already insufficient if Alsace were to be defended effectively, and MacMahon must bear the responsibility for the comprehensive defeat of a force given an inappropriate task and inadequate resources.

It should not have needed the muddle of the approach to Saarbrucken and the inept and unsupported deployment of Abel Douay's division to convince imperial headquarters in Metz that it could not exercise direct command of all the formations in the field and also be responsible for the international aspects of the conduct of the war and the organisation of reinforcement, resupply and the lines of communication. On the day after Wissembourg, the emperor ordered the first of three major changes which were to be made over the next nine days to the French higher command structure. Unfortunately, the initial alteration produced nothing better than the system it replaced. Bazaine and MacMahon were given an imprecise degree of responsibility for the corps respectively in Lorraine and Alsace, while retaining command of their own formation. The two marshals were now empowered to exercise command, during active operations only, in Bazaine's case of II and IV Corps, and in that of MacMahon V and VII Corps. The emperor retained direct command of the guard, now at Metz, and Canrobert's corps, still forming at Chalons. Two days later, VI Corps was ordered up into Lorraine, but a combination of poor staff work, the continuing chaos of the mobilisation arrangements, and inadequate movement resources and organisation east of Chalons caused VI Corps, when committed to battle nine days after its order to move, to be still without its cavalry division, three-quarters of one of its infantry divisions and more than two-thirds of its artillery complement. Although the direct railway line petered out fifty miles short of Metz, west of Verdun, and the link via Nancy was soon under harassment from German cavalry patrols, *Grande Armée* staff and marching abilities would have made short work of the move of the whole formation in the time available.

The command structure ordered on 5th August would be enough to give any present-day staff officer nightmares, not just because of the dual function assigned to Bazaine and MacMahon as both army and corps commander. The circumstances in which command would pass from Metz to St Avold, or to MacMahon's headquarters at Reichshofen, were not strictly and precisely laid down. Imperial headquarters could, and did, continue to send orders to individual corps headquarters without informing the army commanders-in-waiting, and after three weeks of war and one of active operations there was still no design for the campaign to which the principal subordinate commanders could work. The first victim of this system of the madhouse was to be Failly, hero of the defence of the Papal States in 1867. His V Corps had suffered more than the others from the 'prevention of smuggling' deployment arrived at in July, having been strung out over the fifteen miles in parallel with the frontier between Bitche and Sarreguemines, in an effort to provide a link between the forces in Lorraine and those in Alsace. During this time, Failly had answered variously to Bazaine at Metz or St Avold, and to imperial headquarters after the arrival of Le Boeuf. Having been drawn northwards to support Frossard's operation against Saarbrucken, he was now the recipient of an inexact order subordinating him to MacMahon, in circumstances inadequately defined.

FROESCHWILLER

MacMahon, in the fashion of the time, was a fearless front-line commander and the soul of honour and integrity, who on 6th August would fight a good tactical battle against a vastly more numerous and better-armed opponent. But he was no strategist. Although now nominally responsible for three corps, he had in practice barely one. All his divisions were understrength because of the failure of the mobilisation plan, that which had been mauled so badly at Wissembourg, gravely so. Only Conseil-Dumesnil's division of VII Corps was in the field, and even that not yet concentrated. The rest of VII Corps was still non-operational. Failly's nearest division was fifteen miles distant, further away from MacMahon than the leading elements of the crown prince's army, now over the Lauter. To fight a battle on 6th August against an enemy who could deploy over 100,000 men, MacMahon would have no more than 48,000 under his hand.[39] The choice before him was to fight where he stood, or to withdraw and give up Alsace. He chose to fight, and perhaps politically had no other option. His position on the hills north and south of Froeschwiller, one of Frossard's 'positions magnifiques', avoiding Woerth, itself two miles to the east in the depths of the Sauer valley, was well chosen. Quite correctly, on 5th August MacMahon ordered Failly to join him at Froeschwiller.

Meanwhile, on the other side of the hill, the advance of Third Army proceeded at a deliberate pace throughout 5th August, general objective Strasbourg. By evening, its leading elements were closing the line of the Sauer south of Woerth but without cavalry (4th cavalry division was still far to the rear) they had no precise intelligence of the location or the strength of the French forces in front of them. This problem was in part resolved during the night of 5th August. The weather, hitherto fine, broke with a typical Rhineland thunderstorm. The soaked and dispirited French troops, many without greatcoats or the two-man 'tentes d'abri', used, contrary to orders, the plentiful brushwood of the wooded slopes to make campfires, which gave away the limits of the front and flanks of their deployment.[40]

The poor discipline of MacMahon's troops had already made itself apparent. Howard quotes[41] the parish priest of Froeschwiller, whose church on 6th August became a lazarette for the wounded:

> Everyone behaved as he wanted. The soldier came and went as he pleased, wandered off from his detachment, left camp and came back as he saw fit.

And on the following morning, the German V Corps commander felt it necessary to mount a formal assault on Woerth, which MacMahon had left unoccupied. A large number of French troops, after their miserable night in the open, had left their units to seek such comfort as the village had to offer. The point has to be made that MacMahon's army was formed from the best Algerian-recruited units and regular regiments of the line, albeit with a high reserve content.

The Froeschwiller ridge is an E-shape, eastward-facing towards the Sauer. It is five miles in length, wooded at the crests of its northern and southern extremities, with the village at its centre. The ribs of the E form a double re-entrant either side of Woerth. The length of the feature and the risk of being outflanked to the south forced MacMahon to place four of his five divisions forward. The competent and energetic Ducrot was well entrenched on the northern spur, between Langensalzbach and the Froeschwiller forest; Raoult on the more open ground either side of the village; Conseil-Dumesnil, whose second brigade arrived only during the morning, was established around the hamlet of Elsasshausen, on the crest of the southern re-entrant; and Lartigue on his right, at the high point of the southern rib of the E around Morsbronn, but with detachments forward towards the river at Gunstett. The survivors of Wissembourg, now under Pellé, were in reserve north of Froeschwiller and

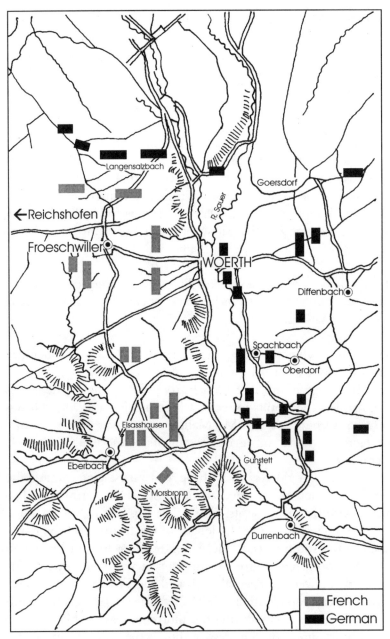

Froeschwiller, 6th August, 1870

Bonnemain's cavalry division likewise in reserve west of the village. It was not entirely MacMahon's fault that the position was too big for the number of troops available to defend it and, the deployment forward of part of Lartigue's division notwithstanding, that the flanks were in the air. Further messages from Reichshofen urged Failly to make haste. Although MacMahon chose not to order any cavalry reconnaissance east of the Sauer, he had the evidence of the battle on 4th August that he was about to be attacked by a much larger force. However, the tidy-minded Failly, confused by contradictory orders from Metz and possibly also by the reports of the battle developing concurrently to the north on the Spicheren feature, thought it unwise to move towards MacMahon until the positions he was holding could be handed over to units of III Corps.

The availability of the electric telegraph between Metz and the corps headquarters had already been responsible for a great deal of wasted movement by the units of the line, sweltering in wholly unsuitable uniforms in an early August heatwave. By the time the machines had sputtered out a four-way discussion in code between Reichshofen, Bitche, Metz and St Avold – order, expostulation, argument, counter-argument, reiterated order and decisions – 5th August had passed. Failly's leading division, that of Guyot de Lespart, did not leave Bitche until mid-morning on 6th August. Moving with no great urgency it took eight hours to cover fifteen miles. By the time Guyot reached Reichshofen, still three miles west of Froeschwiller, the French Army was in full retreat from the ridge, the battle was lost and Alsace, under French rule since 1648, lost with it. For underperforming even D'Erlon on the day of Quatre Bras and Ligny, the decision was taken to dismiss Failly. He remained unaware of this, and such was the incompetence of selection, communications and staff procedures that his replacement did not reach V Corps until the morning of 31st August, with the Battle of Sedan imminent.

The leading element of Third Army, 20th Brigade of V Corps, encountered a fatigue party of Lartigue's division drawing water from the Sauerbach streamlet soon after daybreak, and, in accordance with Moltke's standing doctrine that the enemy should be attacked wherever found, engaged them. Also obeying Moltke's principle that flanking formations should move to the sound of the guns in order to support the troops already in action, the leading elements of XI Corps to the south and II Bavarian Corps to the north joined in. Woerth was occupied and tactical control of the battle taken by von Kirchbach, V Corps commander, in spite of a wound sustained at Wissembourg which prevented him from riding. But the crown prince did not want a battle which had begun without his knowledge. Blumenthal's intentions for the day had been to close up to the line of the Sauer, reorganise for a further advance and allow time for I Bavarian Corps, 4th cavalry division and the army supply train to catch up. Army headquarters ordered Kirchbach to break off the battle. He declined, on the ground that he was too far committed to withdraw, and pressed on regardless. The crown prince, having no other option, accepted the situation and sent peremptory orders to I Bavarian Corps, his only other formation within marching distance, to join the battle on the northern flank.

Initially the superb fields of fire from the Froeschwiller ridge into the double horseshoe either side of Woerth denied the Germans much headway, the Bavarians in particular showing little appetite for a repeat of an unsuccessful first attack on Ducrot's position.[k] But by mid-morning, superior numbers and heavier weight and longer-range artillery began to tell. Kirchbach concentrated the fire of all eighty-four guns of his corps artillery on the French centre. The French guns were outranged and forced to withdraw. Deprived of their support, Raoult's position around Froeschwiller village began to crumble. Raoult himself was killed, as was MacMahon's chief of staff, Colson. Even worse for MacMahon was the success of a full-scale attack by von Bose's XI Corps, which drove a wedge between the divisions of Lartigue and Conseil-Dumesnil, captured the high ground around Morsbronn shortly after noon and posed a threat to the French line of retreat. In an attempt to restore the situation and to gain time for his forward infantry to withdraw up the hill from Gunstett, Lartigue turned to the only local reserve, Michel's brigade of the corps cavalry division, directing them to recapture Morsbronn. Charging over ground badly broken by vines, tree stumps, ditches and boundary walls, and under fire both from XI Corps artillery on the opposite bank of the river and the Hessian infantry, which had wasted no time in extemporising a defence in the stone buildings of the village, Michel suffered a disaster equivalent at least to that of the British Light Brigade at Balaclava. His brigade was destroyed. The fall of Morsbronn enabled the crown prince to mount a converging attack by all four infantry divisions of V and XI Corps on the French position between Elsasshausen and Froeschwiller, supported by the fire of the 168 guns of the two corps artillery groups. Elsasshausen fell in its turn. With his retreat now seriously threatened, MacMahon committed his last infantry reserve, the survivors of Wissembourg. As Pellé's men emerged from dead ground north-east of the village, attacking

---

[k] Although one of the two Bavarian corps was in the battle from the start, V and XI Corps took eighty-five per cent of Third Army's casualties.

southwards along the spine of the E towards Elsasshausen, they came under fire frontally from the infantry which had consolidated around the village and in flank from Kirchbach's corps artillery. This second French counter-attack was blown apart. Only Ducrot was maintaining his position against the unenthusiastic Bavarians.

By early afternoon, even the combination of unbending character and limited intelligence that was the Maréchal Duc de Magenta could comprehend that the battle was lost. It was time for another sacrificial cavalry charge. MacMahon asked Bonnemain to gain him a quarter of an hour so that the infantry could break clean. Armed and equipped as for a battle of the First Empire, the 2,000 sabres of the reserve cavalry division thundered down the re-entrant south of Froeschwiller[l] in two successive waves. But the firepower now in the hands of infantry had developed more than a little in the intervening half century. Bonnemain's division suffered the same fate as Michel's brigade, and not one of his cuirassiers reached the German positions. Nevertheless, this act of desperate gallantry enabled what was left of MacMahon's troops south of Froeschwiller to draw off.

Ducrot by late afternoon was threatened by four German corps. The time needed for him to extricate himself was bought by an equally heroic rearguard action by the left flank unit of Raoult's division. The 2nd Algerian tirailleurs (Turcos) had gone into battle with eighty-four officers and 2,216 other ranks, some twenty-five per cent under its war establishment. The regiment died where it stood in the Froeschwiller forest, firing until all its ammunition was expended. Only eight officers and 441 soldiers emerged to fight again. One was Sergeant Mohammed bin Drakhir. Entrusted with the regimental colours by his colonel, he wandered for three days in a strange land now traversed by German troops before reaching Strasbourg.[m43] Four thousand men of Lartigue's division also reached the same destination.

Once committed to battle, many of the hitherto undisciplined and disaffected regiments of MacMahon's army had fought with the utmost

---

[l] This charge is sometimes described incorrectly as 'the Charge of Reichshofen'. This village, whose château had housed MacMahon's headquarters until the morning of the battle, is three miles west of Froeschwiller. At the end of the day, the leading elements of Guyot de Lespart's division fired a few shots at a German pursuit reaching its limit of exploitation. For further discussion, see Appendix C.

[m] The day after Froeschwiller, the crown prince detached the Baden Division to invest Strasbourg. The first French city to come under a state of siege, Strasbourg was the second to surrender, on 28th September four days after Toul.[42]

bravery. But although a force of 48,000 had, at a cost of around 6,000 killed and wounded, inflicted nearly twice as many casualties on their enemy, the French had lost also another 9,000 as prisoners. Bravery had not been enough. An imprecise command structure and impossibly inept staff work had caused MacMahon to fight a battle with insufficient troops to hold a position of great natural strength. Once battle was joined, the decisive factors were the Prussian battle procedures, which brought all formations within earshot or range of messenger to the sound of the guns, and the overwhelming superiority of the Krupp artillery.

MacMahon's retreat was eased by the fact that after the battle the crown prince advanced with extreme circumspection, taking the next five days to cover the thirty miles which brought Third Army through the Vosges passes at La Petit Pierre and between Saverne and Phalsbourg. Thereafter the country, west of what is now the E25 Euroroute between St Avold and Phalsbourg, becomes much more open, but the crown prince advanced no faster because of concern at both third army and army group headquarters about the risk of an attack in flank from the north. Likewise MacMahon's shattered troops had no place to stand and fight without certainty of annihilation. Strasbourg and Toul, the latter on the Upper Moselle and only fifty miles due south of Metz, were abandoned to be besieged. It was necessary for MacMahon to go sixty miles further back, to Chalons, Aldershot of the army of the Second Empire. An eyewitness described the desperate state of the beaten army as it straggled back into Chalons:

> Disorder reigned supreme in the camp. Instead of begilt generals there were commanders in dirty uniforms, who seemed afraid of showing themselves to their men. Instead of the fine regiments of other days there was a mass of beings without discipline, without cohesion, without rank – the swarm of dirty, unarmed soldiers known as the *isolés*. There, outside the tents and huts – there was no room for them inside – squatting or lying round the bivouac fires, without any regular order, without arms, and with their uniforms in shreds, were the isolés of MacMahon, the fugitives of Reichshofen, the remnants of regiments overwhelmed and dispersed by defeat; soldiers of the line without rifles or [ammunition] pouches, Zouaves in drawers, Turcos without turbans, dragoons without helmets, hussars without sabretaches. It was an inert world, vegetating rather than living, and grumbling at being disturbed from its sleep of the weary.[44]

Nevertheless, the very incompetence of the French mobilisation process saw to it that reinforcements were available.[n] Prodigies of improvisation both at Chalons and in Paris enabled MacMahon to issue forth only fifteen days after Froeschwiller at the head of the Army of Chalons, comprising the reconstituted if poorly equipped I, V[o] and VII Corps, a newly formed XII Corps, and five brigades of reserve cavalry.

SPICHEREN

On the same day as Froeschwiller, what was in many respects a carbon-copy battle was taking place forty miles away, north of the west–east spur of the Vosges, on the Spicheren heights overlooking Saarbrucken. Here, as at Froeschwiller, a position of great natural defensive strength was entrusted to a formation too weak to hold it without reinforcement. Likewise, the imprecise French command structure, unpractised battle procedures and faulty staff work prevented help reaching the defence in time. The reasons Spicheren was a lesser disaster for French arms were, first, that supports were closer at hand and secondly, that the battle was precipitated, in defiance of Moltke's orders, by Steinmetz, whose First Army was the smallest of the three and which did not have any further resources on hand to develop the action.

After his minor success on 2nd August, Frossard had rightly withdrawn from what would have been a death trap in the valley of the Saar, but was forced to deploy one of his three divisions, that of Vergé, in the valley north of the Spicheren feature, in order to deny to the enemy the road from Saarbrucken to Forbach, three miles to the west, where stores were being accumulated to support a future invasion of Germany. As soon as battle was threatened on 6th August, Frossard split his reserve division, under Bataille, to support Vergé and his other forward division, commanded by Laveaucoupet and deployed on one of Frossard's own *positions magnifiques*; the high ground around Spicheren village and the Stiring ironworks on the Rotherburg feature. This eminence overlooked but, in terms of nineteenth-century firepower, did not dominate the road westwards out of Saarbrucken because this was out of range from the heights. Frossard's two combat groupings, each of a division

---

[n] For an analysis of the strength of the French armies in the field between 31st July and the capitulations of Sedan and Metz, see Appendix 1 of Chapter XIII.

[o] Lapasset's brigade of the left division of V Corps, together with some cavalry and artillery, withdrew towards Metz, where it became incorporated into Frossard's II Corps.

and a half, were not therefore within mutual supporting distance and he was left without a reserve.

It was a battle which the German commander nevertheless thoroughly deserved to lose. With I Corps still in East Prussia, whether because of insufficient rail capacity to move it, or as a continuing safeguard against French amphibious operations in the Baltic, Steinmetz had only two infantry corps available. Launching his attack in defiance of Moltke's orders, Steinmetz directed VIII Corps, under von Goeben, to advance westwards from its concentration area. Once across the Saar at Volklingen, VIII Corps might outflank the Spicheren position, but ran the risk of defeat in detail if there were significant French forces north of the road between Forbach and St Avold, because his other Corps, VII under von Zastrow, was directed on a divergent axis, advancing to contact south-westwards. Having crossed the routes given to III Corps, on the right flank of Second Army, thus confusing and delaying the latter in closing the Saar, VII Corps, once over the river, would soon come up against the Spicheren feature.

Von Kamecke, commanding the leading division of VII Corps, was thirsty for distinction and his troops were not yet rendered cautious by direct experience of combat.[p] Not so his corps commander; Zastrow's seniority and an adequate performance as a divisional commander in 1866 had perhaps justified his promotion, but in 1870 he was too old for active campaigning and on 6th August proved to have been promoted beyond his ceiling. Receiving Kamecke's first contact report, Zastrow allowed his thrusting junior to act as he saw fit, whereupon the latter threw in his units and formations piecemeal as they arrived against the almost impregnable Spicheren feature. Even a cavalry regiment attached to his division, the 15th Hanoverian Hussars, was sent in against the Stiring ironworks on the strongest part of the Rotherburg, with disastrous consequences.[q] Until mid-afternoon, II Corps in its two defensive 'boxes' had no trouble in beating off a series of uncoordinated attacks. But Frossard, a sapper and a military academic rather than a combat-arms tactician, made no attempt to exploit a success presented to him by the disobedience of Steinmetz and the rashness of Kamecke. Conceiving his main

---

[p] This division of VII Corps had taken part in the Sadowa campaign. As part of the Army of the Elbe, it was exposed less than any other to the major actions of the campaign and the bloodletting on the morning of 3rd July, 1866. See Chapter VIII.

[q] No equitation school includes instruction in rock-climbing. A present-day visitor needs experience neither of warfare nor horse-management to comprehend the total unsuitability of this task for cavalry.

duty to be the protection of the Forbach stockpile, Frossard contented himself with a static defence from his strong positions, and ordered no local counter-attacks against the successive but increasingly frenzied assaults of the Rhinelanders.

Frossard did, however, seek reinforcements both from Le Boeuf in Metz and directly from Bazaine at St Avold, whose III Corps was nearest to hand. As early as 9.15 a.m., obedient both to letter and spirit of the higher command structure ordered on the previous day, and having even earlier sent a model 'contact' report, Frossard offered to place himself under Bazaine's command if only the latter would come up with some part of his corps, grouped at the time in a tight lozenge formation around St Avold, twelve miles to the rear, and take over the battle.[45] It is beyond question that had either Le Boeuf or Bazaine reacted properly, the Army of the Rhine would have gained an impressive local success far exceeding that won four days earlier.

In the light of the orders given on the previous day, Bazaine's failure to grip the battle is inexcusable. Although command was never transferred formally from Metz to St Avold, a less inhibited personality would not only have ignored this formality but also have gone forward, to see for himself. Having seen, he would have demanded the utmost energy from his subordinate commanders to get themselves into the battle. Bazaine and Le Boeuf were of course participants in the four-way discussion about the tasking and destination of Failly's corps. This, and reports of German cavalry patrols between Sarreguemines and Bitche, induced Bazaine to move his southernmost division, that commanded by Montaudon, away from the Spicheren battlefield to cover the positions being vacated by Failly. Similarly, a second division of III Corps, that of Decaen, was retained, justifiably, north of St Avold to guard against a German thrust from the direction of Volklingen, which was in fact the axis of advance ordered for von Goeben's VIII Corps. But war is an option of difficulties, most particularly at the level of high command, and the triumvirate of Napoleon III, still in supreme command and with the Imperial Guard under his hand in army group reserve, Le Boeuf, who as chief of staff should have had contingency plans prepared, and Bazaine, nearest to the battle, should have cut through the irrelevancies. Three divisions were within easy marching distance of the battlefield, two could be regarded as available and one would probably have been enough to annihilate VII Corps, so mindlessly hazarded. This would not in any way have helped MacMahon in Alsace, though the timely arrival of Failly's corps undoubtedly would have done. The ensuing chaos which such a defeat would have caused to the German right wing might have been unscrambled and the ultimate outcome of the war perhaps not altered. Nevertheless, if, as Clausewitz had taught, the ultimate aim of war is to destroy the will of the enemy to fight, something might have accrued to the benefit of the Second Empire and the end result could not have been any worse.

The sorry failure of the French higher command to grip the battle was matched by the commanders of Bazaine's two other divisions. Castagny, with an initiative unmatched by hardly any other French formation commander during the campaign in Alsace and Lorraine, without waiting for orders, had marched his division towards the sound of the guns, but having reached Theding, no more than an hour's forced march from Spicheren, had become prey to second thoughts and had stopped to await orders which never came. Bazaine actually placed his fourth division, that of Metman, under Frossard's command, but omitted to tell the divisional commander. When, at 4 p.m., he was ordered by Frossard to move, Metman understandably queried the order with his corps headquarters. It took another two and a half hours to resolve the difficulty and to put Metman's division on the road. When he arrived in the area of the battle, he was no more use to Frossard than Failly's dilatory leading division to MacMahon.

The corps commanders of First Army, Zastrow and Goeben, arrived on the battlefield shortly after the massacre of the Hanoverian cavalry, followed soon afterwards by von Alvensleben, commanding III Corps of Second Army, and accompanying those of his leading units, which had emerged from the muddle created by Steinmetz on the routes east of the Saar. Goeben, arriving first, took tactical control of the battle from Kamecke, but transferred it, not to his senior, Zastrow, but to his junior, Alvensleben, on the ground that the latter, unlike his colleagues of First Army, still had fresh troops available to commit. The tactical outcome, despite the initial attacks of the leading formations of III and VIII Corps, remained unchanged for a little longer. The French chassepots continued to fend off frontal attacks, even though these were supported by better artillery. In the end it was German superior numbers rather than tactical brilliance which decided the issue. Von Glumer's division of VII Corps, seeking elbow room to deploy, outflanked to the north Vergé's 'box' astride the road to Forbach, and troops of VIII Corps appeared on the hills north of the important logistic asset there which Frossard had sought to defend. No division of III Corps having yet responded to Frossard's repeated requests for reinforcements, and with Laveaucoupet's division, which had held the Spicheren feature all day, in danger of being cut off, Frossard was forced to order a withdrawal and the battle was lost. The Germans had suffered nearly

5,000 killed or wounded, mostly from Kamecke's division. The II Corps had lost nearly 1,000 fewer, but half of these were unwounded prisoners of war.

The communiqué from imperial headquarters in Metz put the facts of this disastrous day for French arms without embellishment:

> Marshal MacMahon has lost a battle on the Sauer. General Frossard has been obliged to retire. The retreat is being conducted in good order. *'Tout peut se rétablir.'*[r][46]

Notes

[1] Guedalla, *Second Empire*, p.389.

[2] Fisher, op.cit., p.892. The treaty of 1839 was the 'scrap of paper' which brought England into the First World War.

[3] Whitton, op.cit., pp.162–64.

[4] Howard, op.cit., p.42.

[5] Guedalla, *Marshals*, p.151.

[6] Howard, op.cit., p.48.

[7] Howard, op.cit., pp.74–75.

[8] Guedalla, *Second Empire*, p.412.

[9] Whitton, op.cit., p.183.

[10] Taylor, op.cit., p.121, and Howard, op.cit., p.54. Bismarck 'topped and tailed' Abeken's factual account to make it appear that Benedetti's approach had been insolent and that the king had not only dismissed him, but had sent a message to the effect that he would not receive him again.

[11] Howard, op.cit., p.55.

[12] Howard, op.cit., p.56–57.

[13] Guedalla, *Marshals*, p.148.

[14] Von Moltke, *The Franco-German War of 1870–71*, written in 1887, first translated into English in 1907 and published by Harper Bros, London; reprinted London, Greenhill Books, 1992. The order of battle of the French and German armies is set out in an appendix.

[15] Whitton, op.cit., pp.195–96.

---

[r] Untranslatable in this context. Posters of this proclamation were still to be seen on the walls of the citadel of Sedan six weeks later.[47]

[16] Howard, op.cit., p.78.

[17] Whitton, op.cit., p.191.

[18] Ascoli, op.cit., p.53.

[19] Chandler, *Campaigns*, p.1,030.

[20] Whitton, op.cit., pp.195–97. See also Zola, op.cit.

[21] Whitton, op.cit., p.190.

[22] Whitton, op.cit., p.189.

[23] Ascoli, op.cit., p.50.

[24] Howard, op.cit., p.78.

[25] Howard, op.cit., p.35.

[26] Guedalla, *Marshals*, p.155.

[27] Whitton, op.cit., p.185.

[28] Von Moltke, op.cit., p.8.

[29] Whitton, op.cit., p.213.

[30] Von Moltke, op.cit., p.7.

[31] Howard, op.cit., p.66.

[32] Whitton, op.cit., p.194.

[33] Ascoli, op.cit., p.19, and Fuller, op.cit., vol. III, p.99.

[34] Ponsonby, Sir Francis, [ed.] *Letters of the Empress Frederick*, London 1928; quoted Howard, op.cit., p.60.

[35] Von Moltke, op.cit., p.446.

[36] Meissner, H.O., [ed.] *War Diary of the Emperor Frederick III*, by published in Berlin in 1926 and in London in 1927; quoted Howard, op.cit., p.78.

[37] Guedalla, *Marshals*, p.158.

[38] *From Sedan to Saarbrucken*, op.cit., p.90.

[39] Howard, op.cit., p.105.

[40] Taken from the placards on the guided route round the battlefield north of Froeschwiller, May 1995.

[41] Quoted Howard, op.cit., p.71.

[42] Ascoli, op.cit., p.82.

[43] Battlefield guided route, see note 40 above.

[44] Whitton, op.cit., p.202.

[45] Howard, op.cit., p.91.

[46] Ascoli, op.cit., p.92.

[47] *From Sedan to Saarbrucken*, op.cit., p.11.

Chapter XIII
Double Envelopment

Emperor Louis Napoleon was right to try to put a brave face on it, but no one believed him. The consequences of the defeats on 6th August became at once apparent at four critical centres of decision. These were in the perceptions of the remaining potential allies of the empire; in Paris; at Metz; and within the mind of Moltke, who, after having received and evaluated the results of the frontier battles, issued the first of a series of four directives to the armies, the consequence of which was the termination of the Second Empire within a month. In this achievement the forces of the king of Prussia were placed at enormous risk and Moltke's whole design was nearly wrecked by two of the army commanders. The tale of France's potential allies is soon told. The Dual Monarchy and Denmark, both with scores to settle with Prussia, declined involvement. Tsar Alexander II had already threatened to counter any Austrian declaration of war with one of his own, on the side of his uncle by marriage, the king of Prussia; and although Beust, the Saxon foreign minister of the Dual Monarchy, had personal as well as political reasons for supporting France, he could not carry this policy against the Russian threat, the advice of the army chief of staff and Magyar intransigence. The Danish foreign minister told a special envoy sent by Gramont that 'unexpected events' would not allow his government to adopt any attitude other than neutrality.[1] Italy, with no grudge against Prussia, took steps short of mobilisation to place her army on a war footing, but decided to await further developments.

In Paris, the news led to the fall of Ollivier's ministry. And in a Delphic message from the empress regent to her husband, conveyed by telegram on 8th August, based upon the belated realisation that Louis Napoleon was not in a physical condition to command his army, Eugénie suggested that the field command of the armies should be handed over to Bazaine, but warned in the strongest terms that the emperor must not return to Paris without a victory. The questions begged by this wifely direction – what was the emperor to do meanwhile and what if there were to be no victory? – need no emphasis. Trochu was summoned to Paris from his mobilisation appointment on the

Pyrenees frontier. Invited to head a new government, he declined both this post and also that of minister of war, unless he were allowed to publish his opinions on everything which had gone wrong in France's military establishment under the Second Empire. It is as though Churchill in May 1940 had made publication of his view of all the mistakes made by the National Government in the previous eight years a precondition of acceptance of office as prime minister; Trochu was no Churchill but a pedantic and long-winded bore of the 'I told you so' persuasion. This was no time to wash the dirty linen of the Second Empire in public, and Trochu was packed off to Chalons as commander (designate) of the newly forming XII Corps, almost certainly at the behest of the man who did accept the responsibilities Trochu had rejected. This was General Cousin de Montauban, Comte de Palikao. Considered too old at the start of the war for a corps command (he had been commanding the Lyon military district), Palikao in a tenure of office of barely three weeks acted with energy and decision, both in trying to reinforce and refurbish MacMahon's shattered army at Chalons and in raising and organising new forces in Paris. Unfortunately, the reverse side of the coin was that Palikao preferred to rely on wishful thinking rather than evaluated intelligence, which contributed substantially to the next disaster to befall MacMahon.

In Metz, the defeats not only forced the abandonment of any remaining strategic intention to invade Germany but also, on the same day as the telegram from the empress regent, produced a new command structure, the third since the start of the war. The Army of the Rhine was divided into the Army of Chalons and the Army of Lorraine, but without the incorporation of VI Corps and the Imperial Guard in the latter. MacMahon and Bazaine were elevated to the status of army commanders, their former corps going to Ducrot and Decaen. But even this was not the end of the story. In addition to the telegram Louis Napoleon had received from Paris, a tactful enquiry from Pietri, his cabinet secretary, may have precipitated the next alteration to the higher command organisation:

> Do you feel yourself to be physically quite competent to go through the fatigues and hardships of an active campaign, all day long on horseback and all night in the bivouac?[2]

At some time during the next seventy-two hours Napoleon III elected to relinquish chief command of the armies. His successor was arrived at by process of elimination. When the war began, five of the nine living marshals of the empire – Vaillant, Baraguey, Randon, Regnault and Forey – had been considered too old for active service in the field. Of those with the armies, Le Boeuf, reputation in tatters because of the failure of the mobilisation plan and relieved of his post as minister of war on 9th August by the council of regency, was clearly acceptable to no one as commander-in-chief. MacMahon was, to say the least, fully occupied at Chalons. That left Canrobert, by far the senior, and Bazaine. Canrobert, first to be offered the post, declined, perhaps through a sense of his own limitations, perhaps having made a shrewd and realistic estimate of the catastrophe which was to follow. Waiving his seniority, he offered to serve under Bazaine, but bearing in mind the reputations and personalities of both men, it is doubtful whether this offer should have been accepted. In the light of subsequent events it is worth recording that Bazaine, just like Benedek in 1866, had at the time of his appointment the full confidence of his emperor, the council of regency, the politicians who had opposed the war, and the army, to an extent far greater than any other possible contender. It is also noteworthy that, together with MacMahon, he retained much of this confidence into September, Mars La Tour, Gravelotte and Sedan notwithstanding.[3]

No one who rises through every rank in an army from private to field marshal,[a] earning most of his early promotions by documented acts of extreme bravery in hand-to-hand combat, can be either a fool or a coward. Bazaine was a 'soldiers' general'; happiest when leading his troops from the front and destined to give further proof of his controlled physical courage in the forthcoming battles. But, although he was not without tactical sense, nothing can be done to manufacture for him a reputation as a strategist or as a commander-in-chief. The absence of any intellectual discipline in the French Army meant that he had had no theoretical training for the task of commanding over 150,000 men in the field. His practical experience extended to the command of no more than 10,000 men on active operations, 25,000 in the Chalons manoeuvres of the previous summer, and some 40,000 on dispersed operations in Mexico. Even as a corps commander it had been noted of him that he was unable or unwilling to work through a properly constituted staff, and now he was to be denied the staff officers he wanted. He was forced to accept as his chief of staff Jarras, one of Le Boeuf's two deputies, on the ground that Jarras knew more of the wider picture than Bazaine himself or any of his own choices. That the personalities of the two men were entirely

[a] The only comparable equivalent in the history of the British Army is Field Marshal Sir William Robertson.

different should not have mattered since many 'military marriages' are founded upon a multiple of opposites. What did matter, and considerably, was that the (one suspects deliberately) rough and ready former warrant officer in the Foreign Legion made no effort to harness the abilities of the prim and proper staff officer. Bazaine had further serious disadvantages as a commander-in-chief. Although he was the youngest of the contenders, he had become by 1870 a heavy fifty-nine year old, who, unlike the Prussian generals, would end the critical day of 16th August physically drained by the exertions he had seen fit to impose on himself. His failure to grip the situation on the day of Spicheren should have shown that he would be above his ceiling as an army commander. Worst of all was his crushing inferiority complex. Although by no means quite of the lowly background he liked to make out, he was of no more than middle-class origin and there was some doubt about his legitimacy. Having, as we have seen, failed the entrance examination for the *École Polytechnique*, he had enlisted in the ranks of the army of the bourgeois monarchy,[4] but unlike the marshals of the First Empire who had emerged from backgrounds at least as humble as his own – Augereau, Bernadotte, Massena, Murat, Soult – he was incapable of assuming the character of a grand seigneur, in spite of his aristocratic second marriage. Feeling at a disadvantage when placed over his social superiors, the graduates of the *'Écoles Speciales'* to which he had failed to gain entry, and most of all vis-à-vis those who had previously been his seniors in military rank, his orders lacked decisiveness and force, resembling rather the 'advice' of troop sergeant to inexperienced subaltern. But even if he had had none of these failings, it is hard to see what he might have made of the situation on 12th August, when an imperial decree placed him in command of all the armies of France.[b] As Guedalla so aptly puts it: 'it may be doubted if Napoleon himself could have played the cards dealt by Napoleon III to Bazaine.'[5]

Given Bazaine's defects, it was of no help to him that the emperor remained with the Army of Lorraine until the early morning of 16th August. After Spicheren, the three corps (II, III and IV) of this army as constituted on

---

[b] Bazaine never attempted to exercise command of the Army of Chalons. On 18th August, he was to telegraph MacMahon: 'I presume the minister of war will have given you orders, your operations being at the moment entirely outside my zone of action.'[6] And, as Bazaine's defence might have been argued three years later at the court martial which saddled him with the blame for everything from Spicheren up to the capitulation of Metz, his responsibility for MacMahon's operations was removed as early as 21st August. See p.533–34 below.

8th August had been gathered on the line of the River Nied.[c] Rising in the hills south-east of Metz, this river, of little more than trout stream proportions, flows northwards to join the Saar, itself a tributary of the Moselle, at Saarlouis. The Nied is in no sense a major obstacle and because both their flanks were open the French could not offer battle there. Another retreat was ordered on 11th August, and the troops pulled further back towards Metz. Morale plunged to rock bottom. The storm which had drenched MacMahon's troops the night before Froeschwiller had been the precursor of days of heavy rain. Only II Corps had so far been significantly engaged, and the sodden soldiery did not understand why they were retreating. The additional bridges emplaced over the Moselle at Metz either to allow reinforcement and support of the army east of the river or to speed up its further withdrawal were swept away by unseasonable flooding and the meadows on either bank, essential as assembly areas, became swamps.

Meanwhile, on the other side of the hill, Moltke had received during the night of 6th/7th August a report of the crown prince's victory so incomplete that it was necessary for him to telegraph: 'Where was the battle, and in which direction has the enemy retired?'[7]

It was not until 10th August that Moltke had enough information to appreciate that the defeated French forces in Alsace had retreated away from and not towards those in Lorraine. The foundation of his design thus in place, he issued the first of his four critical directives to the army commanders. As he was to write later:

> The German left wing had no enemy before it, and could be brought into closer connection with the centre. To bring the three armies abreast of each other a wheel to the right was requisite. The advance of the First and Second Armies had to be delayed, as the Third Army did not reach the Saar [in the area of Saar-Union] until 12th August. The whole movement was so arranged that the Third Army was to use the roads by Saar-Union and Dieuze and to the southward; the Second, those by St Avold and Nomeny and to the southward: the First, those by Saarlouis and Les Etangs [Boulay], the last also taking the direction of Metz.[8]

---

[c] This was the 'Nied Française'. For further confusion a lesser tributary, the 'Nied Allemande', has its source east of St Avold.

This movement, if unopposed, would place the three German armies on the line of the Moselle and the Upper Saar, on a front of no more than forty miles. But if the Army of Lorraine chose to stand and fight east of the Moselle, Moltke would, before many days had passed, be well placed to overwhelm it. Discounting, as he could afford to do, the forces at Chalons, First Army could hold the enemy frontally while Second Army drove in on its southern flank. Prince Frederick Charles, whose leading elements reached the line of the Moselle at Pont à Mousson on 11th August, proposed just such a battle for the following day, but Moltke, preferring to wait for the arrival of the three corps hitherto retained in Germany,[d] rejected the suggestion. In the event, when First Army patrols closed the line of the Nied, they found that the French Army had withdrawn. On 12th August, Moltke supplemented the directive issued two days previously by ordering all three armies to advance on the broad front along which they were currently dispersed. Prince Frederick Charles secured intact the bridges over the Moselle at Pont à Mousson and Dieulouard, but Steinmetz, in contrast to his early aggression, and sulking at the reprimands for having confused the advance of the German right wing and for bringing on prematurely the Battle of Spicheren, moved with no urgency.

Meanwhile, the confused and rapidly changing French command structure ensured that their strategic design remained in limbo. As early as 8th August, while Bazaine and Le Boeuf were conferring at St Avold about the possibility of a limited counter-offensive, the emperor and Le Brun, co-deputy with Jarras to Le Boeuf, were in Metz, preparing orders to withdraw the whole army to Chalons. Two days later, with the Army of Lorraine on the line of the Nied, Bazaine proposed an even more radical expedient, a withdrawal to the area south of Toul and Nancy, from where he believed the army would be poised to take in flank any German advance westwards from the Moselle. The extreme risk of a lateral movement across the front of Second and Third Armies, even assuming the river would have afforded flank protection, appears not to have occurred to him. And even before the fall of the Ollivier administration, Paris took a hand with a warning about the political consequences of abandoning Lorraine. On 11th August, still in pouring rain, the Army of Lorraine withdrew from the Nied and pulled in under the guns of the fortress of Metz. But although it was by now fully apparent to the

---

[d] The I Corps, destined reinforcement for First Army, was moved from its assembly area in East Prussia to the Rhine in four days, an achievement to be compared and contrasted with the French failure to complete the move of Canrobert's corps from Chalons to Metz. The Prussians moved more men and more than twice as many guns six times the distance in half the time.

emperor and others that the line of the Moselle was already compromised and that a further withdrawal to the Meuse should be set in hand as soon as possible, it was not until Bazaine's first day in command, 13th August, that orders were issued to bring the whole army back across the river and to retreat through Metz to Verdun. Five days had been wasted.

The first step was to withdraw II, III and IV Corps, over 100,000 men, to the west bank of the Moselle and at 4.30 a.m. on 14th August the troops were formed into column of march. But the operation needed a quality of staff work well beyond the capability of the Army of Lorraine. In ideal circumstances, a marching column of 10,000 infantry requires about three and a half miles of road space and will take an hour to pass any given point. Given accurate timings based upon correct strength returns and calculation, even the convergence of routes into a bottle neck such as a bridge can be surmounted. Conversely, if snags are not foreseen and provided for, columns will cross each other's line of march, delays become cumulative and at worst the consequent gridlock requires hours to disentangle. The process cannot be speeded up, but a breakdown of even one wagon can cause a hold-up. Here the circumstances were far from ideal. Responsibility for the movement plan was split between Bazaine's small personal staff at Borny east of the river and the main headquarters in Metz. One of the three permanent bridges was ignored completely in the planning. It was not until mid-afternoon that four pontoon bridges were re-established and the heavy rain of the previous week had turned the approaches and ground nearby into a quagmire, impassable for horses, guns and wagons. Correctly, the supply, baggage and reserve ammunition wagons had been ordered to move first, but poor planning and indiscipline blocked the routes to the permanent bridges and congested the narrow streets of the city. It was only after the temporary bridges had been reopened that the infantry, already under arms for twelve hours, could begin to thin out. The movement table ordered II Corps to withdraw first, then IV, with III Corps, the largest, following last.

All the ingredients were present for a major disaster, from which the French were saved by the sullen non-cooperation of Steinmetz. Cavalry patrols of Second Army were by now operating far west of the Moselle south of Metz, and on 14th August Third Army occupied Nancy, but Moltke wished all the elements of his broad front advance to remain in touch. On the evening of 13th August he had issued orders restraining the leading corps of Second Army from advancing beyond the line of the Moselle. This would allow First Army to close with the position the French had now taken up east of Metz, and perhaps might create the conditions for the kind of battle proposed by the Red Prince on the previous day. But this ideal situation failed to materialise. Even with the certainty of the French evacuation of the Nied position, Steinmetz took Moltke's order holding back the advance of Second Army to apply also to himself. First Army's advance westwards from the Nied was thus set in hand without urgency, and it was mid-afternoon on 14th August before 26th brigade of von Glumer's 13th division of VII Corps came in sight of the valley of the Moselle. Evidence of the chaotic nature of the French retreat was in full view, but III Corps, now under Decaen, was deployed competently as a covering force. What had become the standard pattern then recurred. The 26th brigade, commanded by one of the numerous von der Goltz clan,[e] attacked at once without waiting for higher authority, drawing in the rest of Glumer's division and also the leading elements of the newly arrived I Corps on their right.

Neither army commander wanted the battle, variously entitled, subsequently, Borny or Colombey–Nouilly. Bazaine had chosen to command forward[f] rather than from army headquarters on the west bank of the river and his small personal staff was co-located at Borny with the headquarters of his former corps. He went up to the line, forbade local counter-attacks and insisted that the retreat must continue. Coming into range of the German artillery, he suffered a minor wound.

Although VII Corps had learned restraint from their experience at Spicheren, Manteuffel's I Corps were in their first engagement and attacked vigorously enough to require Bazaine to bring back part of Ladmirault's IV Corps to secure the French left. But Steinmetz, arriving on the battlefield at about eight o'clock, with a good hour's daylight remaining, not only ordered the attacks to be broken off but also directed Zastrow and Manteuffel to withdraw to the line of the Nied. Both corps commanders found ways of failing to comply, and were sustained in their disobedience when the king, reaching the battlefield on the next morning, congratulated von der Goltz and ordered the Westphalian and Prussian regiments to remain where they were. The intractable Steinmetz had presented Bazaine with the time needed to complete his withdrawal to the west bank. The action had cost the French 3,500 casualties, including the newly appointed commander of III Corps. The

---

[e] There were two others in senior command appointments and the future field marshal was present as a junior officer.

[f] Not unreasonably. Most generals of the time would have preferred to command a complicated operation such as this from a position which gave them the best view of the battle, in order to apply fine tuning at the right moment.

attacking Prussians had lost 5,000 in killed and wounded. It was apparent also on the morning of 15th August that the French were continuing their withdrawal. In Moltke's words: 'Immense clouds of dust were observed rising on the further side of the fortress.'[9]

A combination of unconnected circumstances had thus fortuitously created the conditions for a typical Napoleonic 'manoeuvre sur les derrières', or a Moltke encirclement operation. On the afternoon of 15th August, Moltke issued the second of his key directives. Third Army was ordered to secure the line of the Upper Moselle between Nancy and Bayon, and First Army was directed to mask Metz and to cross the river south of the city, out of range of the guns of the fortress, but without interfering with the crossing points reserved for Second Army. From the latter, all restraint was removed. Allocated the bridges at Corny–Noveant, Pont à Mousson and Dieulouard, Prince Frederick Charles was told to block the routes from Metz to Verdun in the neighbourhood of Fresnes and Etain.[g]

> The commander of Second Army is entrusted with this operation which he will conduct according to his own judgement and with the means at his disposal, that is to say, all the corps of his army.[10]

To quote further from Moltke:

> In the Headquarters of Second Army there was the belief that serious fighting with the French was no longer to be anticipated on the Moselle...[11]

The Red Prince took the bit between his teeth. One of his cavalry divisions was already probing far to the west, in spite of some wringing of hands at the risk by its commander, von Rheinbaben. At 11 p.m. on 15th, Second Army commander issued his orders. The V and VI cavalry divisions were to engage the enemy wherever found; the two leading corps, III and X, were to cross the river, moving respectively on axes Corny–Gorze–Étain and Pont à Mousson–Fresnes–Verdun. Based on assumption rather than evaluated information, III Corps on the inside flank was warned that it might make contact with 'some

---

[g] Moltke's planning was assisted and related to reality by plentiful maps of France with the detail updated to May 1870. By contrast, maps in the French Army, both in Lorraine and at Chalons, were in chronic scarcity and from an edition dated 1862, so excluding most of the considerable rail and road expansion undertaken during the Second Empire.

of the enemy tomorrow evening'.[10] The X Corps was given the objective for 16th August of St Hilaire-en-Woevres, twenty miles from its start point at Pont à Mousson and more than half the distance to Verdun, without being given any expectation of contact. Prince Frederick Charles chose to ignore a vital clause in Moltke's directive, 'with all the corps of his army'. The Guard Corps, having been allocated the southernmost of Second Army's crossing points at Dieulouard, three miles upriver from Pont à Mousson, could, given timely and correct intelligence, march to support either of the leading corps, but, if there was going to be a major battle on 16th August, none of the other four corps of Second Army could arrive in time for it. The IV Corps was maintaining the essential link with Third Army on the upper Moselle, IX Corps was a day's march behind III, the Saxon Corps similarly a day's march east of Pont à Mousson on X Corps axis, and Fransecky's II Corps, retasked on 7th August but given a lower movement priority than I Corps, had only just reached the frontier. Only at Leipzig fifty-seven years earlier had any general attempted to control an army of over 200,000 men as a single entity in battle, and, until confronted with the evidence of his own eyes, no German formation commander believed that on 16th August he would have to deal with anything more than the rearguard of the Army of Lorraine; this notwithstanding the eyewitness view which the king and Moltke had had on the morning of 15th August of at least a substantial part of the French Army struggling up the Moselle escarpment and not yet on the Lorraine plateau. In defiance of all the evidence of the campaign so far, the German commanders attributed to the Army of Lorraine a march discipline and capacity far in excess of its capability.

The two divisions of Reserve Cavalry now with the Army of Lorraine, those of the Marquis de Forton and Du Barrail, the latter lacking one of its four regiments, had not been committed east of the Moselle. As early as mid-morning on 15th August, Prince Murat's brigade of Forton's division brushed Rheinbaben's patrols around Puxieux, south of the direct route and about a third of the distance from Metz to Verdun. Rheinbaben had nothing with which to develop a battle and Murat chose not to press the action. Forton's division withdrew towards Vionville, unsaddled and went into bivouac. Bazaine was told, incorrectly, that the German cavalry had had infantry supports. No one, cavalry commander, intelligence officer, chief of staff or commander-in-chief, paused to ask where these horsemen had come from or what might be behind them. During 15th August VI Corps and the Guard, neither of which had been in action beyond the Moselle, established themselves on the eastern edge of the Lorraine plateau, VI Corps north of the small village of Rezonville and the Guard around Gravelotte, where the road westward out of Metz reaches the top of the escarpment.

First to emerge from the chaos in the valley was Frossard's II Corps, with the addition of Lapasset's brigade group from Failly's corps, but without Laveaucoupet's division, because the latter had been detached, for the unenviable task of providing a garrison for the fortress of Metz. The city would soon be isolated if the rest of the army were to withdraw to the Meuse, but, although lying then, as now, mostly east of the Moselle, it could not be abandoned. Not solely for reasons of national prestige and political credibility, important as these were; Metz, a city since Roman times, having withstood a siege in 1552, had remained in French hands ever since. More relevantly, the fortress was an essential *point d'appui* in any French counter-offensive. Frossard of course was furious at the detachment. Making no effort to push on towards Verdun, he deployed around Rezonville south of Canrobert's position, but did not attempt to ascertain by reconnaissance what there might be on his open (southern) flank.[h] Thus the inner prong of the Red Prince's two-corps flanking movement was left to cross the river no more than five miles away at Corny-Noveant undiscovered and undisturbed. Frossard could have blocked its axis of advance at the head of the Gorze defile with the minimum of effort, and one savage blow down the left bank of the Moselle might have caught III Corps at its most vulnerable and overwhelmed it. But Frossard, though a skilled military engineer and academic soldier, was no tactician. The French III and IV Corps, which had taken the brunt of the fighting on the late afternoon of 14th August, had broken clean thanks to Steinmetz' fit of sulks, but needed the following day to regroup and reorganise. By dawn on 16th August, leading elements of III Corps had reached Vernéville, three miles north of Gravelotte, but IV Corps, intending to follow on the same line of march, was still in the valley. The III Corps was now under its third commander in a week. With Decaen killed at Borny, the appointment went to Le Boeuf, now out of both his posts as minister of war and army group chief of staff. .

During the night of 14th/15th August, after the Battle of Borny had smouldered out, Bazaine went to visit the emperor, still in Metz. Napoleon

---

[h] With the result that three corps were jammed into a triangle of no more than five square miles. This was a relic of the tactics of North Africa, where the much smaller columns had closed up tightly at the end of each day for protection. It will have been noted that the German practice followed that of the *Grande Armée* in keeping the corps a day's march apart from each other during the advance to contact.

rejected Bazaine's request to be relieved of his command because of his wound with the encouraging words, '*Vous venez de briser la charme.*'[12]

On the following day, the emperor decided to leave the Army of Lorraine and moved to the little inn at the Gravelotte crossroads. Paris barred from him, his only other possible destination was Chalons, but the route he might take was left for later decision in the light of further information about the whereabouts of the German cavalry.

Late on 15th August, Bazaine issued his own orders for the following day. They are a compound of detail best left to the regimental commanders, unsubstantiated guesswork, and platitude:

> *La soupe sera mangé demain à quatre heures. On se tiendra prêt à se mettre en route à quatre heures et demi, en ayant les chevaux sellés et les tentes abbatués. Les II et VI Corps doivent avoir 30,000 hommes devant eux; ils s'attendent à être attaques demain. Les reconnaissances doivent se faire comme d'habitude.*[13]

Leaving aside the detail, over-fussy at army command level, about a hot meal for the troops before starting and the striking of tents, from where derived the information that II and VI Corps might have 30,000 enemy in front of them? 'Reconnaissances to be carried out as usual'? From the experience of Algeria and Mexico, just what the French Army should have been good at; and the recent commander of the Nancy military district must have known something about the quality of the regiments of the garrisons of metropolitan France which had not seen active service since 1859. The dereliction of Forton and Frossard, whose corps included a cavalry division, beggars belief, but Bazaine should have harried them for information, if only to validate his estimate of 30,000 enemy on the Lorraine plateau.

Early on the morning of 16th August Bazaine rode up to the Gravelotte crossroads, to find the emperor already in his carriage.

> *Je me décide à partir pour Verdun et Chalons; mettez-vous en route pour Verdun dès que vous pourrez... Je vous confie la dernière armée de la France; songez au Prince Impérial.*[14]

Thus he left, on the more roundabout route to Verdun by way of Doncourt and Étain, taking with him as escort a brigade of chasseurs d'Afrique, two-thirds of the available strength of Du Barrail's division. Authorities differ about Bazaine's reaction; was he glad at last to be unquestionably his own master, or did he regret the loss of a higher authority who could take ultimate responsibility? Both viewpoints have adherents and neither is certain. What is definite is that Bazaine, on returning to his own headquarters, and perhaps in the light of up-to-date information about the still confused state of III and IV Corps,[i] countermanded his order of the previous evening.

> *Dès que les reconnaissances sont rentrées et que tout indiquera que l'ennemi n'est pas en force en proximité, on pourra dresser de nouveau les tentes. Nous partirons probablement dans l'après midi dès que je saurai que les III et IV Corps sont arrivés à notre hauteur en totalité. Des ordres, du reste, seront données ultérieurement.*[15]

Bazaine's change of plan, accepting the loss of another day in withdrawing beyond the Meuse, was not only directly contrary to the order given him less than an hour before by the emperor, it was also based upon wishful thinking, because neither Forton nor Valabrègue, commanding II Corps cavalry division, can have carried out any reconnaissance whatsoever. The former was the first to pay the penalty. At about 9 a.m., on a glorious August morning presaging a day of intense heat, two horse artillery batteries of Rheinbaben's division came over the crest of the low ridge between Puxieux and Vionville to find a fat, soft target within easy range. Forton's division, pride of the French Army, had no picquets posted, *tents d'abri* were erected in nice neat lines, horses were unsaddled and being watered in turn at the village pond, and the troops were breakfasting as though it were the prelude to a Chalons field day. The guns unlimbered, came into action and opened fire.

Mars La Tour

By the standards of eighteenth-century warfare, Mars La Tour was a drawn battle which would in all probability have led to an armistice and the discussion of peace terms. The opposing armies ended the day broadly in possession of the ground they had occupied at the start of the battle; casualties on both sides were roughly equal, though the German proportion of loss to number engaged was far higher. But this was no longer the eighteenth century. A single battle, even one which brought over 200,000 men into

---

[i] It would have been wholly in character for Bazaine to have accepted the reports of the corps commanders without probing them, or applying pressure to make them do better.

combat,[j] was no longer an end. The objective Moltke had given to Second Army, to block the enemy retreat to Verdun, was attained in the sense that the French commander-in-chief ended the day convinced that his army could not continue this movement. Most importantly, if, as Clausewitz had taught, the fundamental aim of war is the destruction of the enemy's will to fight, the Germans were the victors beyond question. Bazaine's conduct from the evening of 16th August until he surrendered his army and the fortress of Metz ten weeks later can be explained only in terms of a complete mental and moral collapse, brought about by an overwhelming opposing force. As Ascoli has established in *A Day of Battle*, Mars La Tour was a conclusive strategic victory for Germany and the decisive event of the war. The battle was the second key point in the achievement of Moltke's design – to drive the French Army into 'the confined background of the north.'[k]

It was a battle marked by stupendous incompetence on both sides and, with one notable exception, tactics founded on the presumption that flesh, bone and willpower can get the better of firepower; hence over 26,000 killed and wounded, one in eight of the numbers engaged. Neither army headquarters exercised proper control of the battle. On the Prussian side, royal and army group headquarters began the day at St Avold and ended it at Pont à Mousson, ignorant almost until the end about what was happening. Prince Frederick Charles spent the morning similarly unaware of the desperate struggle which had developed no more than ten miles to the north-west, seeing the follow-up corps of Second Army over the Moselle crossings. When he arrived on the battlefield in the early evening, with the strategic issue no longer in doubt, his intervention was unfortunate. The German senior officers immediately involved, Rheinbaben, Konstantin von Alvensleben commanding III Corps, and Lieutenant Colonel George Leo von Caprivi, Chief of Staff of X Corps, went into battle in the belief that the French Army had 'stole away', and all they had to deal with was a flank guard. The Germans won, not because of tactical brilliance or superior firepower – Krupp artillery and chassepot tended to cancel each other out in engagements fought inside the range of the latter – but because Alvensleben, the corps commander in operational control for much of the day and as long as the outcome remained uncertain, appreciated that the only way in which he might avoid annihilation was to keep attacking. As more troops arrived, his own corps, that of Voigts-Rhetz, the two Second

---

[j] See Appendix 1 to this chapter for a discussion of French strengths, casualties and availability for battle.

[k] Chapter XII, note 28.

Army cavalry divisions, a brigade of the guard cavalry division, the leading units of Manstein's IX Corps and even, late in the day, an infantry brigade from First Army – they were fed into the battle, not just to plug gaps but often as a gigantic bluff to convince the French commanders that it was they who were outnumbered, when the reverse was the case. Von Alvensleben's direction of the battle was a model of its kind. At any time during the day, a resolute and coordinated French attack should have brushed aside what was currently in front of them, and the road to Verdun and temporary safety beyond the Meuse would have been open.

Bazaine's orders already quoted are redolent of a lack of determination and precision. If Verdun were indeed his objective, there was no attempt to impress this on the minds of his subordinate commanders. Moltke, always understated and never openly critical of his opponent, wrote subsequently, 'It is not easy to discern, from a purely military standpoint, why this course was not resorted to.'[16]

The only possible conclusion is that Bazaine was already mesmerised by the security supposedly offered by the fortress of Metz. The extent to which a commander can influence a battle once joined is defined by his ability to create a reserve, and his priorities by where and when he decides to commit it. The orders which Bazaine gave during the battle were all designed to secure not his route of strategic withdrawal towards Verdun, but the purely tactical aim of retreat into Metz.

Bazaine's own conduct during the day was that of a soldier absolutely fearless on the battlefield despite a lifetime of combat experience, but one totally unfitted to be a commander-in-chief. The engagement starting with the stampeding of Forton's division through Frossard's position, there was every reason for Bazaine's initial appearance at Rezonville to steady the line, but thereafter he behaved like Huckleberry Finn playing truant. He distanced himself deliberately from his army headquarters staff, whose workings he appears not to have wanted to understand: '*Ces bougres-là vont me laisseur seul en l'air.*'[17]

Accompanied by no more than his personal staff, two of his own nephews, one of Marshal Soult's and two devoted aides-de-camp, Boyer and Willatte, who had been with him since Mexico, he led battalions into action, directed the fire of single batteries and fought hand-to-hand to avoid capture when surprised by a German cavalry charge. After this last episode, he was lost sight of altogether, for long enough to cause Jarras to warn Bourbaki, commanding the Imperial Guard, and although the junior corps commander the only one both available and uncommitted, to be prepared to take over command of the

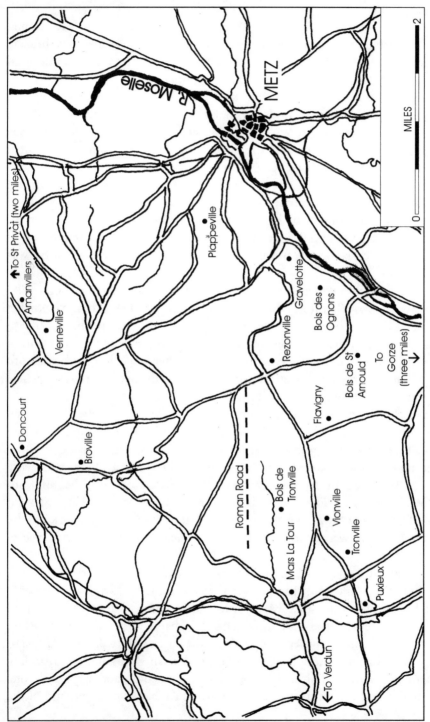

Mars La Tour and Gravelotte, 16th and 18th August, 1870

army. The consequence was that the five corps now comprising the Army of Lorraine never fought as one controlled entity seeking to achieve a single, simple and unequivocal aim. While all of Bazaine's subordinate formations would be engaged to greater or lesser degree at some point during the day, their operations were never coordinated, and when in the afternoon the commanders of III and IV Corps agreed to launch a combined local counter-attack it was purely by chance. Although it was mid-afternoon before Ladmirault's corps, last to extricate itself from Metz, appeared on the battlefield, Bazaine always had a numerical superiority over the troops available to Alvensleben and never fully exerted it.

Absence of positive operational command was compounded on the French side by passive tactics and poor appreciation and use of ground. The option of a thrust at the hinge of Second Army's flanking movement, the inner axis of which was no more than five miles from Metz, appears never to have been even contemplated. On the battlefield itself, the troops deployed as though it were a parade ground. The Battle of Mars La Tour was fought over a parallelogram of about fifty square miles, bounded on the south by the road from Gravelotte through Rezonville to beyond Mars La Tour, to the west by the Yron streamlet, and to north and east by the roads leading from Jarny through Doncourt and Vernéville back to Gravelotte. The terrain resembles the central area of Salisbury plain north of Stonehenge – long, bare ridges and shallow valleys interspersed by copses and coverts. In these circumstances, and particularly when related to the weaponry of the time, relatively small undulations of ground assume enormous tactical significance. The French corps which stood on the defensive all day undoubtedly picked suitable ground, but never sought to occupy the woodlands and villages to their front as covering positions. At the very least, these would have caused considerable nuisance value; and at best a determined defence of the Bois de Tronville, no more than 400 yards north of the road at Vionville, would have prevented the deployment of the German gun line on the ground from which Rheinbaben's batteries had first surprised Forton. It was this gun line, reinforced steadily during the day as additional batteries came up and amounting to 210 guns by evening, which underpinned the whole German conduct of the battle.

Rheinbaben was operating under command of X Corps as its screen. He had come into action much later than Voigts-Rhetz would have wished, and then only as a result of determined urging by X Corps chief of staff. Caprivi, a captain on the general headquarters staff before Sadowa, was now no more than a recently promoted lieutenant colonel, but one in a key appointment and clearly marked for advancement.[l] Determining early in the day to go forward to stiffen and enthuse the somewhat overcautious Rheinbaben, and relying on his subordinates to deal with any problems which might arise during the advance of X Corps towards St Hilaire, Caprivi had brought with him help in the shape of two batteries of X Corps artillery, as well as on-the-spot interpretation of the thrusting orders of the corps commander. He remained on the battlefield throughout the day, for much of it in advance of his own headquarters, and ensured that, as X Corps units arrived, they were fed into the battle as III Corps commander directed.

Shortly after the stampeding of Forton's division, Alvensleben, Rheinbaben and Caprivi met on the gun line west of Vionville. It was by now apparent that a fish far bigger than the French rearguard had been hooked, because 6th Cavalry Division, screening the advance of III Corps, had come upon the infantry of Frossard's corps, deployed earlier in the morning around Flavigny facing southwards, and had been driven off. Caprivi sent off an urgent contact report to Voigts-Rhetz. Alvensleben ordered the division on his right axis, V under von Stulpnagel, advancing northwards up the defile from Gorze, to attack the enemy round Rezonville at once, and that on his left, VI commanded by von Buddenbrock, advancing north-westwards on Mars La Tour, to change direction north-eastwards and attack Frossard's outer, and exposed, flank west of Flavigny. The artillery of III and X Corps expanded the gun line until it formed a three mile concave crescent west and south of Vionville. By the end of the day the guns had fired more than 20,000 rounds.[m] This weight of metal supported a series of determined attacks by the infantry of the Brandenburg Corps, who during the day were to lose a quarter of their strength in killed and wounded.

By midday, Frossard's right flank division, that of Bataille, had been driven out of its position west of Flavigny. With Bataille himself and one of his brigade commanders killed, and the whole corps in some confusion, Frossard was forced to retreat towards Rezonville. The route of strategic withdrawal of the Army of Lorraine was now blocked at Vionville; whether it would remain so would depend upon whether the French could mount an attack strong enough to force III Corps away from the ridges within gun range south of the road. But while Alvensleben understood that to cease attacking was to lose the battle, the thought never entered Bazaine's mind of offensive action along the

---

[l] Twenty years later, he was destined to succeed Bismarck as imperial chancellor.

[m] About an eighth of the total British artillery ammunition expenditure in the three years of the Boer War a generation later.[18]

axis of the road through Mars La Tour, or the alternative of a holding operation which would allow the bulk of his army to take the more roundabout road to Verdun through Doncourt and Étain. Arriving on the battlefield at about the same time as the meeting between Alvensleben and Caprivi, Bazaine's first sight was the wreck of Forton's division, which had carried away with it that of Valabrègue, and his first thought the security of his line of retreat from Rezonville and Gravelotte back into Metz. Having ordered the Imperial Guard to secure Gravelotte from any attack emerging from the south (which order did not, be it noted, include any exhortation to aggressive initiative), Bazaine next ordered Canrobert, deployed north of Rezonville facing westwards, not to remove his reserve division from its current position. The incomplete move of Canrobert's VI Corps from Chalons having left it without most of its artillery, Bazaine detached seven batteries from the army artillery park, which Canrobert deployed at right angles to his infantry, along the line of the Roman road which runs half a mile north of and parallel to the main road west of Rezonville. Thereafter it is a matter of record that for the rest of the battle Canrobert received no orders whatever from his army commander. Bazaine next encountered Le Boeuf, unlike Canrobert his junior in rank but nevertheless one from whom Bazaine had been accustomed to receiving orders, either as minister of war or as army group chief of staff. Bazaine 'suggested', or as Le Boeuf was later to put it, *'m'invité'* that III Corps should prolong Canrobert's open flank along the Roman road. Le Boeuf likewise for the rest of the day received no further orders, apart from one to send Montaudon's division to reinforce the already excessive concentration between Rezonville and Gravelotte,[n] and a further 'suggestion' in late afternoon that a local counter-attack should not be mounted until Ladmirault's corps could take part.

Returning to Rezonville at about midday, Bazaine's next experience was the sight of Frossard's corps in full retreat, between the hammer of Buddenbrock and the gun line and the anvil of Stulpnagel. No thought from either Bazaine or Canrobert of an attack on Buddenbrock's open flank which would have hacked off the head of the German advance. The lancer regiment which Lapasset had brought with him having already charged to disaster,

---

[n] By mid-afternoon, the guard, II Corps, Montaudon's division and Forton's division were crammed into an area of barely three square miles, with Levassor-Sorval's division of VI Corps, anchored by Bazaine's order, within a quarter of an hour's march. Of these 60,000 troops, only Picard's division of the guard, which had taken over the defence of Rezonville, and the guard artillery, fired another shot in the battle.

Bazaine's recourse was the same as that of Lartigue and MacMahon at Froeschwiller: 'We must sacrifice a regiment; we have got to stop them.'[19] The heavy cavalry regiment of the Imperial Guard charged at a strength approximating to that of the light brigade at Balaclava, 698 all ranks, and lost about the same proportion of men, thirty-five per cent casualties.

Alvensleben drove home his temporary advantage by committing his only immediately available reserve; two light cavalry regiments of von Redern's brigade of 5th cavalry division – strictly speaking under command of X Corps. These not only completed the French rout west of Rezonville, but very nearly captured Bazaine himself, who was at the time happily engaged in siting a horse artillery battery on the approach to the village. The German infantry fell back to an extemporised defence east of Vionville, where the 6th Brandenburg infantry regiment memorial records their loss during the day of more than half their officers and a third of their men.

Alvensleben's conduct of the battle had applied rigidly Moltke's doctrine and followed faithfully the design of his army commander. As a result, by early afternoon his corps was at its last gasp. After starting at daybreak an approach march of some fifteen miles, the troops had then been in intense combat for the next three hours in a temperature approaching the mid-thirties centigrade. Only one brigade of X Corps infantry had so far reached the battlefield, Colonel Lehman having marched his Thirty-Seven Brigade to the sound of the guns without waiting for orders. Alvensleben had used it, not to strengthen the tenuous defence line between the head of the Gorze defile and Vionville, by now capable of little more than providing a protection force for the artillery, but to support an attack by Buddenbrock north of the road which had secured the Bois de Tronville. However, these troops were now pinned down by increasingly effective fire from Canrobert's gun line on the Roman road. After the event, both Moltke and Prince Frederick Charles would appreciate how close III Corps had come to disaster, and each would blame the other for it. Now if ever was the time for the senior serving marshal of the empire to act on his own initiative and counter-attack with everything he had available. Such an attack would, at the very least, have obliterated III Corps as a fighting force and opened the road west. It might also have brought on the defeat in detail of X Corps, strung out on its line of march; and, had it been combined with a thrust from Metz directed against the hinge of Second Army's right wheel, might have brought about the conclusive victory some were to claim at the end of the day.[o] The long-term effect is perhaps more debatable. Could the chaotic over-concentration around Rezonville have been sorted out in time for the French to resume their strategic withdrawal before the second wave of the Red Prince's army could develop an attack? Would the destruction of two German corps have seemed sufficient compensation in the eyes of the critics of the empire, and indeed doubting potential allies, for the abandonment of Lorraine? Would a defeat of this magnitude have forced Moltke to abandon his offensive strategy, given the fact that he would still have had an enormous numerical superiority and would not have wished to give MacMahon time to recover? The insight of a Lee combined with the executive skill of a Jackson was needed to grasp the opportunity presented to the Army of Lorraine, but neither Bazaine, lost to sight after his escape from Redern's cavalry, nor Canrobert, was the man to take it. The latter, although a 'bon général d'Afrique', had provided abundant evidence both in the Crimea and the Italian campaign of his hesitancy and timidity as a corps commander.

Canrobert's window of opportunity existed perhaps for half an hour, and was shattered by another last-gasp attack of extreme boldness. III Corps commander yet again threw in his only available reserve, this time two regiments of von Bredow's 12th cavalry brigade, which, like that of Redern committed earlier, was from Rheinbaben's division. Alvensleben ordered Bredow to charge Canrobert's gun line and so disrupt any impending counter-attack which might be intended to drive the Germans out of the Bois de Tronville. Bredow was the one subordinate commander on either side who during the battle combined tactical sense and a proper appreciation of ground. Taking his time for reconnaissance, he identified a shallow valley which leads northwards from Vionville before turning east beyond the Bois de Tronville, so providing a covered approach[p] to Canrobert's open flank, which was as yet unguarded by Le Boeuf's corps. The charge of the 800 horsemen of the 7th Magdeburg cuirassiers and the 16th Altmark uhlans lasted no more than twenty minutes, and only half the men returned, but their achievement was out of all proportion to their numbers. Undiscovered until they were almost on top of the flank gun, a classic of surprise and tactical expertise threw two divisions of Canrobert's corps, with perhaps 20,000 men present for battle, into complete confusion. The memorial marking the limit of their charge lies due north of Rezonville. The VI Corps took no further part in the battle.

---

[o] Including Ladmirault, in a position to know better by reason of his own squandered opportunities later in the day.

[p] Bredow's approach can still be walked today. See Appendix C.

The III Corps, too late, came into line on the Roman road in prolongation of Canrobert's shattered corps, and IV Corps, following in mid-afternoon, extended the line even further westwards, towards the road between Mars La Tour and Bruville (the present D932). Le Boeuf and Ladmirault met. Whether or not appreciating the flimsy nature of what was in front of them and that they had found the German open flank, they decided to attack. Between them they had four fresh divisions to bring into action against one and a half which had by now been in intense combat for four hours. The III Corps drove Lehman's exhausted men out of the Bois de Tronville, and Grenier's division leading Ladmirault's corps was within half a mile of a burning Mars La Tour when, with no coordinated German resistance remaining north of the Rezonville–Mars La Tour road, Grenier inexplicably halted. Alvensleben, reduced to a last-ditch defence, had withdrawn all his infantry to the ridge north and east of Tronville village, prepared to hold this position to the last man and round, or until reinforced. Grenier's fears that he was about to be counter-attacked transmitted themselves to Ladmirault, who elected to await the arrival of the second of his three infantry divisions, that of Cissey, before continuing his attack. Momentum was lost, and yet again a delay of half an hour forfeited another opportunity. By 4 p.m., 20th Division of X Corps was arriving on the battlefield, after a forced march of twenty-five miles in eight hours.[q] Ladmirault drew back on to the defensive, extending the line of III Corps along the Roman road, but with his open flank strongly established around the hamlet and farm buildings of Grisières, at the crest of an eminence dominating its local approaches from the south and west.

Voigts-Rhetz, accompanying his leading infantry, needed little time to appreciate Alvensleben's parlous state. The first three battalions of 20th Division to arrive were thrust into the line at Flavigny to bolster the position held since early afternoon by the Brandenburg infantry, and, with all of X Corps artillery now in action, Aymard's division of III Corps, exposed in the Bois de Tronville by Ladmirault's hesitancy, began to feel the weight of the German gun line. Le Boeuf ordered Aymard to withdraw. As the main body of 20th Division arrived, Voigts-Rhetz ordered it into the Bois de Tronville and the Germans were once again established north of the vital route through

---

[q] To compare and contrast the German and French marching achievements, III Corps earlier in the day and X Corps by late afternoon covered twice the distance demanded of Le Boeuf's and Ladmirault's infantry in half the time. Of the French formations, only III and IV Corps, still in and around Metz on 15th August, had any appreciable distance to march to get themselves into the battle, and they took twice as long as the Germans to do it.

Mars La Tour. But Voigts-Rhetz was after far bigger game than a mere local success and stabilisation of the battlefield. Sending orders to 20th Division to continue to attack northwards, in effect on the junction between III and IV Corps, he ordered 38th Brigade, leading his other infantry division, to attack the right flank of the French line, at the Grisières farmstead. For some reason never afterwards identified, 20th Division did not receive their order and 38th Brigade, after an approach march of twenty-seven miles in ten hours, launched their assault unsupported. Their brigade commander chose to attack over ground which, unlike the covered approach found by Bredow, ran wholly in favour of the defence. Attacking frontally up the ravines leading to the Grisières farm buildings, 38th Brigade, Westphalians who until four years previously had been subjects of the king of Hanover, was destroyed, losing seventy-two out of ninety-five officers and 2,542 out of 4,546 soldiers.[20]

Again, a French commander, presented with the opportunity to gain a local success capable of expansion into one which might have been decisive, hesitated. Just as earlier Ladmirault had chosen to wait for his second infantry division before continuing with an attack which was on the point of success, so now he preferred to await the arrival of his third, that of Lorencez.[r] Voigts-Rhetz, though not in trouble to the extent which Alvensleben had been earlier in the day, but with a quarter of his corps already destroyed and all of it committed to action, called in the only available reserve. There should be no surprise that in the Prussian style the units were neither from X Corps nor III Corps, but two dragoon regiments of the guard cavalry division; no need to seek the authority of the army commander, not yet present on the battlefield; no need to seek the concurrence of the commander of the Guard Corps, Prince Augustus of Wurtemburg. The five squadrons, no more than 600 horsemen,[s] fell on the open flank of the advance resumed belatedly by Ladmirault, stopped it in its tracks and forced its recall back to its start point.

As we have seen, up to now in the war the commitment of cavalry had been the last option of both sides, whether or not ground or mission was appropriate, and so it was to be again. At much the same time, at around 6 p.m., Ladmirault and Voigts-Rhetz each decided to hit their enemy's open flank with cavalry. Ladmirault had under his hand his own cavalry division, commanded by Le Grand, and a brigade of the guard cavalry division, under De France. Voigts-Rhetz had the third brigade of Rheinbaben's division, 11th,

---

[r] Despite a series of hastening messages from IV Corps commander, this division did not reach the battlefield until 10 p.m.

[s] Two of Bismarck's sons took part in this charge; the elder, Herbert, was seriously wounded.

(von Barby), who had been providing a diversion and flank guard throughout the day north and west of Mars La Tour, as part of the deception plan to persuade the French that their route to Verdun was already blocked. Their horses had had a long, hard day but so far 11th Cavalry Brigade had taken few casualties. On this occasion at least, the ground, between the Yron streamlet and the road from Mars La Tour to Jarny, was perfect for a cavalry encounter. Starting at almost the same moment, the two masses of horsemen, 5,000 in all, met head on. There would be few major 'cavalry versus cavalry' actions in future in military history and this one ended in yet another tactical success for the Germans, because of the inhibiting and stultifying nature of the hierarchical French command structure, and confusion arising from lack of training on the French side. Opinions differ about the detail of this phase of the battle: the Germans claimed, inferior numbers notwithstanding, to have driven the French back: the French version is that the recall was sounded and Le Grand broke off the action. But yet again the French had additional resources available which they failed to commit. Two brigades of Clerambault's cavalry division of III Corps, five regiments, were within charging distance and should have joined in, but in the absence of positive orders from Le Boeuf, Clerambault did no more than send forward Maubranche's brigade to cover the withdrawal of Le Grand's squadrons. Bearing in mind what Bredow had achieved earlier in the day, the inhibitions of Clerambault by comparison cost the Army of Lorraine another first-rate opportunity, because if Barby's squadrons had broken, the French cavalry would have been on and even behind the open flank of X Corps, with the German gun line there for the taking.

While the critical area of the battle had since midday moved progressively westwards as successive formations of the Army of Lorraine came on to the line of the Roman road, attacked half-heartedly and were held or gave up just short of breaking through, Stulpnagel's 5th Infantry Division had continued to maintain the pressure on Bazaine's 'hedgehog' position around Rezonville. Although the French had in the area six and a half infantry divisions, two and a half cavalry divisions and the artillery of two corps,[t] there was no attempt at a counter-attack. The opportunity existed for the whole afternoon, but it waned towards evening, because more reinforcements for the Brandenburgers were on their way. Prince Frederick Charles received his first news of the battle in the early afternoon, and at once ordered the nearest available infantry corps of Second Army, IX Corps following up on III Corps axis, to advance as rapidly

---

[t] See note to p.505, above.

as possible by way of Corny-Noveant and Gorze, in order to reinforce the right flank of III Corps. But it was not Second Army which had the men closest to the battlefield. It will be recalled that First Army had been ordered to mask Metz from the south. There seems to have been no contact between the army commanders, either directly or through army group headquarters. Nevertheless, von Goeben, commanding VIII Corps of First Army, once again followed Prussian standing operational procedures and marched his men to the sound of the guns. Having crossed the Moselle on extemporised bridging, Goeben's leading brigade, 32nd commanded by Colonel von Rex, set out for the Lorraine plateau, inevitably through Gorze.

By late afternoon this village, at the bottom of a steep valley, presented a scene of total confusion. The wounded were being brought down from the plateau, the ambulances contesting passage with ammunition replenishment wagons; the large convent had been turned into a field hospital and every building had been taken to provide shelter for the battle casualties; the logistic train of III Corps, miniscule by today's standards but enormous in terms of road space and hard standing available in the village, added to the apparent muddle. Meanwhile two infantry brigades, perhaps 15,000 men, each formation needing nearly some two hours' worth of route space, were converging on Gorze with both wanting the same narrow road leading up the defile to the Lorraine plateau. However good the plan and the training, such a situation can be resolved only by effective positive control on the spot. Some unsung but forceful and well-trained hero saw to it that the two brigades, not just from different corps but from different armies, were fed through the administrative clutter, Rex's brigade leading, followed by 49th Brigade (von Wittich) of Prince Louis of Hesse's 25th Division of IX Corps. Stulpnagel committed Rex as soon as he arrived to a series of spoiling attacks; no thought of breaking through, but in order to maintain the pressure, and pinning down the French concentration round Rezonville. Although not engaged until about the same time as the calamitous attack on the Grisières farm buildings on the other side of the battlefield five miles away, Rex's brigade, which had already fought at Spicheren and Borny, lost some 2,500 men, at least a third of its entry-into-battle strength, in advancing to within a mile of Rezonville. No credit whatsoever to the French for holding off successive attacks and retaining their ground; with the numbers much in their favour even after the arrival of the reinforcements for Stulpnagel, so they should have done; but every blame for not even considering a counterstroke.

The contrast between the German and French commanders who at different times had the result of the battle in their hands is total. On the

German side there appears to have been no more than a minimum need either for consultation between Alvensleben and Voigts-Rhetz or of orders to the subordinate commanders as they reached the battlefield: everything was directed to the same aim – to deny to the French their route of strategic withdrawal. In the Army of Lorraine, Canrobert, Le Boeuf and Ladmirault were presented in turn with clear opportunities to reverse the course of the battle, and perhaps of the future of the war. None possessed the combination of ability to recognise their chance and the moral courage to take it. And the performance of the French subordinate commanders, brave enough in hand-to-hand combat, was tactically inept, and flabby in seeking to impose their will on the enemy.

Meanwhile, what of the commander-in-chief of the Army of Lorraine? After his adventures, he returned to the army headquarters at Gravelotte at around 3 p.m., which he did not leave for the rest of the day. Nor was any staff officer sent to find out about the progress of the battle on the strategically decisive western flank. Bazaine had under his eyes the beaten formations of Frossard and Forton, and in his ears the sound of the artillery of the Guard as they engaged Stulpnagel's successive spoiling attacks. As these grew to a crescendo with the arrival of Rex's Rhinelanders and Wittich's Hessians, Bazaine interpreted the evidently increasing tempo of the battle south of Rezonville as an attempt to cut his army off from Metz. By the end of the day the defeat within his own mind was total: the Army of Lorraine must withdraw towards Metz. He was not alone in having overestimated ever since his order of the previous evening the strength of the enemy opposed to him: there had been positive identifications during the day both of the Guard Corps infantry and the Saxon Corps, neither of which was within a day's march of the battlefield.

So all day long the noise of battle had rolled, but it was not yet over. Second Army commander, having at length arrived on the ridge above Puxieux from where Alvensleben had directed the battle, thought he discerned the opportunity for the *coup de grâce*. It was gathering dark, but nevertheless the Red Prince issued orders for a general advance. Moltke's contempt can still be felt:

> It was clearly most inadvisable to challenge by renewed attacks an enemy who still outnumbered the Germans; which action, since no reinforcements could be hoped for, could not but jeopardise the success so dearly bought. The troops were exhausted, most of their ammunition was spent, the horses had been under the

saddle for fifteen hours without fodder; some of the batteries could move only at a walk, and the nearest Army Corps on the left bank of the Moselle, the XIIth,[u] was distant more than a day's march.[21]

The troops were too exhausted to obey the orders of the army commander, but the increased sound and fury from the gun line, even though heralding an attack which never materialised, served further to convince Bazaine that he was up against overwhelming numbers. With night now fallen the battle should have ended, but the Red Prince was not yet done. The duke of Mecklenburgh-Schwerin's 6th Cavalry Division had played a useful if unspectacular role since bumping Frossard's position at the start of the battle, by providing a flank guard for Stulpnagel and in judicious local and limited attacks which contributed to the success of the gigantic confidence trick perpetrated on the French at Rezonville. As a cavalry officer, the Red Prince should have known better than to order a mounted formation to make a night attack. Nevertheless, the division was launched against the shank of the French position on the Roman road due north of Rezonville. Although the elite Brandenburg Hussar regiment, the Ziethen Hussars, penetrated to the centre of VI Corps' line, throwing this unlucky formation again into confusion, the attack as a whole achieved nothing except to add a further 700 casualties to the 15,000 already suffered during the day by the armies of the king of Prussia.

The casualty figures of the protagonists[22] of Mars La Tour have an eloquence all their own:

TABLE XVII

	Killed	Wounded	Missing	Total	Proportion of number engaged
Germany	4,421	10,402	965	15,788	1 in 5
France	1,367	10,120	5,472	16,959	1 in 9

[u] Not quite; power lies in the hand of he who wields the pen. Moltke's *ex post facto* narrative ignores the fact that the balance of VIII Corps and IX Corps, following up their leading brigades, were much closer than the Saxons. But route congestion alone was reason enough why neither Goeben nor Manstein could reach the battlefield until the next day.

It is clear which side was doing the attacking on the ground, whether well advised or not; and the figures of missing, though much increased on the French side because the wounded still on the battlefield were abandoned when the Army of Lorraine retreated on the following morning, are an indicator of individual motivation and morale.

At about 10 p.m. the battle at last died away and Bazaine assembled his headquarters staff. Orders were to be issued at once for a withdrawal as early as possible on the following morning eastwards, to the dominating ground forming the escarpment on the left bank of the Moselle. It was evidently clear in the mind of the marshal that this was but the preliminary to another retreat, because his words which set the staff to work concluded:

> If anyone thinks there is something better to be done, let him say so. After all, we must save the army, and for that we must go back to Metz.[23]

No one spoke; and it is a matter of record that no corps commander questioned the principle of the orders which were based on this directive. The only query came from Canrobert, a suggestion which, when Bazaine adopted it, reduced further his range of choice. The original French design of an invasion of Germany, if not stillborn, had been killed off by the results of Froeschwiller and Spicheren; and now their second concept, the strategic retreat to the Meuse, was also finished.

Gravelotte–St Privat

Before 1870, very few battles had lasted more than a single day, but some had been resumed after a day's interval for replenishment, reinforcement and regrouping. Second army headquarters, established for the night of 16th August in Gorze, could be under no illusion that the battle was over. Prince Frederick Charles had every reason to expect that he would be attacked on the following day. If the French were to attack at dawn, nothing could arrive in time to support the troops already on the ground, but during the morning he could count on the arrival of the remainder of IX Corps and the Saxon Corps from his own army, and perhaps the rest of VIII Corps from First Army. The Guard Corps was a full day's march away, but II Corps was hastening by forced march towards Pont à Mousson, and might be available by late afternoon. The IV Corps was needed to cover the open flank to the south and to maintain the link with Third Army. Second Army had sent little information about the progress of the battle to royal and army group headquarters, which by evening was established at Pont à Mousson, but as the night drew on the picture began to develop. Von Stiehle, Second Army Chief of Staff, suggested that those corps of Second Army not so far engaged should press on to the Meuse, but Moltke's mind was not made up until after he had ridden with the king to the heights above Flavigny early on the morning of 17th August. Arriving there at around 6 a.m., and joined by First and Second Army commanders, he could see that, though French long-term intentions were no more clear than from the perspective of Pont à Mousson, they were not attacking, which a succession of reports continued to confirm. Having forbidden the army commanders to launch any attack on 17th August and having indicated to them his probable design for the resumption of the battle next day, Moltke returned to his headquarters, and at around 2 p.m. issued his third crucial directive. To a degree, this catered for both the options still, in theory, open to the Army of Lorraine. The marches of the corps of Second Army already in progress were placed equally well either to fight on the same ground as on 16th August, or, if a substantial part of Bazaine's force managed to break through, to give it a running fight as far as the Meuse. In the former case, First Army was well placed to provide the spearpoint of a thrust against the French left; in the latter, to support and cover the flank of Second Army.

But Moltke had read correctly the mind of the French commander-in-chief, and this time evaluated accurately the capacity of the opposing army for marching and offensive action. Deducing that the more likely enemy course would be to wait to be attacked, Moltke's orders swung First and Second Armies into an enormous left hook. His decision was validated during the afternoon by reports that the French were withdrawing eastwards. Pivoting on First Army, which was directed to take up a position between Rezonville and Gravelotte north of the Bois des Ognons, and with III and X Corps remaining on the ground so hard won on 16th August, IX Corps was to come up on the left flank of the arc of the positions ordered for VII and VIII Corps, which would point them eastwards towards Germany, and, of more immediate relevance, directly opposite the centre of the ridge, six miles long, extending parallel with the Moselle from Rozerieulles three miles east of Gravelotte, through Amanvillers and St Privat to Roncourt. If this movement could be completed before the French made any attempt to fight their way through to Verdun by the direct route, their only remaining axis of strategic withdrawal would be northwards, away from the troops reforming at Chalons, which Third Army was ordered to mask, and towards the Luxembourg frontier. If not, there would be a major battle for the St Privat feature. The I Corps of

First Army was ordered to continue to block the exits from Metz on the eastern bank of the Moselle, and IV Corps was told to capture Toul,[v] exploit westwards and prevent any attack against the open flank of Second Army. The guard and the Saxon Corps were directed on a flank march even wider than that of IX Corps, and although the line of march ordered for XII Corps crossed that of the guard, Moltke expected to have all five corps, VII, VIII, IX, Guard and XII, aligned clockwise in an arc south through west to north-west some time during 18th August, with II Corps coming up to support the pivot of his turning movement, and III and X Corps in reserve.

Moltke did his utmost to restrain Steinmetz, whose assaulting corps had no distance to march, from attacking prematurely. The VII Corps, already patrolling aggressively north of the Bois des Ognons, was ordered to do no more than to harass with artillery fire the southern flank of any position taken up around Rozerieulles, and VIII Corps was not to be committed to battle without a positive order from the king. Overall, Moltke's plan moved all but two of the ten corps now comprising First and Second Armies into a position in which the Army of Lorraine was between them and Germany, and from which their line of retreat across the Moselle could, even at this stage, be severed by a determined thrust from either Metz or Chalons. If anything went wrong with the execution of the plan, the risk was likewise increased. As Moltke himself puts it, characteristically without elaboration:

> A peculiar feature of the situation was that both parties had to fight with inverted front, and sacrifice for the time their respective lines of communication. The consequences of victory or defeat would thus be greatly enhanced or exaggerated, but the French had the advantage of having as their base a large place of arms with its resources.[w24]

---

[v] A *coup de main* attempt by IV Corps to capture Toul failed. The fortress city was invested, and capitulated five weeks later, on 23rd September.

[w] In relevant military history up to this point, it had not been unknown for commanders to abandon deliberately their lines of communication; but none had consciously sought a major engagement with the main enemy army between them and home. Valmy (1792) had been fought similarly with opposing fronts reversed, but, compared with August 1870, barely a quarter of the numbers were deployed and the battle, although strategically decisive, was hardly more than an artillery duel.

He might have added that, in any resumption of the battle around Metz, the Army of Lorraine would fight in greater strength than at Mars La Tour in spite of the casualties incurred on 16th August, because of the availability of the formations which had failed to reach that battlefield in time,[x] and of the Metz garrison.

Any German apprehension of a French attack at first light on 17th August was groundless. As we have seen, the orders for a retreat towards Metz had already been issued. Bazaine, when called to account later for his actions, gave differing reasons for his decision. To Baraguey's commission of inquiry in 1871 he declared that his intention had been to fight one or two defensive battles on impregnable ('*inexpugnables*') positions in order to wear down the enemy. Two years later still, at his court martial, he would state that he and the emperor had shared the view that time had to be gained for the Army of Chalons to form and to come to his relief – which implies withdrawal into Metz and acceptance of a siege. On 17th August, Bazaine signalled to the emperor at Chalons and to Palikao in Paris that he had won a battle, but had withdrawn the army to the Rozerieulles–St Privat feature in order to replenish with food and ammunition before resuming the move towards Verdun by way of the northernmost route through Étain. These dispatches, and one to the emperor from General Coffinières de Nordeck, governor of the fortress of Metz and professional pessimist, were not only ambiguous but wrong in fact. The test of victory in battle is ground gained or ground retained. By admitting to a withdrawal, Bazaine himself called into question his claimed victory. Nor had he any need to withdraw to Metz to replenish. Although French artillery ammunition expenditure on 16th August had exceeded the German, it was no more than a quarter of the total stock with the army. Similarly, although over 1,000,000 rounds of chassepot ammunition had been fired,[y] this was less than six per cent of the Army of Lorraine's holding at the start of the battle. The position was the same with regard to rations and forage. Bazaine's army had left Metz with four and a half days' supplies of each – so much that the wagons jammed the road out of Metz up to the plateau. Moltke's acceptance of abandonment of his lines of communication contrasts savagely with

---

[x] See Appendix 1 to this chapter.

[y] This personal weapon ammunition expenditure seems a lot at first sight, but if related to the number of infantrymen available for commitment to battle it is barely ten rounds a man from a weapon capable of a rate of fire of five rounds a minute; further evidence of half-hearted, ineffective and uncoordinated conduct of the battle by a French Army whose questionable fire discipline (see Chapter XI, note 34) would have tended to *increase* ammunition expenditure.

Bazaine's refusal to do the same thing and risk living off the country in a retreat of no more than forty miles across prime farmland with the harvest only just gathered in, irrespective of food and forage stocks with the army.

It is the duty of the logistic staff to warn their commander of constraints which may inhibit his plans, or conversely to confirm that his operations can be supported fully. In the French Army of 1870, accounting, stock monitoring and distribution arrangements for essential combat supplies – ammunition, rations and forage – were all inefficient and the staff inadequate and untrained. Above all, the advice which Bazaine received about ammunition stocks from his artillery commander, General Soleille, was wildly inaccurate and unjustifiably pessimistic. This does nothing to remove Bazaine's ultimate responsibility. A commander, when given staff advice which he is not disposed to accept, has a duty to probe and the authority to override it. Bazaine, mind malletted to jelly by responsibilities for which he was unfitted and by the events of 16th August, did neither.

The Army of Lorraine fell back, in extreme discontent because the regimental officers and soldiers could not understand why they were giving up positions which they had defended successfully, undisciplined because no element of the army except II Corps and the headquarters had received rations, and in much confusion. The movement plan to retire the army through a right angle was a poor one, in that too many divisions were routed across another's line of march, and ill-judged tactically because VI Corps, weakest in terms of hitting power, was given the outside flank of the position soon to become known as the Lines of Amanvillers. Bazaine's design was for a 'shanked' position, with the corps of Frossard, Le Boeuf and Ladmirault on the ridge as far as Amanvillers, the guard in reserve around Plappeville behind the left flank, to which Bazaine was always sensitive, and VI Corps making a right angle on the spur leading westwards towards Vernéville. But Canrobert complained that this deployment would leave his right flank (and thus that of the army) '*en l'air*'. Bazaine made no attempt to enforce his authority over the social superior who had commanded an army in which Bazaine himself had had no more than a brigade. In consequence, with the guard still retained at Plappeville, which was also the location of army headquarters, the other four corps were in a linear deployment (II–III–IV–VI) along the six miles of ridge from Rozerieulles to St Privat, with Canrobert's flank no less '*en l'air*' than it would have been at Vernéville and with no flexibility left in the conduct of the defence. If the Lines of Amanvillers could not be held, the Army of Lorraine would have no course open other than to retreat into Metz.[z]

The enormous natural strength of the Lines of Amanvillers remains apparent today, despite some major environmental surgery round the southern extremity of the position. The Vernéville spur separates the approaches from the Lorraine plateau, and produces for each half of the feature a different but equally effective natural defence, both of which were much sought after by fortress architects. On the southern half of the position, the Mance streamlet originates on the spur and flows south, following the line of the present D11 road for five miles before joining the Moselle at Ars, south of Metz. The stream is at the bottom of a very steep wooded ravine, crossed in 1870 by a causeway between Rozerieulles and Gravelotte and formed a natural moat. In addition, the Point du Jour feature at the southern end of the ridge was a natural redoubt, completely dominating the approaches to the ridge from south to west and, because slightly advanced from the feature, perfectly placed to pour enfilade fire into any frontal attack directed against the positions on the ridge between Rozerieulles and Amanvillers. There is no covered approach.

This position was allotted, quite correctly, to Frossard's corps which, after its bad start to the day, had spent 16th August in Bazaine's 'box' round Gravelotte. Frossard's limitations as a tactician have already been noted, but he had an unquestioned eye for good defensive ground. With more time at his disposal than any of the other corps commanders, his engineer expertise had enhanced the already considerable natural defensive strength of his sector. His troops were dug in, in depth, and placed to provide mutual support, not just to each other but across the fronts of III and IV Corps to the maximum range of their weapons. North of Frossard's position, as far as the village of Amanvillers, the corps of Le Boeuf and Ladmirault had entrenched their positions on the ridge, but neither thought to occupy any of the solid stone farm buildings, hamlets and coverts on the western slope of the feature, which would have added depth to their defence.

The approach to the ridge north of the Vernéville spur has no such obstacle as the Mance ravine, but the ground nevertheless gives the defence a comparable advantage. The Lorraine plateau rises upwards in a long bare

---

[z] The author, having walked the ground when researching for this book, considers that Bazaine's first thoughts were right – especially if Canrobert's corps had been tasked with conducting a fighting withdrawal to St Privat once the Vernéville spur became untenable. See Appendix C.

slope, forming a natural glacis to the crest of the ridge between the villages of Amanvillers and St Privat. North of St Privat the ground falls away, the hamlet of Roncourt less than a mile north of St Privat providing the last of the commanding ground. This sector was entrusted to Canrobert, the worst choice because, without his engineer park and short of artillery which would inhibit both preparation and conduct of a defensive battle, his corps was the weakest. He would also be compelled to refuse his right flank as a precaution against the whole line being outflanked to the north. Apart from loop-holing the western walls of the houses in St Privat, Canrobert did little to strengthen his sector, whether through shortage of time, lack of entrenching tools or contempt for the spade as a weapon of war, but he did have the tactical acumen to secure a natural strong point a mile west of the ridge between St Privat and Roncourt. The hamlet of Ste Marie aux Chênes is a natural outpost, but Canrobert could not afford to allot to it more than one understrength regiment from Lafont's division and a single battery of four pounders. Even this small force was not deployed until the morning of 18th August; too late to do much to improve the natural defensive strength of the village. Canrobert's hitting power was further eroded by the return to army reserve of the seven batteries attached to him on 16th August, and he had no mitrailleuse batteries.[aa]

Bazaine's positioning of his reserve formation, the Imperial Guard, reflected his excessive and unreasonable preoccupation with the security of his left flank and line of retreat into Metz. At Plappeville, Bourbaki was directly behind the strongly-positioned corps of Frossard and Le Boeuf, but an hour's march away from Canrobert. The only order he received from Bazaine during 18th August until too late was one to hold the Guard 'at readiness'. The commander-in-chief of the Army of Lorraine spent the day in and around Plappeville, almost comatose in a state of what might now be diagnosed as stress-induced inertia and extreme battle fatigue. In contrast to his physical courage on 16th August, he never went to see for himself any part of the line nor sent any of his staff to observe and report. He relied for information about what was happening on his right flank upon flag signals transmitted from St Privat via a church tower in Metz. In response to successive messages from early afternoon onwards, first from Ladmirault asking for the Guard to launch a counterstroke, and later, of increasing urgency from Canrobert, pleading for

---

[aa] A more logical movement plan would have placed Canrobert's corps between Frossard and Le Boeuf on the ridge, with Ladmirault taking the outside flank; also, by sandwiching the weakest formation between two stronger ones, far better tactically.

reinforcement to safeguard the open flank clearly about to be enveloped, Bazaine doled out reserves like Scrooge distributing Christmas boxes. The Guard was never committed; at his court martial, Bazaine would advance the incredible proposition that it was for the commander of the reserve to decide where, when and in what strength to commit it. All that Canrobert received was one artillery battery and a small ammunition resupply. Thus, Bazaine's defensive layout for a set-piece battle on ground of his own choice was seriously flawed, and would attract considerable criticism as the first effort of a staff college student; for his conduct of the battle, the kindest award is 'aegrotat'.

Thus the stage was set for the biggest set-piece battle, Leipzig apart, in military history to date. While authorities differ, as for Mars La Tour and for much the same reasons, on the number of troops actually engaged, the two sides together had at least 300,000 infantry and artillerymen on hand and available to be committed. The Army of Lorraine went into battle at much the same strength as had reached the battlefield by the end of 16th August, the casualties of that day being offset by the availability of Lorencez's division of IV Corps. On the German side, Moltke had eight corps available and by the end of the day six had been committed, the exceptions being the heroes of 16th August, III and X Corps. Only the artillery of the latter was engaged on 18th August. Apart from one act of senseless immolation perpetrated on the 1st Pomeranian uhlan regiment of I Corps cavalry division, no cavalry took part on either side. Ignoring therefore all cavalry apart from this regiment, it seems reasonable to suggest starting strength figures of 200,000 Germans and 120,000 French. By early morning on 18th August, the German royal and army group headquarters had established itself on the heights above Flavigny, where Moltke had on the previous day briefed First and Second Army commanders. These orders he had, as we have seen, confirmed subsequently in writing. From that point, there was no more than a landscape view of the French position beyond the Mance ravine, too far away to make out any detail through the battle smoke and heat haze, and no view whatever of the ground north of the Vernéville spur six miles distant.

The working element of the headquarters, fewer than 100 of all ranks in the three staff sections of the 'Demigods', was encumbered as at Sadowa by a crowd of hangers-on. There was the civil administration of Prussia, represented by Bismarck; War Minister Roon; the king's military cabinet and suite; extraneous members of the Prussian royal family, including the titular commander-in-chief of the Prussian navy; foreign observers and members of the ruling families of the lesser German principalities, who, if too old to be at the head of their troops, nevertheless found it prudent to be present. The whole was supported by aides-de-camp, grooms, horseholders and servants; and, an innovation since 1866, war correspondents, welcomed by Moltke and subject to no censorship. Leaving aside this gilded gaggle, the task of the supreme command in what was intended to be a decisive battle was to apply fine tuning, encouragement, restraint or amendment, whichever might be appropriate, to the execution of the design for battle, but, above all, to create, control and commit at the decisive time and place a reserve of adequate strength. Moltke's directives to the army commanders invariably included a rider to the effect that further orders would be issued in the light of events. Two of his aphorisms, that no plan survives contact with the enemy, and that if the enemy is thought to have three courses open he will inevitably choose the fourth, encapsulate his understanding of the uncertainty of battle. Both presuppose comprehension of the necessity to create and maintain in being a reserve, and of the need for a control and communication mechanism to ensure that this is committed at the right place and time. On 18th August, army group headquarters made two decisions only, both negative. One was shown almost at once to be wrong, and the other, taken in panic, was both mistaken and unnecessary. The king was much more than a figurehead, and Moltke something less than a Merovingian mayor of the palace or shogun to the Kyoto emperor. Both must share the responsibility for a grotesque failure of control which risked the whole battle. The arch-planner had totally succeeded in bringing all available forces to the decisive battlefield; but once they were there he made no attempt to command them.

With army group headquarters abdicating control of the action, much depended on the army commanders. Both made mistakes, predictable in terms of character and track record, which would have cost the battle against a more aggressive and tactically aware opponent. Moltke had some inkling of at least part of this, because during the morning of 18th August he repeated his order of the previous day to Steinmetz, which reserved to army group headquarters the decision on when to commit VIII Corps.

Moltke's scythe, five corps at the cutting edge, was designed to place the centre corps, IX, against the right flank of what was thought to be the French defence, with the guard and the Saxons intended to outflank it. Ideally, all five corps would engage simultaneously; hence the restraining orders to Steinmetz, because VII and VIII Corps were already on their start lines. Moltke's intention was frustrated at once by a planning mistake and false assumptions. Given the points they had reached when Moltke issued his written orders on 17th August, the Guard Corps should have been on the outside flank, with XII

Corps between them and Manstein. But whether through oversight or for a political reason, to encourage the Saxons, worthy opponents in 1866 and new adherents now, XII Corps was allotted the post of honour on the open flank, and the march of the Guard Corps was delayed for two hours to allow them to pass.[bb] Inevitably, Manstein's divisions, as well as those of First Army, would be poised to attack long before the two outside corps could support them. The detail of Second Army's orders enjoined a pattern of march never attempted previously on the same scale and never contemplated thereafter. Ignoring roads, and with the ground hardened by five days of baking sunshine, the three assault corps of Second Army advanced in solid divisional phalanxes across country, with the divisional and corps artillery groups filling the gaps between the marching divisions. Thus, the artillery could at any time be ordered to advance ahead of the infantry in order to provide the shock action hitherto considered to be the role of heavy cavalry, but, in the light of improved defensive firepower, demonstrably so no longer. The clouds of dust kicked up on yet another day of intense heat by perhaps 60,000 pairs of feet and 3,000 artillery horses should have left the Army of Lorraine in no doubt regarding what was about to hit it, where and even when, as it is not difficult to estimate the rate of progress of a large body of troops on the march in open country. There was no cavalry reconnaissance in front of Second Army's advance to contact.[cc] The French right wing was assumed, not known, to rest on Montigny, where the Vernéville spur joins the main ridge. It was not until late morning that Manstein discerned in front of Amanvillers, a mile north of Montigny, a French encampment, in Moltke's phrase, 'apparently in negligent repose.'[25] It should have been apparent to Manstein that he had struck not the French right flank, but their centre. Although Prince Frederick Charles endeavoured to restrain Manstein from attacking, the latter, perhaps feeling that what had worked for III Corps commander two days previously would now work for him, had already sent forward nine of his fourteen artillery

---

[bb] It is inconceivable that an order of this importance was not checked before signature and distribution. In the author's opinion, therefore, the decision was deliberate.

[cc] Although 5th Cavalry Division was fought out by its exertions on 16th August, and 6th wasted by the Red Prince at the end of the day, there were still two brigades of the guard cavalry division and the cavalry division of the Saxon Corps, at least 4,000 horsemen even allowing for straggling and detachment, who had not fought on 16th August and so were available to the Second Army commander to screen and gather information in advance of the 'scythe'. He ignored them.

batteries to a point at which they were an hour ahead of his leading infantry. The roar of the guns started at around midday.

An exaggerated use of the Prussian tactic which used artillery to blast a path for the infantry brought Manstein's unprotected gunners within the effective interdiction range of the chassepot. His gun detachments were thus exposed to the risk of heavy casualties before an infantry attack could be mounted. But because the chassepot had twice the range of the needle gun of the German infantry, the latter would have a bad quarter of an hour if their massed frontal assaults, over ground bare of cover and lashed by the fire of the French infantry, were deprived of artillery support. The IX Corps were the first to experience this recurring feature of the battle on 18th August, which, aggravated by the mistakes of the high command, came near to bringing about a comprehensive defeat for the German army. Before Manstein's infantry could come up, the batteries he had sent forward were forced to withdraw. Notwithstanding Ladmirault's unimaginative neglect of using the woods and farm buildings on his front to cause delay and casualties ahead of the battle for his main position, the successive attacks of IX Corps throughout a long hot afternoon were held off without difficulty. Manstein's situation was improved somewhat when the Guard Corps artillery came into action on his left, but it was late afternoon before the guard infantry divisions could develop their attack against a French position clearly extending much further northward than had been expected. By that time, IX Corps, having taken nearly 5,000 casualties and gained not a yard of significant ground, was fought out, held on its start line and long vulnerable to a French counter-attack. Ladmirault's request to Bazaine to launch the Imperial Guard in order to complete the defeat of Manstein's corps was rejected, and, as has already been mentioned, Bazaine never made the twenty minute ride from Plappeville to see for himself. Thus the battle at what was evidently its geographic centre reached a stalemate, which could only be broken by events elsewhere.

Predictably, the noise of the battle three miles to the north was sufficient inducement to Steinmetz to disobey his orders. The VII Corps involvement soon went beyond the artillery interdiction to which they had been limited by Moltke's direction and VIII Corps commander, having already twice, at Spicheren and on the evening of Mars La Tour, gained great credit by marching towards the sound of the guns, now did so again, notwithstanding the repeated orders subordinating him to army group headquarters. As Manstein fruitlessly assaulted Ladmirault's position, so Steinmetz threw in VII and VIII Corps against Frossard and Le Boeuf. If the result in the centre was stalemate, that in the south was slaughter – of German soldiers. The afternoon of Gravelotte was a foretaste of the Somme, but with the French, not the Germans, in dominating defensive positions, able to bring overwhelming firepower to bear against unprotected infantry. Even what was thought to be a local success secured by VIII Corps in mid afternoon was in fact only the prelude to further disaster for German arms.

The farmstead of St Hubert lay on a false crest at the head of a re-entrant leading eastwards from the Mance ravine north of the Point du Jour, where Frossard was strongly established. To the Germans, looking upwards towards St Hubert, the buildings appeared to be the key to the centre of the French position, from which, once secured, their defence could be rolled up in both directions. From the French side, it remains clear to the present-day that they were nothing of the kind. St Hubert was dominated, not only from the natural bastion of Point du Jour, but also by Le Boeuf's positions to the east and north, and any troops attacking it from the re-entrant entered a salient overlooked and beaten by chassepot fire from three sides. The whole of VIII Corps, with the exception of Rex's brigade which had suffered so many casualties forty-eight hours previously, was thrown at St Hubert, notwithstanding the protests of the corps commander. Few reached it; those that did could use the stone buildings for protection and to cobble together a strongpoint defence, but the farm was in no sense the launch pad for the next phase operation which Steinmetz was soon to urge. Having sent back an absurdly incorrect message to army group headquarters that the ridge in front of him had been captured[dd] 'with drums beating and bugles sounding', Steinmetz allowed himself to be deceived by the sight of the French infantry apparently abandoning St Hubert, in fact withdrawing to positions further up the ridge out of sight from the ravine, and a slackening of French artillery fire, in reality for ammunition replenishment. Notwithstanding the objections of von Goeben, whose corps he had all but wrecked, Steinmetz now threw in I Corps cavalry division across the Mance ravine causeway, with the aim of passing VIII Corps artillery across to St Hubert. The ground was totally unsuitable for cavalry action and dominated by the firepower of the defence. The only regiment to cross the causeway, the 1st Pomeranian uhlans, lost half its strength almost at once, and of the four batteries which succeeded in breaking through the curtain of fire only one gun was still in action at nightfall.

[dd] Someone at army group headquarters, the king or Moltke for instance, might have punctured this bombast by enquiring, 'By whom?' in view of the repeated orders given to Steinmetz.

Nothing daunted, Steinmetz next presented himself at army group headquarters, which by late afternoon had come down from the heights above Flavigny to a small eminence north of Gravelotte, where they had a 'front stalls' view[ee] of the southern end of the battlefield, but were even worse placed to comprehend what might be happening north of the Vernéville spur. Notwithstanding the double disobedience of Steinmetz, the king and, by implication, Moltke, agreed that the only available reserve, Fransecky's corps, just arrived on the battlefield by forced march from the Rhine and intended to reinforce Second Army, should consolidate and exploit the opportunity Steinmetz claimed to have gained. For II Corps, it was a classic example of being in the wrong place at the wrong time. Evening was drawing on, the daylight fading but nevertheless II Corps made a significant contribution to the human sacrifice offered up by Steinmetz. Moltke would write later:

> It might have been more proper if the chief of the general staff of the army [i.e. himself], who was on the spot at the time, had not permitted this movement at so late an hour in the evening.[26]

The gathering darkness was enough to cause confusion. The leading elements of II Corps, having picked their way through the carnage in the Mance ravine and run the gauntlet of French artillery fire, were fired on by their own side as they approached St Hubert, in the belief that they were a French counter-attack. It was twenty minutes and cost many casualties before the muddle was sorted out, but it was too much for some of the troops. The Supreme Warlord and his chief of staff were witnesses of the unedifying spectacle of Prussian troops broken and running away in disorder. The exact extent of the disaster to First Army was not immediately clear, but that it was a disaster was beyond doubt. When the casualties came to be counted, First Army had lost 6,000 men, to no purpose whatever. Army group headquarters took its second decision of the battle, and orders were issued to clear all the Moselle crossings in case a retreat had to be set in hand.

But just when it appeared that the French had won a decisive victory south of Amanvillers, the battle was being cast away in the north. However, this was not at once apparent to Moltke. It was midnight before he knew that the disaster to First Army had been retrieved, but not by the skill of Prince Frederick Charles and his corps commanders. Concurrently with the massacre

---

[ee] Too good, because the supreme headquarters came within range of chassepot fire and the sailor-prince Adalbert had his horse killed under him.

of the Pomeranian cavalrymen, the Guard Corps, in the northern half of the battle area, became the next candidates for slaughter. Their commander, Prince Augustus of Wurtemburg, already disgruntled by the preference shown to the Saxon Corps, determined to win the battle on his own before the crown prince of Saxony could intervene in time to earn a share of the glory. Nor did his army commander do anything to restrain him. With IX Corps on his right fought out, the commander of the Guard Corps, from around 4.30 onwards, launched his infantry in a series of attacks against the outpost at Ste Marie aux Chênes and up the open slopes leading to Amanvillers and St Privat. Like Manstein and Steinmetz, Prince Augustus had nothing to show for 8,000 killed and wounded, one-third of the infantry strength of his command, most of whom were lost within forty minutes of commitment to battle.

Description of the action, or rather want of it, must now pass to the French side. From mid-afternoon onwards, Canrobert could see great clouds of dust representing the Saxon Corps moving over the ground to the west, north-west and finally closing in on him from the north. He sent message after message to Bazaine warning that his open flank was about to be turned, but the army commander did nothing until 6 p.m., when he ordered the guard to move northwards from Plappeville to reinforce Canrobert. By then it was too late; those with least spirit for the fight were streaming away from St Privat. But the right wing of the Army of Lorraine did not break; Canrobert's refused flank at Roncourt gave a good account of itself against the Saxons and it was the massed fire of over 200 guns rather than infantry assault which drove Canrobert out of St Privat. Bazaine's concern for his line of retreat by his left proved groundless because VI Corps withdrew by minor roads down the escarpment into Metz, as Canrobert was later to claim, in good order. Nevertheless, the loss of the ridge north of Amanvillers forced the abandonment of the whole position. At a cost of 13,000 casualties in killed, wounded or missing, eighty per cent from IV and VI Corps, the French had inflicted a loss of 20,584 on the Germans.[27] But a defensive battle fought on ground chosen by Bazaine had been not so much lost as thrown away by his inability to grasp the situation. The Army of Lorraine had no option left but to retreat into Metz.

Sedan

Early on the morning of 19th August German patrols, having traversed the carnage in the Mance ravine and on the glacis west of St Privat, found that the positions the Army of Lorraine had held to such effect throughout the

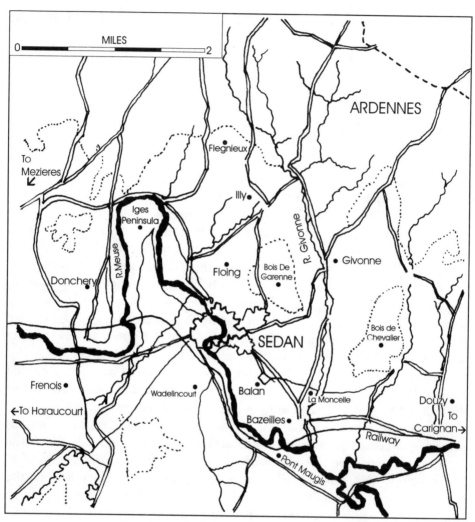

Sedan, 1st September, 1870

previous day had been vacated during the night. Gaining the crest of the ridge, they looked down into the valley of the Moselle and saw the little *tentes d'abri* planted under the guns of the fortifications on the western enceinte of Metz. Moltke lost no time at all in ordering a regrouping to maintain the pressure on the beaten enemy. By eleven o'clock the same morning his fourth critical directive of the campaign had been approved by the king and was on its way to the army commanders.[28] No fewer than seven corps, comprising the three which hitherto had formed First Army and II, III, IX and X from Second Army, were grouped under Prince Frederick Charles, whose headquarters was set up at Corny, and charged with the investment of Metz. They moved fast enough to ensure that 19th August was the last day of uninterrupted communication between Bazaine and his political superiors, whether at Paris or Chalons. Within a week Metz was completely cut off from the outside world, except for such communications as Prince Frederick Charles chose to allow through, and a few brave individuals prepared, on pain of death, to hazard the lines of the besieging army. All the German formations except I Corps were positioned west of the river, in an arc of twenty-five miles. The characteristic attention to detail of the Prussian general staff provided additional pontoon bridges over the river north and south of the city, and unobstructed internal routes on the west bank to ensure the rapid reinforcement of any part of the blockading army, whether attacked by sortie from the garrison or by relieving force from the west. The heights either side of the river allowed the Germans to keep the besieged army under permanent surveillance. Supply depots were established at Pont à Mousson and Remilly.[ff]

Although Metz was fully invested, with earthworks completed on both banks of the river, the city was never formally besieged in the manner of previous centuries, with saps, parallels and breaching operations. But as each week went by the cordon round the city was made increasingly effective by telegraph and railway links, and all the Red Prince had to do was to wait for the population to be starved out. In contrast to an earlier siege (in 1552), the *'bouches inutiles'* had not been removed. On the contrary, the number of civilians had been increased by many of the inhabitants of the villages on the Lorraine plateau, who had perhaps been quicker to appreciate what was about to happen than Bazaine and his staff. The Army of Lorraine began to shed prisoners at once, in the shape of hungry soldiers foraging for potatoes beyond the limits of the fortifications.

[ff] Between St Avold and Metz, and not to be confused with the 'Remilly' on the Meuse five miles south of Sedan.

Leaving the organisation of Third Army unaltered for the moment, Moltke grouped the remaining formations, the Guard Corps, IV and XII Corps and the 5th and 6th cavalry divisions, once reinforced and remounted, into an 'Army of the Meuse'. Command of this was given not to Steinmetz, who was sacked after refusing to accept subordination to Prince Frederick Charles, nor to the senior corps commanders in Prussian service (Manteuffel and Prince Augustus of Wurtemburg), but to the crown prince of Saxony, whose younger brother, Prince George, took over XII Corps.[gg] Moltke directed the Army of the Meuse and Third Army to close the line of the Meuse as soon as possible, on a broad front between Commercy and Verdun, and then, by 26th August, to 'converge' to reach the line Ste Menehould-Vitry le François, the latter on the Marne and no more than twenty miles south-east of Chalons. Royal and army group headquarters moved first from Pont à Mousson to Bar-le-Duc, and then, on 26th August, to Clermont en Argonne, six miles east of Ste Menehould. A glance at the map shows that this 'convergence' claimed by Moltke in his memoirs[29] is very slight, thirty miles down to twenty-seven, but Third Army was kept deliberately a day's march ahead of the Army of the Meuse, so that any counterstroke mounted from Chalons could be met simultaneously both in front and flank by all eight corps of Moltke's hunting pack.

On 24th August, a cavalry patrol from the Rhine Provinces dragoon regiment of 4th cavalry division, screening the advance of Third Army, penetrated to Chalons and the permanent camp at Mourmelon. Both were found deserted and had evidently been abandoned in a hurry. Captured documents indicated that MacMahon had withdrawn north-westwards towards Rheims. From there, his army would be placed to either withdraw further on Paris, cover the approach to the capital from the east or to advance towards any attempt at a breakout from Metz. This information was corroborated[hh] by reports in the uncensored Paris press, sent to Moltke from

---

[gg] It can be argued that the crown prince of Saxony gained this promotion on merit, quite apart from the political arguments in its favour. In the inevitable reaction when the appalling casualty lists of the battle on 18th August became apparent, the king was devastated at the slaughter among the guard corps, and Bismarck stated openly that people had become sickened of the butchery of Steinmetz. The Lion of Nachod was sent to take up the ceremonial and representative functions vacated by Manteuffel when I Corps was ordered from East Prussia to reinforce First Army. Manteuffel, disappointed of promotion on this occasion, was given an army command later in the war.

[hh] But not, of course, confirmed.

London, that MacMahon was already at Rheims, and also by a report of a debate in the chamber which had demanded that MacMahon should march to relieve Bazaine. Moltke accordingly issued orders which realigned the advance of his striking force from westwards to north-west towards Rheims, with Third Army pivoting on the Army of the Meuse. The crown prince of Saxony's cavalry was directed to patrol north of the Argonne to the line Buzancy–Vouziers, on the Aisne, from where, as Moltke claimed, 'a thorough insight into the situation could not but be obtained.'[30]

Thus the week which followed the victory won at such enormous cost on the slopes of Gravelotte–St Privat had done much to bring to fruition Moltke's design for the campaign. He could not have foreseen either that what was the first army of France – not 'the last' as Napoleon III had mourned when he said goodbye to Bazaine on the morning of Mars La Tour – would so soon end up immured in a fortress, or that MacMahon, through a combination of misplaced chivalry and political misdirection, would embark upon a death ride. What was clear at the start of the last week in August was that the element of the French Army still with liberty of movement, unless it withdrew to Paris at once, was being driven back 'from the fertile southern provinces into the more confined background to the north'.[ii] And a much more enticing strategic prospect was beginning to emerge. If MacMahon withdrew to Paris, fair enough; the Germans were now deep into France and, even if the whole of the Red Prince's Army had to remain committed to the siege of Metz, Moltke had still eight corps to deal with the remains of the army beaten at Froeschwiller, however augmented with what had been cobbled together since. But what if MacMahon were to be compelled for political reasons to march towards Bazaine? An advance by the direct route eastwards from Rheims to Metz was precisely the contingency which Moltke's echelonned deployment was best placed to meet. A march by a more roundabout northward route, uncovering Paris, would lead the French dangerously close to the frontier with neutral Belgium and could not on purely military grounds be expected. 'Such a move seemed strange, and indeed somewhat venturesome; but nevertheless it was possible.'[31]

The fine tuning ordered by Moltke on 25th August catered also for this least probable course. He transferred command of the two Bavarian corps from Third Army to the crown prince of Saxony's army, giving the latter five corps should a battle develop on the right bank of the Meuse, which Moltke at the time, and for a few days longer, considered to be the more likely

---

[ii] See Chapter XII note 28.

probability.[31] Their concentration could be achieved very quickly by forced march. And the two reserve corps in the Metz besieging force, IX at Ste Marie aux Chênes and III at Vernéville, also received warning orders. Wherever battle might be joined in the quadrant of country bounded by Vernéville, Ste Menehould forty miles to the west and the small fortress town of Sedan forty miles north on the Meuse and within five miles of the frontier with Belgium, these two corps could reach it in two days' long, but not forced, march. It was on this day also that Moltke first noted the activities of the Francs-Tireurs; there had been no guerrilla operation apparent in Alsace or Lorraine, but this was to become increasingly troublesome as the theatre of war moved westwards.

There was no similar coherent planning on the French side. Napoleon III's roundabout journey from the inn at the Gravelotte crossroads to Chalons ended late on the evening of 16th August, at about the same time as the last shots were being fired north of Rezonville. He found the Army of Chalons in no fit state for operations. The condition of the survivors of Froeschwiller who had found their way to Chalons has already been noted, and their re-equipment was far from complete. Packs and personal kits had been abandoned on the battlefield or in flight, and replacements could be issued only on a scale of one per two men. The reservists who had reported to their regimental depots too late for the frontier battles and had since been sent to Chalons were no better trained and certainly worse motivated than those who had reported on time. The *Gardes Mobiles* of Paris and the department of the Seine were in an even worse state and little short of mutiny. More promising was part of the newly forming XII Corps, whose command had been given to Trochu. This included some of the finest troops of the Second Empire. One of its three divisions was of '*soldats marins*' under General de Vassoigne. Many were veterans of the colonial wars of the 1860s and their hand-picked officers were several cuts above the elderly '*troupier*' company officers who formed too high a proportion in the line regiments. But there were only enough '*soldats marins*' for two understrength brigades. The other two divisions of XII Corps were of a standard comparable to the rest of the regular French Army – nine regiments brought up to war strength with reservists which had not been moved to Metz or Alsace during the concentration process, and two '*régiments de marche*' formed ad hoc.

A conference at Chalons on 17th August attended by the emperor, MacMahon, Trochu, Berthaut, the commander of the *Gardes Mobiles*, and Prince Napoleon was dominated by the latter. The upshot was that Trochu and the national guardsmen were returned to Paris. It was thought that the militiamen would fight better in defence of their own homes, and MacMahon no more than Palikao wanted Trochu as a subordinate. Trochu was appointed military governor of Paris and command of XII Corps went to Lebrun, who until 13th August had been co-deputy (with Jarras) to Le Boeuf. The conference decided that the Army of Chalons would also withdraw to Paris after a few more days for reorganisation and re-equipment, but this was at once contorted by Bazaine's telegrams to the emperor and to Palikao which, as we have seen, told something less than the whole truth about the result of the Battle of Mars La Tour. The emperor, sick and in pain but with instinct unimpaired, responded at once: 'Tell me the truth about your position so that I can act accordingly.'[32]

Palikao on the other hand assumed the worst. He telegraphed the emperor advising strongly against the withdrawal of the Army of Chalons to Paris. The council of regency had taken up the standpoint, which it was never to abandon, that the regime could not survive unless an attempt were made to extricate Bazaine. Notwithstanding this argument, on 21st August MacMahon began his withdrawal to Rheims, three days before the German cavalry patrols entered Chalons – a position which retained for the time being all his strategic options. Palikao, loyal servant of the empire, energetic optimist and big-finger-on-small-scale-map-strategist, persisted. He prepared a plan which relied upon a deception to divide the German armies, to be followed by an attack by MacMahon on the open flank of an enemy 'already worn out by several engagements.' The kindest comment to be made about this idea is that it might have succeeded had the opposing armies exchanged levels of morale and competence. Rouher, President of the Senate and Bonapartist elder statesman, was sent to Rheims on 21st August to reinforce the political will of the council of regency. Having arrived and seen for himself the condition of the troops after their short march from Mourmelon, Rouher needed little convincing that Palikao's plan was impractical. He acquiesced in the further withdrawal of the Army of Chalons towards Paris, drafted an imperial proclamation which appointed MacMahon commander-in-chief of the Army of Chalons and of all troops in and around Paris,[jj] and returned to the capital either to convince the empress regent and his colleagues, or to face their anger at his change of mind.

[jj] Thus, *de jure*, ending Bazaine's responsibility for MacMahon's operations, conferred on him by the imperial decree issued at Metz on 12th August. This nevertheless did not prevent Baraguey's commission of enquiry in 1871 from finding Bazaine responsible for MacMahon's defeat at Sedan, nor did Bazaine's inept defence at his court martial two years later make anything of this point in mitigation.

The correct military decision, having been arrived at, was as promptly reversed, not in Paris but at Rheims, when Bazaine's report of the Battle of Gravelotte–St Privat at length reached MacMahon. After saying that his troops needed two or three days of rest, Bazaine declared his intention of fighting his way northwards out of Metz, by way of Montmedy and then either direct through Ste Menehould and Chalons or through Sedan and Mezières. In either case, Bazaine had by now clearly lost all hope and interest, if indeed he had ever had any, in a withdrawal by the direct route through Verdun and any retreat by way of Montmedy brought the Army of Lorraine perilously close to the Belgian frontier and the penalty, under the accepted laws of war of the time, of internment for any troops crossing it. Even this highly qualified statement of intent was further watered down by a second telegram from Bazaine, to the effect that the enemy was now in such strength around him that he would be compelled to take the northernmost route. One glance at the map makes clear the implicit risks for the breakout force in a combination of a highly vulnerable left flank and at least one day's march within five miles of a violation of Belgian territory on the right of its proposed axis. There is an unresolved conflict of evidence about whether MacMahon saw this second telegram,[33] but whether he did or not the brave, knightly but rather stupid Maréchal Duc de Magenta decided that he had no option but to move to the relief of Metz. On 23rd August he set his army once more on the march, not westwards towards Paris, but north-east towards Rethel – and Sedan.

The events of the next week, the last in the roller-coaster existence of the Second Empire, can be compared to the resolution of a triangle of forces, the only constant element of which was the position of the Army of Lorraine in Metz. Half-hearted attempts to break out were made on 26th and 31st August, both on the less strongly held right bank of the Moselle, in the promised northerly direction towards Montmedy. But the summer weather had broken again, this time finally.[kk] Yet again, the guns and ammunition limbers bogged down in the soggy water meadows by the river, just as they had during the withdrawal from the east bank a fortnight previously. The staff had not learned by their experience: too many units were stood to arms too soon, waiting in the pouring rain while other units cleared their line of march. The very size of the garrison and the enceinte produced a tactical difficulty which the French were to experience again during the four month Siege of Paris. Since bivouac areas and thrust lines were dominated by observation from the surrounding heights, it was impossible for any sortie to achieve surprise

---

[kk] It rained almost continuously until Metz capitulated on 27th October.

because its weight and direction became apparent almost as soon as the attempt was under way. Although he had no siege artillery – the heavy guns in production in the Krupp workshops did not reach the armies until after the fall of Metz[ll] – few army commanders have ever been presented with such an easy task as that given to Prince Frederick Charles in the two months up to the end of October 1870. Bazaine himself was considerably less than enthusiastic about the attempts to break out. It was a decision which required considerable moral courage to take and great energy to execute, and Bazaine by now was bereft of both. His immediate subordinates – the two other marshals, Canrobert and Le Boeuf, the other three corps commanders Frossard, Ladmirault and Bourbaki,[mm] Coffinières the commander of the fortress and Soleille, commanding the army artillery group – at no time tried to urge a more positive and determined design. The two latter in particular provided a Greek chorus of impending doom. All should have been given a share of the execration which Bazaine would ultimately bear in full.

The orders issued by Moltke on 25th August needed three days to become effective on the ground, but at no point during this period of notice could the eight corps under his hand be engaged by the Army of Chalons, and the warning time would be sufficient to bring up the two corps on standby from the Metz besieging force. Moltke was thus poised to counter with superior forces any move MacMahon might make in the direction of Metz. On 26th August, royal and army group headquarters was established at Clermont en Argonne, behind the centre right of the position ordered for the Army of the Meuse, to await the reports of the strong cavalry reconnaissances ordered to comb the ground north of the Argonne, broken by woods and waterways. The reports Moltke received on arrival at Clermont indicated that MacMahon had adopted the course which Moltke had assessed both as least likely and most favourable to his own design. Although it can be argued that for a short time the initiative lay with MacMahon, it was an initiative which would, if he chose any course other than to retreat towards Paris, allow him to do no more than select his own place, method and date of defeat.

The French march performance remained bad over terrain which, until the immediate approaches to the Meuse valley were reached, imposed few inhibitions on movement. On one day the leading elements of Failly's corps

---

[ll] Though some heavy guns from the Sedan fortress surrendered by the capitulation of 2nd September were moved to Metz and used against their recent owners.

[mm] Bourbaki was to be exfiltrated from the garrison in September in circumstances amounting to Whitehall Theatre farce.[34]

achieved an advance of no more than five miles when the whole V Corps was taking up nine miles of road space. Supply arrangements in Rheims had collapsed in panic and disorder, with properly authorised unit ration parties sent away from depots empty-handed while others were allowed to take all they could carry in order to prevent stocks being captured by the Prussians. After the army left Rheims its logistic back-up failed altogether, the troops having to ravage the country. In an operation which would require rapid augmentation of the permanent bridges across the Meuse, and, in the light of Bazaine's expressed intentions, probably the Moselle also, the Army of Chalons had no bridging train. By the evening of 27th August, four days after leaving Rheims, MacMahon's headquarters had moved no more than forty miles, to Le Chêne. Here he again hesitated.

On the previous day, contact had been made with the cavalry patrols of the Army of the Meuse, a contact which the German cavalry was never again to lose. From 26th August onwards, Moltke and the two army commanders had continuous and accurate information about the strengths, dispositions and axis of movement of their enemy, information which, conversely, was denied to MacMahon by the dispositions and operational efficiency of Moltke's cavalry screen. With no further information about Bazaine's intentions, and suspecting if not knowing the extent to which his own formations had been 'placed' since the day before by the German cavalry, MacMahon signalled the council of regency that he was forced to give up the attempt to move towards Bazaine, and planned to retire on Paris, initially by way of Mezières.[nn]

Orders were accordingly issued to the Army of Chalons, but, yet again, no sooner issued than countermanded. MacMahon's telegram to Paris drew immediate responses from Palikao, first in the form of what amounted to political direction to the emperor, still accompanying the Army of Chalons, and then as a direct order to MacMahon. Palikao warned of revolution in Paris if no attempt were made to rescue Bazaine. His telegram continued on the basis of blind guesswork and capped the stream of optimistic information with which he had already bombarded MacMahon, and which he alone discerned. The minister of war in Paris told the army commander in the field that he had

---

[nn] This expressed intention initially to move northward indicates that MacMahon considered the line of the Aisne already compromised and that this river would not therefore protect the flank of a retreat by the direct route due west. And had MacMahon stuck to his proposed course, it was probably too late anyway. An initial movement towards Mezières would have given the two German armies time to close up to the line of the Aisne, from where they would be well placed to take in flank any attempt to bypass them to the north-west.

at least thirty-six hours' start on the crown prince and that there was nothing in front of him but 'a feeble part of the forces blockading Metz.'[35]

MacMahon was also bribed by the promise of reinforcement by Vinoy's XIII Corps, formed ad hoc in Paris and being directed on Rheims. Another telegram received later during the night was expressed as a direct order in the name of the council of regency: 'I require you to aid Bazaine, taking advantage of the thirty-six hours march you have over the crown prince.'[36]

Whether or not this was a legitimate order, it could have been overruled either *de jure* by the emperor as head of state, or both *de jure* and de facto by MacMahon, with the status of a commander-in-chief in the field since Rouher's visit to Rheims a week previously, and as the man in charge on the spot. The absence of bridging equipment already alluded to was a further practical argument in favour of a strategic withdrawal. But a decision on purely military grounds was too much for the hero of the Malakoff Redoubt. He had his orders; he would go on.

MacMahon's own orders issued during the early morning of 28th August directed his four corps towards the Meuse crossings between Sedan and Stenay, but soon had to be amended because French cavalry reconnaissance discovered that the enemy was already established strongly at Stenay.[oo] Their effect by the evening of 29th August was to place XII Corps (Lebrun) safely on the Meuse crossing at Mouzon and I Corps (Ducrot) relatively so at Raucourt et Flabe, no more than three miles from the bridge at Remilly, but still needing to descend the steep and wooded Haraucourt defile, which offered no more than a single route to his four divisions. MacMahon's other two corps were not so well placed. The VII Corps (Douay) was directly behind Ducrot, but needing the same constricted route to the Remilly crossing point. The V Corps (Failly) having reached no further than Buzancy, which had had to be cleared of Prussian cavalry, was dangerously exposed to an attack in flank on the axis of the left bank of the river and its direct route across the Meuse was already blocked. MacMahon's order diverting Failly north-eastwards to the crossing at Mouzon never reached him because the aide-de-camp bearing it – a Captain de Grouchy[pp] – was captured by a German cavalry patrol. Since the order contained the routes allotted to the other three corps, the whole game was delivered into Moltke's hands.

[oo] Verdun was still in French possession, but under siege.

[pp] One of the numerous progeny of the marshal of the First Empire, and no luckier than his ancestor.

Moltke's immediate preoccupation when he arrived at Clermont was the organisation of the logistic support of the Army of the Meuse as it moved northwards across the grain of the difficult country of the Argonne. And while the day-to-day administrative routine of a headquarters can usually be left in the hands of a camp commandant, the galaxy of minor royalty and civilian dignitaries trailing along in the wake of the Supreme Warlord produced problems which obtruded even to the level of the chief of the general staff, particularly when the facilities available to army group headquarters deteriorated with each operational move from country town into a succession of small farming villages. But in the light of the information gained by the cavalry screen, the axis of advance of Third Army required a course correction from that ordered three days before. The crown prince of Prussia was therefore directed to continue his right wheel, in order to come in from the south-west behind the Army of Chalons, now under constant surveillance. So confident was Moltke of the outcome that he stood down the two reserve corps of the army besieging Metz from the commitment he had given them on 25th August. By the morning of 29th August, even before he had seen the orders captured when en route to Failly, it was clear to Moltke that he had the possibility of a decisive battle on the left bank of the Meuse, with MacMahon pinned against the river. This time there was to be no chance of the design being wrecked by a disobedient Steinmetz or a Red Prince burning to prove that he had outgrown tutelage. The strongest orders were sent to both army commanders that, while maintaining contact and continuing to shepherd MacMahon's formations against the Meuse, a general engagement was not to be provoked until both armies were in position. While Third Army hastened north by forced march, and although it soon became apparent that the Army of the Meuse had Failly's corps at its mercy, Moltke sent one of the 'Demigods' to the headquarters of the crown prince of Saxony to ensure that the latter did not exceed his orders.

Failly remained in ignorance not only of his changed orders[qq] but also of the circumstances which had forced their alteration. In consequence V Corps was still, in the late afternoon on 29th August, lumbering along the road from Buzancy towards Stenay when the advance guard 'bumped' not a cavalry patrol but infantry. The whole royal Saxon Corps was deployed for battle at Champy, across Failly's route to Stenay. In a confused fight which continued until nightfall the Saxons held their ground and Failly, deprived of his direct

---

[qq] Berthier – and Moltke – would have seen to it that this vital order was carried by separate 'gallopers' on different routes.

route, was forced to withdraw to Mouzon, the next crossing point to the north, through the Forêt de Belvel, in pitch darkness on forest tracks worsened by rain. The V Corps took six hours to cover as many miles, and as each unit reached Beaumont the soldiers collapsed exhausted to the ground. No sentries were posted, horses were unsaddled and those batteries which had survived the anarchic move from Chalons and been heaved along the muddy forest tracks in darkness were not put into action.

Although the full extent of this chaos was unknown to Moltke, his orders issued on the evening of 29th August are evidence of his decision to spring the trap. Both armies were authorised to attack on the following day, but, in order to give Third Army a little more time to reach the battlefield, the Army of the Meuse was forbidden to start its advance to contact before 10 a.m.[37] and in contrast to the Army of Chalons, which had kept its empty supply wagons in the vain hope that organised resupply might somehow be reconstituted, Moltke forbade the German formations to take with them anything more than would be needed for the decisive battle, now certain within the next seventy-two hours.

Third Army resumed its advance at daybreak on 30th August. This time the Army of the Meuse was established on a line running east–west through Nouart, with its right flank protected by the Meuse, the Saxon Corps on the right, the elder (Gustav) von Alvensleben brother's IV Corps on the left, and with the Guard Corps behind them in reserve. The Forêt de Belval which had so exhausted and confused Failly's men during the night still presented its movement control problems in daylight, but Prussian staff organisation saw to it that the tactical advance to contact through the five miles of woodland was controlled rigidly along four parallel tracks, and each of the columns was directed not to start their attack until all were through the wood. On the left of IV Corps, the two Bavarian corps were advancing north-eastwards from Sommauthe. To their north, Third Army was closing the ring fast, with V Corps advancing towards Oches, XI Corps, together with the division furnished by the principality of Wurtemburg, headed for Le Chêne, and VI Corps for Vouziers. Only the latter was too far distant to reach a general engagement if fought on 30th August. North of the crown prince of Prussia's toiling infantry, a cavalry screen was patrolling beyond the Aisne, between Attigny and Rethel. Nor was the Prussian diplomatic arm idle; it was on this day that Bismarck dispatched what was little short of an ultimatum to King Leopold II of the Belgians, to the effect that if any French troops straying over the border were not interned, the armies of the king of Prussia reserved the right of pursuit. The cautious and avaricious Leopold was preserved from having to make a commitment not by his own diplomatic subtlety, but by the speedy resolution of the issue through the genius of Moltke's planning matched by the marching stamina of the German infantry and the power of their artillery.

Although thoughts of a decisive battle as early as 30th August proved premature because Third Army still had too much ground to cover, the battle between the Army of the Meuse and V Corps was allowed to develop, notwithstanding Moltke's wish that both armies should engage simultaneously. As with Forton at Vionville and Ladmirault at Amanvillers, so now Failly at Beaumont was taken by surprise, in spite of the fact that contact had been broken on the previous evening only by darkness and there could be no great distance between the armies, even on the assumption that the Army of the Meuse had remained static. Yet again, a French formation came under fire with its tents still pitched, its horses unsaddled or being watered, its artillery still limbered up and its camp fires cooking the day's main meal. Moltke's restraining orders of the previous day, the march tables and movement control organisation which had surmounted the problems posed by the Forêt de Belval, together with the luck which attends the winning side, brought XII Corps, IV Corps and I Bavarian Corps into action simultaneously, at around 1.30 p.m. French improvisation, bravery in the face of the enemy and the firepower of the chassepot prevented total annihilation, but in four hours the battle was over. Failly's corps lost nearly 5,000 men, including 3,000 unwounded prisoners, and fifty-one guns. The booty also included the 'military chest' of the intendance, containing FF 150,000.[38] By darkness, the debris of Failly's corps was in full retreat towards the Meuse bridge at Mouzon, held securely by XII Corps, but the fighting value of V Corps, having regard to its losses, henceforward could be rated no higher than that of a division.

Concurrently with the fighting around Champy and at Beaumont, the other three corps of the Army of Chalons were either crossing to the right bank of the Meuse by the existing bridges at Mouzon and Remilly or waiting their turn. Although Third Army's cavalry patrols were hovering round the rearguard of Douay's corps, following behind that of Ducrot on the northern route, and there was a sharp fight at Raucourt, VII Corps passed through the dangerous Haraucourt defile without serious opposition. Nevertheless, I, VII and XII Corps all reached the Meuse valley in considerable disorder and the French had to devote 31st August to unscrambling a turmoil little better than rout. On the same day the Army of Chalons received a reinforcement, though not Vinoy's corps as promised in the exchange of telegrams between Palikao and MacMahon during the night of 27th/28th August.

On 31st August XIII Corps, by some triumph of improvisation, had reached Mezières by rail, administratively loaded,[rr] where, providentially for them, they were delayed for four hours. This was to allow a train bearing the fourteen year old prince imperial, who had accompanied his father throughout, to be moved with his suite to sanctuary in Belgium.[ss] The XIII Corps thus missed the disaster which would unfold on the next day. A further roundabout railway journey returned them to Paris, where they formed the core of the French Army which stood the siege. The reinforcement which did arrive carried rather less firepower than an army corps, but rather more potential to cause damage, unfortunately to his own side. General Emmanuel de Wimpffen,[tt] a veteran of the war of 1859, had been left on mobilisation to command the residual garrison in North Africa. On 22nd August, Palikao summoned him to Paris, possibly as counterweight to Trochu. After some discussion, it was perhaps recalled that Failly had been superseded on 12th August, but had not yet been relieved of his command. Wimpffen was sent to make his way as best he could to the Army of Chalons, furnished with the wrong maps, no doubt plenty of Palikao's unsubstantiated optimism and a dormant commission as army commander, should any untoward accident befall MacMahon. An indirect journey with delays comparable only to those inflicted on their passengers by a twentieth-century railway network when working to rule brought Wimpffen to MacMahon's headquarters in the citadel of Sedan on the morning of 31st August. Making no mention of his dormant commission, he was sent to relieve the hitherto unsuspecting and afterwards bitterly angry Failly.

Had there been enough troops available, a good defensive position might have been established on the hills which encircle Sedan. But a perimeter securing all the crest lines on both sides of the river, together with a reserve to reinforce any threatened sector, would have needed perhaps three times the number at MacMahon's disposal. The obvious corollary is that a defensive position around Sedan in the valley of the Meuse soon becomes untenable once an enemy has secured the dominating ground. Nevertheless, something had to be organised in order to gain time for stragglers to rejoin their units, for

---

[rr] See Chapter II, note 1.

[ss] The emperor, invited to go also, refused.

[tt] Not to be confused with the Austro-German military family of the same name, represented at both Wagram and Solferino.

regiments which had become detached to find their way back to their proper formations, for XIII Corps to catch up and for the army to regroup for the next phase of the advance to Metz. What emerged was an inverted U-shaped position with a perimeter of about eleven miles round the town. The open mouth, from the Meuse due east to Bazeilles, was entrusted to XII Corps, hitherto unblooded but including the elite division of *soldats marins*. The eastern side of the perimeter, along the line of the Givonne stream, was entrusted to I Corps and the north, from Illy to Floing including the Bois de Garenne, to VII Corps. The western arm of the U, along the right bank of the Meuse past Sedan back to Bazeilles, was not continuously held, the remnant of V Corps being placed between the town and the Bois de Garenne in reserve. Five brigades of reserve cavalry were also held in reserve, in the fields south of the Floing hill. It was a perimeter too large to be held by a force amounting to no more than eleven divisions, with each expected to hold an average of a mile of front. Defensive integrity was compromised by the failure to destroy three vital bridges, at Donchery beyond the Iges peninsula west of Floing, at Douzy over the River Chiers which joins the Meuse south of Bazeilles, and at Pont Maugis, leading directly to XII Corps' position. The bridges would have been needed to sustain any further French advance and MacMahon's intentions evidently remained offensive as late as the afternoon of 31st August, when he and the emperor accompanied a reconnaissance in force as far as Carignan, on the right bank of the river and one-sixth of the 100 miles towards the beleaguered Bazaine.

On the previous evening, notwithstanding the disaster during the day at Beaumont, the young bloods of the reserve cavalry had organised an impromptu ball at Douzy.[39] But others were more realistic. Douay ordered his corps to entrench; and Ducrot, whose language frequently employed the choicer epithets of the *grognards* of the *Grande Armée*, having delivered himself of his comment about the chamber-pot nature of the army's position, wrapped himself in his cloak and sat out the night beside the camp fire of one of the Zouave regiments of his late division. But MacMahon still had another option. Even though he had consistently underestimated[uuu] the number of enemy

---

[uuu] There appears to have been no attempt on the French side to make any intelligence assessment of enemy strength by analysis of identified formations in front of them. In the forty-eight hours before the Battle of Sedan opened, elements of the Army of Chalons had been in contact with five of the eight German corps moving to surround them – IV Corps and the Saxons (differently uniformed from the Prussians) at Beaumont, the two Bavarian Corps at Sommauthe, destined to be the scene of another epic clash of French and German arms in May

directly opposing him, he could still withdraw north-westwards through Mezières – until the German Third Army had closed the gap.

On the German side, the enemy had been found and 'fixed'. All that remained was to annihilate him. This was accomplished without the need for any of the suicidal massed infantry attacks of the previous battles. Sedan was an unusually 'surgical' battle, whose three phases can be clearly discerned: first the movement of the chess pieces which completed the encirclement of the French position; secondly, bombardment by massed artillery, which could stand off beyond the range of anything in the hands of their adversary; and thirdly, the blocking of the attempts to break out by elements of a dying army, which, whatever its many failings, once engaged, had fought bravely in all the battles of the previous month until the position was hopeless. The battle was watched throughout, rather than controlled, from army group headquarters situated on the heights of Frenois, west of the river and opposite the town. For the last time in military history, a commander-in-chief had under his own eye the totality of his force engaged in a major battle. Moltke's orders required the Guard Corps, the Saxons with a division of II Bavarian Corps attached, and IV Corps to attack on the east bank of the Meuse. The Guard Corps, with the longest approach march which took it across both the Meuse and the Chiers, was to attack the enemy on the line of the Givonne from the east. The XII Corps, crossing the Chiers by the bridge left intact at Douzy, would support this attack from the south-east. The IV Corps was in immediate sector reserve, following the Saxons. The open mouth of the U was to be attacked frontally by I Bavarian Corps, while II Bavarian Corps, minus its detached division, was to secure the bank of the Meuse below Frenois. Meanwhile, the leading corps of Third Army, XI followed by V, and supported by the Wurtemburg division, were to cross the Meuse at Donchery and wheel right, passing north of the loop of the Meuse round the Iges peninsula. This movement, once completed, would block the last remaining withdrawal route of the Army of Chalons. When the two armies had linked up north of Illy, the French would be in an unbreakable stranglehold. The VI Corps was retained in army group reserve.

1940, and V Corps at Raucourt. Even a cursory assessment would have indicated a strength far larger than MacMahon could hope to attack successfully with his troops at hand. The ration strength of the forces in pursuit of the Army of Chalons, even allowing for casualties and detachments since 19th August, was over 200,000 – nearly double the combined French loss in the battle and the subsequent capitulation.

The German armies were astir early on the morning of 1st September. With ground still to cover, the formations of Third Army began their march at 3 a.m., and an hour later, covered by the morning mists of autumn in the valley of the Meuse, I Bavarian Corps launched its assault against Vassoigne's marines in Bazeilles, who held their ground, beating off the initial Bavarian attacks without difficulty. But the Saxons, whose point of attack fortuitously struck the junction between the positions of Lebrun and Ducrot, achieved some penetration at once. Ducrot's right flank was turned and the Saxon Corps artillery used their longer range to drive off the French batteries.

MacMahon, visiting the outposts at Bazeilles, received at around 6 a.m. a disabling but not fatal wound. Forced to relinquish command, he nominated Ducrot as his successor, appreciating that the latter, although the junior corps commander, was a better fighting general than the disgraced Failly, the fatalistic Douay, the court soldier Lebrun or the egregious Wimpffen. Ducrot received news of his elevation at around eight o'clock, by which time his position along the Givonne was frontally threatened by the Guard Corps[vv] and on its southern flank by the determined assault of the Saxons. In attempting to restore the line at La Moncelle, in order to retain touch with XII Corps, Lartigue, the last surviving divisional commander of those appointed to I Corps on mobilisation six weeks earlier, was killed, together with his chief of staff. Ducrot, without knowledge of MacMahon's intentions,[ww] at once ordered a general retreat towards Illy as a preliminary to further withdrawal on Mezières, a course he had urged without success on MacMahon the previous day. Even now, beyond the eleventh hour, this might have worked if the French could break clean from a running fight, because the German Third Army had not yet closed the gap.

Lebrun, under protest, abandoned Bazeilles, which the Bavarians occupied at around 10 o'clock, and XII and I Corps began the difficult operation of withdrawal when still in contact. Wimpffen had not initially reacted to the news of MacMahon's wound, nor to the assumption of command by Ducrot, but the order to withdraw northwards was too much for him. Encountering Lebrun, he produced the dormant commission signed by Palikao, dashed off a note to Ducrot informing the latter that he had been superseded, countermanded the orders Ducrot had given and enjoined instead a general

---

[vv] It was in this action that Lieutenant Paul von Hindenburg, adjutant of his battalion of foot guards, gained the Iron Cross.

[ww] MacMahon's Chief of Staff, Faure, appears also to have been in ignorance of what his chief had in mind.

movement in entirely the opposite direction. Ordering Lebrun to recapture Bazeilles, Wimpffen concluded with the words: 'I will not have a retirement on Mezières. If the army is to retire[xx] it is to be on Carignan and not on Mezières.'[40]

From this moment dates the final disintegration of the Army of Chalons. The best troops in the world would falter if ordered to recapture a position they had defended successfully and from which they had withdrawn barely an hour before, not as a result of overwhelming enemy force, but only in response to orders. Meanwhile, as the disastrous morning wore on, it became apparent that further German forces were lapping round the north of the defensive perimeter. By ten o'clock the artillery of XI Corps, leading its infantry in the Prussian practice, was in action against the French positions at Illy. Their corps commander, von Bose, exhibited a better understanding of all-arms cooperation than had Manstein on the slopes leading to Amanvillers. His guns had an escort of seven infantry battalions and could not be dislodged when attacked by the French cavalry. An hour later, the illustrious spectators on the hill at Frenois could see that the French position was surrounded. The crown prince had two corps artillery groups – 146 guns – in action firing southwards, crossing the fire of nearly 300 guns supporting the Guard Corps, the Saxons and the Bavarians, and from the west bank of the Meuse. The whole shrinking French position was raked by the German guns.[yy] The only protection for the defence was that provided by the folds in the ground; the Commander of the Guard Corps Artillery, Prince Kraft von Hohenlohe Ingelfingen, was subsequently to write:

> Our superiority over the enemy was so overwhelming that we suffered no loss at all. The batteries fired as if at practice.[41]

Having been successively informed of the wound to MacMahon, the passing of the command first to Ducrot and then to Wimpffen, and the reversal by the latter of the orders given by the former, the emperor rode out to seek death among his troops. Failing, he rode back into Sedan determined to put an end

---

[xx] Given Wimpffen's aim – to relieve the Army of Lorraine – an odd use of the word 'retire'.

[yy] The devastation wrought by the German artillery was still apparent three weeks after the battle. Particularly poignant is the description of the Bois de Garenne, where the musicians of the Army of Chalons had been sent before the battle for safety. The ground was still littered with the mouthpieces of wind instruments and music sheets of, ironically, Strauss and Offenbach.[42]

to the slaughter. But his generals were not yet done. Wimpffen tried to organise an attack towards Carignan, but this forlorn hope fell apart almost as soon as it was mounted. Ducrot, more logically, thought he saw the opportunity of a breakout through Floing, and, like Lartigue at Morsbronn, MacMahon at Froeschwiller and Bazaine at Rezonville, turned to the cavalry. Their senior general, Margueritte, having started the war in command of a brigade in Du Barrail's reserve cavalry division, now found himself with the status of a corps commander. He appears to have been a competent officer who, in contrast to many of the French senior commanders, had gained and retained the loyalty of his troopers. Reconnoitring his line of attack, he was mortally wounded. With a cry of '*Vengez-le!*', the last charge of the Second Empire crashed to its doom. His senior brigadier, the Marquis de Gallifet,[zz] brave beyond the point of rashness, hero of Italy and Mexico, typical over-promoted cavalry subaltern and Second Empire socialite, made two further attempts, both unsuccessful, but drawing a gasp of admiration from the opposing royal commander-in-chief watching from his grandstand view at Frenois: '*Oh les braves gens!*'

All the time the German gunfire continued. A white flag, hoisted over the citadel on the orders of the emperor, was torn down on those of Wimpffen. The corps commanders foregathered in Sedan, where the debris of the army were in a state incorporating panic, despair and rage. The white flag, hoisted for the second time, was not taken down again. Napoleon III sent a short note to King William:

> *Monsieur mon frère,*
> *N'ayant pu mourir au milieu de mes troupes, il ne me reste qu'a remettre*
> *mon epée entre les mains de votre majesté.*
> *Je suis de votre majesté le bon frère.*[43]

There then ensued an unseemly wrangle between the senior French formation commanders about which of them should bear the ignominy, at the time and for ever after, of signing the capitulation. Bismarck, having moved quickly to ensure that Napoleon's submission related only to himself and did not purport to represent that of the Army of Chalons, the other forces still in the field or the French nation, turned the negotiations over to Moltke. Moltke would

---

[zz] The gallant general survived, to become minister of war in 1899, where his blend of loyalty to the army and his class and thick-headedness proved inadequate to cope with the ramifications of the Dreyfus Affair.

accept no terms other than unconditional surrender, of army and fortress. The following morning, a signature extracted under protest from Wimpffen ceded 83,000 men in addition to the 21,000, mostly unwounded, taken prisoner during the battle, 413 field guns including seventy mitrailleuses, 139 fortress guns, some of which were soon brought into use against the garrisons of Metz, Strasbourg, Toul and Verdun, 66,000 chassepots, over 1,000 wagons and 6,000 serviceable horses. The French had also lost 17,000 killed or wounded during the battle, and a further 3,000 who had escaped over the border into Belgium were disarmed. The figures are those of Moltke,[44] who summed up the victory in this critical phase of the Second War of Prussian Supremacy in characteristically unadorned prose: 'With the nullification of this army fell the Empire in France.'

Preussens Gloria

As night fell on the battlefield, the soldiers of the king of Prussia were beyond celebration. The mood was rather of thanksgiving, and the men, predominantly staunch and practising Lutherans except for the Roman Catholic Bavarians, expressed their gratitude for victory and personal survival in chants of the soul-stirring seventeenth-century chorale, *Nun Danket Alle Gott*. The presence of the French emperor with the Army of Chalons had not been known to the Germans; the news that he was in Sedan and had surrendered might have created the belief that the war was over. However, anyone holding this view was soon disabused of it by the fact that Louis Napoleon himself made clear that his surrender to his brother–monarch was personal only, and that thereafter, as a prisoner of war, he did not consider himself competent to negotiate on behalf of his country. The terms discussed between Moltke and Wimpffen on the morning of 2nd September were purely military, dealing with no more than the capitulation of the Army of Chalons and the fortress of Sedan. The war would continue.

When the news of the débâcle and the surrender of the emperor reached Paris, the Second Empire lasted barely another day. The regime was swept away in the anarchic rage of the Paris mob. The leaders of the new provisional government, in the main men of the purest republican and egalitarian principles, swore perpetual defiance. The senior soldiers of the empire still at liberty, some of whose careers had, like that of Trochu, been blighted hitherto for political reasons, placed their duty to France higher than their oath of allegiance to the fallen emperor. The armies of the provisional government fought just as bravely as their predecessors, and, even occasionally, with better success. Paris, invested within a fortnight after Sedan, withstood a siege of over four months until starvation forced an armistice and soon afterwards the acceptance of peace terms which required the surrender of Alsace, including Strasbourg, northern Lorraine including Metz, a German victory march through Paris and payment of an indemnity of FF 5,000,000,000 in gold or agreed bonds, a sum equating to nearly double the total annual national revenue.[45] The new frontier followed the course neither of the Moselle nor the Meuse and was not demarcated by any defined geographic feature. The Amanvillers ridge and most of the battlefield of Mars La Tour, though not the village itself, became German territory. But perhaps the most significant acquisition of the victors was one not appreciated until after its transfer. The rich coal and iron ore deposits east of Briey, barely exploited under the empire, fell into German hands and for the next forty-seven years this invaluable geological resource provided raw materials for the factories of Krupp and not Creusot. The rest of the Lorraine iron basin lay at risk from the first German incursion over the new frontier.

The unconditional surrender of Metz at the end of October freed the seven corps of the besieging force for operations in the field, but the lengthening German lines of communication created conditions for some local successes for the armies raised by the energy of Gambetta, while at the same time spontaneous guerrilla activity caused increasingly bitter conduct of the war. The French railway system was essential for the support both of the German Army besieging Paris and for their field armies, which, as winter drew on, were engaged simultaneously near the Swiss frontier, on the Loire and in Normandy. In any event less developed than the railways east of the Rhine, the French network proved to be highly vulnerable to disruption by ever more effective sabotage. There was a continuous need to bring in more reserve and second line soldiers from Germany to form additional army corps for operations and to protect the lines of communication. By the time of the armistice, Moltke's ration strength in France had expanded to 630,736 men, 1,742 guns and 61,000 cavalry. About one-sixth of the manpower was employed on lines of communication duties.[46]

Moltke refused to accord belligerent status to the Francs-Tireurs, who if captured when bearing arms were executed out of hand. As almost every French peasant household had some sort of gun for shooting game, and with the tenuous 'galloper' and logistic communications of the invaders, the temptation to raise the stakes existed for both sides. When summary executions proved to be ineffective as a deterrent, Moltke authorised reprisals against villages and parishes. The German armies, who at the beginning of the war had been far more scrupulous than the French in their respect for civilian property, ceased to bother about it. Thus, warfare in Europe finally became 'total' in the Clausewitzian sense because the campaign throughout the autumn and winter of 1870–71 came to involve the total resources of both the belligerents, and was only concluded when the national will and ability of one side to continue fighting had been broken completely. Although the European wars of the seventeenth and eighteenth centuries had on occasions produced worse devastation and massacre of civilian populations in battle areas, their conduct fell short of 'total' war as defined by Clausewitz, nor can the 'Bruderkrieg' of 1866 be so described. On the other hand, this condition had been reached by the end of the War Between the States in America. Henceforward, no war would be fought on anything less than an extreme basis, until, in the second half of the twentieth century, the threat of mutually assured destruction if nuclear weapons were used forced the Great Powers into war for limited objectives, and prosecution of surrogate warfare. Though even in these wars, the 'Peoples' War' forecast by Clausewitz remained an ingredient in the composition of the will to fight of at least one protagonist, who, irrespective of relative strength, was often victorious if their opponent lacked equivalent determination.

Proof of the ascendancy of Prussia within Germany, and of Germany within Europe, was manifest before the surrender. On 18th January, 1871, the creation of the German Empire was proclaimed in the Galerie des Glaces at Versailles, with the somewhat reluctant King William of Prussia as emperor. Although the armies of all the German states had contributed to the decisive results of Mars La Tour, Gravelotte and Sedan, there could be no question about which state should lead a united Germany. There followed in the new nation an outpouring of energy and inventiveness. Birth rate, industrial output and development and application of new technologies alike soared. Massive self-confidence, the aggressive spirit already commented upon by one perceptive observer after Sadowa,[a*] and the doctrine of Teutonic supremacy in all fields propounded by the German philosophers,[a*] and apparent as a fact in the quality, quantity and successful innovations of industrial production, gave rise to an overweening arrogance which won few friends. It was self-evident that France, the Dual Monarchy and Russia were all now secondary powers compared with the new empire, but for as long as Germany restricted her ambitions to pre-eminence on the European land mass, no combination of any two of these was likely to secure the adherence of England, and peace was

---

[a*] Chapter VIII, p.354 and Chapter VII, pp.304–5.

assured. It was only when imperial and popular self-confidence in Germany boiled over in the mutually inclusive demands for colonies and a high seas fleet that the long-term possibility of English involvement in a combination against Germany began to emerge.

If the new status quo achieved by the creation of the German Empire and the humiliating peace treaty were to be overturned, France would have to take the initiative, but it was clear that she was too weak to attempt this unilaterally. However, before seeking allies it was first necessary to produce a form of government which would command the approval, at least tacit, of a majority of the population. It was by no means for the first time that, in the wake of Sedan, the Paris mob had overturned a government, but the regime they sought to impose in its place proved far too radical for the temper of the country at large. The national elections during the armistice in February 1871, permitted by Bismarck so that he could obtain a valid and viable signature on the peace treaty, produced a moderate, conservative and cautious body of men who wanted nothing more than a period of peace and retrenchment. Adventurism was at a discount, temporarily at least. Hence the basis for the Third Republic. Its first task was to crush the forces of the Paris Commune. This having been achieved in a fortnight's bloody civil war in and around Paris in May, by an army commanded by MacMahon and composed largely of returned prisoners of war, the country settled down to pay off the indemnity under the presidency, first of Thiers and then MacMahon. The latter provided a quasi-regal figurehead for the Paris Exhibition of 1878, an event designed to prove to the world that capital and nation had found their feet again. But the essential dichotomy in the French body politic remained; fundamental differences were contained within the framework of the Third Republic only because no two parties wishing to replace it – Legitimists, Orléanists, Bonapartists and extreme Republicans – could agree to combine for long enough to do so. The Third Republic endured for sixty-nine years, as long as the combined life of its eight predecessors,[b*] but it was a survival through weakness rather than strength, and one shaken by a series of scandals which discredited its institutions of government both at home and abroad.

There were only two common strands of policy which commanded a majority view in the country between 1871 and 1914. These were the return of Alsace–Lorraine and belief in the army, and both were eroded as time went by. In the beginning, the extreme radical elements of the Third Republic were the

---

[b*] First Empire, first Bourbon Restoration, the One Hundred Days of Napoleon I, second Bourbon Restoration, Orléans monarchy, Second Republic, Prince-Presidency, Second Empire.

harbingers of revenge, taking as truth Gambetta's watchword: '*N'en parlez jamais, y pensez toujours.*'[47]

This process had to be started by restoration of national confidence in the army and of the army's own self-belief, the first step in the attainment which was the court-martial of Bazaine. This took place in the autumn of 1873, on charges of capitulation of the fortress of Metz without exhausting all means of defence and doing everything required by duty and honour, of capitulation with an army in the field and of negotiating with an enemy before doing everything required by duty and honour. In spite of assurances of support given him beforehand by both Thiers and MacMahon, Bazaine, who sacrificed his case in the interests of a possible Bonapartist restoration, was, in one of the least edifying episodes in French military history, found guilty on all counts and condemned to death, at once commuted by MacMahon to imprisonment for twenty years.[48] But France had her scapegoat and the honour and capability of the army could be presented as untarnished. Nevertheless, there were reservations for anyone who wished to see them.

The perceived necessity of maintaining belief in the army as an article of faith, whatever the obvious facts to the contrary, produced during the twelve year long (1894–1906) Dreyfus Affair,[49] a Watergate-scale mountain of 'improved' evidence, half-truths and outright lies, so big as not only to call into question national confidence in the one institution in which all Frenchmen were expected to take some pride, but also to threaten the very existence of the Third Republic. The regime survived, partly by surprisingly effective damage limitation and partly because of the absence of a viable and obvious alternative, but too many senior officers had performed so badly in the witness box in the succession of trials, retrials and appeals that confidence in the army was severely dented. This, successful colonial expansion and French predominance, through the abilities of Jean Jaures and others, in the internationalist thrust of socialism in the first decade of the twentieth century, weakened the demand for the return of the lost territories.

By 1910, there was serious general staff concern about the absentee rate to be expected should it ever be necessary to mobilise the reserves. In the event, war fever and presidential leadership[c*] as strong as was possible under the balanced constitution of the Third Republic caused the estimate of a thirteen per cent shortfall to be nearly ten times too high.[50] But although this particular concern proved to be misplaced, the French Army in 1914 was at a disadvantage because its doctrine and planning were flawed by false lessons

---

[c*] Of Raymond Poincaré, elected in 1913, himself a Lorrainer.

drawn from the war of 1870. While the intellectual elite of the *École Superieure de Guerre* admitted that firepower had been of some importance, and Bonnal, at first instructor and later commandant, published meticulous studies of the two wars of Prussian supremacy, the received wisdom that France had lost in 1870 because of misplaced and undue emphasis on defence became mandatory at every level in the French Army. Apostles of firepower, such as Pétain, found their careers blighted. There developed the principle of attack at all costs, based on a high flown philosophy that attack, whatever the circumstances or consequences, would always succeed because of the unbreakable strength of French offensive spirit. This belief led to the tactical doctrine laid down by the French Army Field Regulations of 1913, which began with the words: 'The French Army, returning to its tradition, henceforward admits no law but the offensive.'[51]

In January 1914, Joffre, commander-in-chief designate on mobilisation, introduced his operational directive in similar terms:

> Whatever the circumstances, it is the commander-in-chief's intention to advance with all forces united to the attack of the German armies.[52]

On the same logic, the commands of Michel at Morsbronn, Bonnemain on the Froeschwiller ridge and De Gallifet at Floing had been shot out of their saddles, and whatever other description may be applied to the march of the Army of Chalons to Sedan it was most certainly not a defensive movement.

Belief in the irresistible power of the offensive had its effect also on equipment policy. Notwithstanding the fundamental lesson which should have been learned about the battle-winning potential deriving from better range and lethality of artillery, the French Army's field gun, the *'soixante-quinze'*, was highly mobile but had negligible hitting power against dug-in troops. Yet again, the French Army would go to war on a plan based upon false assumptions, with battlefield procedures which ignored technological development, and with inferior equipment.

Nevertheless, the crushing German victory gained in the Second War of Prussian Supremacy carried within it the germs of future catastrophe, both diplomatic and military. On the diplomatic front and with the hindsight possible a century later, it can be argued that all Imperial Germany had to do to guarantee her pre-eminence in Europe *sine die* was to avoid giving affront to England, and, if an alliance between France and Russia could not be prevented altogether, to ensure that it remained defensive, to be invoked only in the event of an attack on either by a third party. The conflicting claims of the Romanov and Habsburg empires on the Slavonic lands and peoples made impossible any friendship between Russia and the Dual Monarchy, but Bismarck, who remained imperial chancellor until 1890, saw to it that Germany, if not necessarily at all times and always the friend of both, nevertheless retained influence strong enough to prevent the eruption of a destabilising war on the lower reaches of the Danube. However, after his fall from power, diplomatic and family links with Russia were allowed to cool, in spite of intermittent and over-emotional attempts by the kaiser to resurrect them.[d*]

Russia, needing investment capital, found it on the Paris market. The revanchist element in the French Government, probably at all times a majority, saw the need for an ally. The financial and commercial link became the defensive alliance which brought the European balance *post-1870* to the threshold of German concern.

Until the turn of the century, an alliance, or at least an 'understanding', between Germany and England was by no means an impossibility. Naval rivalry and the German demand for colonies were still containable. But Joseph Chamberlain, the strongest English advocate for friendship with Germany, lost his enthusiasm because of the virulent pro-Boer stance taken by the kaiser for home consumption, by his Chancellor Prince von Bulow, and in the German press, and because of what became his own total preoccupation with the cause of imperial preference. As the twentieth century emerged from infancy, Conservative and Liberal politicians alike in England came to realise that France was a lesser threat to English overseas possessions than Germany. It was a Conservative government which reached a series of agreements with France over outstanding colonial differences, and the two nations made common cause in the crisis over Morocco in 1905. Later, it was a Liberal government which, at the Algeciras Conference of 1908, accorded full diplomatic support to France against Germany, placing Morocco totally within the French sphere of influence. Military conversations between England and France had begun as early as 1905. They were continued under the Liberal administrations, first of Campbell-Bannerman, which came to power the

---

[d*] Particularly at a meeting between Kaiser Wilhelm II and Tsar Nicholas II at Bjorkö in Finland in July 1905. The two monarchs, supposedly on holiday and in the absence of diplomatic advisers, concluded a treaty which neither country could ratify, because it was in conflict with previous commitments, in the case of Russia to France and in that of Germany to the Dual Monarchy.[53]

following year, and then of Asquith, who succeeded as prime minister in 1908 when Campbell-Bannerman became terminally ill. Both parties when in government reiterated at intervals that these discussions, initially between the director of military operations in the War Office and the French military attaché in London, were entirely without commitment. This proposition continued to be maintained even when possible deployment areas for a British expeditionary force in north-eastern France came to be agreed as a result of a meeting of minds between Generals (Henry) Wilson and Foch, at the time commandants of their respective armies' staff colleges, but both marked men for further advancement to the highest military posts.

By 1911 Asquith, and the 'imperial' element in his cabinet, in particular Grey and Churchill, were sufficiently aware of the detail of the staff conversations to decide that reports of them had to be shaded in presentation, as required under the rule of collective cabinet responsibility, to their pacifist and 'Little Englander' colleagues such as Morley, whose viewpoint was, until the Agadir crisis in that year, shared by Lloyd George and probably a majority of the Liberal Party in the House of Commons. While it could be argued that England's assistance would be invoked only if and when Germany invaded France, it is impossible to avoid the conclusion that England had become committed, by everything short of a formal treaty, to supporting France in a war against Germany, because, while such a war might start with an act of German aggression, in French eyes the conflict would at once and inevitably become a crusade for the recovery of the lands lost since 1870. Thus England had an imprecise liability to participate in a war in which the distinction between 'offensive' and 'defensive' aims was blurred from the start.

Years before, and in a quite different context, Bismarck had declared that he would never wish to tie the trim frigate of Prussia's policy to Austria's worm-eaten barque.[54] He had, nevertheless, with his usual pragmatism, concluded in 1879 a defensive alliance with the Dual Monarchy. With Russia and England both driven towards friendship with France, Austria–Hungary had, by the end of the first decade of the new century, reached the status of sole friend of Imperial Germany. The fundamental opposition of the interests of some members of the two alliances of the European Great Powers, Germany and the Dual Monarchy on the one hand and France, Russia and England on the other, created an international situation with all the stability of a house built by a child out of playing cards. When, through a simultaneous failure of diplomatic and governmental machinery among and within all five capitals, Austria's status advanced to that of holder of a blank cheque with unlimited drawing rights, a conflict, always probable by reason of the opposed interests, became inevitable. When it occurred, it was rendered total in Clausewitzian terms by the ability of every major power to bring to bear the whole sum of its national resources, manpower and industrial, on the prosecution of the war. New technologies and improved documentation of people and assets made it far easier than ever before to harness everything to the war effort.

When the war began, it was beyond question that Germany was the world's leading land power, and also had a navy fit to challenge English supremacy at sea, which had remained uncontested since Trafalgar. But, just as France had drawn the wrong lessons from the war of 1870, so had Prussia. That war had been won by a plan of genius and the effective application of superior numbers and better firepower. The supreme planner, especially one without personal experience of direct combat at unit level, might well deduce and pass on to his successors the propositions not only that all that mattered was the doctrine and the plan, but that the plan had worked in spite of and not because of the efforts of the subordinate commanders. As we have seen in consideration of the battles of August 1870, not one decision was required at army group or army command level to alter the course of a battle in progress, and the few which were taken were wrong. For the most part, the battles had been fought either without the knowledge or against the wish of the commanders at the two top levels. It is possible too that the surgical precision of Sedan was taken as the blueprint for the future, rather than the hand-to-mouth scramble of Mars La Tour. Moltke remained as chief of the general staff until 1888, perfecting mobilisation procedures and continuing his impeccable annual appreciations of the military threat to Imperial Germany and the allocation of resources to counter it. The army of course benefited from the expansion and technological progress of an industrial base matched only in the United States, but, as experience of war receded, there was no proper attempt to relate improved weapon capabilities to the conduct of battle. The result was that the German Army went to war in 1914 on a plan perfect in logistic detail but inflexible, because the minds of those who launched it could not conceive of the need to alter it to meet unforeseen circumstances. The plan was assumed to be the master of events. But its means of control, never properly practised in peacetime, proved defective and at point of contact level the troops, committed to advance because the plan required a pre-emptive invasion of France through Belgium, were thrown into attacking with no more tactical subtlety than that displayed by Manstein or Steinmetz on the Lorraine uplands forty-four years earlier.

Appendix 1
French Mobilisation and Battlefield Strengths

The combined strengths of the Armies of Chalons and Lorraine when they capitulated respectively on 2nd September and 29th October was at least 40,000 more than the number of soldiers of the Army of the Rhine who had arrived for duty by 31st July, notwithstanding at least 75,000 battle casualties between 4th August and 1st September.

Calculation

Table XVIII

		Numbers	Source
1.	Ration strength of the Army of the Rhine on 31st July	238,188	a
2.	Surrendered		
	a. At Sedan by the capitulation	83,000	b
	b. At Sedan during the battle	21,000	b
	c. At Sedan interned	3,000	c
	d. At Metz by the capitulation	173,000	d
	e. Fugitives from Froeschwiller, who withdrew to Strasbourg	4,000	
	TOTAL	288,000	

	Numbers	Source
3. Battle casualties, killed, wounded, missing and prisoners, excluding those accounted for above:		
a. Wissembourg and Froeschwiller	16,188[*]	f
b. Spicheren	4,078	g
c. Borny	3,600	h
d. Mars La Tour	16,959	I
e. Gravelotte–St Privat	12,273[*]	j
f. Beaumont	4,800[*]	k
g. Sedan, killed and wounded	17,000	b
TOTAL not less than	75,000	

[*] Incomplete and minimum

Sources, from op.cit.
a. Howard, p.78 b. Moltke, p.100 c. Fuller, p.130.
d. Moltke, p.165 e. Ascoli, p.82 f. Ascoli pp.75 and 83
g. Moltke, p.25 h. Moltke, p.32 i. Ascoli, p.210
j. Howard, p.181 k. Moltke, p.82.

Deduction

It follows that, between 1st August and 1st September, the gross manpower strength of the French armies in the field increased by at least 120,000, i.e. two plus three above minus the original start state, and no reinforcements can have reached the Army of Lorraine in Metz after 18th August. The increased strength was not entirely reservist, because in XII Corps the division of soldats marins had a strength of around 10,000, all 'with the colours' at the start of the war, and this corps also had seven line regiments. Assuming these to have been at fifty per cent strength before mobilisation was ordered, this gives another 10,000 non-reservist infantry and its ten gun and three mitrailleuse batteries produced approximately a further 2,500 artillerymen. Deducting these figures from the total increase in August, it follows that some 100,000 reservists caught up with the field armies in eastern France some time during the month. Still others went to XIII Corps or the Paris garrison. Had they all reported in time, Le Boeuf's postulated ration strength of 385,000 by the fourteenth day of mobilisation would have been achieved.

Battlefield Strengths

Mars La Tour provides an early example of the increasing difficulty, discussed in Chapter I, of assessing the numbers physically engaged in a single battle, principally because it was an 'encounter' battle fought over what, by the standards of the time, was a relatively large area. The yardstick used by the author is to estimate the number of men who were close enough to the scene of fighting to have been committed to operations actually ordered, even though some, for example in the divisions of Montaudon (III Corps) and Levassor-Sorval (VI Corps), did not fire a shot on 16th August. Thus the battle strength of the Army of Lorraine on that day must exclude Laveaucoupet's division, left behind as the garrison of Metz, and that of Lorencez (IV Corps), which did not reach the battle area until 10 p.m., by which time the fighting was over. Bazaine therefore had at his disposal thirteen and three-quarters infantry and five and a quarter cavalry divisions:

TABLE XIX

Formation	Infantry	Cavalry
Imperial Guard	2	1
II Corps	2 and 1/2	1 and 1/4
III Corps	4	1
IV Corps	2	1
VI Corps	3 and 1/4	
Reserve cavalry		1

Allowing for undermanning and the casualties taken at Spicheren and Borny, Bazaine had on the Lorraine plateau, therefore, at 'entry-to-battle' strength, somewhere between 120,000 and 140,000 infantry and not less than 12,000 cavalry. His artillery strength, notwithstanding the deficiency in Canrobert's corps, was not less than sixty field batteries (360 guns) of various calibres and eleven or twelve mitrailleuse batteries (sixty-six or seventy-two guns).

On the German side, III and X Corps were complete except for stragglers and the casualties taken by the former at Spicheren. Committed to action in addition were V and VI Cavalry divisions, a brigade of the guard cavalry division, and, not until early evening, infantry brigades from VIII and IX Corps which together amounted to another division. Thus the German forces available and committed, which unlike on the French side amounted to the same thing, comprised five infantry and two and a half cavalry divisions, giving a manpower strength of between 65,000 and 75,000, and 210 guns. By any method of calculation, the odds in favour of the Army of Lorraine were at least four to one until the arrival in late afternoon of the infantry divisions of X Corps, at least two to one thereafter, and often locally much better.

Notes

[1] Howard, op.cit., p.121.

[2] Ascoli, op.cit., p.48.

[3] *From Sedan to Saarbrucken*, p.17.

[4] Guedalla, *Marshals*, p.15 et seq.

[5] Guedalla, *Marshals*, p.179.

[6] Howard, op.cit., p.185.

[7] Whitton, op.cit., p.204.

[8] Moltke, op.cit., pp.27–28.

[9] Moltke, op.cit., p.33.

[10] Ascoli, op.cit., p.108.

[11] Moltke, op.cit., p.34.

[12] Guedalla, *Marshals*, p.175.

[13] Ascoli, op.cit., p.109.

[14] Guedalla, *Marshals*, p.177.

[15] Ascoli, op.cit., p.119.

[16] Moltke, op.cit., p.37.

[17] Guedalla, *Marshals*, p.184.

[18] Nicholson, *King George the Fifth: His Life and Reign*, London, Constable and Co., 1952; reprinted 1984, p.261.

[19] Guedalla, *Marshals*, p.183.

[20] Ascoli, op.cit., p.189.

[21] Moltke, op.cit., p.45.

[22] Ascoli, op.cit., p.210.

[23] Guedalla, op.cit., p.186.

[24] Moltke, op.cit., p.48.

[25] Moltke, op.cit., p.52.

[26] Moltke, op.cit., p.58.

[27] Moltke, op.cit., p.63.

[28] Moltke, op.cit., p.65.

[29] Moltke, op.cit., p.69.

[30] Moltke, op.cit., p.70.

[31] Moltke, op.cit., p.71.

[32] Howard, op.cit., p.186.

[33] The conflicting evidence is set out by Howard, op.cit., pp.189–90.

[34] For the full story of this bizarre sub-plot, see Guedalla, *Marshals*, pp.207–11.

[35] Howard, op.cit., p.196.

[36] Howard, op.cit., p.197.

[37] Moltke, op.cit., p.76.

[38] Moltke, op.cit., p.82.

[39] Horne, op.cit., p.51.

[40] Fuller, op.cit., p.124.

[41] Fuller, op.cit., p.126.

[42] *From Sedan to Saarbrucken*, p.17.

[43] Whitton, op.cit., p.272.

[44] Moltke, op.cit., p.100.

[45] *One Hundred Years of European Statistics*, Economist Publications, 1989, compiled by Thelma Liesner, gives the total national revenue of France in 1885 as FF 3,057,000,000,000.

[46] Moltke, op.cit., p.403.

[47] Fisher, op.cit., p.1,002.

[48] At the time of his sentence, Bazaine was nearly sixty-three. Ascoli, op.cit. pp.334–37, and Guedalla, *Marshals*, pp.235–43, describe this sorry episode. Bazaine, with the help of his wife and some of his 'military family', contrived to escape from imprisonment to exile in Spain, where he lived on, in extreme poverty, until 1888.

[49] Bredin, *The Affair: The Case of Alfred Dreyfus*, translated into English by Jeffrey Mehlman, London, Sidgwick and Jackson, 1983.

[50] *Thomson, The Twelve Days 24th July to 12th August, 1914*, London, The History Book Club, 1966, p.155.

[51] Tuchman, *The Guns of August: August 1914*, London, Constable and Co., London 1962; Four Square 1964, p.51.

[52] Tuchman, op.cit., p.57.

[53] Massie, *Nicholas and Alexandra*, London, Victor Gollancz, 1968; Gollancz Paperbacks 1985, pp.92–93.

[54] Taylor, op.cit., p.38.

Chapter XIV
Sustainability

Whatever improvements are made to the areas of combat capability already discussed, their effective operation on the battlefield depends entirely upon the continuing ability of a human agency to use them. There is a finite limit to the load the soldier can carry, and also to the length of time he can continue to work without being fed and watered. The development of the crew-served weapon and the mobile weapon platform extend some of the physical limits of the individual, but introduce additional logistic demands. While throughout the decade of the Catalytic Wars these fundamental principles were usually understood, the logistic backing for all the armies engaged faltered on at least one important occasion. For nearly all of the armies and almost all of the time, sustainability was no better than it had been in the armies of the eighteenth century. Disastrous shortages occurred and strategic designs were more than once inhibited because no logistic provision had been made beforehand to support them. Where these lapses happened, the problem was not so much that the supplies did not exist, except in the Confederacy throughout most of the War Between the States; it was far more usually a failure in the organisation of the movement of combat supplies to the place where they were most needed. If the best which can be claimed is that for much of the time the combat units had enough 'beans, bullets and bandages' to see them through, the reason perhaps lies in the additional physical and mental endurance which is brought on by the demands of combat – or self-preservation. But there is a limit to the length of time for which even the best-motivated soldiers can be left to go hungry, and their fighting power ends abruptly when their ammunition runs out.

Battlefield sustainability starts with what the soldier himself can carry, plus what is immediately to hand without the need for him to leave his position in combat or to bring his weapon out of action in order to be resupplied. When his resources run short, the soldier charged with the direct engagement of the enemy must not be looking over his shoulder for replenishment. Starting at the lowest level of combat subunit, the infantry company, cavalry squadron or artillery battery, there must always be one experienced soldier responsible for seeing to it that ammunition stocks are always kept up, and for organising the daily distribution of rations and drinking water. In most armies, this is usually the task of a warrant officer or quartermaster-sergeant. Behind the direct fire zone and also to artillery gun lines, resupply forward to replace consumption must be automatic, but surplus stocks which could impede battlefield mobility must not be allowed to accumulate.

The staff responsible for the forward movement of combat supplies have further problems to overcome. As soon as it is necessary to move commodities on wheels, the motive power creates its own resupply and maintenance demands: there must be a 'continuous loop' system of controlled movement for the vehicles, otherwise the means of transportation will dwindle to nothing; and careful attention must be paid to load and route capacities. For any given carrier, ammunition tends to 'weight-out', in that the load-bearing limit is reached before all the space is filled, while for other commodities, food and forage in particular, the tendency is to 'bulk-out', in that the conveyance is full before it is loaded with the maximum possible weight. The former constraint is the more significant because, given the natural erosion of routes through constant use, poor weather and enemy artillery fire, some additional motive capacity, horse- or engine-power, is always desirable whatever the weight of the load.

The decade of the Catalytic Wars introduced three further factors for which logistic staffs had to allow in their plans. The first was the increase in size of the armies and the second the coming of the railways. These did not cancel each other out, because an entirely new organisation had to be created at railheads, to unload freight wagons, break down bulk cargoes, make up and load unit or formation 'packs' of combat supplies, hold stocks not immediately needed by the combat units and manage two transportation loops, one forward to the combat zone, and one to the rear, to return empty railway trucks for their next load. As we have seen, even the armies of the king of Prussia in 1870, best grounded of any in terms of forethought, planning and training if not actual length of combat experience, failed to resolve this problem satisfactorily. The third new factor derived from the first two. Whatever the number of combat soldiers, their food and forage requirements were constant and could easily be calculated. Much the same continued to apply even after the internal combustion engine replaced the horse. What is never a constant is the consumption of ammunition, and thus its resupply requirement. The need for replenishment on an enormous scale after a major battle was as old as the firearm; what set the pattern for the future was the continuous combat extending over a period of months, first experienced in the American Civil War, most particularly in the eastern theatre from May 1864 onwards. Here, the increase in numbers of manpower was compounded by a firefight conducted over an unprecedented span of time and at an intensity likewise without previous parallel in military history. This level of ammunition consumption would become the norm once comprehension of the 'total' nature of warfare coincided with the ability to harness the entirety of national resources to its conduct.

Subsistence in the Field

Since the fighting power of any army depends in the first instance upon that of the individual soldier, with a whole greater than the sum of the parts brought about by a combination of leadership and planning, it is appropriate to start with the arrangements for his subsistence. If he is to march long distances on metalled roads, his boots and the means for their repair and replacement must be up to the task. The ultimate in provision was reached by the German Army in 1914, which had cobblers' wagons accompanying each infantry regiment to conduct running repairs, a measure undoubtedly deriving from the experience of 1870. If the foot soldier is to remain in the field for any length of time, he can expect to have to carry a load of between sixty and seventy pounds, progressively eaten down by consumption, but which must be built up again by replenishment. A special harness is essential to carry this burden and there is no ideal design. The composition of the load varies according to doctrine and circumstance. Highest priority must be given to the soldier's personal weapon and an appropriate scale of ammunition for it, but the latter cannot be allowed to exclude the need for everything else. Health, hygiene and a basic standard of comfort demand some spare clothing. The rations, issued either on an individual basis or as a proportion of those intended for the basic combat grouping of up to ten men, take up a significant part of the available payload, as does the means to cook them. Because all armies at the time expected to feed themselves by 'group' cooking, which allowed a more economic distribution of rations than individual issue, quite large and heavy cooking utensils had to be carried, either by individuals in turn or on subunit transport. The soldier must also carry enough water for his immediate needs and a 'survival' medical kit. Highly desirable also is the means of producing a rudimentary shelter if there is a halt for any length of time, to keep off the worst of the rain in temperate or tropical climates or to provide shelter from extreme heat. And from the American Civil War onwards, there was some provision of tools, ad hoc at first but scaled in most armies before much of the First World War had run its course, to construct field defences – picks, spades, axes and saws.

The French Army in 1870 was perhaps the victim of previous and recent combat experience more varied than any other. Because it had fought in all climates, from the frozen winter of the Crimea, through the steamy humidity of an Italian summer and the tropical conditions of Mexico and South-East Asia to the dry heat of the North African desert, the French soldier was over-provided, even allowing for individual shortages caused by the chaotic mobilisation process. The full scale of equipment for the mobilised army probably existed, and Le Boeuf's boast to the chamber on the day upon which mobilisation was ordered, that the army was 'ready down to the last gaiter-button', was not empty bombast. What failed, as has been discussed, was the method of distribution. But at least some of the equipment which the *'fantassin'*[a] was expected to carry was wholly unnecessary for a campaign to be fought in a predominantly benign climate over one of the most fertile and best-wooded areas in the world, and more appropriate to the conditions of the bare desert. The soldier has his own time-honoured way of dealing with this problem: if he is required to carry something for which he sees no immediate need, he soon finds a way of discarding it by the wayside, and, unless unit discipline is good, he is allowed to get away with doing so. Soon, more important equipment is also lost.[b] Where in 1870 the French soldier was fully equipped, he was carrying far too much. Worse, many items of his uniform were inappropriate for service in the field, and there was too much rather than too little unit transport,[1] which produced consequent problems of congestion on routes at a time when everything depended upon the marching pace and capacity of the infantry.

Compared with present-day standards of diet and the nutritional levels thought necessary for those engaged in strenuous physical activity, the rations provided for the soldier in the field a century and a quarter ago seem revolting, and fell well short of the necessary calorific value. As is often the case in prolonged wars, the War Between the States was for the individual soldier a succession of long marches to battle leading to short bursts of intense and dangerous action, interspersed with much more lengthy spells when the armies were static, with no activity beyond self-administration, training and

---

[a] Contemporary slang for infantryman.

[b] For a fictional description in all probability very close to events, see Chapter Two of Zola's *La Débâcle*.

providing for local security. The main items in the daily ration scale of a Union soldier in the latter 'camp' conditions were three-quarters of a pound of preserved salt pork or one and one quarter pounds of fresh or preserved beef, and a pound of hard bread. This was issued in the form of large biscuits, each 3" square and 0.5" thick, nine or ten making up a somewhat bulky day's ration. Smaller items in the daily ration scale included a portion of dried vegetables or rice, enough coffee beans to brew up three to four pints a day, pinches of salt and pepper, an ounce or so of sugar and occasionally a ration of a quarter of a pound of potatoes. There was also an occasional issue of anti-scorbutics. Better found or more enterprising regiments, if static for any length of time, established field bakeries and by the end of the war units had mobile bakery wagons. In these circumstances, and when the ingredients were available, the troops received fresh bread instead of the biscuit ration. Fresh beef was kept 'on the hoof' until needed, but the salted meat was in barrels, and required prolonged soaking before it could be cooked. Even then, through venality or incompetence by either contractor or commissary department, the meat might be so aged and rotten as to be inedible, and the biscuits were a natural target for weevil infestation, just like those provided for the crews of Nelson's ships of the line. Human ingenuity being what it is, the soldier soon learned to supplement his ration by foraging, which was permissible, or by looting which was not. Each regiment was authorised to appoint a regimental contractor, called a 'sutler', who would sell tobacco, tinned fruit, sugar and similar delicacies from his wagon, for as long as his stocks and the pay of the soldiers lasted.[2] One variation available to the Union Army later in the war was the tinned meat produced in the new packaging factories of Chicago, which the soldiers termed 'embalmed beef'.[3]

Although the unit cooks were found most usually from soldiers too incompetent, slovenly or stupid to learn the drill movements upon which their survival in battle depended, performance no doubt improved with practice and criticism. Some of the 'contrabands' – escaped slaves – who gravitated towards the Union armies made very good unit cooks. And with the most fertile farmlands in the world providing the raw materials, any shortage of rations stemmed from inadequate distribution arrangements rather than lack of availability. The need to embark upon long marches with the prospect of combat did not usually take commanders, staffs or units by surprise. For a move, the camp scale of rations was converted instantly into a marching scale of from three to ten days, depending upon distance, stocks immediately to hand and prospects for resupply, to be carried by the soldier. There was no special packaging provided for the meat ration, which the soldier was expected to carry in his haversack along with all his other belongings. In the conditions of the continental United States summer, it must soon have become inedible. Cattle on the hoof might accompany the troops on a march, a proportion being slaughtered at the end of each day for immediate consumption.

A contemporary account discloses much about the standards of rationing achieved in the Union Army during the four months' campaign on the James peninsula in the summer of 1862, when troops and commissary department were still new to war. Charles B. Haydon of the 2nd Michigan, who began the war as an elected sergeant and died in March 1864 as a lieutenant colonel, has a diary entry for 22nd August, 1862, when his regiment, part of III Corps, had been returned to the lower Potomac to join the concentration for Second Manassas:

> The men received their first full ration of soft bread since leaving this place in March. I hoped to have remained here for a week or ten days. I have lived so slim for the last two or three months that my strength is perceptibly diminished, but merely need better food for a few days.[4]

The James peninsula was cotton plantation rather than agricultural land, and such farm produce as there might have been would not long have survived the depradations of the two armies, in total over 200,000 men, in presence for three months.

Given the standards and capabilities of the time and the unprecedented scale of the supply problem, most other armies which fought in this decade will have sought to feed themselves in much the same way. The exception was the Confederate armies in the field, which were significantly worse off because of the difficulties of distribution in a collapsing railway network, as well as shortage of food stocks in a country whose primary crops were cotton and tobacco. Both of Lee's invasions of the North were motivated to some extent by the fact that in fertile western Maryland and Pennsylvania his army could live off the land, something which had become impossible in war-ravaged Virginia. Towards the end of the war, the armies of the Confederacy were suffering badly from scarcity of food. One of Lee's officers in Petersburg stated: 'It is hard to maintain one's patriotism on ashcake and water.'[5] When J.E. Johnston capitulated to Sherman nine days after Lee's surrender to Grant at Appomattox Courthouse, his army was saved from starvation by an issue of ten days' rations from Union Army stocks.

The French Army had a system of overnight cooking. Bazaine's orders for the day of battle upon which the whole fate of the Second Empire depended started with the phrase: '*La soupe sera mangée demain matin à quatre heures.*'[6] By 1870 the Prussians appear to have had a more satisfactory marching scale of ration than anyone else.[7] But in both armies in 1870, particularly the French, failure of distribution arrangements rather than lack of supplies caused the shortages of rations, as was often the case thereafter.[c]

All the armies of the decade had a procurement system based upon local purchase for cash at the going rate, or requisition on a signature promising future payment, which the fortunes of war might or might not subsequently allow to be honoured. The commissary department of the United States Army, the intendance of the armies of the Second Empire and the staff of the commissary-general of the Prussian general staff coped as best they might with problems of scale for which there were no previous blueprints to suggest a solution. By far the worst was the French intendance, fighting, as events transpired in their own country, over fertile farmland. The staff were inadequate, the mobilisation arrangements had in some cases neglected to provide them with ready cash, and the situation was made worse by the fact that the intendance was also responsible for replenishment. The French Army had no quartermaster-general's[d] staff of military officers. A combination of requisitions and self-help looting by the troops left unrationed soon exhausted the goodwill of the inhabitants of Alsace and Lorraine.[8] And while in the fortnight between the fall of Sedan and the investment of Paris strenuous efforts were made to provision the city for a siege of unforecastable duration, the number of inhabitants was underestimated by more than one-third, and the need for milk-producing cows overlooked altogether.[9] At the same time, the supply arrangements for the invading Prussian Army also broke down. After their own supplies and captured French stocks had been exhausted, the troops charged with the reduction of the fortresses still holding out in Lorraine were reduced to a requisitioning policy which, according to a contemporary account,[10] left a bare subsistence level for the inhabitants, who displayed absolutely no confidence that the bonds freely issued by the occupying army would ever be redeemed.

---

[c] As, for instance, in the Falklands in 1982. The Argentine soldiers who surrendered on the hills west of Port Stanley showed signs of malnutrition, while in the warehouses six miles away there were enough combat rations to feed their whole invasion force for two months.

[d] This term is used as it would be in the British and United States armies. In the German Army up to 1945 the '*Quartermeisters*' were not logisticians, but general staff officers.

The campaigns of 1866 and 1870 were nevertheless too short for the consequences of malnutrition and impure water to have had any impact, except in the besieged fortress cities. Such was not the case in the four years of the War Between the States, in which disease killed as many men as fell in combat. Without any of the means of water purification a modern army would consider essential, typhoid and dysentery, both water-borne diseases, took an appalling toll, with a consequent multiplication of the load on medical and hospital resources. In the Union Army throughout the war, fifty-five per cent of all deaths were from disease, half from typhoid or dysentery, as against thirty per cent in action or from wounds, and fifteen per cent from other causes. As half of the latter are classified as being 'in captivity', the proportion from disease, including malnutrition, must be increased accordingly. From less accurate and incomplete statistics, the Confederate proportion of deaths caused by combat and disease lies the other way, fifty-seven per cent to forty-three per cent.[11] In all, 250,000 men died of disease while serving.[e] It was, of course, the unseasoned troops who suffered most, particularly at the start of a war in which enthusiasm was allowed to take the place of stringent physical examination of the volunteer before he was accepted for service. It has to be concluded that the best protection of the troops against death from a cause at least as likely as enemy action was their own hardihood, especially those who were country-bred and inured to a life in which survival depended upon physical strength and endurance. If, by the time of the world wars of the twentieth century, the causes of the most prevalent diseases had been identified and protective or remedial antidotes made available, the recruit, at least in the armies of the Western powers, because he was increasingly town-bred, had become a much softer specimen.

Ammunition Resupply

Before the decade of the Catalytic Wars, it had seldom been necessary to think beyond the needs of a single day of battle for an army in the field. The infantryman carried as part of his standard equipment an ammunition pouch or box holding between twenty and sixty complete rounds, cartridge and ball or bullet, quantity depending upon calibre, which was normally enough for the demands of all but the most intense battlefield day. If it were not, the

---

[e] Standards of military health were in any event appalling, irrespective of the toll of combat. In 1860 the number of admissions during the year of soldiers to the military hospital at Aldershot, largest peacetime concentration of troops in England, exceeded (14,949 to 14,875) the average daily strength of the garrison.[12]

immediate recourse of the combat soldier was the ammunition pouch of a dead or seriously wounded comrade. At the end of the day, especially in the War Between the States where the adversaries fought with the same types of weapon, the side left in possession of the field scoured it for anything which might be useful. For the armies of the Confederacy in particular, the best source of resupply throughout the war was captured stocks. After Antietam, Lee's army was able to re-equip itself with weapons and ammunition as well as clothing from the booty surrendered at Harper's Ferry.

Artillery was likewise self-sufficient for a day of battle. The caisson and limber associated with each field gun held ninety-six rounds for the twelve pounder, rising to as many as 150 for six pounders,[13] with up to as many again in the caissons drawn by the spare gun teams of a battery at full establishment. Both resupply and dumping, when they were needed, were ad hoc; as we have seen, everything was subordinated on the afternoon of 16th August, 1870 to the priority of ammunition resupply through the Gorze defile for the embattled German troops around Mars La Tour. Earlier, in the War Between the States, the Army of Northern Virginia, when forced to make more use of field entrenchments, had rudimentary dumping programmes on the gun lines at Spotsylvania, Cold Harbour and around Petersburg, but the stockpiling programmes required to support the artillery concentrations of the First World War lay far in the future. In any event, the ammunition stocks did not exist.

There was, as we have seen, a variety of types of personal weapon in the hands of the Union armies, and the same occurred also in the forces which the provisional government of France put into the field in the winter of 1870–71. The pre-war production line of 1,000,000 chassepots was insufficient to arm the men raised by Gambetta's *levée en masse*.[f14] The logistician's nightmare, resupply of several different types of ammunition with no clear idea either of consumption or of the numbers of different weapons involved, nevertheless seems to have been resolved on the spot, and inevitably, as casualties occurred, the obsolete types of firearm were the first to be discarded. Ammunition resupply in the field was the responsibility of the artillery train, organisations for which varied according to availability of ammunition stocks, horses and carts. The latter were no different from standard heavy-duty farm issue. In the French Army, the caissons and limbers of the field batteries had been redesigned in 1858 to match the introduction of the new rifled cannon,

---

[f] Further evidence of the inability of successive previous French Governments to grapple with the trained military manpower imbalance *vis à vis* Prussia.

but those of the Artillery Park had remained unchanged since 1827.[15] Nor had they needed to be, given the perceived demands of resupply in the field at the time. But the heavy expenditure in the battles of August 1870 required guns to come out of action and withdraw in order to replenish, and the fact that Frossard at Gravelotte, on the afternoon of 18th August, drew a fortuitous advantage from being forced to do this does nothing to justify a bad practice.

The organisations of the artillery trains of even the German armies in 1870 were not standardised. In the Prussian Army, each artillery regiment, numbered the same as its parent corps and of course recruited from the same province of the kingdom, had an 'artillery column' and sometimes an 'artillery train' as well. But Moltke's order of battle for the German armies as on 1st August, 1870[16] groups these sometimes under divisional and sometimes under corps control, for no obvious tactical or logistic reason. The armies of Prussia's more or less unwilling partners in the North German Confederation and allies against France – Saxony, Bavaria, Wurtemburg and Baden – all had different organisations for the logistic support of their artillery, in so far as these existed at all. It has to be concluded that the continuous and high-level ammunition expenditure of later wars had not yet reached the level which required a foundation of standard organisation and replenishment planning, variable at need by exception or expansion.

Similarly, planned peacetime stockpiling was a matter for the future. It was almost non-existent in the army of the United States in 1861, and it is doubtful if any European Great Power held field artillery ammunition stocks beyond the envisaged requirements of a single battle. In any event, military prestige in peacetime derived more from the introduction of new types of cannon rather than from a build-up of the stocks they would fire. It was only in the nuclear age that ammunition stockpiles became a quantity in the equation of deterrence. Nevertheless, at the start of the war of 1870, Alfred Krupp saw the point at once. Before the end of July and without waiting even for an indication from the war ministry in Berlin that new supply contracts were in the offing, he directed round-the-clock shift work in his factories and also gave an unprecedented authorisation for sub-contracting.[17] While some of this was directed towards the production of replacement gun barrels and other main components, the priority was given to ammunition production. But throughout the war and for long afterwards, the logistic requirement was still seen to be more in the organisation of the movement of stocks from production- to gun line, rather than the building up of stocks in peacetime, to support the army in the field through the opening and intense phase of a prolonged war, until additional production resources could be developed to match expenditure rates. Neither England nor France gave any thought to this problem, still less planned any resources to meet it, beyond production for the barest minimum first-line requirements; hence the shell shortages in both armies which became manifest in 1915.

Medical

If ammunition replenishment stocks and procedures were just about capable of supporting the increased scale of the battles of the decade, the medical provision failed totally. Progress in this discipline since 1815 had been slower than in any other major area of human development. Innovative research leading to an improved standard of military medicine had been minimal, and the techniques and remedies of the eighteenth century for the care of wounds had barely altered. Thus, no improvement in medical science had occurred to match the vastly increased lethality of weaponry, most particularly the 'spread' effect of the Minié bullet.[g] There is no reason to doubt the conclusion of the leading modern authority on the American Civil War that as many as fifty per cent of those who survived the treatment for the wound which they had suffered on the battlefield remained too badly crippled to return to any military duty,[19] and thus by extension for any heavy work once the war was over, either on the land or to meet the rapidly increasing manpower demands of the burgeoning industries of the Second Industrial Revolution. The United States avoided a manpower shortage and contained industrial wage costs because of the unending and almost unlimited availability of immigrant labour.

If care of wounds had not advanced in fifty years, the practice of military hygiene fell below the standards laid down in the Old Testament for the armies of the Israelites. The average Union regiment in the War Between the States seldom fought its first action at anything much above half its paper strength, mostly because of the effects of disease, and, with very few exceptions, was never restored even to a fifty per cent strength level because the political advantage lay in the raising of new regiments and not in a coherent replacement system for the incurably sick and the battle casualties. If Confederate unit entry-into-battle strengths were higher, it was because of the greater hardihood derived from a country upbringing.

A more humane age was beginning to force some change. An English gentlewoman, by the application of political influence and the enforcement of

---

[g] But, by 1870, the smaller calibre of the chassepot had tended to reduce the severity of wounds.[18]

the same standards of hygiene she would have insisted upon in her own home, dramatically improved the recovery rate of the sick and wounded who had survived initial treatment and evacuation from the Crimea. A Swiss gentleman, travelling in northern Italy for pleasure, visited by chance the battlefield of Solferino, and was appalled by what he saw of the suffering of 40,000 wounded left on the field, Henry Dunant founded an organisation which by 1870 was internationally based and, according to a contemporary account, was doing much three weeks after Sedan to alleviate the suffering of the wounded. In 1870 the Red Cross deployed in national contingents.[18]

On the other hand, no army expected to fight without casualties and all had made some provision ahead of that of the *Grande Armée*, itself in the forefront for its time, as described for the campaign on the Danube in 1809:

> ... egotistical, beauty-loving Massena had no ambulances in his corps; honest, incompetent Oudinot had a fifty per cent equipment; while the iron, ruthless Davout had his full 100 per cent of ambulances and his 100 per cent of doctors.[20]

A decree four months after Louis Napoleon had taken increased powers as prince-president in December 1851 established the medical services of the French Army under the son of the Baron Larrey, who had been surgeon-in-chief to the army of the First Empire. There was an establishment of three doctors for each regiment of infantry, cavalry and artillery, an embryonic staff of 700 doctors and pharmacists to form the nucleus for fifty military hospitals and even a small military medical school at the Val de Grâce hospital in Paris.[21] In contrast, the total military medical establishment of the army of the United States at the beginning of 1861 numbered 115, twenty-four of whom resigned at once to form the basis of the medical service of the army of the Confederacy.[22] The volunteer spirit nevertheless affected doctors as much as other men, and there seems to have been enough of them to have provided a surgeon with every regiment, the best no doubt as good as any of the time, but at the other end of the scale a fair proportion of backwoods quacks of doubtful qualification and competence. By the end of the war the Union Army had 10,000 surgeons, some two and a half times as many as in the Confederacy.[23]

The length of the War Between the States, combined with the permanent and continuous public audit of government function which is perhaps the best feature of American democracy, combined to force an improvement in military medical care for the sick and wounded of the Union armies. By 1863 there were special ambulance wagons, with a rocking rather than a rigid suspension to provide a less uncomfortable ride for the casualties, and each division had an establishment of forty such vehicles.[24] There was a system of regimental aid posts, and divisional and corps field hospitals, which sought to achieve, then as now, resuscitation from shock and stabilisation of the wound. Bullets were extracted by primitive techniques and damaged limbs amputated at the first suggestion of gangrene. Field hospitals sought to set up in any available stone or brick building, such as the church in Froeschwiller or the Stone House by the Warrenton turnpike at First Manassas, which gave some cover from fire and reduced the risk of conflagration inherent in a wooden structure.[h] Casualties were evacuated, as soon as their condition and the available resources allowed, to the base hospitals. It was these installations which first attracted the attention of the predominantly volunteer US Sanitary Commission, and so forced an improvement both in them and also in camp hygiene. This was done by the provision of direct aid in the form of medical supplies, foods and comforts purchased by public subscription, and also in the application of unremitting pressure on congressmen.[25]

A high sickness and absentee rate is always an indicator of low morale. As has already been noted, after the Battle of Fredericksburg, the mud march and six weeks of unorganised squalor in the camps round Falmouth, something approaching two-thirds of the posted strength of the Army of the Potomac was absent from its place of duty. It was a combination of pressure from the volunteers of the Sanitary Commission and a report on the conditions at Falmouth by an emissary of the surgeon-general of the United States Army which, in the short term, sealed the fate of Burnside and throughout the rest of the war produced a substantial improvement in the conditions of field and base hospitals. In 1864, Grant's staff pooled the resources of five corps hospitals to create the medical facility of the Union Army logistic base at City Point, the first ever composite logistic installation ever established in the field for the long-term support of operations. By then, there were also hospital ships to evacuate the seriously sick and wounded from the war zone. For the North, the problem had lain not in a shortage of resources, but in the proliferation of a bureaucratic accounting system geared to minimising the cost of a small army in peacetime rather than maximising the efficiency of a large one in war. This had been compounded by a failure of distribution arrangements, and corruption.[26] But all was relative; if a contemporary observer could judge the Prussian Army in 1870 to have 'a thorough and minutely [sic] perfect organisation of its ambulance corps,'[27] it has to be

---

[h] The Dunker Church at Antietam was so used nevertheless – and survived.

remembered that the wounded evacuated after Sadowa suffered 'unheard-of tortures'.[i]

Sustaining Prolonged Operations

Grant's redirection of the axis of his campaign in June 1864 led to the establishment of the logistic base at City Point. The size this prototype support installation eventually attained cannot have been foreseen when the Union Army was moved south of the James after the indecisive battle at Cold Harbour. The base was only 'completed', in the sense that it was carrying out all the functions needed to support the commander's operational plan, when the campaign and the war came to an end. Throughout the autumn, Grant set his face against the erection of hutted accommodation, on the ground that any such permanent structures would imply there was no foreseeable end to the break-in battle for Petersburg, and that the Union Army would relax its efforts during the winter months. But the weather was deteriorating; the general was to be absent from his headquarters for two days, during which time the work was set in hand. When Grant returned, he did not object to it.[28]

The 3,500 acre site, situated on the south bank opposite the confluence of the James and Appomattox rivers, was eight miles north-east of Petersburg and linked to it by narrow-gauge railway. The estate had been the property of the Eppes family since 1635. In 1861 the current owner, a doctor, loyal to the Confederacy but by no means an ardent secessionist, enlisted in the 13th Virginia cavalry, but was soon reassigned to duties more related to his professional skills, as a surgeon in a Petersburg hospital. His family joined him there in 1862, when the appearance of federal gunboats on the James in support of McClellan's Peninsula Campaign forced them to abandon the Appomattox Manor House. For the next two years, although outside the path of the fighting, the house had remained unoccupied and the plantation unworked. Now Grant selected the estate as his headquarters, which he established not in the manor house but in the estate buildings augmented by tentage. The land was taken into use as required for the components of a support base, for which it was ideally situated by location. Grant's own quarters, where he was joined by Mrs Grant, were a three-room log cabin.[29]

The army which Grant brought across the James had, as we have seen, suffered heavily, and though the unprecedented battle casualties of the previous six weeks had been replaced, the new men were not of the veteran status of those who had been lost. Half the troops had never heard a shot fired

---

[i] Chapter Ten, note 37.

in anger. Nevertheless, not all the replacements were unwilling draftees or 'bounty men'. There had been a combing-out of the troops which, since 1861, had formed the garrison of the fortifications around Washington. In these units, classified as 'heavy artillery regiments' and at their established strength of 1,800 equivalent in manpower to many a hard-fought brigade of the field army, the men had received some infantry training.[30] But, because of the static nature of their employment over the last three years, they were not battle-hardened and were of limited and unproven combat value. After the failure of a break-in operation in June, with the aim of forcing Lee's lines before they became too strong, the new troops soon became seasoned to combat by continuous trench warfare. The next operation was intended to exploit the detonation of four tons of explosive early on the morning of 30th July. This 'mine' had been placed under a Confederate redoubt in their front line by the mining experts of a regiment recruited from the Pittsburgh coal fields, who had tunnelled for over 500 feet from their own trenches. An original idea was frustrated by incompetent execution and the operation failed, at a cost of another 3,800 casualties.[31]

During July, Grant had three infantry and one cavalry corps south of the Appomattox, and Butler's Army of the James still boxed up in Bermuda Hundred. The two wings of the army were connected by a bridge of boats across the James, and after the failure of the Crater operation two more infantry corps were moved to the south bank of the Appomattox. There was no intention of pausing for rest, replenishment or reassessment of objectives, as might have been the course adopted by some of Grant's predecessors. His stock in trade as commander-in-chief was the continuous application of pressure on the enemy. The troops settled down to what half a century later would be described as a war of attrition – continuous action but no major operation or manoeuvre – and the composite logistic base at City Point began to take shape.

A mile of deep-water wharfage was built along the river bank, and there was a continuous steamer service by way of the Potomac, the Chesapeake and the James, conveying visitors (including Lincoln), reinforcements and the supplies brought by railroad from the munitions factories and granaries of the North to the termini on the lower Potomac. Sometimes there were as many as twenty vessels arriving in a day. Some of these ships returned the sick and wounded on the first stage of their journey to base hospitals in their home states. Warehouses on the wharves and elsewhere on the Eppes estate contained a stockpile of thirty days' rations for the whole army, and twenty days' forage, which were distributed on a daily replenishment basis. There was an ordnance park for field artillery[j] and a main ammunition dump of unquantified size. A bakery produced 100,000 rations of fresh bread daily. Given the stronger stomachs of the time, the rivers provided an unrestricted supply of fresh water. Areas were also provided for sutlers and other tradesmen, who were allocated shipping space to bring in their wares.

As the base developed, so did the distribution arrangements. With five infantry corps south of the river, the lines of circumvallation after the failure of the Crater operation were prolonged ever westwards throughout the summer and autumn. The pre-war rail link towards Petersburg was further developed, and extended by a twenty-one mile spur line supporting the Union forces in the entrenchments round the south-east quadrant of the city. This was built by the US Military Railroad Construction Corps. The line started outside the warehouses on the wharves, twenty-five locomotives and 275 freight wagons were brought down by steamer, and the corps sectors were supported by a daily service to their railheads.[29] Thus there was for the first time a daily replenishment supply system for an army in the field over a prolonged period of combat, from field depot to fighting unit. There was also the ability to build up stocks of combat supplies to support a major operation.

City Point made similar provision for what would now be described as the adjutant general's services. The largest single installation was the Base Hospital, on a 200 acre site, which contained 1,200 hospital tents, and, after the autumn permanent building programme, ninety log cabins. The whole complex could hold 10,000 sick and wounded in conditions which, thanks largely to the US Sanitary Commission, were as good as they could be for the circumstances of the time, including regular changes of bed linen. Much had been achieved compared with the ordeal of the wounded in the Crimea less than ten years before.

Much less well provided for were the military criminals of the army, held for serious civil offences or desertion, who were confined in appalling conditions. There was a court martial in permanent session to try cases, and a contemporary account asserts[29] that on one day five men were led off to be executed by firing squad. There was also a stockade for interim holding of prisoners of war, 1,400 of whom were staged through City Point en route to prison camps in the North.

After the war, the property reverted to Dr Eppes, who was required to pay $641, 50 to the federal government for the structures which the Union Army

---

[j] A photograph in Catton's *Picture History of the Civil War*, [p.404] shows too many 'Napoleon' twelve pounders to be counted.

abandoned when they withdrew from the site in February 1866. The visitors had not been kind to the property of a 'rebel'. Dr Eppes described the place when he returned as:

> desolation personified, a perfect waste, not a house, fence... or scarcely tree of any kind standing, everything destroyed.'[29]

The manor house too had been vandalised. Owners of property requisitioned for military use in England in the Second World War may perhaps discern a parallel. But the logistic installation at City Point was, for a period of at least six months, the forerunner of the field depots upon which the whole support of twentieth-century armies came to depend.

Notes

[1] Guedalla, *The Two Marshals*, London, Hodder and Stoughton, 1943, pp.167 and 174.

[2] Coggins, *Arms and Equipment of the Civil War*, North Carolina, Broadfoot Publishing Co., 1990 pp.120 and 124; and Catton, *Mr Lincoln's Army*, New York, Doubleday and Co., 1951, pp.200–6 describe the arrangements for rationing, cooking and sutlers in the Union Army.

[3] Macdonald, *Great Battles of the Civil War*, New York, Collier Books, 1992, p.121.

[4] Sears,[ed.] *For Country, Cause and Leader: The Civil War Diary of Charles B. Haydon*, New York, Ticknor and Fields, 1993, p.276.

[5] Catton, *Picture History of the Civil War*, New York, American Heritage Publishing Co., 1960, p.475.

[6] Ascoli, *A Day of Battle*, London, Harrap, 1987, p.109.

[7] Ascoli, ibid., p.159

[8] Howard, *The Franco-Prussian War*, London, Rupert Hart-Davis Ltd, 1961; reprinted, St Albans, Granada Publishing Ltd, 1979, p.71.

[9] Horne, *The Fall of Paris*, London, Macmillan and Co., 1965; The Reprint Society, London, 1967, pp.65–67.

[10] 'An Officer of the Royal Artillery', *From Sedan to Saarbrucken*, London, Tinsley Brothers, 1870; reprinted Helion Books, Solihull, 1992, pp.67–68 and 80–81.

[11] Lanier, [ed.] *Armies and Leaders*, New York, Fairfax Press, 1983, p.148, and Catton, *Mr Lincoln's Army*, p.205. The former tabulates casualties from all causes in the War Between the States.

[12] 'The First Soldiers Home', in *The Times*, 15th March, 1961.

[13] Coggins, op.cit., p.69.

[14] Howard, op.cit., pp.246–47.

[15] Willing, *L' Armée de Napoleon III*, Arcueil, Préal, 1993, pp.73 and 79.

[16] Moltke, *The Franco-German War of 1870–71*, London, Harper Brothers, 1907, reprinted Greenhill Books, London, 1992, pp.432–47.

[17] Manchester, *The Arms of Krupp*, Boston, Mass, Little, Brown and Co., 1964, p.119.

[18] *From Sedan to Saarbrucken*, pp.28, 31 and 64.

[19] Catton, *Mr Lincoln's Army*, pp.211–12.

[20] Macdonnell, *Napoleon and His Marshals*, London, Macmillan and Co. Ltd, 1934, p.193. As a front-line soldier on the Western Front in the First World War, Macdonnell is better placed than most to comment on casualty evacuation and the care of wounds.

[21] Willing, op.cit., p.80.

[22] Coggins, op.cit., p.118.

[23] Macdonald, op.cit., p.96.

[24] Coggins, op.cit., p.119.

[25] Catton, *The Glory Road*, New York, Washington Square Press, 1952, p.109.

[26] Catton, ibid., pp.114–16.

[27] *From Sedan to Saarbrucken*, p.28.

[28] Related by the official guide to the author on a visit to City Point, July 1995.

[29] *City Point Unit*, Petersburg National Battlefield leaflet, published by the US Department of the Interior.

[30] Catton, *A Stillness at Appomattox*, New York, Washington Square Press, 1958, p.270.

[31] Catton, ibid., pp.250–53 and 273–86, and also, Catton, *Never Call Retreat*, New York, Doubleday and Co., 1965, p.380, between them give the full story of the Crater operation and its many further implications.

Chapter XV
Blitzkreig 1914 and 1940: Schlieffen and Manstein

From Envelopment to Encirclement

By any objective standard, Imperial Germany in 1871 was unassailable on land, and, having at the time no interest outside Europe and a fleet whose operational capability was limited to the Baltic, was unlikely to come into conflict with the British Empire. For almost the first time since the emergence of the European nation state, England was prepared to tolerate the pre-eminence of another country on the Continent. This was a change of the attitude which, throughout the previous six centuries, had sent England into war at recurrent intervals, either to preserve an altruistic balance of power or out of self-interest to safeguard her trade routes into Europe by way of the Low Countries. Given the extent of the defeat of France in 1870, it seems inconceivable now that within five years of her triumph Germany should have felt threatened. But France had recovered quickly. In 1872, for the first time in peacetime in the history of the nation, legislation enforced a genuine universal liability to military service of two years with the colours, subsequent training as a reservist and commitment up to age forty to recall on mobilisation. Equally important in view of the ramshackle arrangements made in July 1870, a permanent formation structure was decreed which for the first time since the days of the *Grande Armée* gave the army the same peacetime organisation as it would have in war. And in 1875, the *École Superieure de Guerre* was established, with Colonel Lewal as its first commandant.[1] Lewal was the only senior staff officer in the headquarters of the Army of Lorraine in whom Bazaine had had any confidence.

The whole process so worried Moltke that in the winter session of the Reichstag in 1874–5 he broke his habitual silence to state that Germany stood in great danger, sending, as one authority put it, 'a shiver down every patriotic German spine.'[2] In the spring of 1875, tension between Germany and the

Third Republic rose to a level which had not been approached in Europe since the Hohenzollern–Sigmaringen candidacy five summers before. Moltke and Bismarck each played on the fears of the other. On the last day of April, Moltke said to the Belgian minister in Berlin:

> Much as I hate war, I do not see how Germany can avoid it next year unless the Great Powers coalesce to persuade France to reduce her armaments to a reasonable peace establishment.[2]

On this occasion, Tsar Alexander II of Russia, nephew of the old emperor, acted as peacemaker. But Moltke continued to draw the attention of Germany to the danger from across the Moselle, warning in 1877 that:

> ... in France, the army is the spoiled child of the nation – its pride and its hope; in France, the army has long been forgiven for its defeats.[2]

For another ten years, the ascetic and austere old man, bereft of all joy in life since the wife to whom he had been devoted died in 1868, continued to be seen taking his daily walk in the Tiergarten in Berlin. Dressed in the simple cloak and unbraided cap of a Prussian general, he looked more like a professor of philosophy or botany than the pre-eminent strategic planner of the age. He continued to devote meticulous attention to the selection and training of the officers of the general staff, and to his annual appreciations of the threat facing the empire which he had done so much to establish. His worst possible scenario, imposed upon him by the facts of geography, was a combination of Russia and France against Germany. Until 1880, Moltke's strategic design to counter this was to throw the whole weight of an offensive against France, while conducting a holding operation in the East. It had not escaped the attention of the foremost exponent of the use of railways for strategic mobility and logistic support that the expansion of the Russian railway system, now proceeding apace, was on a different gauge from that of Western Europe. Therefore, any advance by either side far beyond the frontier of East Prussia and partitioned Poland would be totally dependent upon horse-drawn logistic support. But in 1880, Moltke reversed his view, because of the growing strength of the French Army – birthrates in the 1850s and 1860s having been similar, there would now be little difference in mobilised strengths – and the development of the fortress system of General Séré de Rivière either side of the forty mile gap deliberately left open between Toul and Epinal.[a] Instead of an offensive against France, Moltke's new design was for a defensive war in the west and an offensive against Russia, but one with strictly limited objectives.

In 1882 Moltke first sought retirement from the post of chief of the general staff, after a tenure of a quarter of a century. He was becoming too frail to sit on a horse, but neither emperor nor country could contemplate a future without the architect of the victories of 1866 and 1870. He was given a deputy, but it was only in 1888, after the death in that year of both William I and his son, the latter prematurely of cancer of the throat after a reign of only ninety-eight days, that the new emperor, Wilhelm II,[b] granted Moltke his release. He retired to Kreisau, the estate in Silesia which he had purchased shortly before the death of his wife, and died there in 1890.

His deputy, Alfred Count von Waldersee, was the obvious successor, by virtue both of appointment and a carefully cultivated friendship with the young emperor, ever since the ultimate heir to the throne had entered the 1st Regiment of foot guards as a twenty-one year old ensign in 1881.[3] Waldersee's military background was impeccable – guard artillery, general staff, military attaché in Paris before the start of the war in 1870, and chief of staff of a corps commanded by a Hohenzollern prince. But his ambition went well beyond the position of professional head of the army. By the mid-1880s, he had set himself up in opposition to Bismarck, seeking involvement in matters of foreign policy, which, under the constitution of the empire, was the sole prerogative of the chancellor, and going far beyond anything Moltke had ever claimed. Whether formal treaty existed or not, Bismarck had, ever since the war of 1866, sought to remain on friendly terms with both the Dual Monarchy and Russia, in spite of the irreconcilable differences between Habsburg and Romanov empires. Waldersee, on a visit to Vienna in 1888, had let it be known publicly that the Dual Monarchy had no need to fear an attack from Russia, whereas the foundation of Bismarck's conduct of policy was to keep the other players guessing. Also, having married a very rich wife, Waldersee had acquired a controlling interest in a Berlin newspaper which was fed regularly with titbits from the press section of the general staff, a department newly established on Waldersee's authority and answerable to him. In 1890, he felt himself strong enough to directly challenge Bismarck's conduct of foreign

[a] See Chapter V.
[b] See Appendix A.

policy in front of Wilhelm II. But by this time, Waldersee's ultimate goal, the chancellorship, had passed beyond his reach.

Wilhelm was already disenchanted with his chief of general staff – his own appointee and less than two years in post. More than any other head of state in history – and there is much competition for the post – Wilhelm II loved to play soldiers. Destined for the throne from birth and succeeding to it when aged only thirty, he had had the most Spartan and demanding upbringing and education at the hands of the Lutheran pastor George Hinzpeter, on a regimen which would have delighted the heart of his maternal grandfather, the Prince Consort.[4] Hinzpeter imposed iron intellectual restraints and from the time of his appointment as tutor demanded total accountability for every minute of a twelve hour working day. Many young men, once free of these shackles, would have run wild. Wilhelm did not. His education gave him a total sense of duty to his position as sovereign and Supreme Warlord, accountable only to God, with a burning desire to excel in whatever field he undertook, possessing total confidence in his own judgement. Notwithstanding an arm that remained withered because it had been damaged at birth and which imposed its own psychological damage, he became an excellent horseman. But he could not tolerate opposition or criticism. When, at the annual manoeuvres in 1890, his proposed tactical solution met with criticism from Waldersee, the days of the latter were numbered; no matter that the chief of general staff was an experienced soldier nearly thirty years the emperor's senior, nor even that he was right and Wilhelm wrong. The general did not succeed Bismarck as Chancellor, but was instead shunted to a corps command. He confided to his diary a comment on his monarch: 'He wants to be his own chief of staff; God help our country.'[5]

The next chief of general staff was the man who had been Waldersee's own deputy since 1889, Alfred Count von Schlieffen. By the 1890s the threat in the mind of Moltke twenty years before and the intellectual worst possible case in his annual strategic appreciations were taking on a tinge of reality, because in 1894 France and Russia concluded an alliance pledging each nation to go to the help of the other if either were attacked by a third party. The threat from this purely defensive alliance was remote, but it became a phobia in the mind of the German people. The flame of *Einkreisung* – encirclement – once lit was fanned by no one more actively than the kaiser himself. He endorsed, when he did not lead actively, the national demand for a high seas fleet, colonies, and a still larger fleet to protect the sea lanes to them. Even though, as late as 1910, the kaiser could still be welcomed by *The Times* in the friendliest of terms[6] when visiting London for the funeral of King Edward VII, the uncle whom he had hated as the architect of *Einkreisung*, the policy inspired by Wilhelm and by then in full swing was the biggest single factor in driving England into an undefined and imprecise alliance with France, and so by extension Russia.

This march of events was reinforced by a series of German diplomatic blunders dating from the dismissal of Bismarck. The effect was that, if Moltke's plans after 1871 had been made against a threat which was little more than academic, the work of Schlieffen and his successors might well become the blueprint from which Germany would have to fight a war on two fronts.

The Dedicated Planner

In many ways, Alfred Count von Schlieffen combined the best qualities of cavalry officer and junker. Wild as a hawk when first commissioned into the guard cavalry in 1854, his fundamentally serious nature took over as he matured, and he became a complete master of his profession. But a blissfully happy marriage to a cousin ended after only four years when Anna von Schlieffen died. Schlieffen never recovered from the loss. The darker side of his Prussian personality took over. Increasingly reserved and introspective, he became totally remote from all but his immediate circle of assistants, and after his wife's death had no solace or interest outside his work. The process went too far. When, during a staff ride in East Prussia, a junior officer exclaimed at the beauty of the River Pregel in the early morning sunshine, the chief could only snap, 'An unimportant obstacle'.[7] The head of one section of the general staff became accustomed to receiving, every Christmas Eve, a staff problem to which the solution had to be returned on the following day.

Schlieffen's career had been that of an outstanding and well-connected officer. Qualifying for entry to the general staff in 1865, he was on the staff of the Cavalry Corps of First Army throughout the campaign in Bohemia, and one authority suggests that Sadowa, a victory won by double envelopment, exercised a dominant influence on his thinking for the rest of his life.[7] In the war of 1870–71 he served on the staff of the Grand Duke of Mecklenburgh-Schwerin, who initially commanded XIII Corps, formed after the fall of Metz, and then an army groupment in the operations on the Loire during the winter. In 1884, Schlieffen was appointed head of the highly rated military history section of the general staff, and deputy (*Oberquartermeister*) to Waldersee five years later. The personalities of the two men could hardly have been more different. As Schlieffen drew in ever further on himself, the last thing he would do was criticise the suggestions of his imperial master and Supreme Warlord – not through weakness of character but through loyalty and the

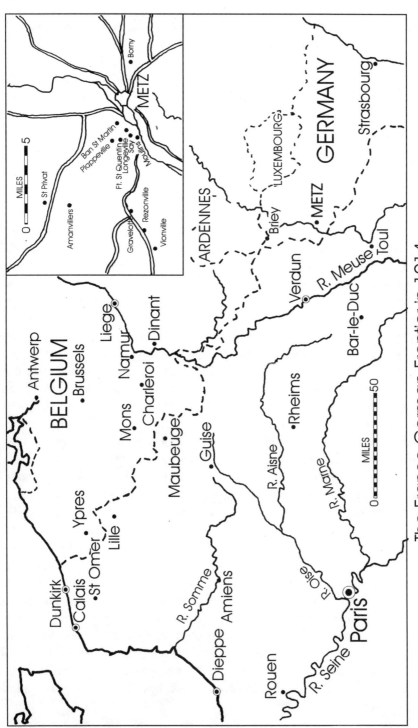

The Franco-German Frontier in 1914

unquestioning obedience to superior authority which he exacted from his own subordinates. At the same time, Wilhelm, impulsive rather than analytical, never gave critical scrutiny to the plans developed by Schlieffen during his fourteen years in post, and neither military cabinet nor Ministry of War had the necessary prestige, resources or even a watching brief to do so. The general staff had become supreme, and its plans were not subject to evaluation, still less stringent analysis.

As a planner, Schlieffen was the supreme technocrat. His method was to seek the ideal solution, which would define the resources needed to achieve the desired result. The requirements thus established, the plan itself became the case for the necessary provision to be made. There was no element of resource constraint. Between 1891 and 1905 the German Army never had the troops available to carry out Schlieffen's plan, the final variant of which appeared in his last year in office. Between 1906 and 1914 the design did not alter. What changed, as more soldiers became available, was the proportion allocated to each task. Schlieffen's underlying assumption was that the necessary manpower would at length be provided for the number of corps-sized formations his plan demanded. This was not necessarily invalid, in spite of the priority and provision given after 1890 to the Imperial Navy. The governmental structure of Wilhelmine Germany and the prestige and position of the army within the nation were powerful factors in his favour. However much the Reichstag might balk at ever-rising defence appropriations, the money would ultimately be forthcoming thanks to a booming economy. In addition, the necessary manpower did exist. From the 1880s the German birth rate soared ahead of that of France and by the turn of the century Imperial Germany was in the same position as the kingdom of Prussia forty years earlier before the appointment of von Roon as war minister. Although military service remained the first duty of every fit adult male, apart from a few specifically exempted categories such as Krupp workers, many young men were escaping the call-up altogether because the German Army did not have enough units in which they could be enlisted and trained.

Strategy is limited by the availability of resources and by topography. The fifteen first-line corps mobilised in 1870 had been increased by two during the war, and a further two were added in 1884.[8] Fourteen of the 1870 formations, all except the Guard Corps, drew their manpower from a single province of the empire, and fourteen including the Guard Corps could produce a reserve corps from the manpower not needed on mobilisation by the first-line formations, either because it was surplus or because it was superannuated, but nevertheless, under the Roon mobilisation laws, still subject to recall. It was only during the time of Schlieffen as chief that the reserve corps became written into the plans for immediate commitment to battle once mobilised, thus making them, at least on paper, the equivalent of their first-line counterparts. This stroke of the pen gave Schlieffen a total of thirty-three infantry corps,[c] nineteen first line, fourteen reserve. Three more first-line corps had been formed by the date of his retirement, and a further three were established in 1912.[9] Still this was not enough.

The plans continued to be refined after the younger von Moltke, Helmuth like his uncle, succeeded Schlieffen at the beginning of 1906, but in spite of the additions the master plan in 1912 was still deficient of three corps. The case for these was made by Colonel Ludendorff, head of the operations section of the general staff and so nominally one of four co-equals as heads of sections answerable to the chief. Ludendorff, by reason of his considerable abilities, mania for work and personality, had become both the most influential of the four and the most disliked. This time he overreached himself and his enemies seized the opportunity to engineer his posting away from Berlin, to command a regiment in the Rhine Provinces Corps. Nevertheless, even in a Reichstag in which, after the election of 1912, the internationalist and anti-war Social Democrats had become the largest single party, the three additional corps which were the subject of the argument were agreed in principle, for establishment between 1916 and 1921.[10] And in the event, on the outbreak of war, after the mobilisation of all the reserves, a further six corps were authorised and formed in mid-August.[11] It is therefore beyond question that the manpower existed.

It remained fashionable in the higher strata of the British and French armies, right up to 1914, to decry the quality of reservists. In the German Army, the excess of available manpower at the peak of potential physical attainment raised the quality of the reserve formations. The guard reserve corps had an active division, and the Reserve V, VI and VII Corps, from Polish Prussia, Silesia and Westphalia, each had an active brigade.

---

[c] These corps all had a basic organisation of two infantry divisions, little changed from the 1870 structure. By 1914 the much smaller cavalry divisions were grouped separately in cavalry corps, and the number and variety of corps troops had increased, owing to the increasing demands of new weapons, communications systems and logistic complexities. Each first-line corps included an aviation detachment. The organisation and strength of first line and reserve corps were similar, except that the latter had less artillery and thus fewer ammunition columns.[11] The manpower strength of each corps was between 40,000–45,000, predominantly infantry riflemen. Battalions had no more than two machine-guns, the same as in the British Army.

Soon after his appointment, Schlieffen changed the priority arrived at by Moltke in 1880 and maintained by Waldersee. German temperament and philosophy alike caused France to be seen as the primary enemy. Unlike the Dual Monarchy, Germany had no source of perpetual tension with Russia. Also, by the end of the century, Clausewitz had become the sage worldwide of military thought, and nowhere was the prophet more honoured than in his own country. A new edition of *On War* published in 1905 contained a foreword by Schlieffen himself.[12] The whole logic of the first two chapters of this work is to establish the proposition that the maximum possible force must be brought to bear in order to destroy the will of the enemy to fight – an argument which leads inexorably to the conclusion that, if the enemy is an alliance, the stronger partner must be destroyed. This conclusion was reinforced by the continuing incompatibility of the German and Russian railway systems and by the knowledge that in 1812 even the capture of Moscow had led the *Grande Armée* to nothing but destruction.

It was of course open to the planners in Berlin to produce a defensive strategy on both eastern and western frontiers. The events of 1914 were to confirm that the four corps allocated by Schlieffen to the defence of East Prussia, a provision Moltke left unaltered, were adequate to beat a Russian army greatly outnumbering them, always provided that the army commander kept his nerve. The armies of the tsar in 1914 were too badly equipped, short of ammunition, poorly coordinated and incompetently commanded to conduct a sustained offensive. In the west, if the Second Empire in 1870 had found it impossible to arrive at a design for the invasion of Germany, the difficulties for the Third Republic were now incomparably greater. The post-1871 frontier provided a buffer zone for Germany west of the valley of the Moselle, thus denying to the French Army this oblique axis of invasion to threaten the Ruhr. Strasbourg and Metz were now German cities, making them *points d'appui* for a German and not a French strategic design. The only course open to France which did not involve violation of neutral territory was a tactical as well as a strategic frontal offensive to force crossings over the Moselle, which would then come up against the north–south grain of the Vosges, ideal defensive country. In this scenario, the whole advantage would lie with the defence, as was also proved in August 1914 when the French offensive in Alsace towards Morhange and Sarrebourg failed at enormous cost.

And yet, while all the logic implied that Germany should remain on both strategic and tactical defensive, at least until after the Russian threat had been beaten off, there is no evidence that this course was even contemplated. Perhaps such thoughts were impossible in the cauldron of expansionist and aggressive pressures building up in the Second Reich. The two leading living military philosophers in Germany in the first decade of the century were Friedrich von Bernhardi and Colmar von der Goltz, both veterans of the war of .1870, and both generals who had had careers of the highest military distinction. In a book published in 1910, Bernhardi[13] claimed that Germany had a right and a duty to make war, that to demand new spheres of influence and new territories was 'the first and foremost duty of the state' and that conquest was a law of necessity. And von der Goltz, in his *Nation in Arms* wrote: 'To make war means to attack'; and:

> In describing a battle, we have been led, in spite of ourselves, to depict an offensive battle. What German soldier could do otherwise?[14]

The intellectual drive towards a strategic offensive turned into a general staff planning assumption which was never challenged, still less validated.

If the design was for an offensive against France, and the plan was not to be constrained because the men needed to implement it had not yet been enrolled, the only remaining limitation was geographic. Again, Clausewitz provided the necessary doctrine:

> The centre of gravity of France lies in the armed forces and in Paris. The allied[d] aim must therefore be to defeat the army in one or more battles, capture Paris and drive the remnants of the enemy's troops across the Loire. The most vulnerable area of France is that between Paris and Brussels, where the frontier is only 150 miles from the capital.[15]

---

[d] All writers are to some degree the prisoners of their experience, and Clausewitz was writing in the afterglow of personal involvement in the success of the Grand Coalition which had defeated Napoleon and captured Paris in 1814 and 1815. He was thinking in terms of an alliance to which Prussia would contribute an army of 200,000 men. A total of 725,000 would be made up by a further 250,000 from Austria, 150,000 from 'the rest of Germany', 75,000 from the Netherlands and 50,000 from England. As we have seen in Chapter XIII, Moltke's ration strength at the end of the war in 1871 was of the order of 630,000 and the German armies had lost 130,000 men, killed.[16] The Dual Monarchy had remained neutral and there were no contributions from the Netherlands or England, but in terms of force level the only mistake which Clausewitz made was to underestimate the German birth rate.

An offensive by way of the inviting gap between Toul and Epinal did nothing to achieve this aim. The attention of the planners was drawn, perforce and at once, towards an approach march through Belgium.

The Plan Becomes Master

It was entirely in accordance with both his temperament and training that Schlieffen discarded at once the idea of a frontal attack on the French fortress system. He was also bound to seek a replica of Moltke's achievement in August 1870: to pin the French Army against either a neutral frontier or its own fortress system with its front reversed. He ruled out an attack through Switzerland because of the difficulty of the terrain, the shortage of good routes and inadequate linkage with the German railway system. Thus Schlieffen was drawn by force of circumstances to the cockpit of Europe – the pennant-shaped triangle of ground with its vertical axis running from Aachen to Luxembourg, and the longer sides closing on the Channel coast at Calais. This territory had been fought over in most centuries since the time of Julius Caesar. Writing in 1934, even after the recovery of the lands lost in 1870, Charles de Gaulle assessed the strategic vulnerability of this approach into France as greater than any other possible invasion route:

> Just as a portrait may arouse in the observer the impression of a personal destiny, so does the map of France reveal our lot. The main body of the fatherland provides at its centre a stronghold, a rugged massif of aged mountains, flanked by the plateau of Languedoc, the Limousin and Burgundy; all around, immense glacis most of which are difficult of access for any threatening invader, being protected by trenches, the Saone, Rhone and Garonne, barred by ramparts, the Jura, Alps and Pyrenees, or plunging far away into the Channel, the Atlantic and the Mediterranean; but with a terrible breach in the north-east, that links up with the Germanic regions the vital basins of the Seine and Loire. Though nature indicated to the Gauls that the Rhine was their limit and their protection, scarcely did it touch on France than it became remote, leaving the country exposed.
>
> It is true that the Vosges provide a broad partial rampart, but it can be circumvented by the Belfort Gap of the Salt Marshes. It is true that the banks of the Moselle and of the Meuse, supported on the one side by the Lorraine plateau, and on the other by the

Ardennes, constitute obstacles which, although not negligible, are lacking in depth, so that one blunder, or surprise or piece of carelessness is enough to lose them, and which the first withdrawal in Hainaut or Flanders renders liable to a setback. Now it so happens that in these low-lying plains there is neither a barrier nor a trench to which resistance might cling; there are no lines of surmounting heights, and no rivers parallel to the front. Even worse, here geography organises invasion by numerous penetrating routes, the valleys of the Meuse, the Sambre, the Scheldt, the Scarpe, the Lys, along which streams, roads, rails undertake to guide the enemy.

Distressing when viewed in relief, the north-east frontier is no less so with respect to its projecting ground plan. The adversary who attacks simultaneously in Flanders, in the Ardennes, Lorraine, Alsace and Burgundy, is striking concentric blows. If he succeeds at one point, the whole system of the French defences crumbles. The first steps forward lead him to the Seine, the Aube, the Marne, the Aisne or the Oise, and then he need only make his way downstream to strike at the heart of France, Paris, where all these rivers come together.

This gap in the girdle of fortifications is the country's age-old affliction. Through it Roman Gaul saw the barbarians fling themselves on its riches. There the monarchy stood up with difficulty against the empire. There, Louis the Great defended his power against the European coalition. The Revolution almost expired there. Napoleon succumbed there. In 1870, disaster and disgrace took no other road. In this fatal avenue we have just buried one-third of our youth.[17]

The question which the German general staff had to answer, in 1891 and later, was just how much violation of foreign territory would be needed. Routes through Luxembourg, now independent of the crown of Holland, were inadequate for the movement of the mass assault now necessary, and the grand duchy, together with adjoining southern Belgium, was heavily wooded. Germany did not want to mount an advance to contact over this ground in 1914. In May 1940 it was a different matter: the woods provided cover from aerial reconnaissance, and German traffic control, though operating in an area far from ideal for large-scale coordinated movement of armoured vehicles, achieved a technical success as great as that through the Forêt de Belvel before the Battle of Beaumont in August 1870, but on an incomparably larger scale. Thus, part at least of Belgium had to be overrun. The question, as it remained in some minds up to the last minute, was whether the need to use Belgian territory could be restricted to the right bank of the Meuse. If so, there was a chance that the avaricious King Leopold II could be bought off, and the south–north course of this great river between Dinant and Namur, together with the curve north-westwards towards Maastricht beyond the border with Holland, would protect the open flank of the advance. But if it were necessary to go west of the Meuse in order to gain more space so that the great right hook could be uncoiled, the likelihood of Belgian acquiescence was reduced, and that of international concern possibly leading to intervention increased. After the accession of King Albert I to the throne in 1910, there was no possibility of Belgian co-operative neutrality. From a purely military standpoint, a broad swing west of the Meuse improved the chance of striking the bulk of the French Army in flank and rear – a manoeuvre always sought by Moltke, as it had been by Napoleon before him. An even wider swing, through the Maastricht Appendix, involved the invasion of yet one more country. Throughout more than twenty years of planning and refinement,[e] the operational and logistic considerations were provided for down to the last detail. But there was never any consultation with the German Foreign Office, still less acceptance by what passed for the political leadership of the empire, about the wider implications of invading one, two or three neutral countries, or about the unilateral abrogation of treaty guarantees.

Until as late as 1899, the movement plan was restricted to the east bank of the Meuse, but thereafter the routes beyond the river were added. In 1905, the year of Schlieffen's retirement, the plan for the right hook reached its final version. Sixteen corps, nine first line, seven reserve, would advance into Belgium from a concentration area bounded by Cologne–Dusseldorf–Aachen, force the line of the Meuse, capture Brussels, and only then swing south, with the weight of the punch directed through Lille. Schlieffen's directive to his staff was 'When you march into France, let the last man on the right brush the Channel with his sleeve.'[19] After the turn southwards, the rate of advance of the formation on the right wing was expected to regulate that of the whole of the swing of the scythe. Concurrently with the move of the sixteen corps into Belgium, fourteen more would cover their inside flank by a short right hook pivoting on Thionville. The intention was to produce an advance on a continuous front of about 125 miles, with the heaviest manpower density

---

[e] A planning period probably only exceeded during the span of the Cold War.[18]

allocated to the corps on the extreme right. Five corps only were allocated to cover the 100 miles of front between Thionville and the Swiss border east of Belfort, a density which precluded anything other than a tactical defensive, but on ground well suited to it.

The concept for the four corps provided for the defence of East Prussia was slightly different. They were expected to be capable of conducting a holding operation against anything Russia could mount against them within forty days. This was the time limit Schlieffen set for the defeat of France, because thereafter the Russian numbers mobilised and concentrated would render essential the reinforcement of the German forces in East Prussia. The superb latitudinal railway system across Germany would allow the rapid transfer of troops once a quick victory over France had been won. It was, of course, a prime weakness in Schlieffen's planning technique – go for the ideal – that no one stopped to ask what would happen if France had not been defeated by the end of the fortieth day after mobilisation.

The routes over the Meuse were expected to have been secured by the twelfth day, Brussels, at the northern limit of the great flank march, was expected to fall on M+19, and the frontier into France was to be crossed three days later. The first phase of the plan, to secure a continuous line from Thionville to Abbeville on the Somme estuary, was to be achieved by M+31. The plan depended upon German mobilisation and concentration being at least concurrent with that of France, and preferably ahead of it. Also essential was a phenomenal marching performance by the troops on the right wing, and the successful conduct of the holding operations south of Thionville and in East Prussia. This was by no means the end of the story. The second phase of the plan required another right hook to be unleashed once the line of the lower Somme had been secured. Thirteen corps were to advance to close Paris on the north, and to encircle it from west and south, on exactly the same principle as the envelopment of Mack at Ulm by the *Grande Armée* a century earlier. The decisive battle was expected to have been won by M+39, on the ground between the Oise and the Aisne, with the French field army crushed between pincers closing on these two tributaries of the Seine east of the capital.

Until 1899, Schlieffen worked under the implicit assumption that France would be the first to invade Belgium, a contingency which suited the basis of his design – victory in the west as soon as possible. After that year, the assumption, such as it was, lapsed. If the plan required the invasion of Belgium as well as Luxembourg, so be it. No imperial chancellor between 1900 and 1914, neither Hohenlohe, Bulow nor Bethmann-Hollweg, had the standing to question this foundation. Had the French been the first to invade Belgium, the whole diplomatic scenario at the start of the First World War would have been completely different, because it needed the invasion of Belgium and the violation by Germany of the 1839 treaty to persuade at least a third of the members of Asquith's Liberal cabinet that England should enter the war; this notwithstanding the very detailed planning which had been completed by 1911 to bring almost the whole of the British regular army stationed at home, six divisions of infantry and one of cavalry, to a concentration area around Maubeuge in north-eastern France, on the left of the initial French deployment, on the thirteenth day following British mobilisation.[20] At this stage there was no thought that, within two months of the outbreak of war, stalemate would have been reached, with continuous lines of trenches opposite each other from the Channel coast to the Swiss frontier. As we have seen,[f] the French design for the campaign was an all-out offensive, to which the British Army was committed by the thrust of one particular phrase in the somewhat imprecise directive to Field Marshal Sir John French, commander-in-chief of the British Expeditionary Force: '... to assist the French government... to restore the neutrality of Belgium.'[21]

Schlieffen demanded a rigid understanding of the plan by all subordinate formation commanders and chiefs of staff. This time there was to be no place for individual initiative by a Steinmetz unamenable to higher authority, or a Blumenthal wishing to prove he knew better. The plans were worked out in the most complete logistic detail, with daily march tables, routes and distances calculated for each day and every formation. Enforced by the method of conduct of staff rides, map exercises and manoeuvres, the plan became supreme. To question its authority was not encouraged. A junior staff officer, seeking to put forward his own ideas, was told, perhaps ruefully, by his corps commander: 'His Majesty keeps only one strategist, and neither you nor I is that man.'[22]

The German Army would go to war with another disadvantage. Triumph in the field followed by decades of an assumption of supremacy, unchallenged either at home or abroad, was not the climate in which innovative technology was likely to be properly evaluated, any more than in the contemporary Royal Navy still living off the reputation of Trafalgar. The procurement of new equipment was in any event the responsibility of the Ministry of War, not the general staff. France led Germany in seeing a military use for aviation; no one had any idea about what use to make of three prototype armoured cars which

---

[f] See Chapter XIII, notes 51 and 52.

took the field on the annual formation manoeuvres in 1908, or was prepared to follow through a paper design for an armoured machine-gun carrier with caterpillar tracks.[23] And as we have seen, Schlieffen himself, writing in 1909, could even question whether new technology had anything more to offer.[g]

Following a riding accident, Schlieffen retired as chief of the general staff at the end of 1905, but continued to write about the plan and related strategic topics until he died in 1912. His last words, reminiscent of those of King Frederick William I in 1740,[h] were to growl: 'See you make the right wing strong.'[24] He had drawn much from Clausewitz, and even more from Moltke. But one critical point in the philosophy of the latter had not been absorbed:

> It is a delusion to imagine that a plan of campaign can be laid down far ahead and fulfilled with exactitude. The first collision with the enemy creates a new situation in accordance with its result. Some things intended will have become impracticable; others, which originally seemed impossible, become feasible. All that the leader of an army can do is to form a correct estimate of the circumstances, to decide for the best for the moment, and carry out his purpose unflinchingly.[25]

The plan continued to be refined over the next eight years, and reached as near perfection as any plan can. Eleven thousand trains were to move on four routes east to west, at a steady nineteen miles per hour and at ten minute intervals. One hundred and eighty trains were allotted to each corps, and in all nearly 1,500,000 men had to be moved from peacetime barracks and mobilisation centres over four days to railheads from Aachen to Strasbourg. Thereafter, the advance would be at marching pace. Supporting the railway timetables was a framework of subsidiary plans for kitting out, loading and unloading, and assembly areas for each railhead where the units would emerge from logistic train load into tactical column of march, ready to go into battle as soon as the frontiers had been crossed.

The Reluctant Executant

The younger Helmuth von Moltke was a very different man, both from his predecessor and his uncle and namesake. He was undoubtedly a competent and well-trained officer even by the exacting Prussian standards, because, had

[g] Chapter VII, note 1.

[h] Chapter V, note 37.

he not been, his name alone would not have carried him to the top strata of the army, let alone brought him into contention for the succession to Schlieffen. He was a wholly untypical junker: a man of sensitivity and self-doubt, with a breadth of intellectual interests well beyond the range of most soldiers. He had cultured nineteenth-century tastes in music and literature. He was a man who would question rather than accept. His career had followed the predictable pattern for an officer of ability with impeccable connections. Appointed ADC to his uncle in 1882, he had later, during Waldersee's tenure as chief, served as a military assistant to the emperor, during which time he edited his uncle's account of the war of 1870–71. Later he commanded a foot guards regiment, and in 1902 he was appointed to command the 1st Guard infantry division. When it was first suggested to him that he should succeed Schlieffen, he tried to decline the appointment. He had none of the supreme and evident self-confidence which is the hallmark of every great political or military leader, and he would claim later, when it was all over for him, that when he was offered the post his conscience had warned him against acceptance, suggesting that he did not have the strength to carry the burden of supreme command in war because:

> I lack the power of rapid decision. I am too reflective, too conscientious. I have not the temperament that can risk all on a single throw.[26]

He warned the kaiser that making the appointment was not the same as buying a lottery ticket, in the hope that the same number would come up twice, but his reservations were overcome by the unique imperial combination of authoritarian brusqueness and compelling charm:

> You can look after what work there is in peacetime; in war, I am my own chief of staff.[26]

And Wilhelm would continue, for a few more years at least, to reiterate that if war came he would personally command the army in the west.[27]

Thus Waldersee's fears, expressed more than a decade before, were well on their way towards fulfilment. The state of Moltke's health was also relevant. A heavy fifty-eight year old on appointment, by 1911 his health had begun to break down, to the point at which he and his physician discussed the need for his retirement on medical grounds.[28] He remained in post, but, like Napoleon

III in 1870, he would prove to be not physically fit enough to cope with the demands of supreme command in war.

With the strength of a new appointee, Moltke challenged successfully the long-standing tradition that the side commanded by the kaiser should always win the two-sided formation manoeuvres which brought to a climax the annual training cycle of the active army. But his speculative mind stopped short of questioning the flawed basis of the plan, which continued to be worked upon by a dedicated and competent band of staff officers. This included the application of lateral thinking when the kaiser, impressed by the speed at which Barnum and Bailey's circus could set up and strike, sent officers to observe the techniques used in loading and unloading railway freight wagons.[29] More significantly, the negotiating methods of Schlieffen continued to be followed, in that the requirements of the plan continued to be used to bludgeon the Reichstag into providing the money to pay for the hitherto surplus manpower, to be conscripted into new formations. But as the new corps became operational, Moltke's capacity for second thoughts caused him to use them to strengthen not the right wing as Schlieffen had continued to demand on his deathbed, but the centre and left of the German concentration in the west. Moltke had three reasons. The first was an appreciation, pre-dating that of Colonel de Gaulle by a quarter of a century, of the benefit which might be gained if simultaneous blows were struck across the whole front. The second was intended to take advantage of a previous French move into Belgium. This would locate the decisive battle not in the pastoral countryside east of Paris, but in Flanders; perhaps a battle similar to Sedan, with the French caught between two German armies, one moving westwards from the Meuse, the other in a powerful thrust launched from the concentration area between Metz and Thionville, and the frontier of neutral Holland. Moltke's third scenario was a strike at and behind the left (northern) flank of a French offensive to recover the lands lost in 1870. In this case, the corps concentrating between Thionville and Metz would attack south-westwards. The plan as it existed was constrained when, in 1911, Moltke ruled out any violation of Dutch territory,[30] so placing additional emphasis upon early capture of the Meuse crossings at Liège. And on the Staff Ride in 1912 Moltke said:

> From the moment when it is known that the mass of the French
> Army is taking the offensive between Metz and the Vosges, the
> movement of the German right wing becomes without object.[31]

Thus the options, which were not entirely mutually exclusive, were kept open – a flexibility mirrored in the allocation of the new formations. Sixteen corps continued to be allotted to the right hook through Belgium as Schlieffen had planned, but the new formations as they were raised were not grouped into a reserve to provide fresh troops for the westward swing round Paris after M+31. They went instead to the centre and left. Thus the weight of assault when the plan was implemented in August 1914 was quite different from what Schlieffen had intended.

The Corps were grouped into seven armies:[32]

TABLE XX

| Army | Commander | Corps | | | Army | Concentration |
		Line	Res	Cav	Strengths in '000s	Area
First	von Kluck	4	3		320	Dusseldorf–Cologne
Second	von Bulow	3	3		260	Cologne–Aachen Blankenheim
Third	von Hausen	3	1	2*	180	Southern Eifel (Ardennes)
Fourth	Duke Albrecht of Wurtemburg	3	2		180	Trier–Luxembourg border
Fifth	Imperial Crown Prince	3	2	1	200	Thionville–Metz
Sixth	Crown Prince Rupprecht of Bavaria	4	1	1	220	Metz–Sarrebourg
Seventh	von Heeringen	2	1		125	Strasbourg–Colmar Mulhouse

* For concentration only. These two cavalry corps were transferred to Second Army at the start of the operation.

Schlieffen's original allocation of four corps to East Prussia was left unaltered. The critical change was the provision for the three southern armies, increased from five infantry corps to thirteen – the eight corps intended by Schlieffen for the second phase of the campaign.

War and Rumour of War

From 1906 onwards, the work of the planners in the general staff building on the Konigsplatz continued against a most uneasy background. War between France and Germany nearly broke out on at least two occasions over spheres of influence in North Africa, and from 1911 onwards there was an almost uninterrupted state of war in the Balkans, which fell short of involving Russia and the Dual Monarchy by the narrowest of margins. Had either been drawn in, so would the other and in all probability their stronger partners would have followed.

In France, the birth rate had fallen well below that in Germany. Between 1890 and the outbreak of the First World War, the population of the Reich increased by fifty per cent,[33] while that of France remained nearly static. This had obvious consequences regarding the number of young men available for conscription, and by 1910 alarm bells were ringing in the Ministry of War in Paris. Apart from the politicians of the Left, all members of a succession of typically weak coalition governments of the Third Republic came to accept the need for an increase in the term of service with the colours from two years to three. The received wisdom of the general staff that '*Les réserves, c'est zéro*' was accepted without question and the necessary measures passed into law in August 1913. While immediate readiness for war improved because there would now be half as many men again present for duty with the regiments, the increased term of service, as 'peace at any price' politician Joseph Caillaux observed, kept 200,000 young men away from production for another year, and gave France not a single soldier more in time of war.[34]

The contribution of the kaiser to this brew was twofold and contradictory. A constant series of bellicose statements bordering on the hysterical and a series of diplomatic initiatives usually to the extreme embarrassment of his chancellor, actively encouraged the belief that Germany would go to war to achieve her objectives, not as a last resort but willingly, almost as the solution of first choice. The kaiser was never seen out of uniform except when hunting,[i] and the army retained its pre-eminent position in Wilhelmine society and the structure of the nation. At the Hague Peace Conference in 1899, called on the initiative of the tsar with the aim of limiting the scale of proposed armament increases, a move which would have been of benefit to Russia and the reverse to the Dual Monarchy, the German delegate, Count Munster, declared that his country could not accept third-party arbitration of international disputes. To do so would be against her interests because the nation was prepared for war better than any other, and could mobilise in ten days.[35] On the other hand, as the first decade of the new century unfolded, Wilhelm's own self-confidence was destroyed. Glaringly obvious diplomatic disasters and gaffes such as the report of an interview with him published by

---

[i] Game shooting in English parlance.

the London *Daily Telegraph* in October 1908, and scandals involving his closest friend, Prince Philip von Eulenberg, and others in the court circle close to the throne,[36] not only tarnished Wilhelm's reputation but also induced a constant self-doubt which had not previously formed part of his make-up. The bombast continued, but abdication was hinted at more than once and the determination to take personal command of his armies, as his grandfather had done, drained away. When Germany went to war, imperial self-confidence had waned to the point that the German armies had, in effect, no human commander-in-chief. The plan was in supreme command. Worse, control and the ability to make variations as events might require was not only unsatisfactory in itself but also depended upon a communications system totally inadequate for the task. The distances had become too great for either personal contact or trusted 'galloper' to cover effectively, and the telephone and the radio were at too early a state of development to cope.

There was a serious war scare in the winter of 1912, stemming from the situation in the Balkans. At a well-documented conference on 8th December at the Berliner Schloss, the imperial residence in the capital, the chief of the kaiser's Naval Cabinet records Moltke as saying, 'I believe war is inevitable, and the sooner the better.' Tirpitz, Secretary of the Navy, advised that a delay of a year and a half would be preferable, to which Moltke replied that the navy would not be ready even then, and that the position of the army could only get worse.[37]

Moltke was right. The Imperial Navy needed at least two more years of shipbuilding to bring its number of battleships nearer to the strength of the Royal Navy, and with the tonnages of the all-big gunships having increased from the 18,000 tons of the first German Dreadnought-type in 1906 to 26,000 tons for the class of 1912,[38] the Kiel Canal required deepening. This work was not finished until August 1914.[39]

Blitzkreig on Foot

The story of the approach to war in July 1914 does not need to be repeated. What is relevant to any analysis of the influence of the elder Moltke on the plan made by Schlieffen and executed by his nephew is the last-minute decision-taking process in Berlin and the ordering of the changes which contributed to the failure to achieve Schlieffen's aim of a decisive victory in the west before Russia had had time to mobilise. The planned mobilisation times of each power are relevant. Every general staff, having calculated the capabilities of their probable enemies, would inevitably press their political leadership for the decision. The gain of a day might be invaluable; any more was unlikely because the process could not be kept secret. Once one protagonist had mobilised, its opposition would follow suit. Germany required only thirteen days to move all first-strike formations to concentration areas on the frontiers and a further four to complete the mobilisation process. France required eighteen days, the Dual Monarchy seventeen to twenty-one and Russia twenty-one to twenty-five.[40] England, as we have seen, needed only thirteen days to concentrate her expeditionary force in north-eastern France, but the numbers were less than a tenth of those of the continental powers.

During the second half of July 1914, at the centres of authority in Vienna, St Petersburg, Berlin, Paris and London the military case against being forestalled was tempered by intermittent political realisation of the probable horrors of the approaching conflict, and punctuated by diplomatic efforts to find a solution. The two latter never coincided for long enough or were prosecuted with sufficient energy to prevent the outbreak of war.

In Berlin, at 5 p.m. on 1st August, after preliminary steps had been set in hand on the previous day, a signature ordering the start of full mobilisation on 2nd August was wrung from a reluctant kaiser. No sooner given than revoked: Moltke, on his way back to the Konigsplatz with the order in his pocket, was recalled. A report had arrived from the German ambassador in London, Prince Lichnowski, to the effect that England would prevent France from carrying out any aggressive acts against Germany on condition that Germany did not attack Russia. The kaiser had changed his mind:

> Now we need only wage war against Russia. So we simply advance with the whole army in the east.[41]

Moltke was aghast. Did the Supreme Warlord really not realise that plans to deploy the armies were so interwoven that it was impossible to implement part only of the master plan? Did he not understand that what in late twentieth-century parlance would be styled 'M-Nought measures' were already in hand? These included one which was irreversible: the plan required the immediate seizure of a railway junction in Luxembourg. This was significant because, since 1871, the territory of the grand duchy formed a salient in Fourth Army's area, and the lateral north–south communications between the two army railheads at Cologne and Thionville were regarded as essential.

In the ensuing argument, perhaps reminiscent of those between Bismarck and King William I which the chancellor had always won, Moltke found himself alone. Ranged against him were the kaiser, the chancellor, the ministers of war and the navy, the chiefs of the kaiser's military and naval cabinets and the state secretary for foreign affairs, deputy in this area of responsibility to Chancellor Theobald von Bethmann-Hollweg. Moltke warned the gathering of the impossibility of altering the plan, and of the need to secure the railway junction north of Clervaux, known to the Germans as Ulflingen and in Luxembourg as Trois Vierges. The kaiser was at his most brutal: 'Your uncle would have returned me a different answer'; adding as an afterthought that Moltke might care to use 'some other railway'. The argument was unnecessary on two counts: first because there came in during the evening a second telegram from London, this one monarch to monarch. King George V dashed to the ground the hopes erroneously raised earlier in the day by Lichnowski. And secondly, Moltke himself was wrong: in a study published years later, after the war, General von Staab, chief of the railway section of the General Staff, demonstrated that from the start state on 1st August he could have deployed four of the seven armies on the Eastern Front in a fortnight, leaving the other three in a defensive posture in the west.[42]

Moltke, having spent the evening in a *crise des nerfs* in his office, was summoned again to the schloss and told that he could now, after all, proceed as planned. The incident was significant not only in exposing that Imperial Germany had no war aim. In addition, the diplomatic implications of the Schlieffen Plan had never been considered, and it was evident that the Supreme Warlord had at best a child's grasp of the logistic complexities of a deployment plan on an unprecedented scale, involving five times as many men as in 1870 and perhaps comparable in later military history to the plan for the invasion of Normandy in 1944. The damage to Moltke's confidence in himself and faith in his *de jure* supreme commander was total. He began the war as a beaten general.

The Dual Monarchy had declared war on Serbia on 28th July, but without previously having ordered full mobilisation. The other European powers ordered the irreversible process to begin as soon as it was evident that they risked conceding an irrevocable advantage if they delayed longer. M-Day in Russia was 31st July, 1st August in France, 2nd August in Germany and 5th August in England. For over a fortnight, apart from the battle for Liège,[j] there was no major clash of arms. This should have come as a surprise to no one. Although all the protagonists had implemented some pre-mobilisation

---

[j] See Chapter IX.

measures, time was needed to arm and equip reservists and to move them to concentration areas. On 16th August, German supreme headquarters, *Ober Heeresleitung* or OHL, accompanied by kaiser and court as though it were 1870 all over again, moved to Coblenz. Up to this point arrangements had worked without a hitch, but, as the great Moltke had taught, no plan survives contact with the enemy. It is a debatable proposition that Schlieffen's plan was already incapable of fulfilment because of the diversion to the front in Alsace of the eight corps needed for the west-about envelopment of Paris.

After the plan was set in motion it is possible to identify three critical spans of time, none longer than forty-eight hours. Within each, decisions were taken and events occurred which between them ensured that there would be no German victory in the west in forty days. In discussion of what happened, it has to be remembered that the standard of communications imposed its own time delays and confusion factors. The telephone provided the primary means, but was insecure. There were no dedicated circuits, amplifiers or any of the technology which the late twentieth century takes for granted. It might need hours to establish a link for a bellowed conversation liable to be broken off at any moment. The radio network had few sets or stations, and relays had to be established almost at intervisible distance. The vast increase in the size of the battle area had rendered the mounted galloper out of date, but the staff officer, travelling in a car which was neither fast, comfortable nor reliable by modern standards, could be delayed for hours if he had to cross lines of march, casualty evacuation or resupply.

The first of the three vital time-spans was from 20th to 22nd August, and the location supreme headquarters in Coblenz. The 20th August began badly with the suicide of the master of the horse, distraught because circumstances of war prevented the achievement of his absolute standards of peacetime. Over the next forty-eight hours, Moltke had to take three critical decisions. The first was forced on him by the fact that the Belgian Army had not been deployed to support the Liège forts. Had it been, it is possible that a stand-off distance could have been bought, beyond the range of the Krupp super-heavy guns, which might have won the time for the French Army to have come up into Belgium. But on a deployment plan prepared before the war, the one cavalry and six infantry divisions of the Belgian Army[k] had been concentrated in the centre of the country. This was because neutrality carried with it the requirement to fight the first invader, which could be any of France from the

---

[k] Coincidentally the same formations and almost exactly the same strength (117,000) as the BEF (110,000).[43]

south, Germany from the east, the Netherlands from the north or even England from the sea. After the German invasion on the morning of 4th August, the Belgian Army deployed on the line of the River Gette through Tirlemont (Tienen), towards the battlefield of Ramillies and Namur, twenty-five miles west of Liège and so unable to influence the battle for the Meuse crossings. By 18th August, fighting under the personal command of King Albert I, they had been forced back to a line facing south-east between Mechelen (Malines) and Aalst (Alost), abandoning Brussels, which the German Army entered two days later, on M+19 as planned. Beaten but in good order, the Belgian Army completed, also on 20th August, a controlled withdrawal into the fortress complex surrounding Antwerp, forcing Moltke to approve the detachment of two corps to mask the city. This at once reduced the front First Army could cover at the tip of the scythe blade.

The second crisis to emerge during the day was a report, overstated, as was soon proved, and excitable in tone, of a disaster in East Prussia.[44] There, the army commander, von Prittwitz, had neither executed his directive nor controlled his subordinates. It could have been relevant that two of his four corps, First and First Reserve, recruited from East Prussia and so were possibly reluctant to surrender territory in the controlled withdrawal which the overall plan demanded. Indeed, the commander of I Corps, von François, son of one of von Kamecke's brigade commanders at Spicheren who had been killed in that battle, launched his formation on an advance towards the Russian frontier. In their planning, the Russian general staff had yielded to French importunity to mount an offensive as soon as possible, in order to take pressure and perhaps divert troops from the west. Consequently a group of two armies, potentially 450,000 strong and so three times the strength of the German Eighth Army, was formed to invade East Prussia well before the completion of Russian mobilisation. The northern army, commanded by Rennenkampf, was in assembly areas and in a position to open the attack on 17th August, except that its own logistic support would not be in place for another three days and the southern formation, under Samsonov, could not be ready for another six. Rennenkampf attacked nevertheless, with some success, including routing the German XVIII Corps, commanded by Mackensen, caught unsupported on the wrong side of the River Angerapp. Prittwitz panicked and ordered a retreat behind the Vistula, which, had it been implemented, would have abandoned the whole of East Prussia and most of Prussian Poland. He telephoned Moltke in Coblenz; Moltke, preoccupied by the battles in the west and in no condition to stiffen a failing subordinate, acquiesced. But there were stronger characters than the chiefs both at Eighth

Army headquarters and in Coblenz. The operations staff at OHL obtained a less hysterical and more factual report from their opposite numbers. The retired General von Hindenberg was nominated to succeed Prittwitz, with Ludendorff, hero of the *coup de main* operations at Liège, as his chief of staff. Ludendorff, en route via Coblenz and Hanover, where Hindenburg joined the train, and Hoffman, head of the operations section at Eighth Army headquarters, proved the academic excellence of Prussian staff training by arriving independently at the same design, which annihilated the whole Russian army group. This victory had been accomplished by the time the customary staff processes in Coblenz had ground out two corps, the guard reserve from Second Army and the XIth from Hausen's Saxons, to reinforce the army in East Prussia, despite Ludendorff's report that the additional troops originally demanded by Prittwitz were not needed. The two corps were detached on 25th August, released by the fall of Namur.[45] They were not necessarily the most appropriate on operational grounds. The selection process had not been immune from imperial and court influence and it was a further mark of weak leadership that the two corps were taken from the two army commanders worst placed both by temperament and status to object. Thus two further corps were detached from the right wing, and the diversion of staff effort in Coblenz and the drain on the *'Innere Fuhrung'*[1] of the chief of staff were considerable and unnecessary distractions from concentration on the main objective.

The third matter requiring decision in Coblenz, at the point in the campaign at which the plan was inevitably coming under the pressure of events, stemmed from success all along the line in the west. In Alsace, a French advance to contact had begun on 15th August, and in obedience to the overall design the German Sixth and Seventh Armies, grouped under the command of Crown Prince Rupprecht of Bavaria, had fallen back, not without protest. Mulhouse fell to the advance, to the delight of those inhabitants who had remained French at heart ever since 1871. The city was lost again three days later, to remain in German hands for another four years. On 20th August, Rupprecht received permission to counter-attack after the slaughter of the French assaults on the long-prepared defensive positions around Morhange and Sarrebourg. As early as the same evening he was

---

[1] Literally, 'inner leadership'; a phrase often on the lips of a later German military philosopher, General von Senger und Etterlin, who commanded Allied Forces Central Europe towards the end of the Cold War. An essential component in the character of anyone who seeks to lead soldiers, it is a combination of self-belief, motivation and personal morale.

reporting victory and pressing for permission to pass over to the offensive. With the fall of Brussels and the repulse also of attacks by the French Third and Fourth Armies across the River Semois towards Virton and Neufchâteau in the Ardennes, Moltke could perceive the grail of victory on all fronts. On 22nd August, Rupprecht was authorised to 'Pursue direction Epinal'.[46]

Thus, instead of reverting to the aggressive defence which would have limited Sixth and Seventh Armies to the holding operation required by the plan, they were committed to an attack on the French fortress systems. Later in the month, as the German attacks up the long, open slopes of southern Lorraine failed in their turn, Rupprecht and his chief of staff, Krafft von Dellmensingen, would become as importunate for reinforcement as the other army commanders. Moltke had no one but himself to blame. It is always easier for a character whose reserves have been drained by previous events to give in to pressure from a vociferous (and in this instance royal) subordinate than to overrule him. At the same time as the defensive successes in the Ardennes and the Vosges, the German Fifth Army, commanded by the imperial crown prince, had done more than was expected of it west of Thionville. Longwy fell on 23rd August, and another frontal assault was authorised, to try to head off the French armies in the centre from the Meuse crossings at Verdun.

The army group command and communications structure was already beginning to appear fallible. As the operations of Kluck and Bulow's armies could not be coordinated from Coblenz, Bulow, on the inside flank and also by far the less thrusting character, was given overall charge, producing another variant on the plan. And because there was no army group commander on the spot to coordinate a combined attack by the German First, Second and Third Armies, a golden opportunity was missed to annihilate the French Fifth Army, trapped in the angle of the Sambre and the Meuse, with Bulow driving in on its front between Charleroi and Namur, and Kluck and Hausen lapping round its flanks. The French, with the BEF on their left, made good their escape, but there followed a further and excessive detachment from the German right wing, in the shape of a corps to mask Maubeuge.

The decisions taken by Moltke between 20th and 22nd August, and those which followed in consequence, were no more than acquiescence to pressure from subordinates. On the other hand, the directive he issued on 27th August, his first of the campaign, was positive, in that an entirely new design replaced that of Schlieffen. The concept of a west-about encirclement of Paris was abandoned. First Army's role was effectively reduced to that of flank guard to the whole army group, along the axis of the Oise, with the exploitation limited to the confluence of that river with the Seine, north-west of Paris. The

Second, Third, Fourth and Fifth Armies were directed to advance to contact from a start line La Fere–Laon–Vouziers on parallel axes south-south-west, with a view to bringing the French Army to battle between the Aisne and the Marne. Sixth and Seventh Armies were directed primarily to contain any resumption of the French attack into Alsace. But:

> if the enemy falls back, the Sixth Army will cross the Moselle between Toul and Epinal and advance in the general direction of Neufchâteau.[m47]

While this order paid lip-service to Schlieffen, in that the two armies on the left were given a containing role, the lapse of control by a weak commander over a strong subordinate was explicit. In view of their track record, Rupprecht and Krafft were bound to construe the directive as tacit permission to attack.

This directive, coming nearly four weeks after Mobilisation Day and ten days since the start of the frontier battles, took twelve hours to reach the headquarters of First and Second Armies. From the time it arrived at the executive headquarters, the Schlieffen Plan became an incident of history, except for two considerations. One was the battle positions reached in obedience to the plan; the other was its conditioning effect on the minds of the senior commanders, who had progressed up the higher echelons of the army in the expectation that the Master Plan would guide their every action. On 29th August, OHL moved from Coblenz to Luxembourg, to a headquarters building extemporised in a girls' school, but was no better placed there than at Coblenz to command seven armies operating on a concave front 300 miles in circumference and 200 miles distant from the headquarters of the main striking force, as well as the operations in the east. In the absence of a plan, OHL would now have to control the armies, but the directive initiating this process was outdated by circumstance as soon as issued. Too many corps had been detached: the continuous front could not be maintained and dangerous gaps had opened between the armies. Kluck was already edging eastwards from the course of the Oise in order to maintain contact with Bulow, a movement heartily endorsed by Bulow himself when, after a sharp encounter at Guise on 29th August, he called for help from First Army. Kluck obliged. As a result of this manoeuvre, Kluck's axis of advance was drawn due

---

[m] Neufchâteau in the Department of the Vosges, not to be confused with the town of the same name in the Ardennes.

south from Compiègne towards the Marne rather than south-west. Moltke, when informed of this manoeuvre, approved: 'The movements carried out by First Army conform to the intentions of OHL.'[48]

This statement could not have been more wrong. There was still a gap between First and Second Armies, and, because Kluck could in no sense be said to be containing any formation capable of mounting an operation from Paris, his right flank was wide open to attack. Thus the decisions promulgated on 29th August produced an unworkable design, which could be amended only by a control system which was incapable of timely response to events. The situation on the ground was potentially dangerous, and would become actively so if Kluck were drawn further west, so widening the gap between his army and that of Bulow in the picturesque countryside between the Marne and the Seine.

Meanwhile the advance continued. Rheims fell on 3rd September, and two days later German troops were over the Marne.

On the evening of 4th September, Moltke issued a second general directive. Recognising the danger looming both from the dispersion of the armies of the right wing and of a counterstroke from Paris, he ordered a temporary halt to the advance of Kluck and Bulow, and transferred the emphasis of attack to Sixth Army's attempt to break through between Toul and Epinal. The outline of these orders reached Kluck and Bulow by radio at 7.15 a.m. the next morning. They were already out of date because the hard-driving von Kluck was two days' march south of where Moltke had assumed him to be, and where the directive required him to halt. It was another twenty-four hours before its momentum could be stopped and First Army turned round. During the evening there arrived at First Army headquarters an emissary from OHL, Lieutenant Colonel von Hentsch, head of the foreign armies section of the headquarters staff. Carrying Moltke's full orders, he gave a most depressing description of the campaign as a whole, but, nevertheless, in staff-to-staff discussion, stated that the OHL directive could be carried out without undue haste. This was another statement out of date as soon as made, because Kluck's flank guard was already engaged to the north-west. First Army was only saved by faultless staff work and the marching power of troops who had already tramped nearly 400 miles in three weeks, and been exposed to combat for the previous two. First Army was withdrawn forty miles through difficult country, turning ninety degrees as they did so to take up a defensive position on the line of the Ourcq, facing west. Although the open flank of the army group had been secured, always provided that First Army could hold against whatever attack was mounted from Paris, the gap between First and

Second Armies was now some forty miles wide, and covered only by II Cavalry Corps and a regimental group of infantry and artillery. Into this gap the BEF was advancing, turned round after retreating for over a fortnight.

On 8th September, there was a staff conference in Luxembourg. Information was scanty, but it was clear that an allied offensive had been launched, both from Paris and into the gap between First and Second Armies, and that Rupprecht's attempt to break through the Trouée des Charmes had failed. The events of the past six weeks had reduced Moltke to a state of moral collapse comparable to that of Bazaine after Mars La Tour. The decision was taken to send Hentsch round the army headquarters again, this time armed with full plenipotentiary powers, to order either a continuation of the defensive battle on ground currently held or a retreat. Visiting each headquarters in turn as he drove westwards from Luxembourg, Hentsch had to cross lines of communication clogged with unorganised transport and the novelty of wounded, chaotic to the tidy general staff mind without previous combat experience. Arriving at Second Army headquarters on the evening of 8th September, the natural pessimism of Hentsch, reinforced by his experiences of the day, was complemented by the gloom of Bulow and his chief of staff, von Lauenstein, about the situation of Second Army. Continuing his journey on the following morning, Hentsch took a further seven hours to reach Kluck's headquarters, through scenes for which no peacetime manoeuvres could have prepared him. Instant communications when on the move lying far in the future, Hentsch was out of contact throughout his journey. He was greeted by the news that while he had been on the road Bulow had issued orders for a withdrawal. Although First Army was holding its positions, and strong direction from Hentsch to Bulow, even though from a lieutenant colonel to an army commander, might have saved the situation, Hentsch saw no option other than to order First Army also to go back. On 12th September, Moltke ordered the armies to entrench north of the Aisne, a withdrawal of fifty miles from the positions they had reached four days earlier.

It was the forty-first day after mobilisation. Although Germany was left in a position of enormous strategic advantage, with her armies deep inside France and all the onus of attack to extract them resting on the allies, France had not been totally defeated as the plan had required. The plan had failed; failed because of diversion of resources, failed because of lack of comprehension and inadequate means of control and modification, failed possibly also because the whole design was beyond the capability of troops moving at marching pace. The strength of any blow is a combination of mass and force. Although the term '*blitzkreig*' lay a quarter of a century in the future, it describes adequately enough a design for battle intended to destroy the will to fight of an alliance with a million and a quarter men in the field. But, for all their marching prowess, the German soldiers on foot could not move fast enough. If the battle had to be fought again, something different would have to be tried.

Blitzkreig 1940 – the Opposing Philosophies

In the light of hindsight more than half a century later, the Second World War was inevitable from the moment Hitler came to power in Germany. Nevertheless, the opening months of the conflict, apart from the annihilation of Poland, developed almost on eighteenth-century lines, without any major clash of arms. In 1939, Hitler had no intention of fighting an all-out war in the West. After the obliteration of the Polish Army in barely a fortnight and yet another partition of that unfortunate nation with Russia, he had hoped to negotiate a general peace on the basis that the immediate *casus belli* had been resolved. The German general staff thus had no plan when the war began for anything other than defensive operations in the west, and there was no element of the preparatory work of Moltke for 1870 or of Schlieffen for 1914. Nevertheless, the superb latitudinal railway network, undamaged by the First World War, still existed and was reinforced by the new fast motor roads. The eternal verities of topography were unchanged, most particularly the vulnerability of France by way of the frontier in Flanders. Also, as in 1914, Belgium and Holland insisted upon maintaining neutrality until the last possible moment and the French Army provided the bulk of the force available for the war on land.

However, as the autumn of 1939 drew into winter, it became increasingly apparent in Berlin that neither France nor Great Britain was interested in agreeing to a negotiated peace, even though operations on the Rhine or in Flanders could do nothing to help Poland. During the winter, most of the formations which had taken part in the Polish campaign were moved west, to lie up in assembly areas along the borders with France, Luxembourg and Belgium, just as had happened as part of the mobilisation process in 1914. It was, however, a very different sort of army.

At the start of the First World War, there had been more points of similarity with the armies of 1870 than of difference, but the armies of 1939 were very much changed from those of 1914. The armoured fighting vehicle and the combat aircraft had introduced new dimensions to the conduct of the land battle. In Germany, the comprehensive defeat of 1918 had forced a review of battle procedures, which, together with the restrictions on the size, structure and weaponry of the army imposed by the peace settlements, had led to a fundamental examination of all national resources which might possibly be used in war. The doctrines developed by the British military philosophers about the nature of a future war, and especially the employment of armoured vehicles capable of cross-country movement, had been thought through further in Germany than in any other country, even though such weapons were forbidden to the army of the Weimar Republic. Although in 1939 the bulk of the German Army still moved on foot, with nine out of ten of its divisions requiring five tons of forage for horses for every two of fuel for motor vehicles, a new doctrine had been evolved for the elite armoured formations. Tanks, integrated with mechanised infantry, artillery and logistic vehicles, coordinated with ground-support aircraft, were expected to break through a continuous front. Having done so, the task of the armoured combat groupings was to blast on at will through unprotected rear areas, leaving prepared linear defence systems high and dry and destroying gun lines and logistic assets. This would spread a confusion intended to break the will of the enemy to fight, by demoralising in turn refugees, civilian population, army and government. In the campaign in Poland, the first combat trial of this method of war, though not without its tactical hitches, had achieved total success.

The number and complexity of new weapon systems, together with their counters, was compounded by vastly increased ammunition tonnages for infantry support weapons and artillery, a requirement deriving from First World War experience. It followed that for the first time the number of combat soldiers in any formation larger than a brigade would now be exceeded by the number needed to support and sustain them. This, together with an even further improved ability to identify, enrol and direct all military-age manpower, caused a further increase in the size of the basic strategic counter. In the War Between the States and the war of 1866 this had been the division, usually the smallest combat grouping to integrate elements of all types of combat and logistic unit. If by 1870 strategic planners had come to think in terms of corps, and in 1914 of armies, it had by 1939 become necessary for them to base their considerations upon the army group. Though much larger by the end of the war, even in 1940 these formations would have a manpower strength of over half a million, but they were never of the same size, structure or composition. Nor were the component formations, from brigade upwards, any longer broadly similar. There were many different kinds of armoured brigade and division, and while in the German army tanks, broadly of the same type, were all concentrated in armoured mechanised formations, in the French and British armies there was a multiplicity of designs and a tendency to disperse those with the best hitting power and strongest protection (and thus poorest mobility) in small numbers or even singly to the direct support of infantry battalions.

The disparity in manpower between France and Germany which existed at the start of the century had widened even further by 1939, in spite of the return of Alsace–Lorraine to France as an integral part of the peace settlement. De Gaulle, writing in 1934, could assert that for every Frenchman between the ages of twenty and thirty, there were now two Germans.[49] Worse, and by no means for the first time in military history, victory inhibited forward thinking and proper evaluation of new ideas and emerging technology. It was beyond question that the fundamental lesson emerging from the First World War had been the predominance of firepower, a superiority which in France after 1918 was thought to be permanent. The point that every weapon has its counter was missed. Pétain, a principal exponent of the importance of firepower before 1914, when it had been almost sacrilege to challenge the belief in the overwhelming power of the offensive at all costs, had been conditioned by continuous formation command on the Western Front throughout the war. In 1916 he had saved France by his mastery of the science of the application of artillery fire. His experience in dealing with the mutinies in the French Army in 1917 and recognition of the long-term damage inflicted by the enormous casualty lists ingrained in him a determination to safeguard the young manpower of the nation at almost any cost.

In one position or another, Pétain had a primary responsibility for French defence policy from the end of the war until 1934.[50] Although he was never solely responsible, this continuity and his wartime achievements combined to give him an influence approached by no one else. If the Maginot Line came to bear the name of the minister of war in office at the time of its inception, the philosophy, the military statement of requirement, the prestige to undertake this super-defensive project and the willpower to sustain it through time- and cost-overruns of more than sixty per cent were provided by the senior surviving marshal of France of the First World War.[n]

After some years of debate, construction of the Maginot Line began in 1930 and after another seven years the Third Republic had bought, for FF 7,000,000,000, an illusion of security provided by a defensive system

---

[n] Pétain, who received his baton at a unique ceremony in Metz in December 1918, in front of Foch and the British and American commanders-in-chief in France, Haig and Pershing, outlived both Joffre (d.1931) and Foch (d.1929). In contrast to Pétain, neither played much active part in either forming policy or conducting the operation of the French Army after 1919.

directly descended in concept from the Great Wall of China. The Maginot Line was a continuous belt of fortifications, reinforced concrete and steel sunk into the ground to provide total protection against the heaviest contemporary artillery fire. The line extended for eighty-seven miles along the common frontier with Germany, to a maximum depth of twelve miles. It was complete with strong points, steel cupolas for observation and gun turrets, underground railways and logistic self-sufficiency for up to three months.[51] But the 250 mile stretch of common frontier with Luxembourg and Belgium was left unprotected, except by field fortifications thrown up after the start of the war. Prolongation of Maginot was denied, partly on the ground of cost in its own right,° partly because of the political and financial difficulty of leaving the industrial area round Lille and the Borinage of Belgium either within or outside the system, and partly because the more immediate length of frontier north-west of Sedan was held to be impassable. Perhaps too there was a degree of political wishful thinking, on the lines that Germany, having lost one war because of the violation of Belgian territory, would not repeat the mistake. After mobilisation and deployment to battle positions, the sector of front from Longwy through Sedan, Charleville-Mezières, Valenciennes and Lille to the Channel, was entrusted to one of the three allied army groups responsible for the defence of the frontier as far as the border with Switzerland. The No. 1 Army Group (Billotte) comprised four French armies and the nine division strong British Expeditionary Force, under Lord Gort. The three army groups were subordinated to General Georges, Commander-in-Chief, North-East Front, who answered to Gamelin, Supreme Commander French Land Forces.ᴾ

The allied design for the campaign was that, as soon as politically possible and with Belgian compliance, the BEF and two French armies were to advance into Belgium to the line of the River Dyle, which runs northwards from Charleroi through Louvain towards Antwerp. The Belgian Army, initially deployed on the Meuse, was expected in due course to withdraw, to

---

° If eighty-seven miles of fortification cost FF 7,000,000,000, it is a simple enough calculation to arrive at a crude first estimate of what a further 250 miles might have cost. At the time, the total annual national revenue amounted to FF 50,000,000,000, of which over 8,000,000,000 was spent on the army.[52]

ᴾ Gort's directive, like that to Sir John French in 1914, gave him right of appeal to his home government if he felt that the safety of the British Army was endangered. Fortunately for the future course of the war, Gort had the moral courage to exercise this right when it became necessary, bypassing three higher levels of command.

form part of a defensive line held successively from the north by the Seventh French Army (Giraud) and the Belgian, British and First French armies, the last commanded by Blanchard. A strict interpretation of neutrality by Belgium precluded any pre-planning on the ground. The army group front from Sedan to the northern limit of the Maginot Line around Longwy was held by the other two armies in the group, Ninth under Corap and Second under Huntziger. But the area facing the Ardennes, the line of the Meuse from Sedan to Dinant and by extension to Namur, was thinly held, by a combination of French light armour, cavalry and frontier guards. The Ardennes were thought to be impassable.

The campaign in the last three weeks of May 1940 shattered most of the preconceptions deriving from the First World War and taught many lessons. Perhaps the most important of these, because it applies at all levels from platoon minor tactics to national defence policy, is that, unless an obstacle is covered permanently by observation and can be dominated at any time by fire, it is no obstacle. Until the battle opened, the French high command was little concerned about this area. At least one contemporary authority, in direct contact at cabinet level in both London and Paris and with all the higher strata of the allied command structure, implies that the French were more worried about an attack through Switzerland which would turn the southern flank of the Maginot Line.[53]

The Advent of Manstein

In no area of human endeavour does time stand still, least of all in the conduct of war. Although, in the face of Allied inactivity all the military advice to Hitler was urging a defensive stance in the west and search for an early peace, on 19th October Hitler issued a planning directive for an attack. *Fall Gelb* (Case Yellow) required the occupation of Holland, Belgium and the Channel coast as far as the Somme estuary, and the defeat of any French and British forces moved into Belgium.

A short digression is necessary here to explain the German military command structure at the start of the war. Hitler was at this stage the supreme commander of all the German armed forces, in which capacity he was served by *Oberkommando der Wehrmacht*, (OKW), high command of the armed forces, whose chief of staff was Keitel. Subordinate to OKW were the three single service headquarters, that for the army entitled *Oberkommando des Heeres*, (OKH), translated as 'high command of the army.' Though Hitler himself was later to assume the post, the army still had a professional soldier as commander-in-chief, in 1940 von Brauchitsch, and the chief of staff at OKH was Halder.

OKH transmuted Hitler's directive into a framework plan for expansion by the headquarters of the three German army groups now in the west. As the formation strength built up throughout the winter and spring, these eventually came to comprise ninety-three divisions, ten of which were armoured ('Panzer'), with a further forty-five divisions in theatre reserve. The three army groups were aligned B (von Bock) opposite the Dutch border, A (von Rundstedt) in the area Dusseldorf–Aachen–Cologne, and C (von Leeb) covering the Maginot Line. The OKW framework plan gave them tasks reminiscent of Schlieffen. Army Group B, having secured the Dutch border, was to capture the Meuse crossings at Liège, violating the Maastricht Appendix only if necessary. This achieved, Army Group B would regulate the pace of an advance through Belgium into northern France, with Army Group A on its left, defeating the French, British and Belgian forces in front of them; in short, an exact repetition of the tasks given to von Kluck and von Bulow in the first phase of the Master Plan a quarter of a century earlier. Similarly, Army Group C was limited to a holding operation against any assault mounted from the Maginot Line. The army groups were directed to complete all preparations and to submit their own detailed plans by 5th November.[54]

Army Group A at once raised an objection. Decisions of this sort still followed the principles established by Moltke, in that formation commander and chief of staff shared responsibility for all plans and orders emanating from their headquarters, and although the Army Group A alternative went to OKH in the name of the commander, von Rundstedt, the idea and the work were that of his chief of staff, Lieutenant General Erich von Manstein. This was a run-in military marriage, Rundstedt and Manstein having served together in Poland.

Manstein was at this time fifty-three years old. He was born Erich von Lewinski, the tenth child of a typical junker family, impoverished notwithstanding the fact that his father reached in due course the rank of full general. One of Frau von Lewinski's sisters was married to the future field marshal and president Paul von Hindenburg und Beneckendorff, and another to General Georg von Manstein, son of the von Manstein who had questioned the existence of 'General von Moltke' on the morning of Sadowa, and who had commanded IX Corps on the afternoon of slaughter in front of the Lines of Amanvillers on 18th August, 1870. The Mansteins having no children, they adopted Erich, who assumed their surname. With these connections, there was a degree of inevitability about his term of service as a page at the court of

Wilhelm II, and his commission as an ensign in his Hindenburg uncle's regiment, the third foot guards, in 1906. Thereafter, ability took over. He was an outstanding officer from the first. Adjutant of his battalion in 1911, he was, three years later, attending the Kriegsakademie well below the average age when his course was cut short by the outbreak of war. Highly promising peacetime achievement though this was, Manstein was not the youngest student of his year. A thrustful subaltern of Jagers (light infantry), Heinz Guderian, who already had training experience in the use of radio for battlefield communications, was a year younger. On a long staff course, friendships are formed which often become of great future benefit to service and country, because, apart from shared combat experience, there are few better environments than a long course, competitive and requiring the highest standards, to instil mutual trust and assessment of reaction to any given situation. Both young officers received very good appointments when the Kriegsakademie closed on mobilisation. Manstein became regimental adjutant, in British Army terms brigade major, of the second guard reserve regiment, and Guderian signals officer of 5th Cavalry Division. Both started the war on the Western Front, Guderian serving through the whole process from the advance, through the opening battles and the Battle of the Marne, to retreat and petrification of the front north of the Aisne. Manstein, in the guard reserve corps, was transferred to the eastern front after the fall of Namur, arriving too late for Tannenburg. Seriously wounded in November, he recovered in time to take part in the marathon operations of marching and fighting which were characteristic of the war in the east. Both Manstein and Guderian emerged from the First World War with outstanding records as combat formation staff officers. They continued to ascend the upper levels of the truncated army of the Weimar Republic, and rose further and faster with the expansion of the army after Hitler came to power. Between the wars, Guderian translated into practical terms the theories of armoured warfare propounded by Fuller and Liddell Hart. Manstein had a more conventional career. In a series of exemplary performances in increasingly important command and staff appointments by 1939 he had established himself as a contender for the very highest posts in the army of the Third Reich. He had at the same time acquired a reputation for an inability to suffer fools gladly, particularly those senior to him. Gossip also had it that he was not too popular with Hitler. The uneducated, and to Prussian eyes uncouth, Bohemian corporal, come to power by way of despised Bavaria, was thought to consider the original surname, Lewinski, and the strong nose in the firm, soldierly face, as evidence of a Jewish connection.[55]

Manstein had two fundamental objections to the OKH plan. On the deduction that force levels in the west would be about equal,[q] and that the Allied armies had the advantage of the defence, Germany had to concentrate a superior force at the decisive point and achieve surprise while doing so. The means was the tank, but those available, although organised into ten panzer divisions, had been given no primary role. The OKH concept for their employment was inadequate in doing no more than grouping them in mass. Secondly, a repetition of Schlieffen in circumstances which failed to achieve the surprise element of August 1914 seemed likely to lead to nothing but a head-on clash with sizeable Allied armies in Flanders, on ground which favoured the defence. Manstein's alternative proposal suggested an approach march for the majority of the armoured formations through the difficult Ardennes country, known to be only lightly defended. This would precede the forcing of crossings over the Meuse between Dinant and Sedan, the latter on the boundary between the areas of responsibility of the French Ninth and Second Armies, and, as we have seen, the whole sector for the planned break-in phase lay beyond the northern limit of Maginot. Having broken through, Manstein envisaged the panzer and motorised divisions continuing on two separate axes. The northern thrust was to head due west across the open country of Champagne, seeking to strike the Channel north of the Somme estuary, thus cutting across the rear of the BEF, the Belgians and the other two French armies in Billotte's army group. The southern prong, having broken through at Sedan and bypassed the close country of the Argonne, was then to swing south and south-east, to take the Maginot Line in rear, pinning any supporting French forces against the fortress system. The design was purest Moltke, but in no way a slavish imitation. Manstein's understanding of principle and evaluation of the known facts placed great emphasis upon the initial deployment, concentration in time at the decisive point followed by a manoeuvre of envelopment, and, apart from the initial break-in operation, the avoidance of a strategic design based upon frontal attack. His proposal also took account of the lessons of the Polish campaign – the potential of massed tanks to achieve the shock action which had been lost from the battlefield since the development of firepower had terminated this role for cavalry, and the confusion implicit in a rampage across lines of communication. The design in itself was unlikely to appeal to Army Group B, because it gave the

---

[q] See Appendix 1 to this chapter for an assessment of the relative strengths of the German and Allied armies.

critical role to von Rundstedt instead of von Bock, and grouped the majority of the armoured divisions under Army Group A.[r]

The design was far too bold for the liking of Brauchitsch and Halder at OKH, who initially rejected it out of hand. Rundstedt and Manstein continued to press the plan throughout the last two months of 1939, some at least of the arguments deriving from consultation between Manstein and Guderian, who was at this point commanding XIX Panzer Corps, and determined to secure an appropriate role for the weapon he had done so much to forge.

Nevertheless, despite all the Army Group A pressure, and the prestige of the Panzer lobby reinforced by its recent success, all that had been achieved by the turn of the year was an OKH decision to retain some of the armoured divisions initially in theatre reserve, for commitment as the situation might indicate; a good idea in principle, but one which, in this particular instance, tended to obscure the immediate aim and also removed the centre of decision for the commitment of a large proportion of the critical asset too far from events. An OKH warning order that the offensive would start on 17th January was countermanded by another, on 12th January, which directed a postponement. This was partly because of particularly severe winter weather and of the risk of compromise. Two days previously, two Luftwaffe staff officers, travelling by light aircraft and bearing, in breach of standing orders, the air element only of the overall plan, had been forced to land in Belgium. It became known, by way of the German military attaché in The Hague, that part at least of the document had fallen into Allied hands.

There is a difference of opinion between authorities about the amount of damage caused by the compromise. Goerlitz goes so far as to say that, 'the plan was never forwarded to the French'. Manstein himself subsequently considered that the incident had had little influence in the adoption of his own design. On the other hand, Fuller, Horne, Keegan and Carver all suggest varying degrees of damage.[56] On principle, even the bare risk of serious compromise should have been enough to force a change. What is certain is that the general commanding the air army to which the aircraft had belonged was dismissed out of hand, and that on 17th January Hitler himself ordered an indefinite postponement of *Fall Gelb*.

On 25th January, Brauchitsch visited the headquarters of Army Group A at

---

[r] In the event, after the adoption of Manstein's design, Army Group A had seven of the panzer divisions and Army Group B only three.

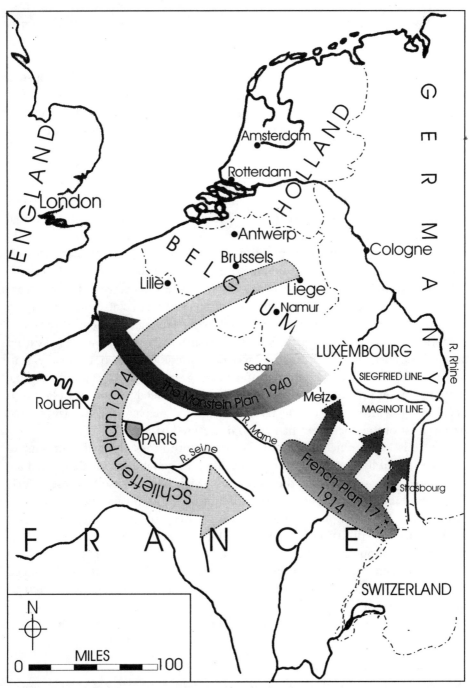

The Schlieffen and Manstein Plans

Coblenz. There had by now been six formal submissions of Manstein's design to OKH, and in the circumstances a visit by the commander-in-chief was essential to try to resolve the difference. The attempt was a failure. Manstein was at his most forceful in presentation, and two days later received his reward, in the form of a posting to command 38th Corps, at Stettin. Given the German Army custom that officers should alternate between command and staff appointments in each rank, Manstein was due for command of a corps, and had indeed already been warned for it. But, on the other hand, key appointments should not be changed when a major operation is pending, and it is hard to avoid the conclusion that Brauchitsch and Halder had taken the classic way out of the weak character in a superior position, in disposing of a tiresome and intractable subordinate. Manstein remained at Coblenz until 9th February, engaged no doubt in handing over to his successor. Two days before his departure, Halder attended an Army Group A map exercise of the forthcoming operation. As a result of what he heard, he agreed to one of the fundamental points in Manstein's design, that a panzer corps should be ready at hand to exploit the forcing of the crossing at Sedan. Guderian's command was duly reassigned, to the displeasure of von Bock, but OKH was still a long way from accepting the Guderian doctrine that the armoured thrust should, from the first, be tasked to penetrate so deep that there would be no need to worry about its flanks. Halder was still thinking in First World War terms, of a set-piece forcing of the Meuse by infantry and artillery.

En route to Stettin, Manstein paid the customary courtesy call on Hitler, whose intuitive understanding of strategic concepts was fired by Manstein's ideas. It is also possible that, in spite of his alleged personal prejudice against Manstein, and Manstein's own impeccable general staff background, Hitler was attracted by a proposal which went counter to the formal advice he had received from OKW and OKH. He was already distrustful of his generals, and a more radical course was likely to appeal. Having been convinced, Hitler summoned the OKH hierarchy to Berlin. Presenting Manstein's ideas to them without due attribution, he directed that they should be adopted. Brauchitsch and Halder were in no position to refuse. On 24th February, a fresh OKH directive went to the army groups, directing the preparation of an entirely new plan based on the Manstein design.

Manstein himself took part in the campaign as a corps commander, 38th Corps having followed the redeployment to the west which continued throughout the spring of 1940, while Denmark and Norway fell to German arms. The detailed course of the Second Battle of Sedan and the subsequent operations across France are not relevant to this book. Within six weeks of the start of the campaign on 10th May, all of the *Fall Gelb* objectives had been achieved: Belgium and Holland had been overrun; France had sued for an armistice which would leave the whole Channel and Atlantic coasts in German hands; the BEF was back in England, having left behind nearly all its heavy equipment – tanks, artillery and logistic vehicles. And had the panzers not been restrained by a direct order from Hitler when poised to drive in from the south-west to the evacuation perimeter around Dunkirk, the victory over the Allied armies which had advanced into Belgium might well have been one of annihilation by double envelopment.

Appendix 1
Allied and German Strengths in the West – May 1940

Until the era of the Catalytic Wars, assessment of relative strengths needed to be little more than the computation of men and guns present for battle. By the mid-nineteenth century, it became necessary also to take into account the quality of the weaponry. By the start of the Second World War the opposing methods of organisation and tactical employment had become critical considerations which tended to accentuate rather than cancel out differences in imponderables such as generalship, training, level of battlefield experience, morale and motivation. This appendix seeks to establish that in May 1940 the numerical strength levels of the opposing armies in France and Flanders were broadly equal; history has established beyond doubt which side had the advantage in non-quantifiable areas. There are also some discrepancies between sources about the number of divisions on each side. These are not significant; while there is little argument about the similar numerical value of opposing infantry divisions, there were many different types of armoured and mechanised division, and also different methods of combining independent brigades to create division equivalents.

The difficulty in defining a common base line, to establish the number of infantry battalions and armoured and artillery regiments in the order of battle of the British Army, was not unknown in the UK Ministry of Defence in the succession of defence reviews and studies in the 1970s and 1980s.

Allies

Horne[57] produces a total of forty-nine infantry divisions for No. 2 and No. 3 Army Groups, holding the Maginot Line. For Billotte's No. 1 Army Group on the critical front between the Channel coast and Longwy, he credits the Seventh Army with seven divisions, including one Division Legère Mechanique (DLM), which had an establishment of 174 tanks. The BEF had nine divisions and one army tank brigade. The French First Army had ten divisions and the Cavalry Corps under command, which included two DLMs. Ninth Army and Second Army are credited altogether with thirteen infantry divisions and four Divisions Legère Cavalerie (DLC), the latter a combination of light armour and horsed cavalry. Horne also enumerates a theatre reserve of eighteen divisions, three of which were armoured, but only formed between January and April 1940. A fourth came into existence on 15th May, command going to the newly promoted Général de Brigade Charles de Gaulle.[58] Horne also credits the Belgian Army with twenty divisions and the Dutch with ten, but Holland was overrun before the latter could come into action.

We deduce therefore from this source a start state of divisions as follows:

TABLE XXI

Command	Divisions		
	Infantry	Armoured/DLM	DLC
2 and 3 Army Groups	49		
1 Army Group			
– Seventh Army	6	1	
– BEF	9	1/3	
– First Army and Cavalry Corps	10	2	
– Ninth and Second Armies	13		4 1/3
Theatre Reserve	15	3 + 1	
Belgian Army	20		
Dutch Army	10		
TOTAL North Eastern Front	136	6 1/3 + 1	4 1/3

In addressing the extremely complicated relationship between the quality and number of tanks, Horne[59] quotes a total of 3,100 for the French Army, 'of which 2,285 were modern.' The remainder dated back to World War I. But only 800 of the modern tanks, plus the 100 'infantry' tanks of the BEF had the requisite combination of hitting power and protection to enable them to compete with the most recent panzer marque. Their mobility and reliability were far inferior, the German Army having learned lessons about the latter from the occupations of Austria and Czechoslovakia and the campaign in Poland.

Horne[57] gives a total of 1,320 tanks in the five DLM in No. 1 Army Group (174 each) and the three armoured divisions (150 each).

Fuller's figures[60] are slightly different:

TABLE XXII

Army	Divisions		
	Infantry	Armoured	Light Armoured
Holland	8		
Belgium	10		
Great Britain	10	1/3	1 2/3
France	90[*]	3	8[+]
TOTAL	118	3 1/3	9 2/3

[*] Excludes the theatre reserve.
[+] Plus twenty-seven independent tank battalions, split up for infantry close support

Four-fifths of the French tanks had no radio sets, thus rendering the light tanks almost useless for reconnaissance, and the heavy tanks incapable of anything but the most rudimentary coordinated tactical action.

Both sources make the point about the variable quality of the French infantry divisions. There were four categories. Active divisions maintained in peacetime, largely of two year conscripts: Series A, First Line Reserve; Series B, Second Line Reserve; and Fortress, purely defensive. Ninth and Second Armies, upon whom the avalanche was to fall, had between them only three active divisions.[61]

Germany

Horne[62] gives a start state for the German army on 12th May, 1940 of 125 infantry and ten panzer divisions; Army Group B twenty-six and three, Army Group A thirty-eight and seven, Army Group C nineteen infantry, theatre reserve forty-two infantry. The seven panzer divisions of Army Group A are credited with an opening strength of 1,816 tanks.

Fuller[60] credits the German army in the west with a strength of 134 infantry, ten panzer and four motorised divisions, and a *total* tank strength of 2,439.

Artillery and Combat Aircraft

If it is difficult to assess the relative infantry and tank strengths, it is even more so to relate those of artillery and aircraft. Horne[63] gives the French a numerical superiority in field artillery, 11,200 guns to 7,710, but only the German armoured and mechanised divisions and the BEF were motor-drawn. In aircraft, Germany had a small superiority in number of fighters and a very large one in ground-support bombers, including dive-bombers. In this area, the previous combat experience of the Luftwaffe in Spain and Poland gave them a very big advantage.

Notes

[1] De la Gorce, *The French Army*, translated by Douglas, London, Weidenfeld and Nicholson, 1963, pp.8–9.

[2] Whitton, *Moltke*, London, Constable and Co., 1921, pp.304–5.

[3] For the full story of Waldersee's rise and eclipse, see Goerlitz, *The German General Staff*, translated by Battershaw, London, Hollis and Carter, 1953, Chapter V.

[4] Massie, *Dreadnought*, London, Pimlico Press, 1992, pp.28–29.

[5] Goerlitz, op.cit., p.122.

[6] Tuchman, *The Guns of August*, London, Constable, 1962; Four Square Edition, p.33.

[7] Goerlitz, op.cit., pp.128–29.

[8] Goerlitz, op.cit., p.101.

[9] Tuchman, *The Proud Tower*, London, Hamish Hamilton, 1966; Folio Society, London 1995, p.426.

[10] Goerlitz, op.cit., p.149, and Tuchman, *Proud Tower*, p.426.

[11] Spears, *Liaison 1914*, London, Eyre and Spottiswoode, 1930, Appendix V.

[12] Clausewitz, *On War*, Everyman's Library Edition, London 1993; Professor Sir Michael Howard, *The Influence of Clausewitz*, p.34.

[13] Tuchman, *Guns of August*, pp.25–26.

[14] Clausewitz/Howard op.cit., p.36.

[15] Clausewitz, op.cit., pp.766–67.

[16] Moltke, *The Franco-German War of 1870–71*, first published in England by Harper Brothers, 1907, London, Greenhill Books, 1992, p.409.

[17] De la Gorce, op.cit., pp.149–50, quoting de Gaulle, *Vers l'Armée de Métier*, 1934.

[18] For comparative analyses of the Schlieffen Plan, see Goerlitz, op.cit., Chapter VI; Tuchman, *August 1914*, Chapter 2, and Barnett, *The Swordbearers*, London, Eyre and Spottiswoode, 1963, Chapter 2. Spears, *Liaison 1914*, Appendices V and VI, is authoritative about the organisation of the German Army in 1914.

[19] Tuchman, *Guns of August*, p.41.

[20] Tuchman, ibid., pp.68–70.

[21] Spears, *Liaison 1914*, gives the directive in full at Appendix XXIX.

[22] Goerlitz, op.cit., p.134.

[23] Goerlitz, ibid., p.145.

[24] Goerlitz, ibid., p.142.

[25] Moltke, op.cit., p.8.

[26] Thomson, *The Twelve Days*, London, The History Book Club, 1966, pp.142–43.

[27] Goerlitz, op.cit., p.144.

[28] Barnett, op.cit., pp.45–46

[29] Tuchman, *Proud Tower*, p.284.

[30] Barnett, op.cit., p.28.

[31] Barnett, op.cit., p.35.

[32] Spears, op.cit., Appendix V.

[33] Tuchman, *Proud Tower*, p.224.

[34] Thomson, op.cit., pp.31–32.

[35] Tuchman, *Proud Tower*, p.246.

[36] Massie, op.cit., gives the detail of the Eulenberg scandal and the *Daily Telegraph* interview in Chapters 36 and 37.

[37] A full account of the December 1912 war scare is given in Röhl, *The Kaiser and his Court*, Cambridge University Press, 1994, Chapter 7.

[38] Massie, op.cit., appendix.

[39] Churchill, *World Crisis*, London, Odhams Press Ltd, 1938 edition, vol. I, p.73.

[40] Crankshaw, *The Fall of the House of Habsburg*, London, Longmans, 1963; Sphere Books Edition, London, 1970, p.411.

[41] The sequence of events which destroyed Moltke's confidence in both himself and the kaiser is analysed by Barnett in *The Swordbearers*, pp.15–21.

[42] Tuchman, *Guns of August*, p.100.

[43] Spears, op.cit., Appendix IV.

[44] Tuchman, *Guns of August*, pp.299–312, describes the start of the battle in East Prussia.

[45] Fuller, *Decisive Battles of the Western World*, vol. III, first published 1956 Spa Books Ltd, London, 1994, p.211.

[46] Tuchman, *Guns of August*, p.265.

[47] Barnett, op.cit. p.72, quotes Moltke's directive of 29th August.

[48] Barnett, op.cit., p.75.

[49] De la Gorce, op.cit., p.256, quoting de Gaulle, *Vers l'Armée de Métier*.

[50] Guedalla, *The Two Marshals*, London, Hodder and Stougton Ltd, 1943, pp.323–33.

[51] For a full description of the Maginot Line, see Horne, *To Lose a Battle*, first published Macmillan 1969; 1990 edition pp.70–76.

[52] Keesing's *Contemporary Archives 1931–34*, pp.58 F and 277 F.

[53] Spears, *Assignment to Catastrophe*, London, William Heinemann Ltd, 1956, p.14 for French concern before the war, and p.165 for the same French assessment even after the attack had started.

[54] Goerlitz, op.cit., pp.362–63.

[55] For the early careers of Manstein and Guderian, see in particular, Barnett, [ed.] *Hitler's Generals*, first published London, Weidenfeld and Nicholson, 1989; Phoenix, London, 1995; also *Manstein*, by Field Marshal Lord Carver and *Guderian*, by Kenneth Mackesy. See also Paget, *Manstein: His Campaigns and Trial*, London, Collins, 1951.

[56] For the arguments, see Goerlitz, op.cit., p.368, Fuller, op.cit., p.388, Horne, op.cit., pp.202–3, Carver, op.cit. pp.226–28 and Keegan, *The Second World War*, Arrow Books Ltd, London, 1990, p.57.

[57] Horne, op.cit., Table A.

[58] Crawley, *De Gaulle*, London, Literary Guild, 1969, pp.95–99.

[59] Horne, op.cit., p.230.

[60] Fuller, op.cit., p.390.

[61] Fuller, ibid., p.385.

[62] Horne, op.cit., Table B.

[63] Horne, op.cit., pp.232–33.

Chapter XVI
Afterword

The conflicts of the decade of the Catalytic Wars showed that the whole nature of warfare had changed, and the results of the two wars of Prussian Supremacy produced a structure for Europe which endured until 1914. Some of the repercussions remain apparent a century later. In the United States, the influence of the War Between the States had considerable effect on the preparation for war of the armies which came to Europe in 1917, and similarly on the organisation and motivation of United States forces for the Second World War. Even today, visitors to the United States, in particular to Washington, Virginia and Pennsylvania, soon come to recognise that the psychological trauma of the conflict still endures.

What the wars of the decade between 1860 and 1870 did not change was the belief that war was the continuation of policy by other means. It was only after two world wars and the invention of terminal weaponry that every sane head of state or government came to realise that he had to do all he could to avoid Clausewitzian total war, because if he embarked on it his own country risked annihilation from enemy nuclear, biological or chemical weaponry. After 1945, the peace of Europe was maintained because of the mutually deterrent capabilities of the nuclear arsenals of the United States and the Soviet Union. Tension eased only when internal strains in the Soviet Union made it impossible to continue with existing levels of expenditure on the defence and related space programmes, coinciding with a leadership which was prepared to take a serious risk for peace. But in the half century since the end of the Second World War, wars have continued nevertheless. The underlying reasons have been either a failure of deterrence at a level below the nuclear threshold or because an advantage, however short-term, has been perceived by a national leadership if attention can be diverted from internal difficulties by external adventure or intervention by another country in a civil war, in furtherance of its own interests.

The potentially devastating nature of modern war was appreciated long before the start of the First World War in many quarters, some of considerable influence. The unprecedented casualty lists of the Catalytic Wars were caused by the development of more efficient bureaucracy which could identify men of military age, the application of the railway networks which could bring more men to battle, and the effect of rifled barrels and breech-loading for artillery and personal weapons, which increased their range, accelerated their rate of fire and improved their accuracy. The corresponding improvement in the lethality of munitions occurred after the critical decade and derived from the invention of dynamite by Alfred Nobel. Already rich as early as 1873 from the manufacture of explosives, he said:

> I wish I could produce a substance or a machine of such frightful efficacy for wholesale devastation that wars should become thereby altogether impossible. [1]

There could hardly have been a more precise definition of the role of the nuclear weapon after 1945, the year which saw its only use in war. But because an invention on this scale eluded Nobel, because the two peace conferences at The Hague in 1899 and 1907 attracted the whole-hearted support of none of the Great Powers and because no national peace movement was taken up by any individual or party with any prospect of responsibility for government, there was no way of avoiding war if any country considered that vital interests had to be protected, or if a compelling benefit might be obtained. The two peace conferences produced nothing positive apart from restrictions on the employment of some new potential weapons, such as the dropping of explosive projectiles from balloons, which were out of date almost as soon as they had been invented, and a very much qualified agreement that international disputes should, wherever possible, be settled by arbitration. Neither conference impeded for a day either the manufacture of any existing weapon of war or the continuous and unending quest for product improvement. Nor did either conference delay the conscription of one single soldier in those countries, including all the Great Powers except Great Britain and the United States, which imposed a universal obligation for military service on their young adult males. Likewise, international socialism proved powerless as an influence for peace in the approach to war in the summer of 1914. The Social-Democratic Party in Germany was at the time not only the largest of its kind in any country; they had, after 1912, more seats in the Reichstag than any other political party. Nevertheless, German socialists accepted the need to go to war as readily as had the recently elected members of the chamber of the liberalised Second Empire in 1870. The Reichstag voted war credits unanimously.[2] There was thus no influence, moral, diplomatic, dread of consequences or common sense, to prevent Europe going to war in 1914. When the conflict which had always threatened could no longer be restrained, the nations had formed alliances which stemmed directly from the outcome of the Catalytic Wars, and they fought using plans, organisations, weaponry and techniques which were also in direct descent from those of the wars of the ten years up to 1870.

The appalling losses of the First World War should have been enough to convince any sane individual that the same thing must never be allowed to recur. There was much impetus towards making collective security work, and a high level of belief in the potential for good of the League of Nations, notwithstanding the absence of the United States from this body for reasons of domestic politics. Perhaps the high point of confidence in the league was reached in 1931 when the British representative, Viscount Cecil, a younger son of the marquess of Salisbury who had been Queen Victoria's last prime minister, ennobled in his own right, having held cabinet posts during and after the First World War, could echo Emile Ollivier in 1870 by saying to the Assembly of the League: 'There has scarcely been a period in the world's history when war seems less likely than it does at present.'[3]

There then followed, within the month, the Japanese invasion of Manchuria and the start of fourteen years of war with China. In Europe, the attainment of power in Germany by Hitler marked the start of a series of unilateral abrogations of the Treaty of Versailles. These were at first related to matters internal to Germany, about which no two of the former allies of the 1914 war ever felt strongly enough to take effective joint action. But after the redeployment of German troops to the west bank of the Rhine, a matter forbidden by the peace settlement, France and Great Britain submitted successively to the Anschluss with Austria, the takeover of the Sudetenland and the absorption of the rest of Czechoslovakia with no reaction beyond ineffective protests. Similar responses to Italian adventures in Africa and massive German and Italian intervention in the Spanish Civil War were equally futile. The league was proved to be powerless.

Some saw the danger. Churchill had started to publish *The World Crisis*, his massive history of the First World War, in 1923, and began to warn publicly about the menace of Nazi Germany as early as May 1932,[4] eight months before Hitler was appointed chancellor of Germany by the failing President Hindenburg. On 16th March, 1933, Hitler announced his intention to rearm, and reintroduced conscription to Germany. Eight days later, the Reichstag voted complete emergency powers to Hitler for a period of four years, The penultimate section of Churchill's 1938 edition of *The World Crisis* concludes with the words: 'Surely, Germans, for history it is enough?'[5]

It is doubtful if by 1938 Churchill himself had anything more than hope that war could be avoided. Those who thought differently made insufficient allowance for both the evil genius of Hitler and an outstanding propaganda machine adept at the two most effective uses of this art form; first, telling those listening what they most wanted to hear and, secondly, the constant reiteration of succinct statements, whether truthful or not. The vast majority of the population of Germany was convinced because it wanted to be convinced. In addition, there was a carefully concerted programme of youth motivation geared entirely towards eager and zealous service in the armed forces of the Third Reich.[6] Whether the same methods applied today would be equally effective, in a more cynical age with very many other available distractions, may be debated. But their success in the 1930s is unquestionable. If the mass enthusiasm in Berlin which greeted the start of the war in 1914 were absent in 1939, most of the army marched willingly enough.

If the attempt in this book to analyse the forces let loose by the Catalytic Wars started with a lesson taught by one brave man, it ends with the story of another. The breakout battle from the Meuse crossings on the morning of 15th May, 1940 did not by any means go wholly the way of the German Army. Although the B series reserve divisions of Huntziger's Second Army had failed to hold the river line, the gap had been plugged by the French 3rd Armoured Division and 3rd Motorised Division, notwithstanding their commitment to battle piecemeal. A French military historian would state subsequently that General Brocard, the commander of 3rd Armoured Division, 'no longer commanded anything. He had simply become a provider of tanks.'[7]

The subunits of the two divisions fought bravely and well to defend the heads of the defiles leading up from the Meuse valley to the villages of Raucourt and Stonne, where, in the last days of August 1870, disaster for the Army of Chalons had been no more than postponed.

In May 1940, once these two villages had been secured, the tanks and motorised infantry of Guderian's corps could roam free westwards over the open ground of the Champagne plateau, and the French Army had no more reserves to commit. The elite troops of Guderian's leading formations, 10th Panzer Division and the Grossdeutschland motorised infantry regiment, had the scent of victory. But a tank company commander in the former told his crew that his grandfather had been killed on the same ground in the war of 1870, as had his father in the war of 1914. Now, if he were to 'buy it', it would be the end of a military dynasty.[8] It was not just the generals in the German

Army who had a tradition of service from father to son. Ten minutes later he was beaten to the punch by a French anti-tank gun and killed outright.

So long as mankind continues to regard the use of force as its ultimate sanction and men can be motivated to risk their lives for a cause, warfare in one form or another will continue.

Notes

[1] Tuchman, *The Proud Tower*, first published London, Hamish Hamilton, 1966; Folio Society edition, London, 1995, p.215.

[2] Thomson, *The Twelve Days*, London, History Book Club, 1966, pp.196–97.

[3] Taylor, *English History 1914–1945*, Oxford University Press, 1965; paperback edition 1995, pp.298–99.

[4] Churchill, *The Gathering Storm*, London, Cassell, 1950; Reprint Society, 1950, p.73.

[5] Churchill, *The World Crisis*, London, Odhams Press Ltd, 1938, vol. II, p.1,402.

[6] The indoctrination process of the youth of Germany from age ten upwards is described by Horne, *To Lose a Battle*, first published London, Macmillan, 1969; 1990 edition pp.94–97.

[7] le Goyet, quoted by Horne, op.cit., pp.419.

[8] Horne, op.cit., p.420.

Appendix A:
Terminology – Countries, Places and People

The time-span relevant to this book starts with the creation of The Army of the Coasts of the Ocean by Napoleon I in 1803, and ends with the Second World War. Throughout nearly a century and a half, treaty, law and usage changed the names of most of the countries involved, and also those of many of the places of importance. The names and styles of individuals changed, usually as a result of ennoblement, and contemporary and current nomenclature are sometimes at variance. This appendix seeks to explain the changes and to resolve inconsistencies.

Austria

No country changed its name more frequently. At the start of the nineteenth century the archduchy of Austria was a state in the Holy Roman Empire which happened to be the patrimony of the family who for long had held the imperial title, still in theory elective. The only other 'emperor' at the time was the tsar of Russia. Peter the Great had had the title conferred on him by the Senate of Russia in 1721, but this was not recognised at once by many of the European powers. At the time of Austerlitz, when most Europeans spoke of 'the emperor', they meant the head of the house of Habsburg and not Napoleon I or Alexander I. After Austerlitz the Holy Roman Empire ceased to exist, and the lands acquired by the Habsburgs over the centuries became the empire of Austria. After Sadowa, with all northern Italy lost and the Magyars of Hungary exercising a political stranglehold, Austria and Hungary became hyphenated and became known as the 'Dual Monarchy', which at once implied inferior status for all the peoples of the Habsburg realms who were neither German–Austrians nor Magyars. This endured until 1918, with the head of the house of Habsburg as emperor.

Belgium

Belgium became independent in 1830. Until the upsurge of Flemish culture in the second half of the twentieth century, most maps and histories referred to places by their French names. Of the sources drawn upon for this book, Spears, *Liaison 1914*, and Tuchman, *The Guns of August*, use French names almost exclusively. A present-day map of Belgium gives either both French and Flemish names or only the one more relevant to the region, which, over the ground covered by the westward march of the Schlieffen Plan, is more likely to be Flemish. This book gives both in the text where appropriate, particularly in Chapter XV.

Czechoslovakia

Throughout the decade of the Catalytic Wars, the provinces of Bohemia and Moravia were part of the Habsburg Empire, and until 1918 place names on all the maps were in German. Thereafter, Slav place names were used. Site visits conducted for this book in connection with Chapters III and VIII have related the two.

France

Sometimes mentioned in the text according to its contemporary form of government, e.g. Second Empire, Third Republic. *Ancien régime* nobility are referred to by their titles, First and Second Empire creations more usually by family name.

Germany

The mass of states in 1815, already much reduced in number from pre-Revolutionary times, are mentioned as appropriate by name, those allied to Prussia for the war of 1870 as the 'North German Confederation' and after 1871 as the 'German Empire'. Seldom described as 'the Second Reich' during its forty-seven years' existence, nevertheless this is what Imperial Germany was, if Hitler's Germany was the Third. The names of the kings of Prussia, and of Queen Victoria's son-in-law who reigned briefly as emperor in 1888, are given in English. The last emperor (kaiser) is styled Wilhelm in this book, tending to follow usage in most of the source material. The German title *'Graf'* is translated as 'Count'.

Holland

Referred to indiscriminately as 'Holland' or 'The Netherlands'.

Italy

After 1815 the multiplicity of states of the Renaissance reduced to the kingdoms of Sardinia (or Piedmont) and the Two Sicilies, the Papal States, the republic of Venice and a few surviving duchies. The description 'kingdom of Italy' begins to come into use after 1859 and is a correct description after 1871, when the whole of present-day Italy became united under the ruling house of the kingdom of Piedmont.

The United Kingdom

Given present-day emphasis on Scottish and Welsh nationalism especially now that Scotland is becoming devolved, it is strange to have to record the fact that until well into the twentieth century the realm now known as the United Kingdom was invariably referred to as 'England', not necessarily only by foreigners. This book has sought to follow contemporary practice.

The United States

Remained in existence throughout the War Between the States. The seceding states were known throughout their four year life as 'The Confederate States of America' (CSA).

Appendix B:
Military Organisations and Glossary

Organisation and Rank Structure

The smallest tactical organisation of interest in this book is the infantry company, cavalry squadron (subunit troop) and artillery battery, all at the time of the Catalytic Wars usually commanded by captains. Each had an established strength of between 100–150 men, deriving from the Roman century. By the time of the Second World War, the rank of command was usually major. Ranks in the British Army tended to be one higher than in others, particularly the Prussian/German.

The 'unit' of infantry is the battalion, commanded at the time by a major, in the French Army chef de battalion, now usually by a lieutenant colonel. Battalions of the Catalytic Wars era had an establishment of about 1,000 all ranks. Cavalry squadrons and artillery batteries were grouped in regiments, the latter in the British Army until 1938 in 'brigades' of artillery.

The infantry regiment, usually of three battalions, was a tactical grouping in all armies but the British, and was usually commanded by a colonel. In the French Army, the equivalent organisation was sometimes styled 'demi-brigade'.

All the above may be styled 'units'. Anything larger falls into the category of 'formation' because it tends to be a grouping of more than one combat arm and integral logistic services.

A brigade of infantry consisted of two regiments, except in the British Army where there were a number of battalions. A cavalry brigade, usually either 'light' or 'heavy', usually had at least three regiments. Command level was sometimes colonel, more usually brigadier general, (French Army général de brigade) or, after a long period of peace with too many senior officers chasing too few appointments, major general. The British Army dropped the rank of 'brigadier general' after the First World War as a piece of political window dressing. Since then, the one star rank in the British Army has been known as 'brigadier', in some continental armies the designation of a junior NCO.

Brigades are grouped into divisions, command level major general, in the French Army général de division. These are 'two star' generals in modern parlance. Divisions are grouped into *corps d'armée*, commanded by a lieutenant general, except in the French Army, which has three star generals. Corps are grouped into armies, commanded by three or four star generals, the latter in the Prussian Army generals of infantry or cavalry.

The five star rank is field marshal in the British and German armies and marshal of France, except that under both empires these officers of high distinction were styled 'marshals of the empire'. The first Napoleon dismissed one for describing himself incorrectly.

Glossary

STRATEGY AND TACTICS

These terms can mean different things at different levels. What is a strategic decision at one level of command may have been one of tactics or organisation higher up. In broad terms, strategy is the plan and design for a campaign or battle. Tactics is how it is fought. Definitions:

Enfilade	Usually in connection with firepower, the ability to bring fire to bear on a vulnerable flank.
Point d'appui	Strong point or firm base upon which to craft a design for battle.
Refused flank	Usually related to a defensive position, in which the 'refused' flank is at an angle to the main front, in order to provide a line of fire against an outflanking movement.

Reverse slope	Either a defensive position, or a forming-up point for an attack, which is behind a crest line and so concealed from enemy observation and aimed direct fire.
En rase campagne	Literally, in the open field.

ORGANISATION

Equipment table	The full list of all equipment, by type and quantity, to which a unit is entitled. Usually a matter of financial cover, and in the best circumstances related to the tactical task of the unit and the terrain and climate in which it is expected to operate.
Establishment	The authorised maximum strength of a unit, usually related to the budget for it.
Scale	The number of each item of equipment in the unit equipment table, for example a 'scale' of two machine-guns per battalion.
Strength	The number of men present for duty. While a unit always has a numerical strength, it is below establishment as soon as one man is absent from duty.

SIEGES, FORTIFICATIONS AND FIELD ENTRENCHMENTS

Abbati	A breastwork of stone or logs in an extemporised field fortification. Rendered out of date when bursting charges for artillery shells became powerful enough to blow the construction apart.
Bastion	An arrow-shaped fortification, usually mutually supporting and thus without the blind spots of a round or square tower. Part of the main fortification.
Cheveux de frises	Stakes of wood or iron, and thus by extension a line of bayonets, emplaced to defend the approach to a fortified position.
Glacis	The open ground in front of a fortification which an attacking force is compelled to cross.
Lines of circumvallation and contravallation	The former are established by a besieging force to contain the fortress or city under siege. The latter are also established by the besiegers, to guard the troops conducting the siege against attack by a relieving force.
Redoubt	A strong point usually, but not always, part of the outer line of fortification.

Ravelin	A tower or similar fortification detached from the main construction but capable both of supporting and being supported from it.

GUNS

Breech	The portion of the gun at the base of the barrel, which, on equipments post-1870, opens to load the projectile, propellant charge and means of initiation.
Calibre	The internal diameter of the barrel at the muzzle.
Carriage	The part of the cannon related to its movement and deployment – wheels, attachment to method of traction, platform.
Chamber	The portion of the barrel in which the round is seated before firing.
Muzzle	The mouth of the barrel.
Ordnance	The part of the cannon involved in the firing process – barrel, recoil system; sights and firing mechanism.

Appendix C:
Battlefields Then and Now

Tactical success in battle depends fundamentally upon achieving a correct relationship between the proper use of ground, optimisation of weapon capabilities, and good battlefield technique. Given present-day quality of contour maps based upon proper survey and air photographs, the skilled map reader can describe from a large-scale map much of what he would see if he were to visit any particular point. Nevertheless, commanders at all levels will invariably wish to see the ground for themselves. Napoleon was insistent upon this principle and followed it to the last. Marbot attributes the decline in Massena's performance when sent to command in the peninsula after Wagram to the fact that he no longer undertook reconnaissances personally – as well as to the limited travelling stamina of his *maîtresse en campagne*, disguised rather fetchingly as a cornet of dragoons. Likewise, a proper understanding of tactics can only be achieved by practice under instruction on the ground. The training medium of the Tactical Exercise Without Troops (TEWT), developed for combat-arm officer training by the British Army in the Second World War, remains an integral part of such training, and indeed practical promotion examination, to the present. The TEWT is the direct descendant of the 'staff ride' instituted by Moltke and developed by Schlieffen for the German general staff, and of the 'Allez, allez' schemes of Foch which he devised when commandant of the French staff college. The purpose of these exercises was practical instruction and, wherever possible, to familiarise officers with ground over which they might have to fight.

Similarly the military historian will wish to see with his own eyes the battlefields he seeks to describe, particularly those whose course of events provide the basis for his arguments. Given late twentieth-century industrial sprawl and suburbanisation, particularly in Western Europe, this necessary practice becomes ever harder to achieve. Little distorts perspective more completely than a motorway embankment. Fifty years after the end of the Second World War, the progressive expansion of Caen in all directions makes it increasingly difficult to follow the course of at least two of the critical phases of the Battle of Normandy, the attempted infantry-based breakout west of the city in June 1944 (Operation Epsom) and the armour-heavy thrust east of the city three weeks later (Operation Goodwood). The autoroutes and hypermarket sites, and the traffic so generated, render attempts to walk the ground intellectually unsatisfying and physically dangerous. Similarly, at Arnhem the spread of the town has left little of the original battle area except the dropping zone, the military cemetery and a few buildings devotedly maintained as memorials. Nevertheless, where the lie of the ground can still be determined, a visit to the site assists the understanding of most battles. In spite of the cosy villas on the Borguebus Ridge, it remains possible to trace the layout and conduct of the extempore defence thrown together by Oberst von Lutz when Goodwood was on the point of achieving the long-sought breakthrough into open country. Von Lutz himself must rank as one of the all-time masters of the practice of war at regimental group level. Unless totally built over, or changed drastically by environmental surgery, a visit to the scene of the fighting assists comprehension, which can be enhanced by the study of the work of military historians who wrote before constructional development took over. F. Loraine Petre's definitive study of the campaign of 1809, entitled *Napoleon and the Archduke Charles*, and drawn upon extensively for Chapter III of this book, remains invaluable as a guide when visiting the battlefields in the Danube valley and on the Marchfeldt. Colonel Petre wrote in 1909, exactly 100 years after Wagram. Basing his work upon impeccable research and thorough personal examination of the ground, he benefited in a way seldom possible for the late twentieth-century historian by seeing the terrain at a time when it can have changed little since the events he describes so ably. It is also perhaps worth noting that a historian writing in the first decade of the present century is better equipped to understand the limitations of movement at foot pace than is the child of the motor car and aeroplane age.

Today's battlefield visitor, professional historian, soldier or layman may be further distracted by an excess of memorialisation, or worse, theme park. The Butte de Lion mound at Waterloo puts the battlefield completely out of scale. Had it been there at the time, the commanding view from the summit would have resolved much sooner Wellington's uncertainty about the arrival of Blucher. The author, when conducting tours of Waterloo, endeavours whenever possible to place his audience with their backs to this historical monstrosity. On the other hand, the regimental and other memorials at Gettysburg and Mars La Tour can be useful landmarks when seeking to define precisely the site of particular phases of the battle – who was doing what to whom, and sometimes even when, bearing in mind that we are considering an era before precisely synchronised time was available to all.

Subject to these considerations, the reader may be interested in the state of the battlefields when visited in the course of research for this book, in 1994 and 1995.

Austerlitz

The railway from Vienna to Brno probably follows much the same course as the epic approach march of Davout's Corps, described so graphically by Jean-Pierre Blaise (Chapter III). The country remains very much like Wiltshire or Pennsylvania downland, open and rolling, perhaps less wooded than the latter. The western edge of the battle area lies three miles east of the limit of present day Brno, and it is a twenty minute trolley bus ride from Brno railway station to Slapanice, at the time of the battle Lapanz Markt and the centre of the French defensive position. The lakes which blocked the retreat of the allied left at the end of the battle, of which so much is made in Napoleon's post action report and by Marbot, have since been filled in and the whole area is now prime arable land and orchard. The villages on the line of the Goldbach streamlet, though now much larger than at the time of the battle, remain separate communities. There is a monument at the summit of the Pratzen resembling a miniature version of the Eiffel Tower and containing the obligatory museum and memorial crypt. This was completed in 1925, having been built as an anti-war memorial at the urging of Fr Slovak, a Brno priest. The summit of the Zuran hill (The Santon) which was the initial location of Napoleon's headquarters during the battle, has been designated French national territory in perpetuity.

These apart, there is little other evidence of the battle on the ground, although Cedok, the Czech national tourist office, has produced a useful map. The reason is not far to find. The Habsburg Empire, which continued to rule Bohemia and Moravia until the founding of Czechoslovakia after the First World War, had no reason to commemorate a battle in which it had been so thoroughly humiliated. The allied army at Austerlitz was, in any case, predominantly, Russian and few Czech soldiers can have taken part. Those that did so fought as subjects of the Austrian emperor. The battle thus had no place in the tradition of Czechoslovakia, which sought to eradicate all Austro-Germanic influence, and still less in that of the Czech Republic.

This is not necessarily to the disadvantage of the present day student of the battle because he can walk the ground undistracted. The dominating nature of the Pratzen is at once apparent, as is the negligence of the Austro-Russian high command in failing to appreciate the importance of this feature as the lynchpin of their whole position. What is less easy to understand is the failure of the allies to identify the developing threat of the two assault divisions of Soult's corps. For an averagely fit man in late middle age, lightly loaded with a 'day' rucksack, the route taken by the divisions of Vandamme and St Hilaire, 16,000 men, takes an hour to walk, from the point east of Lapanz Markt where it comes into full view from the Pratzen, to where the divisions formed up for the assault. A dank December morning, black powder smoke and a convenient re-entrant would have afforded some measure of concealment but the route can be followed from the summit of the heights for most of the way. And if this mass of manpower were not sighted from there, what was the allied cavalry doing ?

The name given to the battle is also of interest, and the possibilities are discussed by Manceron. Would it be 'The Battle of the Three Emperors' (Napoleon, Francis, Alexander), or 'The Battle of the Anniversary', (of Napoleon's coronation a year previously)? It was left to the victor to decide. Brunn, although a garrison town of some significance, was considered unsuitable because it had been secured by the French ten days before the battle. 'The Battle of the Pratzen', notwithstanding the tactical importance of the feature, would have no significance if so reported in France and across Europe. The fifth option was 'Austerlitz'. This village is three miles east of the battlefield, and formed part of the estates of Prince Kaunitz, Imperial Chancellor under Maria Theresa. The allied emperors had stayed in his manor-house château on the night before the battle and Napoleon slept there the night after it. There was, therefore, no doubting the fact that this otherwise unremarkable village had changed hands as a result of the battle, and so Austerlitz was the best choice for reasons both of prestige and propaganda. Further, Napoleon reserved to himself the whole credit for the victory. As with Marengo, Jena and Friedland, Austerlitz was never granted as a ducal or princely title to any of the marshalate, in spite of some heavy hints from Soult, both at the time and later.

Aspern–Essling and Wagram

The outcome of both these battles depended upon a successful forcing of the crossing of the Danube. The course of the river has been altered totally within this century in order to provide permanently navigable channels for barge traffic and to domesticate and control the dramatic rise and fall of the river level in early summer. This factor, ignored by Napoleon, impeded disastrously the build-up for Aspern–Essling. Lobau is no longer an island, but the bridgehead site at Muhlau remains identifiable. Aspern and Essling have become 'ribbon development' villages on the main road inland from the north bank of the river between industrial Vienna and the frontier with Hungary at Bratislava. The Lobgrund is now, as it was then, fertile market garden land. The only evidence remaining of the desperate battle in May 1809 is a small museum in Aspern churchyard and the granary at Essling, stoutly defended by Boudet's division of Massena's corps. The sturdy strength of this stone building rendered it impervious to contemporary artillery fire. It is now at greater risk of being submerged, by ultra-modern townhouse development, under construction in September 1994.

Looking northwards from the granary, and back over the same ground from the natural rampart formed by the ridge between Wagram and Markgrafneusiedl, the peacetime importance of this broad sweep of country as the source of grain for the population of Vienna is obvious, as is its highly combustible nature in a hot summer. For war, it would in current parlance be described as 'good tank country'. The western half of the Wagram battlefield is now much built over. Sussenbrunn, objective of Macdonald's massed frontal attack on the second day of the battle, is now a residential suburb and a station on the excellent railway network which serves the area. Deutsch Wagram clearly acquired additional cachet when the first railway link from Vienna to Brunn and Prague was routed through the village in 1837. The hamlet of Aderklaa, focal point of the battle on the first evening and early on the second morning, remains identifiable.

The Russbach is little changed from contemporary descriptions by Marbot and others. Although the stream is fordable on foot, the steep banks would have constituted a formidable obstacle to movement for formed bodies of cavalry and horse-drawn artillery. As with the Goldbach at Austerlitz, the attacking force would have to secure the existing bridges. The three miles between Wagram and Markgrafneusiedl is a pleasant country walk, flanked to the north throughout by a rise in the ground, never of more than fifty feet, but quite enough in terms of the firepower of the time to give the defence a considerable advantage in terms of local observation and weapon siting. The Russbach acquired geographical significance in 1866 as the armistice line after Sadowa. It is hard to identify from the map any defence line between the Elbe and the Russbach which the badly beaten Austrian Army could have taken up without the risk of having its flanks turned in an archetypal Moltke design for battle.

The importance of the Bisamberg as the anchor for the Austrian right flank and as an observation post commanding the whole battle area is absolutely clear. Today's visitor can gain a similar view by ascending the Donauturm at the International Conference Centre and United Nations office building on Donaustadt Island. Likewise, a walk up the hill through Grinzing to Nussdorf on the southern bank, upriver from the city, validates Marbot's story of the wealthy and important citizens watching the battle from their summer villas.

The Eastern Theatre of the American Civil War

The battlefields of the American Civil War visited in the course of research for this book are uniformly maintained in superb order by the National Park Service of the US Department of the Interior. Each has its visitors centre, with state-of-the-art audio-visual displays at all the most important sites, and guided tours by staff with formidable knowledge of every detail of the battle. The biggest war ever fought by the United States is commemorated appropriately, not just on the battlefields but in many places elsewhere, such as the Lee family home at Arlington, in Richmond, where the Confederate White House is maintained in perfect preservation, the site of Lee's surrender of the Army of Northern Virginia at Appomattox Courthouse, and at City Point east of Petersburg, where the Appomattox River joins the James. This was the logistic base for the Union stranglehold on Lee's army and on Richmond, the only industrial centre left to the Confederacy, which Grant developed throughout the summer of 1864. It is the first example of such a base in size and scale (see Chapter XIV) and a study of its organisation has much to teach any logistic staff officer.

The battlefields of the James peninsula, Chancellorsville and the Wilderness are now much overgrown. Except at Malvern Hill there is no good view of any site. However a short walk on a summer day is enough to indicate the problems of heat, humidity and mosquitoes which would have plagued both armies in this natural swampland.

Antietam, fought in September 1862, is of more interest to the professional soldier. Harper's Ferry is at the bottom of a steep valley at the confluence of the Potomac and Shenandoah, and any garrison established there is ready prey for an opposing army which can move fast enough – unless set there as bait. Lee took a very considerable risk in dispersing his forces in order to converge on Harper's Ferry and a commander with more drive than McClellan would have taken full advantage of the opportunity presented to him when Lee's operation order fell into his hands less than four days after it had been issued.

Approaching the battlefield along Interstate 270 which runs north-west from the Washington beltway, the antennae of the communication centre of Camp David proud of the skyline on the Catoctin Hills are more apparent to today's visitor than 'the clustered spires of Frederick'. But although the most obvious commemoration of Barbara Frietchie seems to be a fast food restaurant on the motor road leading towards Hagerstown over the spur of South Mountain, Whittier's wholly apocryphal poem is still required learning in the schools of Maryland.

The Amish and the Mennonites still farm the country round Sharpsburg and are still to be seen in their traditional garb, but the land no longer has the trim appearance which it presented in the mid-nineteenth century. The reasons are that the non-mechanised farming methods of these strict sects are no longer cost-effective, the farms are too small to be profitable and many of the young have been lured away. The consequence is that woodland and undergrowth have taken over. However, the white wooden Dunker church has been reconstructed in its original form, and it needs little imagination when standing on the ridge between the North and West Woods, 400 yards north of the church, to appreciate the hair's-breadth margin by which Jackson held this position, critical in securing the line of the Confederate retreat across the Potomac, and the vital importance of the forced march of A.P. Hill's division from Harper's Ferry. At the southern end of the battlefield, the solid stone bridge which Burnside considered to be his only route across the sluggish little Antietam Creek, then as now no more than three feet deep and twenty-five yards wide in summer, remains a focal point for visitors. The stream is steep banked but at the time of the battle would have been fordable at any point. Burnside, on the day a combination of sulks and torpor, failed to realise this.

The significance of Antietam was political rather than military. Since the Army of the Potomac had not lost the battle, Lincoln could issue his Emancipation Proclamation; because they had not won it he could at last dismiss McClellan. The chosen replacement was Burnside, who took the Army of the Potomac south-eastwards beyond Washington, to attempt a head-on attack involving an assault river crossing of the Rappahannock at Fredericksburg, in the depths of winter. This site is now almost entirely subsumed in the modern town. Nevertheless, the lie of the ground remains apparent enough to establish the strength of Lee's defensive position and the suicidal nature of the successive brute-force frontal attacks ordered by Burnside in this classic set-piece battle.

Gettysburg is maintained as a national shrine, and receives 2,000,000 visitors annually. A balance has to be struck between the sacred nature of the memorial, and mass tourism superbly organised for the greatest good of the greatest number. The recent film *Gettysburg* was allowed 'still' shots of the battlefield, but the live scenes had to be shot elsewhere on neighbouring ground, a ruling which also applies to the re-enactments which take place every year on the anniversary of the battle. Nothing is lost as a result, because the terrain is no different. Gettysburg is the classic example of an 'encounter' battle and occurred where it did because of the convergence of important roads at what up to that point had been no more than a small farming town. The surrounding country is prosperous and lush farmland, and the Army of Northern Virginia, logistically ill-found as it was, would have relished living off it.

Gettysburg battlefield now has over 1,000 state, formation and regimental memorials, forty miles of well-signed roads, twenty museums in and near the town and observation towers at such places as Culp's Hill, where the growth of woodland has obliterated the fields of fire which existed in 1863. The atmosphere of the battle can be regained only in the early morning, before the tourist coaches arrive. It is an interesting experience to walk the ground of Pickett's attack on the third day of the battle. The ground rises gently towards Cemetery Ridge and it is beyond question that the defence had the advantage of position. But while the Round Tops which anchored the left of the Union line are formidable *points d'appui*, Cemetery Ridge as such is not. Given the moral ascendancy Lee had established over McClellan, Pope, Burnside and Hooker, successively commanders of the Union Army before Meade was appointed in the week before Gettysburg, it is not too surprising that everything was staked on this last throw; and from where Lee stood, the proposition does not look impossible.

Sadowa

The battle is known indiscriminately as both 'Sadowa' and 'Koniggratz', with Prussian/German sources preferring the former name and Austrian the latter. The long-established Habsburg garrison town of Koniggratz, which changed its name to Hradec Králové after the foundation of Czechoslovakia, is very similar to present-day Brno and Olomouc: some architectural traces of a more gracious age surrounded by dreary 'Sovbloc' slab concrete and ever-expanding post-*détente* futuristic-build business construction. The battle was fought on ground almost equidistant from Koniggratz and Sadowa.

There is little to commemorate it. A small plaque on a house in Hradec Králové indicates the location of Benedek's headquarters before the battle and a very few signs off Euroroute 442 show the way to the Chlum Ridge east of the road. The modern autoroute leads through Jičín to the Iser crossing at Mlada Boleslav into south-east Germany, in other words the exact reverse of the axis of advance of the Prussian First Army. A small museum in Chlum village has about it the air of permanent closure, but the memorial to the commander of the Prussian First Guard infantry division still stands, surmounted by stone eagles, to mark the point at which his formation met and broke the desperate attempt of the Austrian I Corps to restore the refused right of the position compromised by the disobedience of Festetics.

For the same reasons which apply to Austerlitz, but perhaps even stronger, neither the Habsburg Empire nor the Republic of Czechoslovakia had any reason to commemorate the battle. Since the site did not remain in the hands of the victors after the peace settlement there is only the one memorial, and none of the regimental and formation stones which proliferate at Gettysburg and Mars La Tour. There has been little development; perhaps the villages are slightly larger than they were in 1866 and the ground remains, as it was then, prime agricultural land, but more efficient farming methods evidently have caused most of the increased population to work in the town – a fact confirmed by the bus timetables. If the Marchfeldt and the Lorraine plateau resemble Salisbury Plain, the ground over which Sadowa was fought is more like Sussex downland and the country round Gettysburg – broad slopes with good commanding views, probably with the woods thicker now than then, and intersected by streams providing obstacles to coherent formation movement by nineteenth-century armies. The country between Chlum and Koniggratz is closer than that of the battlefield, and would have assisted the sacrificial rearguard actions by the Austrian cavalry and horse artillery, fought at the end of the day to cover Benedek's withdrawal south of the Elbe (Labe). This river, throughout the whole area relevant to the campaign, is only to be crossed by existing bridges or pontoon construction – hence the emphasis in Benedek's operation order (see Chapter VIII, Appendix 1).

By any standards, the whale-back ridge from Chlum to Maslowed could be developed into a formidable defensive position. Had the approach of the Prussian Second Army been further delayed, and the action on 3rd July indecisive, Benedek might well have brought off a notable defensive success in a renewal of the battle on the same ground.

Although by no means impenetrable, the Riesengebirge passes do present serious constraints to movement. Given the speed and efficiency of Prussian mobilisation and the availability of railway links from west and north to Breslau, it is hard to see how the strategy of an advance into Silesia, urged on Benedek by Franz Joseph, could possibly have succeeded. Moltke could have reinforced the army of the crown prince much more quickly than Benedek could have developed a coherent attack from the passes. The ground on the Czech side of the Riesengebirge is similar to the England–Scotland border region and a properly coordinated defence should have made far more of it than was achieved by the disparate actions of the five Austrian corps committed separately to engagements there between 26th and 30th June. But in all probability the issue would still have been decided by the needle gun. Another Euroroute, the E67, leads north and north east from Hradec Králové by way of Jaroměř and Nachod to the Polish frontier, towards Wroclaw (Breslau) and Warsaw. In what is now a drive of less than an hour there is no apparent trace of the series of battles in the closing days of June 1866 which completed the destruction of Benedek's self-confidence.

On the other side of the hill, the expansion of woodland, exactly as at the Frenois eminence on the left bank of the Meuse at Sedan, has almost eliminated the grandstand view which the king of Prussia, his military staff and cabinet ministers and international observers would have had on the day from the Hill of Dub above Sadowa. Thus, claims of what could and could not be seen then cannot be absolutely validated now. Study of map and the lie of ground indicates it is highly probable that the anxious observers on the Hill of Dub would have seen, and with considerable relief, some of the Austrian artillery changing target in mid morning, to fire northwards at what could only have been the leading elements of Second Army. It is, of course, a further flaw in Benedek's conduct of the battle that he did not use one of his cavalry divisions as a covering force in front of the positions he had ordered for IV and II Corps. But although Whitton, and by inference from him Malcolm, claims intervisibility between the Hill of Dub and two prominent trees still standing forty years after the battle on the crest of the Hill of Horenowes nearly five miles away, it is impossible to give any credence to the claim of Bismarck, made years afterwards, that it was he who was first to notice the infantry of the crown prince's army advancing southwards from the latter feature. 3rd July 1866 was a day of poor visibility, steamy after the heavy overnight rain. Even with the best of the optical instruments of the time, it is hard to credit that individual movement could have been identified at this distance.

Alsace–Lorraine

The state of the battlefields of the war of 1870 varies, from total preservation on the good agricultural land of the Lorraine plateau between Gravelotte and the Plain of Woevre, to complete extinction by Eurosprawl overdevelopment. There is now no trace of the siege in Metz, Borny (Colombey–Nouilly in Moltke's account), where the French III Corps fought its delaying action on 14th August, Ban St Martin, where Bazaine had his headquarters throughout the siege, and Scy, his ancestral village, are all now suburbs of this highly prosperous industrial city. Metz has lost completely the 'garrison town' atmosphere it must have exuded for centuries since Roman times, as has Charleville–Mezières, where Zola's Capitaine Beaudoin and the flighty Madame Gilberte Maginot, later Delaherche, enjoyed their first passage of arms. St Privat, Amanvillers and Plappeville, in 1870 solid stone farming villages, are now part of the city's wealthy commuter belt.

At the other end of the prosperity scale is the Briey region. This was not the scene of any significant engagement in 1870 but, because of its enormous mineral resources, it proved to be by far the most valuable of all the prizes exacted from the Third Republic by the victorious German Empire. The assets remained of the most enormous importance throughout their forty-seven years in German possession, to the Krupp production lines in particular. But with the iron industry at the end of the twentieth century in what appears to be terminal decline, Briey now has the same atmosphere as a former mining town in South Wales; nor is the surrounding region dissimilar.

There are some surprising survivals. *'Ils tombent comme à Gravelotte'* is a proverb, at least in Thionville, for a total disaster or collapse. At the Gravelotte crossroads, there is a plaque on the wall of what was then the inn and is now the combined office of a lawyer and undertaker, to mark the fact that Napoleon III spent the night there on 15th August. There is also a small museum of the battle in the village, which, as far as the author knows, is unique in allowing the name of Bazaine to be commemorated.

Cars and lorries thunder up the hill from Metz through the Mance ravine. Having skirted Point du Jour at the southern end of the Gravelotte–St Privat ridge, local traffic continues westwards on the good road through Rezonville, Vionville and Mars La Tour towards Verdun. That going further afield turns north in the village towards the autoroute to Paris. This feeder road traverses the east–west spur of the St Privat feature at Vernéville. This ground was Bazaine's first choice for the position to be taken up by Canrobert's corps, when he decided on the night of 16th August to withdraw towards Metz.

Canrobert talked Bazaine out of it, on the ground that his right flank would be 'en l'air'. It is beyond question that the position taken up in the event by Canrobert for the battle on 18th August was a very strong one, but his withdrawal as far as St Privat compounded the 'option of one' of retreat into the fortress of Metz if the Lines of Amanvillers could not be held, and his right flank was as much exposed there as it would have been on the Vernéville spur. The latter would have been by no means a bad defensive position.

The names of the battles vary depending upon which national source is used. The French tend to use 'Woerth', 'Rezonville' or 'Vionville' and 'The Lines of Amanvillers'. German accounts prefer 'Froeschwiller', 'Mars La Tour' and 'Gravelotte–St Privat.' What is particularly apparent at Spicheren, Froeschwiller and Gravelotte–St Privat is the enormous potential defensive strength of these features, with excellent command of ground and fields of fire out to the maximum range of infantry and artillery weapons. Wisdom after the event indicates that the Spicheren and Froeschwiller 'positions magnifiques' were held in insufficient strength. Had Bazaine reinforced Frossard at Spicheren, and if MacMahon had had available to him at Froeschwiller all the three corps nominally under his command instead of one and a half, the immediate outcome of the frontier battles might well have been different, with a consequent effect on what followed. But probably nothing in the long term could have compensated for the Prussian superiority in artillery and in numbers. Moltke had fifteen full-strength army corps against the initial French eight, all under strength and deficient in essential equipment because of the chaotic mobilisation process (see Chapter XII).

Froeschwiller and Mars La Tour are particularly well-demarcated sites. At Froeschwiller there is a signed walk which covers the left flank of MacMahon's defensive position, north of the road between Woerth and Reichshofen. The chateau in the latter village still stands, unchanged from the painting hanging in the Invalides, of MacMahon and his staff in the courtyard on the morning of the battle. There is a memorial to the heroic 7th Regiment of Algerian tirailleurs, who as much as Bonnemain's cavalry division bought the time for MacMahon to break clean at the end of the battle. An observation tower at Elsasshausen, built by the Prussians partly from captured cannon, gives a fine panoramic view of the southern half of the battle area, including the scenes of the two sacrificial French cavalry charges, by Michel's brigade at Morsbronn over ground then as now broken by vines, and by Bonnemain at the end of this disastrous day for French arms. The Euromonument built to commemorate Bonnemain's charge and the centenary of the battle is on the wrong side of the hill.

Mars La Tour is memorialised almost to the same degree as Gettysburg, but in the era of the European Union attracts only a fraction of Gettysburg's visitors. Some come upon it by mistake, when visiting the scenes of the great American feats of arms in the nearby Argonne in 1918, and between the Meuse and the Moselle in the winter of 1944–45. Mars La Tour itself, unlike Sedan, was not fought over again after 1870. The monuments at Mars La Tour are in the main to German units and formations, because the ground remained in their hands from 1871 until 1918, the frontier after the forced French cession of Alsace–Lorraine running very slightly east of Mars La Tour. It is a curiosity that many of the memorials are attributed to Metz stonemasons, presumably loyal subjects of the empire up to 1870. The atmosphere of the battle is pervasive, and, although the woods are probably much thicker now than they were on the blazing August day of the battle, all the main features of the ground are readily discernible. It remains impossible to understand why Bazaine, whose concern was always for his left flank, did not throw out a blocking force to cover the Bois des Ognons and the defile leading up from the village of Gorze, which would then have become a death trap for any Prussian advance from that direction. And it is even less comprehensible why not even one cavalry patrol, or, failing, that a pre-breakfast canter by a few of the young bloods of Forton's division, did not take the twenty minute ride to the heights above Flavigny. Had they done so they would have brought back intelligence very much to their army commander's advantage.

There is no massive feature within the eight by six mile rectangle within which Mars La Tour was fought, but there are many undulations of ground which provided cover for the attacking Prussians and, conversely, advantages of height, observation and weapon-siting for the defence, had the French used them properly. The intelligent use of terrain which allowed a mere 800 sabres of von Bredow's 12th Cavalry Brigade to disrupt totally the conduct of the defence by Canrobert's corps, with perhaps 20,000 men present for battle, is an object lesson in proper use of ground. Canrobert was aligned east–west on the line of the Roman road, now a farm-cart track, which lies about a mile north and parallel with the main road between Rezonville and Vionville. Bredow formed up in dead ground south of the latter village, and followed a re-entrant north and then east beyond the Bois de Tronville to burst upon Canrobert's open right flank. It will be remembered that Canrobert's corps had no cavalry division to act as flank guard, but there was plenty of Reserve Cavalry available for regrouping. The dominating nature of the ground around the Grisières farmstead, still a sturdy stone construction, which overlooked the approach of von Wedell's 38th Infantry Brigade and so caused the annihilation of this formation, remains obvious. The open ground around the Yron streamlet west of the road from Jarny to Mars La Tour provided perfect cavalry country for the entr'acte-like encounter in late afternoon between von Barby's and von Redern's cavalry brigades of the 5th Cavalry Division, and the cavalry division of Ladmirault's corps.

Rezonville has to be regarded as the centre of gravity of the French position because of the mass of troops retained there by Bazaine throughout the day. The unaggressive and unimaginative nature of the French defence is indicated by two memorials very close to these massed troops, on the Roman road at the eastern end of the wood due north of Rezonville. One, to the Schleswig–Holstein Dragoon Regiment, marks the limit of Bredow's charge. The other, to the 3rd Brandenburg Uhlan Regiment, the Ziethen Hussars, commemorates the point reached by a charge by part of the other (6th) reserve cavalry division of the Prussian Second Army, in a night attack ordered by Prince Frederick Charles when, belatedly, he reached the battlefield. The left flank of von Alvensleben's gun line, on the roadside 200 yards west of Vionville, is marked by a memorial to the Hanover Artillery regiment of X Corps. This position would hardly have been tenable if the French had occupied and held the Bois de Tronville.

The approaches from the west to the Gravelotte–St Privat feature are completely open and resemble the glacis of a fortress. The French infantry and artillery could not have wished for better fields of fire. The murderous disregard for their men's lives implicit in the frontal attacks ordered throughout 18th August by the Red Prince, von Steinmetz and subordinate corps commanders, all desperate for glory, seems to the author worse than anything imputed to any First World War commander. Perhaps most horrifying of all in this context is the ground over which Prince Augustus of Wurtemburg ordered a sequence of attacks by the Prussian Guard Corps throughout the afternoon of 18th August. The long slope up to St Privat is completely open and the chassepots, mitrailleuses and artillery were presented with a succession of unmissable targets by massed infantry attacking frontally over bare ground, using the tactics of Waterloo. It is as if the German commanders had actively sought the slaughter of their men.

It is the contention of the author that battlefields only remain well demarcated provided that the ground is not taken subsequently for urban or industrial development and also that it remains in the hands of the victors, who have an interest in the commemoration of their achievement. Neither proposition is true of Sedan. Although the general lie of the ground remains readily apparent and validates fully the mordant comment of General Ducrot –

'*Nous sommes dans un pot de chambre, et nous y sommes emmerdés*' and the citadel of Sedan still stands, the land either side of the Meuse is now a mass of industrial development. Some traces of the battle remain. The poignant Maison de la Dernière Cartouche in Bazeilles is well worth a visit and there is a memorial in the village square to those killed in this particular segment of the French defensive perimeter. The names are in the main from the heroic marine division of XII Corps, and include four out of the eight battalion commanders. Another monument at Floing bears the praise wrung from the king of Prussia – '*Oh, les braves gens*' – as he witnessed the desperate attempts at a breakout made by the French reserve cavalry division. But it is impossible to reach the top of the hill at Frenois, where king and hierarchy of what would soon be the German Empire had their panoramic view of the battle. Approaches from the north and west are blocked by a French Army field firing range, and the hilltop itself is impenetrable second-growth woodland. However, there are some pillboxes on the hillside overlooking the Meuse. Intended as part of the Maginot Line to deny passage of the river, they mark the point where the panzers broke through in May 1940.

Index

A

Aachen, 452, 589, 591, 594, 597, 614
Abbeville, 592
Abd-el-Kader, 416–17
Abeken, 451
Abensberg, 88
Aberdeen, Earl of, 113, 393
Aderklaa, 101–3, 645
Agincourt, 24
Agram, 287, 323
Aire, River, 406
Aisne, River, 122, 385, 531, 539, 590, 592, 606, 608, 615
Alabama, 115, 177, 183, 389, 398
Alaska, 171
Albert I, King of the Belgians, 591, 603
Albert, Crown Prince of Saxony, 320, 325, 334, 353, 467, 468
Albrecht, Archduke, 318, 323, 332, 350, 455
Alexander I, Emperor of Russia, 57, 69, 77, 80
Alexander II, 278, 286, 434, 487, 580
Alexander, Lt Col., 229, 232, 240, 260
Alexandria, Va, 179, 185, 191, 200, 389, 399, 401
Algeria, 305, 414–18, 420–22, 427, 428, 432, 433, 455, 461, 465, 471, 475, 479, 498
Algiers, 416, 458
Alleghenies, 170
Aller, River, 78, 79
Alma, 26
Alps, 36, 423, 589
Alsace, 120, 131, 132, 428, 430, 446–85, 491, 532, 548, 567, 587, 590, 602, 604, 606
Alsace–Lorraine, 404, 446–85, 550, 611, 446–85
Alvensleben, General Gustav von, 320, 467, 469, 539

Alvensleben, General Konstantin von, 467, 469, 484, 500, 501, 503, 504, 505, 506, 507, 508, 509, 512, 654
Amanvillers, Lines of, 122, 518, 519, 614, 652
Anderson, R.H., Confederate general, 205, 206, 215, 229, 238, 241, 242, 256, 259
Andrew, Governor, 193
Angerapp, River, 603
Angoulême, Duc d', 415
Ansbach, 63, 64
Antietam, 130, 148, 176, 180, 185, 195, 196, 202, 206, 211, 213, 215, 217, 218, 219, 221, 223, 224, 225, 227, 233, 236, 245, 247, 251, 253, 254, 261, 264, 265, 329, 401, 569, 646, 647
Antwerp, 603, 613
Aosta, 394, 426
Appalachian Chain, 225, 385, 389
Appomattox, 182, 194, 566, 646
    River, 371, 372, 574, 575, 646
Aquia Creek, 200, 223, 228, 233, 399
Ardennes, 141, 452, 590, 597, 605, 613, 616
Argonne, 126, 530, 531, 535, 538, 616, 653
Arlington, 185, 187, 188
Arnau, 331
Artois, Comte d', later King Charles X of France, 412
Aspern–Essling, 90, 94, 95, 98, 99, 104, 644–46
Asquith, Prime Minister, 281, 554, 593
Atlanta, 266, 269, 389, 398, 400
Auerstadt, 40, 52–53, 76–77, 99, 100, 342
Augereau, Marshal, Duke of Castiglione, 38, 39, 63, 64, 69, 78, 99, 278, 490
Augsburg, 63, 64, 86
Augustus of Wurtemburg, Prince, 321, 349, 467, 469, 509, 527, 530, 654
Aumale, Duc d', 417
Austerlitz, 24, 45, 48, 53, 67–77, 84, 89, 99, 100, 104, 326, 333, 379, 421, 459, 633, 643–44, 645, 649
Austria, 23, 33, 65, 69, 70, 76, 77, 80, 84, 85, 86, 91, 153, 189, 274, 276, 277, 284–

G